HURRY!

HURRY!

HURRY!

365 days

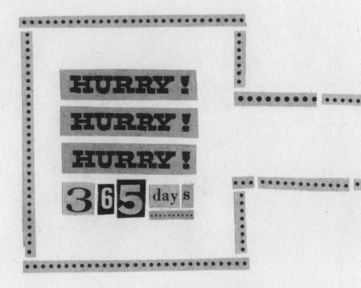

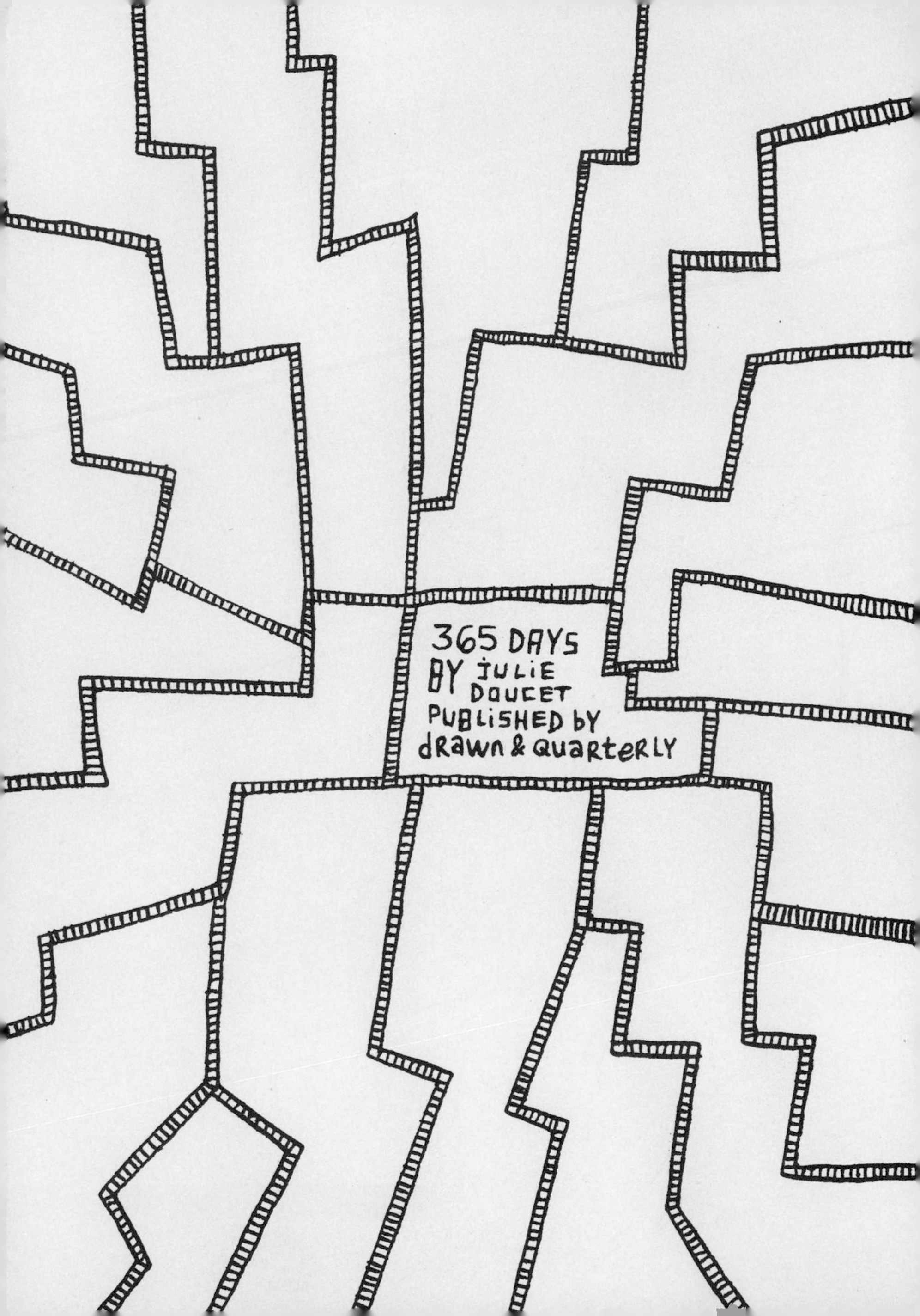
365 DAYS
BY JULIE DOUCET
PUBLISHED BY
drawn & quarterly

TRANSLATED BY JULIE DOUCET.
HAND LETTERING BY DIRK REHM, CHRIS WARE, and RICH TOMMASO.

DRAWN AND QUARTERLY
POST OFFICE BOX 48056
MONTREAL, QUEBEC
CANADA H2V 4S8

www.drawnandquarterly.com

FIRST EDITION: OCTOBER 2007.
PRINTED IN CANADA.

10   9   8   7   6   5   4   3   2   1

LIBRARY AND ARCHIVES CANADA CATALOGUING IN PUBLICATION
DOUCET, JULIE, 1965–
       365 DAYS: a diary / by Julie Doucet
TRANSLATION OF: JOURNAL. ORIGINALLY PUBLISHED IN FRENCH BY
L'ASSOCIATION (Paris, 2004).

   ISBN 978-1-897299-15-9
           I. TITLE.   II. TITLE: THREE HUNDRED AND SIXTY-FIVE DAYS.
PN6733.D6824613 2007   741.5'971   C2007-901213-2

DRAWN & QUARTERLY ACKNOWLEDGES THE FINANCIAL CONTRIBUTION OF THE
GOVERNMENT OF CANADA THROUGH THE BOOK PUBLISHING INDUSTRY DEVELOPMENT
PROGRAM (BPIDP) AND THE CANADA COUNCIL FOR THE ARTS FOR OUR
PUBLISHING ACTIVITIES AND FOR SUPPORT OF THIS EDITION.

DISTRIBUTED IN THE U.S.A. by:
FARRAR, STRAUS and GIROUX
19 UNION SQUARE WEST
NEW YORK, NY 10003

Orders: 888.330.8477

DISTRIBUTED IN CANADA by:
RAINCOAST BOOKS
9050 SHAUGHNESSY STREET
VANCOUVER, BC V6P 6E5

Orders: 800.663.5714

PRINTED BY IMPRIMERIE TRANSCONTINENTAL IN LOUISEVILLE, QUEBEC,
OCTOBER 2007

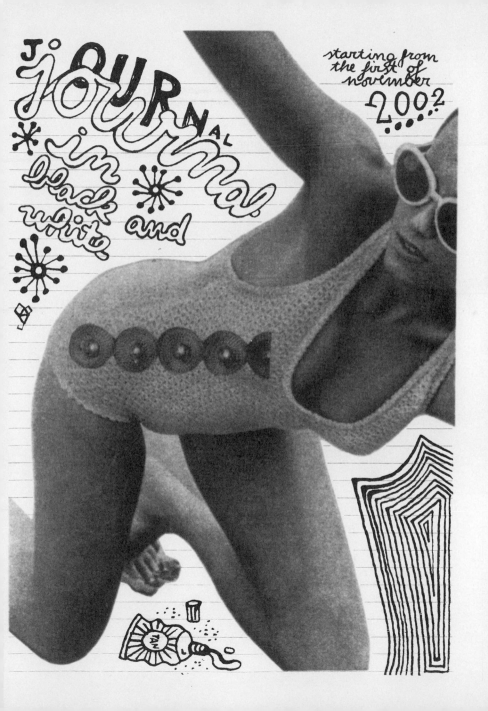

JOURNAL in black and white

starting from the first of november 2002

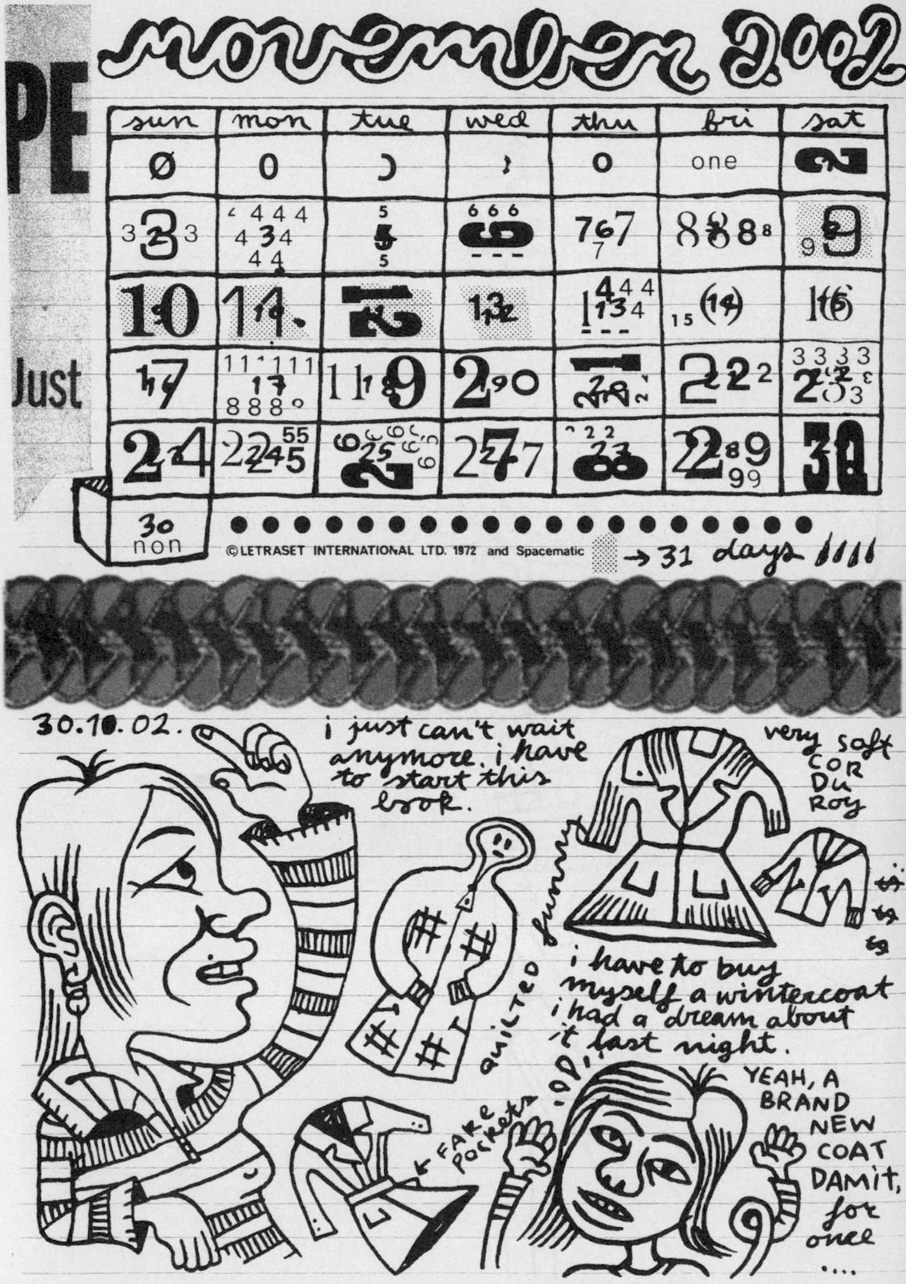
PE
Just
november 2002
sun mon tue wed thu fri sat
one
30 non
©LETRASET INTERNATIONAL LTD. 1972 and Spacematic
→ 31 days
30.10.02.
i just can't wait anymore. i have to start this book.
very soft COR DU ROY
funny
QUILTED
i have to buy myself a wintercoat
i had a dream about it last night.
FAKE pockets
YEAH, A BRAND NEW COAT DAMIT, for once ....

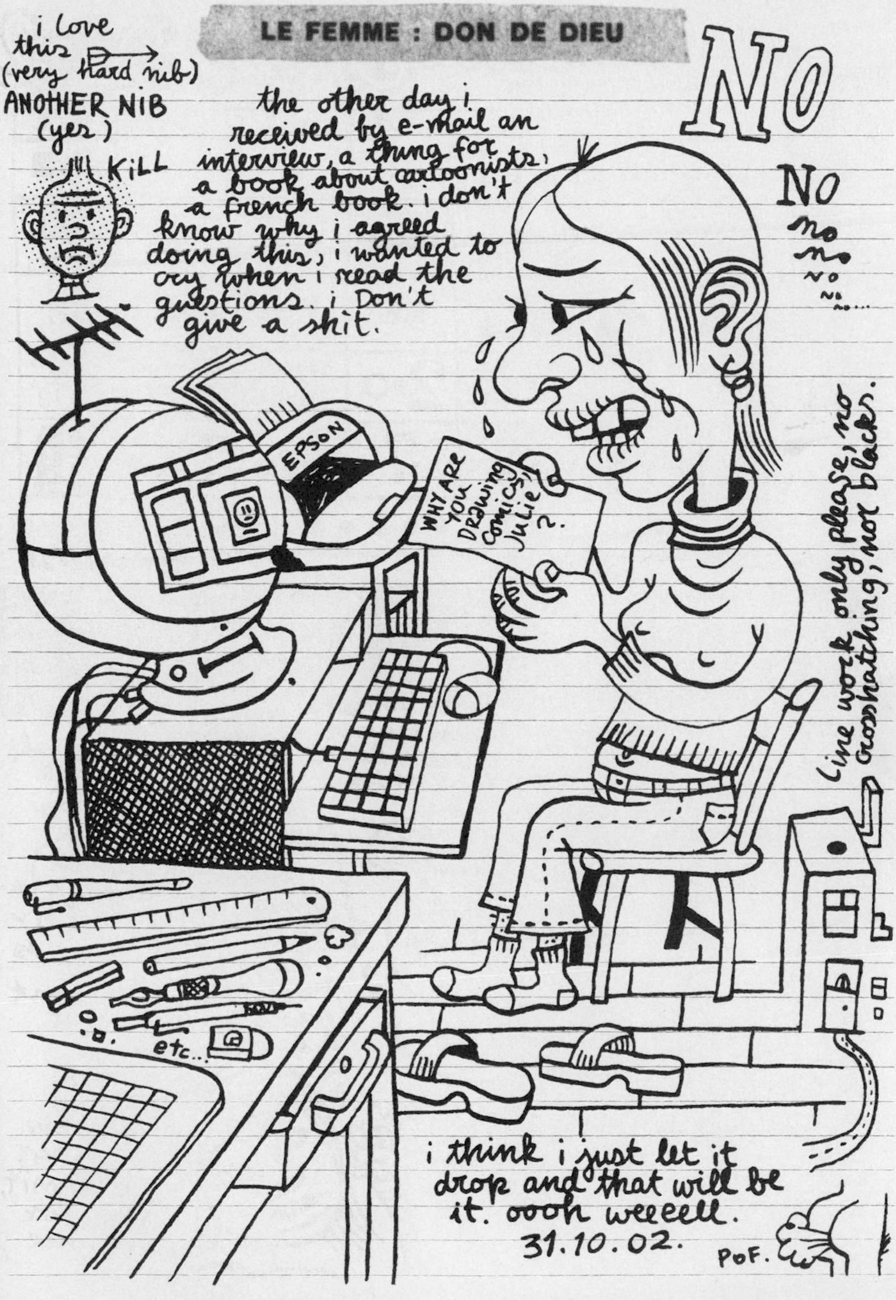

LE FEMME : DON DE DIEU
i love this (very hard nib)
ANOTHER NIB (yes)
KILL
the other day i received by e-mail an interview, a thing for a book about cartoonists, a french book. i don't know why i agreed doing this, i wanted to cry when i read the questions. i Don't give a shit.
NO
NO
no
no
no
no....
EPSON
WHY ARE YOU DRAWING COMICS, JULIE ?
line work only please, no crosshatching, not blacks.
etc...
i think i just let it drop and that will be it. oooh weeeell.
31.10.02.
PoF.

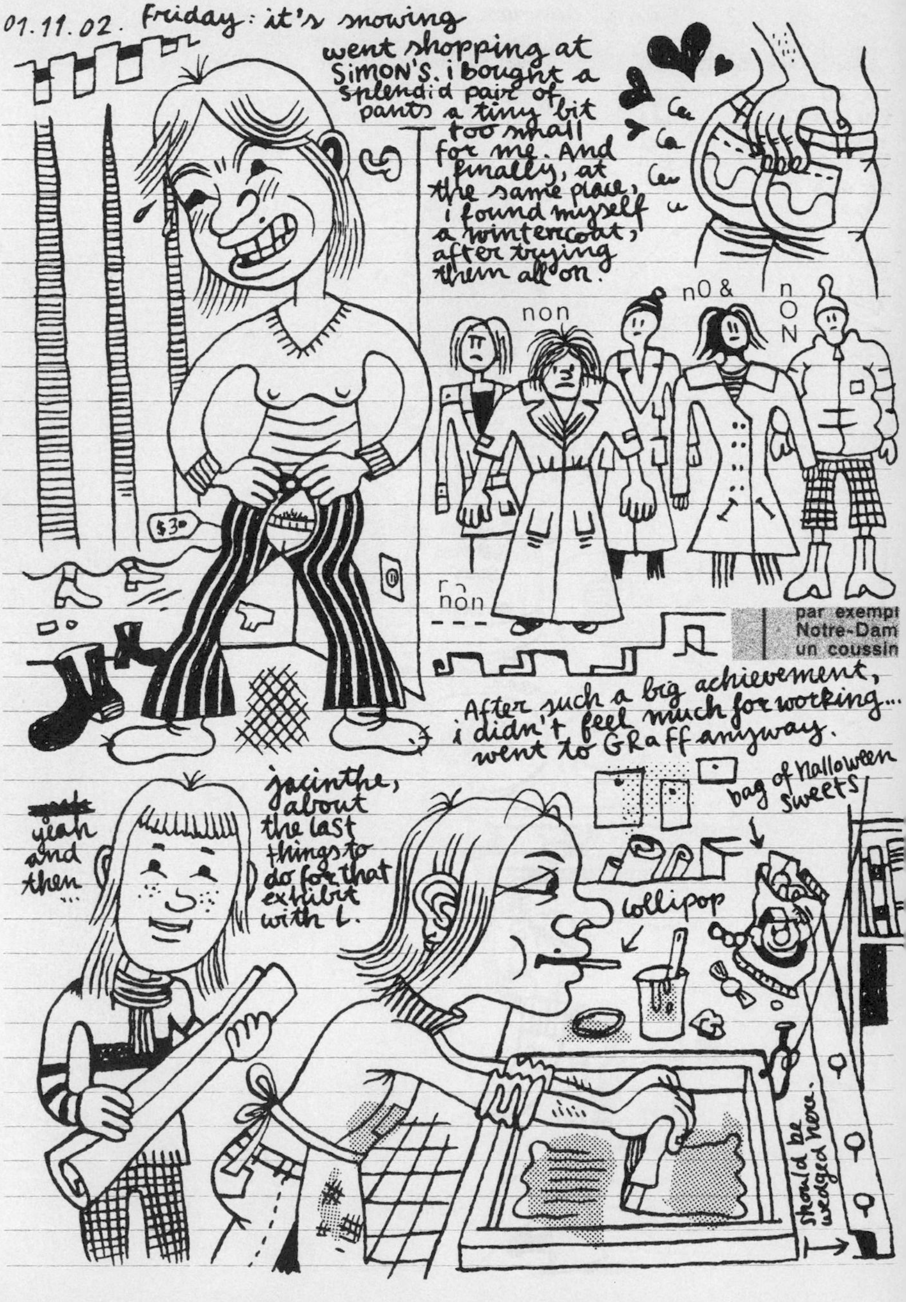
01.11.02. Friday: it's snowing
went shopping at SIMON'S. i bought a splendid pair of pants a tiny bit too small for me. And finally, at the same place, i found myself a wintercoat, after trying them all on.
Ca
Ca
Ca
u
$30
non
n0 &
n O N
non
par exempl
Notre-Dam
un coussin
After such a big achievement, i didn't feel much for working... went to GRaff anyway.
yeah and then ...
jacinthe, about the last things to do for that exhibit with L.
bag of Halloween sweets
lollipop
should be wedged here.

02.11.02. friday: dinner at home which starts late.

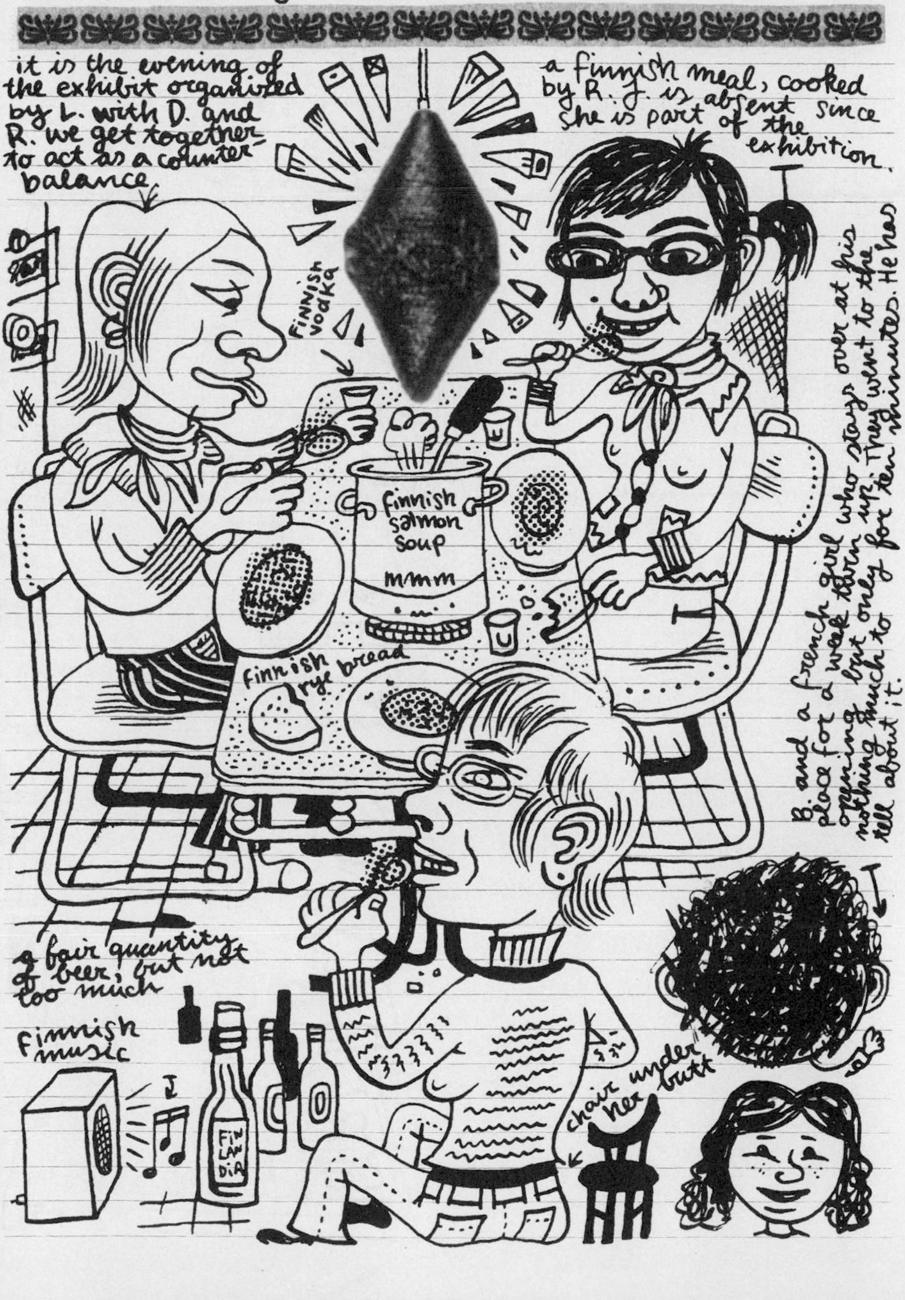
it is the evening of the exhibit organized by L. with D. and R. we get together to act as a counter balance
a finnish meal, cooked by R. J. is absent since she is part of the exhibition.
FINNISH VODKA
finnish salmon soup
mmmm
finnish rye bread
B. and a french girl who stays over at his
place for a week turn up. They went to the
opening but only for ten minutes. He has
nothing much to tell about it.
a fair quantity of beer, but not too much
finnish music
FIN LAN DIA
chair under her butt

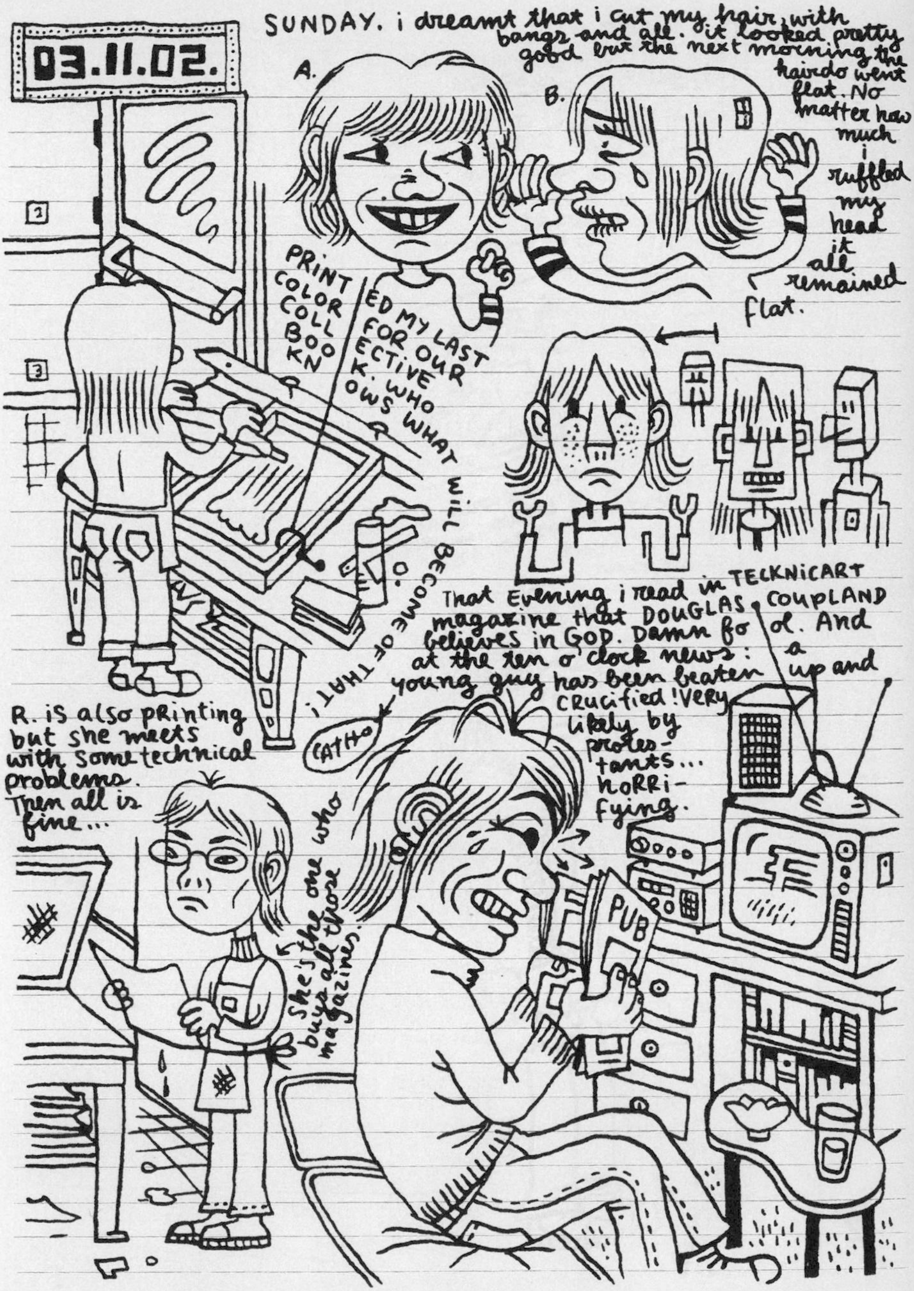
03.11.02.
SUNDAY. i dreamt that i cut my hair, with bangs and all. it looked pretty good but the next morning the hairdo went flat. No matter how much i ruffled my head it all remained flat.
A.
B.
PRINTED MY LAST COLOR FOR OUR COLLECTIVE BOOK. WHO KNOWS WHAT WILL BECOME OF THAT!
CATHO
That Evening i read in TECKNICART magazine that DOUGLAS COUPLAND believes in GOD. Damn fool. And at the ten o'clock news: a young guy has been beaten up and crucified! VERY likely by protestants... horrifying.
R. is also printing but she meets with some technical problems. Then all is fine...
She's the one who buys all those magazines.
PUB

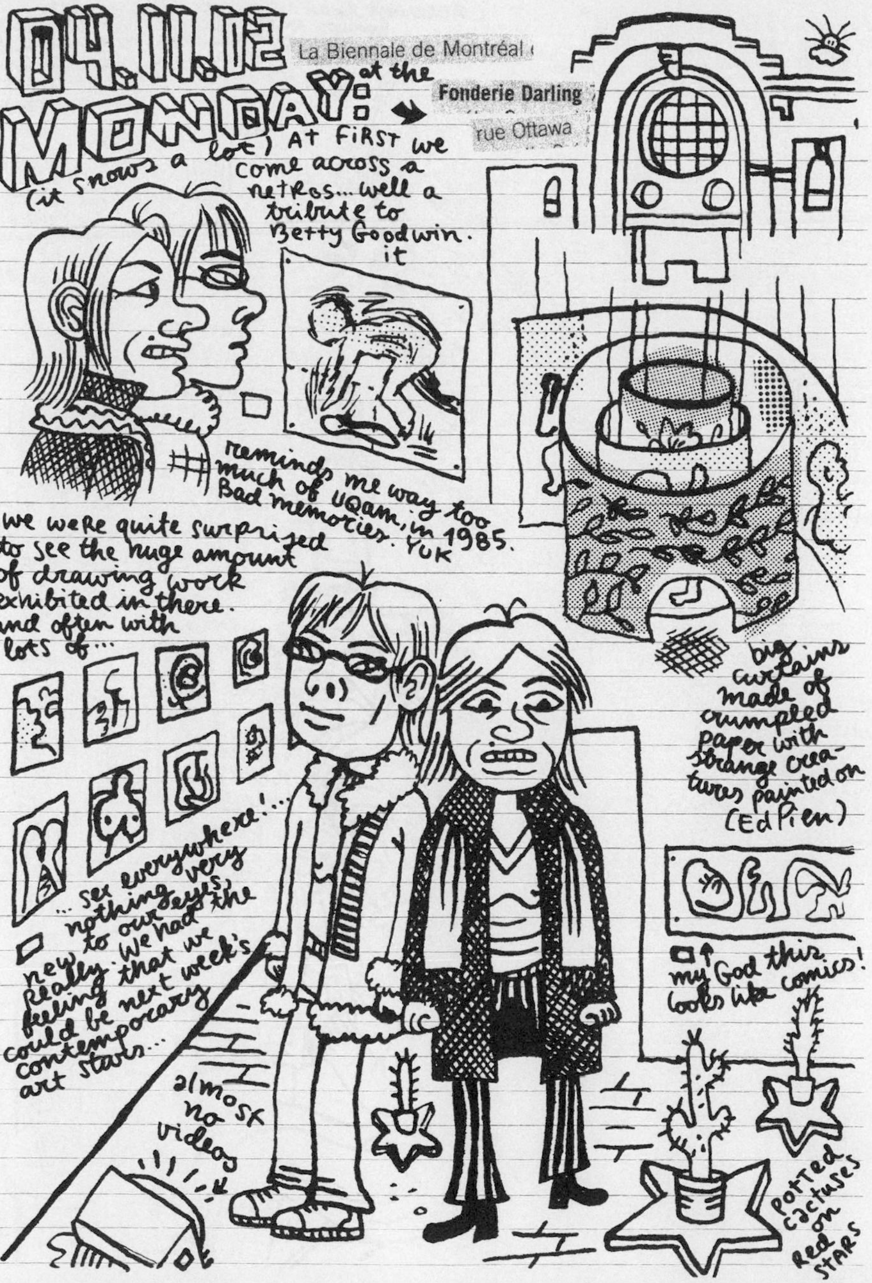

04.11.02
MONDAY:
La Biennale de Montréal
at the
Fonderie Darling
rue Ottawa
(it snows a lot) AT FIRST we come across a retros... well a tribute to Betty Goodwin. it
reminds me way too much of UQAM, in 1985. Bad memories. YUK
we were quite surprised to see the huge amount of drawing work exhibited in there. and often with lots of...
... sex everywhere!... nothing very new to our eyes, really. We had the feeling that we could be next week's contemporary art stars...
almost no videos
big curtains made of crumpled paper with strange creatures painted on (Ed Pien)
my God this looks like comics!
potted cactuses on red stars

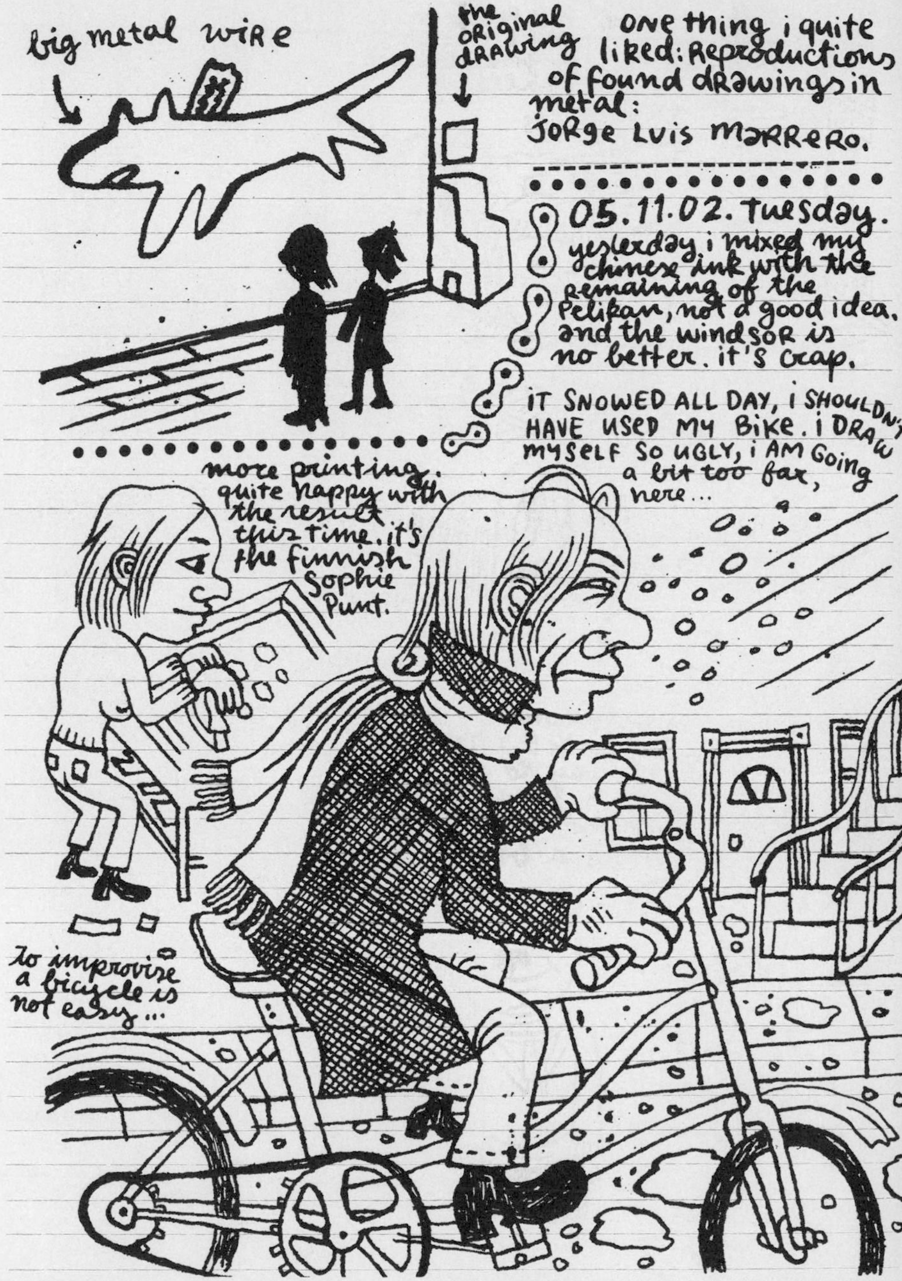

big metal wire
the original drawing
one thing i quite liked: Reproductions of found drawings in metal: Jorge Luis Marrero.
05.11.02. tuesday.
yesterday i mixed my chinese ink with the remaining of the Pelikan, not a good idea. and the windsor is no better. it's crap.
IT SNOWED ALL DAY, I SHOULDN'T HAVE USED MY BIKE. I DRAW MYSELF SO UGLY, I AM GOING a bit too far, here...
more printing. quite happy with the result this time. it's the finnish Sophie Punt.
to improvise a bicycle is not easy...

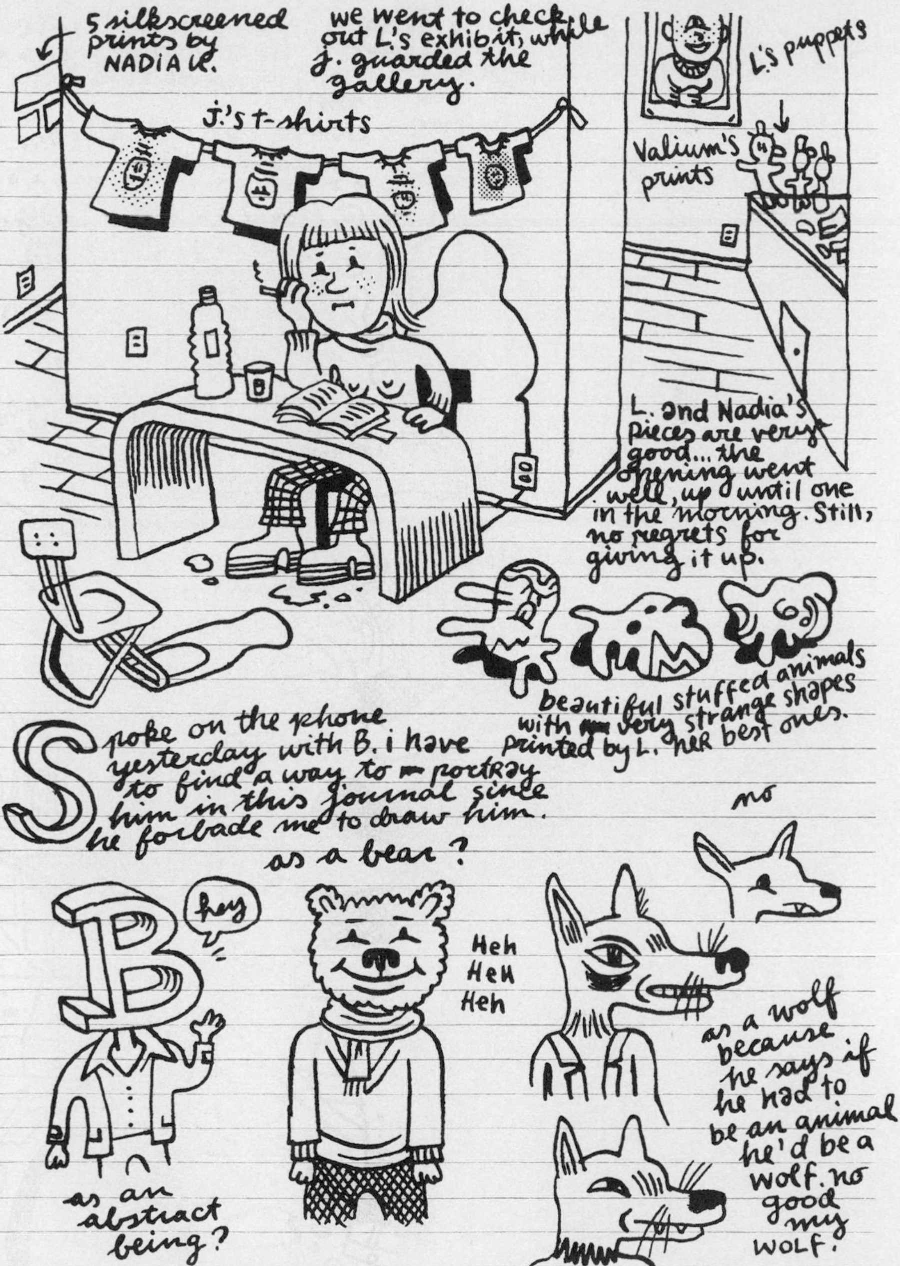
5 silkscreened prints by NADIA K.
we went to check out L.'s exhibit, while J. guarded the gallery.
L.'s puppets
J.'s t-shirts
Valium's prints
L. and Nadia's pieces are very good... the opening went well, up until one in the morning. Still, no regrets for giving it up.
beautiful stuffed animals with very strange shapes printed by L. her best ones.
Spoke on the phone yesterday with B. i have to find a way to portray him in this journal since he forbade me to draw him.
as a bear?
hey
as an abstract being?
Heh
Heh
Heh
no
as a wolf because he says if he had to be an animal he'd be a wolf. no good my WOLF.

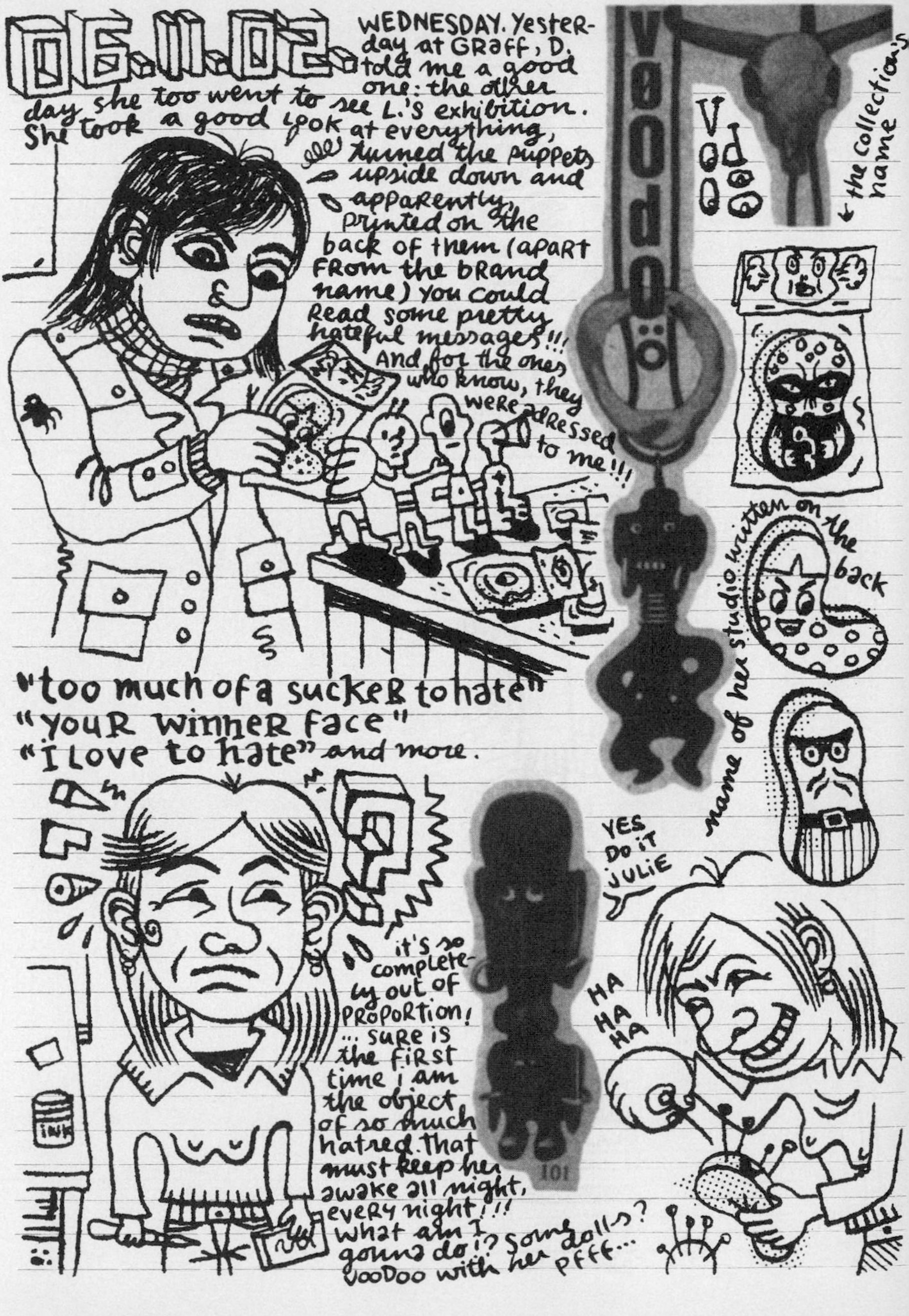
06.11.02.
WEDNESDAY. Yesterday at GRAFF, D. told me a good one: the other day she too went to see L.'s exhibition. She took a good look at everything, turned the puppets upside down and apparently, printed on the back of them (apart from the brand name) you could read some pretty hateful messages!!! And for the ones who know, they were dressed to me!!!
VOODOO
Voodoo
← the collection's name
name of her studio written on the back
"too much of a sucker to hate"
"your winner face"
"I love to hate" and more.
YES DO IT JULIE
it's so completely out of proportion! ... sure is the first time i am the object of so much hatred. That must keep her awake all night, every night!!! What am I gonna do!? Some voodoo with her dolls? pfff...
HA HA HA
INK
101

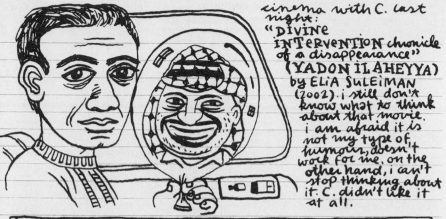

cinema with C. last night:
"DIVINE INTERVENTION chronicle of a disappearance"
(YADON ILAHEYYA)
by ELIA SULEIMAN
(2002). i still don't know what to think about that movie. i am afraid it is not my type of humour, doesn't work for me. on the other hand, i can't stop thinking about it. C. didn't like it at all.

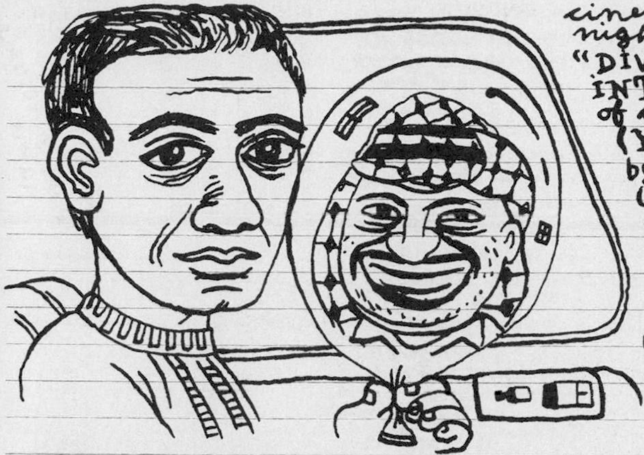

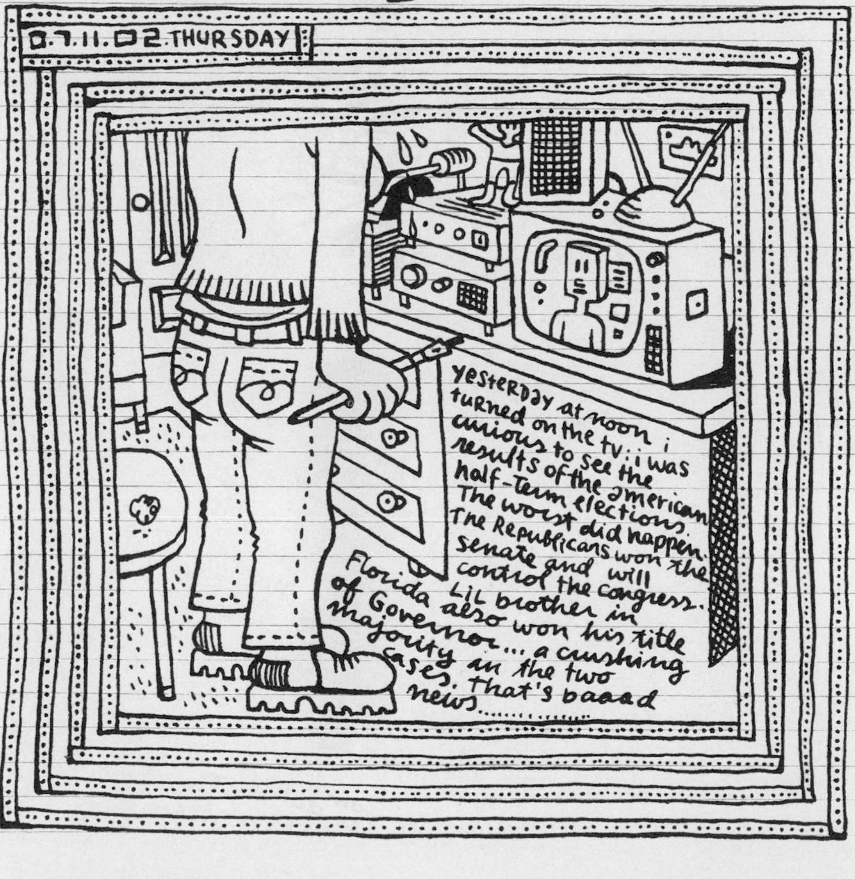
07.11.02 THURSDAY
yesterday at noon i turned on the tv. i was curious to see the results of the american half-term elections. The worst did happen. The Republicans won the senate and will control the congress. Lil brother in Florida also won his title of Governor... a crushing majority in the two cases. that's baaad news........

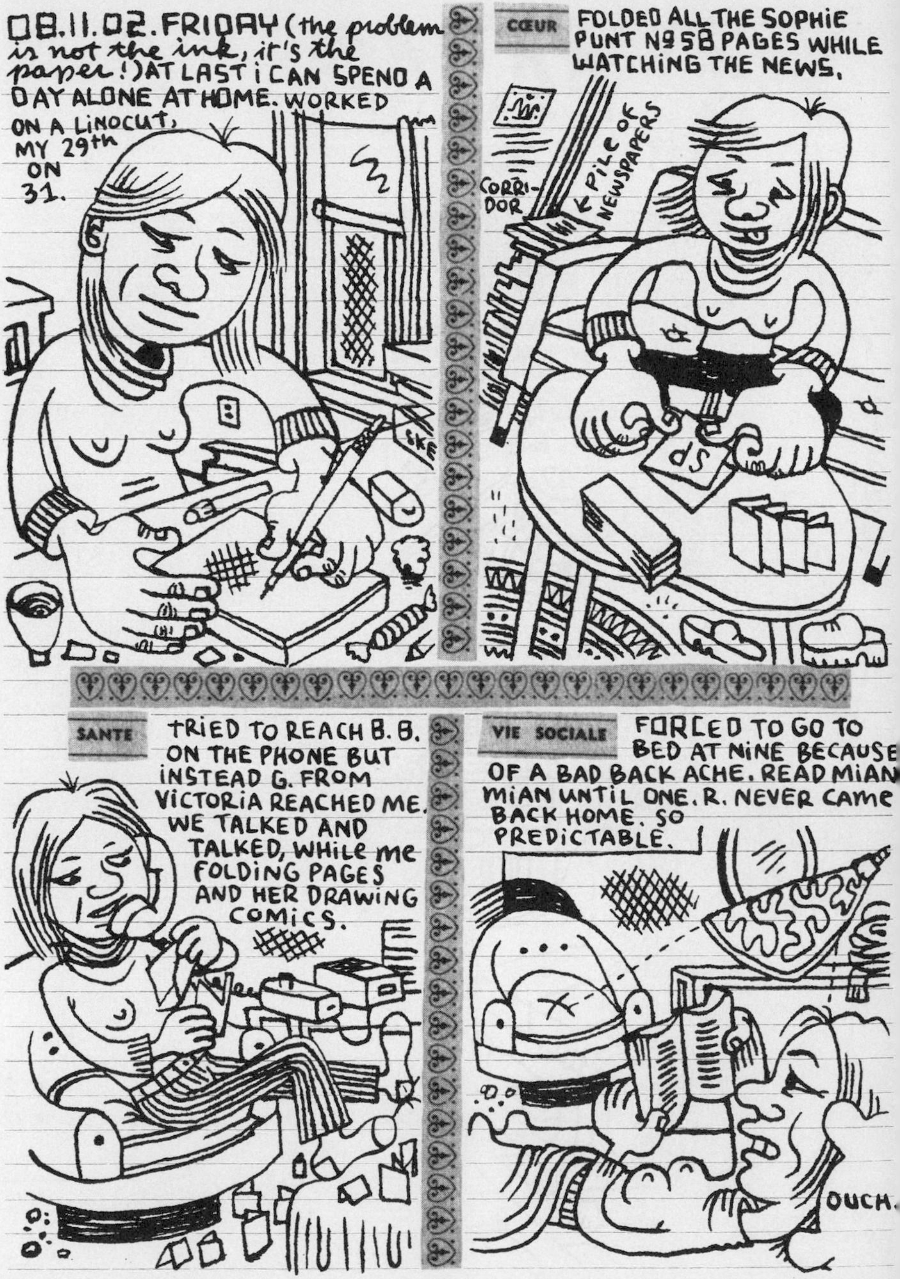
08.11.02. FRIDAY (the problem is not the ink, it's the paper!) AT LAST i CAN SPEND A DAY ALONE AT HOME. WORKED ON A LiNOCUT, MY 29th ON 31.
SKE
CŒUR
FOLDED ALL THE SOPHIE PUNT № 58 PAGES WHILE WATCHING THE NEWS.
CORRI-DOR
PiLE OF NEWSPAPERS
SP
SANTE
TRiED TO REACH B. B. ON THE PHONE BUT iNSTEAD G. FROM ViCTORiA REACHED ME. WE TALKED AND TALKED, WHiLE me FOLDiNG PAGES AND HER DRAWiNG COMiCS.
VIE SOCIALE
FORCED TO GO TO BED AT NiNE BECAUSE OF A BAD BACK ACHE. READ MiAN MiAN UNTiL ONE. R. NEVER CAME BACK HOME. SO PREDiCTABLE.
OUCH.

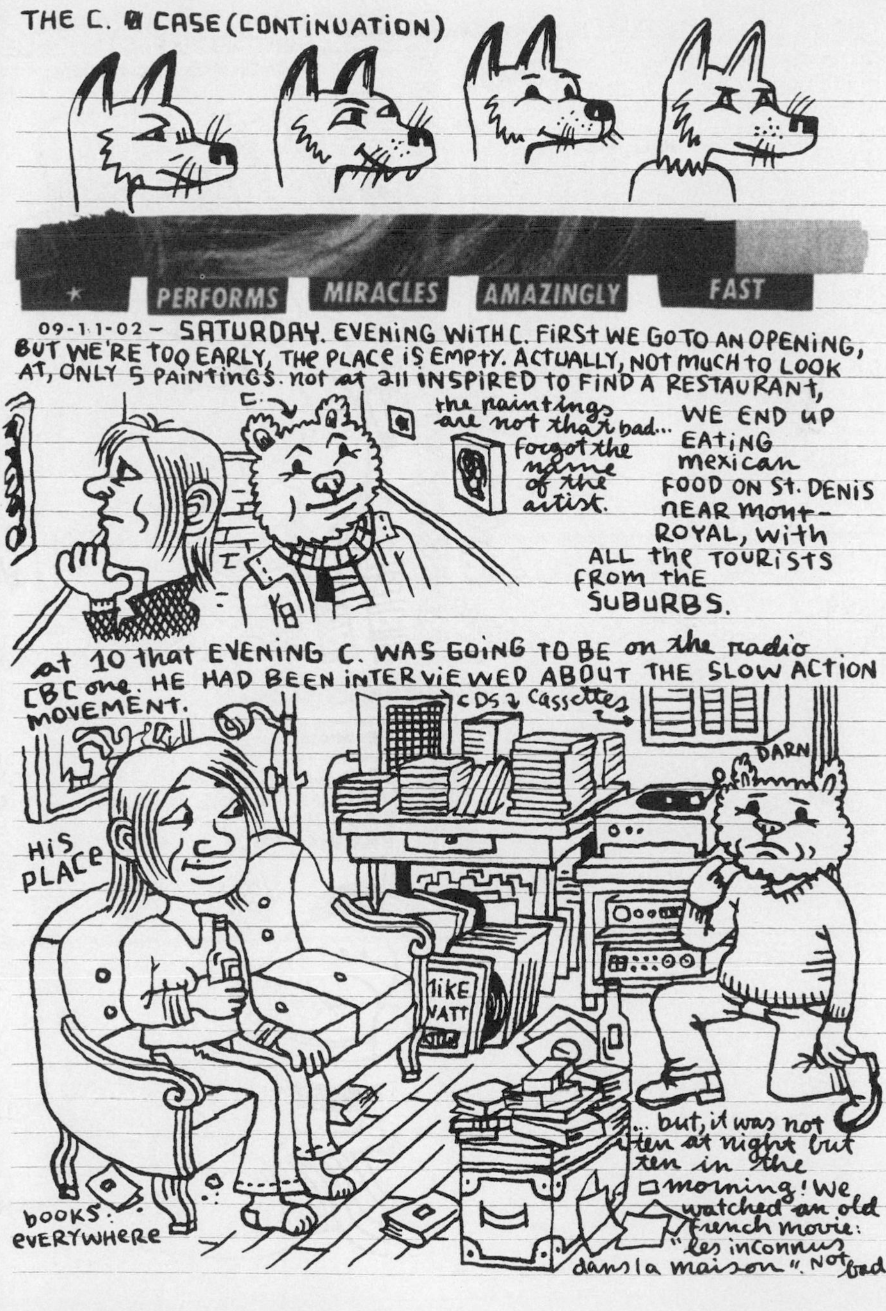
THE C. [redacted] CASE (CONTINUATION)
PERFORMS MIRACLES AMAZINGLY FAST
09-1.1-02 – SATURDAY. EVENING WITH C. FIRST WE GO TO AN OPENING, BUT WE'RE TOO EARLY, THE PLACE IS EMPTY. ACTUALLY, NOT MUCH TO LOOK AT, ONLY 5 PAINTINGS. not at all INSPIRED TO FIND A RESTAURANT,
C.
the paintings are not that bad... forgot the name of the artist.
WE END UP EATING mexican FOOD ON ST. DENIS NEAR MONT-ROYAL, with ALL the TOURISTS FROM THE SUBURBS.
at 10 that EVENING C. WAS GOING TO BE on the radio CBC one. HE HAD BEEN INTERVIEWED ABOUT THE SLOW ACTION MOVEMENT.
CDS
cassettes
DARN
HIS PLACE
MIKE WATT
books: EVERYWHERE
... but, it was not ten at night but ten in the morning! We watched an old french movie: "les inconnus dans la maison". Not bad.

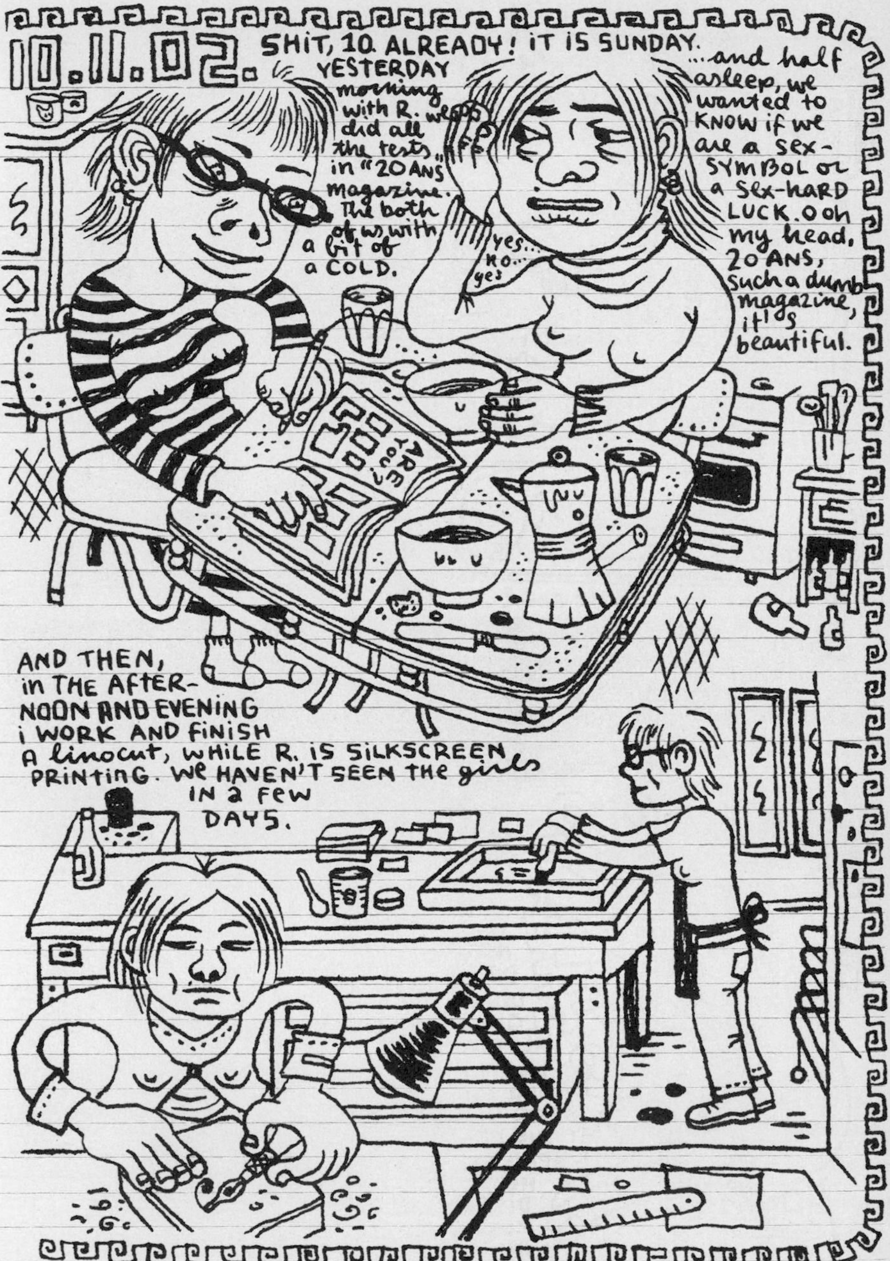
10.11.02.
SHIT, 10 ALREADY! IT IS SUNDAY.
YESTERDAY morning with R. we did all the tests in "20 ANS" magazine. The both of us with a bit of a COLD.
...and half asleep, we wanted to KNOW if we are a SEX-SYMBOL or a SEX-HARD LUCK. Ooh my head, 20 ANS, such a dumb magazine, it's beautiful.
yes... no... yes
ARE YOU?
AND THEN, in THE AFTER-NOON AND EVENING i WORK AND FINISH A linocut, WHILE R. IS SILKSCREEN PRINTING. WE HAVEN'T SEEN THE girls IN A FEW DAYS.

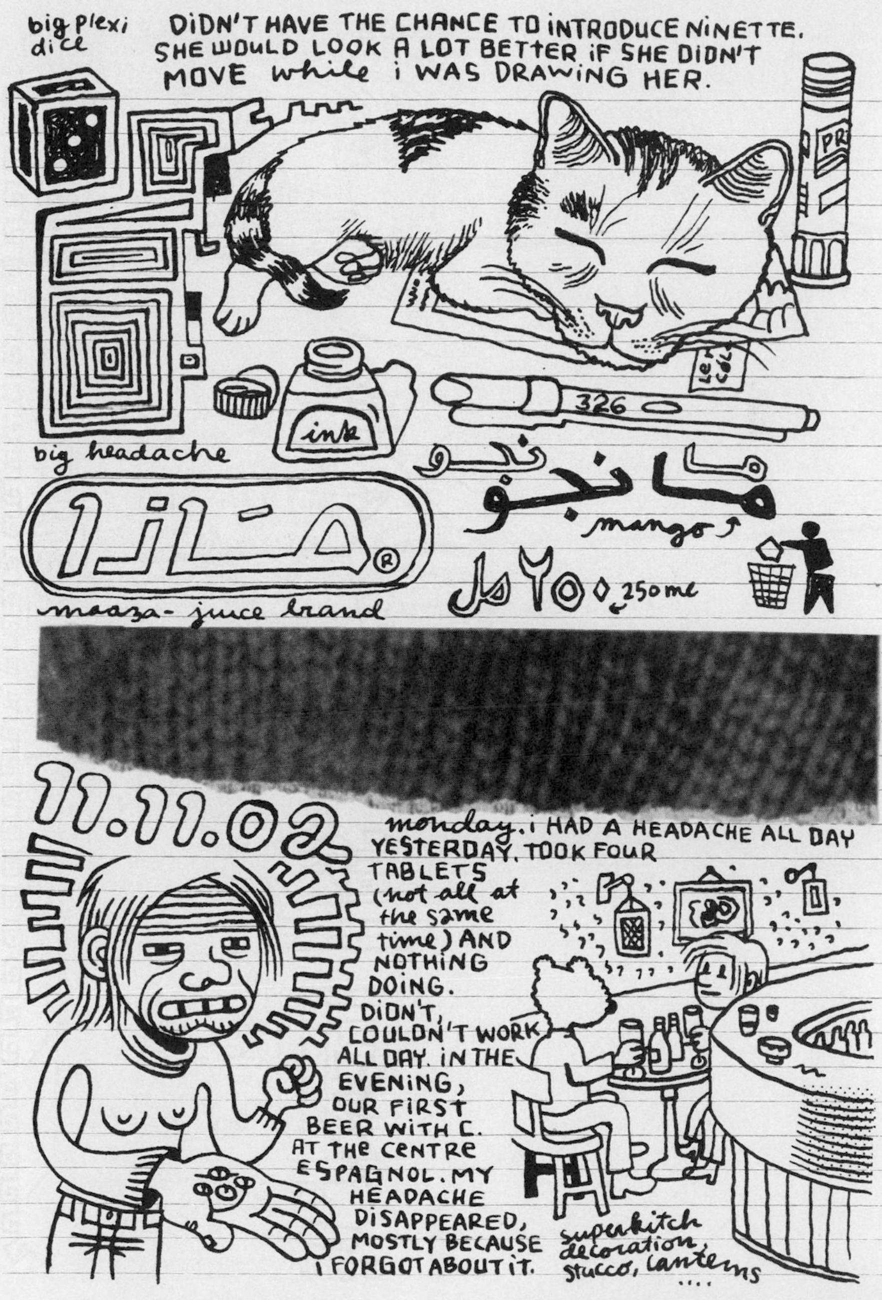
big plexi dice
DIDN'T HAVE THE CHANCE TO INTRODUCE NINETTE. SHE WOULD LOOK A LOT BETTER IF SHE DIDN'T MOVE while I WAS DRAWING HER.
ink
326
big headache
مانجو
mango
٢٥٠ مل
250 ml
maaza- juice brand
11.11.02
monday. I HAD A HEADACHE ALL DAY YESTERDAY. TOOK FOUR TABLETS (not all at the same time) AND NOTHING DOING. DIDN'T, COULDN'T WORK ALL DAY. IN THE EVENING, OUR FIRST BEER WITH C. AT THE CENTRE ESPAGNOL. MY HEADACHE DISAPPEARED, MOSTLY BECAUSE I FORGOT ABOUT IT.
superkitch decoration, stucco, lanterns ....

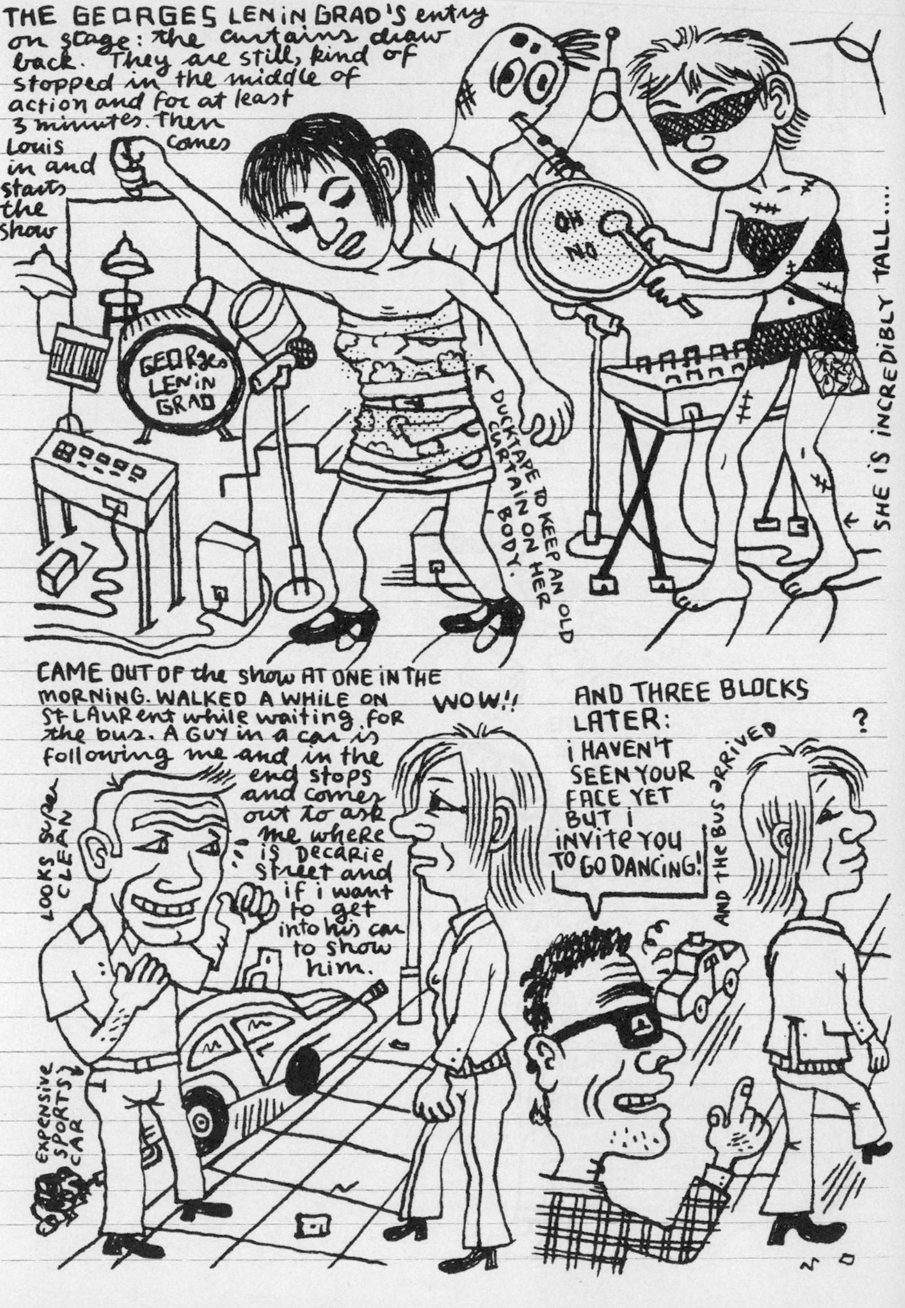
THE GEORGES LENINGRAD'S entry on stage: the curtains draw back. They are still, kind of stopped in the middle of action and for at least 3 minutes. Then Louis comes in and starts the show
GEORGES LENINGRAD
OH NO
DUCKTAPE TO KEEP AN OLD CURTAIN ON HER BODY.
SHE IS INCREDIBLY TALL....
CAME OUT OF the show AT ONE IN THE MORNING. WALKED A WHILE ON St LAURent while waiting for the bus. A GUY in a car is following me and in the end stops and comes out to ask me where is Decarie street and if i want to get into his car to show him.
WOW!!
LOOKS super CLEAN
EXPENSIVE SPORTS CAR
AND THREE BLOCKS LATER:
i HAVEN'T SEEN YOUR FACE YET BUT i INVITE YOU TO GO DANCING!
AND THE BUS ARRIVED
?

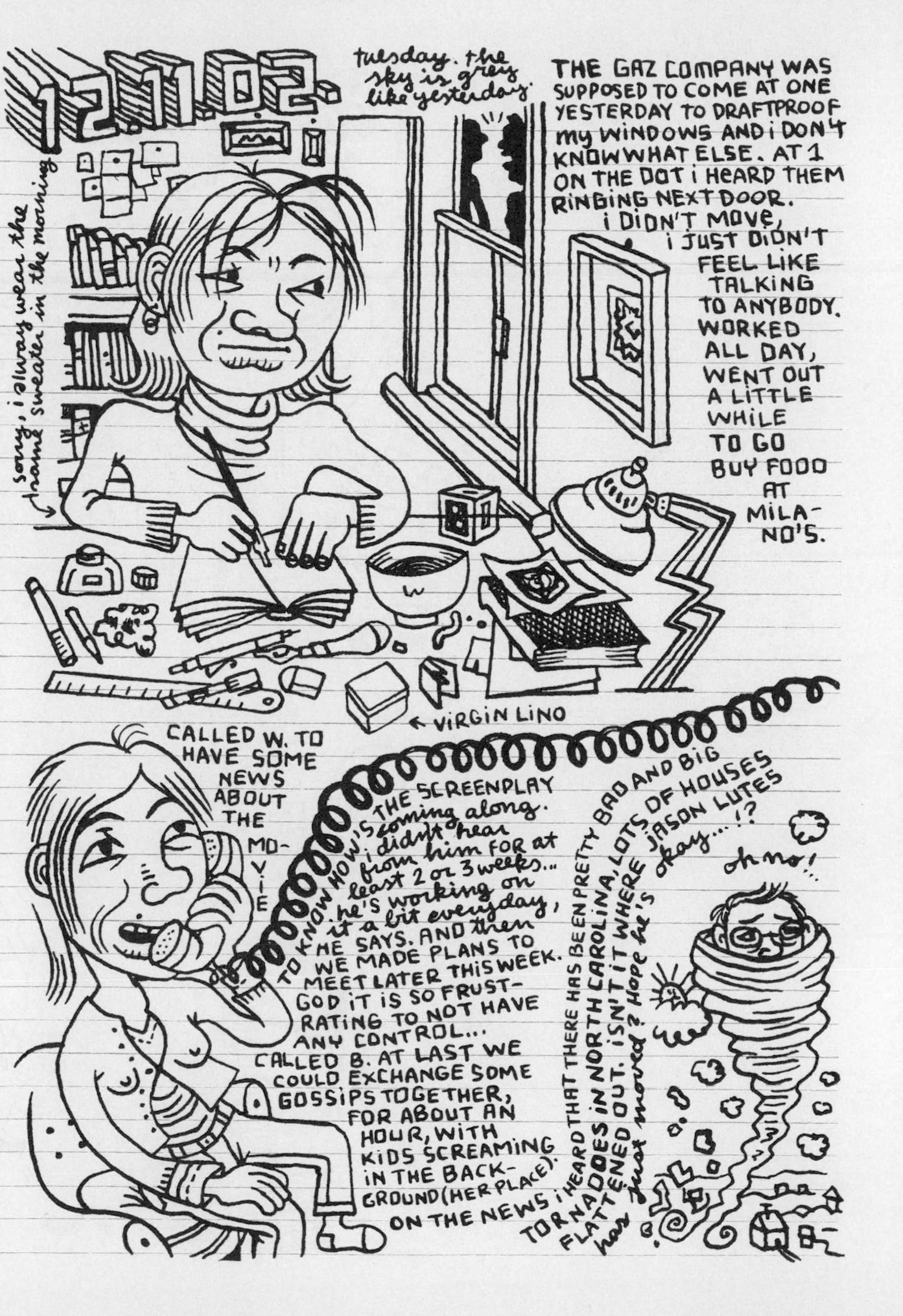
12.11.02.
tuesday. the sky is grey like yesterday.
THE GAZ COMPANY WAS SUPPOSED TO COME AT ONE YESTERDAY TO DRAFTPROOF my WINDOWS AND i DON'T KNOW WHAT ELSE. AT 1 ON THE DOT i HEARD THEM RINGING NEXT DOOR. i DIDN'T MOVE, i JUST DIDN'T FEEL LIKE TALKING TO ANYBODY. WORKED ALL DAY, WENT OUT A LITTLE WHILE TO GO BUY FOOD AT MILANO'S.
sorry, i always wear the same sweater in the morning
VIRGIN LINO
CALLED W. TO HAVE SOME NEWS ABOUT THE MOVIE
TO KNOW HOW'S THE SCREENPLAY coming along. i didn't hear from him FOR at least 2 or 3 weeks... he's working on it a bit everyday, HE SAYS. AND then WE MADE PLANS TO MEET LATER THIS WEEK. GOD iT IS SO FRUSTRATING TO NOT HAVE ANY CONTROL...
CALLED B. AT LAST WE COULD EXCHANGE SOME GOSSIPS TOGETHER, FOR ABOUT AN HOUR, WITH KIDS SCREAMING IN THE BACKGROUND (HER PLACE).
ON THE NEWS i HEARD THAT THERE HAS BEEN PRETTY BAD AND BIG TORNADOES IN NORTH CAROLINA, LOTS OF HOUSES FLATTENED OUT. iSN'T IT WHERE JASON LUTES has just moved? Hope he's okay...!?
oh no!

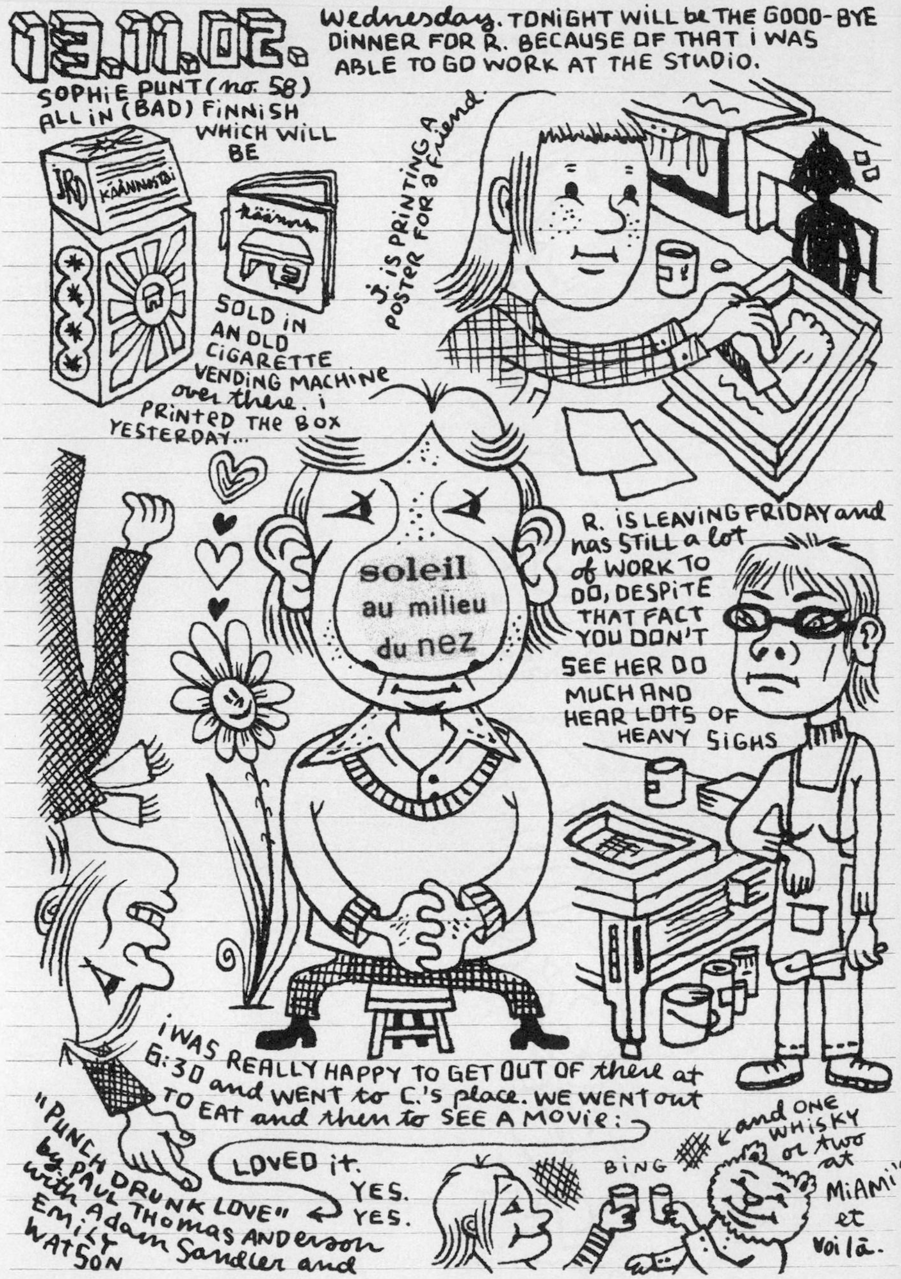
13.11.02.
Wednesday. TONIGHT WILL be THE GOOD-BYE DINNER FOR R. BECAUSE OF THAT i WAS ABLE TO GO WORK AT THE STUDiO.
SOPHiE PUNT (no. 58) ALL iN (BAD) FiNNiSH WHiCH WiLL BE
KÄÄNNöSTä
SOLD iN AN OLD CiGARETTE VENDiNG MACHiNE over there. i PRiNTED THE BOX YESTERDAY...
J. iS PRiNTiNG A POSTER FOR a friend.
soleil au milieu du nez
R. iS LEAViNG FRiDAY and has STiLL a lot of WORK TO DO, DESPiTE THAT FACT YOU DON'T SEE HER DO MUCH AND HEAR LOTS OF HEAVY SiGHS
i WAS REALLY HAPPY TO GET OUT OF there at 6:30 and WENT to C.'s place. WE WENT out TO EAT and then to SEE A MOViE:
"PUNCH DRUNK LOVE" by PAUL THOMAS ANDerson with Adam Sandler and EmiLY WATSON
LOVED it. YES. YES.
BING
and ONE WHiSKY or two at MiAMi'S et voilà.

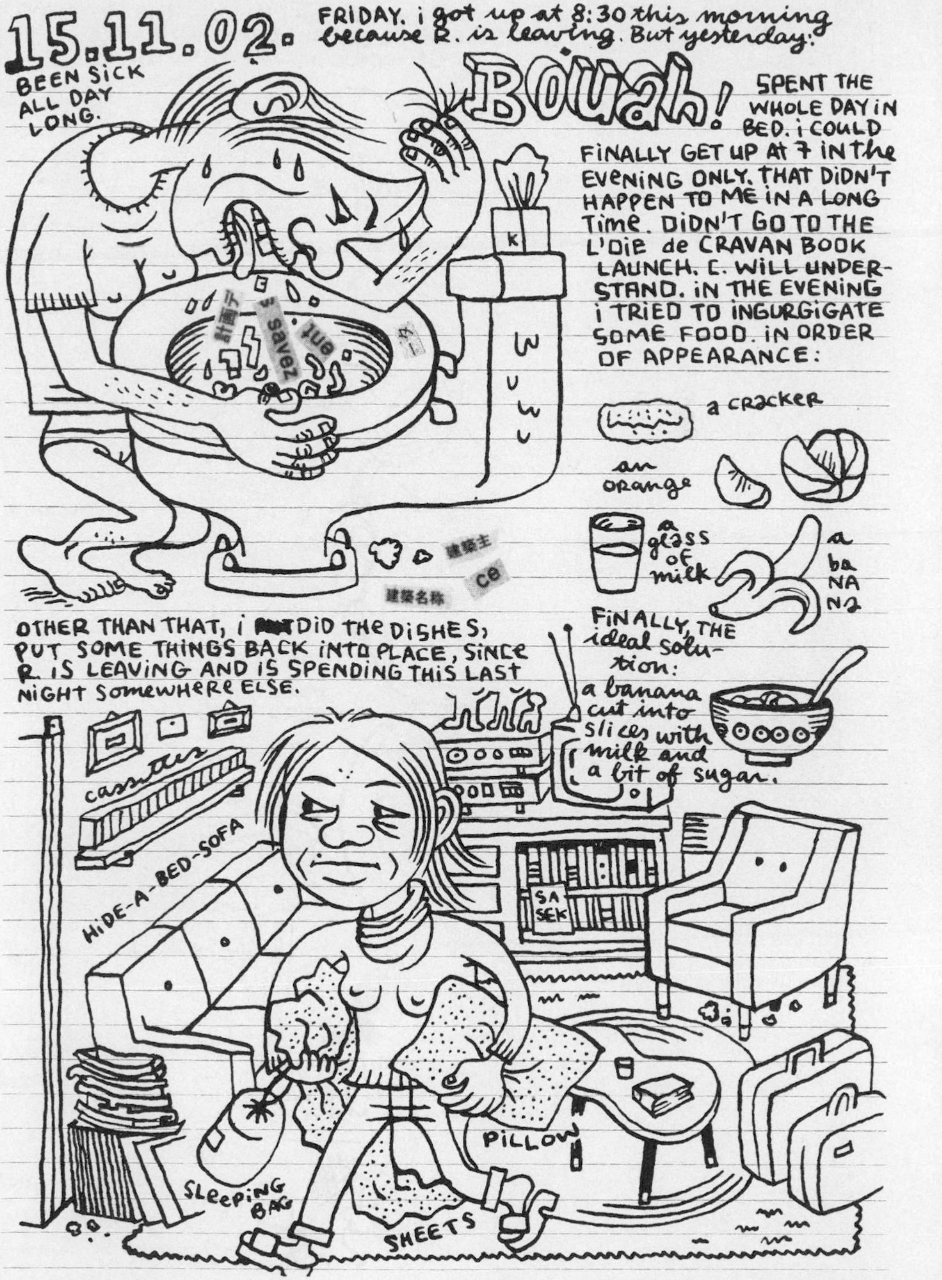
15.11.02.
FRIDAY. i got up at 8:30 this morning because R. is leaving. But yesterday:
BEEN SICK ALL DAY LONG.
Bouah!
SPENT THE WHOLE DAY iN BED. i COULD FiNALLY GET UP AT 7 iN the EVENiNG ONLY. THAT DiDN'T HAPPEN TO ME iN A LONG Time. DiDN'T GO TO THE L'OIE de CRAVAN BOOK LAUNCH. C. WiLL UNDERSTAND. iN THE EVENiNG i TRiED TO iNGURGiGATE SOME FOOD. iN ORDER OF APPEARANCE:
a cracker
an orange
a glass of milk
a banana
FiNALLY, THE ideal solution: a banana cut into slices with milk and a bit of sugar.
OTHER THAN THAT, i [redacted] DID THE DiSHES, PUT SOME THiNGS BACK iNTO PLACE, SiNCE R. iS LEAViNG AND iS SPENDiNG THiS LAST NiGHT SomewHERE ELSE.
cassettes
HiDE-A-BED-SOFA
SA SEK
PiLLOW
SLEEPiNG BAG
SHEETS

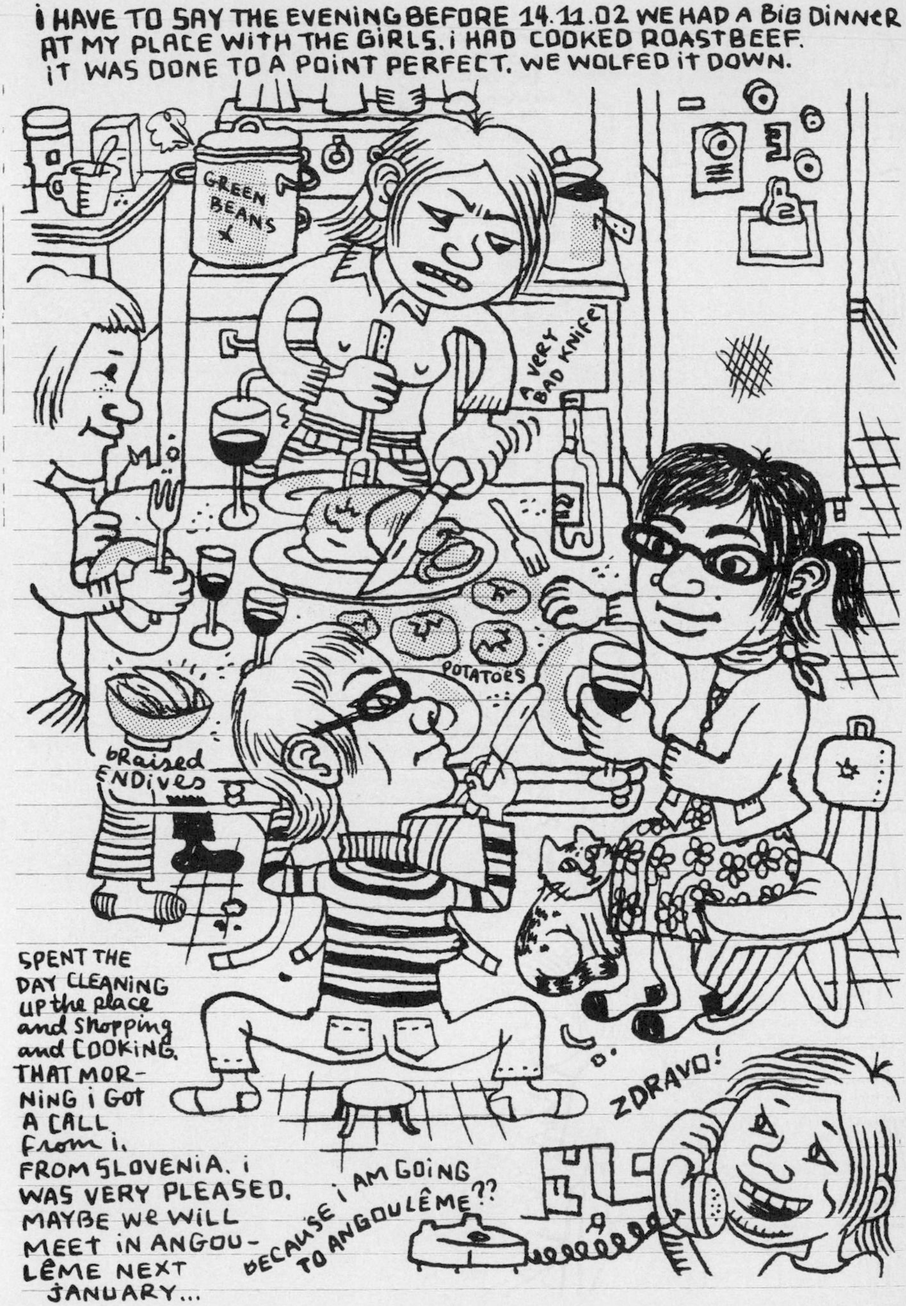
i HAVE TO SAY THE EVENING BEFORE 14.11.02 WE HAD A BiG DiNNER AT MY PLACE WITH THE GiRLS. i HAD COOKED ROASTBEEF. iT WAS DONE TO A POINT PERFECT. WE WOLFED iT DOWN.
GREEN BEANS
A VERY BAD KNIFE
POTATOES
bRaised ENDives
SPENT THE DAY CLEANiNG up the place and shopping and COOKiNG. THAT MORNiNG i GOT A CALL from i. FROM SLOVENiA. i WAS VERY PLEASED. MAYBE WE WiLL MEET iN ANGOULÊME NEXT JANUARY...
ZDRAVO!
BECAUSE i AM GOiNG TO ANGOULÊME??

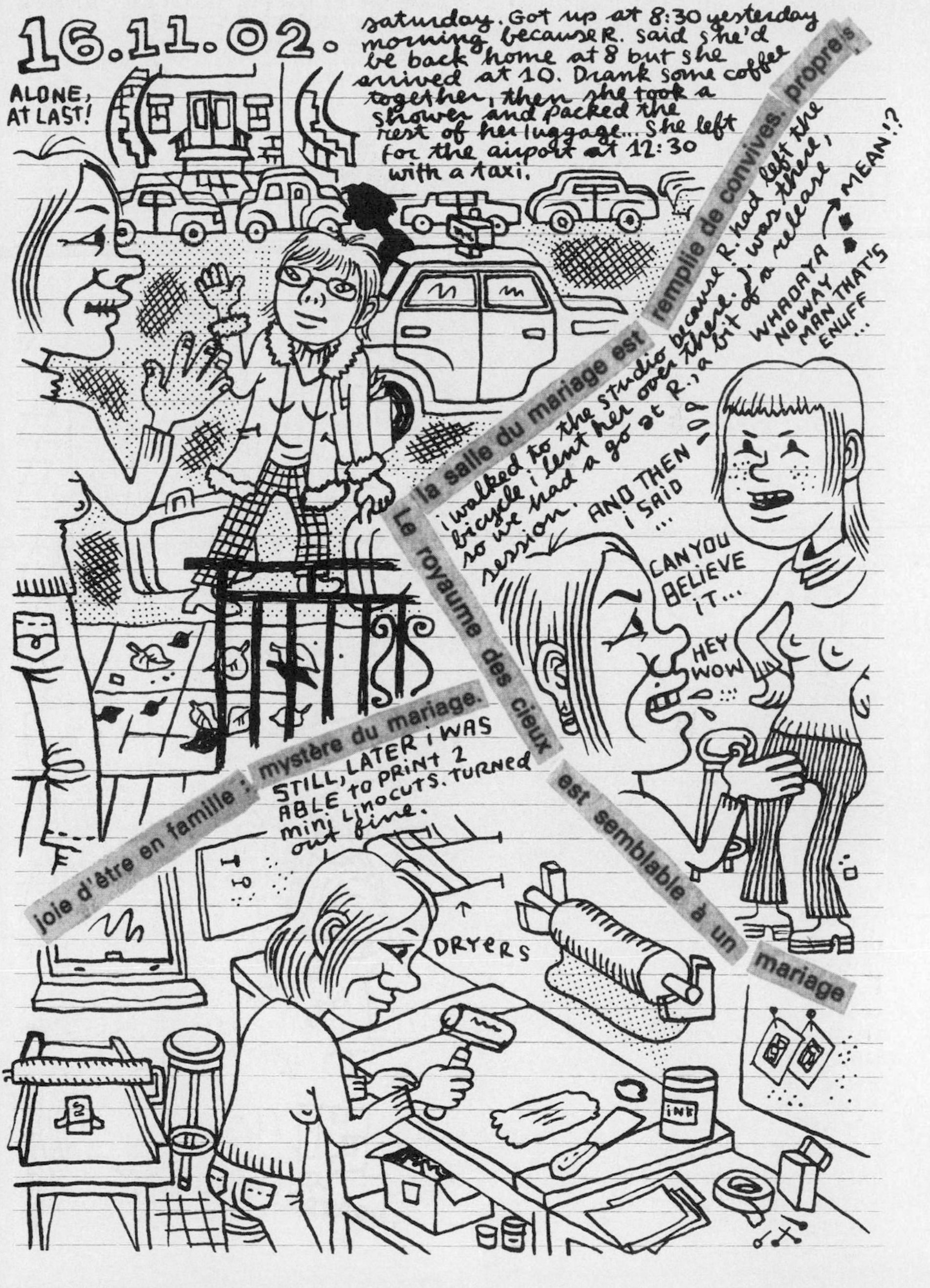
16.11.02.
saturday. Got up at 8:30 yesterday morning because R. said she'd be back home at 8 but she arrived at 10. Drank some coffee together, then she took a shower and packed the rest of her luggage... She left for the airport at 12:30 with a taxi.
ALONE, AT LAST!
la salle du mariage est remplie de convives. propres,
i walked to the studio because R. had left the bicycle i lent her over there. J. was there, so we had a go at R., a bit of a release session.
WHADAYA MEAN!?
NO WAY MAN THAT'S ENUFF...
AND THEN i SAID...
CAN YOU BELIEVE iT...
HEY WOW
Le royaume des cieux est semblable à un mariage
joie d'être en famille : mystère du mariage.
STILL, LATER i WAS ABLE TO PRINT 2 mini Linocuts. TURNED out fine.
DRYERS
iNK

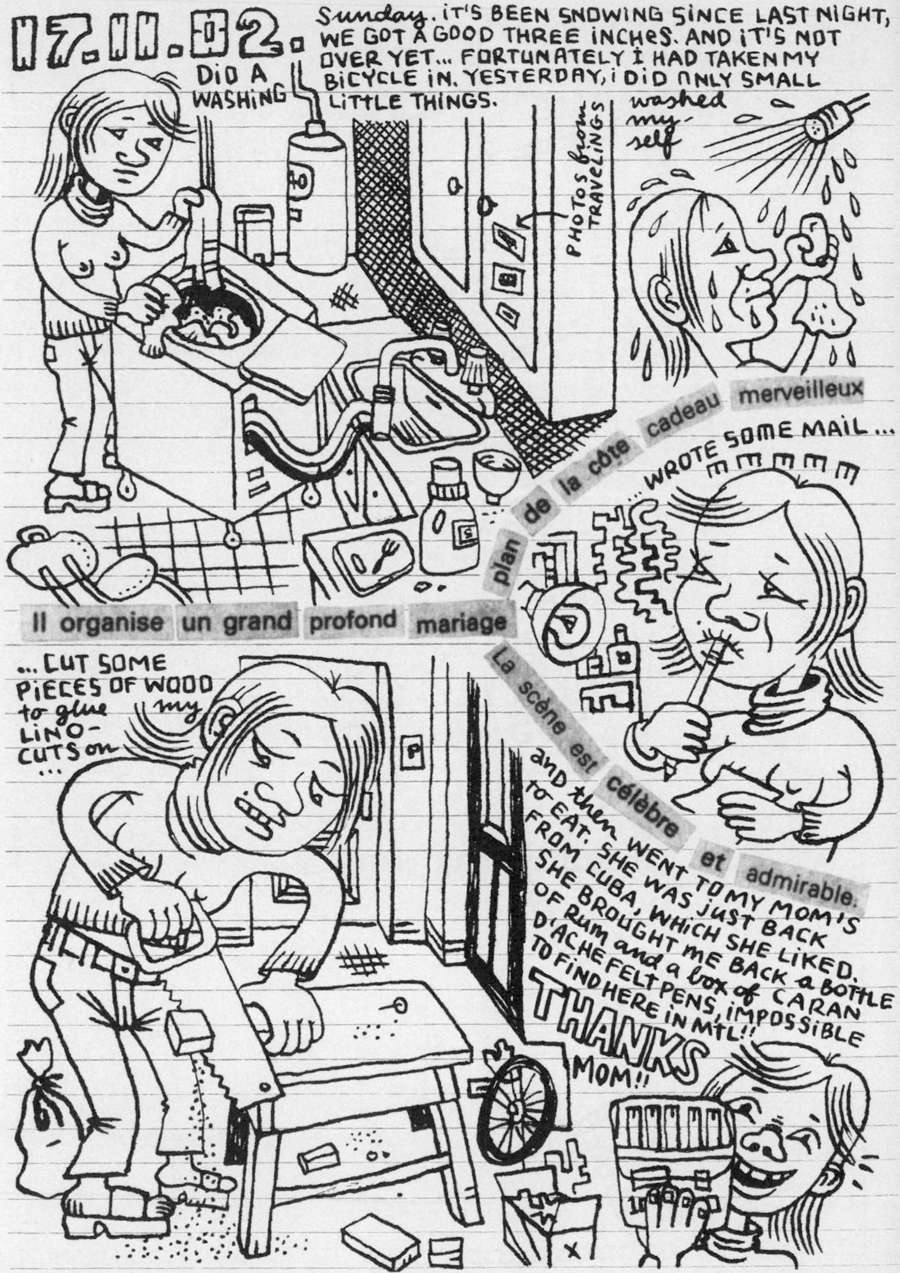
17.11.02.
Sunday. IT'S BEEN SNOWING SINCE LAST NIGHT, WE GOT A GOOD THREE INCHES. AND IT'S NOT OVER YET... FORTUNATELY I HAD TAKEN MY BICYCLE IN. YESTERDAY, I DID ONLY SMALL LITTLE THINGS.
DID A WASHING
PHOTOS from TRAVELINGS
washed my-self
merveilleux cadeau de la côte
...WROTE SOME MAIL...
MMMMMM
Il organise un grand profond mariage plan de la côte cadeau merveilleux
...CUT SOME PIECES OF WOOD to glue my LINO-CUTS on ...
La scène est célèbre et admirable.
and then WENT TO MY MOM'S TO EAT. SHE WAS JUST BACK FROM CUBA, WHICH SHE LIKED. SHE BROUGHT ME BACK a BOTTLE OF Rum and a box of CARAN D'ACHE FELT PENS, IMPOSSIBLE TO FIND HERE IN MTL!!
THANKS MOM!!

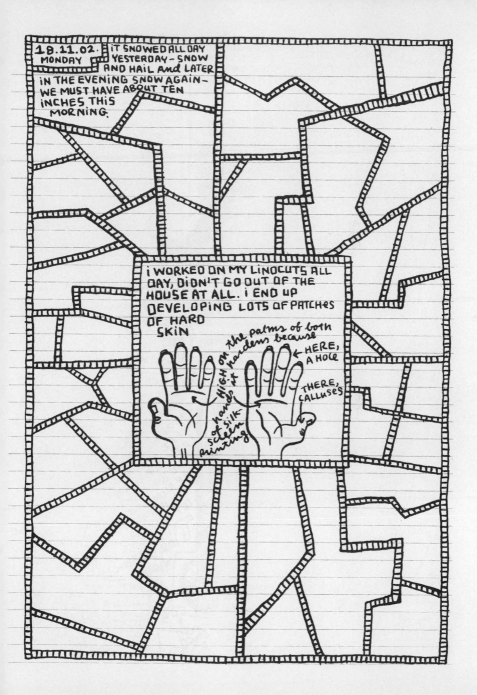

18.11.02.
MONDAY
iT SNOWED ALL DAY YESTERDAY - SNOW AND HAIL and LATER IN THE EVENING SNOW AGAIN - WE MUST HAVE ABOUT TEN INCHES THIS MORNING.

i WORKED ON MY LINOCUTS ALL DAY, DIDN'T GO OUT OF THE HOUSE AT ALL. i END UP DEVELOPING LOTS OF PATCHES OF HARD SKIN

HIGH on the palms of both hands - it hardens because of silk-screen printing

← HERE, A HOLE

THERE, CALLUSES

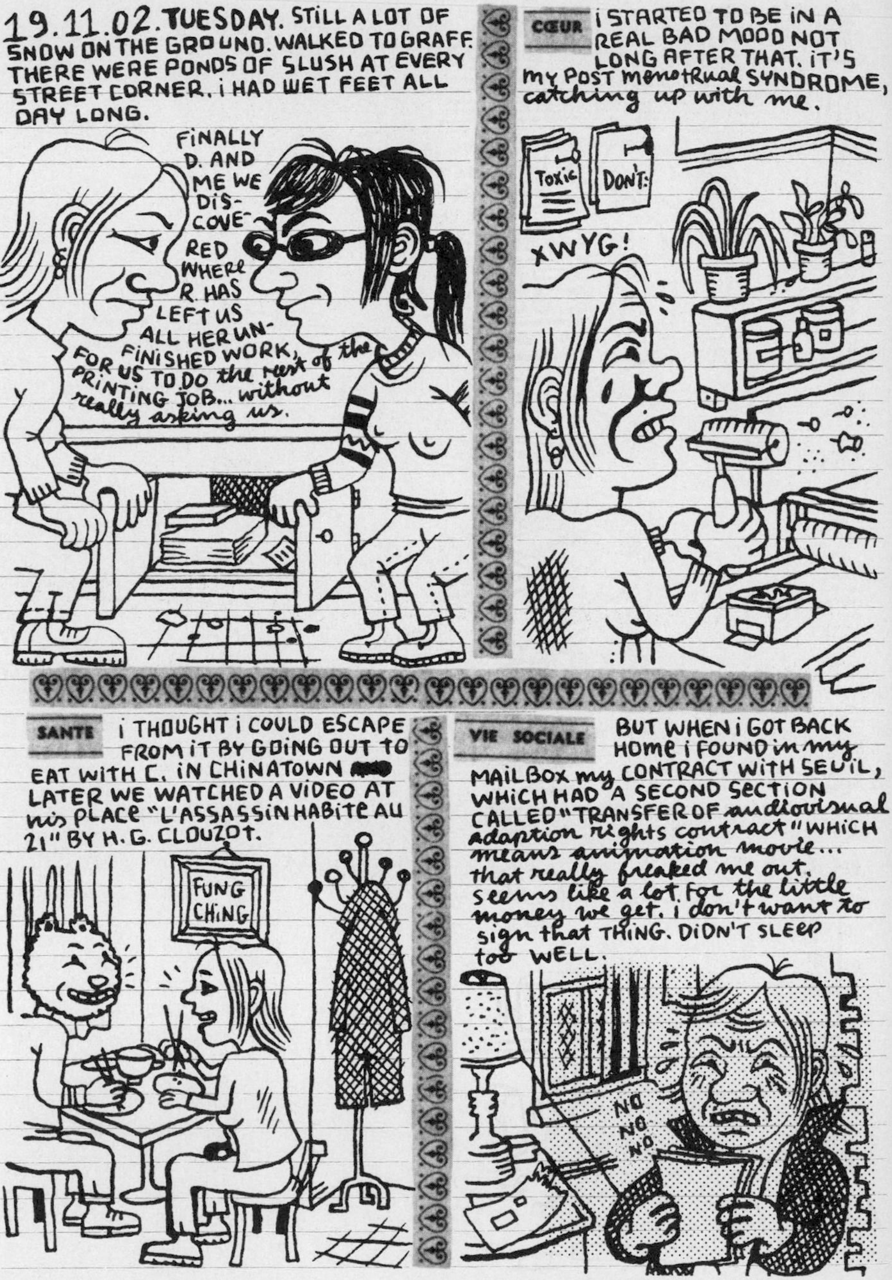

19.11.02. TUESDAY. STILL A LOT OF SNOW ON THE GROUND. WALKED TO GRAFF. THERE WERE PONDS OF SLUSH AT EVERY STREET CORNER. i HAD WET FEET ALL DAY LONG.
FiNALLY D. AND ME WE DiS-COVE-RED WHERE R. HAS LEFT US ALL HER UN-FiNISHED WORK, FOR US TO DO the rest of the PRiNTiNG JOB... without really asking us.
CŒUR
i STARTED TO BE iN A REAL BAD MOOD NOT LONG AFTER THAT. iT'S my POST menstrual SYNDROME, catching up with me.
Toxic
DON'T:
XWYG!
SANTE
i THOUGHT i COULD ESCAPE FROM iT BY GOiNG OUT TO EAT WiTH C. iN CHiNATOWN [redacted] LATER WE WATCHED A ViDEO AT his PLACE "L'ASSASSiN HABiTe AU 21" BY H. G. CLOUZOT.
FUNG CHiNG
VIE SOCIALE
BUT WHEN i GOT BACK HOME i FOUND in my MAiLBOX my CONTRACT WiTH SEUiL, WHiCH HAD A SECOND SECTION CALLED "TRANSFER OF audiovisual adaption rights contract" WHiCH means animation movie... that really freaked me out. seems like a lot for the little money we get. i don't want to sign that THiNG. DiDN'T SLEEP too WELL.
NO NO NO

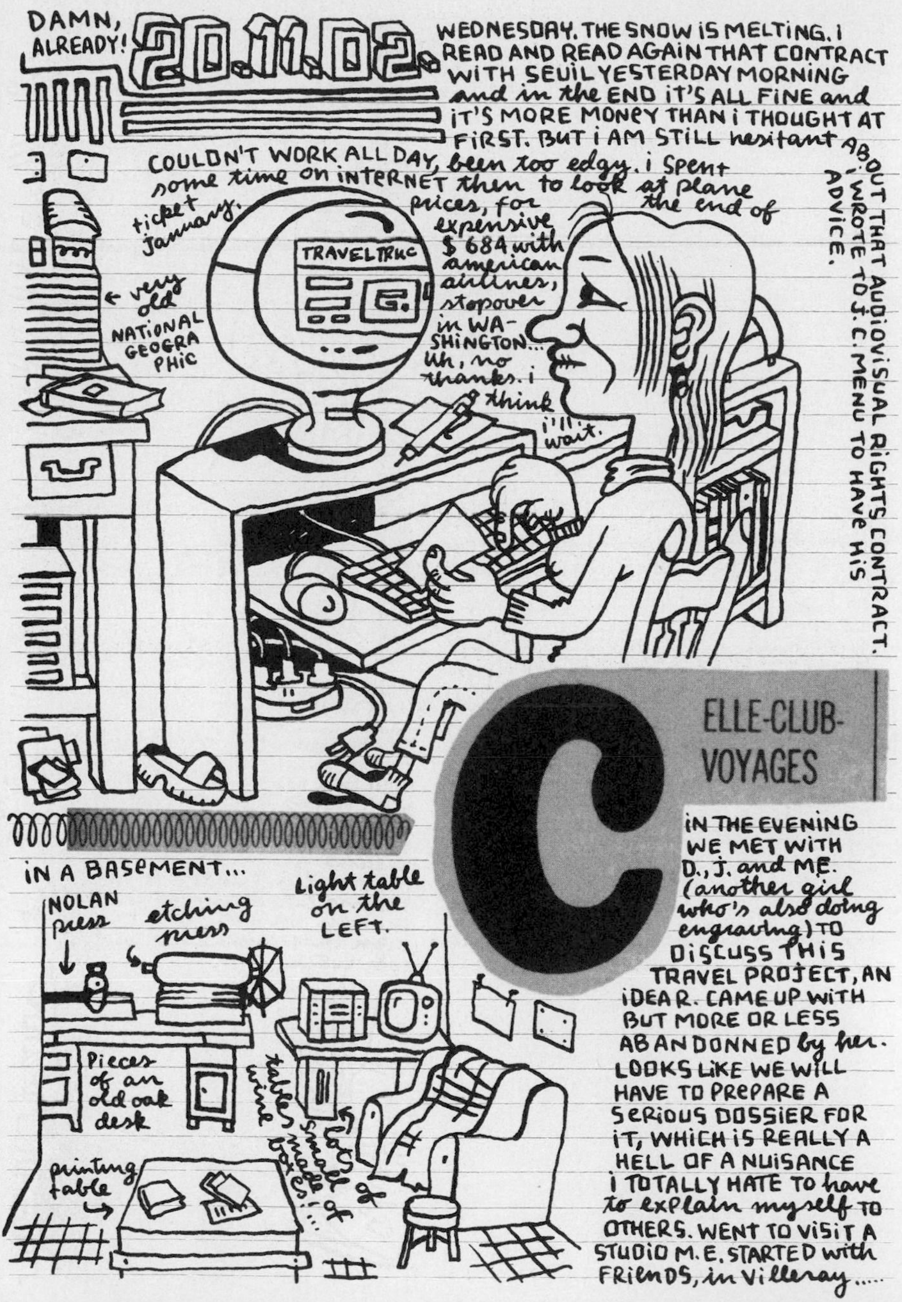
DAMN, ALREADY!
20.11.02.
WEDNESDAY. THE SNOW IS MELTING. I READ AND READ AGAIN THAT CONTRACT WITH SEUIL YESTERDAY MORNING and in the END IT'S ALL FINE and IT'S MORE MONEY THAN I THOUGHT AT FIRST. BUT I AM STILL hesitant ABOUT THAT AUDIOVISUAL RIGHTS CONTRACT. I WROTE TO J. C. MENU TO HAVE HIS ADVICE.
COULDN'T WORK ALL DAY, been too edgy. I Spent some time on INTERNET then to look at plane ticket prices, for the end of January. expensive $ 684 with american airlines, stopover in WASHINGTON... uh, no thanks. i think i'll wait.
TRAVELTRUC
very old NATIONAL GEOGRAPHIC
ELLE-CLUB-VOYAGES
IN THE EVENING WE MET WITH D., J. and M.E. (another girl who's also doing engraving) TO DISCUSS THIS TRAVEL PROJECT, AN IDEA R. CAME UP WITH BUT MORE OR LESS ABANDONNED by her. LOOKS LIKE WE WILL HAVE TO PREPARE A SERIOUS DOSSIER FOR IT, WHICH IS REALLY A HELL OF A NUISANCE I TOTALLY HATE TO have to explain myself TO OTHERS. WENT TO VISIT A STUDIO M.E. STARTED with FRIENDS, in Villeray.....
IN A BASEMENT...
NOLAN press
etching press
Light table on the LEFT.
Pieces of an old oak desk
lots of small table made of wine boxes!...
printing table

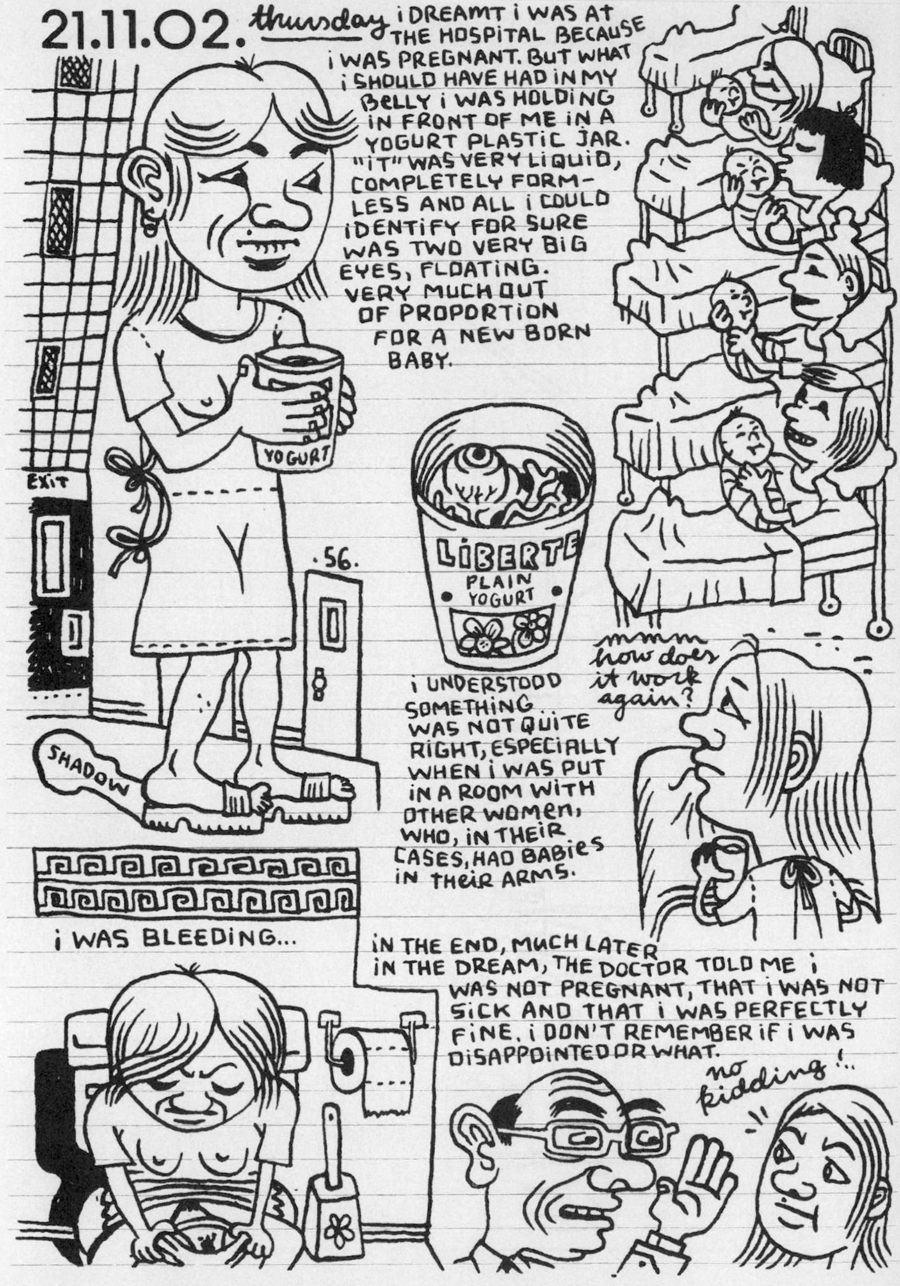
21.11.02. thursday
i DREAMT i WAS AT THE HOSPITAL BECAUSE i WAS PREGNANT. BUT WHAT i SHOULD HAVE HAD IN MY BELLY i WAS HOLDING IN FRONT OF ME iN A YOGURT PLASTIC JAR. "iT" WAS VERY LiQUiD, COMPLETELY FORM-LESS AND ALL i COULD iDENTiFY FOR SURE WAS TWO VERY BiG EYES, FLOATiNG. VERY MUCH OUT OF PROPORTION FOR A NEW BORN BABY.
YOGURT
EXIT
.56.
SHADOW
LiBERTE
PLAIN YOGURT
i UNDERSTOOD SOMETHiNG WAS NOT QUITE RiGHT, ESPECiALLY WHEN i WAS PUT iN A ROOM WiTH OTHER WOMEN, WHO, iN THEIR CASES, HAD BABiES iN THEiR ARMS.
mmm how does it work again?
i WAS BLEEDiNG...
iN THE END, MUCH LATER iN THE DREAM, THE DOCTOR TOLD ME i WAS NOT PREGNANT, THAT i WAS NOT SiCK AND THAT i WAS PERFECTLY FiNE. i DON'T REMEMBER iF i WAS DiSAPPOiNTED OR WHAT.
no kidding!...

23.11.02. saturday. i SKIPPED ONE DAY BECAUSE MY DAD CAME to PICK ME UP WAY TOO EARLY. WE WERE GOING TO HIS place at FRELIGHSBURG, WITH M. OF COURSE.

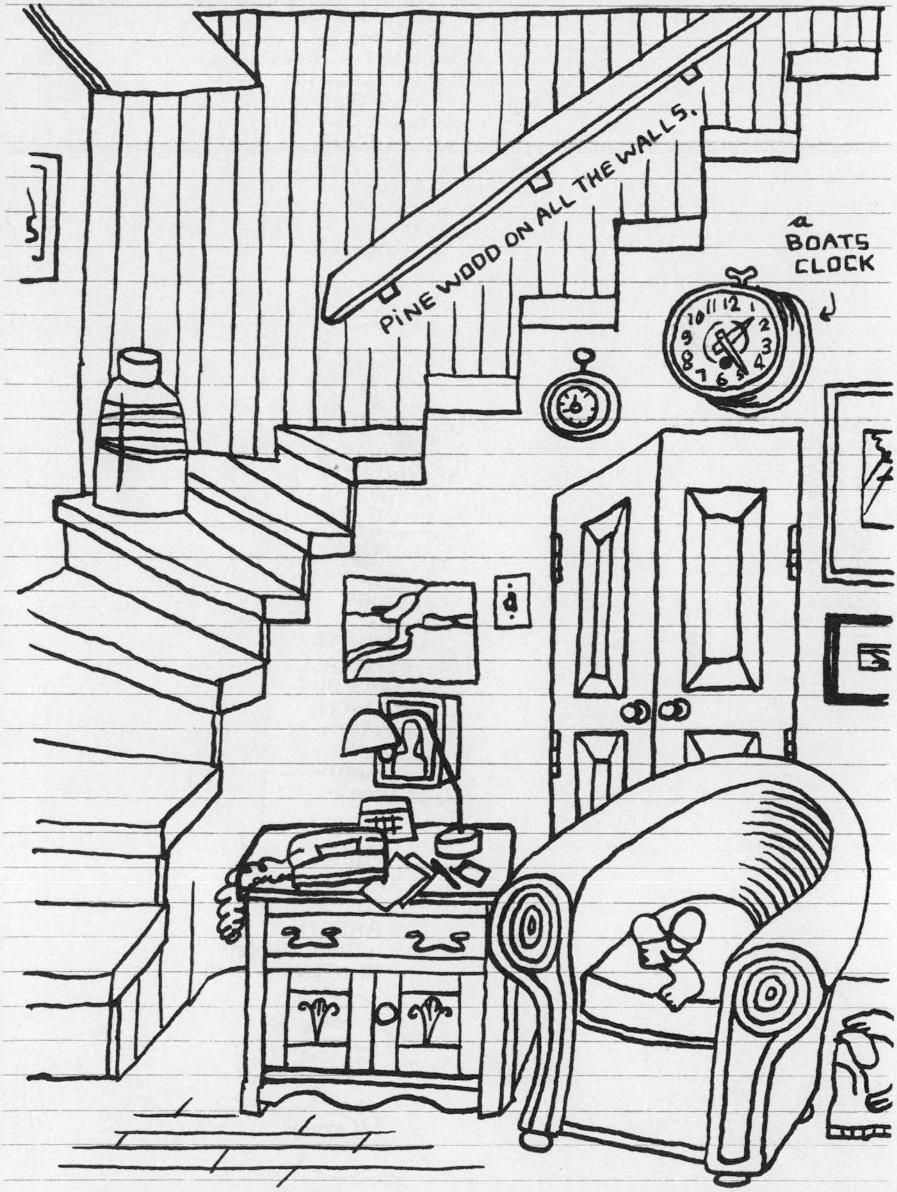

PINE WOOD ON ALL THE WALLS.
a BOATS CLOCK

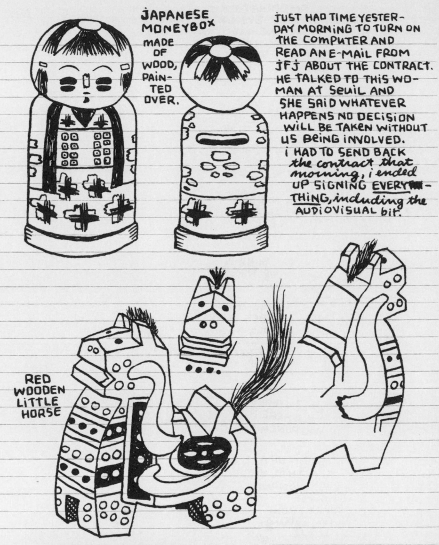

JAPANESE MONEYBOX MADE OF WOOD, PAINTED OVER.

JUST HAD TIME YESTER-DAY MORNING TO TURN ON THE COMPUTER AND READ AN E-MAIL FROM JFJ ABOUT THE CONTRACT. HE TALKED TO THIS WOMAN AT SEUIL AND SHE SAID WHATEVER HAPPENS NO DECISION WILL BE TAKEN WITHOUT US BEING INVOLVED. i HAD TO SEND BACK *the contract that morning, i ended* UP SIGNING EVERY-THING, *including the* AUDIOVISUAL *bit.*

RED WOODEN LITTLE HORSE

i FIGURED, AND THAT'S WHAT i WROTE TO JFJ (SOMETHING LIKE THAT, ANYWAY), WE HAVE MORE TO GAIN THAN TO LOSE. THURSDAY AFTERNOON i WALKED ALL THE WAY DOWNTOWN TO HAVE THOSE GOVERNMENT PAPERS SIGNED TO PROVE THAT i PAY MY TAXES IN CANADA. IT IS SIGNED, AND SENT.

24.11.02. Sunday. i AM GOING BACK TO MTL ONLY TOMORROW MORNING:
THERE'S NO BUS ON SUNDAY EVENINGS AND i CAN'T BE BOTHERED. iT
SNOWED FRIDAY DURING THE NIGHT, the landscape looks amazing.
ALL iS COVERED WiTH SNOW iN THE FOREST, the slightest blade of
grass has two inches OF SNOW ON iT.

VERY STRANGE BLACK WOODEN OBJECT (EXCEPT for the wheel, in
plain wood). i remembered i was told it was a machine
TO MAKE iNK. BUT, iN FACT, iT'S A CARPENTER'S DRAWING PAN
(i DiDN'T MENTION, the thing is japanese).

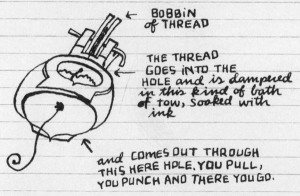

← BOBBiN
of THREAD

THE THREAD
GOES iNTO THE
HOLE and is dampered
in this kind of bath
of tow, soaked with
ink

and COMES OUT THROUGH
THiS HERE HOLE, YOU PULL,
YOU PUNCH AND THERE YOU GO.

25.11.02. monday. GOT UP AT 6:00 THiS MORNING TO CATCH THE BUS TO
GO BACK iN TOWN, WiTH M. YESTERDAY, WE WALKED in the FOREST
AGAiN. GORGEOUS. THEN WE
COOKED, BAKED SOME
FRUiTCAKES...APART FROM
walking, cooking, eating,
i DiD nothing at all.
THEY ASKED ME
WHAT i WANTED FOR
CHRiSTMAS, the
only concrete thing
i could THiNK OF
WAS A PEPPER
SHAKER...

Hot, hot,
hotter!

CRRR
CRRR

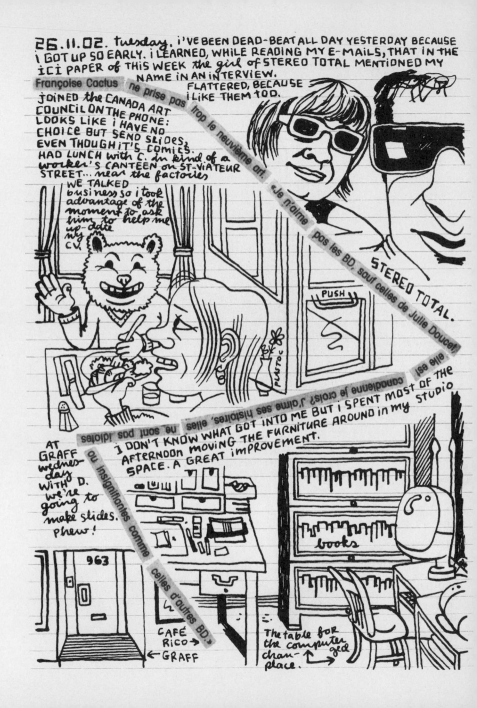

26.11.02. tuesday. i've been DEAD-BEAT ALL DAY YESTERDAY BECAUSE i GOT UP SO EARLY. i LEARNED, WHILE READING MY E-MAILS, THAT IN THE iCi PAPER of THIS WEEK *the girl* of STEREO TOTAL MENTIONED MY NAME IN AN INTERVIEW.

Françoise Cactus

ne prise pas trop le neuvième art.

Je n'aime pas les BD, sauf celles de Julie Doucet, elle est canadienne je crois? J'aime ses histoires, elles ne sont pas idiotes ou insignifiantes comme celles d'autres BD.

FLATTERED, BECAUSE i LiKE THEM tOO.

STEREO TOTAL.

JOINED the CANADA ART COUNCIL ON THE PHONE: LOOKS LiKE i HAVE NO CHOICE BUT SEND SLiDES, EVEN THOUGH iT'S COMiCS. HAD LUNCH with C. in kind of a worker's CANTEEN on ST-ViATEUR STREET... near the factories

WE TALKED business so i took advantage of the moment to ask him to help me up-date my C.V.

PUSH

PLASTIC

i DON'T KNOW WHAT GOT iNTO ME BUT i SPENT MOST OF THE AFTERNOON MOViNG THE FURNiTURE AROUND in my studio SPACE. A GREAT iMPROVEMENT.

AT GRAFF wednesday WiTH D. we're going to make slides. phew!

963

books

CAFÉ RiCO →
← GRAFF

The table for the computer changed place.

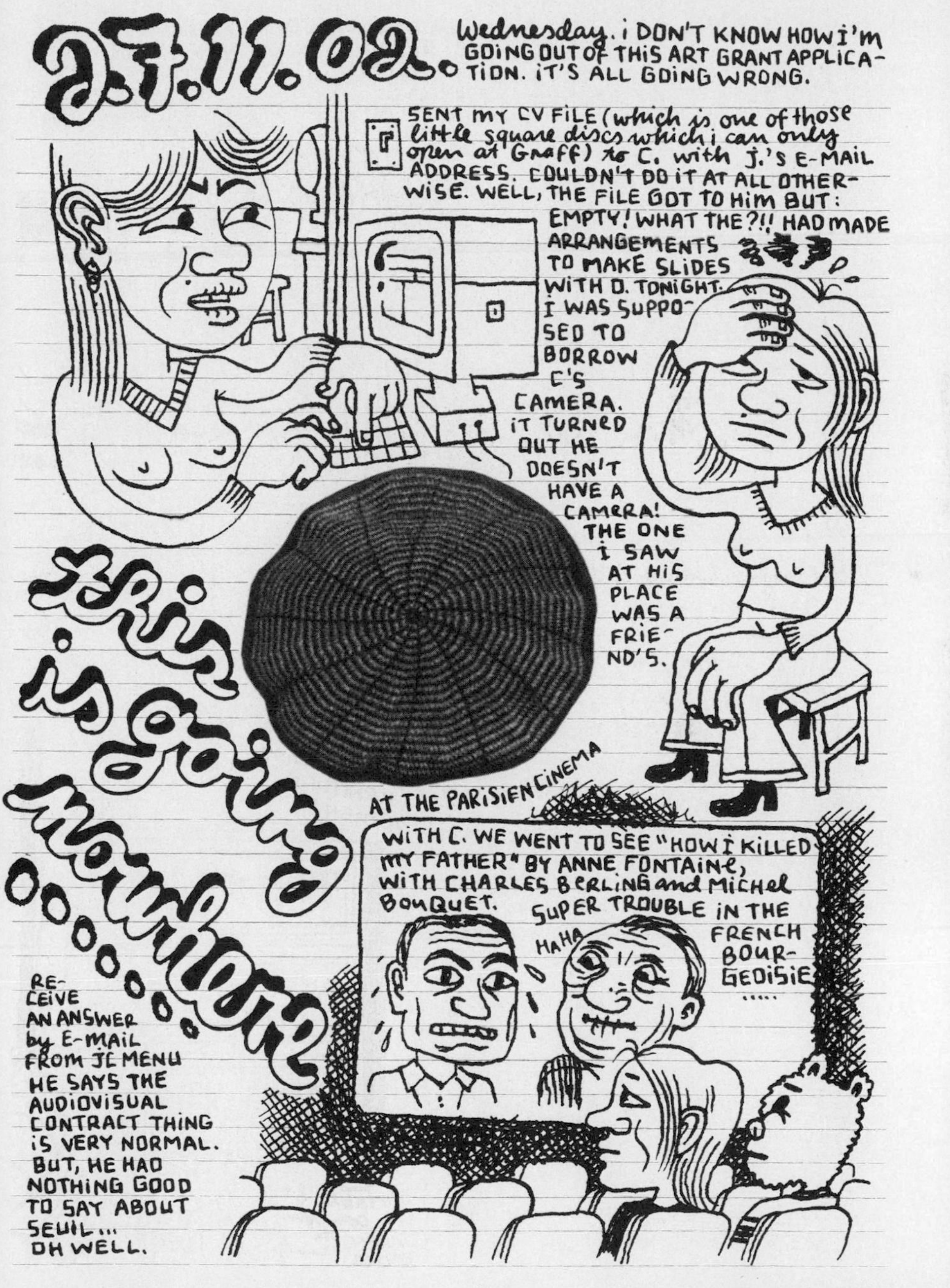
27.11.02.
Wednesday. i DON'T KNOW HOW i'M GOING OUT OF THIS ART GRANT APPLICATION. iT'S ALL GOING WRONG.
SENT MY CV FILE (which is one of those little square discs which i can only open at Graff) to C. with J.'S E-MAIL ADDRESS. COULDN'T DO IT AT ALL OTHERWISE. WELL, THE FILE GOT TO HIM BUT: EMPTY! WHAT THE?!! HAD MADE ARRANGEMENTS TO MAKE SLIDES WITH D. TONIGHT. I WAS SUPPOSED TO BORROW C'S CAMERA. iT TURNED OUT HE DOESN'T HAVE A CAMERA! THE ONE I SAW AT HIS PLACE WAS A FRIEND'S.
this is going nowhere ooo...
AT THE PARiSiEN CINEMA
WiTH C. WE WENT TO SEE "HOW i KILLED MY FATHER" BY ANNE FONTAiNE, WITH CHARLES BERLiNG and MiCHEL BOUQUET.
SUPER TROUBLE IN THE FRENCH BOURGEOiSiE .....
HAHA
RECEIVE AN ANSWER by E-MAIL FROM JC MENU HE SAYS THE AUDIOVISUAL CONTRACT THING iS VERY NORMAL. BUT, HE HAD NOTHING GOOD TO SAY ABOUT SEUIL... OH WELL.

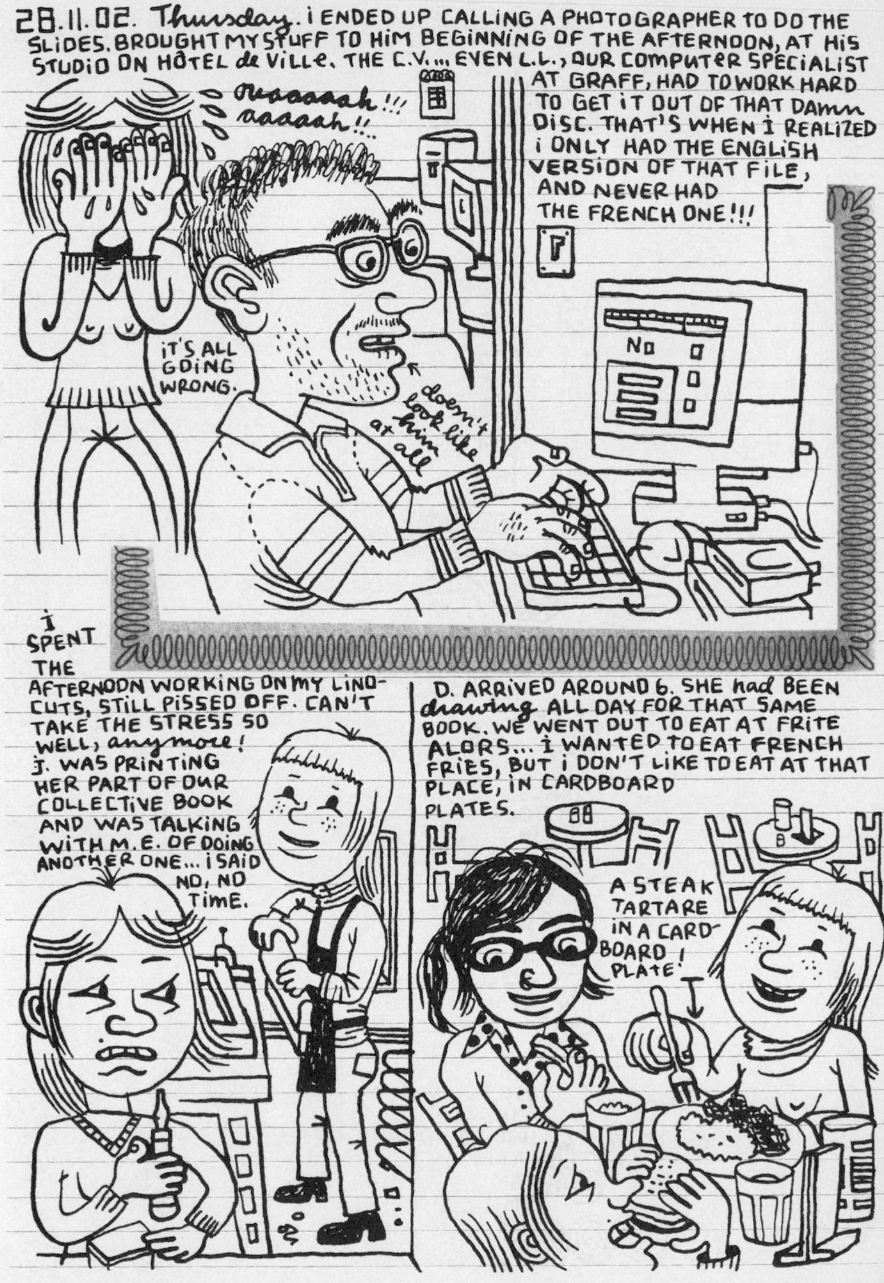
28.11.02. Thursday. I ended up calling a photographer to do the slides. Brought my stuff to him beginning of the afternoon, at his studio on Hôtel de Ville. The C.V. ... even L.L., our computer specialist at Graff, had to work hard to get it out of that damn disc. That's when I realized I only had the English version of that file, and never had the French one!!!
Ouaaaaah!!! aaaaah!!...
It's all going wrong.
doesn't look like him at all
No
I spent the afternoon working on my lino-cuts, still pissed off. Can't take the stress so well, anymore! J. was printing her part of our collective book and was talking with M.E. of doing another one... I said no, no time.
D. arrived around 6. She had been drawing all day for that same book. We went out to eat at Frite Alors... I wanted to eat French fries, but I don't like to eat at that place, in cardboard plates.
A steak tartare in a card-board plate!

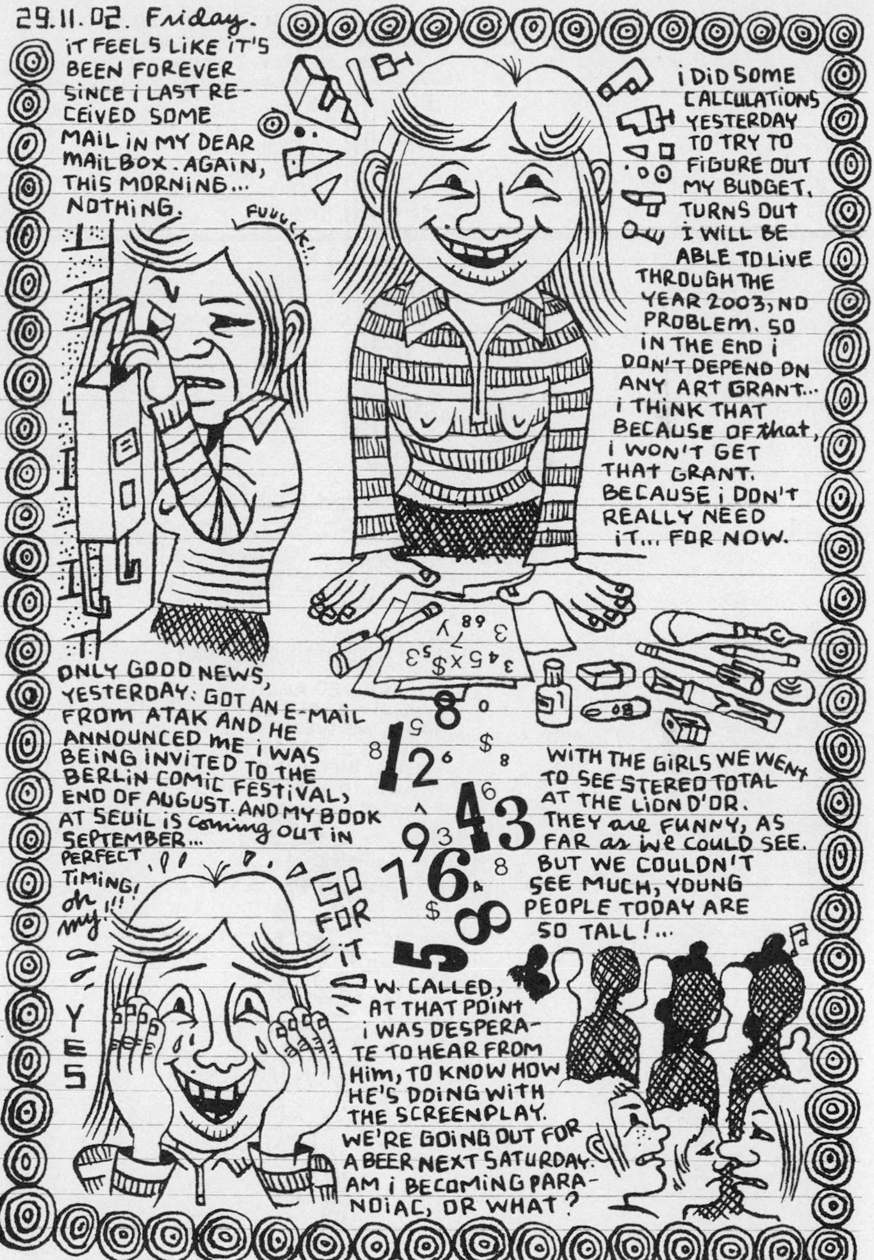
29.11.02. Friday.
IT FEELS LIKE IT'S BEEN FOREVER SINCE I LAST RECEIVED SOME MAIL IN MY DEAR MAILBOX. AGAIN, THIS MORNING... NOTHING.
FUUUCK!
I DID SOME CALCULATIONS YESTERDAY TO TRY TO FIGURE OUT MY BUDGET. TURNS OUT I WILL BE ABLE TO LIVE THROUGH THE YEAR 2003, NO PROBLEM. SO IN THE END I DON'T DEPEND ON ANY ART GRANT... I THINK THAT BECAUSE OF that, I WON'T GET THAT GRANT. BECAUSE I DON'T REALLY NEED IT... FOR NOW.
ONLY GOOD NEWS, YESTERDAY: GOT AN E-MAIL FROM ATAK AND HE ANNOUNCED ME I WAS BEING INVITED TO THE BERLIN COMIC FESTIVAL, END OF AUGUST. AND MY BOOK AT SEUIL IS coming OUT IN SEPTEMBER... PERFECT TIMING! oh my!!!
GO FOR IT
YES
WITH THE GIRLS WE WENT TO SEE STEREO TOTAL AT THE LION D'OR. THEY are FUNNY, AS FAR as we COULD SEE. BUT WE COULDN'T SEE MUCH, YOUNG PEOPLE TODAY ARE SO TALL!...
W. CALLED, AT THAT POINT I WAS DESPERATE TO HEAR FROM HIM, TO KNOW HOW HE'S DOING WITH THE SCREENPLAY. WE'RE GOING OUT FOR A BEER NEXT SATURDAY. AM I BECOMING PARANOIAC, OR WHAT?

30.11.02. *saturday*. NOT SO MUCH TIME TO WRITE/DRAW THIS MORNING BECAUSE i HAVE TO WORK ON THAT GRANT APPLICATION.

YESTERDAY, ANOTHER INCREDIBLE NEWS: GOT AN E-MAIL FROM CAROLINE SURY SHE WRITES THAT NEXT SPRING THEY WILL BE TOO BUSY BUT THAT NEXT SUMMER YES, OKAY, WE CAN COME AND WORK AT THEIR STUDIO. THAT IS JUST ABOUT THE LAST THING i EXPECTED. DOES THIS MEAN BIG TROUBLE? AND WHEN, IN THE SUMMER?

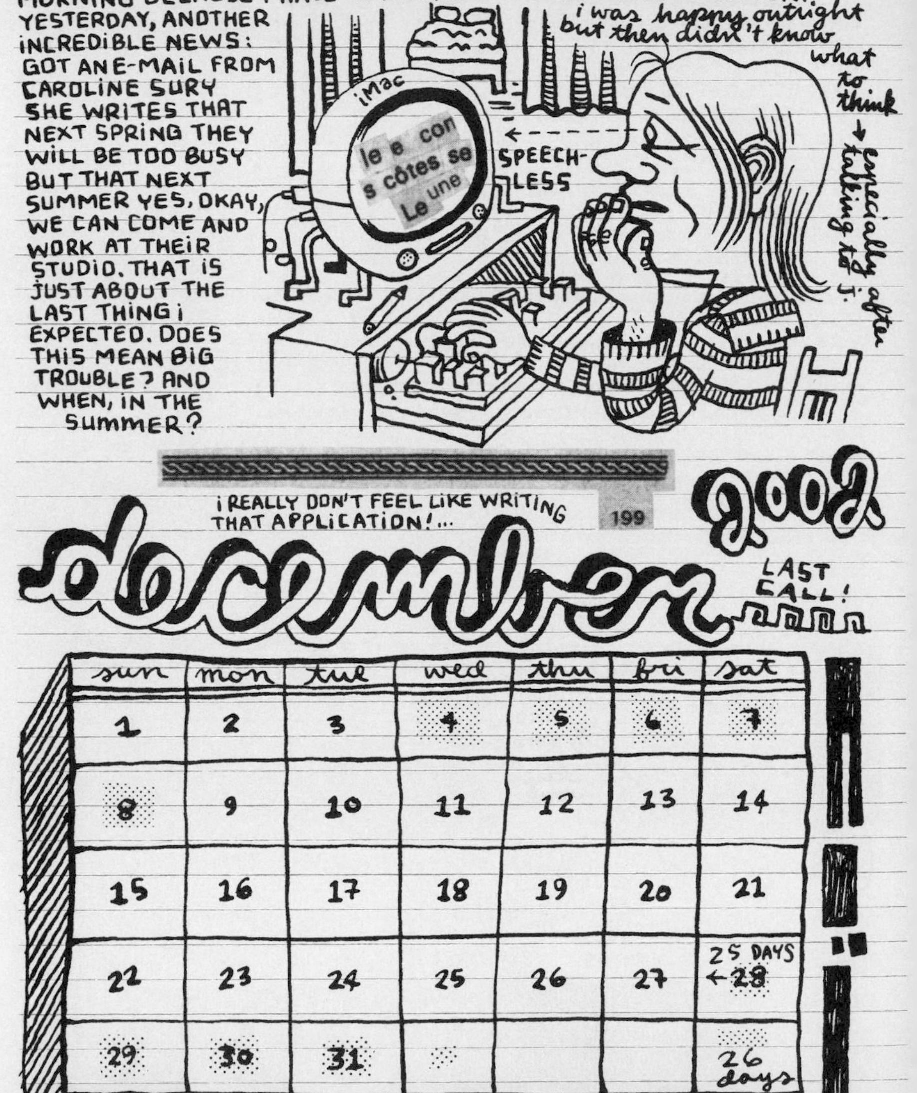
i was happy outright but then didn't know what to think → especially after talking to J.
iMac
le e con
s côtes se
Le une
SPEECH-LESS

i REALLY DON'T FEEL LIKE WRITING THAT APPLICATION!...

199

december 2002

LAST CALL!

sun	mon	tue	wed	thu	fri	sat
1	2	3	4	5	6	7
8	9	10	11	12	13	14
15	16	17	18	19	20	21
22	23	24	25	26	27	25 DAYS ← 28
29	30	31				26 days

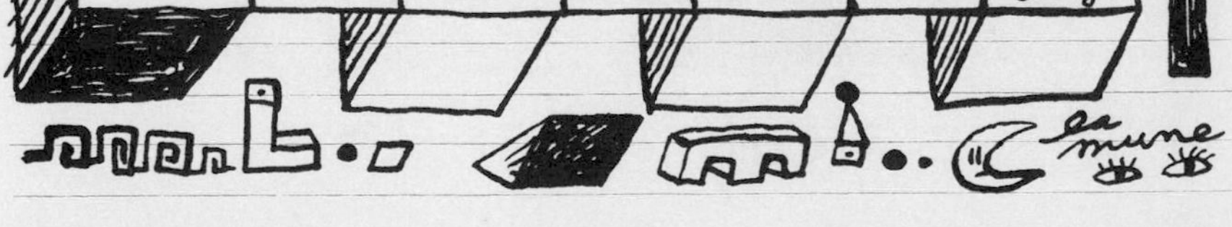
la lune

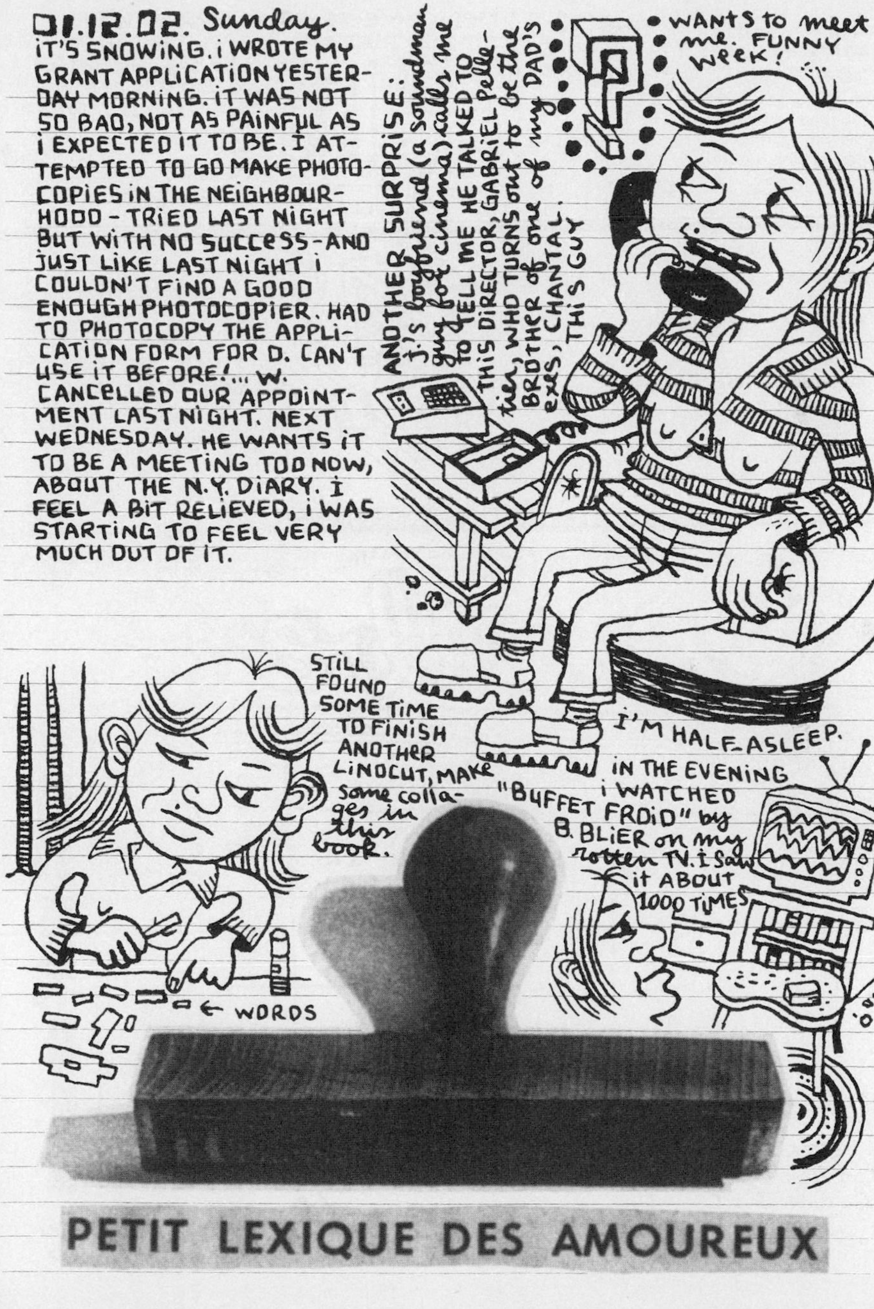
01.12.02. Sunday.
IT'S SNOWING. i WROTE MY GRANT APPLICATION YESTERDAY MORNING. IT WAS NOT SO BAD, NOT AS PAINFUL AS i EXPECTED IT TO BE. I ATTEMPTED TO GO MAKE PHOTOCOPIES IN THE NEIGHBOURHOOD - TRIED LAST NIGHT BUT WITH NO SUCCESS - AND JUST LIKE LAST NIGHT i COULDN'T FIND A GOOD ENOUGH PHOTOCOPIER. HAD TO PHOTOCOPY THE APPLICATION FORM FOR D. CAN'T USE IT BEFORE!... W. CANCELLED OUR APPOINTMENT LAST NIGHT. NEXT WEDNESDAY. HE WANTS iT TO BE A MEETING TOO NOW, ABOUT THE N.Y. DIARY. I FEEL A BIT RELIEVED, i WAS STARTING TO FEEL VERY MUCH OUT OF iT.
ANOTHER SURPRISE: J.'s boyfriend (a soundman guy for cinema) called me to TELL ME HE TALKED TO THIS DIRECTOR, GABRIEL Pelletier, WHO TURNS out to be the BROTHER of one of my DAD'S exes, CHANTAL. THIS GUY
WANTS to meet me. FUNNY week!
STILL FOUND SOME TIME TO FINISH ANOTHER LINOCUT, MAKE some collages in this book.
← WORDS
I'M HALF-ASLEEP.
IN THE EVENING i WATCHED "BUFFET FROID" by B. BLIER on my rotten TV. I saw it ABOUT 1000 TIMES
PETIT LEXIQUE DES AMOUREUX

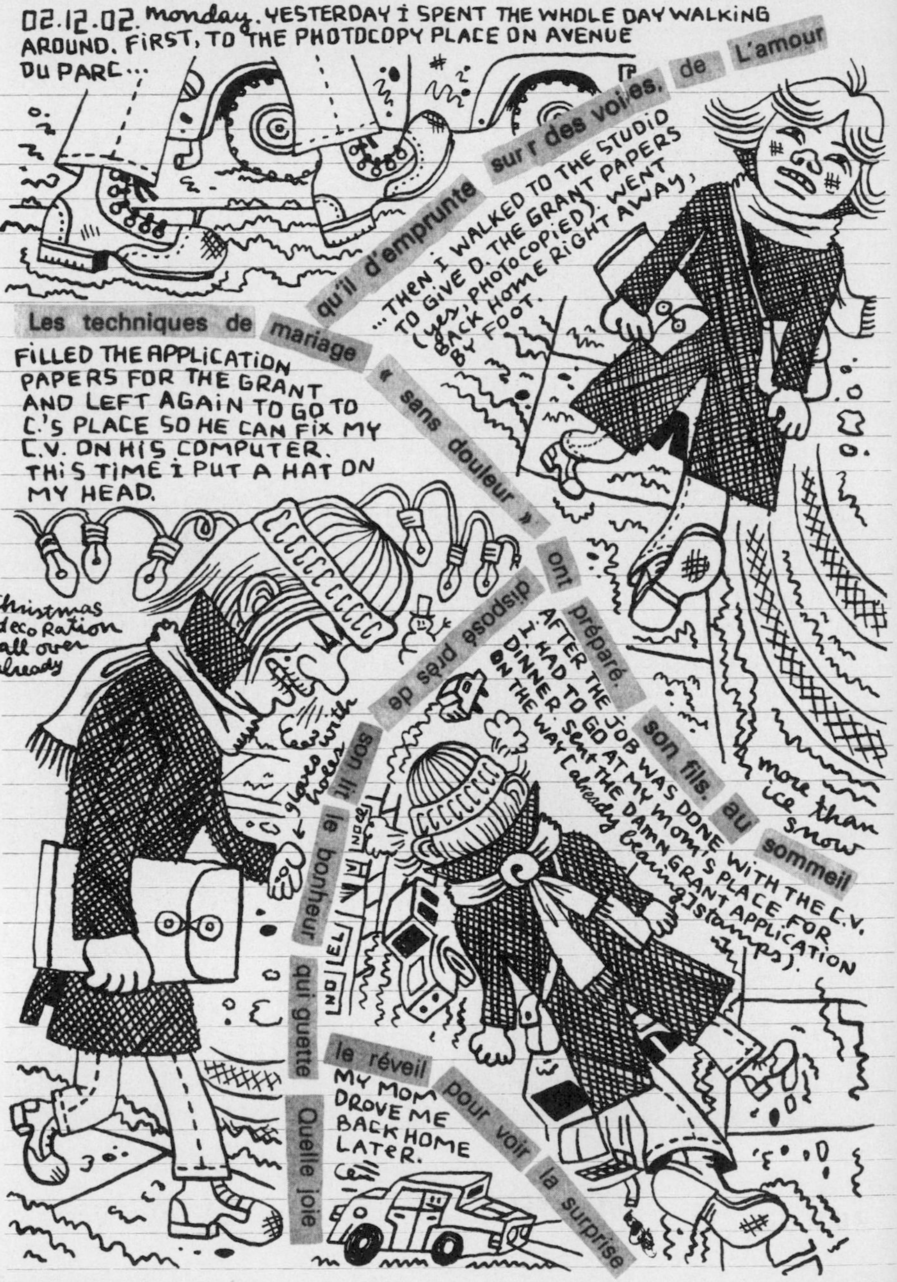
02.12.02. monday. YESTERDAY I SPENT THE WHOLE DAY WALKING AROUND. FIRST, TO THE PHOTOCOPY PLACE ON AVENUE DU PARC...
L'amour de
des voi/es, sur r
qu'il d'emprunte
...THEN I WALKED TO THE STUDIO TO GIVE D. THE GRANT PAPERS (yes, PHOTOCOPIED). WENT BACK HOME RIGHT AWAY, BY FOOT.
Les techniques de
mariage
« sans douleur »
ont
préparé.
son fils.
au
sommeil
FILLED THE APPLICATION PAPERS FOR THE GRANT AND LEFT AGAIN TO GO TO C.'S PLACE SO HE CAN FIX MY C.V. ON HIS COMPUTER. THIS TIME I PUT A HAT ON MY HEAD.
Christmas decoration all over already
dispose près de
son lit
le bonheur
qui guette
le réveil
pour voir
la surprise
Quelle joie
gloves with holes
AFTER THE JOB WAS DONE WITH THE C.V. I HAD TO GO AT MY MOM'S PLACE FOR DINNER. SENT THE DAMN GRANT APPLICATION ON THE WAY [already bearing stamps].
more ice than snow
MY MOM DROVE ME BACK HOME LATER.

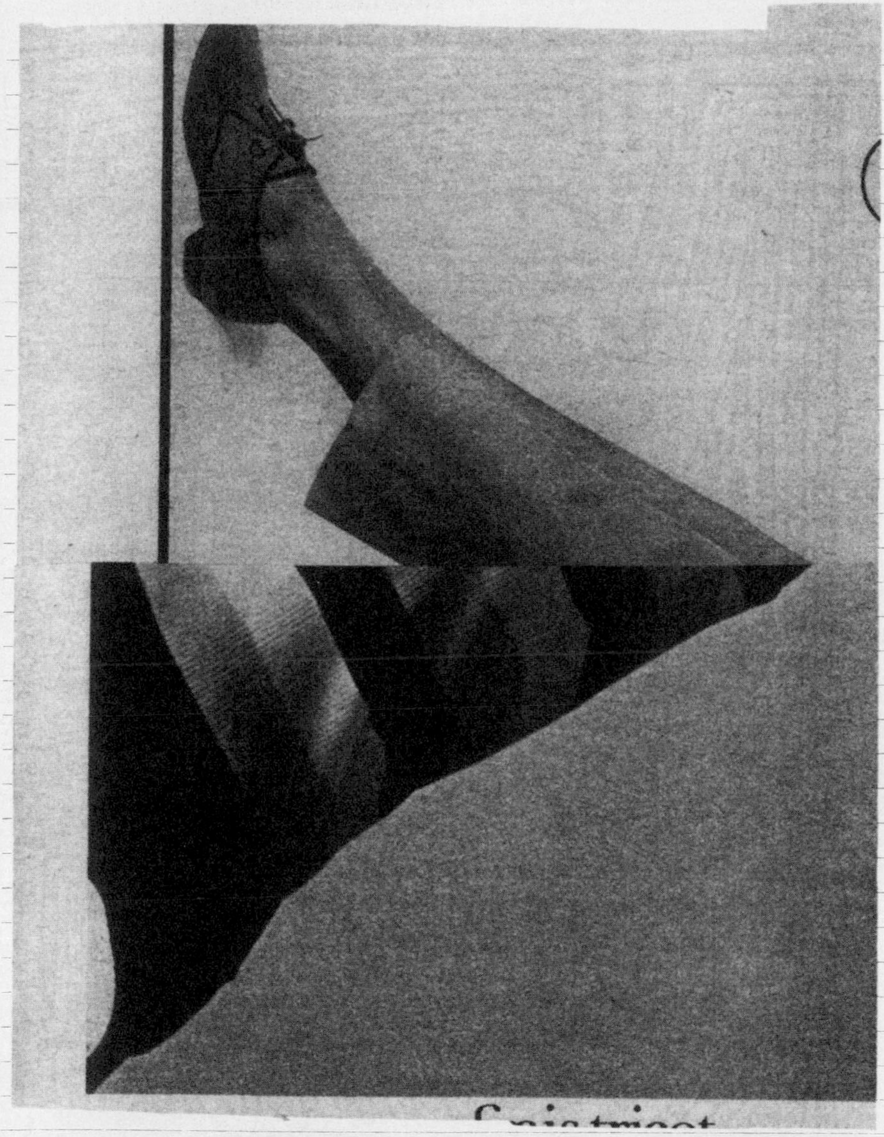

30.11.02.

EN MARCHE VERS L'AMOUR

J.R.Doucet

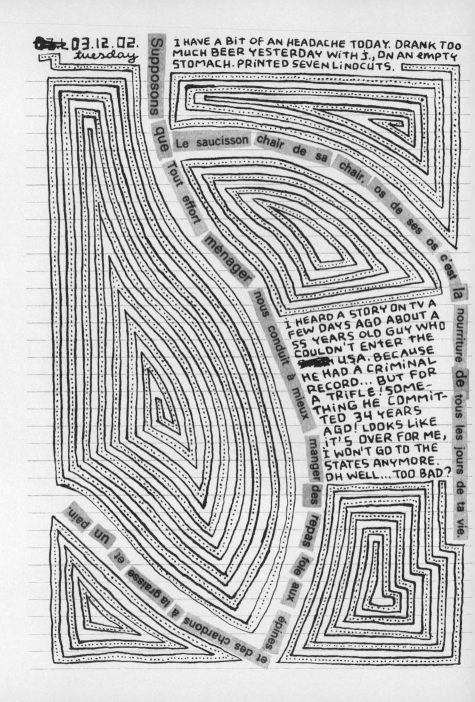

03.12.02. tuesday

I HAVE A BIT OF AN HEADACHE TODAY. DRANK TOO MUCH BEER YESTERDAY WITH J., ON AN EMPTY STOMACH. PRINTED SEVEN LINOCUTS.

Supposons que Tout effort ménager nous conduit à mieux manger des repas foie aux épines et des chardons à la graisse et un pain.

Le saucisson chair de sa chair, os de ses os c'est la nourriture de tous les jours de ta vie.

I HEARD A STORY ON TV A FEW DAYS AGO ABOUT A 55 YEARS OLD GUY WHO COULDN'T ENTER THE USA. BECAUSE HE HAD A CRIMINAL RECORD... BUT FOR A TRIFLE! SOMETHING HE COMMITTED 34 YEARS AGO! LOOKS LIKE IT'S OVER FOR ME, I WON'T GO TO THE STATES ANYMORE. OH WELL... TOO BAD?

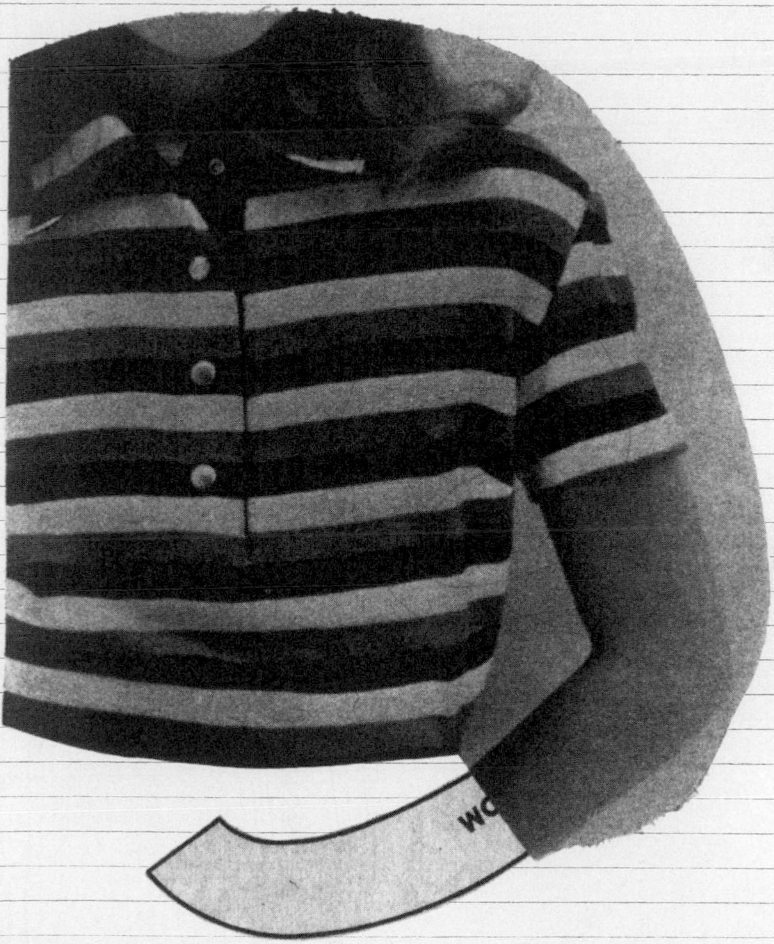
WO

03.12.02.

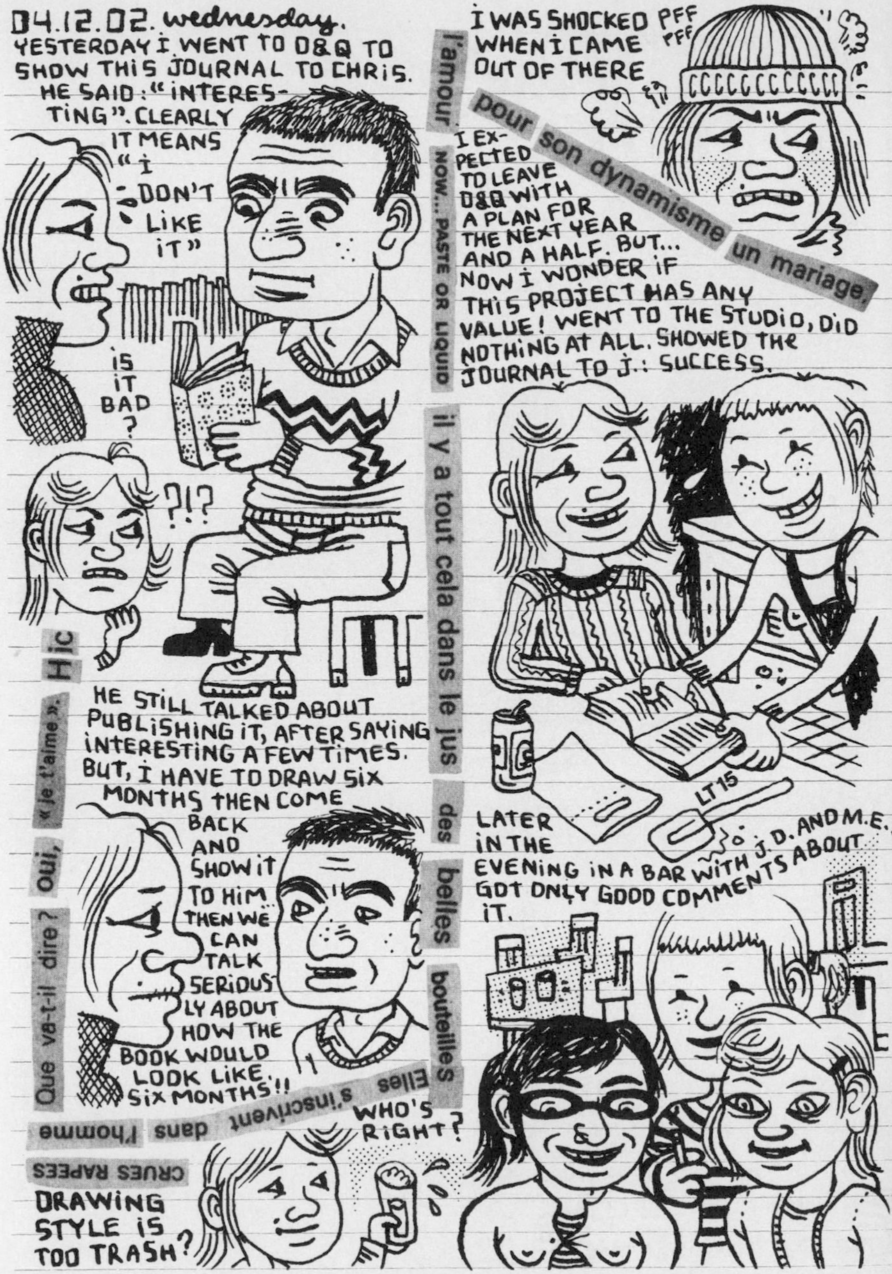

04.12.02. wednesday.
YESTERDAY I WENT TO D&Q TO SHOW THIS JOURNAL TO CHRIS. HE SAID: "INTERESTING". CLEARLY IT MEANS "I DON'T LIKE IT"
IS IT BAD?
?!?
HE STILL TALKED ABOUT PUBLISHING IT, AFTER SAYING INTERESTING A FEW TIMES. BUT, I HAVE TO DRAW SIX MONTHS THEN COME BACK AND SHOW IT TO HIM THEN WE CAN TALK SERIOUSLY ABOUT HOW THE BOOK WOULD LOOK LIKE. SIX MONTHS!!
WHO'S RIGHT?
DRAWING STYLE IS TOO TRASH?
I WAS SHOCKED WHEN I CAME OUT OF THERE
PFF PFF
I EXPECTED TO LEAVE D&Q WITH A PLAN FOR THE NEXT YEAR AND A HALF. BUT... NOW I WONDER IF THIS PROJECT HAS ANY VALUE! WENT TO THE STUDIO, DID NOTHING AT ALL. SHOWED THE JOURNAL TO J.: SUCCESS.
LATER IN THE EVENING IN A BAR WITH J.D. AND M.E.: GOT ONLY GOOD COMMENTS ABOUT IT.
LT15
l'amour
NOW... PASTE OR LIQUID
pour son dynamisme un mariage.
il y a tout cela dans le jus des belles bouteilles
Que va-t-il dire ? oui, « je t'aime ». Hic
Elles s'inscrivent dans l'homme
CRUES RAPEES

i will carry on anyway

GODDAMN IT.

05.12.02. thursday.

i AM REALLY FRUSTRATED. BECAUSE: IF THIS BOOK IS PUBLISHED AT D&Q, IT WON'T BE OUT BEFORE TWO YEARS.!!! WHAT AM i GOING TO BE LIVING OFF, IN THE MEANTIME? FROM ART GRANTS, LIKE HALF OF THE COUNTRY? NO THANK YOU!! NOT FULL TIME!!!

i SUPPOSE i AM PISSED OFF ALSO BECAUSE i TRIED TO DRAW MY PAGES FOR "VAGINA MUSHROOM" BUT NOTHING IS WORKING, TOTAL ARTIST BLOCK. i FEEL THEY ARE JUDGING ME, THAT'S WHY.

this is shit i suck so bad!!!

CŒUR

VIE SOCIALE

SANTE

i WENT OUT ONLY END OF AFTERNOON, TO GO TALK ABOUT THE N.Y. DIARY WITH W. HE SAID IN THE END HE DIDN'T HAVE TIME TO WORK ON IT BECAUSE OF THE RENOVATION BEING MADE AT HIS HOME, AND ALL THE NOISE IT MAKES... SO WE TALKED ABOUT EVERYTHING EXCEPT WHAT WE WERE SUPPOSED TO TALK ABOUT.

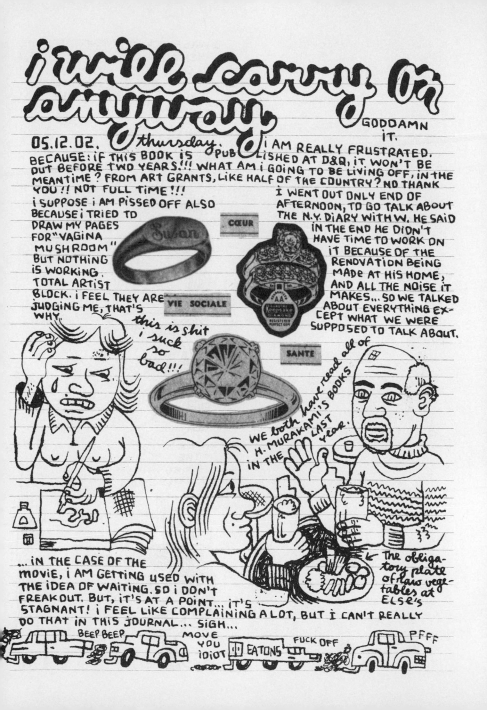

WE both have read all of H. MURAKAMI'S BOOKS IN THE LAST YEAR.

The obligatory plate of raw vegetables at ELSE'S

... IN THE CASE OF THE MOVIE, i AM GETTING USED WITH THE IDEA OF WAITING. SO i DON'T FREAK OUT. BUT, IT'S AT A POINT... IT'S STAGNANT! i FEEL LIKE COMPLAINING A LOT, BUT i CAN'T REALLY DO THAT IN THIS JOURNAL... SIGH...

BEEP BEEP

MOVE YOU iDiOT

EATONS

FUCK OFF

PFFF

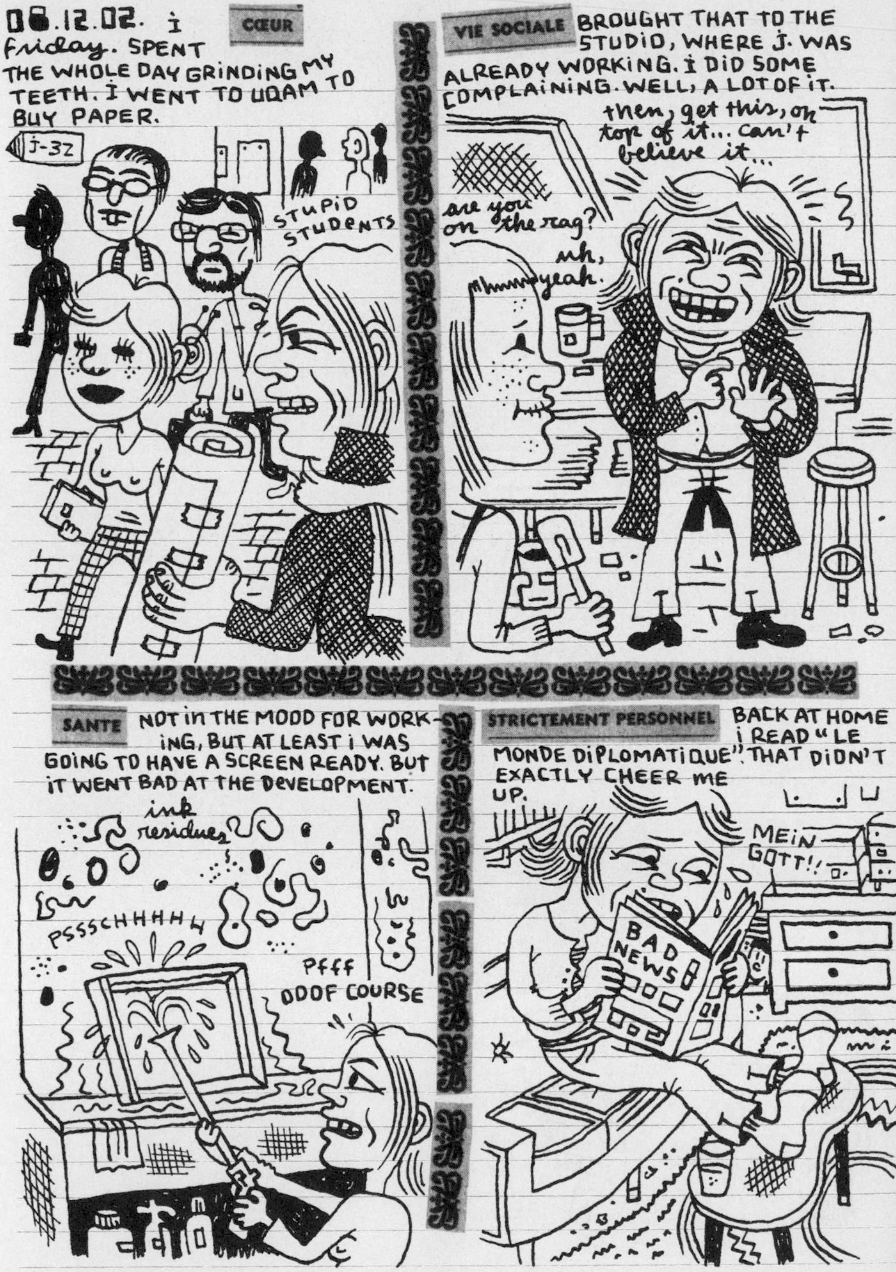
06.12.02. i
friday. SPENT THE WHOLE DAY GRINDING MY TEETH. I WENT TO UQAM TO BUY PAPER.
CŒUR
J-32
STUPID STUDENTS
VIE SOCIALE
BROUGHT THAT TO THE STUDIO, WHERE J. WAS ALREADY WORKING. I DID SOME COMPLAINING. WELL, A LOT OF IT.
then, get this, on top of it... can't believe it...
are you on the rag?
uh, yeah.
SANTE
NOT IN THE MOOD FOR WORKING, BUT AT LEAST I WAS GOING TO HAVE A SCREEN READY. BUT IT WENT BAD AT THE DEVELOPMENT.
ink residues
PSSSCHHHHH
Pfff
OOOF COURSE
STRICTEMENT PERSONNEL
BACK AT HOME I READ "LE MONDE DIPLOMATIQUE". THAT DIDN'T EXACTLY CHEER ME UP.
MEIN GOTT!!
BAD NEWS

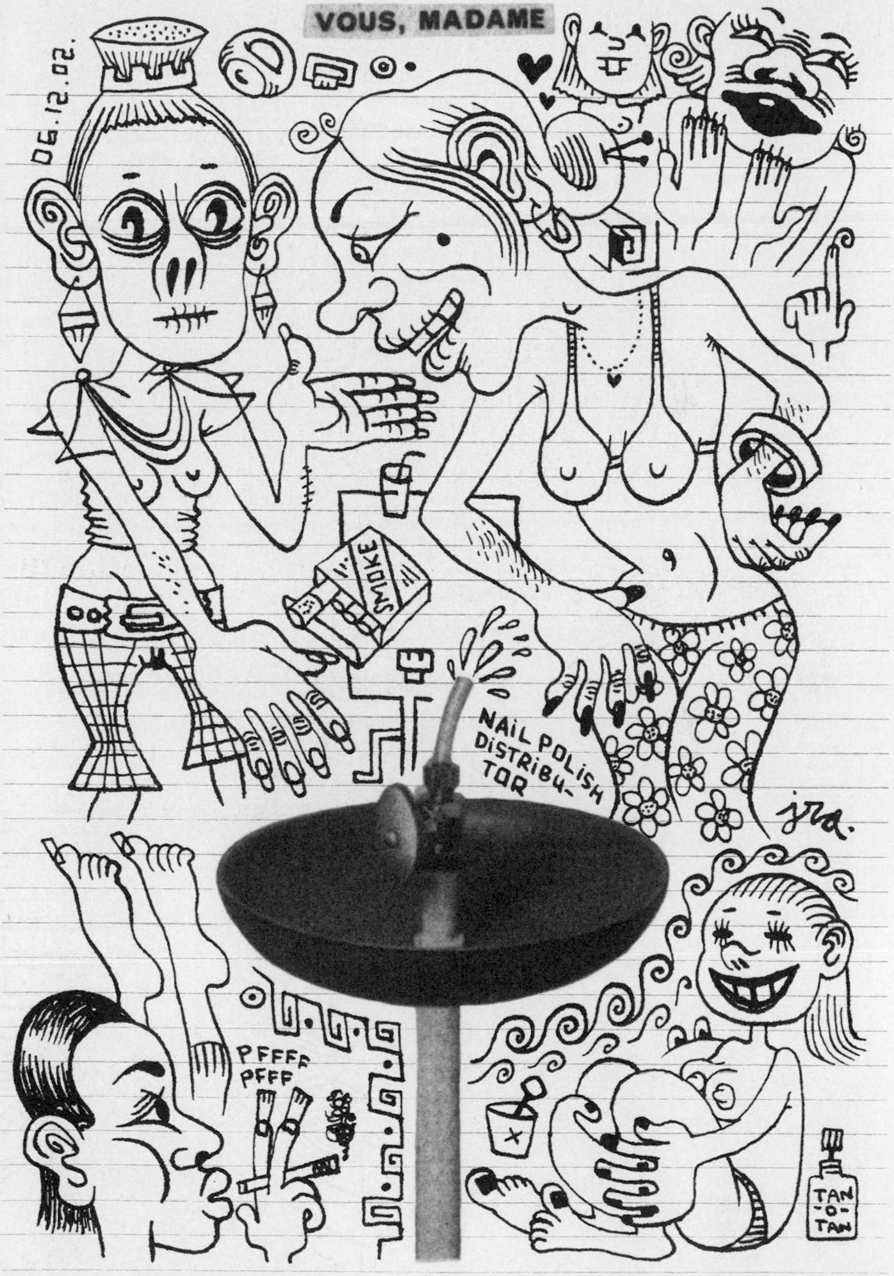
VOUS, MADAME
06.12.02.
SMOKE
NAIL POLISH DISTRIBU-TOR
jra.
PFFFF PFFF
TAN-O-TAN

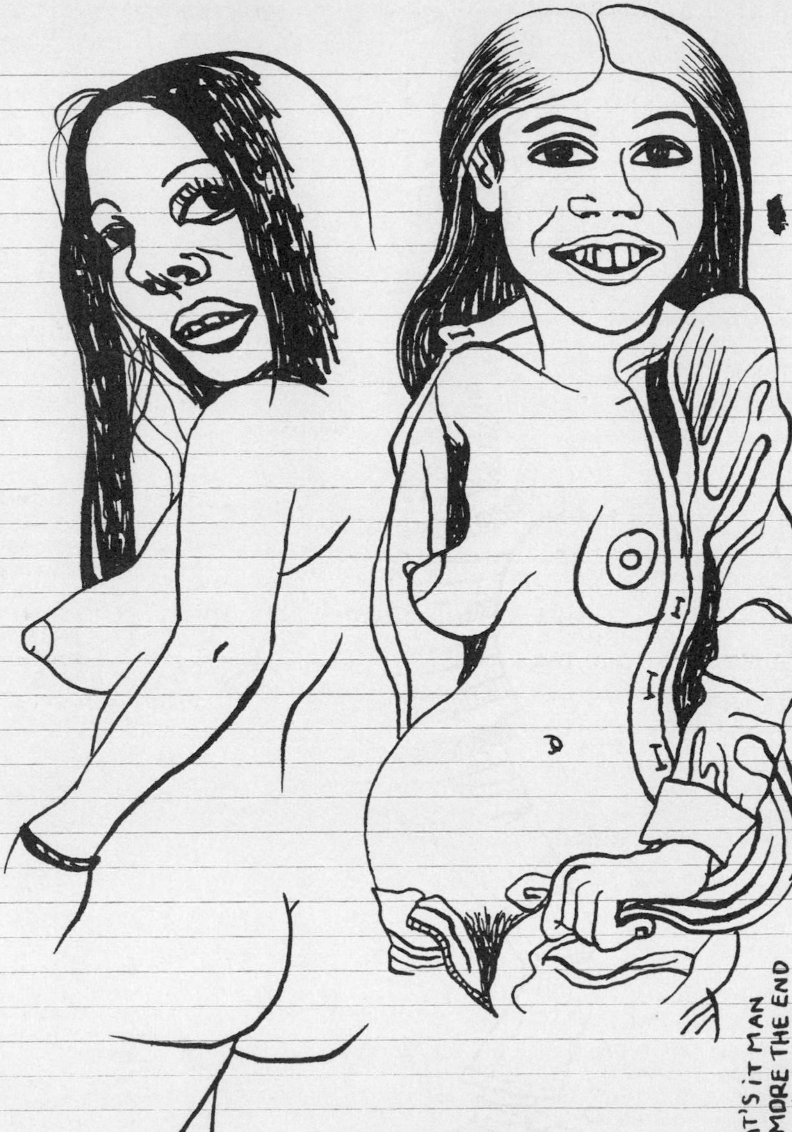

06.12.02. ⋙ NO, OK THAT'S ENOUGH. i JUST CAN'T DRAW AT ALL. i CAN'T STAND MYSELF. i'LL JUST SEND THE NICEST PAGES of this journal

THAT'S iT MAN
NO MORE THE END

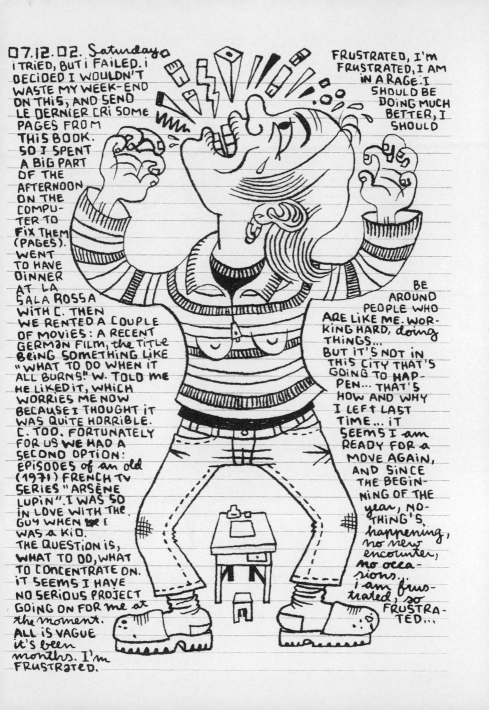

07.12.02. Saturday. i tried, but i failed. i decided i wouldn't waste my week-end on this, and send Le Dernier Cri some pages from this book. So i spent a big part of the afternoon on the computer to fix them (pages). Went to have dinner at La Sala Rossa with C. Then we rented a couple of movies: a recent German film, the title being something like "What to do when it all burns." W. told me he liked it, which worries me now because i thought it was quite horrible. C. too. Fortunately for us we had a second option: episodes of an old (1971) French TV series "Arsène Lupin". I was so in love with the guy when i was a kid. The question is, what to do, what to concentrate on. It seems i have no serious project going on for me at the moment. All is vague it's been months. I'm frustrated.

Frustrated, i'm frustrated, I am in a rage. I should be doing much better, I should be around people who are like me. Working hard, doing things... But it's not in this city that's going to happen... that's how and why i left last time... it seems i am ready for a move again, and since the beginning of the year, nothing's happening, no new encounter, no occasions... i am frustrated, so FRUSTRATED...

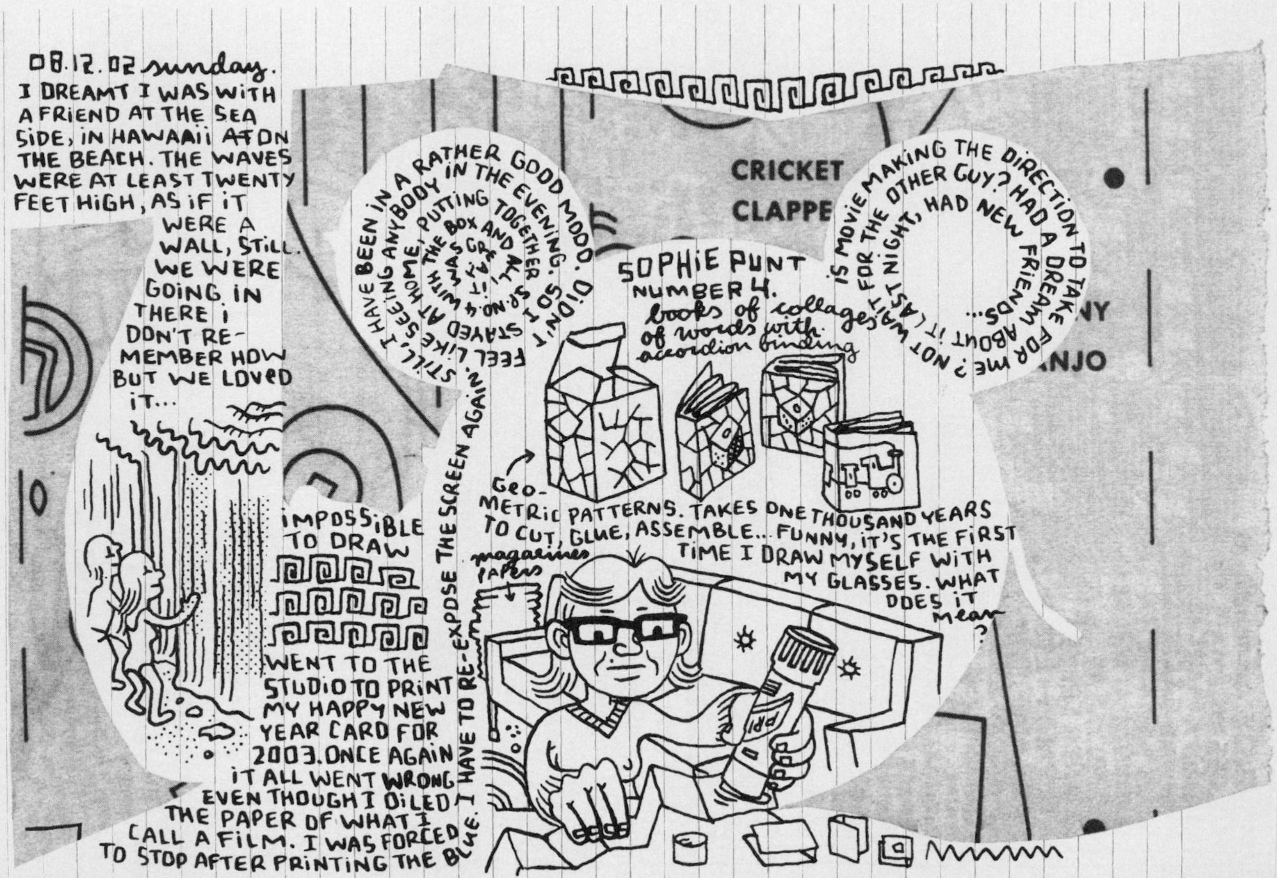
08.12.02 sunday.
I DREAMT I WAS WITH A FRIEND AT THE SEA SIDE, IN HAWAAII AT ON THE BEACH. THE WAVES WERE AT LEAST TWENTY FEET HIGH, AS IF IT WERE A WALL, STILL. WE WERE GOING IN THERE I DON'T REMEMBER HOW BUT WE LOVED IT...
STILL, I HAVE BEEN IN A RATHER GOOD MOOD. DIDN'T FEEL LIKE SEEING ANYBODY IN THE EVENING. SO I STAYED AT HOME, PUTTING TOGETHER S.P. NO. 4 WITH THE BOX AND ALL, IT WAS GREAT.
CRICKET
CLAPPE
IS MOVIE MAKING THE DIRECTION TO TAKE FOR ME ¿ NOT WAIT FOR THE OTHER GUY? HAD A DREAM ABOUT IT LAST NIGHT, HAD NEW FRIENDS...
SOPHIE PUNT NUMBER 4.
books of collages of words with accordion binding
GEO-METRIC PATTERNS. TAKES ONE THOUSAND YEARS TO CUT, GLUE, ASSEMBLE... FUNNY, IT'S THE FIRST TIME I DRAW MYSELF WITH MY GLASSES. WHAT DOES IT mean ?
magazines papers
IMPOSSIBLE TO DRAW
WENT TO THE STUDIO TO PRINT MY HAPPY NEW YEAR CARD FOR 2003. ONCE AGAIN IT ALL WENT WRONG EVEN THOUGH I OILED THE PAPER OF WHAT I CALL A FILM. I WAS FORCED TO STOP AFTER PRINTING THE BLUE. I HAVE TO RE-EXPOSE THE SCREEN AGAIN.

09.12.02

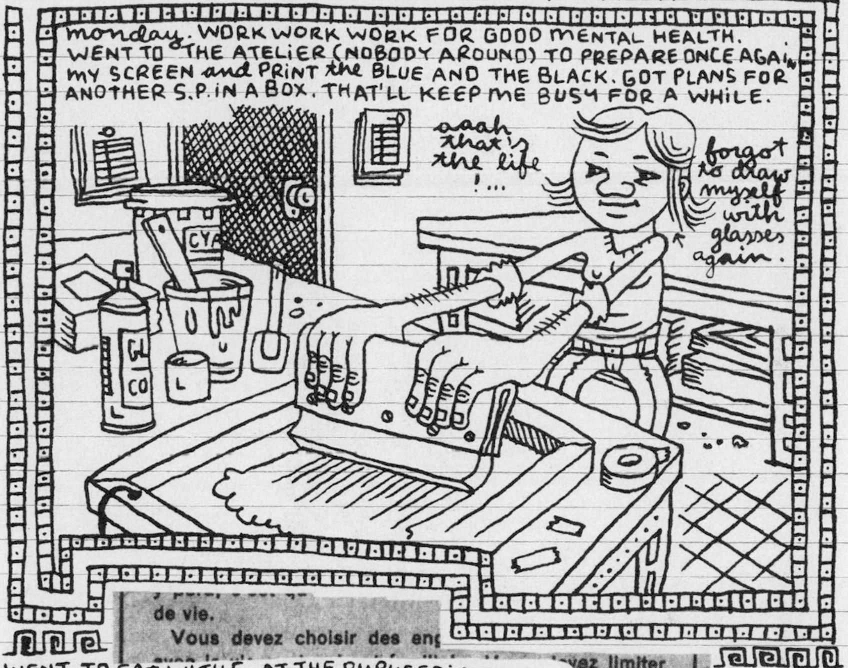
monday. WORK WORK WORK FOR GOOD MENTAL HEALTH. WENT TO THE ATELIER (NOBODY AROUND) TO PREPARE ONCE AGAIN MY SCREEN and PRINT the BLUE AND THE BLACK. GOT PLANS FOR ANOTHER S.P. IN A BOX. THAT'LL KEEP ME BUSY FOR A WHILE.
aaah that's the life !...
forgot to draw myself with glasses again.
de vie.
Vous devez choisir des eng
devez limiter

WENT TO EAT WITH C. AT THE PUPUSERIA AT THE CORNER OF MY STREET. FOR ONCE I DIDN'T FORGET TO CALL H. IT'S BEEN A WHILE. HE'S COMPLETELY SNOWED UNDER WITH WORK BECAUSE OF HIS CAFÉ IN ST. LAMBERT. TWO OF HIS CATS (ON FIVE) DIED, INCLUDING TOUTOUNE. WE TALKED A BIT ABOUT L. SHE'S GOING TO MARSEILLE IN DECEMBER! WE ARE GOING IN SEPTEMBER, FOR ONE MONTH (WE ARE WAITING FOR A CONFIRMATION from caroline). I GET THE FEELING LOTS OF THINGS CAN HAPPEN, in TEN MONTHS!... SPENT ANOTHER EVENING ON THOSE BOXes, AND ON the next S.P. FILMS.

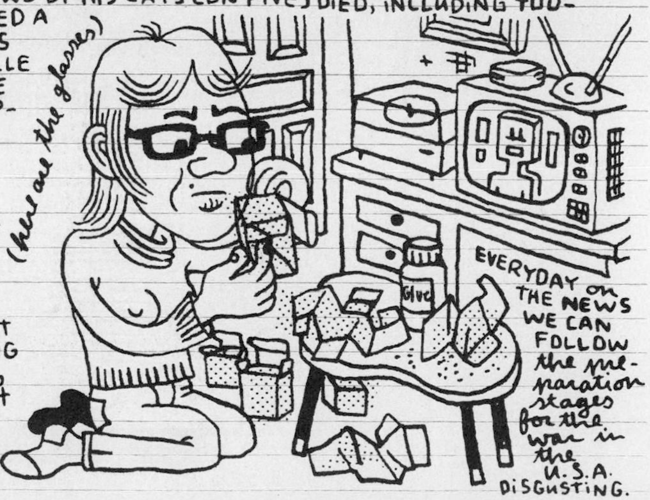
(here are the glasses)
EVERYDAY on THE NEWS WE CAN FOLLOW the preparation stages for the war in the U.S.A. DISGUSTING.

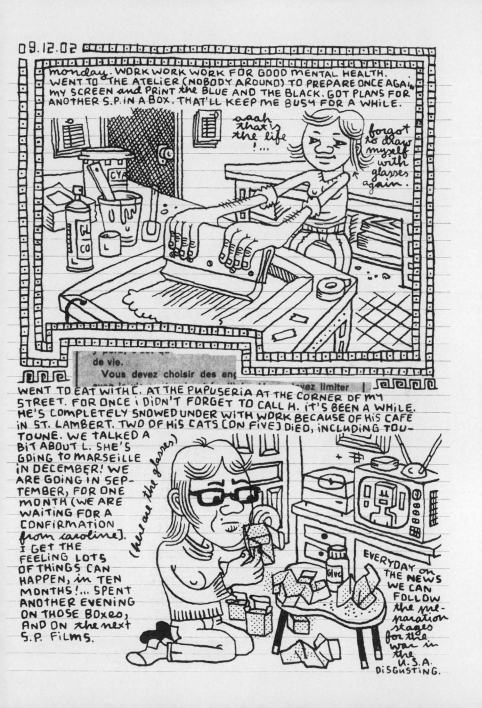

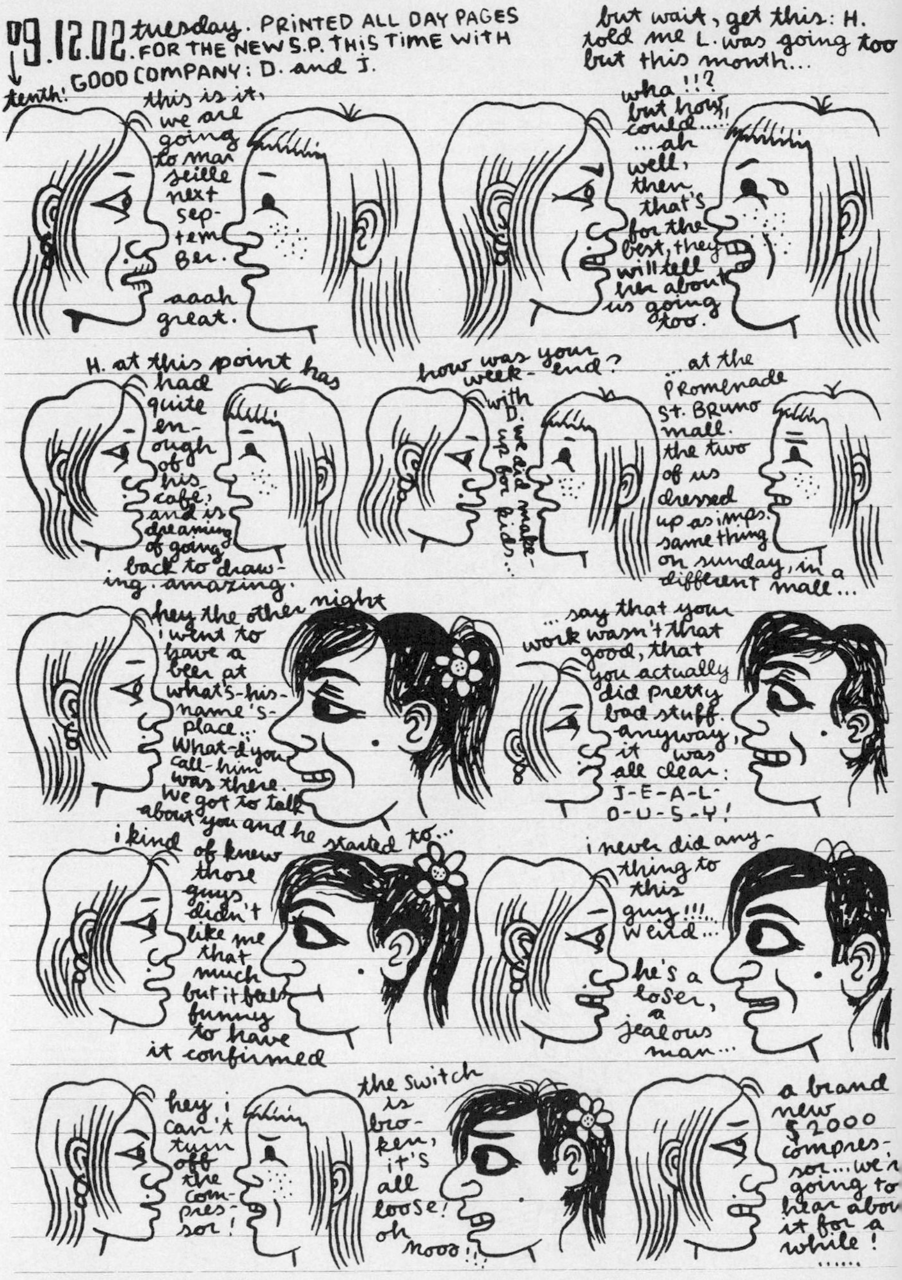

09.12.02 tenth! tuesday. PRINTED ALL DAY PAGES FOR THE NEW S.P. THIS TIME WITH GOOD COMPANY: D. and J.
this is it, we are going to marseille next september.
aaah great.
but wait, get this: H. told me L. was going too but this month...
wha!!? but how could.....
...ah well, then that's for the best, they will tell her about us going too.
H. at this point has had quite enough of his café, and is dreaming of going back to drawing. amazing.
how was your week-end?
with D. we did make-up for kids...
...at the promenade St. Bruno mall. the two of us dressed up as imps. same thing on sunday, in a different mall...
hey the other night i went to have a beer at what's-his-name's place... What-d'you-call-him was there. We got to talk about you and he started to...
...say that your work wasn't that good, that you actually did pretty bad stuff. anyway, it was all clear: J-E-A-L-O-U-S-Y!
i kind of knew those guys didn't like me that much but it feels funny to have it confirmed
i never did anything to this guy!!!... weird...
he's a loser, a jealous man...
hey! can't turn off the compressor!
the switch is broken, it's all loose! oh nooo!!
a brand new $2000 compressor... we're going to hear about it for a while! ......

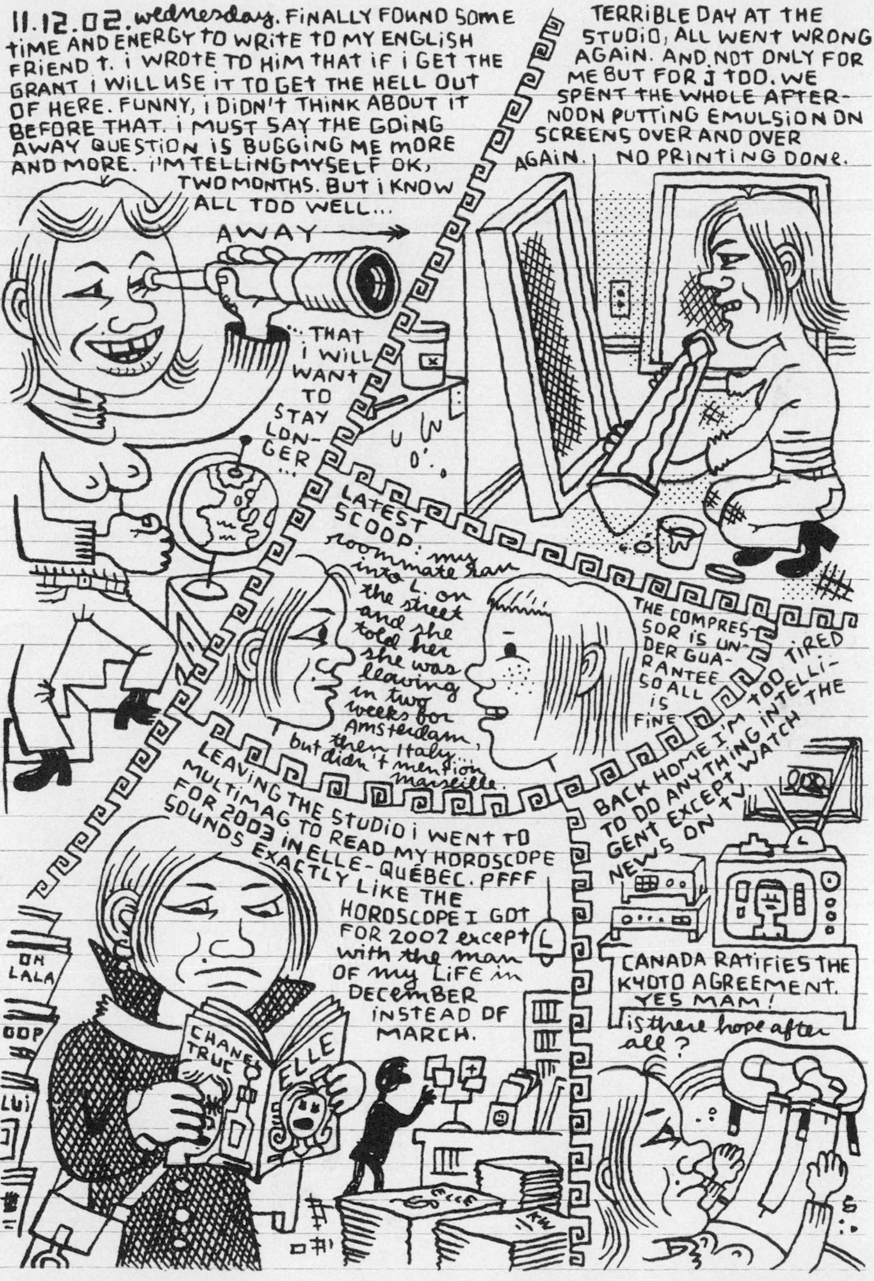
11.12.02. wednesday. FINALLY FOUND SOME TIME AND ENERGY TO WRITE TO MY ENGLISH FRIEND T. I WROTE TO HIM THAT IF I GET THE GRANT I WILL USE IT TO GET THE HELL OUT OF HERE. FUNNY, I DIDN'T THINK ABOUT IT BEFORE THAT. I MUST SAY THE GOING AWAY QUESTION IS BUGGING ME MORE AND MORE. I'M TELLING MYSELF OK, TWO MONTHS. BUT I KNOW ALL TOO WELL...
AWAY
...THAT I WILL WANT TO STAY LONGER...
TERRIBLE DAY AT THE STUDIO, ALL WENT WRONG. AGAIN. AND NOT ONLY FOR ME BUT FOR J TOO. WE SPENT THE WHOLE AFTERNOON PUTTING EMULSION ON SCREENS OVER AND OVER AGAIN. NO PRINTING DONE.
LATEST SCOOP: my roommate ran into L. on the street and she told her she was leaving in two weeks for Amsterdam, then Italy... but didn't mention Marseille.
THE COMPRESSOR IS UNDER GUARANTEE SO ALL IS FINE
BACK HOME I'M TOO TIRED TO DO ANYTHING INTELLIGENT EXCEPT WATCH THE NEWS ON TV.
LEAVING THE STUDIO I WENT TO MULTIMAG TO READ MY HOROSCOPE FOR 2003 IN ELLE-QUÉBEC. PFFF SOUNDS EXACTLY LIKE THE HOROSCOPE I GOT FOR 2002 except with the man of my life in DECEMBER INSTEAD OF MARCH.
OH LALA
OOP
LUI
CHANEL
TRUC
ELLE
CANADA RATIFIES THE KYOTO AGREEMENT.
YES MAM!
is there hope after all?

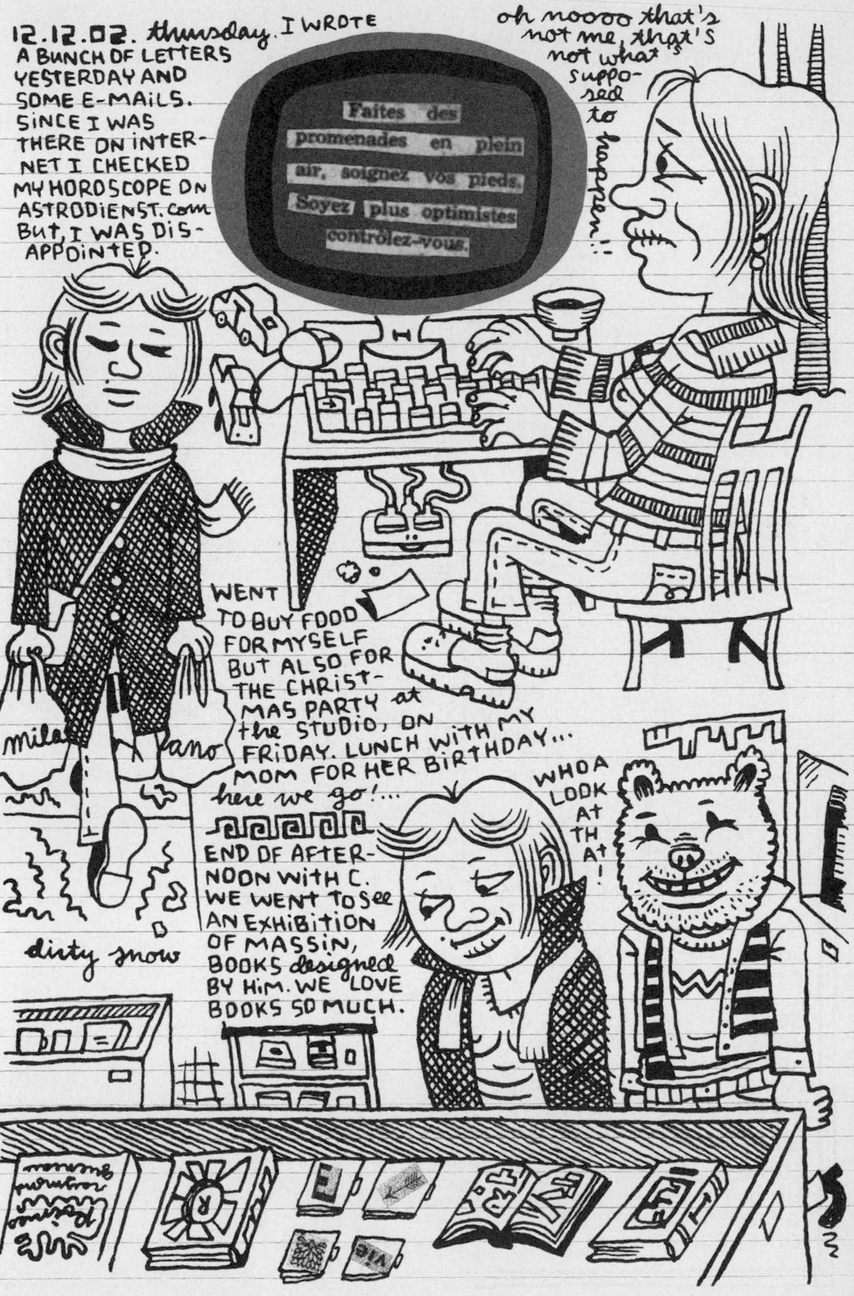

12.12.02. thursday. I WROTE A BUNCH OF LETTERS YESTERDAY AND SOME E-MAILS. SINCE I WAS THERE ON INTERNET I CHECKED MY HOROSCOPE ON ASTRODIENST.com BUT, I WAS DISAPPOINTED.
Faites des promenades en plein air, soignez vos pieds. Soyez plus optimistes contrôlez-vous.
oh noooo that's not me, that's not what's supposed to happen!!
WENT TO BUY FOOD FOR MYSELF BUT ALSO FOR THE CHRISTMAS PARTY at the STUDIO, ON FRIDAY. LUNCH WITH MY MOM FOR HER BIRTHDAY... here we go!...
mila
ano
dirty snow
END OF AFTERNOON WITH C. WE WENT TO SEE AN EXHIBITION OF MASSIN, BOOKS designed BY HIM. WE LOVE BOOKS SO MUCH.
WHOA LOOK AT THAT!

13.12.02. *friday*. FRIDAY THE THIRTEENTH. GOOD THING I TOOK AN ASPIRIN BEFORE GOING TO BED LAST NIGHT BECAUSE I'M SURE I WOULDN'T FEEL SO GOOD OTHERWISE THIS MORNING. THOSE LITTLE PLASTIC GLASSES YOU FILL UP *and* UP AGAIN... I STOPPED COUNTING. GOT NO TIME *and* NO COURAGE TO DRAW THIS MORNING.

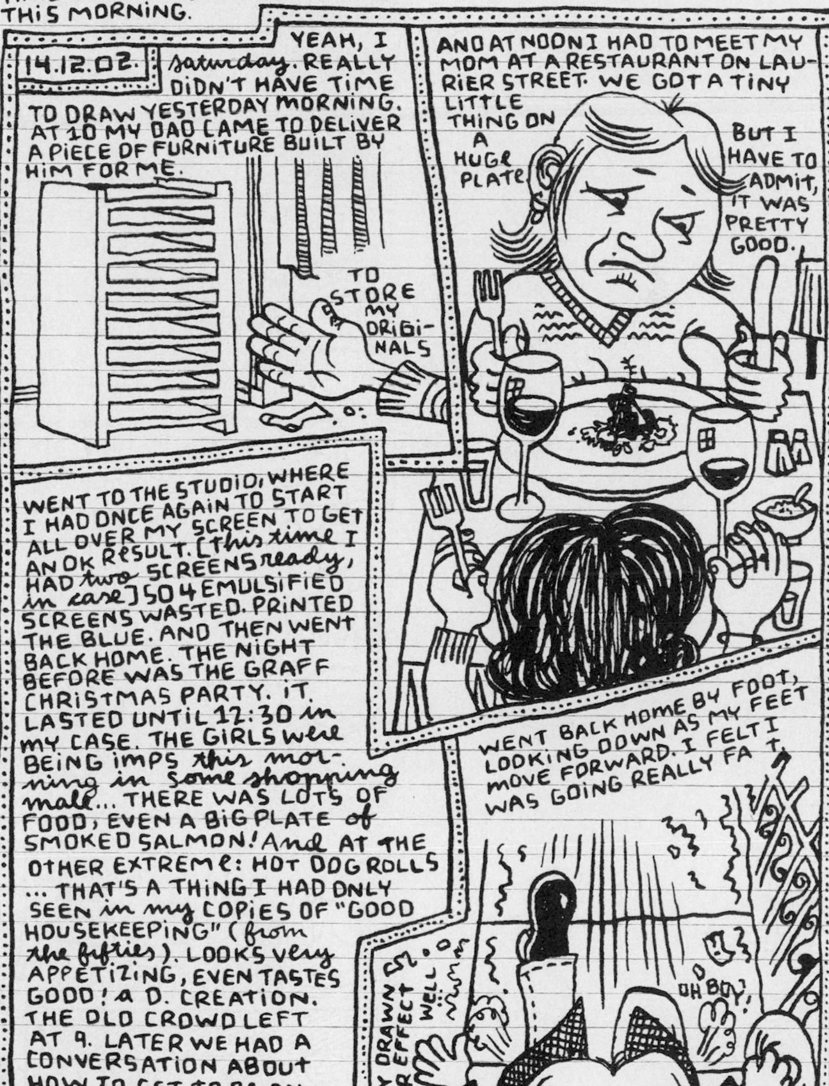
14.12.02.
YEAH, I *saturday*. REALLY DIDN'T HAVE TIME TO DRAW YESTERDAY MORNING. AT 10 MY DAD CAME TO DELIVER A PIECE OF FURNITURE BUILT BY HIM FOR ME.
TO STORE MY ORIGINALS
AND AT NOON I HAD TO MEET MY MOM AT A RESTAURANT ON LAURIER STREET. WE GOT A TINY LITTLE THING ON A HUGE PLATE.
BUT I HAVE TO ADMIT, IT WAS PRETTY GOOD.
WENT TO THE STUDIO, WHERE I HAD ONCE AGAIN TO START ALL OVER MY SCREEN TO GET AN OK RESULT. [*this time I* HAD *two* SCREENS *ready, in case*] SO 4 EMULSIFIED SCREENS WASTED. PRINTED THE BLUE. AND THEN WENT BACK HOME. THE NIGHT BEFORE WAS THE GRAFF CHRISTMAS PARTY. IT LASTED UNTIL 12:30 *in* MY CASE. THE GIRLS *were* BEING *imps this morning in some shopping mall*... THERE WAS LOTS OF FOOD, EVEN A BIG PLATE *of* SMOKED SALMON! *And* AT THE OTHER EXTREME: HOT DOG ROLLS ... THAT'S A THING I HAD ONLY SEEN *in my* COPIES OF "GOOD HOUSEKEEPING" (*from the fifties*). LOOKS *very* APPETIZING, EVEN TASTES GOOD! *a* D. CREATION. THE OLD CROWD LEFT AT 9. LATER WE HAD A CONVERSATION ABOUT HOW TO GET TO BE ON GRAFF'S BOARD *of* DIRECTORS.
WENT BACK HOME BY FOOT, LOOKING DOWN AS MY FEET MOVE FORWARD. I FELT I WAS GOING REALLY FA T.
OH BOY!
BADLY DRAWN
SUPER EFFECT
OH WELL

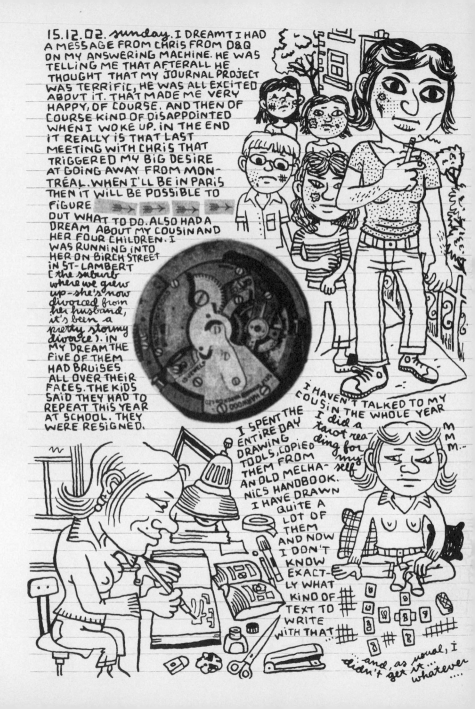

15.12.02. sunday. I DREAMT I HAD A MESSAGE FROM CHRIS FROM D&Q ON MY ANSWERING MACHINE. HE WAS TELLING ME THAT AFTER ALL HE THOUGHT THAT MY JOURNAL PROJECT WAS TERRIFIC, HE WAS ALL EXCITED ABOUT IT. THAT MADE ME VERY HAPPY, OF COURSE. AND THEN OF COURSE KIND OF DISAPPOINTED WHEN I WOKE UP. IN THE END IT REALLY IS THAT LAST MEETING WITH CHRIS THAT TRIGGERED MY BIG DESIRE AT GOING AWAY FROM MON- TRÉAL. WHEN I'LL BE IN PARIS THEN IT WILL BE POSSIBLE TO FIGURE →→→ →→→ →→→ →→→ OUT WHAT TO DO. ALSO HAD A DREAM ABOUT MY COUSIN AND HER FOUR CHILDREN. I WAS RUNNING INTO HER ON BIRCH STREET IN ST-LAMBERT (the suburb where we grew up - she's now divorced from her husband, it's been a pretty stormy divorce). IN MY DREAM THE FIVE OF THEM HAD BRUISES ALL OVER THEIR FACES. THE KIDS SAID THEY HAD TO REPEAT THIS YEAR AT SCHOOL. THEY WERE RESIGNED.

I HAVEN'T TALKED TO MY COUSIN IN THE WHOLE YEAR

I did a tarot rea- ding for my- self

MMM...

I SPENT THE ENTIRE DAY DRAWING TOOLS, COPIED THEM FROM AN OLD MECHA- NICS HANDBOOK. I HAVE DRAWN QUITE A LOT OF THEM AND NOW I DON'T KNOW EXACT- LY WHAT KIND OF TEXT TO WRITE WITH THAT...

...and, as usual, I didn't get it... whatever....

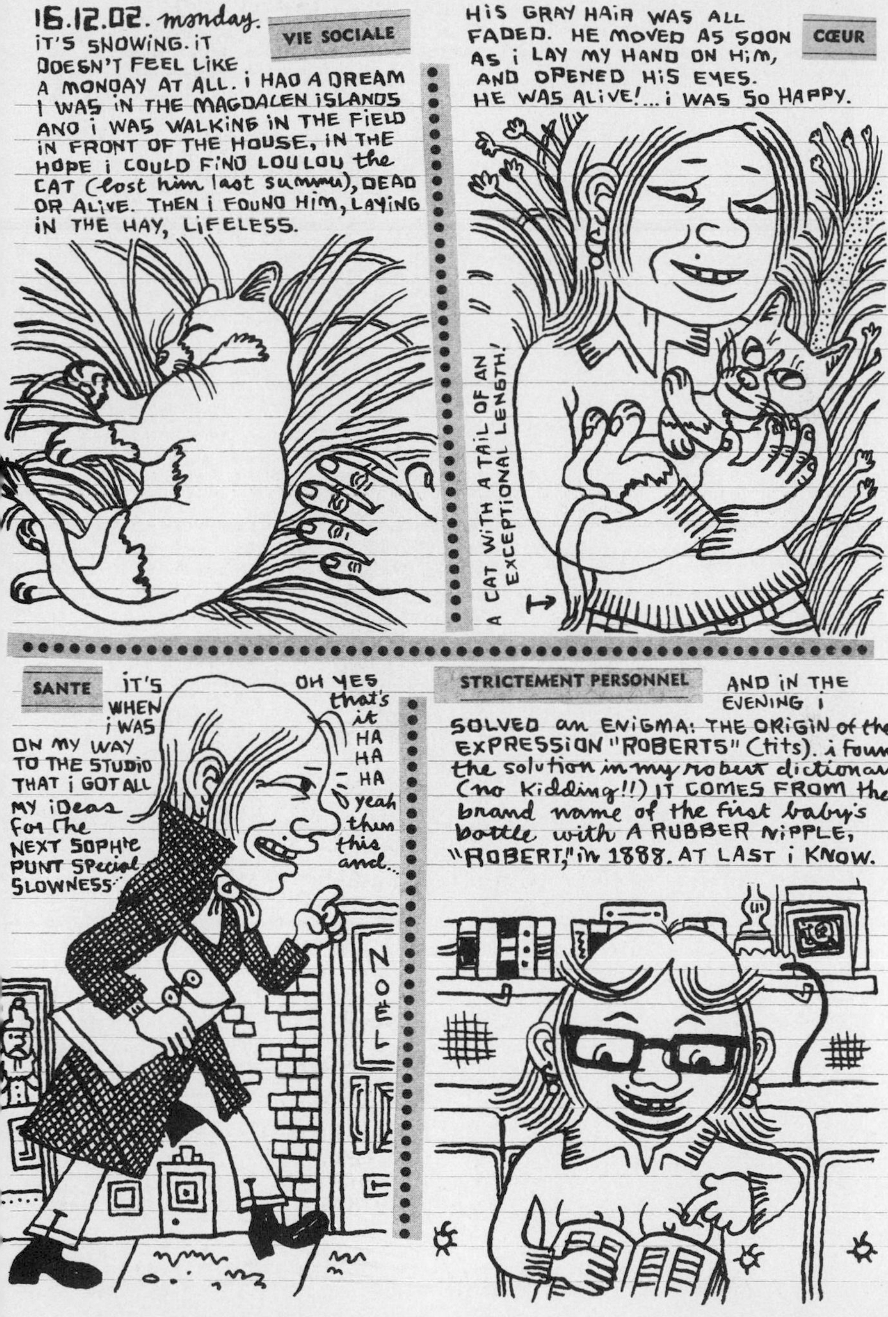
16.12.02. monday.
VIE SOCIALE
IT'S SNOWING. IT DOESN'T FEEL LIKE A MONDAY AT ALL. I HAD A DREAM I WAS IN THE MAGDALEN ISLANDS AND I WAS WALKING IN THE FIELD IN FRONT OF THE HOUSE, IN THE HOPE I COULD FIND LOULOU the CAT (lost him last summer), DEAD OR ALIVE. THEN I FOUND HIM, LAYING IN THE HAY, LIFELESS.
CŒUR
HIS GRAY HAIR WAS ALL FADED. HE MOVED AS SOON AS I LAY MY HAND ON HIM, AND OPENED HIS EYES. HE WAS ALIVE!... I WAS SO HAPPY.
A CAT WITH A TAIL OF AN EXCEPTIONAL LENGTH!
SANTE
IT'S WHEN I WAS ON MY WAY TO THE STUDIO THAT I GOT ALL MY IDeas for the NEXT SOPHIE PUNT Special SLOWNESS...
OH YES that's it HA HA HA yeah then this and...
NOËL
STRICTEMENT PERSONNEL
AND IN THE EVENING I SOLVED an ENIGMA: THE ORIGIN of the EXPRESSION "ROBERTS" (tits). I found the solution in my robert dictionary (no kidding!!) IT COMES FROM the brand name of the first baby's bottle with A RUBBER NIPPLE, "ROBERT," in 1888. AT LAST I KNOW.

17.12.02. tuesday. i WOKE UP AROUND FIVE, AND i COULDN'T GET BACK TO SLEEP. GOT UP A BIT BEFORE SEVEN. iT HAPPENS TO ME ONCE iN A WHILE. i'M GONNA HAVE TIME TO DO TONS OF THINGS THIS MORNING. WRITE SOME LETTERS...

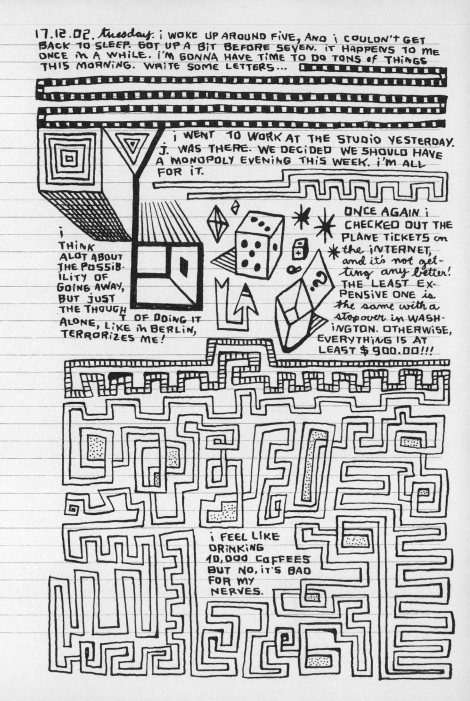

i WENT TO WORK AT THE STUDIO YESTERDAY. J. WAS THERE. WE DECIDED WE SHOULD HAVE A MONOPOLY EVENING THIS WEEK. i'M ALL FOR iT.

i THINK ALOT ABOUT THE POSSIBILITY OF GOING AWAY, BUT JUST THE THOUGHT OF DOING iT ALONE, LiKE iN BERLIN, TERRORIZES ME!

ONCE AGAIN i CHECKED OUT THE PLANE TICKETS on the iNTERNET, and it's not getting any better! THE LEAST EXPENSIVE ONE is the same with a stopover in WASHINGTON. OTHERWISE, EVERYTHING iS AT LEAST $ 900.00!!!

i FEEL LiKE DRiNKiNG 10,000 COFFEES BUT NO, iT'S BAD FOR MY NERVES.

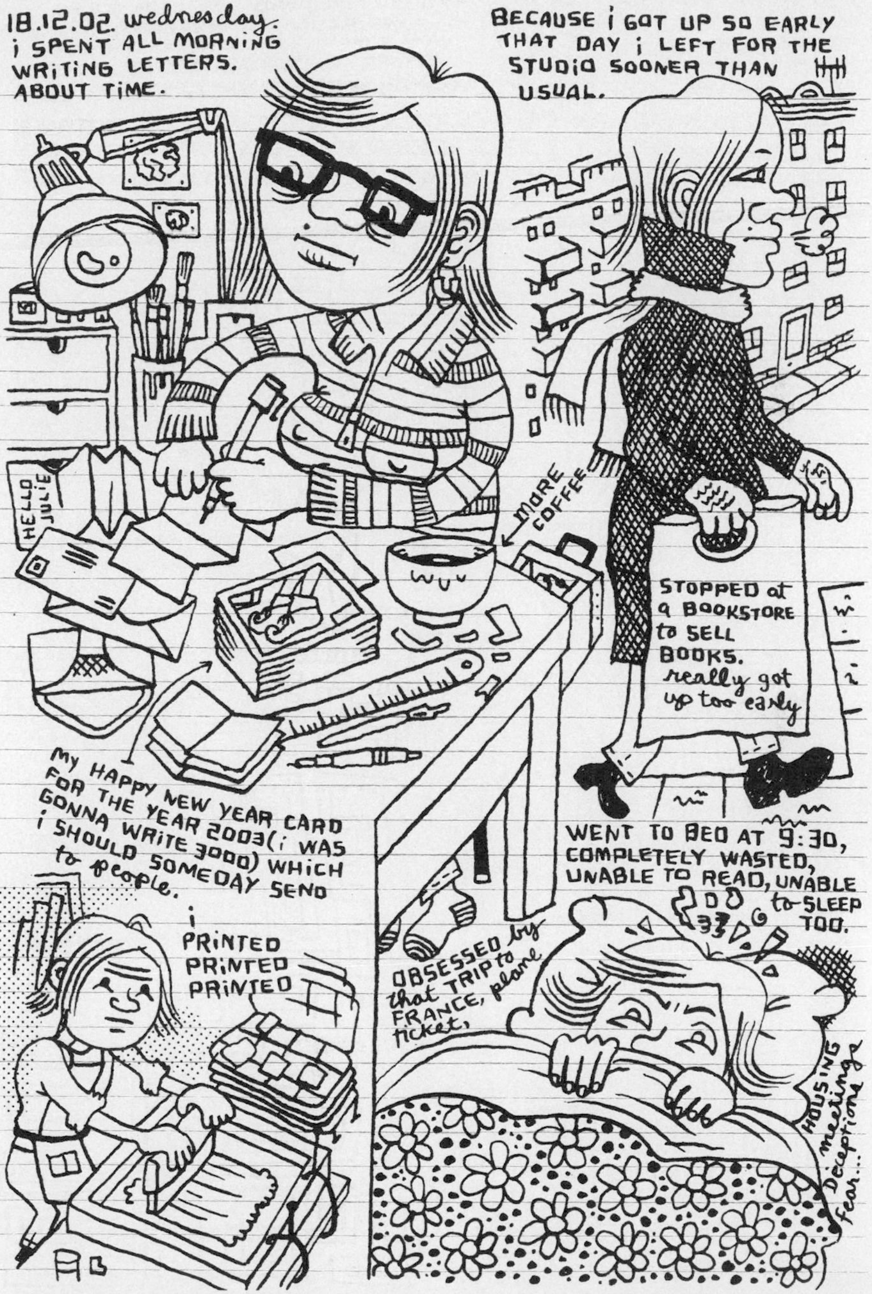
18.12.02. wednesday.
i SPENT ALL MORNING WRITING LETTERS. ABOUT TIME.
HELLO JULIE
MORE COFFEE
MY HAPPY NEW YEAR CARD FOR THE YEAR 2003 (i WAS GONNA WRITE 3000) WHICH i SHOULD SOMEDAY SEND to people.
BECAUSE i GOT UP SO EARLY THAT DAY i LEFT FOR THE STUDIO SOONER THAN USUAL.
STOPPED at a BOOKSTORE to SELL BOOKS. really got up too early
i PRINTED PRINTED PRINTED
WENT TO BED AT 9:30, COMPLETELY WASTED, UNABLE TO READ, UNABLE to SLEEP TOO.
OBSESSED by that TRIP to FRANCE, plane ticket,
HOUSING meetings Deceptions fear...
AB

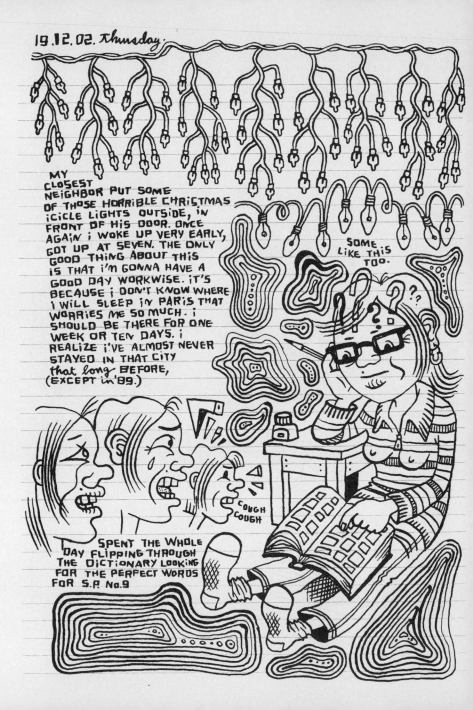

19.12.02. thursday.

MY CLOSEST NEIGHBOR PUT SOME OF THOSE HORRIBLE CHRISTMAS iCiCLE LIGHTS OUTSIDE, IN FRONT OF HIS DOOR. ONCE AGAiN i WOKE UP VERY EARLY, GOT UP AT SEVEN. THE ONLY GOOD THiNG ABOUT THiS IS THAT i'M GONNA HAVE A GOOD DAY WORKWISE. iT'S BECAUSE i DON'T KNOW WHERE I WILL SLEEP iN PARiS THAT WORRiES ME SO MUCH. i SHOULD BE THERE FOR ONE WEEK OR TEN DAYS. i REALiZE i'VE ALMOST NEVER STAYED iN THAT CiTY that long BEFORE, (EXCEPT iN '89.)

SOME LIKE THIS TOO.

COUGH COUGH

SPENT THE WHOLE DAY FLIPPING THROUGH THE DiCTiONARY LOOKiNG FOR THE PERFECT WORDS FOR S.P. No.9

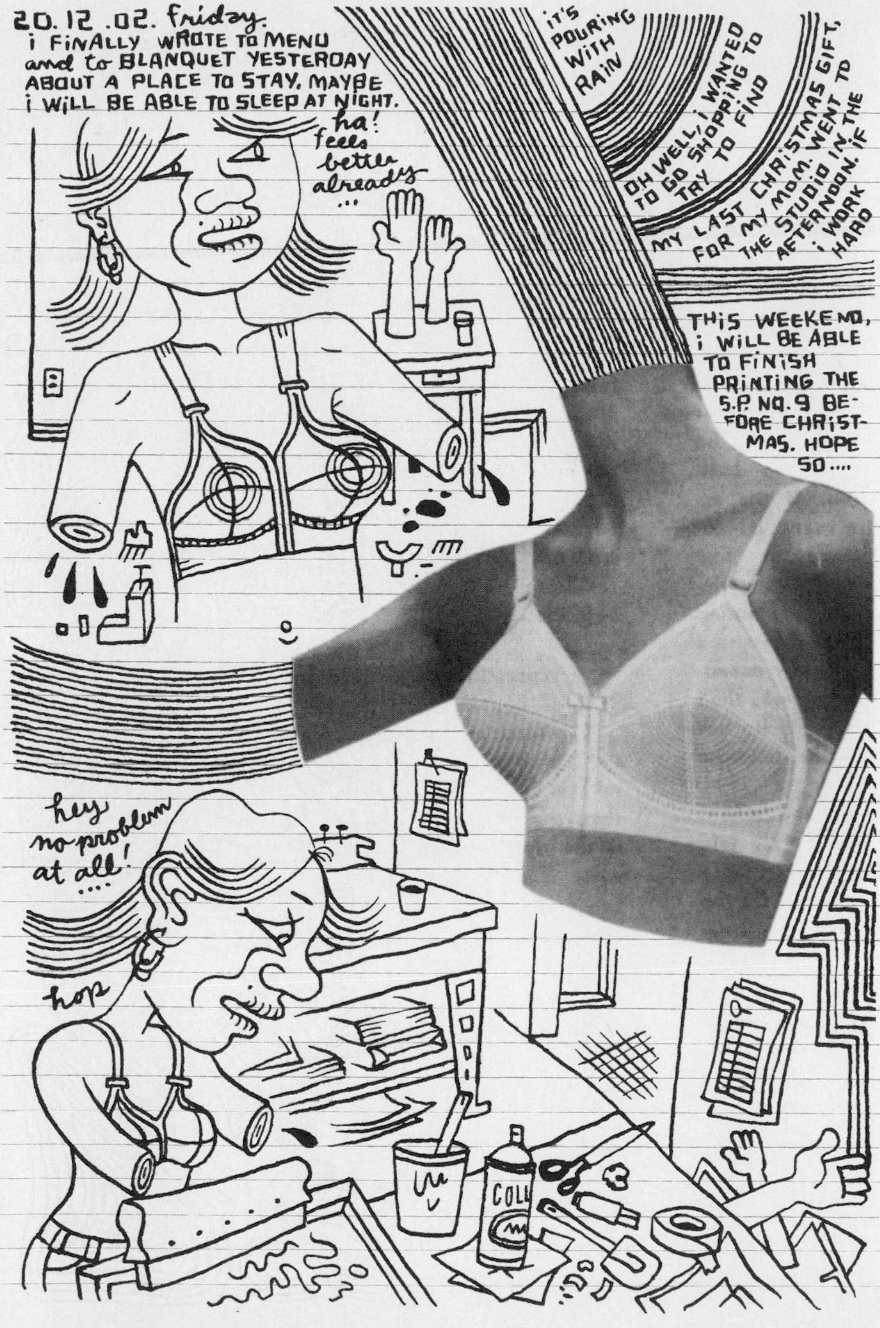
20.12.02. friday.
i FINALLY WROTE TO MENU and to BLANQUET YESTERDAY ABOUT A PLACE TO STAY. MAYBE i WILL BE ABLE TO SLEEP AT NIGHT.
ha! feels better already...
IT'S POURING WITH RAIN
OH WELL, i WANTED TO GO SHOPPING TO TRY TO FIND MY LAST CHRISTMAS GIFT, FOR MY MOM. WENT TO THE STUDIO IN THE AFTERNOON. IF i WORK HARD
THIS WEEKEND, i WILL BE ABLE TO FINISH PRINTING THE S.P. NO. 9 BEFORE CHRISTMAS. HOPE SO....
hey no problem at all! ....
hop

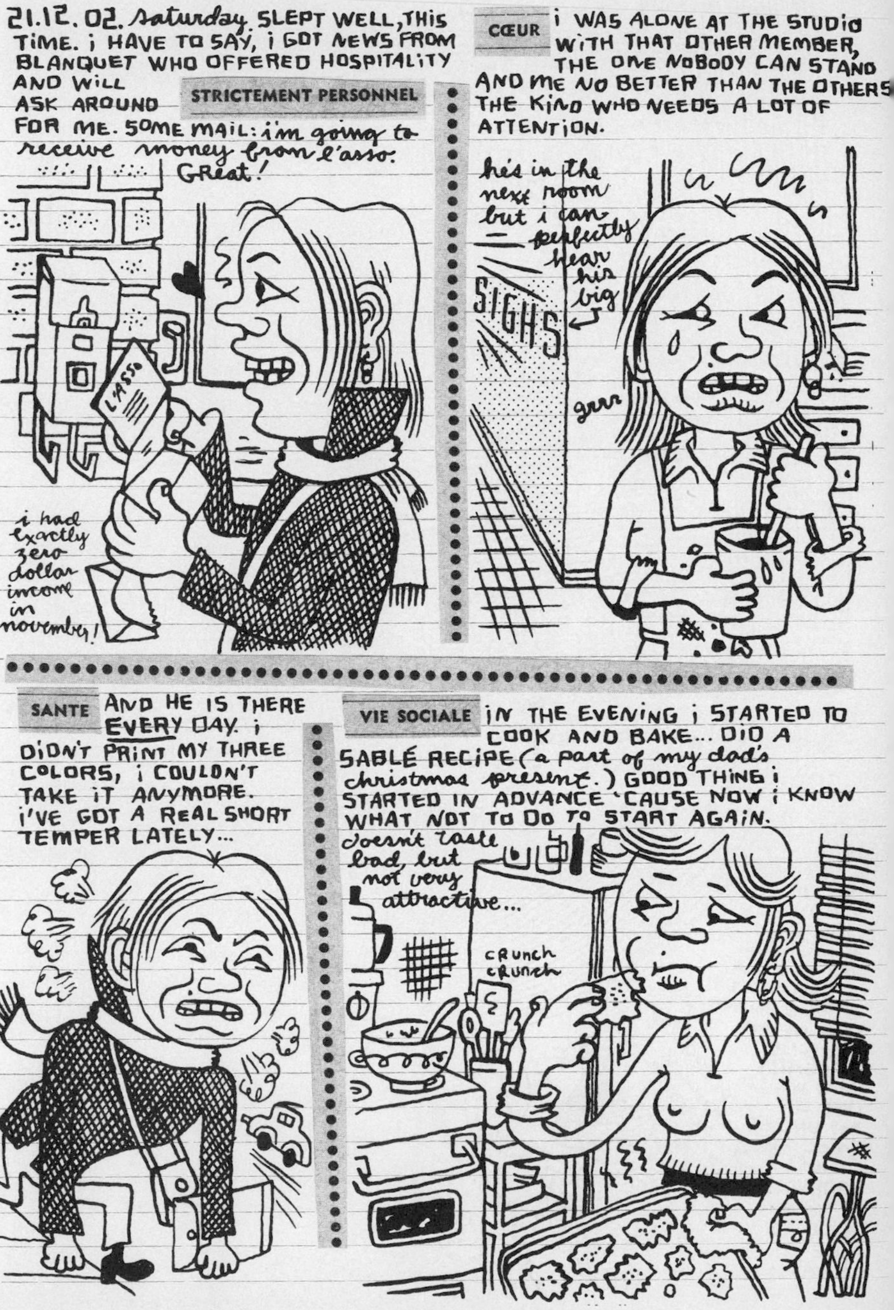
21.12.02. saturday SLEPT WELL, THIS TIME. i HAVE TO SAY, i GOT NEWS FROM BLANQUET WHO OFFERED HOSPITALITY AND WILL ASK AROUND FOR ME. SOME MAIL: i'm going to receive money from l'asso: GREAT!
STRICTEMENT PERSONNEL
L'ASSO
i had exactly zero dollar income in november!
CŒUR
i WAS ALONE AT THE STUDIO WITH THAT OTHER MEMBER, THE ONE NOBODY CAN STAND AND ME NO BETTER THAN THE OTHERS THE KIND WHO NEEDS A LOT OF ATTENTION.
he's in the next room but i can perfectly hear his big
SIGHS
grrr
SANTE
AND HE IS THERE EVERY DAY. i DIDN'T PRINT MY THREE COLORS, i COULDN'T TAKE iT ANYMORE. i'VE GOT A REAL SHORT TEMPER LATELY...
VIE SOCIALE
iN THE EVENING i STARTED TO COOK AND BAKE... DID A SABLÉ RECIPE (a part of my dad's christmas present.) GOOD THING i STARTED IN ADVANCE 'CAUSE NOW i KNOW WHAT NOT TO DO TO START AGAIN.
doesn't taste bad, but not very attractive...
crunch crunch

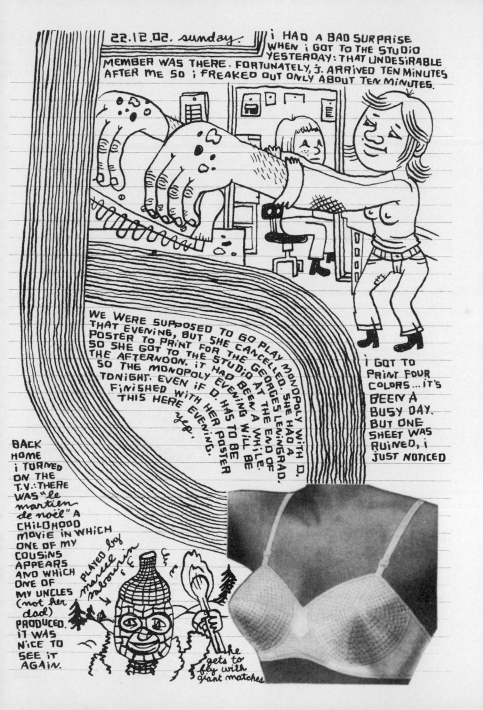

22.12.02. sunday. i HAD A BAD SURPRISE WHEN i GOT TO THE STUDIO YESTERDAY: THAT UNDESIRABLE MEMBER WAS THERE. FORTUNATELY, J. ARRIVED TEN MINUTES AFTER ME SO i FREAKED OUT ONLY ABOUT TEN MINUTES.

WE WERE SUPPOSED TO GO PLAY MONOPOLY WITH D. THAT EVENING, BUT SHE CANCELLED. SHE HAD A POSTER TO PRINT FOR THE GEORGES LENINGRAD, SO SHE GOT TO THE STUDIO AT THE END OF THE AFTERNOON. IT HAD BEEN A WHILE. SO THE MONOPOLY EVENING WILL BE TONIGHT. EVEN IF D. HAS TO BE FINISHED WITH HER POSTER THIS HERE EVENING. yep.

i GOT TO PRINT FOUR COLORS...IT'S BEEN A BUSY DAY. BUT ONE SHEET WAS RUINED, i JUST NOTICED

BACK HOME i TURNED ON THE T.V.: THERE WAS "le martien de noël" A CHILDHOOD MOVIE IN WHICH ONE OF MY COUSINS APPEARS AND WHICH ONE OF MY UNCLES (not her dad) PRODUCED. IT WAS NICE TO SEE IT AGAIN.

PLAYED by marcel sabourin

he gets to fly with giant matches

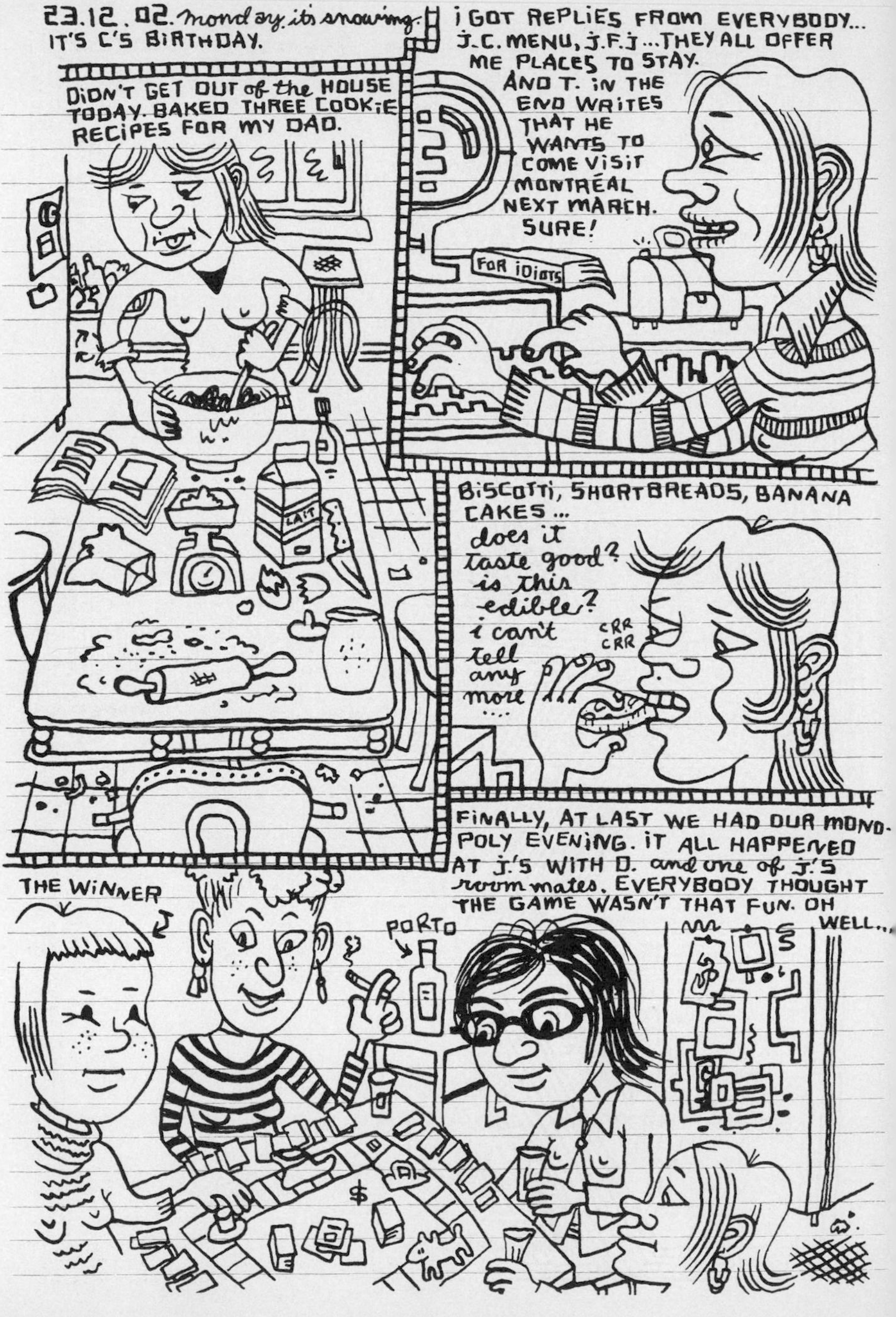
23.12.02. monday. it's snowing. IT'S C'S BIRTHDAY.
DIDN'T GET OUT of the HOUSE TODAY. BAKED THREE COOKIE RECIPES FOR MY DAD.
LAIT
I GOT REPLIES FROM EVERYBODY... J.C. MENU, J.F.J... THEY ALL OFFER ME PLACES TO STAY.
AND T. IN THE END WRITES THAT HE WANTS TO COME VISIT MONTRÉAL NEXT MARCH. SURE!
FOR IDIOTS
BISCOTTI, SHORTBREADS, BANANA CAKES...
does it taste good? is this edible? i can't tell any more....
CRR CRR
FINALLY, AT LAST WE HAD OUR MONOPOLY EVENING. IT ALL HAPPENED AT J.'S WITH D. and one of J.'S room mates. EVERYBODY THOUGHT THE GAME WASN'T THAT FUN. OH WELL...
THE WINNER
PORTO
$

24.12.02. tuesday.

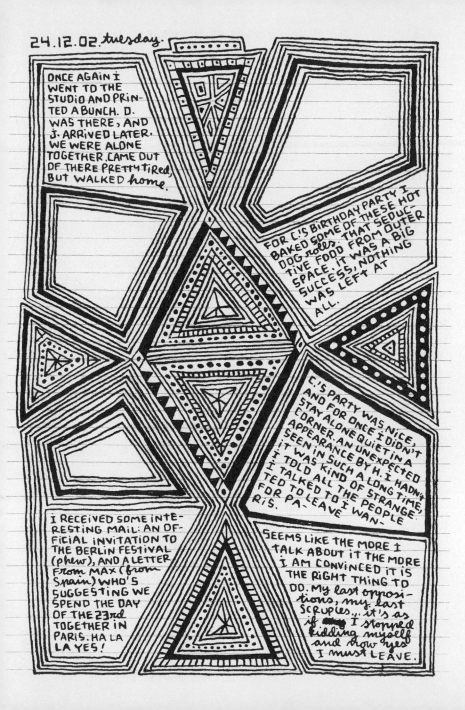

ONCE AGAIN I WENT TO THE STUDIO AND PRINTED A BUNCH. D. WAS THERE, AND J. ARRIVED LATER. WE WERE ALONE TOGETHER. CAME OUT OF THERE PRETTY TIRED, BUT WALKED home.

FOR C.'S BIRTHDAY PARTY I BAKED SOME OF THESE HOT DOG rolls. THAT SEDUC-TIVE FOOD FROM OUTER SPACE. IT WAS A BIG SUCCESS, NOTHING WAS LEFT AT ALL.

C.'S PARTY WAS NICE, AND FOR ONCE I DIDN'T STAY ALONE QUIET IN A CORNER. AN UNEXPECTED APPEARANCE BY H. I HADN'T SEEN IN SUCH A LONG TIME. IT WAS KIND OF STRANGE. I TOLD ALL THE PEOPLE I TALKED TO I WAN-TED TO LEAVE FOR PA-RIS.

I RECEIVED SOME INTE-RESTING MAIL: AN OF-FICIAL INVITATION TO THE BERLIN FESTIVAL (phew), AND A LETTER from MAX (from Spain) WHO'S SUGGESTING WE SPEND THE DAY OF THE 23rd TOGETHER IN PARIS. HA LA LA YES!

SEEMS LIKE THE MORE I TALK ABOUT IT THE MORE I AM CONVINCED IT IS THE RIGHT THING TO DO. My last opposi-tions, my last scruples... it's as if I stopped kidding myself and now yes I must LEAVE.

25.12.02. wednesday
IT DOESN'T FEEL LIKE CHRISTMAS AT ALL. IT'S GREY AND DESERTED.

VERY DELICIOUS DINNER AT MY MOM'S LAST NIGHT.

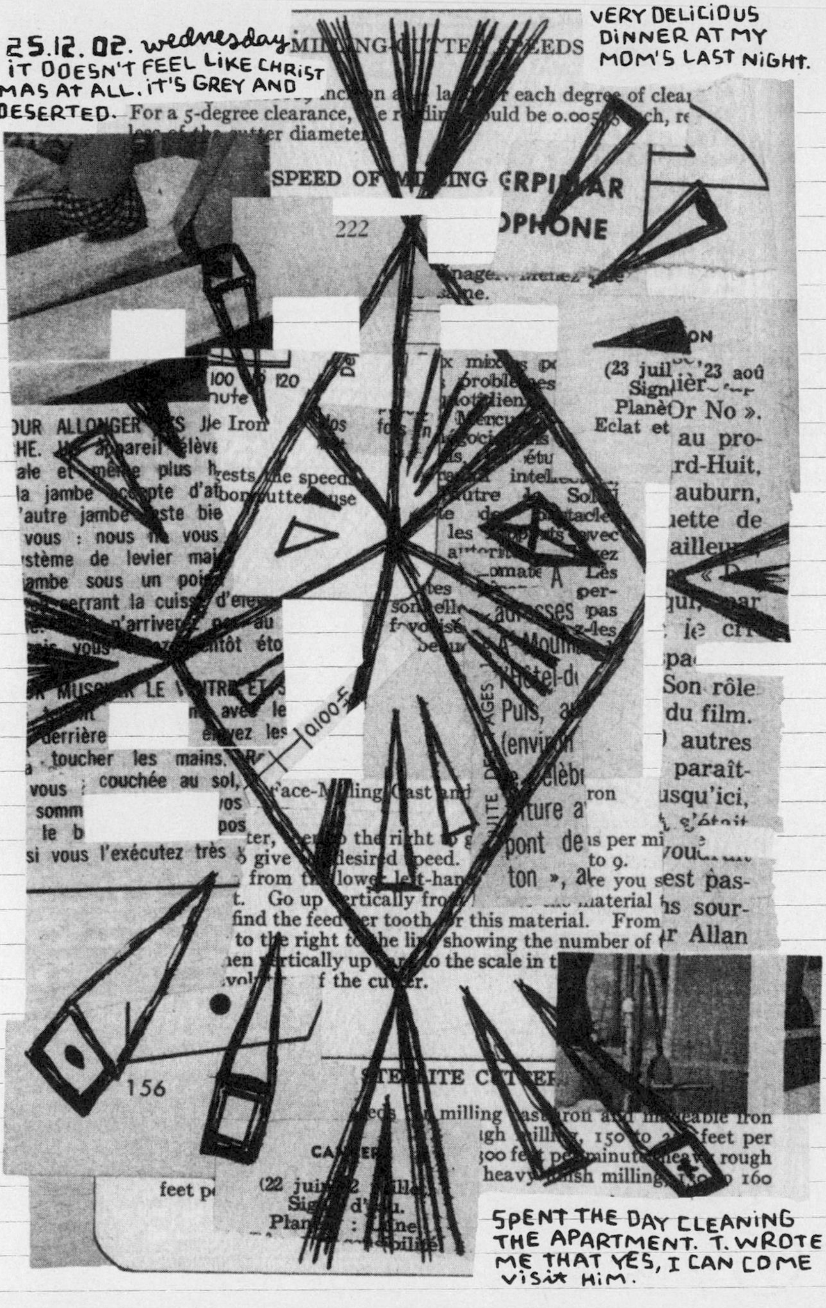

For a 5-degree clearance,
SPEED OF
OPHONE
222
(23 juil
Signe
Planè
Eclat et
Or No ».
au pro-
rd-Huit,
auburn,
uette de
Son rôle
du film.
autres
paraît-
usqu'ici,
toucher les mains.
couchée au sol,
si vous l'exécutez très
Face-Milling Cast
to 9.
find the feed per tooth for this material.
the right to the line showing the number of
f the cutter.
156
milling
heavy
feet p
Signe d'eau.

SPENT THE DAY CLEANING THE APARTMENT. T. WROTE ME THAT YES, I CAN COME VISIT HIM.

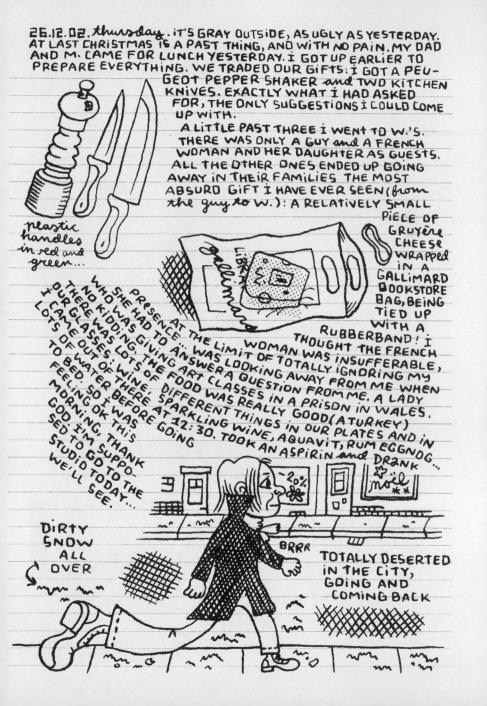

26.12.02. thursday. IT'S GRAY OUTSIDE, AS UGLY AS YESTERDAY. AT LAST CHRISTMAS IS A PAST THING, AND WITH NO PAIN. MY DAD AND M. CAME FOR LUNCH YESTERDAY. I GOT UP EARLIER TO PREPARE EVERYTHING. WE TRADED OUR GIFTS: I GOT A PEUGEOT PEPPER SHAKER and TWO KITCHEN KNIVES. EXACTLY WHAT I HAD ASKED FOR, THE ONLY SUGGESTIONS I COULD COME UP WITH.

A LITTLE PAST THREE I WENT TO W.'S. THERE WAS ONLY A GUY and A FRENCH WOMAN AND HER DAUGHTER AS GUESTS. ALL THE OTHER ONES ENDED UP GOING AWAY IN THEIR FAMILIES. THE MOST ABSURD GIFT I HAVE EVER SEEN (from the guy to W.): A RELATIVELY SMALL

plastic handles in red and green...

PIECE OF GRUYÈRE CHEESE WRAPPED IN A GALLIMARD BOOKSTORE BAG, BEING TIED UP WITH A RUBBERBAND! I THOUGHT THE FRENCH WOMAN WAS INSUFFERABLE, TOTALLY IGNORING MY PRESENCE AT THE LIMIT OF... WAS LOOKING AWAY FROM ME WHEN SHE HAD TO ANSWER A QUESTION FROM ME. A LADY WHO WAS GIVING ART CLASSES IN A PRISON IN WALES. NO KIDDING. THE FOOD WAS REALLY GOOD (A TURKEY) AND IN OUR GLASSES: LOTS OF DIFFERENT THINGS IN OUR PLATES AND IN OUR GLASSES: WINE, SPARKLING WINE, AQUAVIT, RUM EGGNOG... I CAME OUT OF THERE AT 12:30. TOOK AN ASPIRIN and DRANK LOTS OF WATER BEFORE GOING TO BED. SO I WAS FEELING OK THIS MORNING, THANK GOD. I'M SUPPOSED TO GO TO THE STUDIO TODAY... WE'LL SEE.

-20%

noël **

DIRTY SNOW ALL OVER

BRRR

TOTALLY DESERTED IN THE CITY, GOING AND COMING BACK

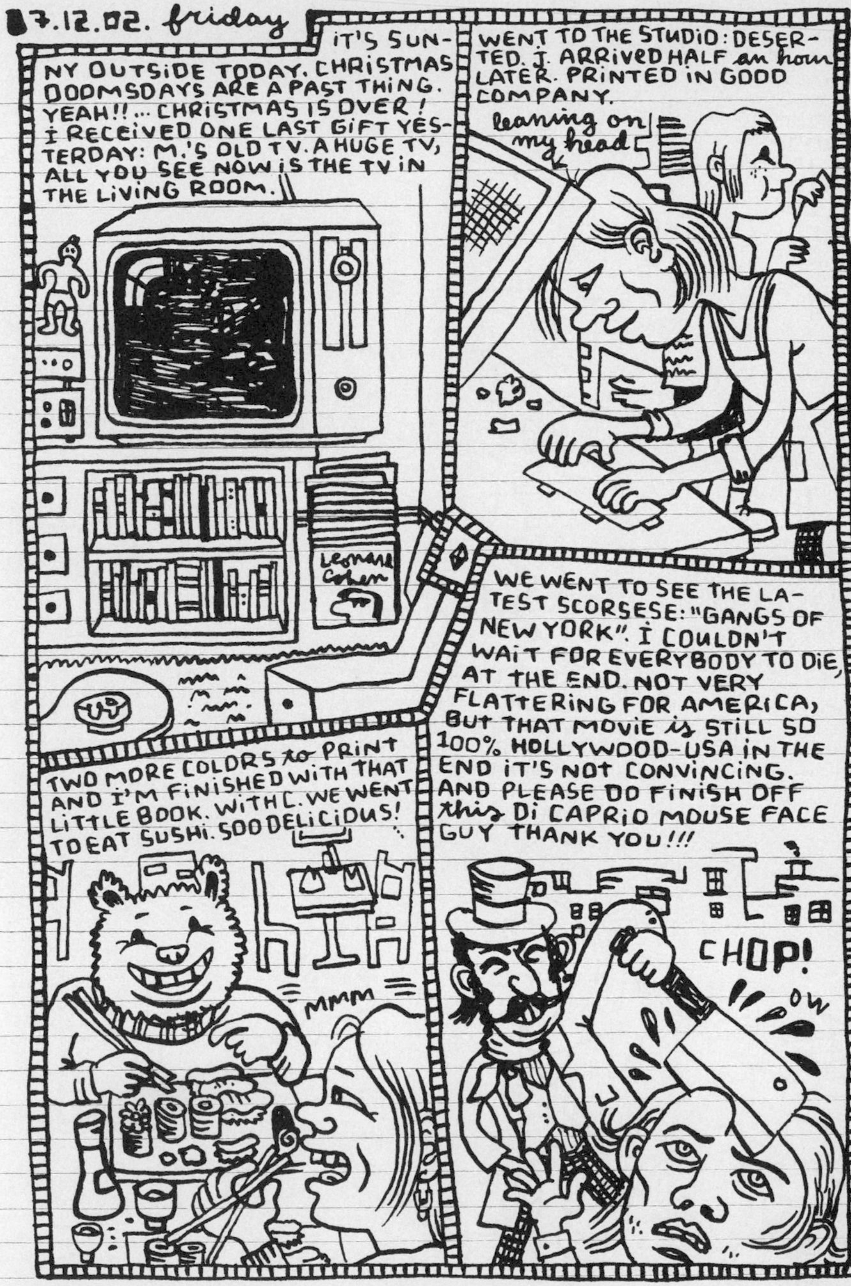
7.12.02. friday
IT'S SUNNY OUTSIDE TODAY. CHRISTMAS DOOMSDAYS ARE A PAST THING. YEAH!! ... CHRISTMAS IS OVER! I RECEIVED ONE LAST GIFT YESTERDAY: M.'S OLD TV. A HUGE TV, ALL YOU SEE NOW IS THE TV IN THE LIVING ROOM.
Leonard Cohen
WENT TO THE STUDIO: DESERTED. J. ARRIVED HALF an hour LATER. PRINTED IN GOOD COMPANY.
leaning on my head
TWO MORE COLORS to PRINT AND I'M FINISHED WITH THAT LITTLE BOOK. WITH C. WE WENT TO EAT SUSHI. SOO DELICIOUS!
MMM
WE WENT TO SEE THE LATEST SCORSESE: "GANGS OF NEW YORK". I COULDN'T WAIT FOR EVERYBODY TO DIE, AT THE END. NOT VERY FLATTERING FOR AMERICA, BUT THAT MOVIE is STILL SO 100% HOLLYWOOD-USA IN THE END IT'S NOT CONVINCING. AND PLEASE DO FINISH OFF this DI CAPRIO MOUSE FACE GUY THANK YOU!!!
CHOP!
OW

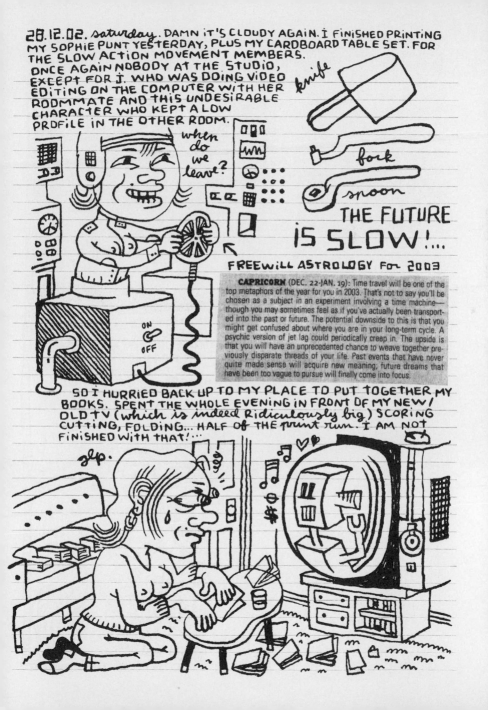

28.12.02. *saturday*. DAMN IT'S CLOUDY AGAIN. I FINISHED PRINTING MY SOPHIE PUNT YESTERDAY, PLUS MY CARDBOARD TABLE SET. FOR THE SLOW ACTION MOVEMENT MEMBERS.

ONCE AGAIN NOBODY AT THE STUDIO, EXCEPT FOR J. WHO WAS DOING VIDEO EDITING ON THE COMPUTER WITH HER RODMMATE AND THIS UNDESIRABLE CHARACTER WHO KEPT A LOW PROFILE IN THE OTHER ROOM.

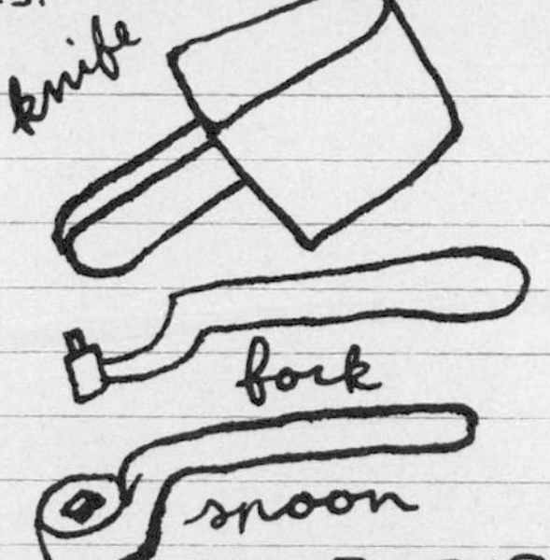

knife
fork
spoon

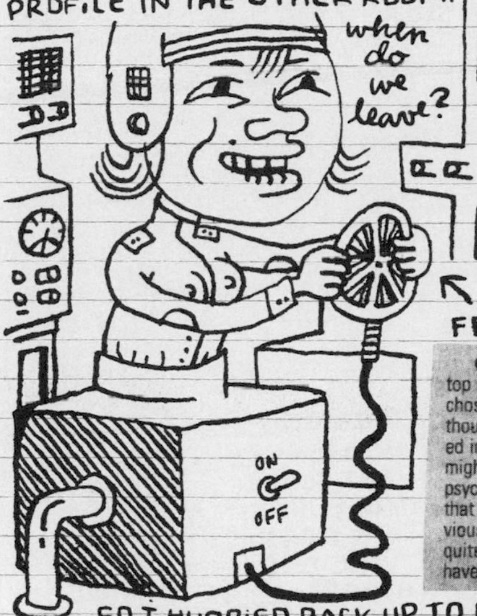

when do we leave?
ON
OFF

THE FUTURE IS SLOW!...

FREEWILL ASTROLOGY FOR 2003

CAPRICORN (DEC. 22-JAN. 19): Time travel will be one of the top metaphors of the year for you in 2003. That's not to say you'll be chosen as a subject in an experiment involving a time machine—though you may sometimes feel as if you've actually been transported into the past or future. The potential downside to this is that you might get confused about where you are in your long-term cycle. A psychic version of jet lag could periodically creep in. The upside is that you will have an unprecedented chance to weave together previously disparate threads of your life. Past events that have never quite made sense will acquire new meaning; future dreams that have been too vague to pursue will finally come into focus.

SO I HURRIED BACK UP TO MY PLACE TO PUT TOGETHER MY BOOKS. SPENT THE WHOLE EVENING IN FRONT OF MY NEW/OLD TV (*which is indeed Ridiculously big*) SCORING CUTTING, FOLDING... HALF OF THE *print run*. I AM NOT FINISHED WITH THAT!...

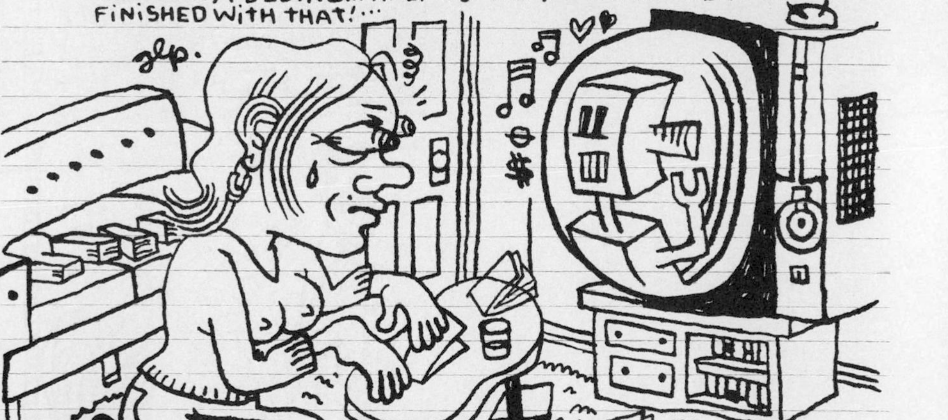

glp.

29.12.02. sunday. PHEW! IT'S SUNNY ONCE AGAIN. ALL THIS GRAY MESS IS HARD TO TAKE. NOTHING MUCH TO TELL: I WENT TO DO SOME SHOPPING IN THE AFTERNOON AND I SPENT ANOTHER EVENING PUTTING TOGETHER THE S. PUNT BOOK. FOLDED the rest OF THEM. I SEWED AND GLUED THREE COPIES. the RESULT IS NOT BAD, I LIKE IT. BUT WHAT A PAINSTAKING ASSEMBLING!!!

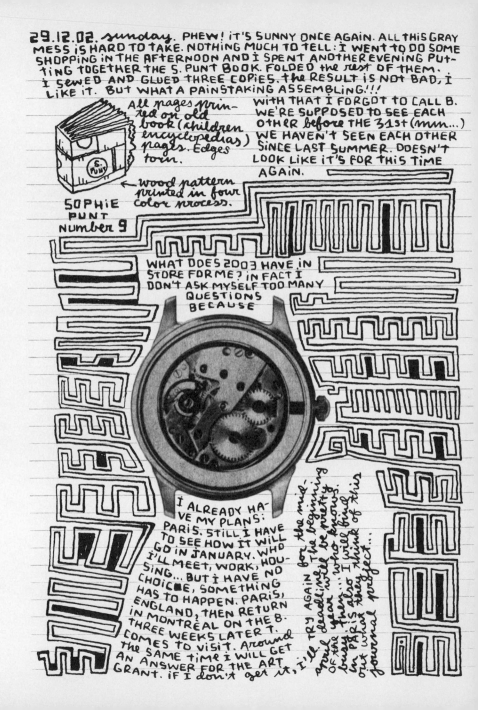

All pages printed on old book (children encyclopedias) pages. Edges torn.

← wood pattern printed in four color process.

SOPHIE PUNT Number 9

WITH THAT I FORGOT TO CALL B. WE'RE SUPPOSED TO SEE EACH OTHER before THE 31st (mm...) WE HAVEN'T SEEN EACH OTHER SINCE LAST SUMMER. DOESN'T LOOK LIKE IT'S FOR THIS TIME AGAIN.

WHAT DOES 2003 HAVE IN STORE FOR ME? IN FACT I DON'T ASK MYSELF TOO MANY QUESTIONS BECAUSE

I ALREADY HAVE MY PLANS: PARIS. STILL I HAVE TO SEE HOW IT WILL GO IN JANUARY. WHO I'LL MEET, WORK, HOUSING... BUT I HAVE NO CHOICE, SOMETHING HAS TO HAPPEN. PARIS, ENGLAND, THEN RETURN IN MONTREAL ON THE 8. THREE WEEKS LATER T. COMES TO VISIT. Around THE SAME TIME I WILL GET AN ANSWER FOR THE ART GRANT. IF I don't get it, I'll TRY AGAIN for the middle of the year... who knows, deadlines will be pretty busy then... I will find out what they think of this in Paris also journal project...

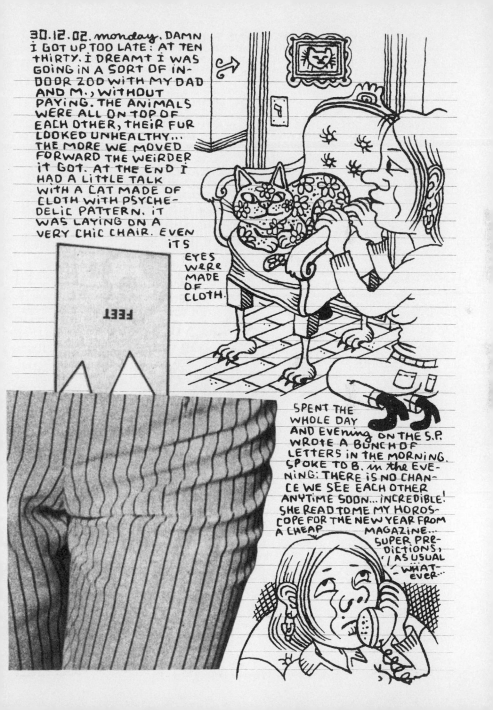

30.12.02. monday. DAMN I GOT UP TOO LATE: AT TEN THIRTY. I DREAMT I WAS GOING IN A SORT OF INDOOR ZOO WITH MY DAD AND M., WITHOUT PAYING. THE ANIMALS WERE ALL ON TOP OF EACH OTHER, THEIR FUR LOOKED UNHEALTHY... THE MORE WE MOVED FORWARD THE WEIRDER IT GOT. AT THE END I HAD A LITTLE TALK WITH A CAT MADE OF CLOTH WITH PSYCHEDELIC PATTERN. IT WAS LAYING ON A VERY CHIC CHAIR. EVEN ITS EYES WERE MADE OF CLOTH.

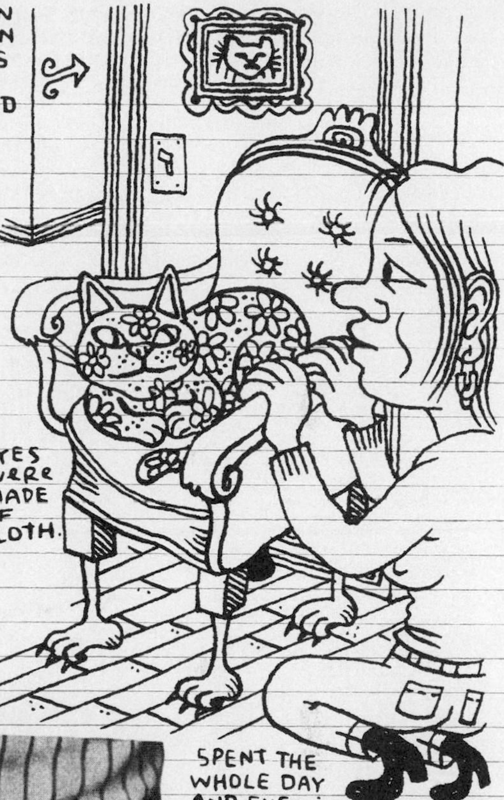

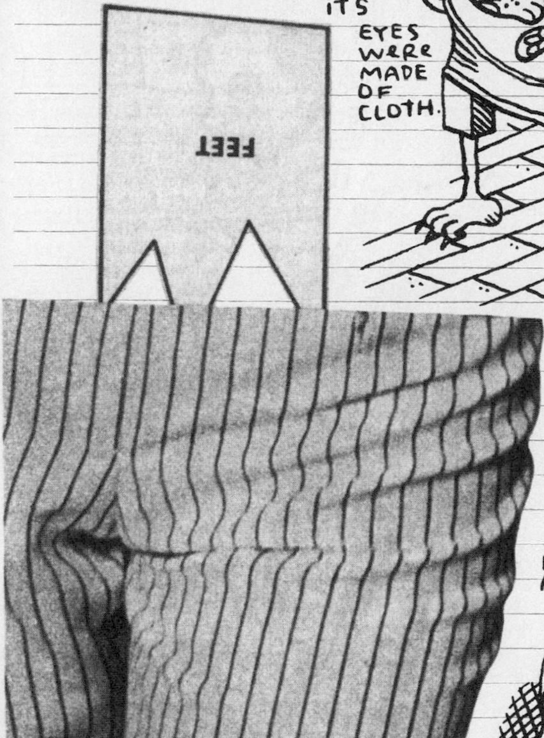
FEET

SPENT THE WHOLE DAY AND EVENING ON THE S.P. WROTE A BUNCH OF LETTERS IN THE MORNING. SPOKE TO B. in the EVENING: THERE IS NO CHANCE WE SEE EACH OTHER ANYTIME SOON... INCREDIBLE! SHE READ TO ME MY HOROSCOPE FOR THE NEW YEAR FROM A CHEAP MAGAZINE... SUPER PREDICTIONS, AS USUAL... WHATEVER...

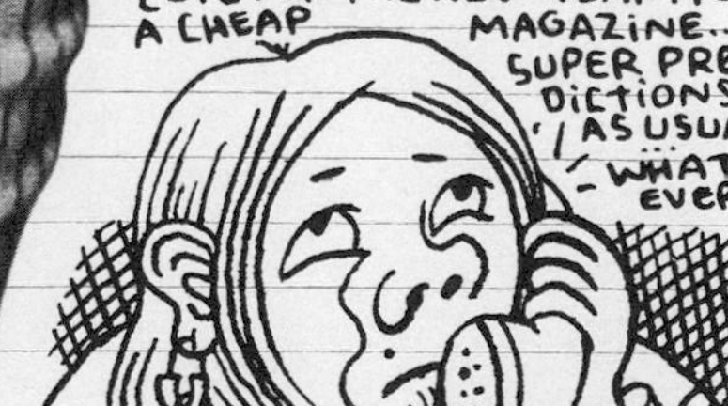

31.12.02. *tuesday*. THE LAST DAY OF THE YEAR AND MY BIRTHDAY: 37 YEARS OLD. NO SURPRISE... I HAVE THOUGHT SO MUCH ABOUT IT DURING THIS PAST YEAR... IT'S RAINING, EVERYTHING IS COVERED WITH ICE. I DID MY PLANE RESERVATION YESTERDAY. TO HAVE A STOPOVER IN LONDON IT'S GOING TO COST ME $928.00. OTHERWISE, PARIS FOR 20 DAYS IS $750.00, WITH A STOP OVER IN QUEBEC CITY [!] LOOKED ON INTERNET: A ONE WAY BY TRAIN *is 223 euros*. SO... LOOKS LIKE I'M GOING TO TAKE THE FIRST PROPOSITION. I'M RELIEVED... LOOKED FOR A BIRTHDAY GIFT FOR MATTI, BUT WITH NO SUCCESS *at all*. ON THE OTHER HAND I *found a* BUNCH OF OLD PHOTOS. *I couldn't* RESIST THAT. C. HAD ORGANIZED A PARTY FOR ME, INVITED ALL HIS FRIENDS, BUT FORGOT TO INVITE... ME!

RECENT BAD NEWS: A HUMAN CLONE IS BORN, THANKS TO CLONE-AID. AN ORGANISATION *created* BY... RAËL. NO LESS.

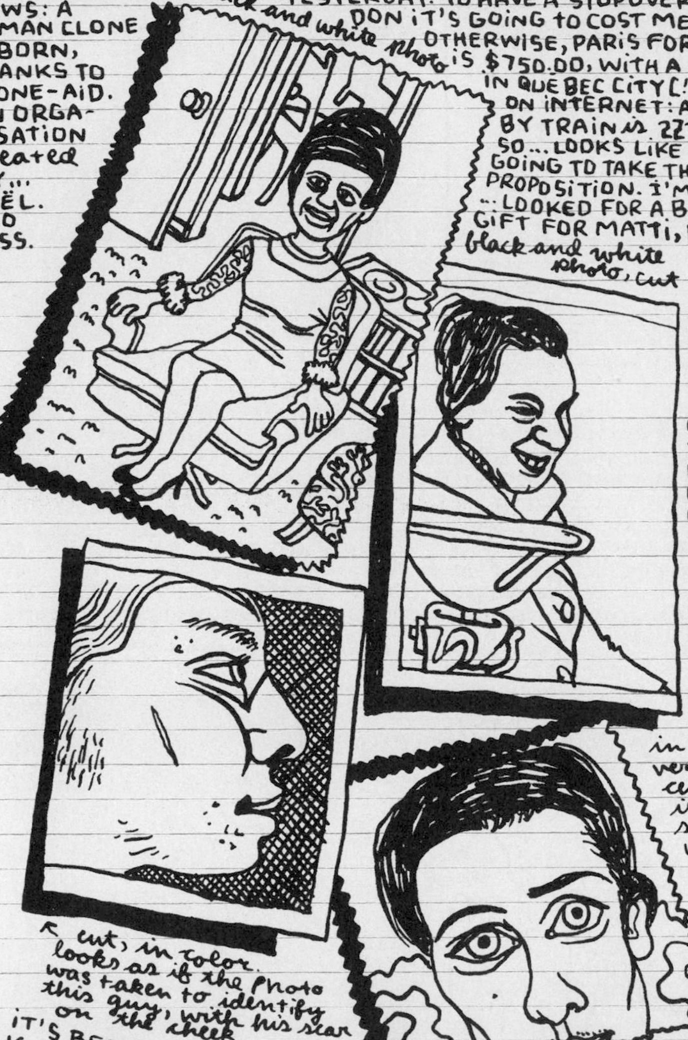

black and white photo
black and white photo, cut
in color, very badly centered. is it the same woman on the 3 photos? (of course, with these drawings...)
← cut, in color. looks as if the photo was taken to identify this guy, with his scar on the cheek

IT'S BEEN WEEKS SINCE I KNOW I'M INVITED FOR DINNER AT J.'S SO THERE'S NOTHING I CAN DO FOR THAT. HE BOUGHT OYSTERS, MY ONLY REGRET. ON FRIDAY I'M GOING TO PAY MY PLANE TICKET, NOW THAT I HAVE THE OK FOR THE DATES, FROM T. I SWEAR, I ALREADY *have a* FOOT *in the* PLANE!!... I CAN'T WAIT...

january 2003

sun	mon	tue	wed	thu	fri	sat
•	•	•	1	2	3	4
5	6	7	8	9	10	11
12	13	14	15	16	17	18
19	20	21	22	23	24	25
26	27	28	29	30	31	•

02.01.03. thursday. I TOTALLY MISSED THE FIRST DAY OT THE YEAR, BECAUSE I HAVE BEEN SO SIIIIICK, SICK LIKE A DOG. TO TAKE IT ON THE GOOD SIDE, LET'S SAY IT WAS THE BIG CLEAN-UP BEFORE STARTING THE NEW YEAR. I VOMITED ALL DAY LONG (first of all the orange juice I just drank then nothing but bile: very painful). LATE IN THE DAY I FINALLY FELL ASLEEP, AND WOKE UP at 8:30 at NIGHT. HAD TO WAIT UNTIL 10:30 TO BE ABLE TO SWALLOW ANYTHING. INDEED I HAVE MORE AND MORE TROUBLE TO RECOVER FROM THESE KIND OF EXCESSES.

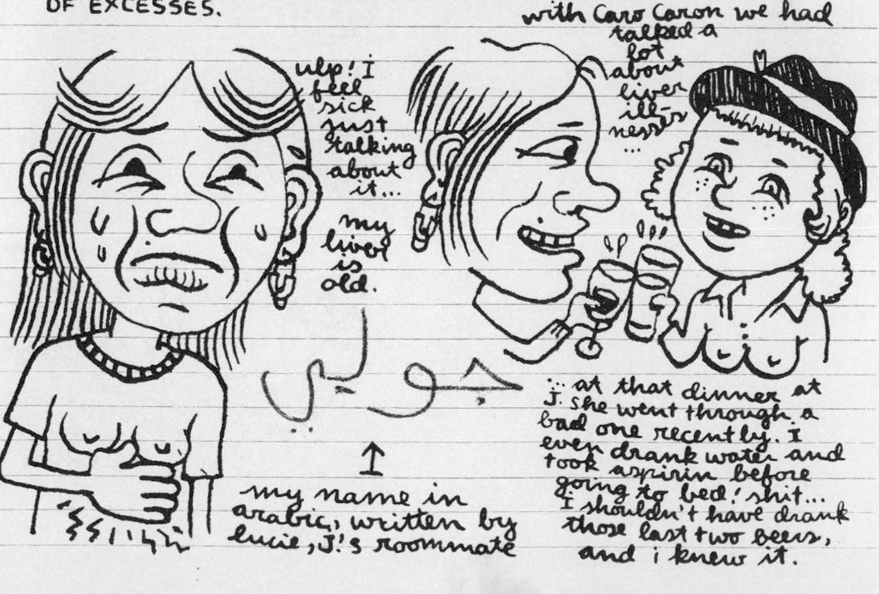
with Caro Caron we had talked a lot about liver ill-nesses...
ulp! I feel sick just talking about it... my liver is old.
my name in arabic, written by lucie, J.'s roommate
... at that dinner at J. she went through a bad one recently. I even drank water and took aspirin before going to bed! shit... I shouldn't have drank those last two beers, and i knew it.

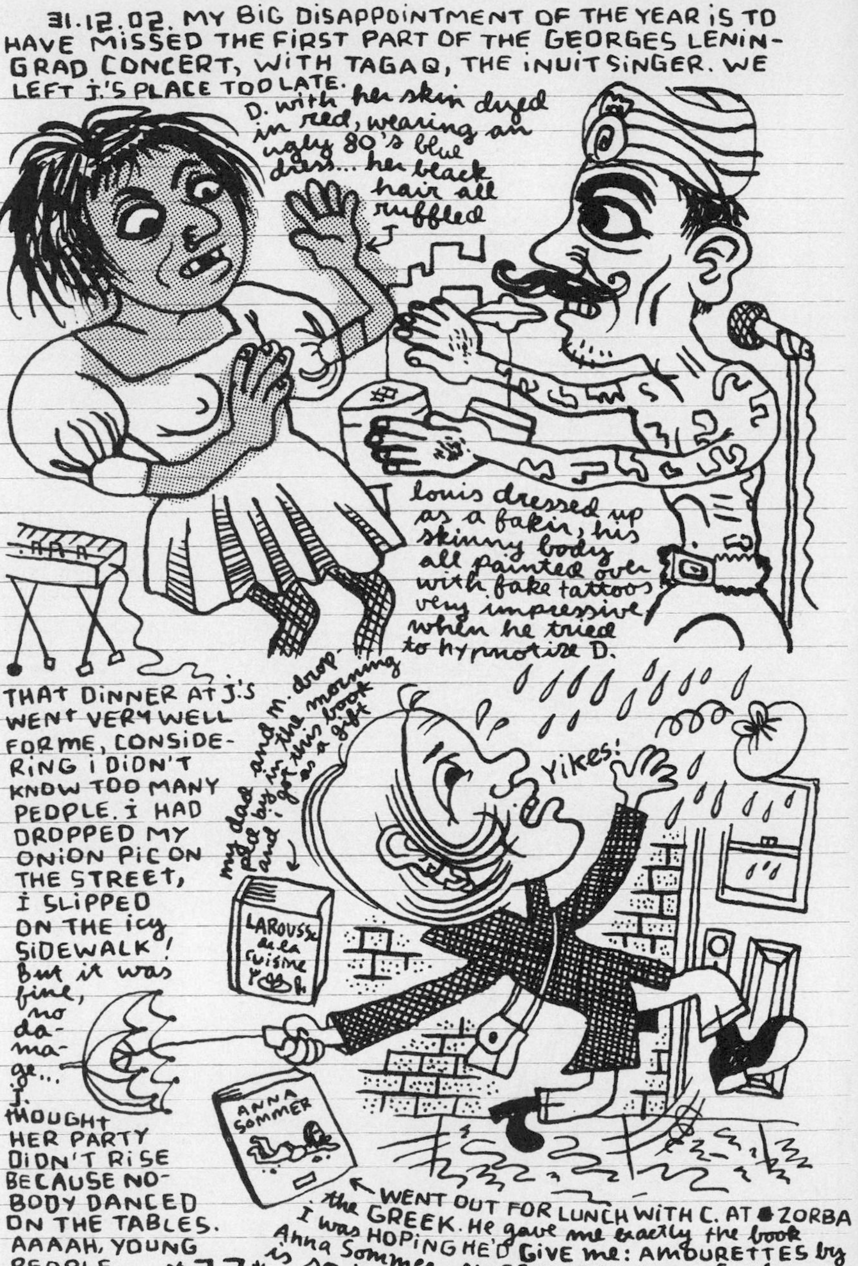
31.12.02. MY BIG DISAPPOINTMENT OF THE YEAR IS TO HAVE MISSED THE FIRST PART OF THE GEORGES LENIN-GRAD CONCERT, WITH TAGAQ, THE INUIT SINGER. WE LEFT J.'S PLACE TOO LATE.
D. with her skin dyed in red, wearing an ugly 80's blue dress... her black hair all ruffled
Louis dressed up as a fakir, his skinny body all painted over with fake tattoos very impressive when he tried to hypnotize D.
THAT DINNER AT J.'S WENT VERY WELL FOR ME, CONSIDE-RING I DIDN'T KNOW TOO MANY PEOPLE. I HAD DROPPED MY ONION PIE ON THE STREET, I SLIPPED ON THE ICY SIDEWALK! But it was fine, no da-ma-ge... J. THOUGHT HER PARTY DIDN'T RISE BECAUSE NO-BODY DANCED ON THE TABLES. AAAAH, YOUNG PEOPLE...
my dad and m. drop-ped by in the morning and i got this book as a gift
LAROUSSE de la cuisine
YIKES!
ANNA SOMMER
WENT OUT FOR LUNCH WITH C. AT ZORBA the GREEK. He gave me exactly the book I was HOPING HE'D GIVE me: AMOURETTES by Anna Sommer. AWESOME!!! Anna S. she is so incredible.

03.01.03. friday. SHIT! IT'S INCREDIBLE! I GOT UP AT QUARTER PAST ELEVEN: THAT'S WAY TOO LATE!!! IT'S STILL CLOUDY OUTSIDE. DIDN'T GO OUT AT ALL YESTERDAY.
HAVEN'T SEEN ANYBODY, DIDN'T TALK TO NOBODY. I HAD TO CATCH UP WITH MY JOURNAL.
"...and i vomited."
I HADN'T TURNED ON MY DEAREST COMPUTER FOR A COUPLE OF DAYS. I HAD A FUNNY MESSAGE FROM CHRIS FROM D&Q: HE WAS WRITING TO ASK ME TO FIND A TITLE FOR MY JOURNAL PROJECT, TO ANNOUNCE IT FOR 2003 IN THE CATALOGUE! THAT I DIDN'T EXPECT AT ALL. I THOUGHT THAT BOOK WOULD COME OUT IN A VERY DISTANT FUTURE...
was i being a Princess? i feel very silly, now...
MORE MAIL TO WRITE. WASHED MY HAIR, WASHED MY BED SHEETS, WASHED TWO WOOL SWEATERS BY HAND...
scratch scratch
IN THE EVENING I READ THE EIGHTBALL NO. 22 THAT ALVIN B. SENT ME AS A GIFT. I DON'T BUY COMICS ANYMORE SO IT'S been A WHILE SINCE I READ D. CLOWES. WELL, IT IS Really GOOD!!... VERY IMPRESSED BY HIS STORY-TELLING.
gasp!
EIGHTBALL

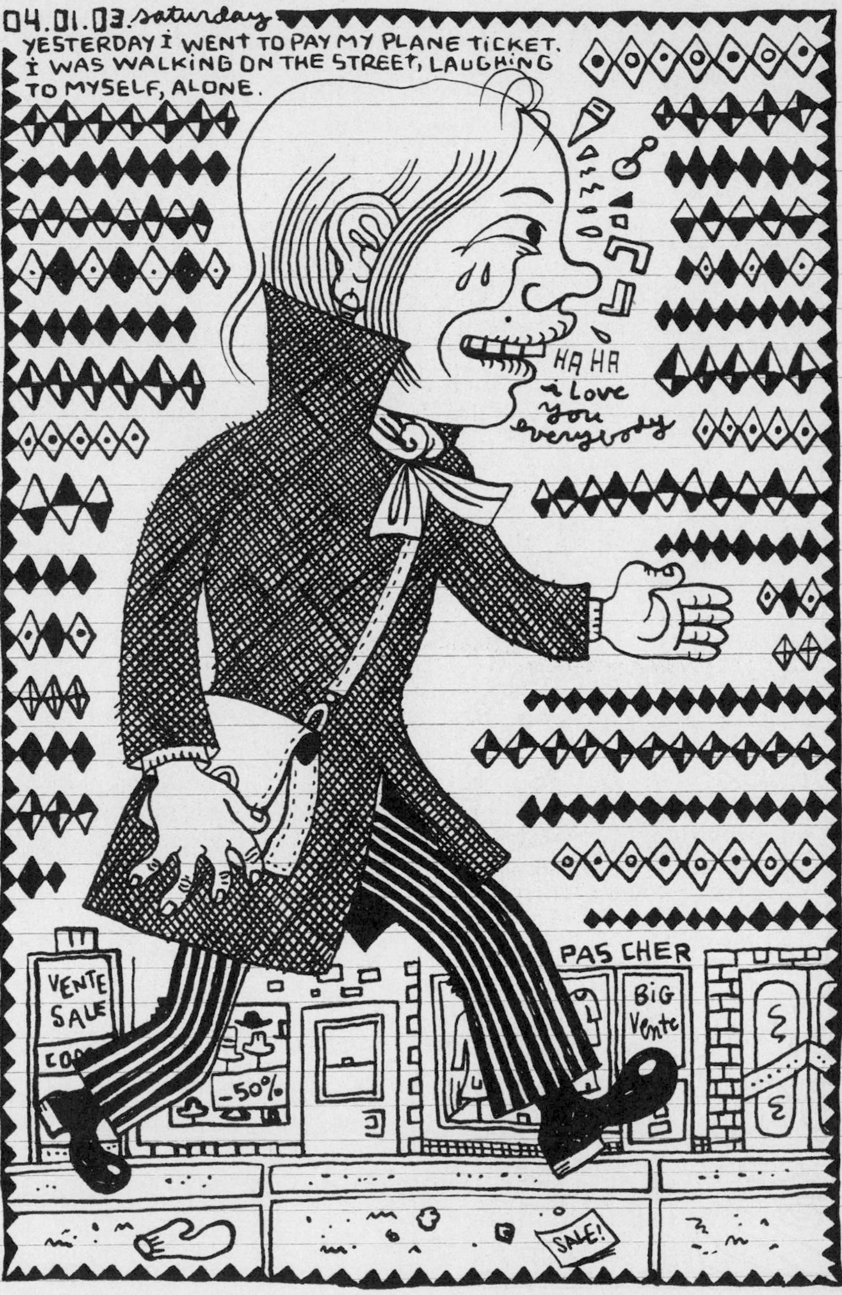
04.01.03. saturday
YESTERDAY I WENT TO PAY MY PLANE TICKET. I WAS WALKING ON THE STREET, LAUGHING TO MYSELF, ALONE.
HA HA
i love you everybody
VENTE SALE
-50%
PAS CHER
BIG Vente
SALE!

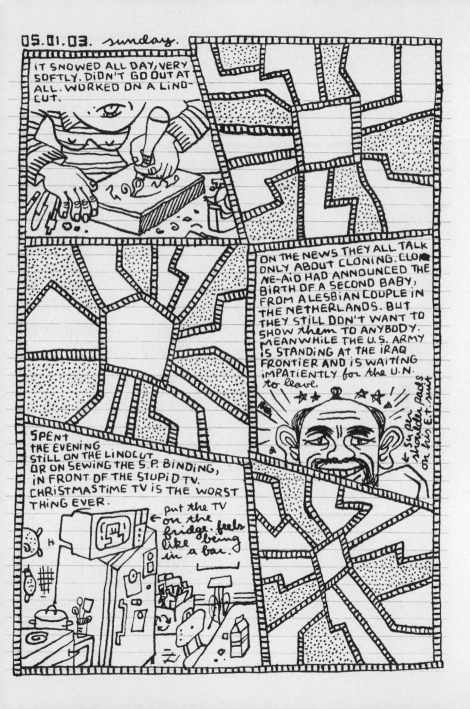

05.01.03. sunday.

IT SNOWED ALL DAY, VERY SOFTLY. DIDN'T GO OUT AT ALL. WORKED ON A LINO-CUT.

ON THE NEWS THEY ALL TALK ONLY ABOUT CLONING. CLONE-AID HAD ANNOUNCED THE BIRTH OF A SECOND BABY, FROM A LESBIAN COUPLE IN THE NETHERLANDS. BUT THEY STILL DON'T WANT TO SHOW *them* TO ANYBODY. MEANWHILE THE U.S. ARMY IS STANDING AT THE IRAQ FRONTIER AND IS WAITING IMPATIENTLY *for the* U.N. *to leave.*

← *su pa shoulder pads on his E.T. suit*

SPENT THE EVENING STILL ON THE LINOCUT OR ON SEWING THE S.P. BINDING, IN FRONT OF THE STUPID TV. CHRISTMASTIME TV IS THE WORST THING EVER.

put the TV ← *on the fridge. feels like being in a bar.*

06.01.03. *monday*. YESTERDAY WAS THE CHRISTMAS/NEW YEAR/TWELFTH NIGHT PARTY IN THE DOUCET FAMILY. I CAN SAY MY EARS COLLECTED SOME FUNNY STORIES! FIRST, MY COUSIN (*the one with four kids*): SHE TOLD ME ALL *about* HER BAD YEAR WITH HER (*ex*) HUSBAND FROM HELL. SHE CAN BE SURE OF ONE THING, 2003 CAN ONLY BE A BETTER YEAR! ANOTHER COUSIN (*her brother, in fact*)

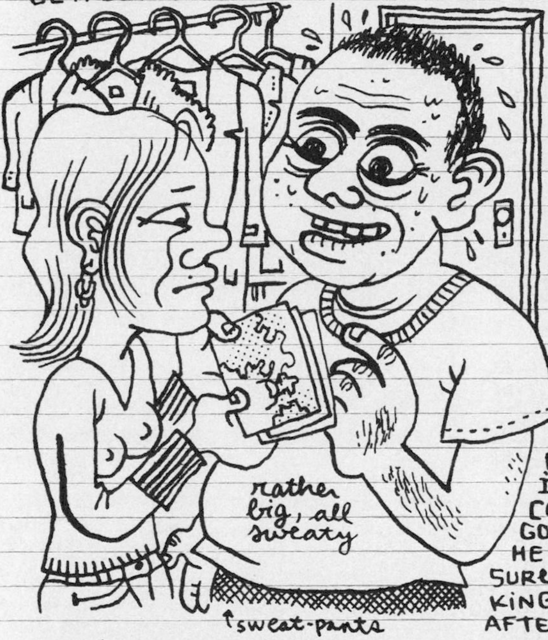

rather big, all sweaty
sweat-pants

TOOK ME TO THE HALL TO SHOW ME SOMETHING "VERY INTERESTING". HE GAVE ME A SERIES OF PHOTOS HE TOOK HIMSELF IN A CEMETERY AT NIGHT: PHOTOS OF... ECTOPLASMS!!! ACCORDING TO HIM THE SKY WAS CLEAR, BUT STILL ON THE PICTURES YOU CAN SEE THOSE KIND OF WHITE CLOUDS OF MIST. HE TOLD ME HE WAS A MEMBER OF A GHOSTBUSTERS CLUB AND THE WOMAN WHO'S *in* CHARGE OF THE ORGANIZATION CAN "READ" THOSE ECTOPLASM PICTURES. AND I CLEARLY HEARD MY COUSIN USE THE WORD GOBLIN, AT SOME POINT! HE SEEMED EXTREMELY SURE OF HIMSELF, WAS WINKING AT ME ALL THE TIME AFTER THAT.

AND I TALKED A BIT ABOUT "MY MOVIE" WITH MY UNCLE WHO'S A RETIRED FILM PRODUCER (*and the two other's dad. very good reputation in the film industry, one of the founders of the Québécois independent cinema... produced* M.A. FORCIER). HE CONFIRMED ONE THING I KIND OF KNEW ALREADY: YOUR MOVIE HAS TO BE JUST LIKE YOU WANT IT TO BE. OTHERWISE, IT'S NOT EVEN WORTH IT TO EVEN THINK ABOUT IT (*something like that*) AND, ABOUT THE FACT THAT THERE IS NO DIRECTOR YET: IT'S A BAD SIGN. IT'S GOING TO BE A PRODUCER'S MOVIE. CAME OUT IN A FUNNY MOOD.

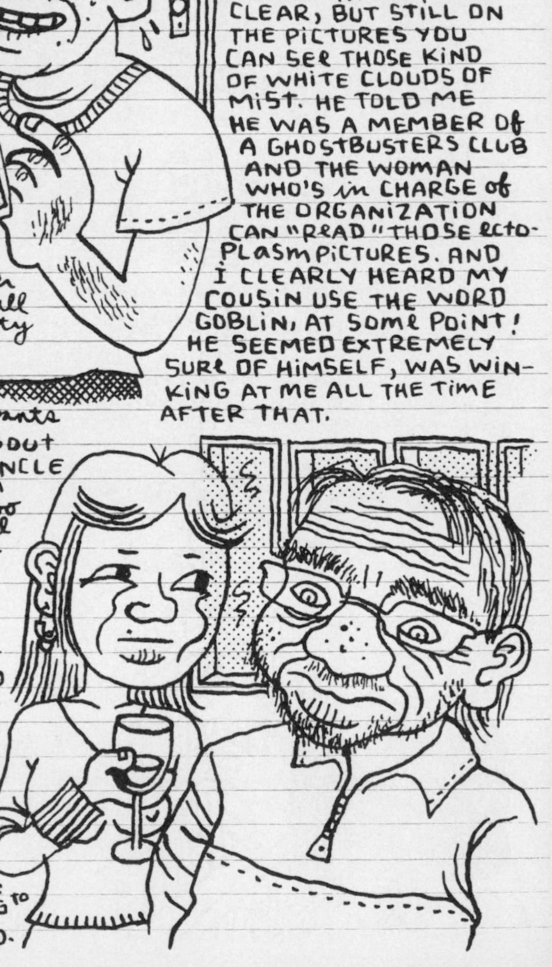

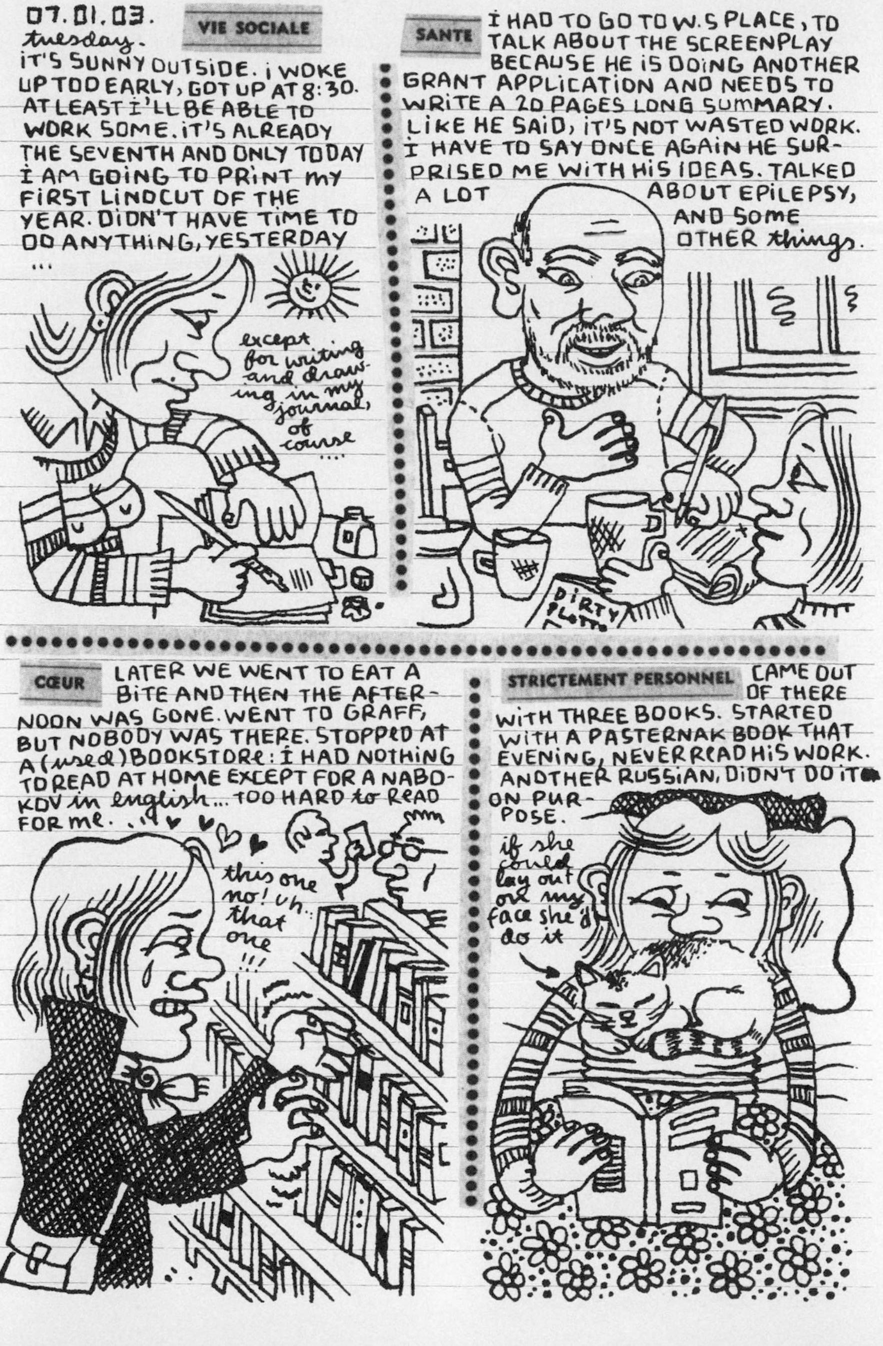
07.01.03.
tuesday.
VIE SOCIALE
IT'S SUNNY OUTSIDE. I WOKE UP TOO EARLY, GOT UP AT 8:30. AT LEAST I'LL BE ABLE TO WORK SOME. IT'S ALREADY THE SEVENTH AND ONLY TODAY I AM GOING TO PRINT MY FIRST LINOCUT OF THE YEAR. DIDN'T HAVE TIME TO DO ANYTHING, YESTERDAY ...
except for writing and drawing in my journal, of course ....
SANTE
I HAD TO GO TO W.S PLACE, TO TALK ABOUT THE SCREENPLAY BECAUSE HE IS DOING ANOTHER GRANT APPLICATION AND NEEDS TO WRITE A 20 PAGES LONG SUMMARY. LIKE HE SAID, IT'S NOT WASTED WORK. I HAVE TO SAY ONCE AGAIN HE SURPRISED ME WITH HIS IDEAS. TALKED A LOT ABOUT EPILEPSY, AND SOME OTHER things.
DIRTY PLOTTO
CŒUR
LATER WE WENT TO EAT A BITE AND THEN THE AFTERNOON WAS GONE. WENT TO GRAFF, BUT NOBODY WAS THERE. STOPPED AT A (used) BOOKSTORE: I HAD NOTHING TO READ AT HOME EXCEPT FOR A NABOKOV in english... TOO HARD to READ FOR ME.
this one no! uh.. that one !!!
STRICTEMENT PERSONNEL
CAME OUT OF THERE WITH THREE BOOKS. STARTED WITH A PASTERNAK BOOK THAT EVENING, NEVER READ HIS WORK. ANOTHER RUSSIAN, DIDN'T DO IT ON PURPOSE.
if she could lay out on my face she'd do it

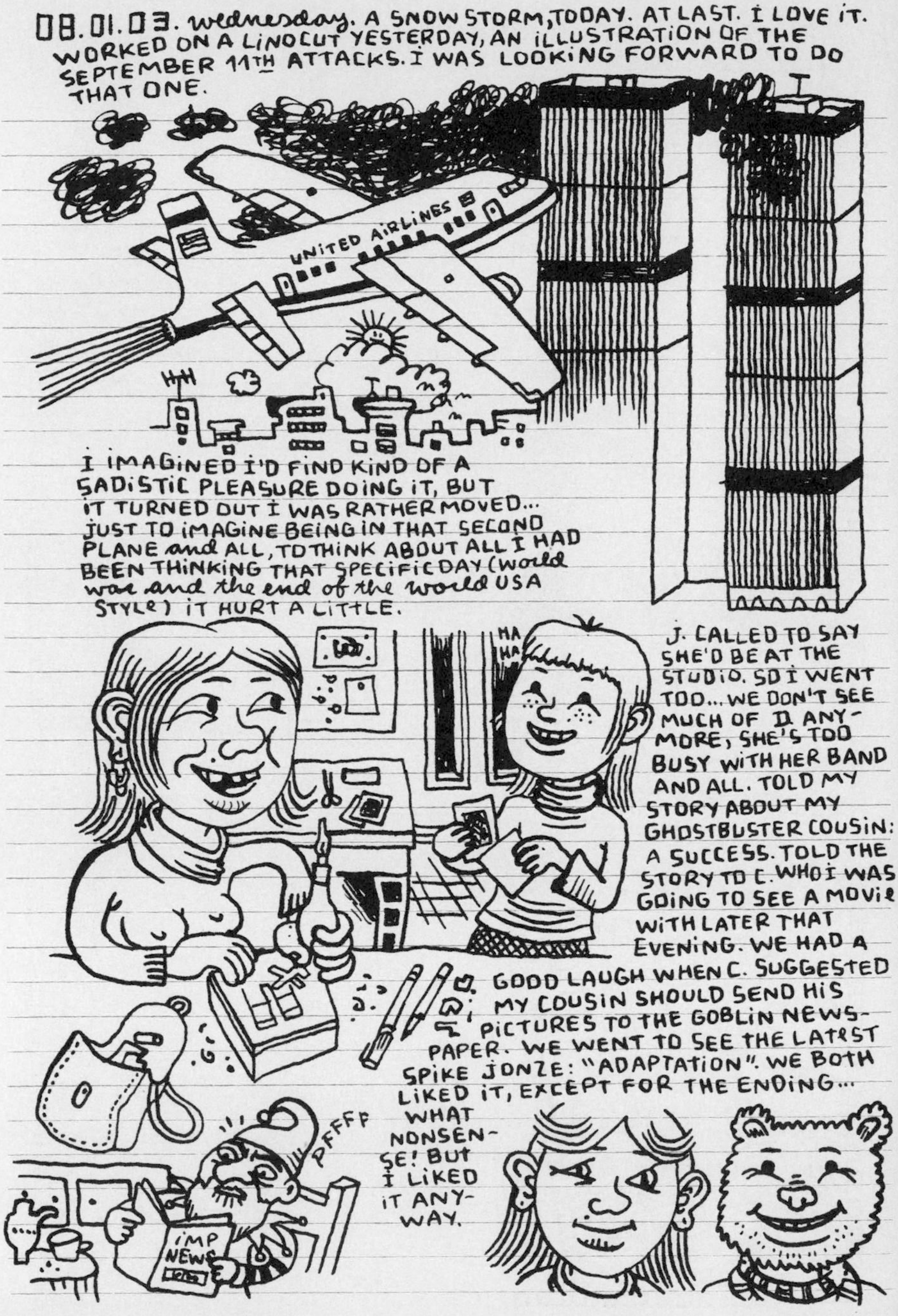
08.01.03. wednesday. A SNOW STORM, TODAY. AT LAST. I LOVE IT. WORKED ON A LINOCUT YESTERDAY, AN ILLUSTRATION OF THE SEPTEMBER 11TH ATTACKS. I WAS LOOKING FORWARD TO DO THAT ONE.
UNITED AIRLINES
I IMAGINED I'D FIND KIND OF A SADISTIC PLEASURE DOING IT, BUT IT TURNED OUT I WAS RATHER MOVED... JUST TO IMAGINE BEING IN THAT SECOND PLANE and ALL, TO THINK ABOUT ALL I HAD BEEN THINKING THAT SPECIFIC DAY (world war and the end of the world USA STYLE) IT HURT A LITTLE.
HA HA
J. CALLED TO SAY SHE'D BE AT THE STUDIO. SO I WENT TOO... WE DON'T SEE MUCH OF D ANYMORE, SHE'S TOO BUSY WITH HER BAND AND ALL. TOLD MY STORY ABOUT MY GHOSTBUSTER COUSIN: A SUCCESS. TOLD THE STORY TO C. WHO I WAS GOING TO SEE A MOVIE WITH LATER THAT EVENING. WE HAD A GOOD LAUGH WHEN C. SUGGESTED MY COUSIN SHOULD SEND HIS PICTURES TO THE GOBLIN NEWSPAPER. WE WENT TO SEE THE LATEST SPIKE JONZE: "ADAPTATION". WE BOTH LIKED IT, EXCEPT FOR THE ENDING... WHAT NONSENSE! BUT I LIKED IT ANYWAY.
PFFFF
IMP NEWS

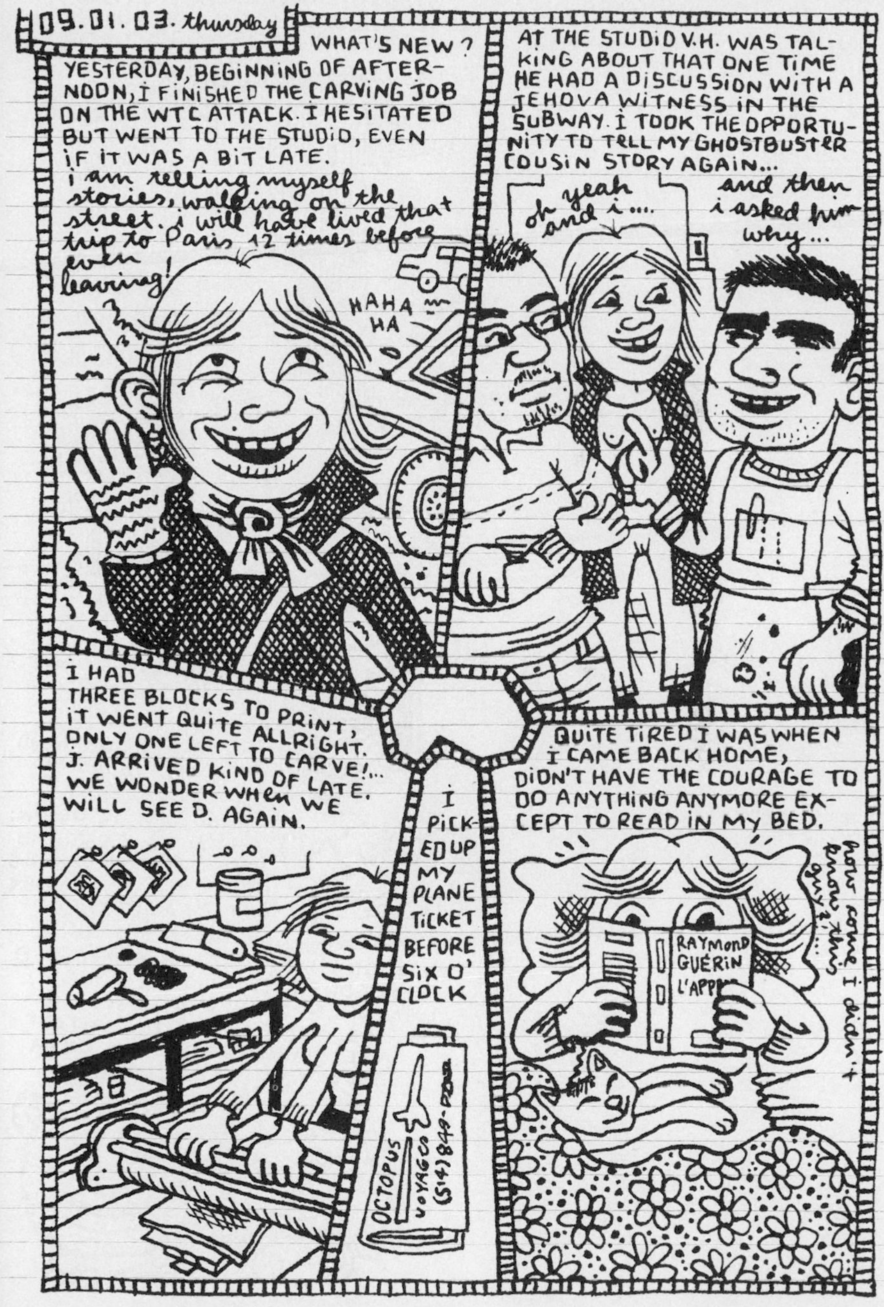
09.01.03. thursday
WHAT'S NEW?
YESTERDAY, BEGINNING OF AFTERNOON, I FINISHED THE CARVING JOB ON THE WTC ATTACK. I HESITATED BUT WENT TO THE STUDIO, EVEN IF IT WAS A BIT LATE.
i am telling myself stories, walking on the street. i will have lived that trip to Paris 12 times before even leaving!
HAHA HA
AT THE STUDIO V.H. WAS TALKING ABOUT THAT ONE TIME HE HAD A DISCUSSION WITH A JEHOVA WITNESS IN THE SUBWAY. I TOOK THE OPPORTUNITY TO TELL MY GHOSTBUSTER COUSIN STORY AGAIN...
oh yeah and i....
and then i asked him why...
I HAD THREE BLOCKS TO PRINT, IT WENT QUITE ALLRIGHT. ONLY ONE LEFT TO CARVE!... J. ARRIVED KIND OF LATE. WE WONDER WHEN WE WILL SEE D. AGAIN.
I PICKED UP MY PLANE TICKET BEFORE SIX O' CLOCK
OCTOPUS VOYAGES (514) 849-
QUITE TIRED I WAS WHEN I CAME BACK HOME, DIDN'T HAVE THE COURAGE TO DO ANYTHING ANYMORE EXCEPT TO READ IN MY BED.
RAYMOND GUÉRIN L'APP
how come I didn't know this guy?...

10.01.03. *friday*. COULDN'T WORK YESTERDAY. I HAD TO MEET MY
GODMOTHER AT THE MODERN ART MUSEUM. I DIDN'T REALIZE IT, BUT I
HAVEN'T SEEN HER SINCE THE MONTH OF APRIL. SHE SURE REMEM-
BERED THAT. WE SAW A PHOTO AND VIDEO EXHIBITION BY SAM
TAYLOR-WOOD (*from England*). ON THE CARD IT SAID HER
WORK PROVOKED A SENSATION OF STRANGENESS AND OF DIS-
COMFORT. I THOUGHT IT WAS VERY MUCH TRUE, IT DID MAKE
ME FEEL A BIT SICK IN MY STOMACH. BUT IT WAS MOSTLY BE-
CAUSE OF HER CREEPING CYNICISM. STILL I LIKED SOME OF HER
PIECES. I LIKED HER VIDEOS BEST. LATER WITH MY AUNT
WE WENT FOR A COFFEE... IN A SHOPPING MALL. NOT EXACTLY
MY KIND OF PLACE. I LISTENED TO HER TALKING ABOUT
THE ARABS, ABOUT HOW THEY NEVER GOT OVER THE HOLY
CRUSADES, HOW *their* RELIGION IS BARBARIC AND KEEPS
THEM FROM EVOLVING. CURIOUSLY, SHE TOTALLY
ENCOURAGED ME TO MOVE TO PARIS! I DON'T HEAR THAT
TOO OFTEN.

I HAD TO DO SOME SHOPPING, AND THAT'S WHAT I DID SINCE
I WAS ALREADY DOWNTOWN. BUT I WAS NOT INSPIRED AT ALL,
DIDN'T *feel* LIKE IT. FAMILY. HAD ENOUGH OF IT. READ ALL
EVENING.

11.01.03. *saturday*. I DREAMT THAT D. HAD DECIDED TO SPEND THE NIGHT AT THE STUDIO, BECAUSE SHE HAD SO MUCH WORK TO DO. ONCE SHE WAS TOO TIRED TO KEEP ON WORKING, SHE PUT HERSELF IN THE FRIDGE TO SLEEP. THE NEXT MORNING, WHEN I ARRIVED AT THE STUDIO, I FOUND HER FROZEN TO DEATH. I WAS HORRIFIED, DEEPLY DISTRESSED. BUT BECAUSE THERE WAS LOTS OF PEOPLE AROUND THAT DAY, I DIDN'T DARE TO TAKE HER OUT OF THERE.

● ● ● ● ● ● ● ● ● ● ● ●

IT'S ONLY LATER THAT I TOLD J. ABOUT IT. SHE WAS REALLY PISSED OFF AT ME FOR NOT TELLING HER RIGHT AWAY. I SPENT THE REST OF THE TIME CRYING, UNTIL I GOT A PHONE CALL FROM D., WHO WAS NOT DEAD, AFTER ALL.

BUTTER
LAIT
M

I SPENT THE WHOLE DAY AND EVENING AT THE STUDIO WITH J. AND D.

IT'S BEEN A WHILE SINCE WE'VE SEEN D. SHE ALSO HAS TRAVEL PROJECTS: WITH HER BAND THEY ARE GOING TO NEW YORK-LONDON-PARIS-BERLIN. WOW!

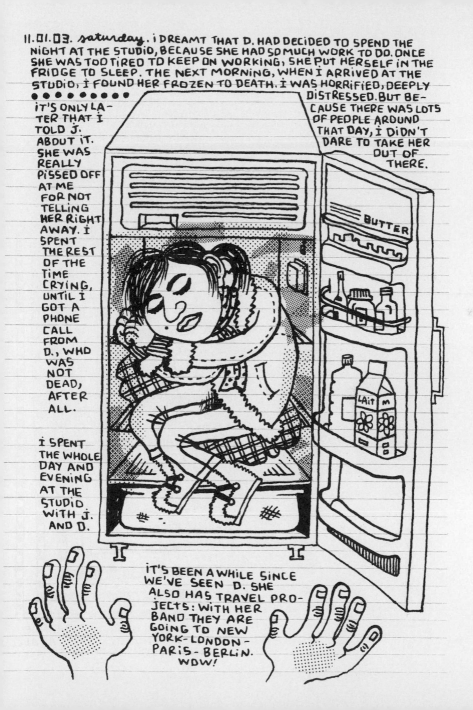

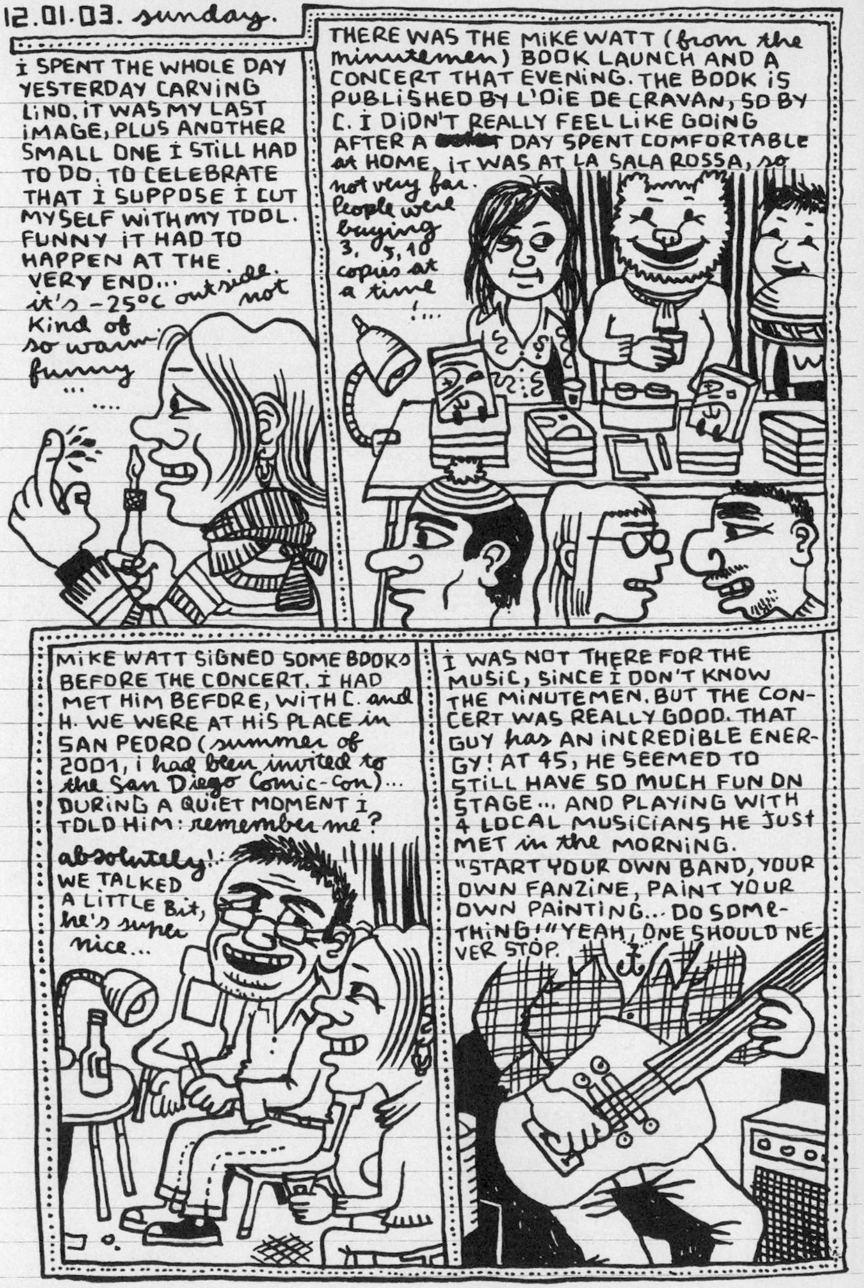
12.01.03. sunday.
I SPENT THE WHOLE DAY YESTERDAY CARVING LINO. IT WAS MY LAST IMAGE, PLUS ANOTHER SMALL ONE I STILL HAD TO DO. TO CELEBRATE THAT I SUPPOSE I CUT MYSELF WITH MY TOOL. FUNNY IT HAD TO HAPPEN AT THE VERY END...
it's -25°C outside. not so warm.
Kind of funny ... .
THERE WAS THE MIKE WATT (from the minutemen) BOOK LAUNCH AND A CONCERT THAT EVENING. THE BOOK IS PUBLISHED BY L'OIE DE CRAVAN, SO BY C. I DIDN'T REALLY FEEL LIKE GOING AFTER A DAY SPENT COMFORTABLE at HOME, IT WAS AT LA SALA ROSSA, so not very far.
People were buying 3, 5, 10 copies at a time !...
MIKE WATT SIGNED SOME BOOKS BEFORE THE CONCERT. I HAD MET HIM BEFORE, WITH C. and H. WE WERE AT HIS PLACE in SAN PEDRO (summer of 2001, i had been invited to the San Diego Comic-Con)... DURING A QUIET MOMENT I TOLD HIM: remember me?
absolutely!
WE TALKED A LITTLE BIT, he's super nice...
I WAS NOT THERE FOR THE MUSIC, SINCE I DON'T KNOW THE MINUTEMEN. BUT THE CONCERT WAS REALLY GOOD. THAT GUY has AN INCREDIBLE ENERGY! AT 45, HE SEEMED TO STILL HAVE SO MUCH FUN ON STAGE... AND PLAYING WITH 4 LOCAL MUSICIANS HE JUST MET in the MORNING.
"START YOUR OWN BAND, YOUR OWN FANZINE, PAINT YOUR OWN PAINTING... DO SOMETHING!" YEAH, ONE SHOULD NEVER STOP.

13.01.03. *monday*. GOT UP TOO LATE YESTERDAY, DIDN'T HAVE TIME TO HANG AROUND I HAD TO LEAVE FOR THE STUDIO. I STILL HAD A LITTLE BIT OF LINO TO CARVE, AND I GOT TO PRINT MY LAST BLOCKS... SO I'M FINISHED WITH THAT JOB!!!

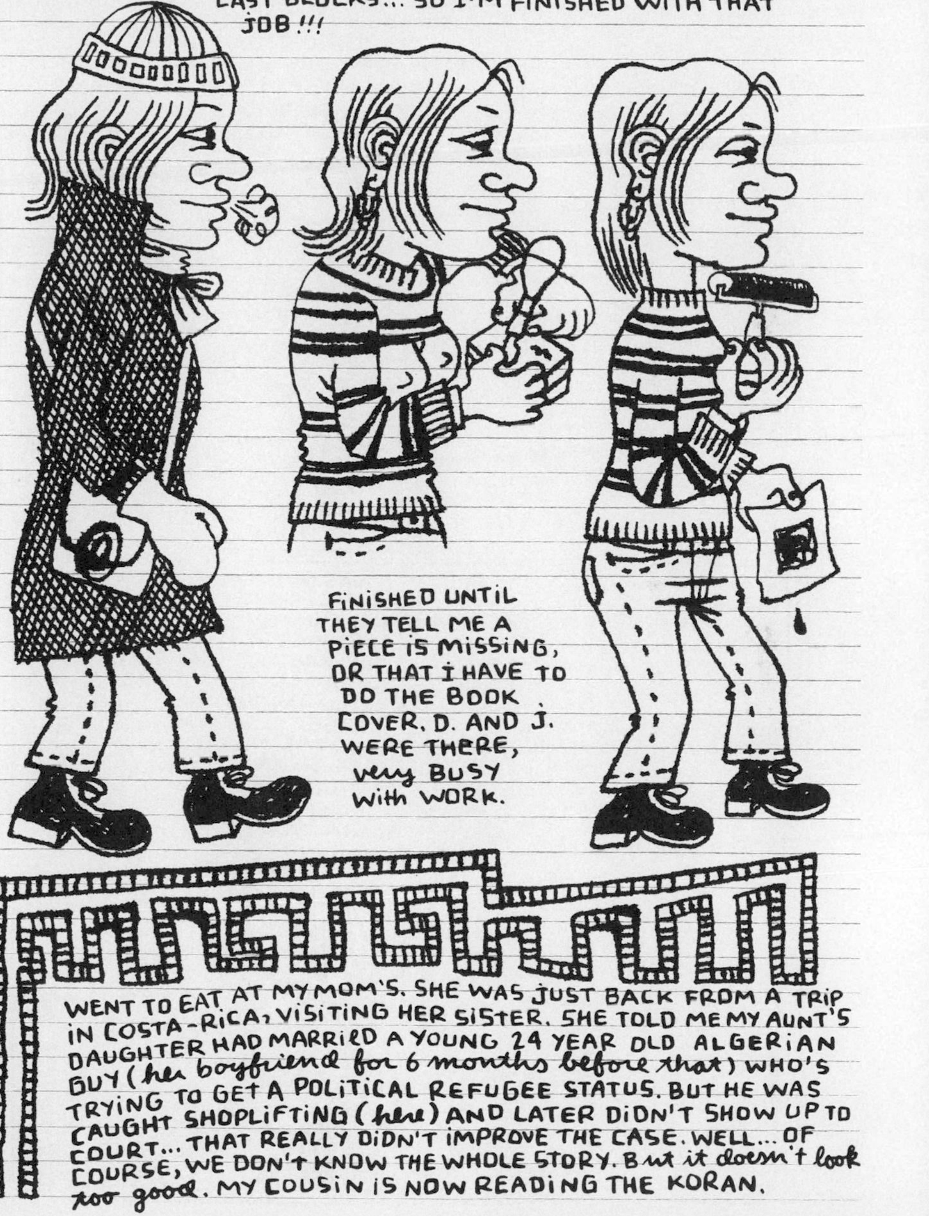

FINISHED UNTIL THEY TELL ME A PIECE IS MISSING, OR THAT I HAVE TO DO THE BOOK COVER. D. AND J. WERE THERE, *very* BUSY *with* WORK.

WENT TO EAT AT MY MOM'S. SHE WAS JUST BACK FROM A TRIP IN COSTA-RICA, VISITING HER SISTER. SHE TOLD ME MY AUNT'S DAUGHTER HAD MARRIED A YOUNG 24 YEAR OLD ALGERIAN GUY (*her boyfriend for 6 months before that*) WHO'S TRYING TO GET A POLITICAL REFUGEE STATUS. BUT HE WAS CAUGHT SHOPLIFTING (*here*) AND LATER DIDN'T SHOW UP TO COURT... THAT REALLY DIDN'T IMPROVE THE CASE. WELL... OF COURSE, WE DON'T KNOW THE WHOLE STORY. B*ut it doesn't look too good*. MY COUSIN IS NOW READING THE KORAN.

14.01.03 tuesday. I AM LEAVING IN ONE WEEK. SPENT THE DAY YESTERDAY WORKING ON THAT PAGE FOR AN ART MAGAZINE FROM MARSEILLE. I'M DOING A COLLAGE. IT'S GOING TO TAKE A COUPLE OF DAYS. the theme is "the castration of the universe" no problem ......

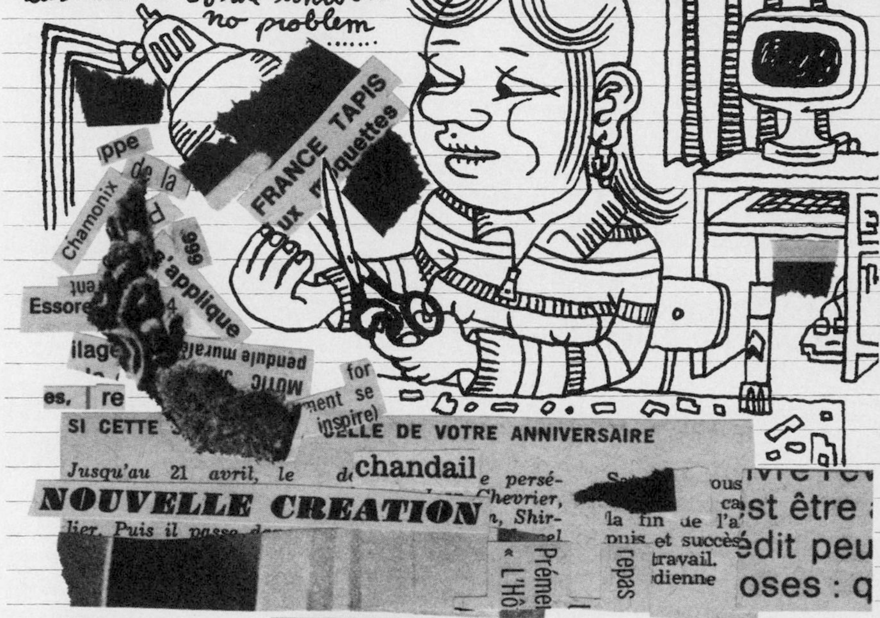

ppe
de la
chamonix
FRANCE TAPIS
ux m
quettes
Essore
'applique
ilage
pendule murale
for
ment se
inspire)
es, | re
SI CETTE S
ELLE DE VOTRE ANNIVERSAIRE
Jusqu'au 21 avril, le
chandail
e persé-
Chevrier,
n, Shir-
NOUVELLE CREATION
lier. Puis il passe
la fin de l'a
puis et succès
travail.
dienne
repas
Prémé
L'Hô
st être
édit peu
oses : q

WITH C. WE WENT TO THE CINEMA TO SEE "CHICAGO" BY ROB MARSHALL. A MUSICAL... WE DIDN'T FEEL LIKE ANYTHING TOO SERIOUS. IT WAS NOT BAD, NO MORE, NO LESS. LATER WE WENT TO EAT AT LA CABANE. HE WAS STILL TALKING ABOUT THE MIKE WATT evening BOOK LAUNCH. AND CONCERT. IT'S TRUE THAT IT WAS A PRETTY GOOD ONE.

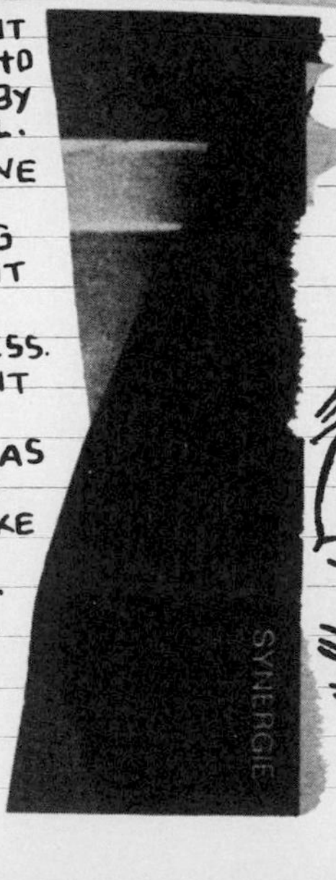

SYNERGIE

...ALSO TALKED ABOUT HIS NEWSPAPER PROJECT. HE WANTS US TO START WORKING ON IT WHEN I COME BACK FROM MY TRIP. BUT IT'S TOO LATE to MAKE PLANS, I'M GOING AWAY!... I'VE WAITED SO MANY TIMES FOR EVERYBody to do THINGS...

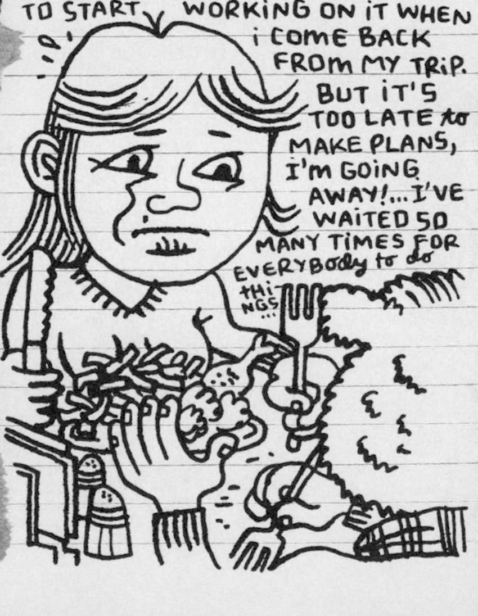

15.01.03.
wednesday.
I SPENT THE WHOLE DAY WORKING ON THAT COLLAGE, YESTERDAY, AND I AM ALMOST DONE WITH IT. ONE LAST DETAIL TO SETTLE.

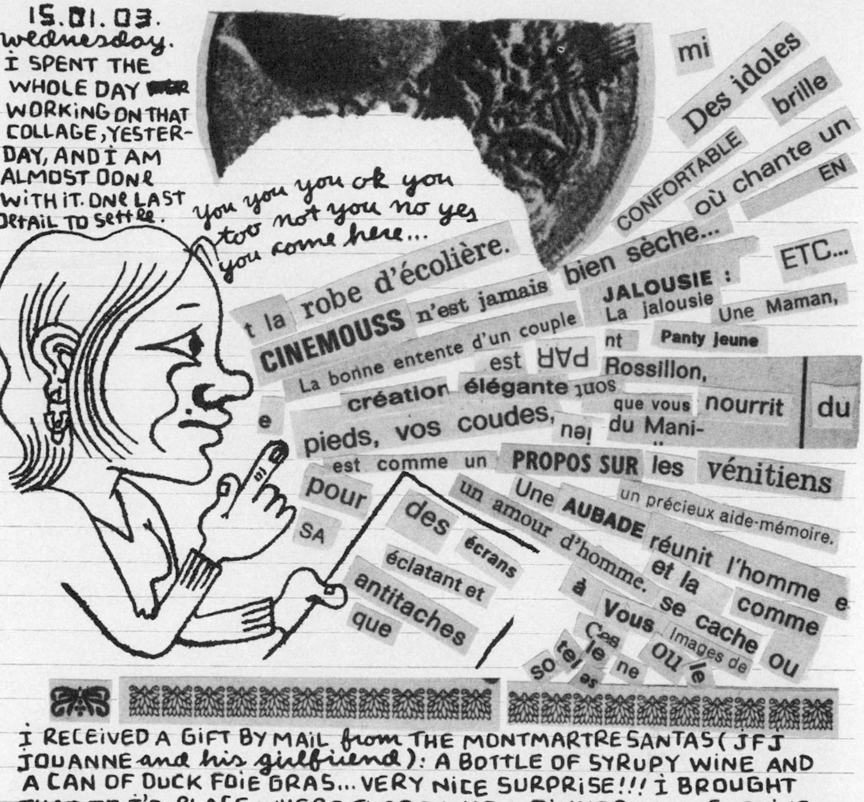

you you you ok you too not you no yes you come here...
mi
Des idoles
brille
CONFORTABLE
où chante un
EN
ETC...
bien sèche...
t la robe d'écolière.
CINEMOUSS n'est jamais
JALOUSIE :
La jalousie
Une Maman,
La bonne entente d'un couple
nt
Panty jeune
est PAR
Rossillon,
création élégante
que vous
nourrit
du
e
pieds, vos coudes,
du Mani-
est comme un
PROPOS SUR les vénitiens
pour
Une AUBADE
un précieux aide-mémoire.
un amour d'homme.
des
SA
écrans
réunit l'homme e
éclatant et
et la
antitaches
comme
que
à
se cache
Vous
Images de
ou

I RECEIVED A GIFT BY MAIL from THE MONTMARTRE SANTAS (JFJ JOUANNE and his girlfriend): A BOTTLE OF SYRUPY WINE AND A CAN OF DUCK FOIE GRAS... VERY NICE SURPRISE!!! I BROUGHT THAT TO J.'S PLACE WHERE THERE WAS A DINNER THAT EVENING WITH D. and M.E. IT WAS DELICIOUS. NOT TO MENTION the RABBIT J. HAD COOKED FOR US. LATER WE PLAYED A GAME OF "RISK". I LOST.

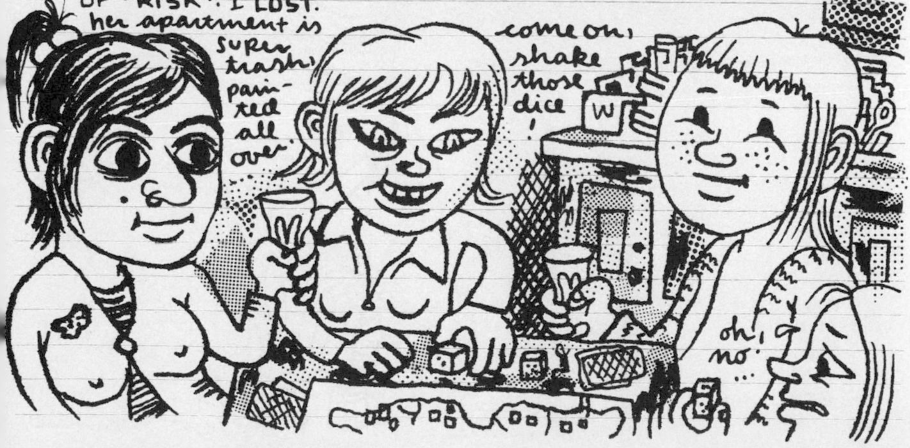

her apartment is super trash: painted all over
come on, shake those dice!
oh, no!...

16.01.03. *thursday*. A QUIET DAY YESTERDAY. WENT SHOPPING. MISSION IMPOSSIBLE TO FIND A BOTTLE OF BLACK INK WATERPROOF IN THIS NEIGHBOURHOOD. HANGED ABOUT AT THE SALVATION ARMY STORE, WHERE I FOUND THIS:

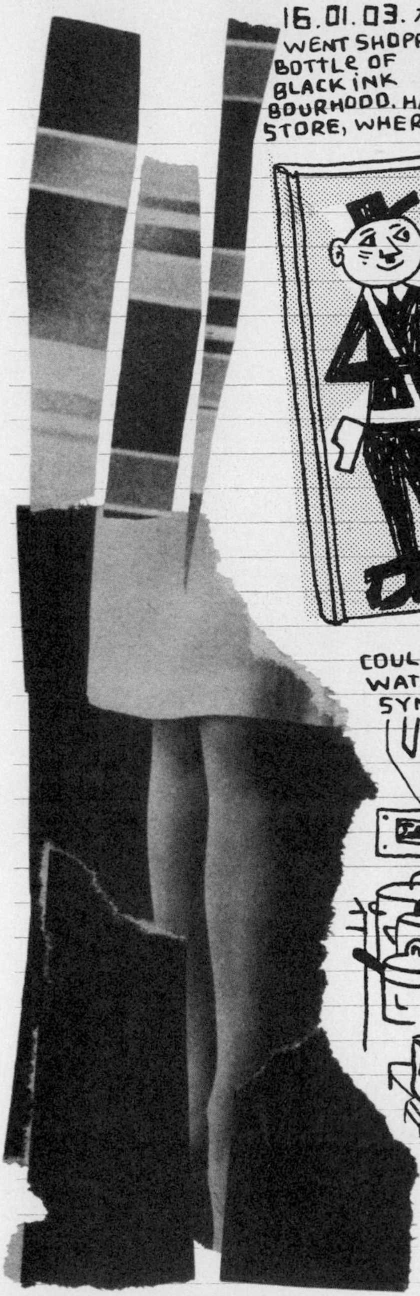

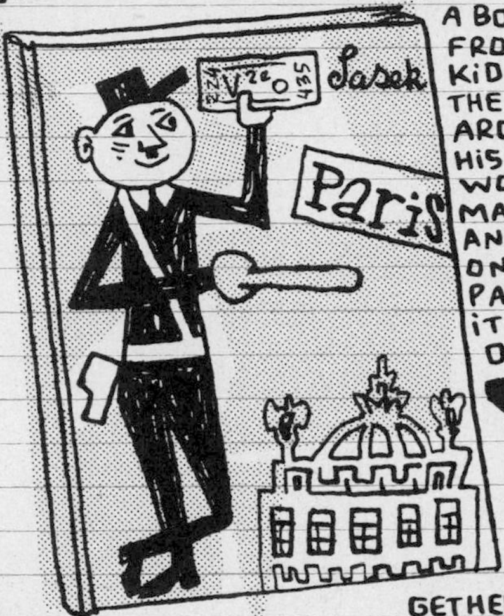
Sasek
Paris

A BOOK BY M. SASEK, FROM A SERIES OF KIDS BOOKS *about* THE BIG CAPITALS AROUND THE WORLD. HIS ILLUSTRATION WORK IS SIMPLY MAGNIFICENT. AND I FOUND THE ONE ABOUT.... PARIS!... LET'S TAKE IT AS A GOOD OMEN.

THEN:

I SPENT THE EVENING PUTTING TOGETHER THE SOPHIE PUNT NO. 9. I COULDN'T IMAGINE I COULD FINISH THE JOB BUT I DID. WHILE WATCHING A DOCUMENTARY ON TV ABOUT SYNTHETIC DIAMONDS.

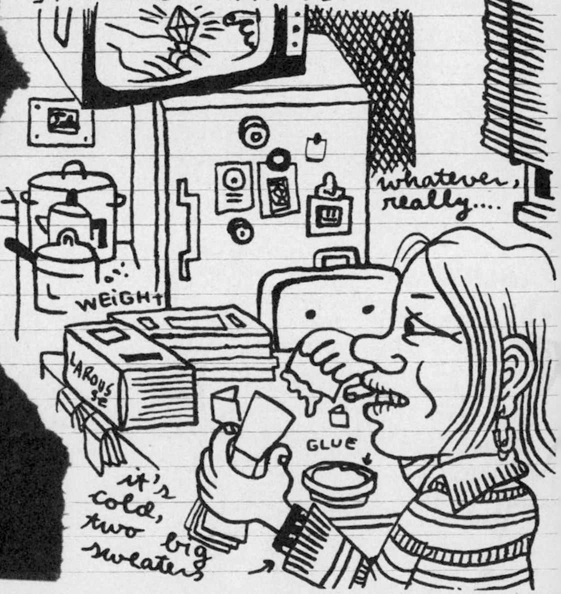
whatever, really....
WEIGHT
LAROUSSE
GLUE
it's cold, two big sweaters

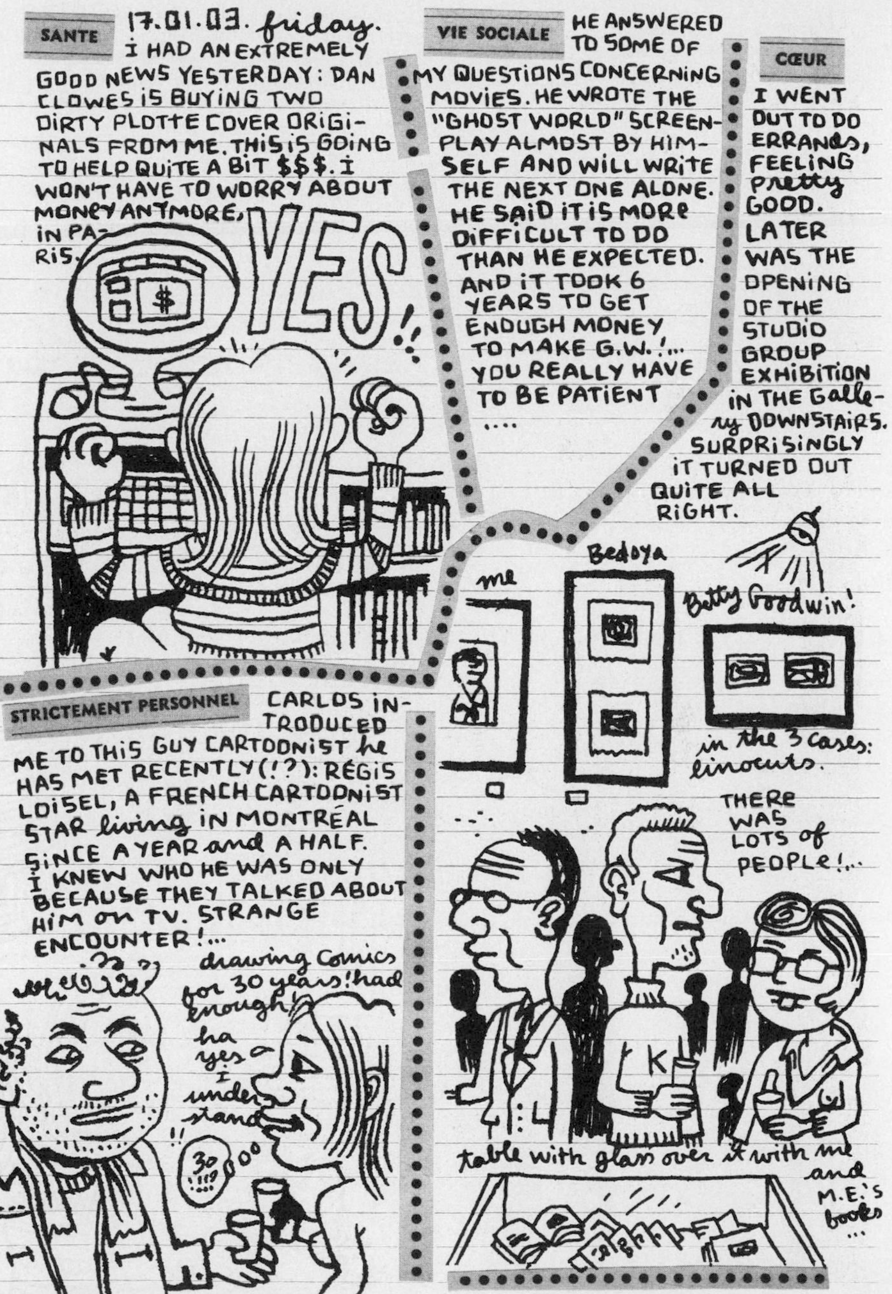
SANTE
17.01.03. friday.
I HAD AN EXTREMELY GOOD NEWS YESTERDAY: DAN CLOWES IS BUYING TWO DIRTY PLOTTE COVER ORIGINALS FROM ME. THIS IS GOING TO HELP QUITE A BIT $$$. I WON'T HAVE TO WORRY ABOUT MONEY ANYMORE, IN PARIS.
$
YES
!!
VIE SOCIALE
HE ANSWERED TO SOME OF MY QUESTIONS CONCERNING MOVIES. HE WROTE THE "GHOST WORLD" SCREENPLAY ALMOST BY HIMSELF AND WILL WRITE THE NEXT ONE ALONE. HE SAID IT IS MORE DIFFICULT TO DO THAN HE EXPECTED. AND IT TOOK 6 YEARS TO GET ENOUGH MONEY TO MAKE G.W. !... YOU REALLY HAVE TO BE PATIENT ....
CŒUR
I WENT OUT TO DO ERRANDS, FEELING pretty GOOD. LATER WAS THE OPENING OF THE STUDIO GROUP EXHIBITION IN THE GALLERY DOWNSTAIRS. SURPRISINGLY IT TURNED OUT QUITE ALL RIGHT.
me
Bedoya
Betty Goodwin!
in the 3 cases: linocuts.
THERE WAS LOTS OF PEOPLE!...
K
table with glass over it with me and M.E.'s books ...
STRICTEMENT PERSONNEL
CARLOS INTRODUCED ME TO THIS GUY CARTOONIST he HAS MET RECENTLY(!?): RÉGIS LOISEL, A FRENCH CARTOONIST STAR living IN MONTRÉAL SINCE A YEAR and A HALF. I KNEW WHO HE WAS ONLY BECAUSE THEY TALKED ABOUT HIM on TV. STRANGE ENCOUNTER!...
drawing Comics for 30 years! had enough!
ha yes a I understand
!!
30
!!!?

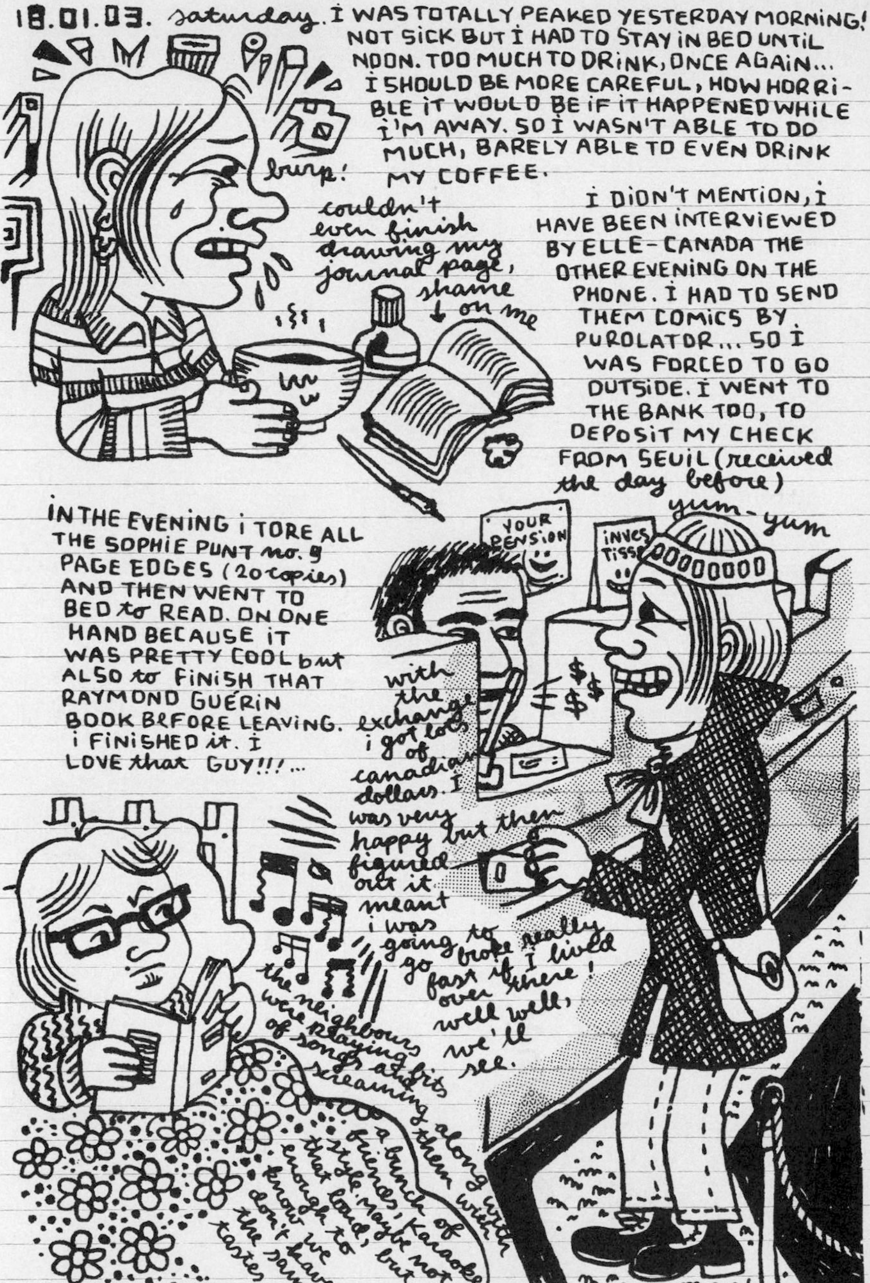
18.01.03. saturday. I WAS TOTALLY PEAKED YESTERDAY MORNING! NOT SICK BUT I HAD TO STAY IN BED UNTIL NOON. TOO MUCH TO DRINK, ONCE AGAIN... I SHOULD BE MORE CAREFUL, HOW HORRIBLE IT WOULD BE IF IT HAPPENED WHILE I'M AWAY. SO I WASN'T ABLE TO DO MUCH, BARELY ABLE TO EVEN DRINK MY COFFEE.
burp!
couldn't even finish drawing my journal page, shame on me
I DIDN'T MENTION, I HAVE BEEN INTERVIEWED BY ELLE-CANADA THE OTHER EVENING ON THE PHONE. I HAD TO SEND THEM COMICS BY PUROLATOR... SO I WAS FORCED TO GO OUTSIDE. I WENT TO THE BANK TOO, TO DEPOSIT MY CHECK FROM SEUIL (received the day before)
yum-yum
YOUR PENSION
INVES TISS
IN THE EVENING I TORE ALL THE SOPHIE PUNT no. 9 PAGE EDGES (20 copies) AND THEN WENT TO BED to READ. ON ONE HAND BECAUSE IT WAS PRETTY COOL but ALSO to FINISH THAT RAYMOND GUÉRIN BOOK BEFORE LEAVING. I FINISHED it. I LOVE that GUY!!!...
with the exchange i got lots of canadian dollars. I was very happy but then figured out it meant i was going to go broke really fast if I lived over there! well well, we'll see.
the neighbours were playing lots of songs and screaming along with them with a bunch of friends, karaoke style. Maybe not that loud, but enough to know we don't have the same tastes.

19.01.03. *sunday*. i DREAMT THAT i WAS ARRIVING AT L'ASSOCIATION OFFICES AND THAT IT HAD ALL CHANGED, i DIDN'T KNOW ANYBODY ANYMORE. THE OFFICES WERE HUGE AND SUPER MODERN, ALL METAL AND GLASS. THERE WAS LOTS OF PEOPLE WORKING. I SAT IN A CORNER, DIDN'T DARE TO TALK TO ANYBODY. EVENTUALLY A GIRL WORKING THERE TOLD ME MENU WAS DOING FINE.

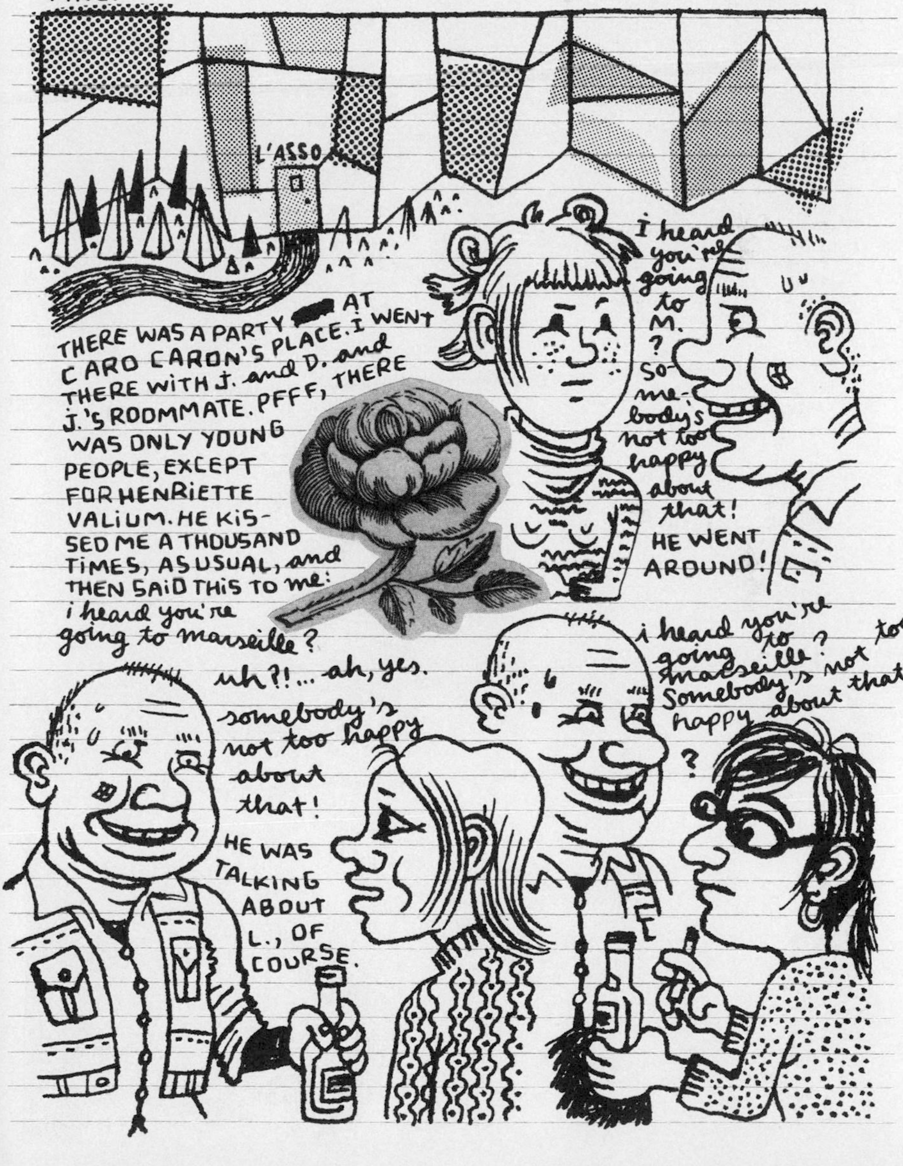
L'ASSO
THERE WAS A PARTY [redacted] AT CARO CARON'S PLACE. I WENT THERE WITH J. and D. and J.'S ROOMMATE. PFFF, THERE WAS ONLY YOUNG PEOPLE, EXCEPT FOR HENRIETTE VALIUM. HE KISSED ME A THOUSAND TIMES, AS USUAL, and THEN SAID THIS TO me:
i heard you're going to marseille?
uh?!... ah, yes.
somebody's not too happy about that!
HE WAS TALKING ABOUT L., OF COURSE.
I heard you're going to M.?
Somebody's not too happy about that!
HE WENT AROUND!
i heard you're going to marseille? Somebody's not too happy about that!
?

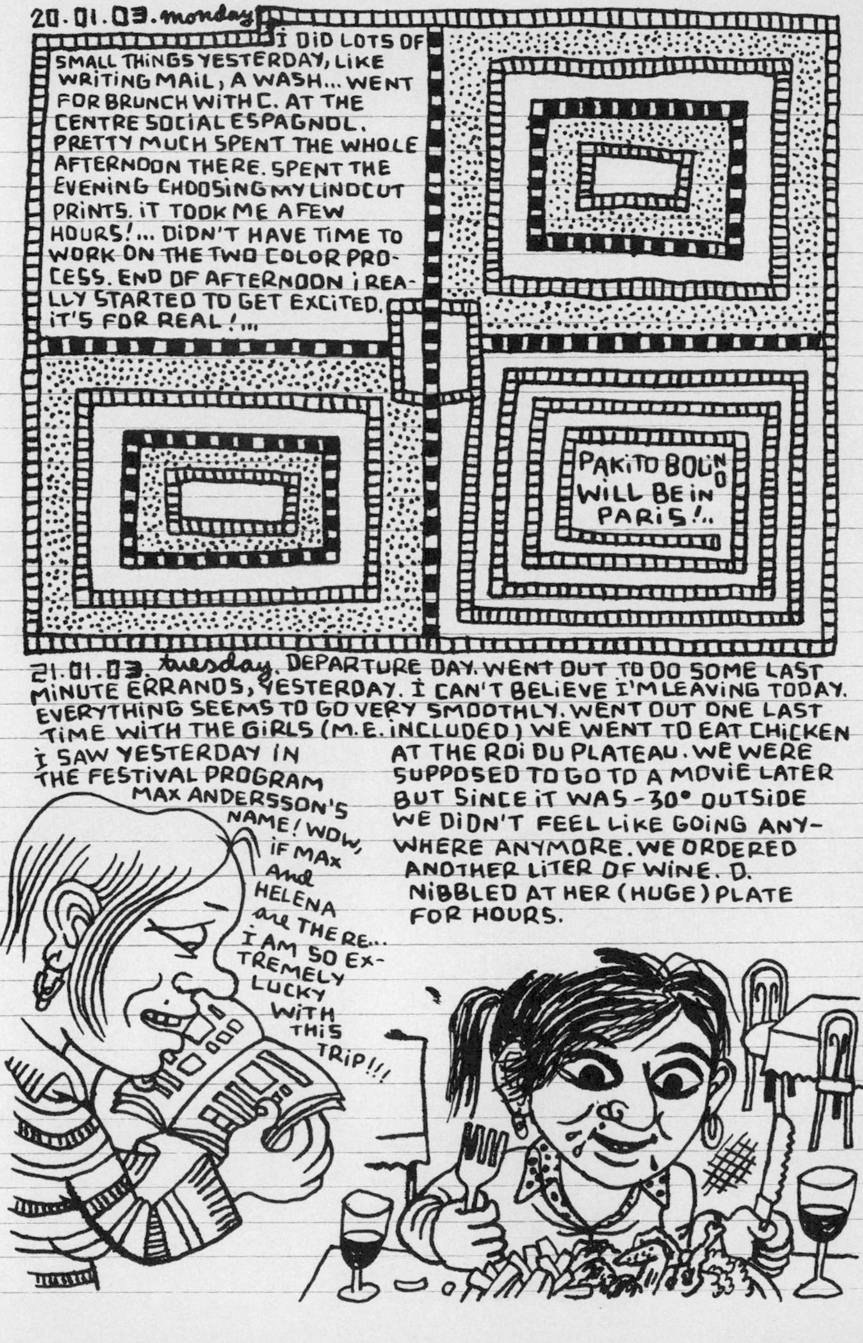
20.01.03. monday
I DID LOTS OF SMALL THINGS YESTERDAY, LIKE WRITING MAIL, A WASH... WENT FOR BRUNCH WITH C. AT THE CENTRE SOCIAL ESPAGNOL. PRETTY MUCH SPENT THE WHOLE AFTERNOON THERE. SPENT THE EVENING CHOOSING MY LINOCUT PRINTS. IT TOOK ME A FEW HOURS!... DIDN'T HAVE TIME TO WORK ON THE TWO COLOR PROCESS. END OF AFTERNOON I REALLY STARTED TO GET EXCITED. IT'S FOR REAL!...
PAKITO BOLINO WILL BE IN PARIS!..
21.01.03. tuesday. DEPARTURE DAY. WENT OUT TO DO SOME LAST MINUTE ERRANDS, YESTERDAY. I CAN'T BELIEVE I'M LEAVING TODAY. EVERYTHING SEEMS TO GO VERY SMOOTHLY. WENT OUT ONE LAST TIME WITH THE GIRLS (M.E. INCLUDED) WE WENT TO EAT CHICKEN AT THE ROI DU PLATEAU. WE WERE SUPPOSED TO GO TO A MOVIE LATER BUT SINCE IT WAS -30° OUTSIDE WE DIDN'T FEEL LIKE GOING ANYWHERE ANYMORE. WE ORDERED ANOTHER LITER OF WINE. D. NIBBLED AT HER (HUGE) PLATE FOR HOURS.
I SAW YESTERDAY IN THE FESTIVAL PROGRAM MAX ANDERSSON'S NAME! WOW, IF MAX and HELENA are THERE... I AM SO EXTREMELY LUCKY WITH THIS TRIP!!!

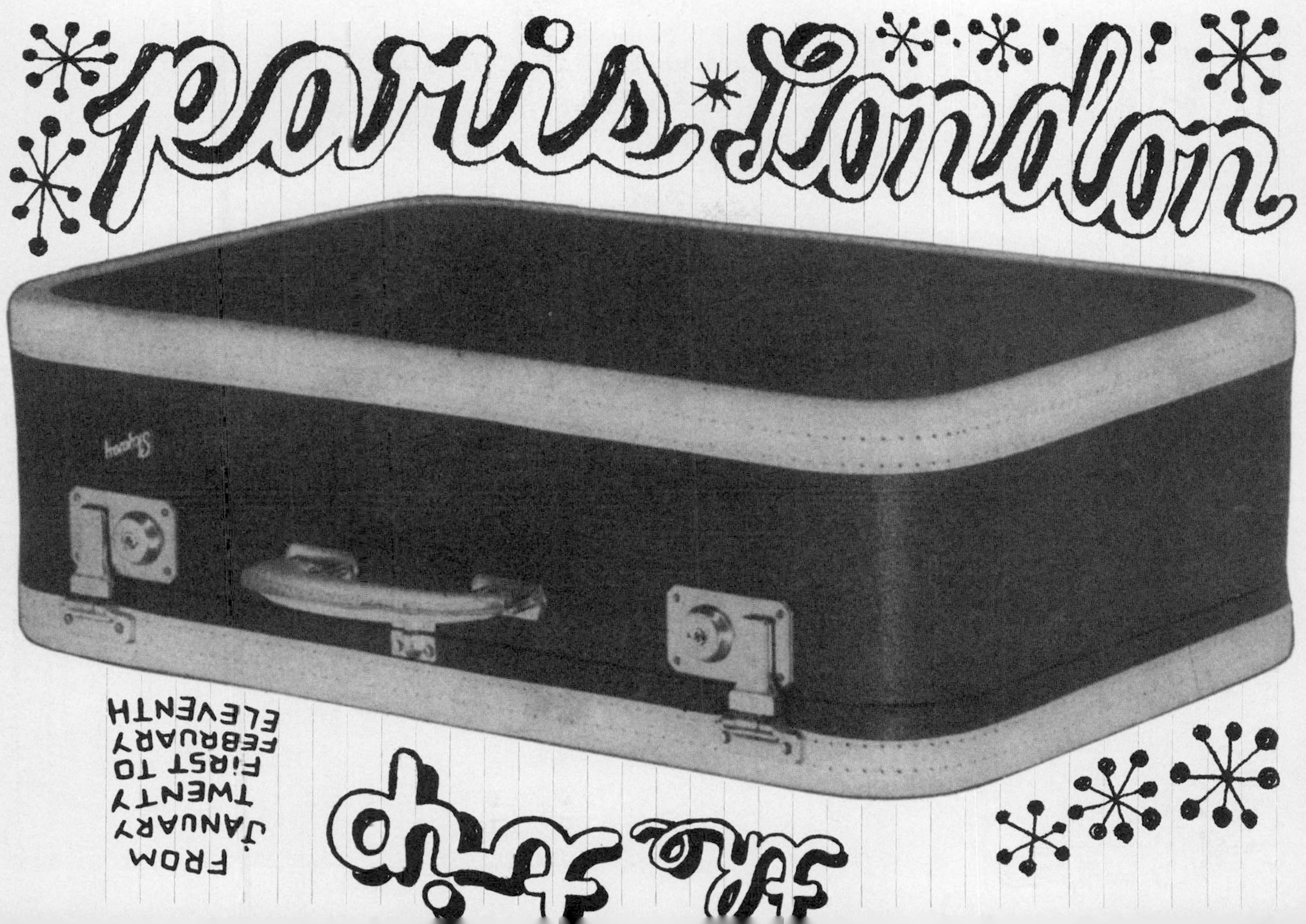
paris london
the trip
FROM JANUARY TWENTY FIRST TO FEBRUARY ELEVENTH

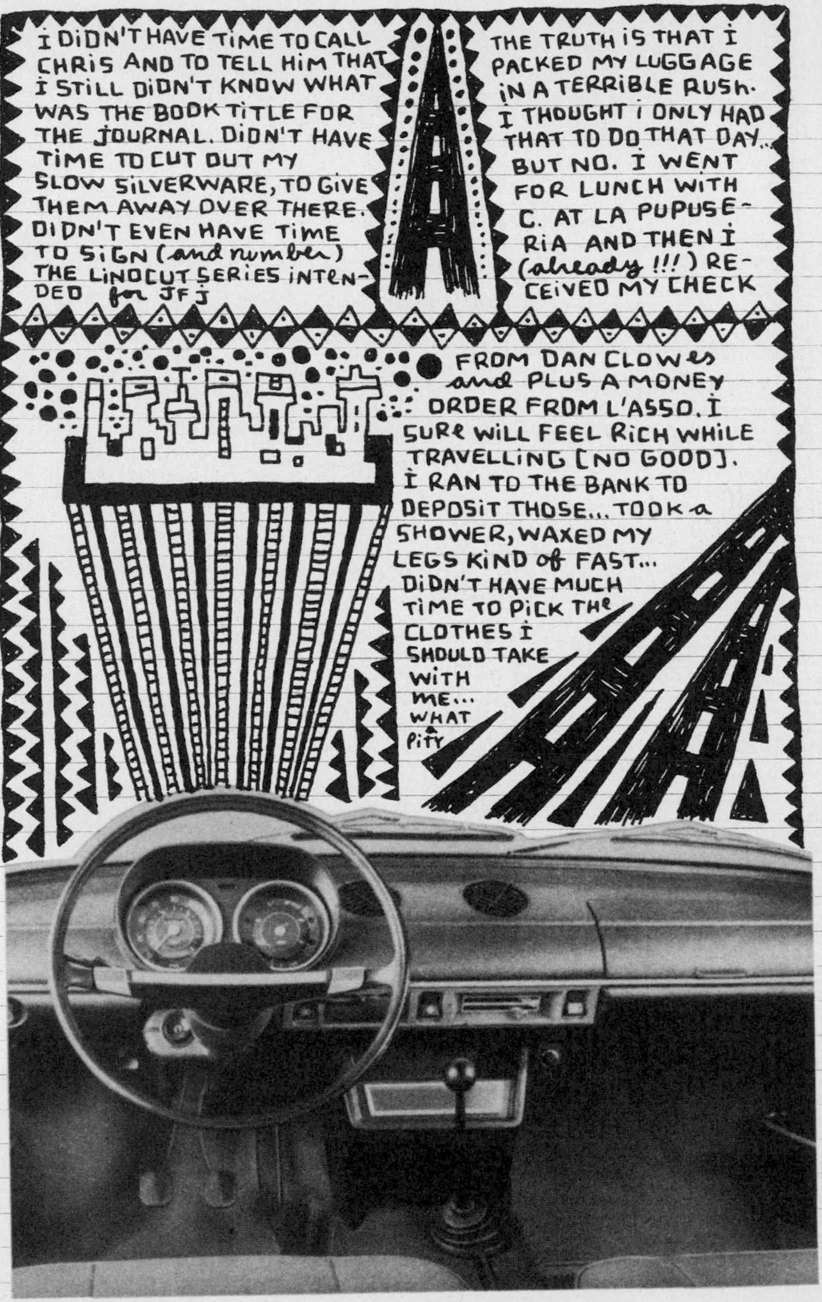
I DIDN'T HAVE TIME TO CALL CHRIS AND TO TELL HIM THAT I STILL DIDN'T KNOW WHAT WAS THE BOOK TITLE FOR THE JOURNAL. DIDN'T HAVE TIME TO CUT OUT MY SLOW SILVERWARE, TO GIVE THEM AWAY OVER THERE. DIDN'T EVEN HAVE TIME TO SIGN (and number) THE LINOCUT SERIES INTENDED for JFJ
THE TRUTH IS THAT I PACKED MY LUGGAGE IN A TERRIBLE RUSH. I THOUGHT I ONLY HAD THAT TO DO THAT DAY... BUT NO. I WENT FOR LUNCH WITH C. AT LA PUPUSERIA AND THEN I (already !!!) RECEIVED MY CHECK
FROM DAN CLOWES and PLUS A MONEY ORDER FROM L'ASSO. I SURE WILL FEEL RICH WHILE TRAVELLING [NO GOOD]. I RAN TO THE BANK TO DEPOSIT THOSE... TOOK a SHOWER, WAXED MY LEGS KIND of FAST... DIDN'T HAVE MUCH TIME TO PICK THE CLOTHES I SHOULD TAKE WITH ME... WHAT a PITY

21.01.03. at dorval airport

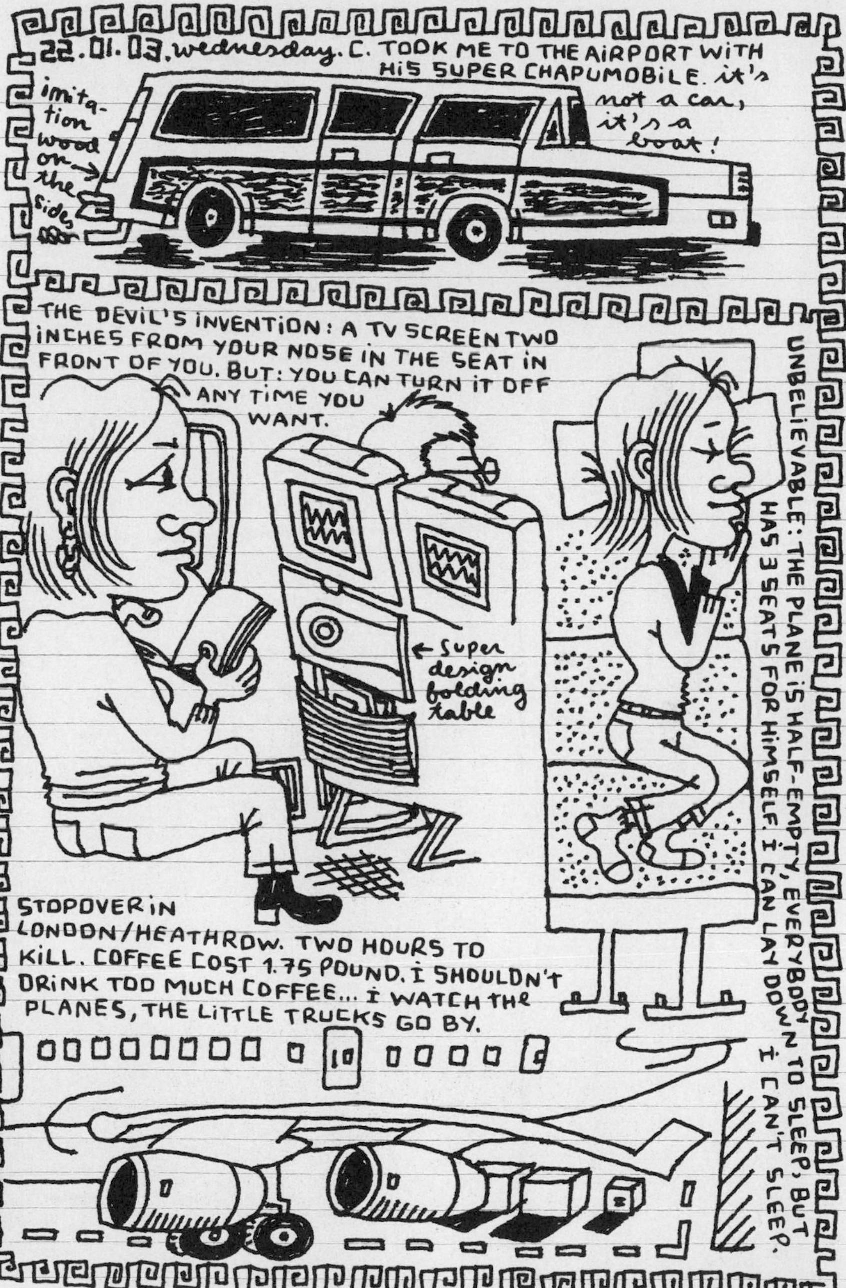
22.01.03. wednesday. C. TOOK ME TO THE AIRPORT WITH HIS SUPER CHAPUMOBILE. it's not a car, it's a boat!
imitation wood on the sides
THE DEVIL'S INVENTION: A TV SCREEN TWO INCHES FROM YOUR NOSE IN THE SEAT IN FRONT OF YOU. BUT: YOU CAN TURN IT OFF ANY TIME YOU WANT.
super design folding table
UNBELIEVABLE: THE PLANE IS HALF-EMPTY, EVERYBODY HAS 3 SEATS FOR HIMSELF. I CAN LAY DOWN TO SLEEP, BUT I CAN'T SLEEP.
STOPOVER IN LONDON/HEATHROW. TWO HOURS TO KILL. COFFEE COST 1.75 POUND. I SHOULDN'T DRINK TOO MUCH COFFEE... I WATCH THE PLANES, THE LITTLE TRUCKS GO BY.
10

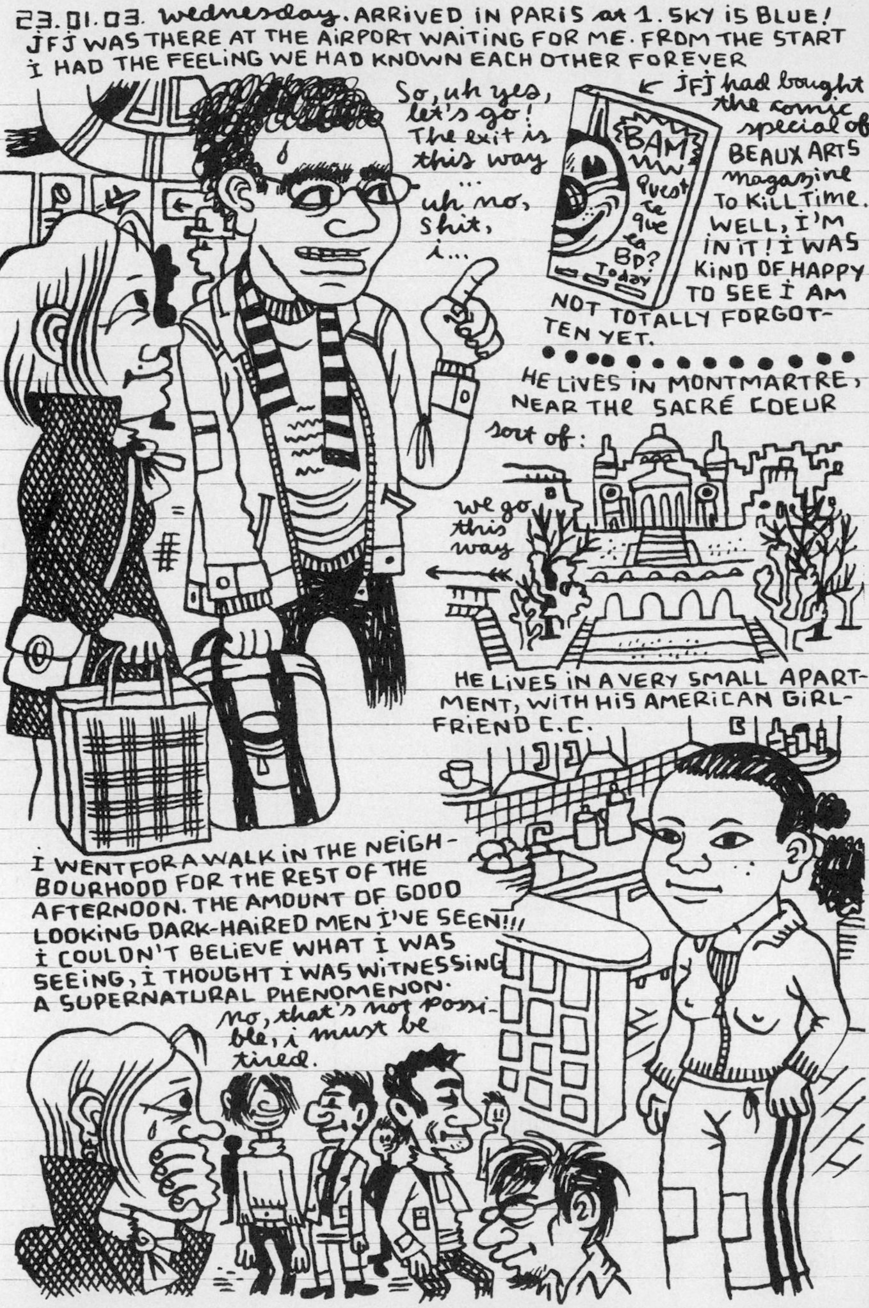
23.01.03. wednesday. ARRIVED IN PARIS at 1. SKY IS BLUE! JFJ WAS THERE AT THE AIRPORT WAITING FOR ME. FROM THE START I HAD THE FEELING WE HAD KNOWN EACH OTHER FOREVER
So, uh yes, let's go! The exit is this way ... uh no, Shit, i...
← JFJ had bought the comic special of BEAUX ARTS magazine to KILL TIME. WELL, I'M IN IT! I WAS KIND OF HAPPY TO SEE I AM NOT TOTALLY FORGOTTEN YET.
BAM
Qu'est ce que ça BD?
Today
HE LIVES IN MONTMARTRE, NEAR THE SACRÉ COEUR
sort of:
we go this way
HE LIVES IN A VERY SMALL APARTMENT, WITH HIS AMERICAN GIRLFRIEND C.C.
I WENT FOR A WALK IN THE NEIGHBOURHOOD FOR THE REST OF THE AFTERNOON. THE AMOUNT OF GOOD LOOKING DARK-HAIRED MEN I'VE SEEN!!! I COULDN'T BELIEVE WHAT I WAS SEEING, I THOUGHT I WAS WITNESSING A SUPERNATURAL PHENOMENON.
no, that's not possible, i must be tired.

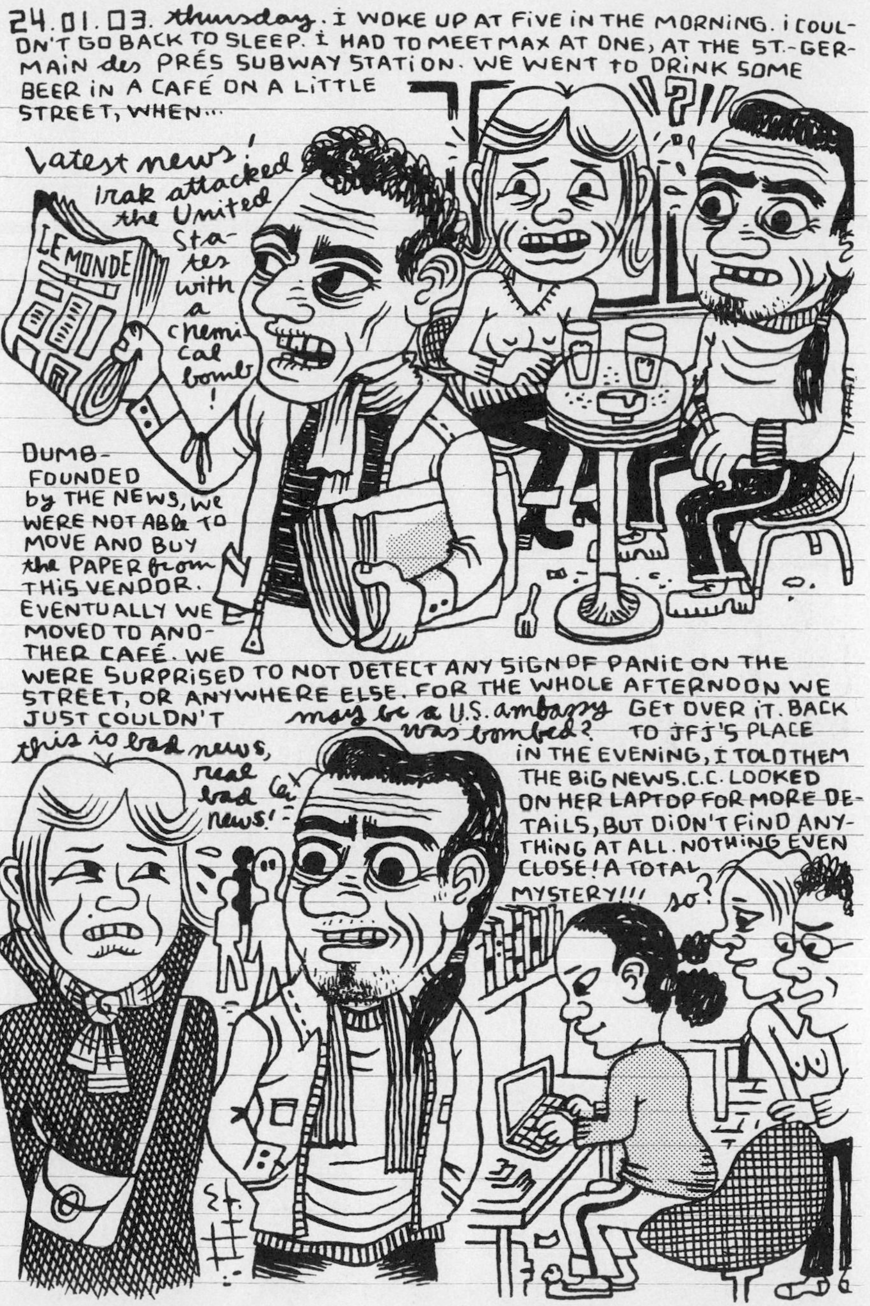
24.01.03. thursday. I WOKE UP AT FIVE IN THE MORNING. I COULDN'T GO BACK TO SLEEP. I HAD TO MEET MAX AT ONE, AT THE ST.-GERMAIN des PRÉS SUBWAY STATION. WE WENT TO DRINK SOME BEER IN A CAFÉ ON A LITTLE STREET, WHEN...
Latest news! Irak attacked the United States with a chemical bomb!
LE MONDE
?!
DUMBFOUNDED by THE NEWS, WE WERE NOT ABLE TO MOVE AND BUY the PAPER from THIS VENDOR. EVENTUALLY WE MOVED TO ANOTHER CAFÉ. WE WERE SURPRISED TO NOT DETECT ANY SIGN OF PANIC ON THE STREET, OR ANYWHERE ELSE. FOR THE WHOLE AFTERNOON WE JUST COULDN'T GET OVER IT. BACK TO JFJ'S PLACE IN THE EVENING, I TOLD THEM THE BIG NEWS. C.C. LOOKED ON HER LAPTOP FOR MORE DETAILS, BUT DIDN'T FIND ANYTHING AT ALL. NOTHING EVEN CLOSE! A TOTAL MYSTERY!!!
this is bad news, real bad news!
maybe a U.S. ambassy was bombed?
so?

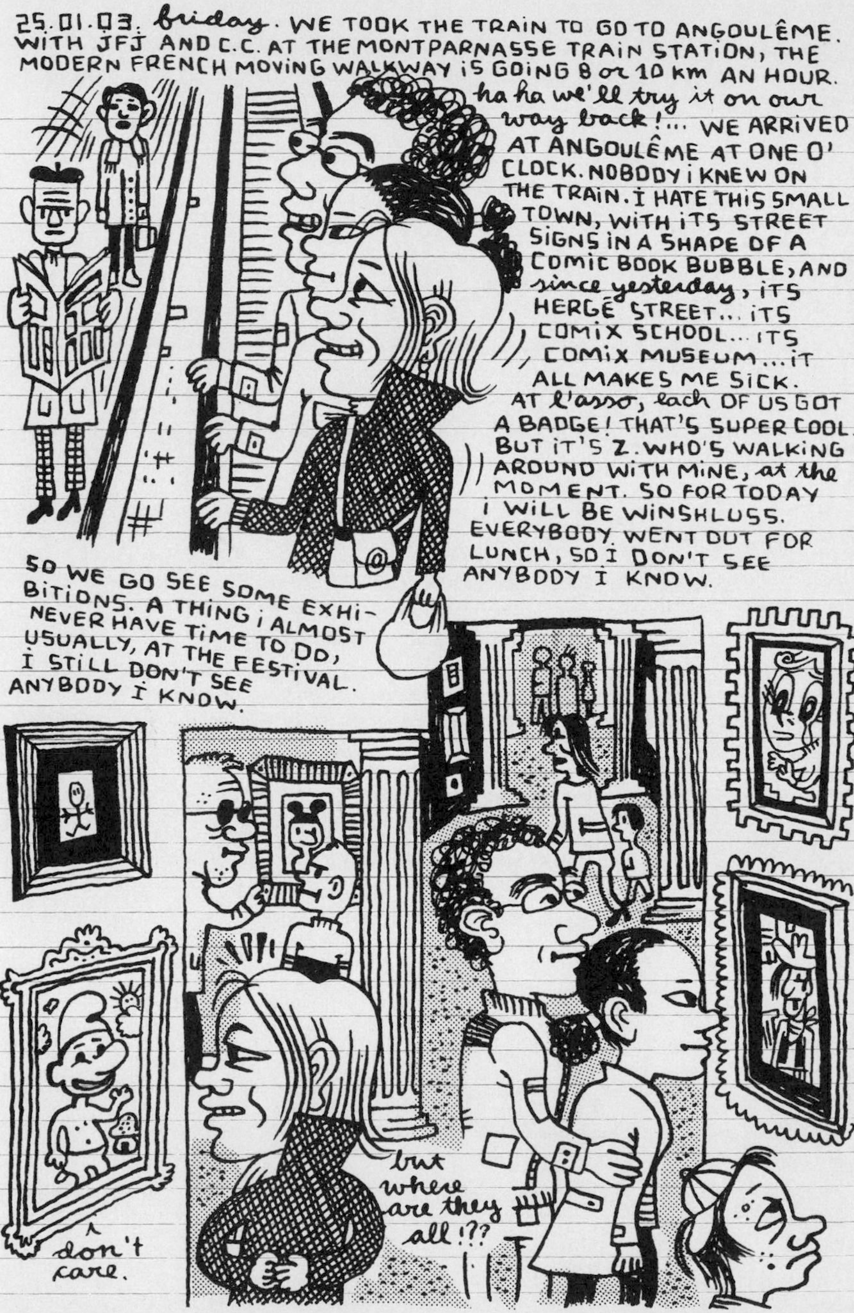
25.01.03. friday. WE TOOK THE TRAIN TO GO TO ANGOULÊME. WITH JFJ AND C.C. AT THE MONTPARNASSE TRAIN STATION, THE MODERN FRENCH MOVING WALKWAY IS GOING 8 or 10 km AN HOUR. ha ha we'll try it on our way back!... WE ARRIVED AT ANGOULÊME AT ONE O' CLOCK. NOBODY I KNEW ON THE TRAIN. I HATE THIS SMALL TOWN, WITH ITS STREET SIGNS IN A SHAPE OF A COMIC BOOK BUBBLE, AND since yesterday, ITS HERGÉ STREET... ITS COMIX SCHOOL... ITS COMIX MUSEUM... IT ALL MAKES ME SICK.
AT l'asso, each OF US GOT A BADGE! THAT'S SUPER COOL. BUT IT'S Z. WHO'S WALKING AROUND WITH MINE, at the MOMENT. SO FOR TODAY I WILL BE WINSHLUSS. EVERYBODY WENT OUT FOR LUNCH, SO I DON'T SEE ANYBODY I KNOW.
SO WE GO SEE SOME EXHIBITIONS. A THING I ALMOST NEVER HAVE TIME TO DO, USUALLY, AT THE FESTIVAL. I STILL DON'T SEE ANYBODY I KNOW.
I don't care.
but where are they all !??

AT 5 WE GO TO THE CHAT NOIR (a detestable café in that detestable town) TO DRINK A BEER. IT'S THE CAFÉ WHERE EVERYBODY MEETS, USUALLY. BUT IT'S TOO EARLY, NOBODY IS THERE. AT 6 WE GO TO THE L'ASSOCIATION BOOTH: EVERYBODY IS THERE.

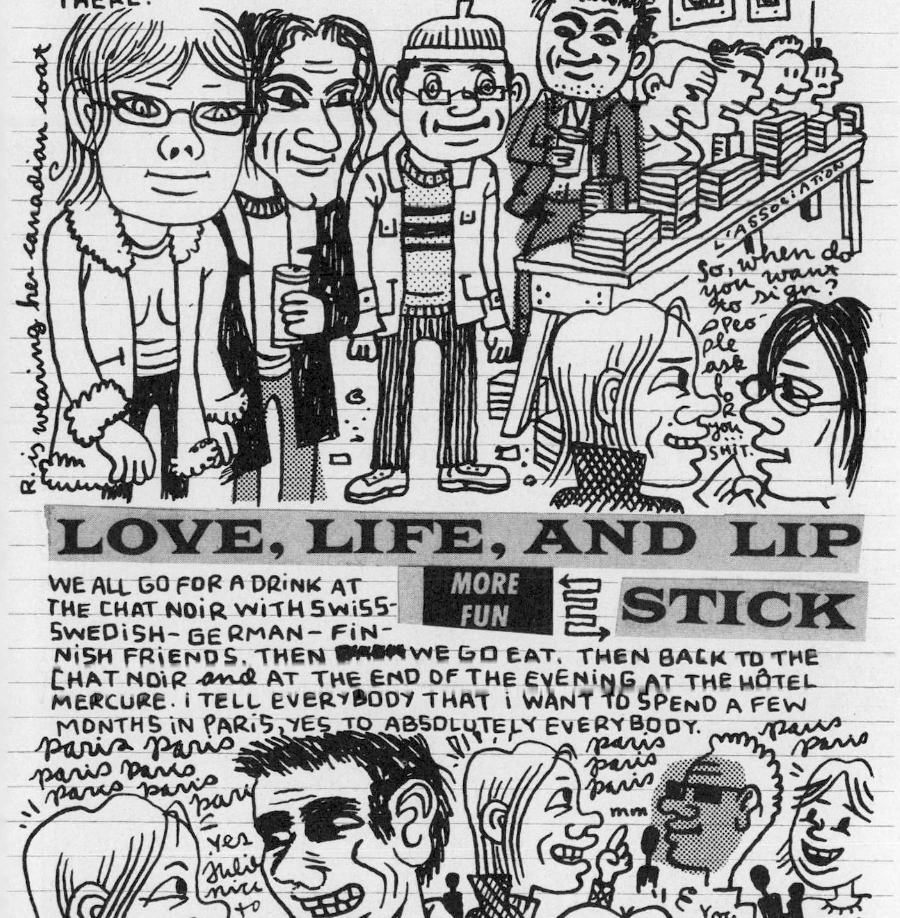
R. is wearing her canadian coat
L'ASSOCIATION
So, when do you want to sign?
people ask for you...
SHIT.

LOVE, LIFE, AND LIP MORE FUN STICK

WE ALL GO FOR A DRINK AT THE CHAT NOIR WITH SWISS-SWEDISH-GERMAN-FINNISH FRIENDS, THEN [redacted] WE GO EAT. THEN BACK TO THE CHAT NOIR and AT THE END OF THE EVENING AT THE HÔTEL MERCURE. I TELL EVERYBODY THAT I WANT TO SPEND A FEW MONTHS IN PARIS, YES TO ABSOLUTELY EVERYBODY.

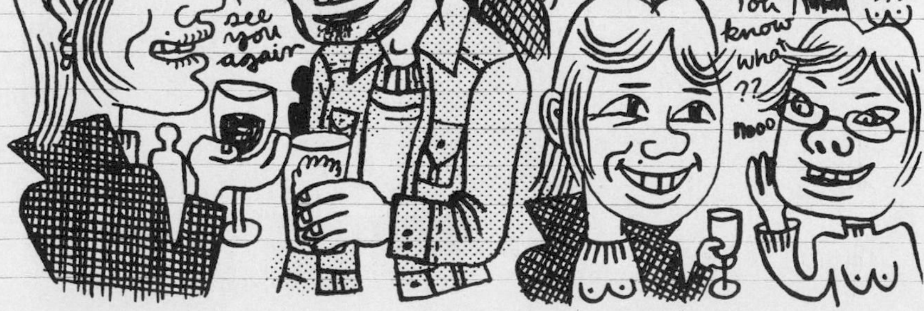
paris paris
paris paris
paris paris
pari
yes Julie nice to see you again
paris paris paris
mm
paris paris
You know what ??
nooo

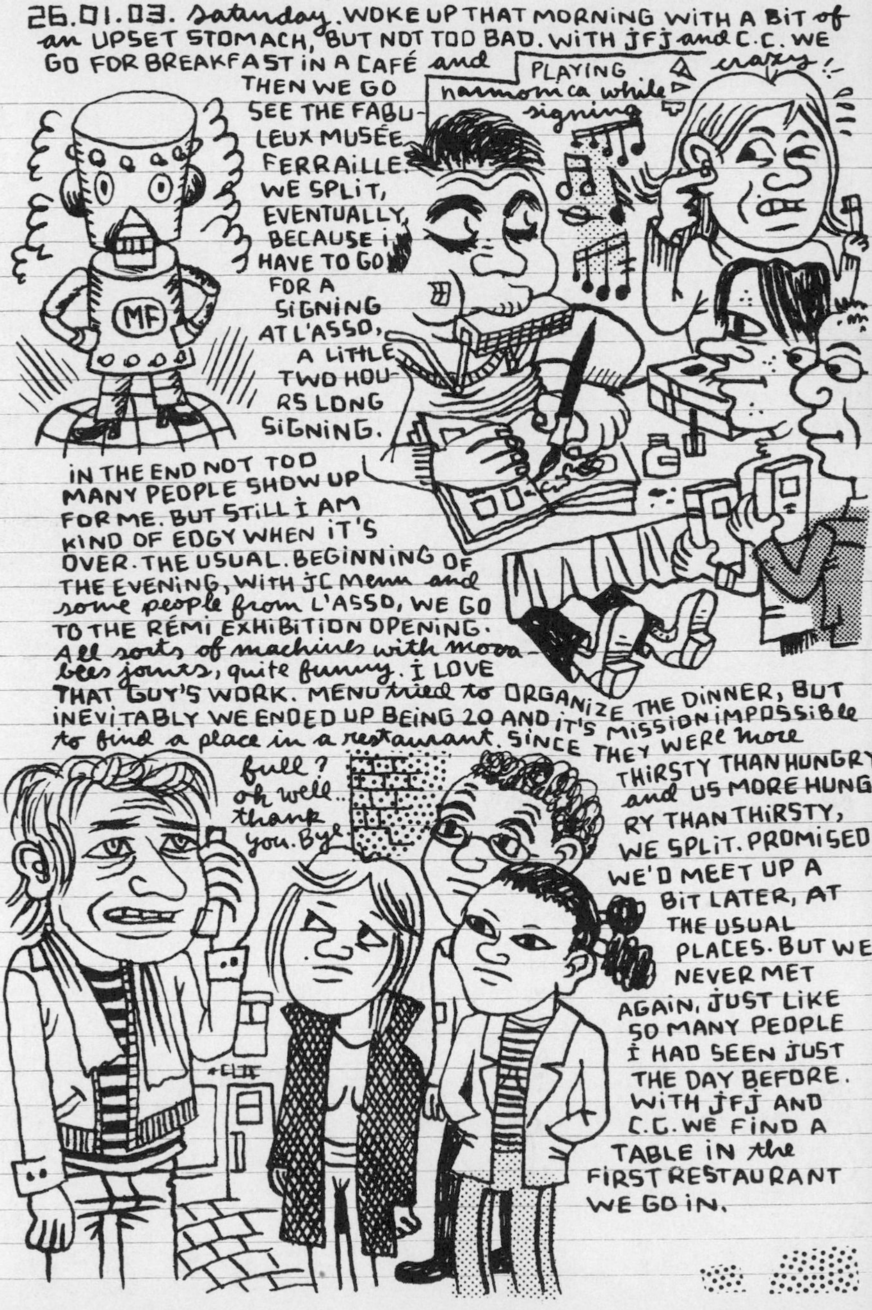
26.01.03. saturday. WOKE UP THAT MORNING WITH A BIT of an UPSET STOMACH, BUT NOT TOO BAD. WITH JFJ and C.C. WE GO FOR BREAKFAST IN A CAFÉ and THEN WE GO SEE THE FABULEUX MUSÉE FERRAILLE. WE SPLIT, EVENTUALLY, BECAUSE I HAVE TO GO FOR A SIGNING AT L'ASSO, A LITTLE TWO HOURS LONG SIGNING.
MF
PLAYING harmonica while signing
crazy!
IN THE END NOT TOO MANY PEOPLE SHOW UP FOR ME. BUT STILL I AM KIND OF EDGY WHEN IT'S OVER. THE USUAL. BEGINNING OF THE EVENING, WITH JC Menu and some people from L'ASSO, WE GO TO THE RÉMI EXHIBITION OPENING. All sorts of machines with movabees joints, quite funny. I LOVE THAT GUY'S WORK. MENU tried to ORGANIZE THE DINNER, BUT INEVITABLY WE ENDED UP BEING 20 AND IT'S MISSION IMPOSSIBLE to find a place in a restaurant. SINCE THEY WERE more THIRSTY THAN HUNGRY and US MORE HUNGRY THAN THIRSTY, WE SPLIT. PROMISED WE'D MEET UP A BIT LATER, AT THE USUAL PLACES. BUT WE NEVER MET AGAIN, JUST LIKE SO MANY PEOPLE I HAD SEEN JUST THE DAY BEFORE. WITH JFJ AND C.C. WE FIND A TABLE IN the FIRST RESTAURANT WE GO IN.
full? oh well... thank you. Bye

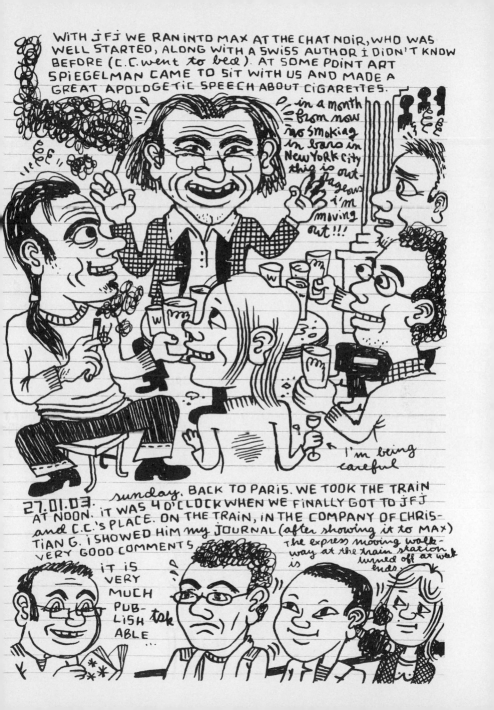

WITH JFJ WE RAN INTO MAX AT THE CHAT NOIR, WHO WAS WELL STARTED, ALONG WITH A SWISS AUTHOR I DIDN'T KNOW BEFORE (C.C. went to bed). AT SOME POINT ART SPIEGELMAN CAME TO SIT WITH US AND MADE A GREAT APOLOGETIC SPEECH ABOUT CIGARETTES.

in a month from now no smoking in bars in New York City this is outrageous i'm moving out!!!

I'm being careful

27.01.03. sunday. BACK TO PARIS. WE TOOK THE TRAIN AT NOON. IT WAS 4 O'CLOCK WHEN WE FINALLY GOT TO JFJ and C.C.'s PLACE. ON THE TRAIN, IN THE COMPANY OF CHRISTIAN G. I SHOWED HIM my JOURNAL (after showing it to MAX) VERY GOOD COMMENTS

IT IS VERY MUCH PUB- LISH ABLE tsk ...

the express moving walk-way at the train station is turned off at week ends

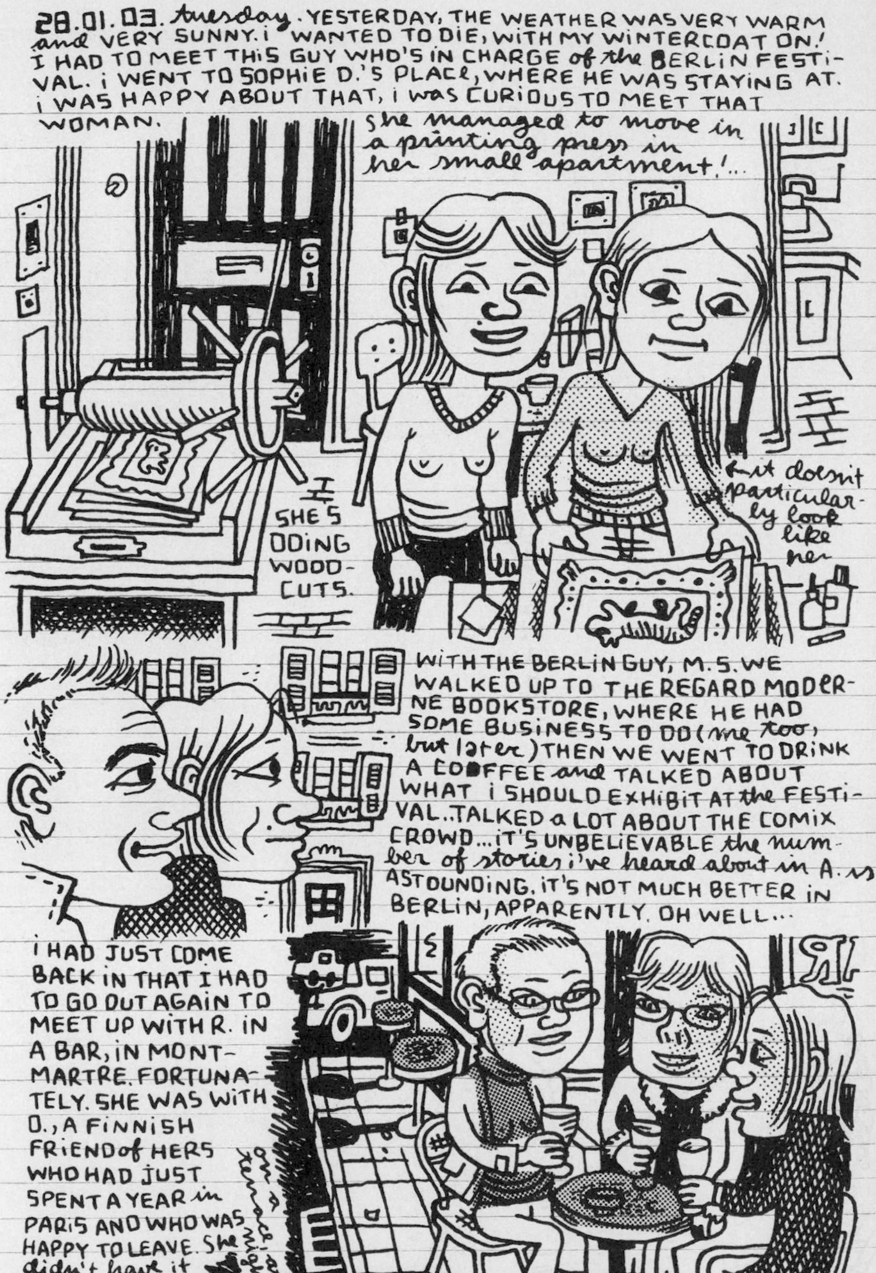
28.01.03. tuesday. YESTERDAY, THE WEATHER WAS VERY WARM and VERY SUNNY. i WANTED TO DIE, WITH MY WINTERCOAT ON! I HAD TO MEET THIS GUY WHO'S IN CHARGE of the BERLIN FESTIVAL. i WENT TO SOPHIE D.'S PLACE, WHERE HE WAS STAYING AT. i WAS HAPPY ABOUT THAT, i was CURIOUS TO MEET THAT WOMAN.
She managed to move in a printing press in her small apartment!...
SHE'S DOING WOODCUTS.
it doesn't particularly look like her
WITH THE BERLIN GUY, M.S. WE WALKED UP TO THE REGARD MODERNE BOOKSTORE, WHERE HE HAD SOME BUSINESS TO DO (me too, but later) THEN WE WENT TO DRINK A COFFEE and TALKED ABOUT WHAT i SHOULD EXHIBIT AT the FESTIVAL.. TALKED a LOT ABOUT THE COMIX CROWD... iT'S UNBELIEVABLE the number of stories i've heard about in A. is ASTOUNDING. iT'S NOT MUCH BETTER iN BERLIN, APPARENTLY. OH WELL...
i HAD JUST COME BACK IN THAT I HAD TO GO OUT AGAIN TO MEET UP WITH R. IN A BAR, IN MONTMARTRE. FORTUNATELY. SHE WAS WITH O., A FiNNiSH FRIEND of HERS WHO HAD JUST SPENT A YEAR in PARIS AND WHO WAS HAPPY TO LEAVE. She didn't have it easy...
on a Renoir - at night!...

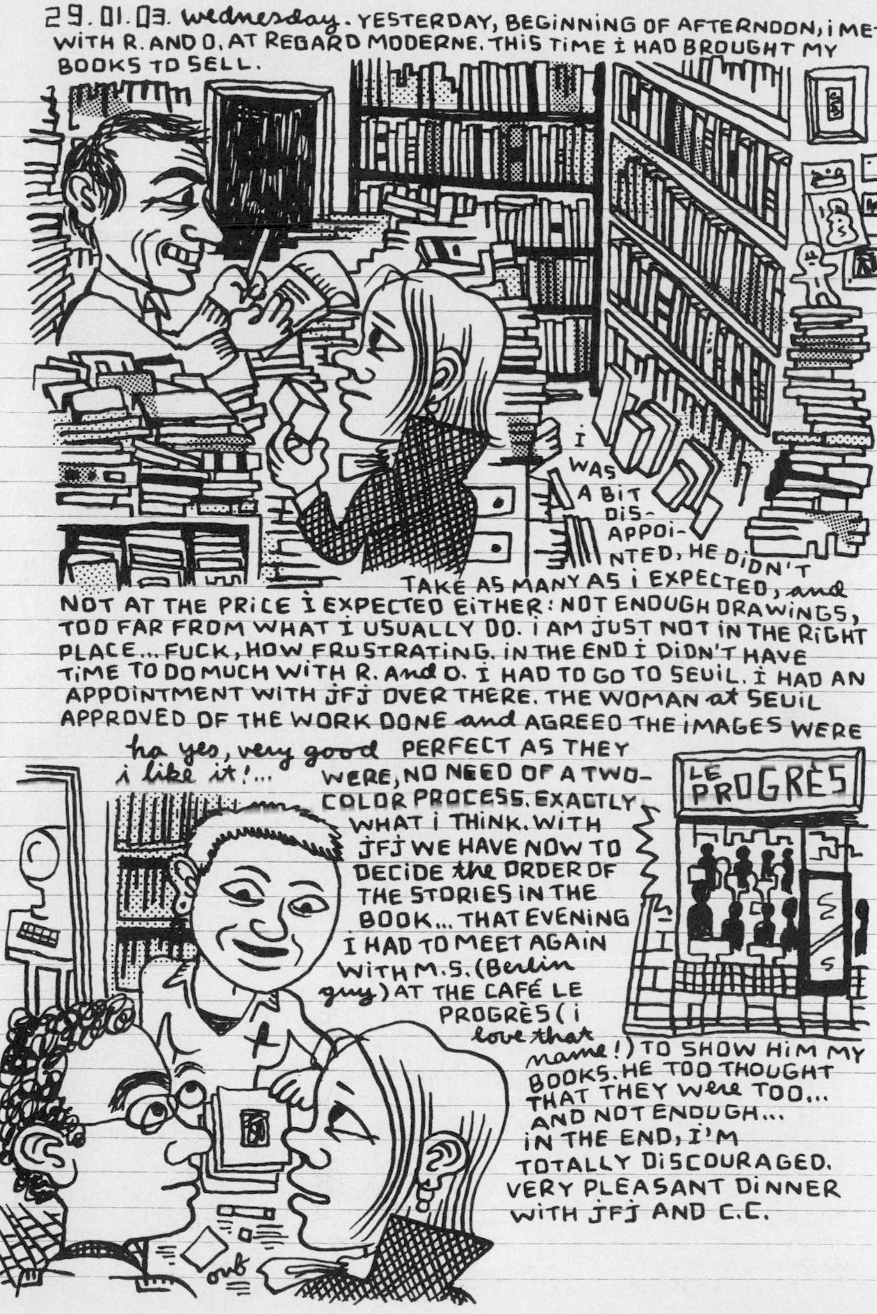
29.01.03. wednesday. YESTERDAY, BEGINNING OF AFTERNOON, i MET WITH R. AND O. AT REGARD MODERNE. THIS TIME I HAD BROUGHT MY BOOKS TO SELL.
I WAS A BIT DIS-APPOINTED, HE DIDN'T TAKE AS MANY AS i EXPECTED, and NOT AT THE PRICE I EXPECTED EITHER: NOT ENOUGH DRAWINGS, TOO FAR FROM WHAT I USUALLY DO. i AM JUST NOT IN THE RIGHT PLACE... FUCK, HOW FRUSTRATING. IN THE END I DIDN'T HAVE TIME TO DO MUCH WITH R. and O. I HAD TO GO TO SEUIL. I HAD AN APPOINTMENT WITH JFJ OVER THERE. THE WOMAN at SEUIL APPROVED OF THE WORK DONE and AGREED THE IMAGES WERE PERFECT AS THEY WERE, NO NEED OF A TWO-COLOR PROCESS. EXACTLY WHAT i THINK. WITH JFJ WE HAVE NOW TO DECIDE the ORDER OF THE STORIES IN THE BOOK... THAT EVENING I HAD TO MEET AGAIN WITH M.S. (Berlin guy) AT THE CAFÉ LE PROGRÈS (i love that name!) TO SHOW HIM MY BOOKS. HE TOO THOUGHT THAT THEY were TOO... AND NOT ENOUGH... IN THE END, I'M TOTALLY DISCOURAGED. VERY PLEASANT DINNER WITH JFJ AND C.C.
ha yes, very good
i like it!...
LE PROGRÈS

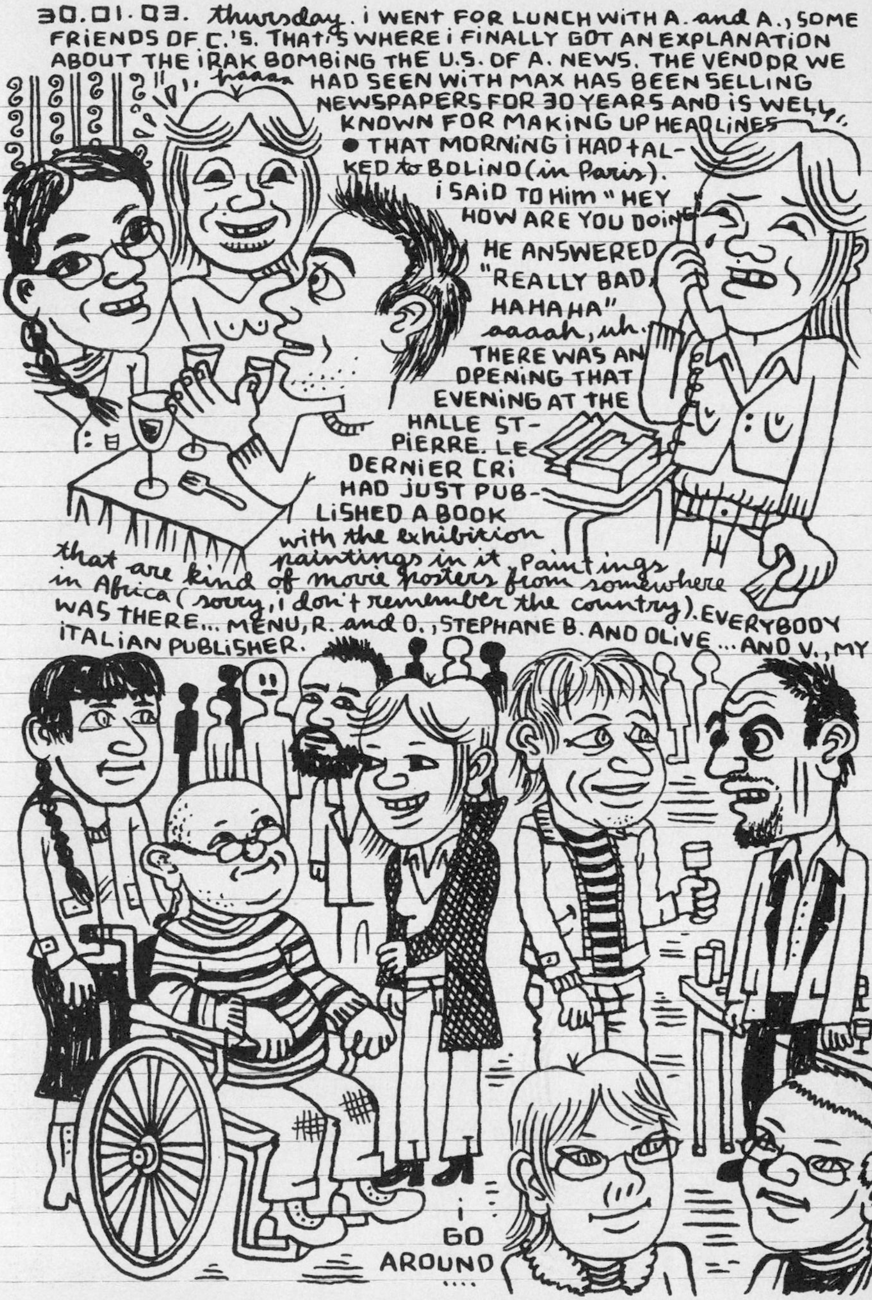
30.01.03. thursday. i WENT FOR LUNCH WITH A. and A., SOME FRIENDS OF C.'S. THAT'S WHERE i FINALLY GOT AN EXPLANATION ABOUT THE iRAK BOMBING THE U.S. OF A. NEWS. THE VENDOR WE HAD SEEN WITH MAX HAS BEEN SELLING NEWSPAPERS FOR 30 YEARS AND IS WELL KNOWN FOR MAKING UP HEADLINES.
• THAT MORNING i HAD TALKED to BOLINO (in Paris). i SAID TO Him "HEY HOW ARE YOU DOING?"
HE ANSWERED "REALLY BAD, HAHAHA"
aaaah, uh.
THERE WAS AN OPENING THAT EVENING AT THE HALLE ST-PIERRE. LE DERNIER CRi HAD JUST PUBLiSHED A BOOK with the exhibition paintings in it. Paintings that are kind of movie posters from somewhere in Africa (sorry, i don't remember the country). EVERYBODY WAS THERE... MENU, R. and O., STEPHANE B. AND OLIVE... AND V., MY ITALIAN PUBLISHER.
i GO AROUND....

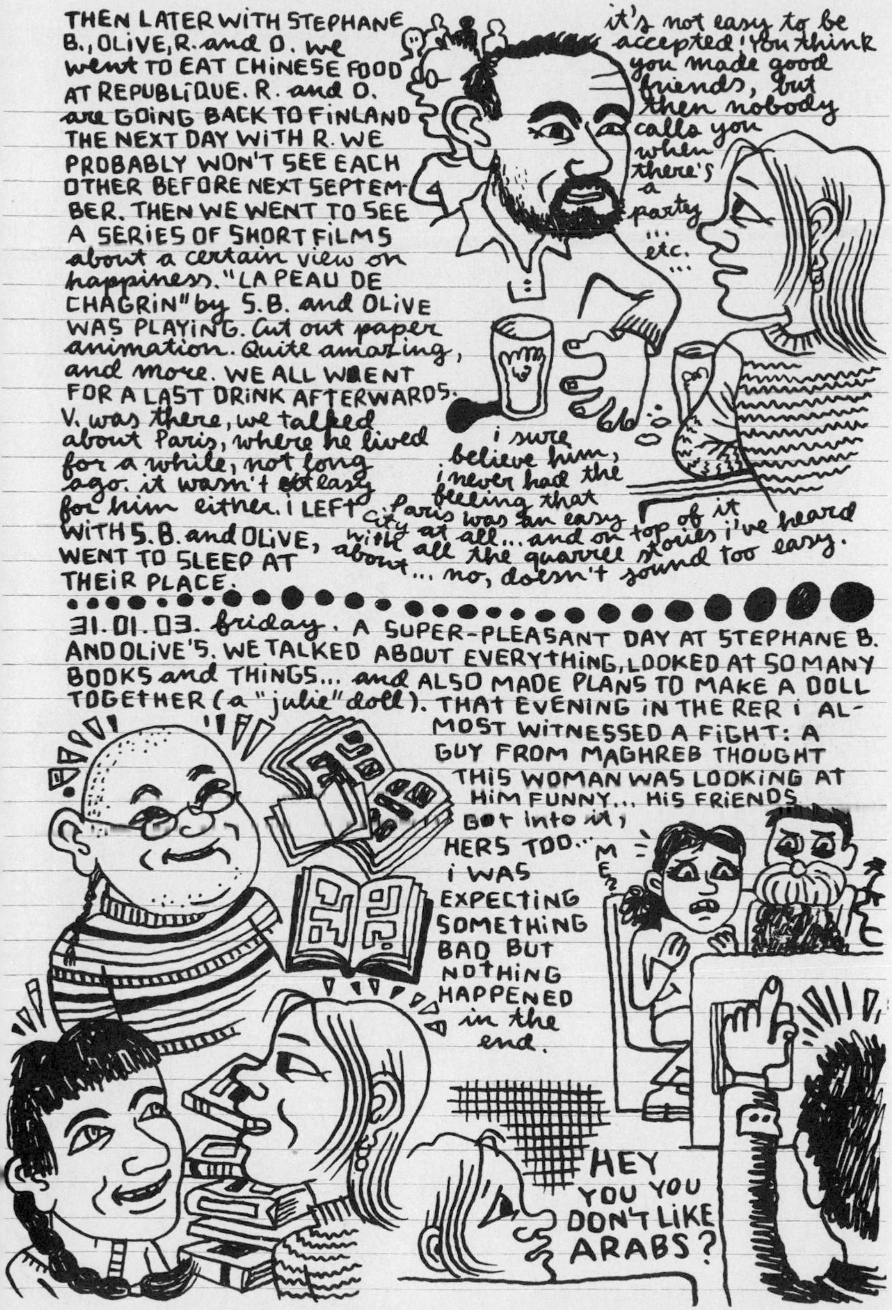
THEN LATER WITH STEPHANE B., OLIVE, R. and O. we went TO EAT CHINESE FOOD AT REPUBLIQUE. R. and O. are GOING BACK TO FINLAND THE NEXT DAY WITH R. WE PROBABLY WON'T SEE EACH OTHER BEFORE NEXT SEPTEMBER. THEN WE WENT TO SEE A SERIES OF SHORT FILMS about a certain view on happiness. "LA PEAU DE CHAGRIN" by S.B. and OLIVE WAS PLAYING. Cut out paper animation. Quite amazing, and more. WE ALL WENT FOR A LAST DRINK AFTERWARDS. V. was there, we talked about Paris, where he lived for a while, not long ago. it wasn't easy for him either. I LEFT WITH S.B. and OLIVE, WENT TO SLEEP AT THEIR PLACE.
it's not easy to be accepted! You think you made good friends, but then nobody calls you when there's a party ... etc. ...
i sure believe him, i never had the feeling that Paris was an easy city at all... and on top of it with all the quarrel stories i've heard about... no, doesn't sound too easy.
31.01.03. friday. A SUPER-PLEASANT DAY AT STEPHANE B. AND OLIVE'S. WE TALKED ABOUT EVERYTHING, LOOKED AT SO MANY BOOKS and THINGS... and ALSO MADE PLANS TO MAKE A DOLL TOGETHER (a "julie" doll). THAT EVENING IN THE RER I ALMOST WITNESSED A FIGHT: A GUY FROM MAGHREB THOUGHT THIS WOMAN WAS LOOKING AT HIM FUNNY... HIS FRIENDS GOT into it, HERS TOO... I WAS EXPECTING SOMETHING BAD BUT NOTHING HAPPENED in the end.
ME
HEY YOU YOU DON'T LIKE ARABS?

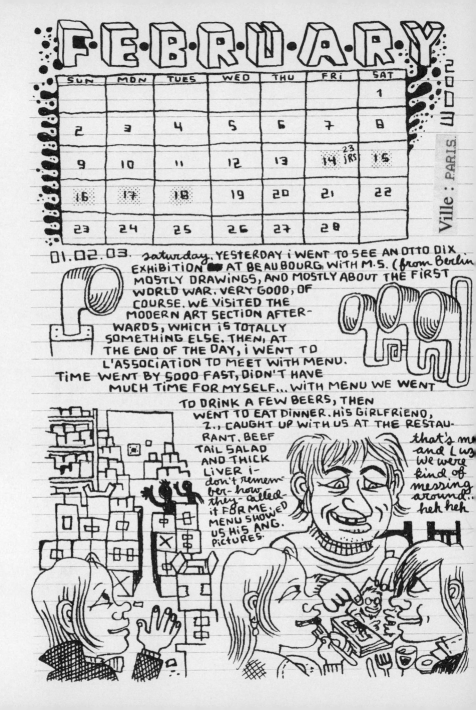

F·E·B·R·Ü·A·R·Y

SUN	MON	TUES	WED	THU	FRI	SAT
						1
2	3	4	5	6	7	8
9	10	11	12	13	14 23 iRS	15
16	17	18	19	20	21	22
23	24	25	26	27	28	

2002

Ville : P.ARI.S.

01.02.03. saturday. YESTERDAY i WENT TO SEE AN OTTO DIX EXHiBiTiON ➡ AT BEAUBOURG, WITH M.S. (from Berlin MOSTLY DRAWINGS, AND MOSTLY ABOUT THE FIRST WORLD WAR. VERY GOOD, OF COURSE. WE ViSiTED THE MODERN ART SECTION AFTER-WARDS, WHiCH iS TOTALLY SOMETHING ELSE. THEN, AT THE END OF THE DAY, i WENT TO L'ASSOCiATiON TO MEET WiTH MENU. TiME WENT BY 5000 FAST, DiDN'T HAVE MUCH TIME FOR MYSELF... WITH MENU WE WENT TO DRiNK A FEW BEERS, THEN WENT TO EAT DiNNER. HiS GIRLFRIEND, Z., CAUGHT UP WiTH US AT THE RESTAU-RANT. BEEF TAIL SALAD AND THICK LIVER i-don't remem-ber-how-they-called it FOR ME. MENU SHOWED US HiS ANG. PiCTURES.

that's me and Luz we were kind of messing around... heh heh

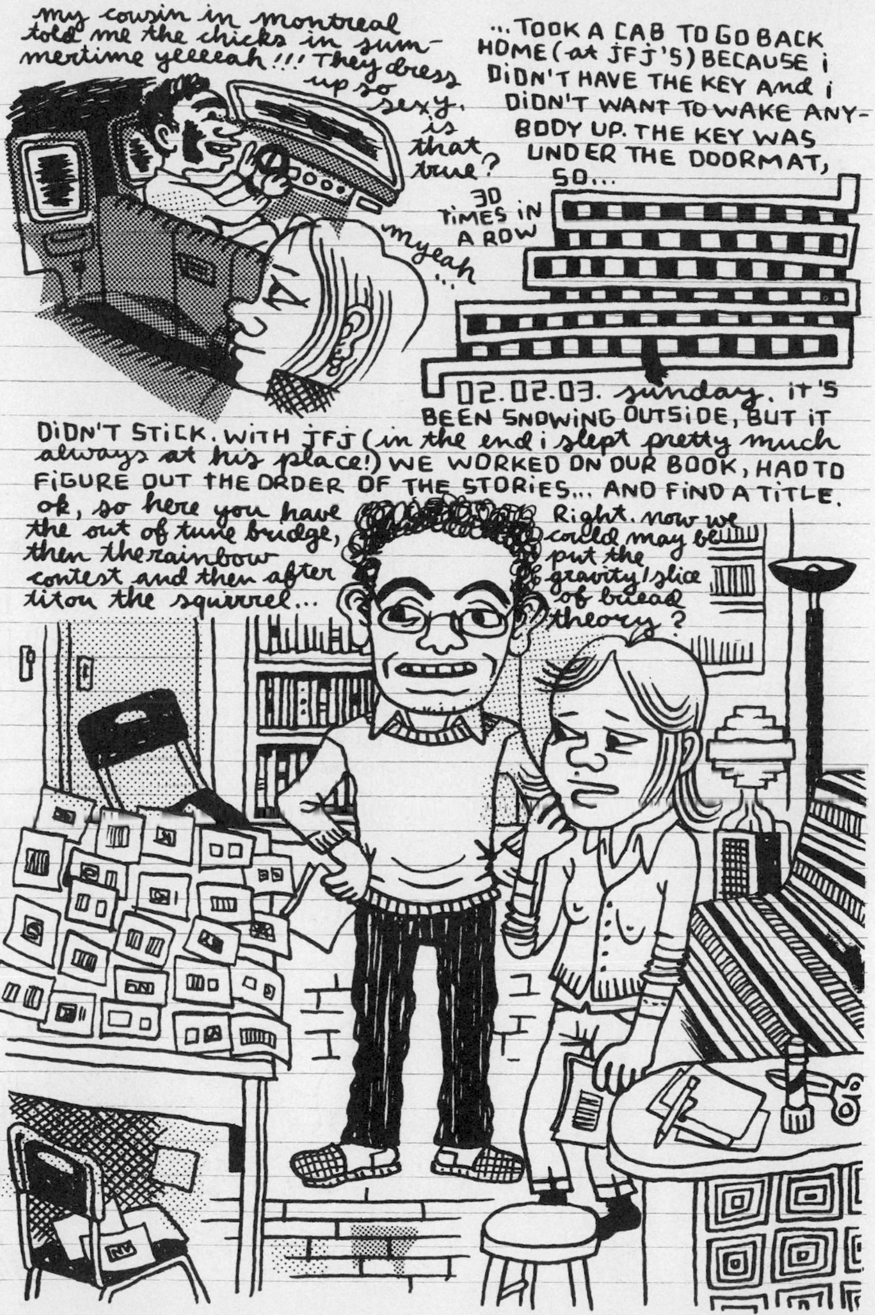
my cousin in montreal told me the chicks in summertime yeeeeah!!! They dress up so sexy. is that true?
myeah...
...TOOK A CAB TO GO BACK HOME (at JFJ'S) BECAUSE i DIDN'T HAVE THE KEY and i DIDN'T WANT TO WAKE ANYBODY UP. THE KEY WAS UNDER THE DOORMAT, SO...
30 TIMES IN A ROW
02.02.03. sunday. IT'S BEEN SNOWING OUTSIDE, BUT IT DIDN'T STICK. WITH JFJ (in the end i slept pretty much always at his place!) WE WORKED ON OUR BOOK, HAD TO FIGURE OUT THE ORDER OF THE STORIES... AND FIND A TITLE.
ok, so here you have the out of tune bridge, then the rainbow contest and then after titou the squirrel...
Right. now we could maybe put the gravity/slice of bread theory?

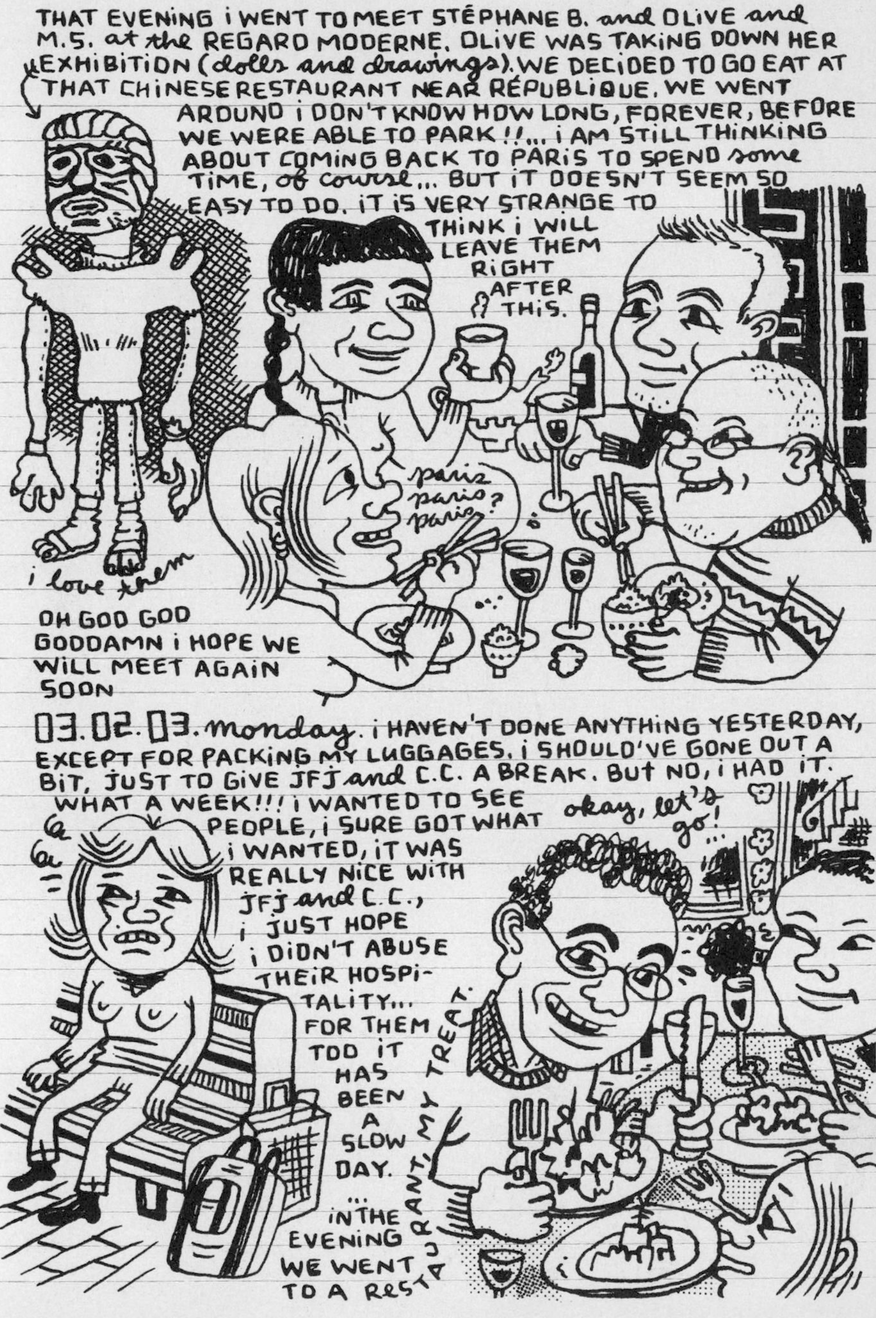
THAT EVENING i WENT TO MEET STÉPHANE B. and OLIVE and M.5. at the REGARD MODERNE. OLIVE WAS TAKING DOWN HER EXHIBITION (dolls and drawings). WE DECIDED TO GO EAT AT THAT CHINESE RESTAURANT NEAR RÉPUBLIQUE. WE WENT AROUND i DON'T KNOW HOW LONG, FOREVER, BEFORE WE WERE ABLE TO PARK!!... i AM STILL THINKING ABOUT COMING BACK TO PARIS TO SPEND some TIME, of course... BUT iT DOESN'T SEEM SO EASY TO DO. iT iS VERY STRANGE TO THINK i WILL LEAVE THEM RIGHT AFTER THIS.
i love them
paris paris? paris
OH GOD GOD GODDAMN i HOPE WE WILL MEET AGAIN SOON
03.02.03. monday. i HAVEN'T DONE ANYTHING YESTERDAY, EXCEPT FOR PACKING MY LUGGAGES. i SHOULD'VE GONE OUT A BiT, JUST TO GIVE JFJ and C.C. A BREAK. BUT NO, i HAD iT. WHAT A WEEK!!! i WANTED TO SEE PEOPLE, i SURE GOT WHAT i WANTED, iT WAS REALLY NiCE WiTH JFJ and C.C., i JUST HOPE i DiDN'T ABUSE THEiR HOSPi-TALITY... FOR THEM TOO iT HAS BEEN A SLOW DAY. ... iN THE EVENING WE WENT TO A RESTAURANT, MY TREAT.
okay, let's go!...

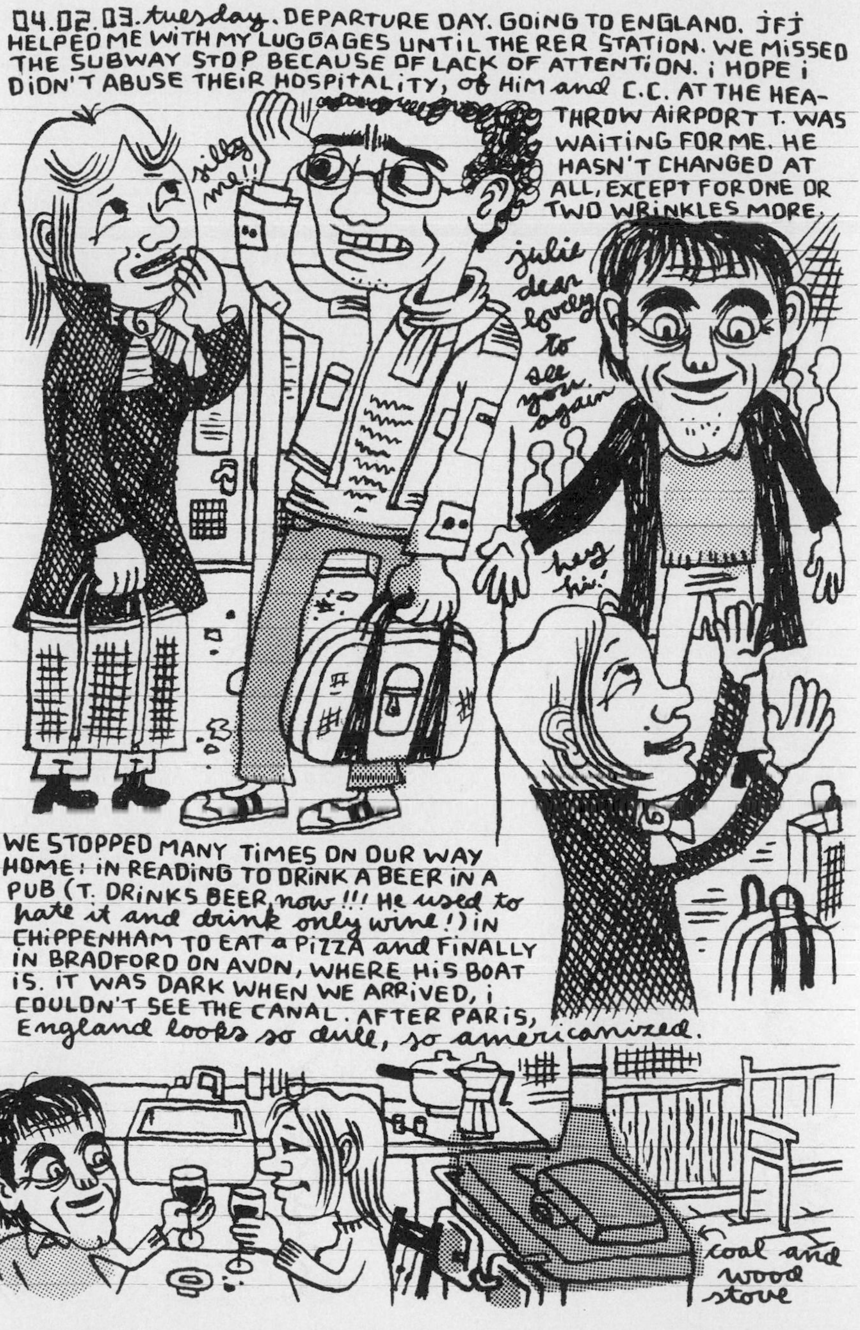
04.02.03. tuesday. DEPARTURE DAY. GOING TO ENGLAND. JFJ HELPED ME WITH MY LUGGAGES UNTIL THE RER STATION. WE MISSED THE SUBWAY STOP BECAUSE OF LACK OF ATTENTION. i HOPE i DIDN'T ABUSE THEIR HOSPITALITY, of HIM and C.C. AT THE HEATHROW AIRPORT T. WAS WAITING FOR ME. HE HASN'T CHANGED AT ALL, EXCEPT FOR ONE OR TWO WRINKLES MORE.
silly me!!
julie dear lovely to see you again
hey hi!
WE STOPPED MANY TIMES ON OUR WAY HOME: IN READING TO DRINK A BEER IN A PUB (T. DRINKS BEER now!!! He used to hate it and drink only wine!) IN CHIPPENHAM TO EAT a PIZZA and FINALLY IN BRADFORD ON AVON, WHERE HIS BOAT IS. IT WAS DARK WHEN WE ARRIVED, i COULDN'T SEE THE CANAL. AFTER PARIS, England looks so dull, so americanized.
coal and wood stove

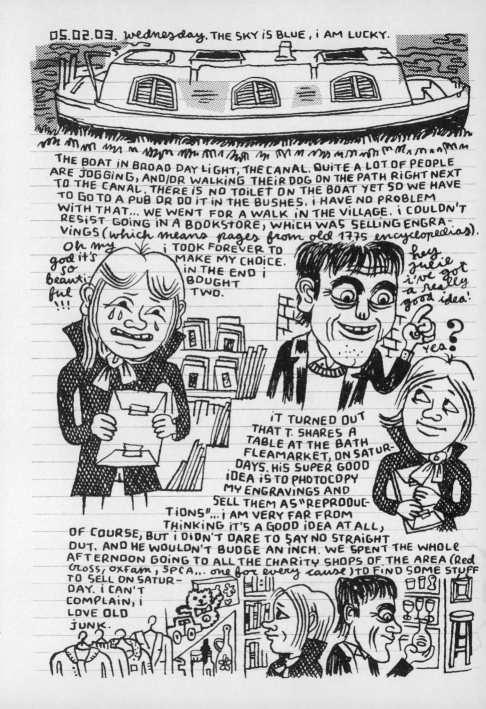

05.02.03. Wednesday. THE SKY IS BLUE, i AM LUCKY.

THE BOAT IN BROAD DAY LIGHT, THE CANAL. QUITE A LOT OF PEOPLE ARE JOGGING, AND/OR WALKING THEIR DOG ON THE PATH RIGHT NEXT TO THE CANAL. THERE IS NO TOILET ON THE BOAT YET SO WE HAVE TO GO TO A PUB OR DO IT IN THE BUSHES. i HAVE NO PROBLEM WITH THAT... WE WENT FOR A WALK IN THE VILLAGE. i COULDN'T RESIST GOING IN A BOOKSTORE, WHICH WAS SELLING ENGRA-VINGS (which means pages from old 1775 encyclopedias).

Oh my god it's so beautiful!!!

i TOOK FOREVER TO MAKE MY CHOICE. IN THE END i BOUGHT TWO.

hey juelie i've got a relly good idea!

yes?

iT TURNED OUT THAT T. SHARES A TABLE AT THE BATH FLEAMARKET, ON SATUR-DAYS. HiS SUPER GOOD iDEA iS TO PHOTOCOPY MY ENGRAVINGS AND SELL THEM AS "REPRODUC-TIONS"... i AM VERY FAR FROM THiNKING iT'S A GOOD iDEA AT ALL, OF COURSE, BUT i DiDN'T DARE TO SAY NO STRAIGHT OUT. AND HE WOULDN'T BUDGE AN INCH. WE SPENT THE WHOLE AFTERNOON GOING TO ALL THE CHARITY SHOPS OF THE AREA (Red Cross, Oxfam, SPCA... one for every cause) TO FIND SOME STUFF TO SELL ON SATUR-DAY. i CAN'T COMPLAIN, i LOVE OLD JUNK.

IN THE EVENING, HE COOKED DINNER. T. IS A VEGAN, DOESN'T EAT FISH OR DAIRY PRODUCTS. WE FINISHED OUR BOTTLE OF WINE WHILE DISCUSSING POLITICS. I FELL OFF MY CHAIR, WAS STUNNED, FLABBERGASTED AND SO ON: T. IS ALL FOR THE WAR IN IRAK, HE THINKS EVERYBODY IS BEING TOO TOUGH ON THE AMERICANS... A TOTAL PARANOID DELIRIUM. I KNOW HE JUST LOVES TO BE IN

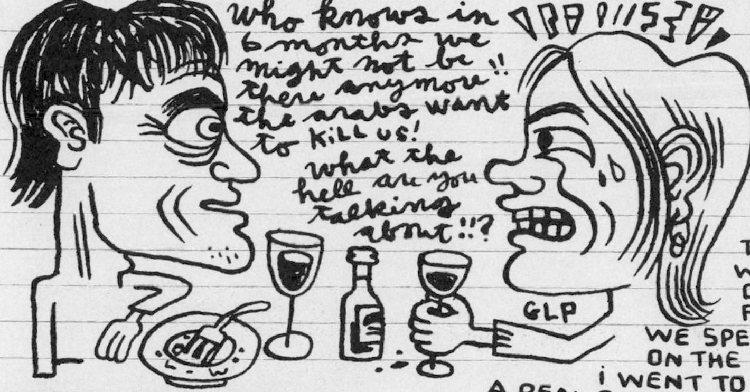
Who knows in 6 months we might not be there anymore!! the arabs want to kill us!
what the hell are you talking about!!?
GLP

OPPOSITION WITH ALL THE PEOPLE AROUND HIM... BUT HE IS GOING A BIT TOO FAR TO MY TASTE WITH THAT ONE. UNFORTUNATELY WE SPENT HOURS ON THE SUBJECT. I WENT TO BED IN A REAL BAD MOOD.

06.02.03. *thursday.* WE GOT UP EARLY TO GO TO AN AUCTION IN A NEARBY VILLAGE. QUITE AN AMAZING BRIC-A-BRAC ALL PILED UP IN TWO BIG WAREHOUSES. RIGHT NEXT TO A LIVESTOCK MARKET. IN THE END THERE WAS MOSTLY FURNITURE, NOTHING SUITABLE FOR T. AND HIS FLEAMARKET GIG. IT WAS FUNNY TO LOOK AT PEOPLE'S FACES, IT ALL FELT LIKE BEING IN A DICKENS NOVEL....

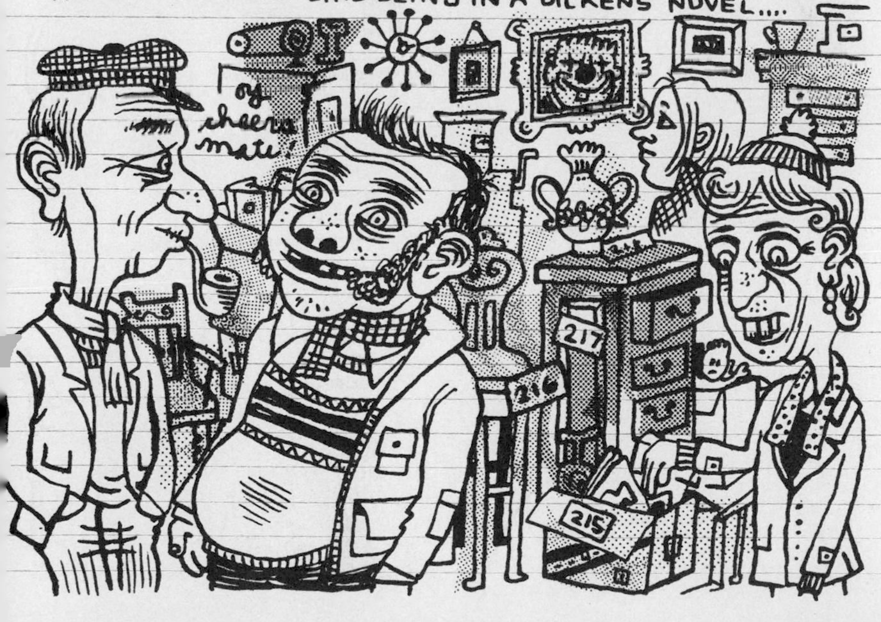
oy cheers mate!
217
216
215

... AND TO LISTEN TO THEM IS LIKE A MONTY PYTHON EPISODE. I AM STILL IN A HIGHLY EMOTIONAL STATE BECAUSE OF LASTNIGHT. OH WELL, BUT... LET'S NOT THINK ABOUT IT. WE WENT TO BATH, HAD LUNCH WITH ONE OF T.'S FRIENDS, A CANADIAN FROM VANCOUVER WHO LIVED IN England FIFTEEN YEARS WITH HIS GIRLFRIEND AND NOW THEY ARE MOVING BACK TO CANADA, THIS COMING SPRING, AND WE WENT SHOPPING (more shopping! i forgot how much shopping we do with T.) WE HAD TO BUY CARDBOARD TO MAKE a PASSE-PARTOUT FOR THE FUTURE FAKE ENGRAVINGS... AT THE END OF THE DAY WE WENT TO THE CANADIAN GUY'S PLACE WHO HAD SOME STUFF TO GIVE T. FOR THE FLEAMARKET.

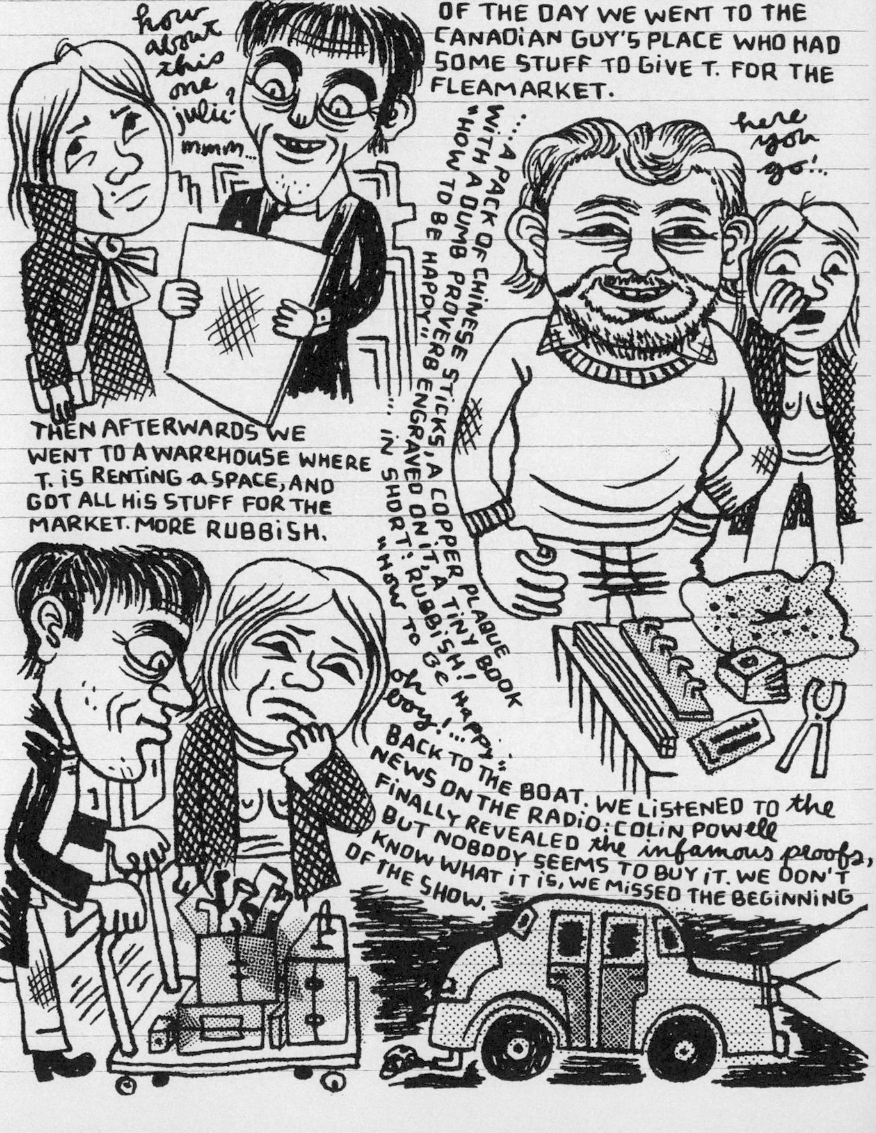
how about this one julie?
mmm...
here you go!..
...A PACK OF CHINESE STICKS, A COPPER PLAQUE WITH A DUMB PROVERB ENGRAVED ON IT, A TINY BOOK "HOW TO BE HAPPY"... IN SHORT: RUBBISH! "HOW TO BE HAPPY"...
oh boy!...

THEN AFTERWARDS WE WENT TO A WARRHOUSE WHERE T. IS RENTING a SPACE, AND GOT ALL HIS STUFF FOR THE MARKET. MORE RUBBISH.

BACK TO THE BOAT. WE LISTENED TO the NEWS ON THE RADIO: COLIN POWELL FINALLY REVEALED the infamous proofs, BUT NOBODY SEEMS TO BUY IT. WE DON'T KNOW WHAT IT IS, WE MISSED THE BEGINNING OF THE SHOW.

07.02.03. *Friday*. WE LEFT BRADFORD ON AVON TO GET CLOSER TO BATH. THE CANAL WAS FROZEN, WE HAD SOME TROUBLE TO CLEAR THE WAY FOR THE BOAT. AT LEAST AT THE BEGINNING.

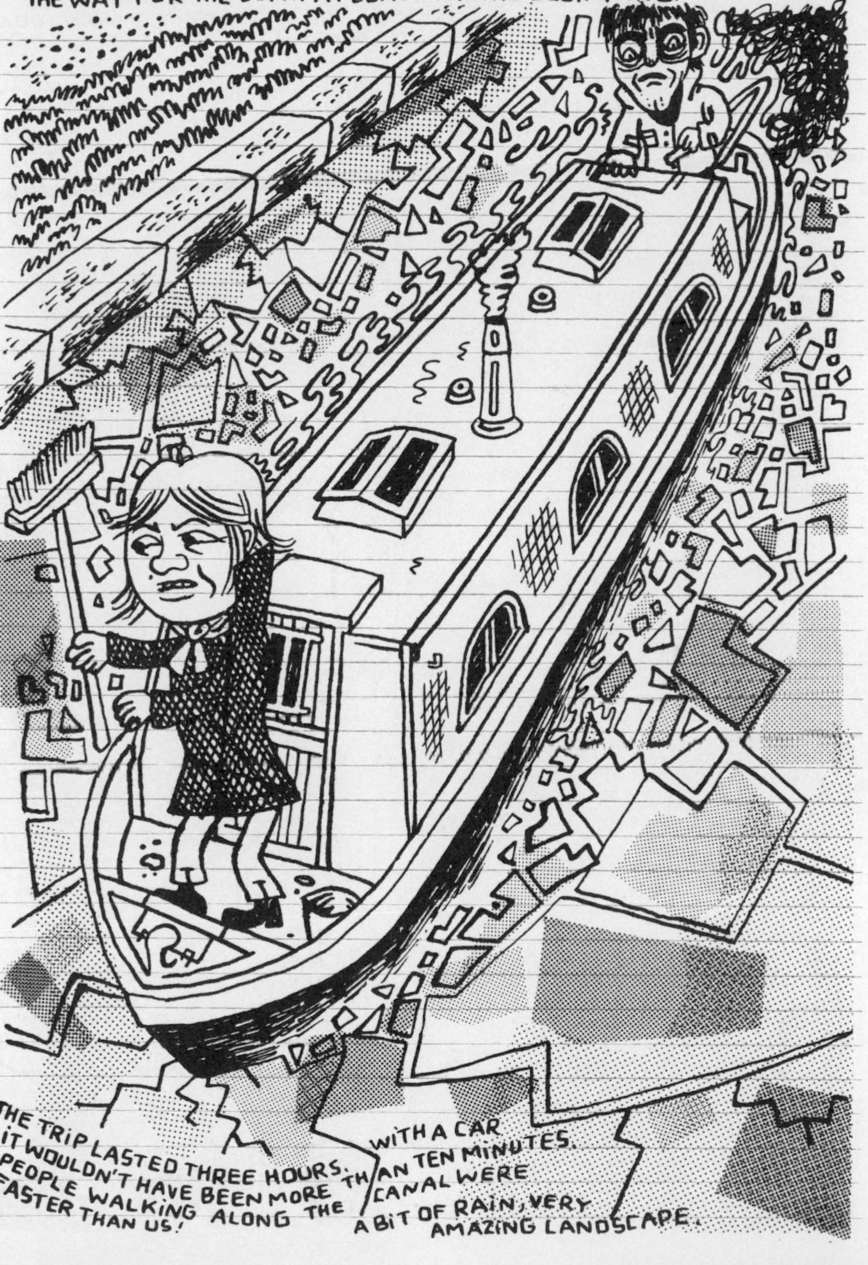
THE TRIP LASTED THREE HOURS.
IT WOULDN'T HAVE BEEN MORE THAN TEN MINUTES WITH A CAR.
PEOPLE WALKING ALONG THE CANAL WERE FASTER THAN US!
A BIT OF RAIN, VERY AMAZING LANDSCAPE.

08.02.03. *saturday*. T. WENT TO SEE HIS HOMEOPATHIC DOCTOR. HE IS ON A SPECIAL TREATMENT TO TRY TO HEAL HIS INTOLERANCE TO NOISE... WHICH MEANS TO SWALLOW LITTLE PILLS MADE OF POISONNED PLANTS EXTRACTS. HE CAN'T STAND THE NOISE OF *the* OTHER BOATS ENGINES, OR THE DOGS BARKING.
THE THING IS, THERE ARE LOTS OF DOGS ON THE CANAL. AND TO HAVE ELECTRICITY *and* HOT WATER ON THOSE BOATS YOU HAVE TO LET YOUR ENGINE RUN (*sailing or not*) AT LEAST.... TWO HOURS A DAY. NO, T. IS NOT CONVINCED THAT LIFE ON A BOAT IS FOR HIM... WHILE HE WAS AWAY I TOOK A WALK ALONG THE CANAL. FOUND OUT THAT THE BOAT PEOPLE ARE HIPPIES (*young and old*) OR RETIRED.

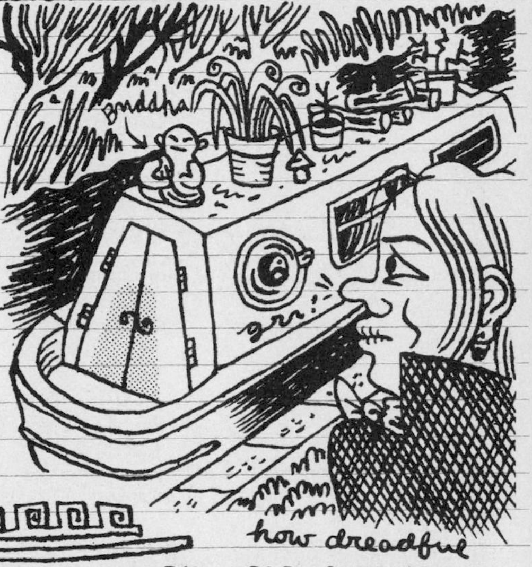
Buddha
grr!
how dreadful

WE WENT FOR A STROLL WITH T., BOUGHT FRESH SUPPLIES, MADE PHOTOCOPIES... WE SPENT THE EVENING MOUNTING THOSE DAMNED AWFUL "REPRODUCTIONS" I ONLY HOPE HE'S NOT GOING TO SELL ANY

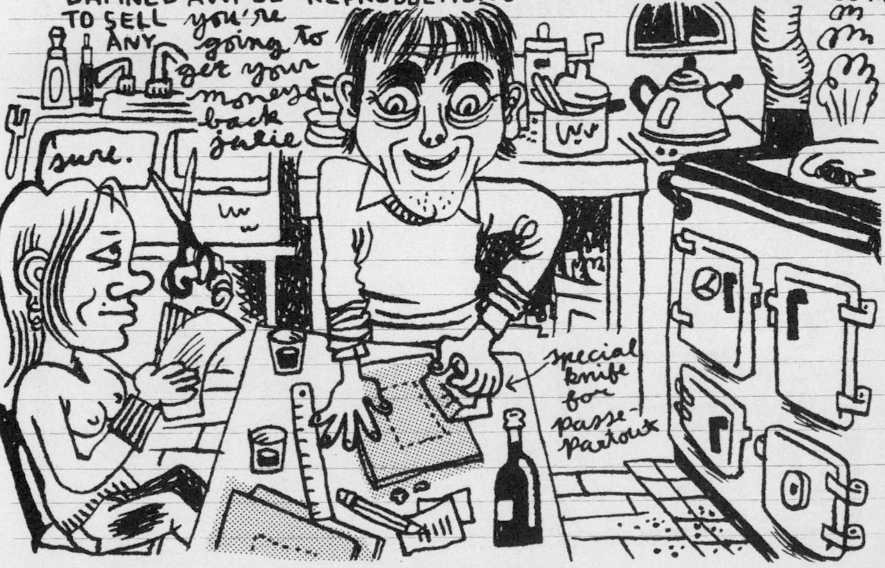
you're going to get your money back julie
sure.
special knife for passe-partout

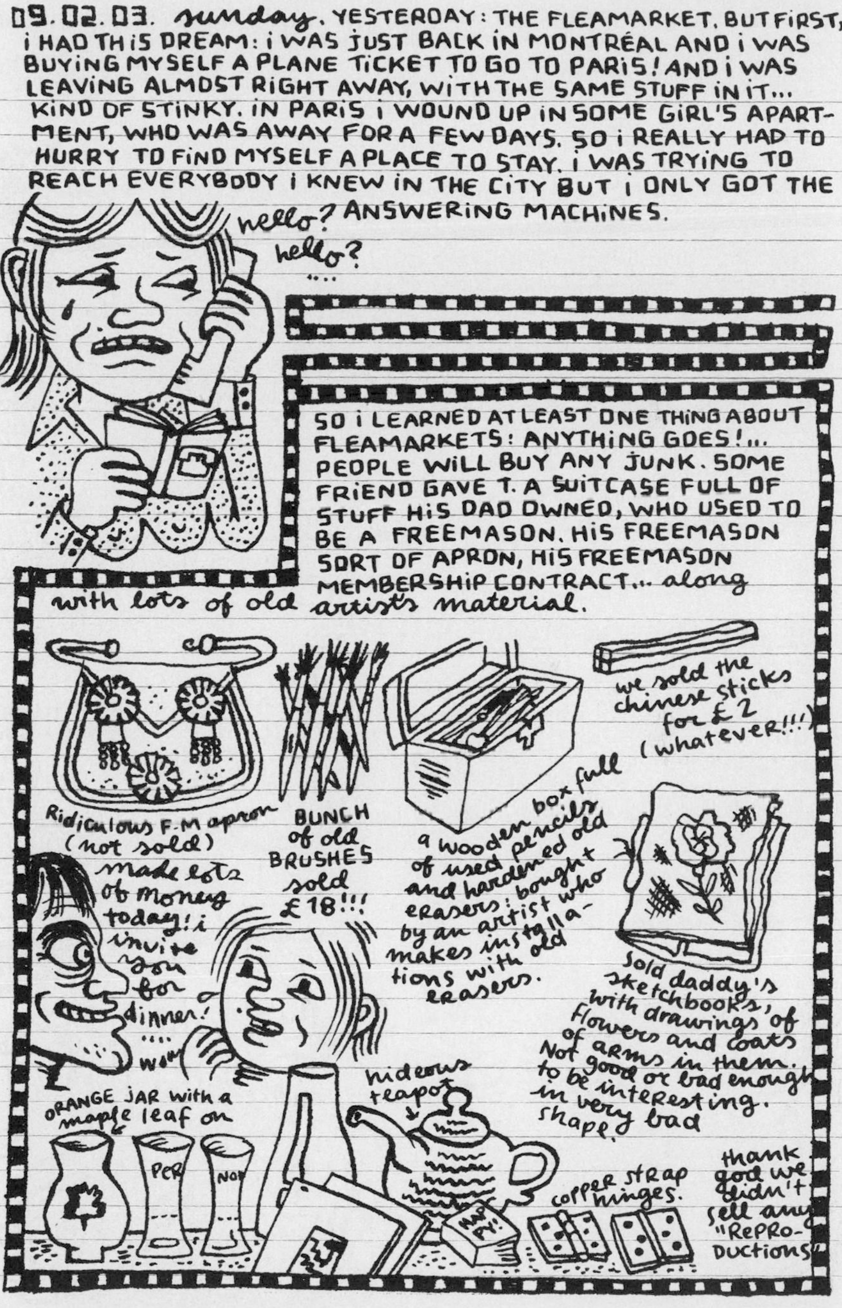
09.02.03. sunday. YESTERDAY: THE FLEAMARKET. BUT FIRST, i HAD THiS DREAM: i WAS JUST BACK iN MONTRÉAL AND i WAS BUYiNG MYSELF A PLANE TiCKET TO GO TO PARiS! AND i WAS LEAViNG ALMOST RiGHT AWAY, WiTH THE SAME STUFF iN iT... KiND OF STiNKY. iN PARiS i WOUND UP iN SOME GiRL'S APARTMENT, WHO WAS AWAY FOR A FEW DAYS. SO i REALLY HAD TO HURRY TO FiND MYSELF A PLACE TO STAY. i WAS TRYiNG TO REACH EVERYBODY i KNEW iN THE CiTY BUT i ONLY GOT THE ANSWERiNG MACHiNES.
hello?
hello?
...
SO i LEARNED AT LEAST ONE THiNG ABOUT FLEAMARKETS: ANYTHiNG GOES!... PEOPLE WiLL BUY ANY JUNK. SOME FRiEND GAVE T. A SUiTCASE FULL OF STUFF HiS DAD OWNED, WHO USED TO BE A FREEMASON. HiS FREEMASON SORT OF APRON, HiS FREEMASON MEMBERSHiP CONTRACT... along with lots of old artist's material.
we sold the chinese sticks for £2 (whatever!!!)
Ridiculous F-M apron (not sold)
BUNCH of old BRUSHES sold £18!!!
a wooden box full of used pencils and hardened old erasers: bought by an artist who makes installations with old erasers.
Sold daddy's sketchbooks, with drawings of flowers and coats of arms in them. Not good or bad enough to be interesting. in very bad shape.
made lots of money today! i invite you for dinner!
....
wow
ORANGE JAR with a maple leaf on
PER
NO
hideous teapot
copper strap hinges.
thank god we didn't sell any "REPRODUCTIONS"

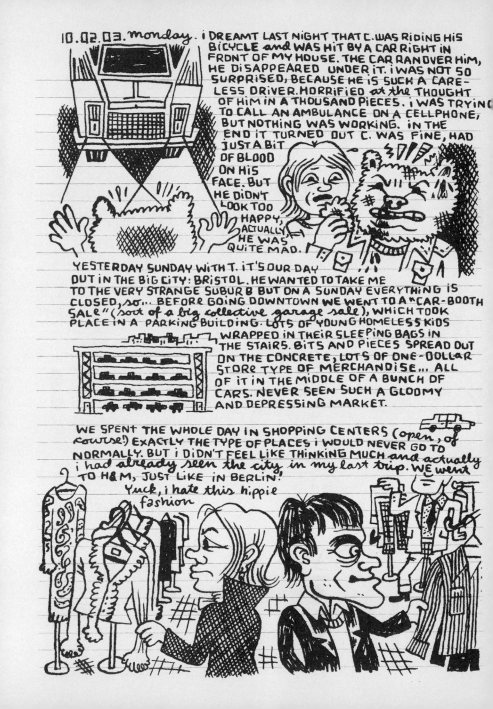

10.02.03. monday. i DREAMT LAST NIGHT THAT C. WAS RIDING HIS BICYCLE and WAS HIT BY A CAR RIGHT IN FRONT OF MY HOUSE. THE CAR RAN OVER HIM, HE DISAPPEARED UNDER IT. i WAS NOT SO SURPRISED, BECAUSE HE IS SUCH A CARELESS DRIVER. HORRIFIED at the THOUGHT OF HIM IN A THOUSAND PIECES. i WAS TRYING TO CALL AN AMBULANCE ON A CELLPHONE, BUT NOTHING WAS WORKING. IN THE END IT TURNED OUT C. WAS FINE, HAD JUST A BIT OF BLOOD ON HIS FACE. BUT HE DIDN'T LOOK TOO HAPPY, ACTUALLY HE WAS QUITE MAD.

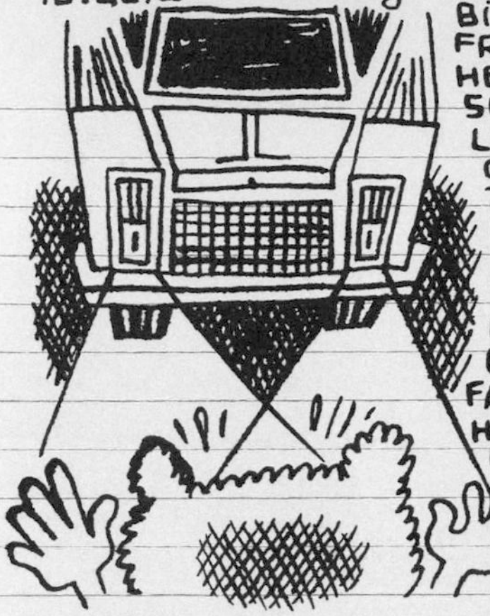

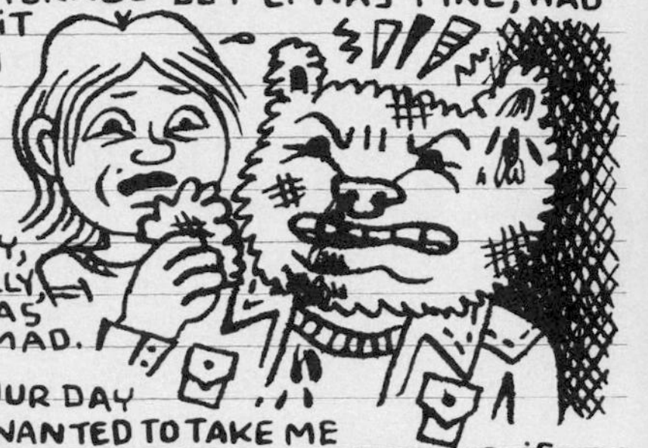

YESTERDAY SUNDAY WITH T. IT'S OUR DAY OUT IN THE BIG CITY: BRISTOL. HE WANTED TO TAKE ME TO THE VERY STRANGE SUBURB BUT ON A SUNDAY EVERYTHING IS CLOSED, so... BEFORE GOING DOWNTOWN WE WENT TO A "CAR-BOOTH SALE" (sort of a big collective garage sale), WHICH TOOK PLACE IN A PARKING BUILDING. LOTS OF YOUNG HOMELESS KIDS WRAPPED IN THEIR SLEEPING BAGS IN THE STAIRS. BITS AND PIECES SPREAD OUT ON THE CONCRETE, LOTS OF ONE-DOLLAR STORE TYPE OF MERCHANDISE... ALL OF IT IN THE MIDDLE OF A BUNCH OF CARS. NEVER SEEN SUCH A GLOOMY AND DEPRESSING MARKET.

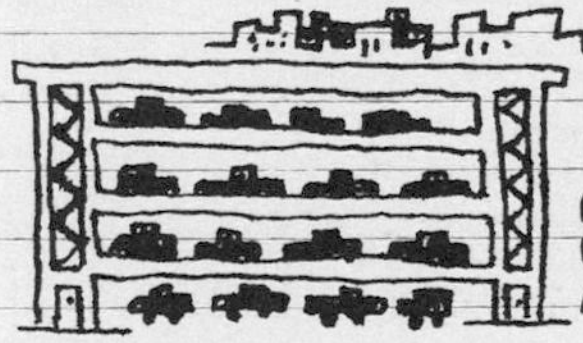

WE SPENT THE WHOLE DAY IN SHOPPING CENTERS (open, of course!) EXACTLY THE TYPE OF PLACES i WOULD NEVER GO TO NORMALLY. BUT i DIDN'T FEEL LIKE THINKING MUCH and actually i had already seen the city in my last trip. WE went TO H&M, JUST LIKE IN BERLIN!

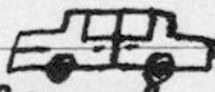

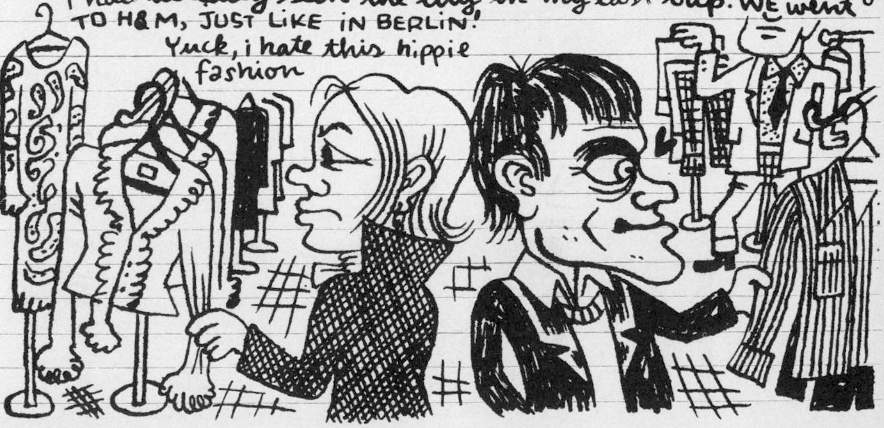
Yuck, i hate this hippie fashion

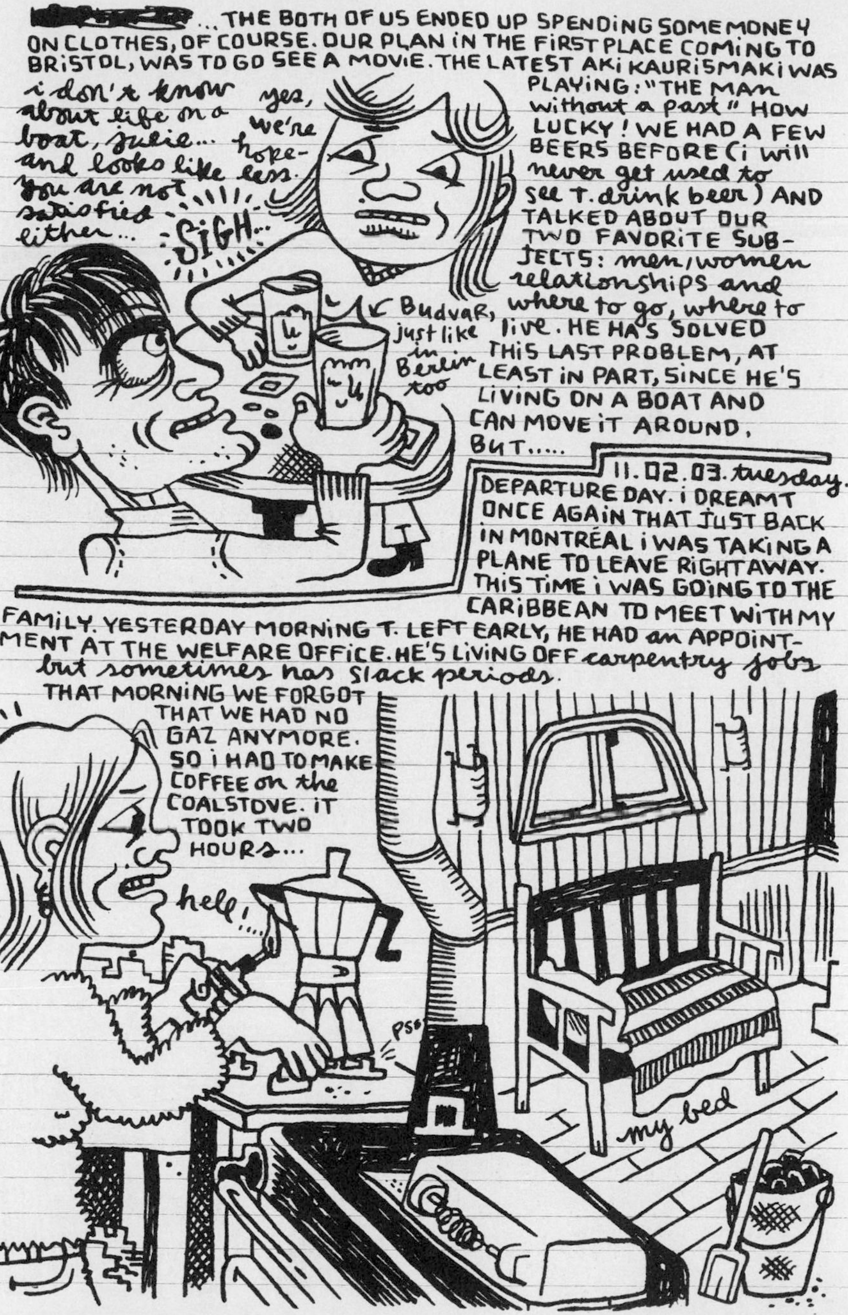
[redacted]... THE BOTH OF US ENDED UP SPENDING SOME MONEY ON CLOTHES, OF COURSE. OUR PLAN IN THE FIRST PLACE COMING TO BRISTOL, WAS TO GO SEE A MOVIE. THE LATEST AKI KAURISMAKI WAS PLAYING: "THE MAN without a past" HOW LUCKY! WE HAD A FEW BEERS BEFORE (i will never get used to see T. drink beer) AND TALKED ABOUT OUR TWO FAVORITE SUBJECTS: men/women relationships and where to go, where to live. HE HAS SOLVED THIS LAST PROBLEM, AT LEAST IN PART, SINCE HE'S LIVING ON A BOAT AND CAN MOVE IT AROUND, BUT.....
i don't know about life on a boat, julie... and looks like you are not satisfied either...
yes, we're hopeless.
SIGH...
Budvar, just like in Berlin too
11.02.03. tuesday.
DEPARTURE DAY. i DREAMT ONCE AGAIN THAT JUST BACK IN MONTRÉAL i WAS TAKING A PLANE TO LEAVE RIGHT AWAY. THIS TIME i WAS GOING TO THE CARIBBEAN TO MEET WITH MY FAMILY. YESTERDAY MORNING T. LEFT EARLY, HE HAD an APPOINTMENT AT THE WELFARE OFFICE. HE'S LIVING OFF carpentry jobs but sometimes has slack periods.
THAT MORNING WE FORGOT THAT WE HAD NO GAZ ANYMORE. SO i HAD TO MAKE COFFEE on the COALSTOVE. IT TOOK TWO HOURS...
hell...
PSS
my bed

WITH T. IN THE AFTERNOON WE WENT TO BATH, TO BUY MY BUS TICKET FOR THE NEXT DAY. And then we wandered around THE CITY, IN THE STORES. AT THAT POINT I DIDN'T CARE WHATEVER WE DO. MY MIND IS SOMEWHERE ELSE, IN PARIS. OR HOW TO GO BACK THERE? SOON it WILL BE VALENTINE'S DAY, THERE ARE LITTLE HEARTS EVERYWHERE: HELLISH.

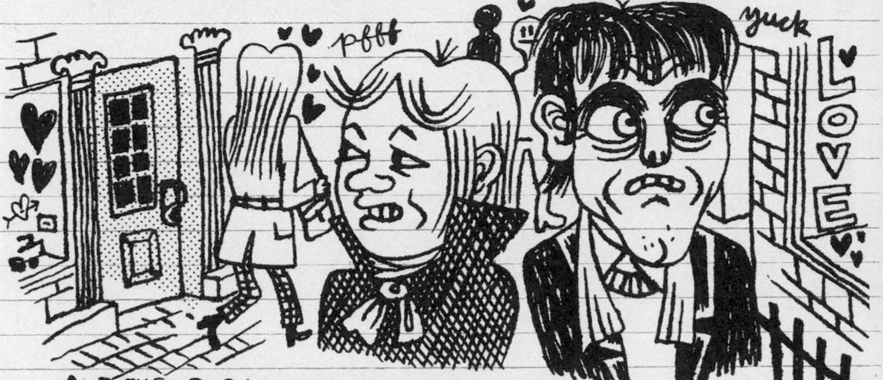
pfff
yuck
LOVE

AND THEN OUR LAST DINNER AT THE BOAT, and our
LAST BOTTLE OF WINE. T. HAD INSISTED THAT WE BUY
A DESSERT, WANTED TO EAT A CHERRY PIE REALLY BAD.
BUT, HE BOUGHT A FROZEN CHERRY PIE... THE UN-COOKED
TYPE OF THING, That you have to bake in the oven at
a very high temperature. WE GOT it EVENTUALLY...
Kind of late

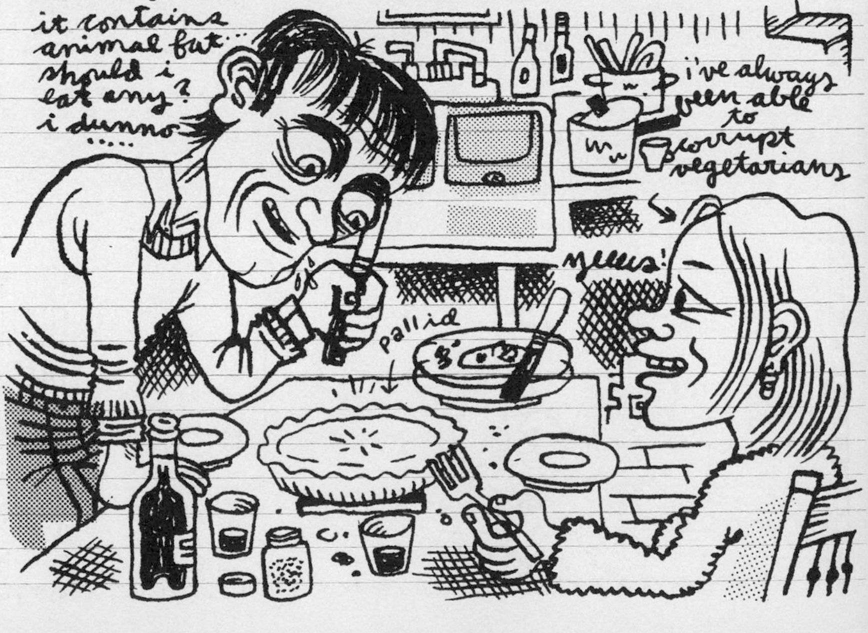
it contains animal fat... should i eat any? i dunno.....
i've always been able to corrupt vegetarians
yeees!
pallid

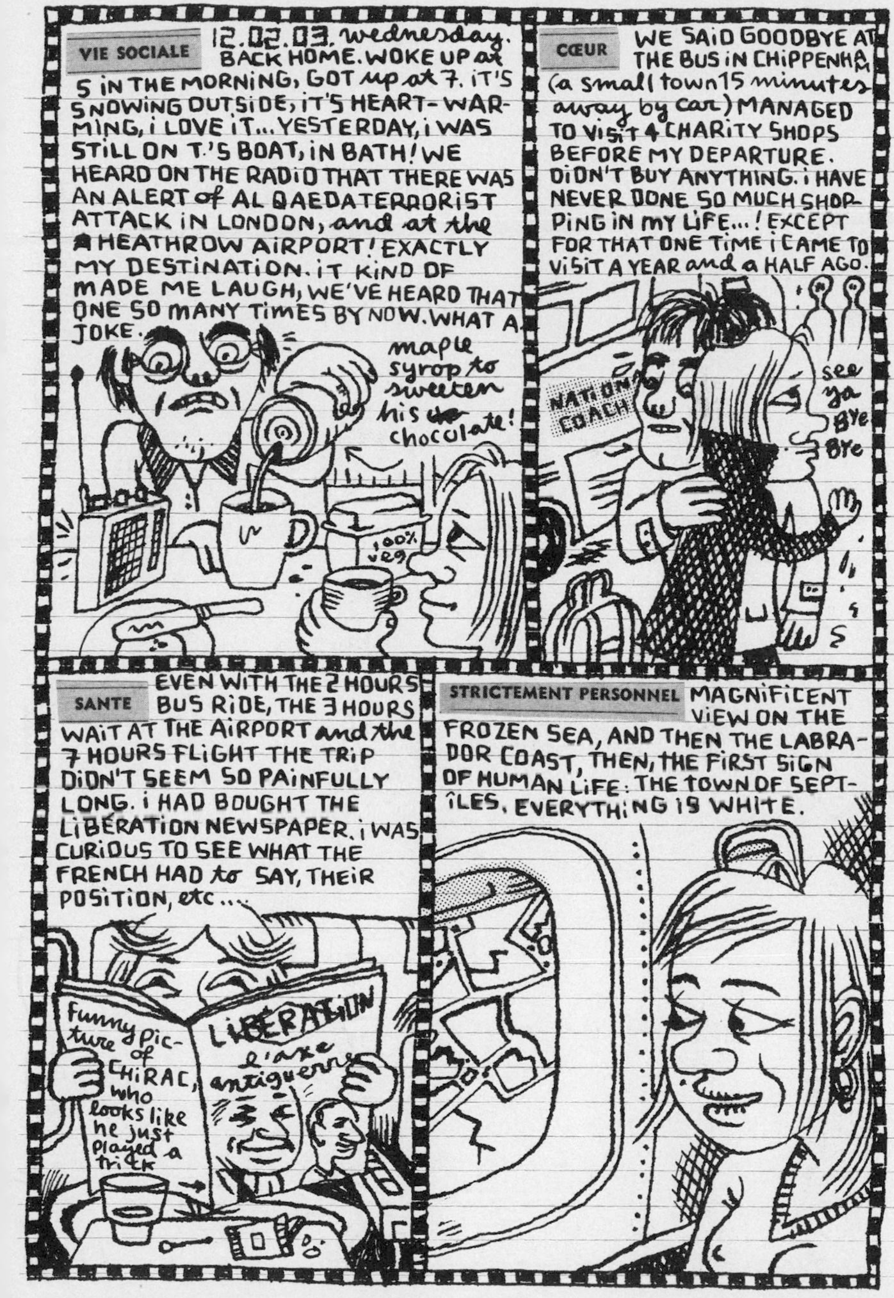

VIE SOCIALE
12.02.03. wednesday. BACK HOME. WOKE UP at 5 IN THE MORNING, GOT up at 7. IT'S SNOWING OUTSIDE, IT'S HEART-WARMING, I LOVE IT... YESTERDAY, I WAS STILL ON T.'S BOAT, IN BATH! WE HEARD ON THE RADIO THAT THERE WAS AN ALERT of AL QAEDA TERRORIST ATTACK IN LONDON, and at the HEATHROW AIRPORT! EXACTLY MY DESTINATION. IT KIND OF MADE ME LAUGH, WE'VE HEARD THAT ONE SO MANY TIMES BY NOW. WHAT A JOKE.
maple syrop to sweeten his chocolate!
100% veg
CŒUR
WE SAID GOODBYE AT THE BUS IN CHIPPENHAM (a small town 15 minutes away by car) MANAGED TO VISIT 4 CHARITY SHOPS BEFORE MY DEPARTURE. DIDN'T BUY ANYTHING. I HAVE NEVER DONE SO MUCH SHOPPING IN MY LIFE...! EXCEPT FOR THAT ONE TIME I CAME TO VISIT A YEAR and a HALF AGO.
COACH
see ya Bye Bye
SANTE
EVEN WITH THE 2 HOURS BUS RIDE, THE 3 HOURS WAIT AT THE AIRPORT and the 7 HOURS FLIGHT THE TRIP DIDN'T SEEM SO PAINFULLY LONG. I HAD BOUGHT THE LIBERATION NEWSPAPER. I WAS CURIOUS TO SEE WHAT THE FRENCH HAD to SAY, THEIR POSITION, etc....
Funny picture of CHIRAC, who looks like he just played a trick
LIBERATION
l'axe antiguerre
STRICTEMENT PERSONNEL
MAGNIFICENT VIEW ON THE FROZEN SEA, AND THEN THE LABRADOR COAST, THEN, THE FIRST SIGN OF HUMAN LIFE: THE TOWN OF SEPT-ÎLES. EVERYTHING IS WHITE.

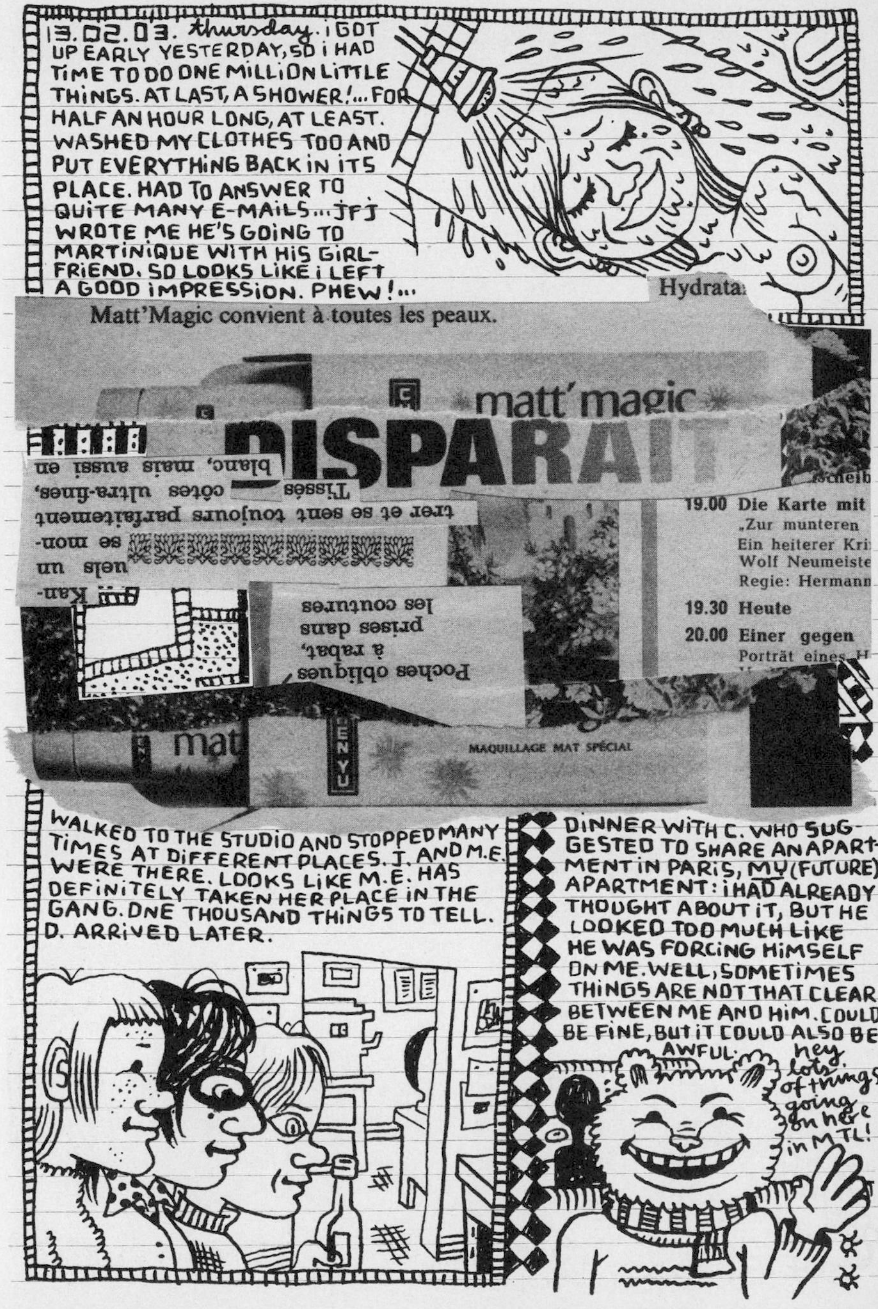
13.02.03. thursday. i GOT UP EARLY YESTERDAY, SO i HAD TiME TO DO ONE MILLiON LiTTLE THiNGS. AT LAST, A SHOWER!... FOR HALF AN HOUR LONG, AT LEAST. WASHED MY CLOTHES TOO AND PUT EVERYTHiNG BACK iN iTS PLACE. HAD TO ANSWER TO QUiTE MANY E-MAiLS... JFJ WROTE ME HE'S GOiNG TO MARTiNiQUE WiTH HiS GiRL-FRiEND. SO LOOKS LiKE i LEFT A GOOD iMPRESSiON. PHEW!...
Hydrata
Matt'Magic convient à toutes les peaux.
matt' magic
DISPARAIT
blanc, mais aussi en
Tissés côtés ultra-fines,
trer et se sent toujours parfaitement
se mon-
uels un
Kan-
les coutures
prises dans
à rabat,
Poches obliques
19.00 Die Karte mit
„Zur munteren
Ein heiterer Kri
Wolf Neumeiste
Regie: Hermann
19.30 Heute
20.00 Einer gegen
Porträt eines H
matt
MAQUILLAGE MAT SPÉCIAL
WALKED TO THE STUDiO AND STOPPED MANY TiMES AT DiFFERENT PLACES. J. AND M.E. WERE THERE. LOOKS LiKE M.E. HAS DEFiNiTELY TAKEN HER PLACE iN THE GANG. ONE THOUSAND THiNGS TO TELL. D. ARRiVED LATER.
DiNNER WiTH C. WHO SUG-GESTED TO SHARE AN APART-MENT iN PARiS, MY (FUTURE) APARTMENT: i HAD ALREADY THOUGHT ABOUT iT, BUT HE LOOKED TOO MUCH LiKE HE WAS FORCiNG HiMSELF ON ME. WELL, SOMETiMES THiNGS ARE NOT THAT CLEAR BETWEEN ME AND HiM. COULD BE FiNE, BUT iT COULD ALSO BE AWFUL.
hey lots of things going on here in MTL!

14.03.03. *friday*. IT HAS BEEN TERRIBLY COLD YESTERDAY, AND IT'S ONLY THE BEGINNING, I'VE HEARD. THE SKY IS BLUE. MY FIRST DAY ALONE, YESTERDAY. DIDN'T SEE ANYBODY AT ALL. STRANGE, VERY STRANGE, AFTER THAT TRIP SO FULL OF PEOPLE. I DON'T KNOW WHY, I HAD AN HEADACHE ALMOST ALL DAY. I HOPE I AM NOT GOING TO HAVE A COLD.

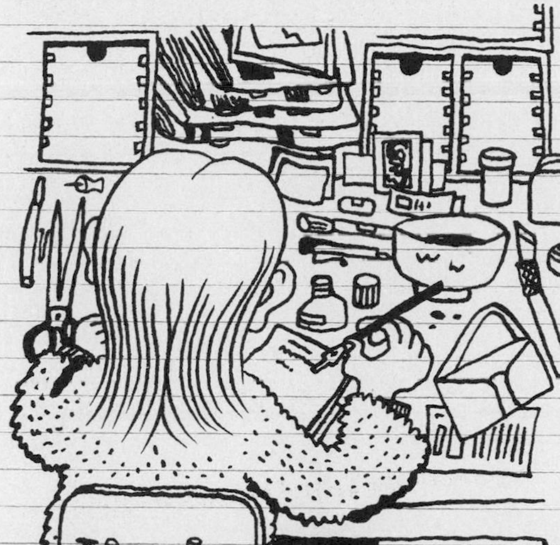

I DREW, I WROTE SOME MAIL, WROTE SOME STUPID E-MAILS. I WENT OUT FOR HALF AN HOUR TO MAKE PHOTOCOPIES, AND GO TO THE POST OFFICE. SOOO COLD!

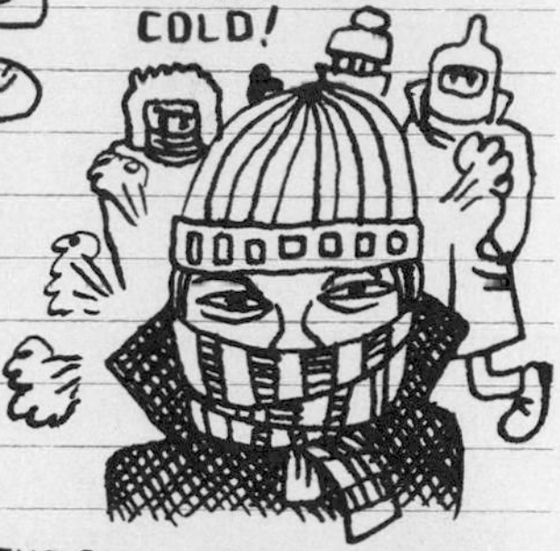

THE ONLY THING TO DO WHEN IT'S COLD SO IS GO TO BED AND READ, WHICH I DID, STARTING AT 6:30. I WAS SUPPOSED TO CALL MY DAD, M. *and* B. BUT I DIDN'T DO IT: AT 8 I HAD TROUBLE TO KEEP MY EYES OPEN. I LASTED UNTIL 10, THANKS TO WILLEM.

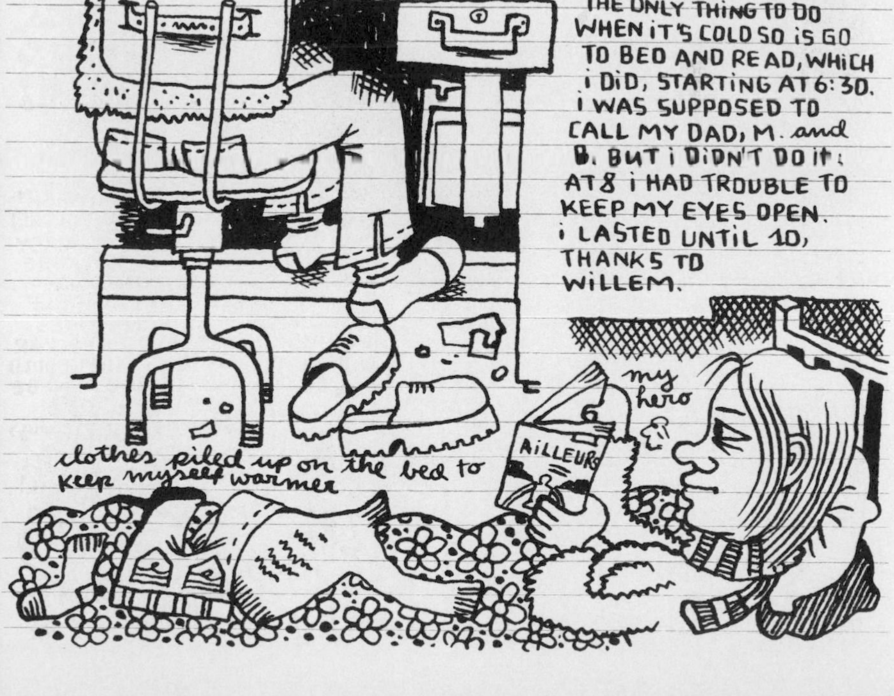

my hero
AILLEURS
clothes piled up on the bed to keep myself warmer

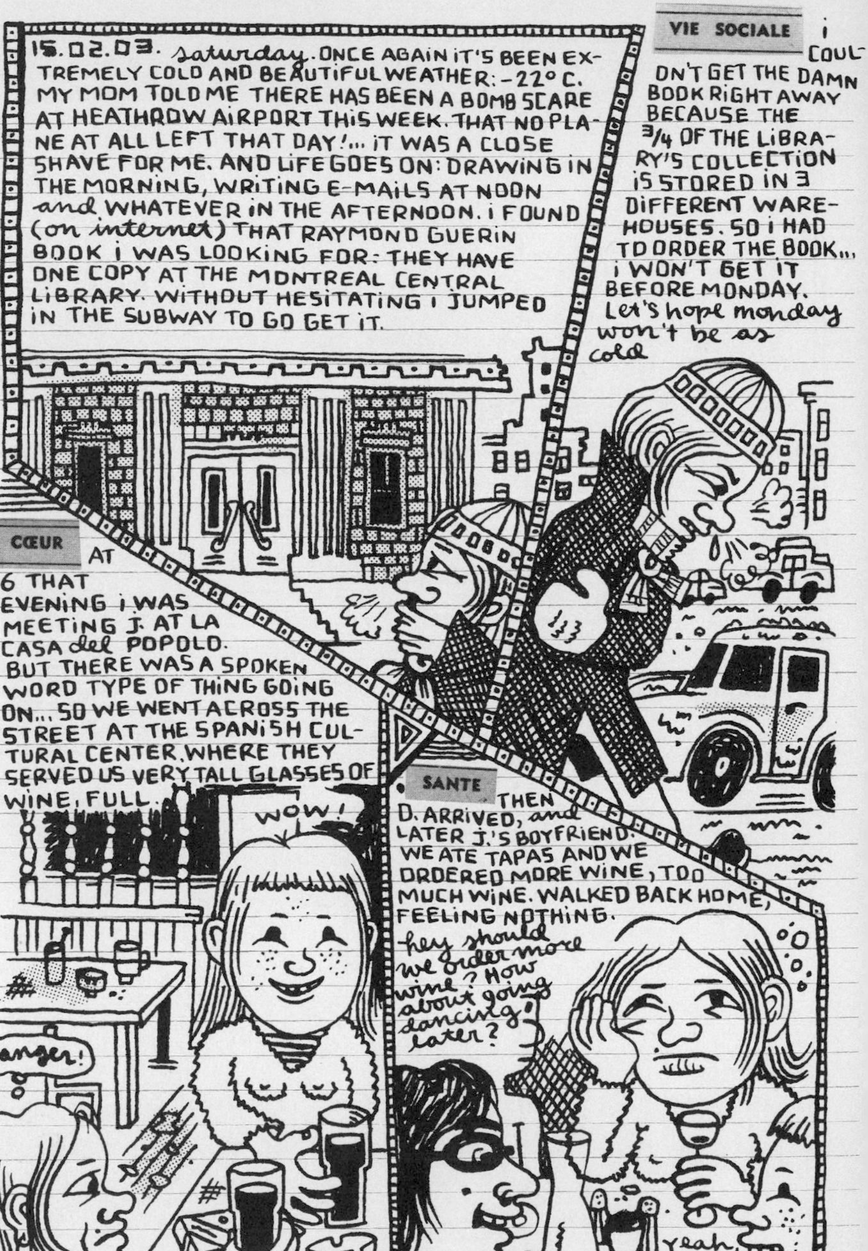
15.02.03. saturday. ONCE AGAIN IT'S BEEN EXTREMELY COLD AND BEAUTIFUL WEATHER: -22° C. MY MOM TOLD ME THERE HAS BEEN A BOMB SCARE AT HEATHROW AIRPORT THIS WEEK. THAT NO PLANE AT ALL LEFT THAT DAY!... IT WAS A CLOSE SHAVE FOR ME. AND LIFE GOES ON: DRAWING IN THE MORNING, WRITING E-MAILS AT NOON and WHATEVER IN THE AFTERNOON. I FOUND (on internet) THAT RAYMOND GUERIN BOOK I WAS LOOKING FOR: THEY HAVE ONE COPY AT THE MONTREAL CENTRAL LIBRARY. WITHOUT HESITATING I JUMPED IN THE SUBWAY TO GO GET IT.
VIE SOCIALE
I COULDN'T GET THE DAMN BOOK RIGHT AWAY BECAUSE THE 3/4 OF THE LIBRARY'S COLLECTION IS STORED IN 3 DIFFERENT WAREHOUSES. SO I HAD TO ORDER THE BOOK... I WON'T GET IT BEFORE MONDAY. Let's hope monday won't be as cold
CŒUR
AT 6 THAT EVENING I WAS MEETING J. AT LA CASA del POPOLO. BUT THERE WAS A SPOKEN WORD TYPE OF THING GOING ON... SO WE WENT ACROSS THE STREET AT THE SPANISH CULTURAL CENTER, WHERE THEY SERVED US VERY TALL GLASSES OF WINE, FULL.
WOW!
danger!
SANTE
THEN D. ARRIVED, and LATER J.'S BOYFRIEND. WE ATE TAPAS AND WE ORDERED MORE WINE, TOO MUCH WINE. WALKED BACK HOME, FEELING NOTHING.
hey should we order more wine? How about going dancing later?
yeah, ok

16.02.03. sunday.

YESTERDAY DEMONSTRATIONS AGAINST THE WAR IN IRAK ALL OVER THE WORLD. THE BIGGEST CROWD EVER IN LONDON, IN NEW YORK, THEY DIDN'T SEE THAT AGAIN SINCE THE VIET-NAM WAR. IN MONTRÉAL, THEY HAD NEVER SEEN SO MANY PEOPLE ON THE STREET EXCEPT FOR A SPORT'S EVENT (like when the Canadians win the Stanley Cup). POLITICIANS JOINED IN TOO ... AMAZING BIG CROWDS IN PARIS, in BERLIN ... LOOKS LIKE SOMETHING IS HAPPENING. MEANWHILE, I HAVE BEEN SOOOO SICK! ONCE AGAIN I'VE BEEN PEAKED ALL DAY

DOWN WITH BUAAAH

AND PART OF THE EVENING. I REALLY CAN'T TAKE IT ANY MORE, I CAN'T DRINK ... FORTUNATELY THAT NEVER HAPPENED TO ME WHILE I WAS AWAY!

17.02.03. monday. AT LAST THE SKY IS GRAY AND A MORE HUMAN TEMPERATURE. IT'S SUPPOSED TO SNOW, I HOPE IT'S TRUE. SPENT THE DAY DRAWING YESTERDAY, AND SORTED OUT PAPERS FOR MY TAXES AND STUFF. I SAW A CURIOUS THING ON TV in the EVENING, in a SCIENTIFIC DOCUMENTARY (a serious TV show in general, no nonsense stuff ever) THE SUBJECT: SEXUAL IDENTITY. ACCORDING TO THEM THE BRAIN (well, some parts of it) IS SEXED AND WHAT WE THOUGHT WAS LEARNED BEHAVIOUR, IS NOT NECESSARILY. WOMEN have 1/10th OF THE MEN'S AMOUNT OF TESTOSTERONE in their BODY. IF SHE HAPPENS to HAVE MORE, SHE BECOMES a TOMBOY, MORE ACTIVE, WHO PREFERS TO HANG OUT and PLAY WITH THE GUYS. SO, THEY SAY:

THE RINGFINGER SHOWS THE TESTOSTERONE influence
the FOREFINGER shows the estrogen influence
SO, in general:

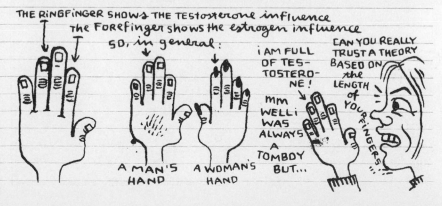

A MAN'S HAND

A WOMAN'S HAND

I AM FULL OF TES-TOSTERO-NE!

mm WELL I WAS ALWAYS A TOMBOY BUT...

CAN YOU REALLY TRUST A THEORY BASED ON the LENGTH of YOUR FINGERS

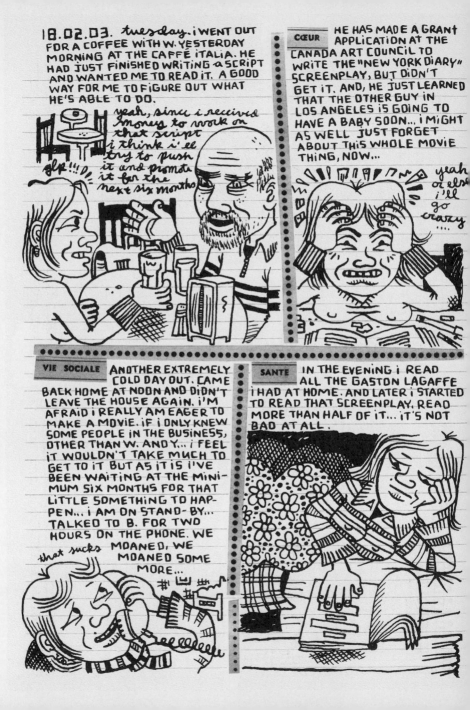

18.02.03. tuesday. i WENT OUT FOR A COFFEE WITH W. YESTERDAY MORNING AT THE CAFFÈ ITALIA. HE HAD JUST FINISHED WRITING a SCRIPT AND WANTED ME TO READ IT. A GOOD WAY FOR ME TO FIGURE OUT WHAT HE'S ABLE TO DO.

yeah, since i received money to work on that script i think i'll try to push it and promote it for the next six months

glk!!!

CŒUR HE HAS MADE A GRANT APPLICATION AT THE CANADA ART COUNCIL TO WRITE THE "NEW YORK DIARY" SCREENPLAY, BUT DIDN'T GET IT. AND, HE JUST LEARNED THAT THE OTHER GUY IN LOS ANGELES IS GOING TO HAVE A BABY SOON... I MIGHT AS WELL JUST FORGET ABOUT THIS WHOLE MOVIE THING, NOW...

yeah or else i'll go crazy ....

VIE SOCIALE ANOTHER EXTREMELY COLD DAY OUT. CAME BACK HOME AT NOON AND DIDN'T LEAVE THE HOUSE AGAIN. I'M AFRAID I REALLY AM EAGER TO MAKE A MOVIE. IF I ONLY KNEW SOME PEOPLE IN THE BUSINESS, OTHER THAN W. AND Y... I FEEL IT WOULDN'T TAKE MUCH TO GET TO IT BUT AS IT IS I'VE BEEN WAITING AT THE MINI- MUM SIX MONTHS FOR THAT LITTLE SOMETHING TO HAP- PEN... I AM ON STAND-BY... TALKED TO B. FOR TWO HOURS ON THE PHONE. WE MOANED, WE MOANED SOME MORE...

that sucks

#!@!

SANTE IN THE EVENING I READ ALL THE GASTON LAGAFFE I HAD AT HOME. AND LATER I STARTED TO READ THAT SCREENPLAY. READ MORE THAN HALF OF IT... IT'S NOT BAD AT ALL.

19.02.03. wednesday. JUST A FEW SNOWFLAKES ARE FALLING DOWN THIS MORNING. AND MEANWHILE THE EAST OF THE UNITED STATES IS BURIED UNDER ONE METER OF SNOW... IT AIN'T FAIR. YESTERDAY THE WEATHER WAS PRETTY MILD, IT DOESN'T HELP.

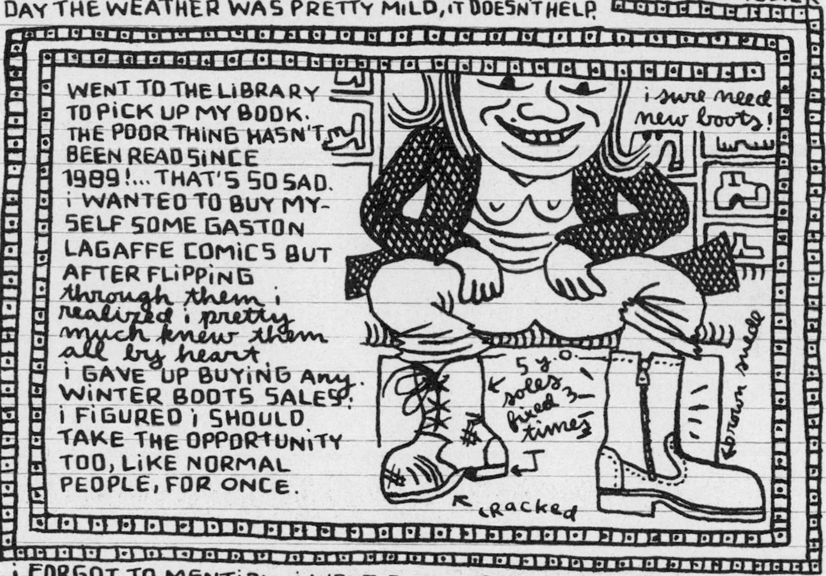

WENT TO THE LIBRARY TO PICK UP MY BOOK. THE POOR THING HASN'T BEEN READ SINCE 1989!... THAT'S SO SAD. I WANTED TO BUY MYSELF SOME GASTON LAGAFFE COMICS BUT AFTER FLIPPING through them i realized i pretty much knew them all by heart. I GAVE UP BUYING ANY. WINTER BOOTS SALES: I FIGURED I SHOULD TAKE THE OPPORTUNITY TOO, LIKE NORMAL PEOPLE, FOR ONCE.
i sure need new boots!
5 y.o.
soles fixed 3 times
cracked
brown suede

I FORGOT TO MENTION: I WENT ON THE QUEBEC ART COUNCIL WEBSITE FOR MORE INFORMATION ABOUT THEIR STUDIO IN PARIS... WELL IT'S NOT AVAILABLE UNTIL 2004 IF I APPLY. FOR IT NEXT APRIL. WAY TOO LATE FOR ME. ICH MUSS GEHEN. NO KIDDING

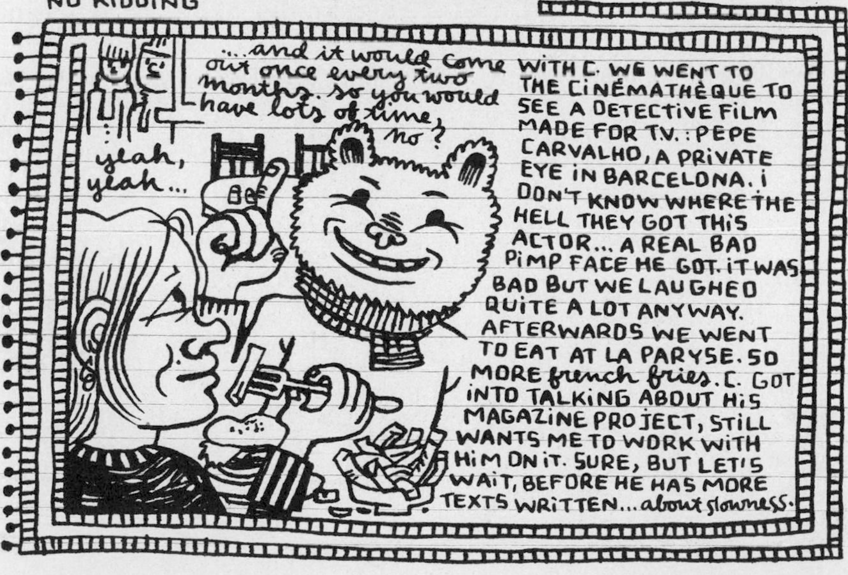

...and it would come out once every two months, so you would have lots of time, no?
yeah, yeah...
WITH C. WE WENT TO THE CINÉMATHÈQUE TO SEE A DETECTIVE FILM MADE FOR T.V.: PEPE CARVALHO, A PRIVATE EYE IN BARCELONA. I DON'T KNOW WHERE THE HELL THEY GOT THIS ACTOR... A REAL BAD PIMP FACE HE GOT. IT WAS BAD BUT WE LAUGHED QUITE A LOT ANYWAY. AFTERWARDS WE WENT TO EAT AT LA PARYSE. SO MORE french fries. C. GOT INTO TALKING ABOUT HIS MAGAZINE PROJECT, STILL WANTS ME TO WORK WITH HIM ON IT. SURE, BUT LET'S WAIT, BEFORE HE HAS MORE TEXTS WRITTEN... about slowness.

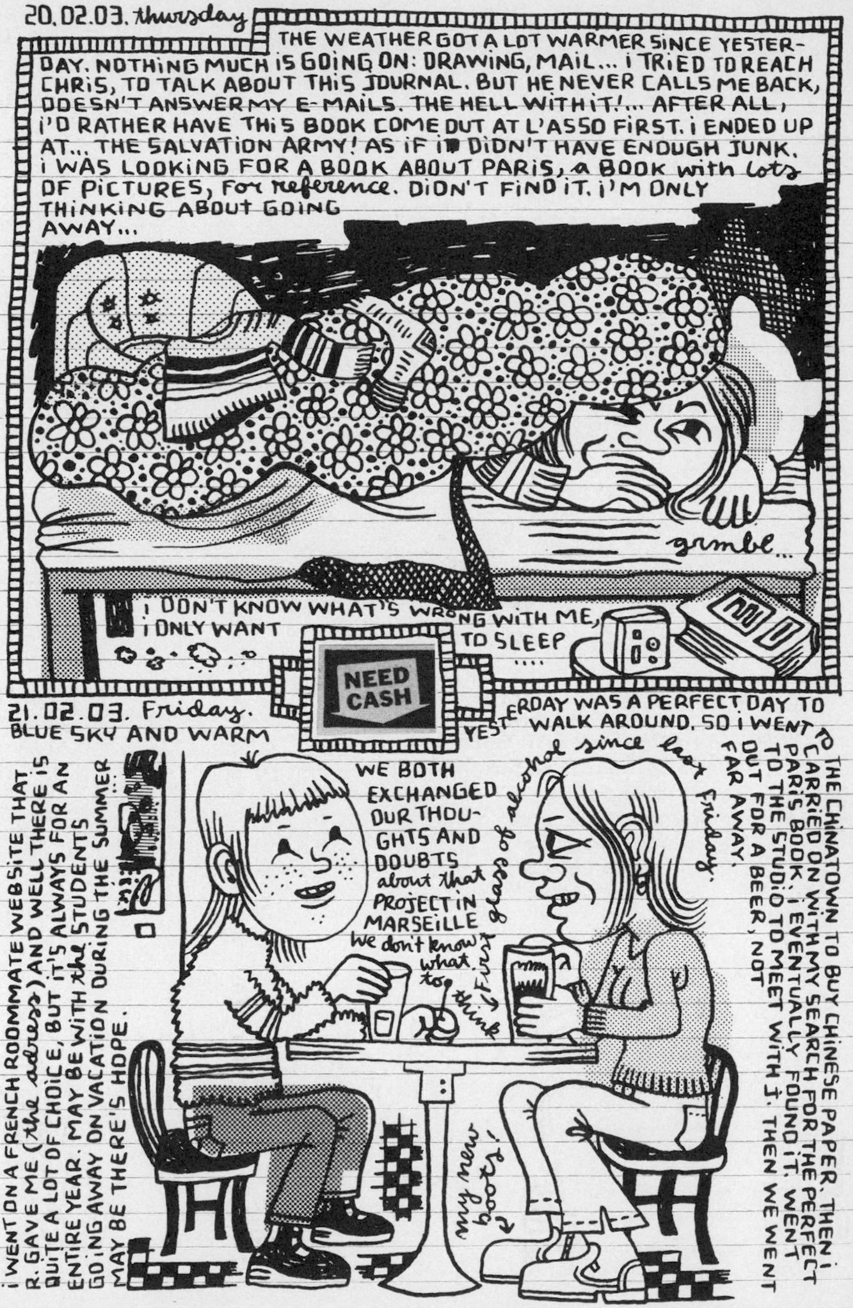
20.02.03. thursday
THE WEATHER GOT A LOT WARMER SINCE YESTERDAY. NOTHING MUCH IS GOING ON: DRAWING, MAIL... i TRIED TO REACH CHRIS, TO TALK ABOUT THIS JOURNAL. BUT HE NEVER CALLS ME BACK, DOESN'T ANSWER MY E-MAILS. THE HELL WITH IT!... AFTER ALL, i'D RATHER HAVE THIS BOOK COME OUT AT L'ASSO FIRST. i ENDED UP AT... THE SALVATION ARMY! AS IF I DIDN'T HAVE ENOUGH JUNK. i WAS LOOKING FOR A BOOK ABOUT PARIS, a BOOK with lots OF PICTURES, for reference. DIDN'T FIND IT. i'M ONLY THINKING ABOUT GOING AWAY...
grmbl...
i DON'T KNOW WHAT'S WRONG WITH ME, i ONLY WANT TO SLEEP ....
NEED CASH
21.02.03. Friday.
BLUE SKY AND WARM
YESTERDAY WAS A PERFECT DAY TO WALK AROUND, SO i WENT TO THE CHINATOWN TO BUY CHINESE PAPER. THEN i CARRIED ON WITH MY SEARCH FOR THE PERFECT PARIS BOOK. i EVENTUALLY FOUND IT. WENT TO THE STUDIO TO MEET WITH J. THEN WE WENT OUT FOR A BEER, NOT FAR AWAY.
WE BOTH EXCHANGED OUR THOUGHTS AND DOUBTS about that PROJECT IN MARSEILLE
We don't know what to think
First glass of alcohol since last Friday.
my new boots!
i WENT ON A FRENCH ROOMMATE WEBSITE THAT R. GAVE ME (the adress) AND WELL THERE IS QUITE A LOT OF CHOICE, BUT IT'S ALWAYS FOR AN ENTIRE YEAR. MAY BE WITH the STUDENTS GOING AWAY ON VACATION DURING THE SUMMER... MAY BE THERE'S HOPE.

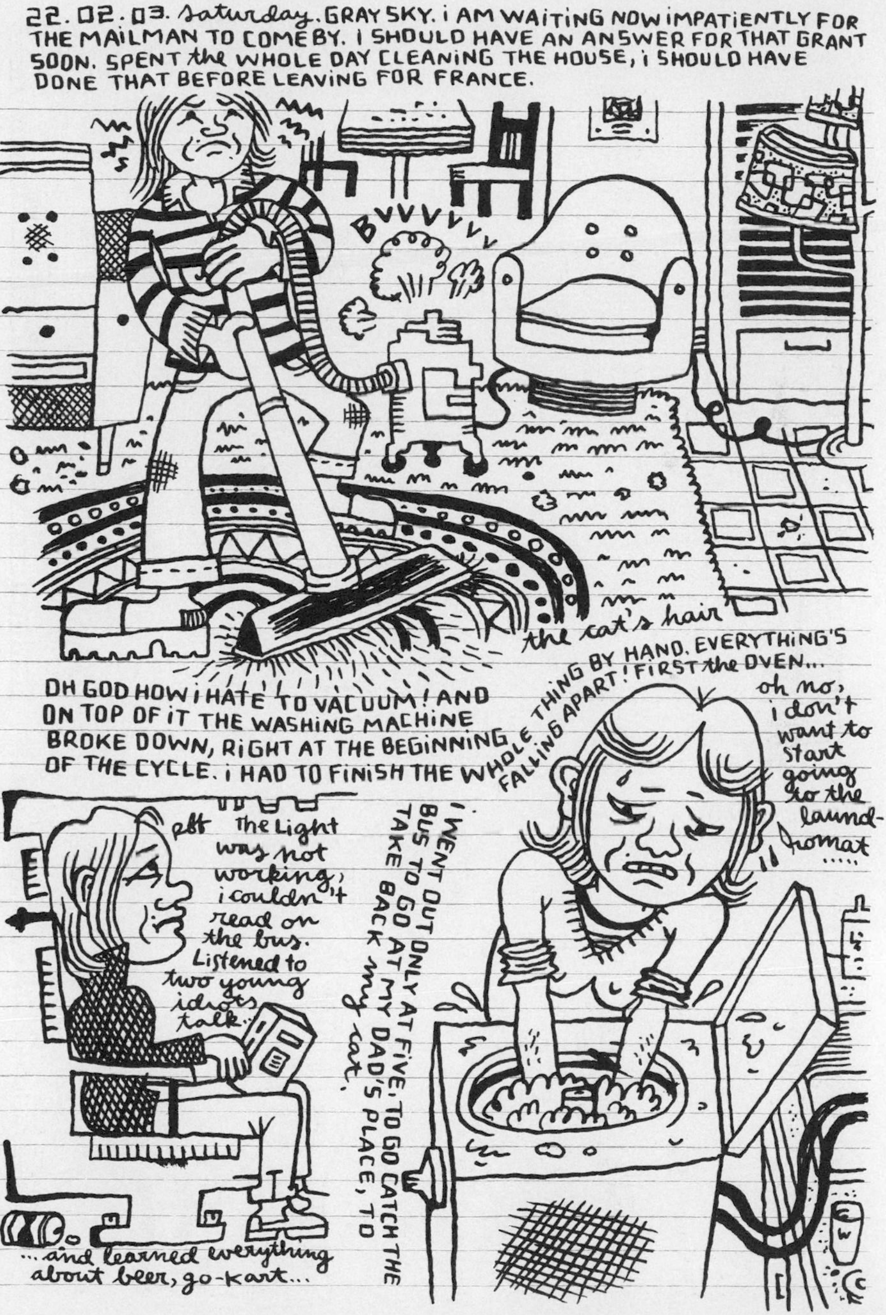
22.02.03. saturday. GRAY SKY. i AM WAITING NOW IMPATIENTLY FOR THE MAILMAN TO COME BY. I SHOULD HAVE AN ANSWER FOR THAT GRANT SOON. SPENT the WHOLE DAY CLEANING THE HOUSE, i SHOULD HAVE DONE THAT BEFORE LEAVING FOR FRANCE.
BVVVVVVV
the cat's hair
OH GOD HOW i HATE TO VACUUM! AND ON TOP OF iT THE WASHING MACHINE BROKE DOWN, RIGHT AT THE BEGINNING OF THE CYCLE. i HAD TO FiNiSH THE WHOLE THING BY HAND. EVERYTHING'S FALLING APART! FIRST the OVEN...
oh no, i don't want to start going to the laundromat .....
i WENT OUT ONLY AT FIVE, TO GO CATCH THE BUS TO GO AT MY DAD'S PLACE, TO TAKE BACK my cat.
pbt The Light was not working, i couldn't read on the bus. Listened to two young idiots talk...
...and learned everything about beer, go-kart...

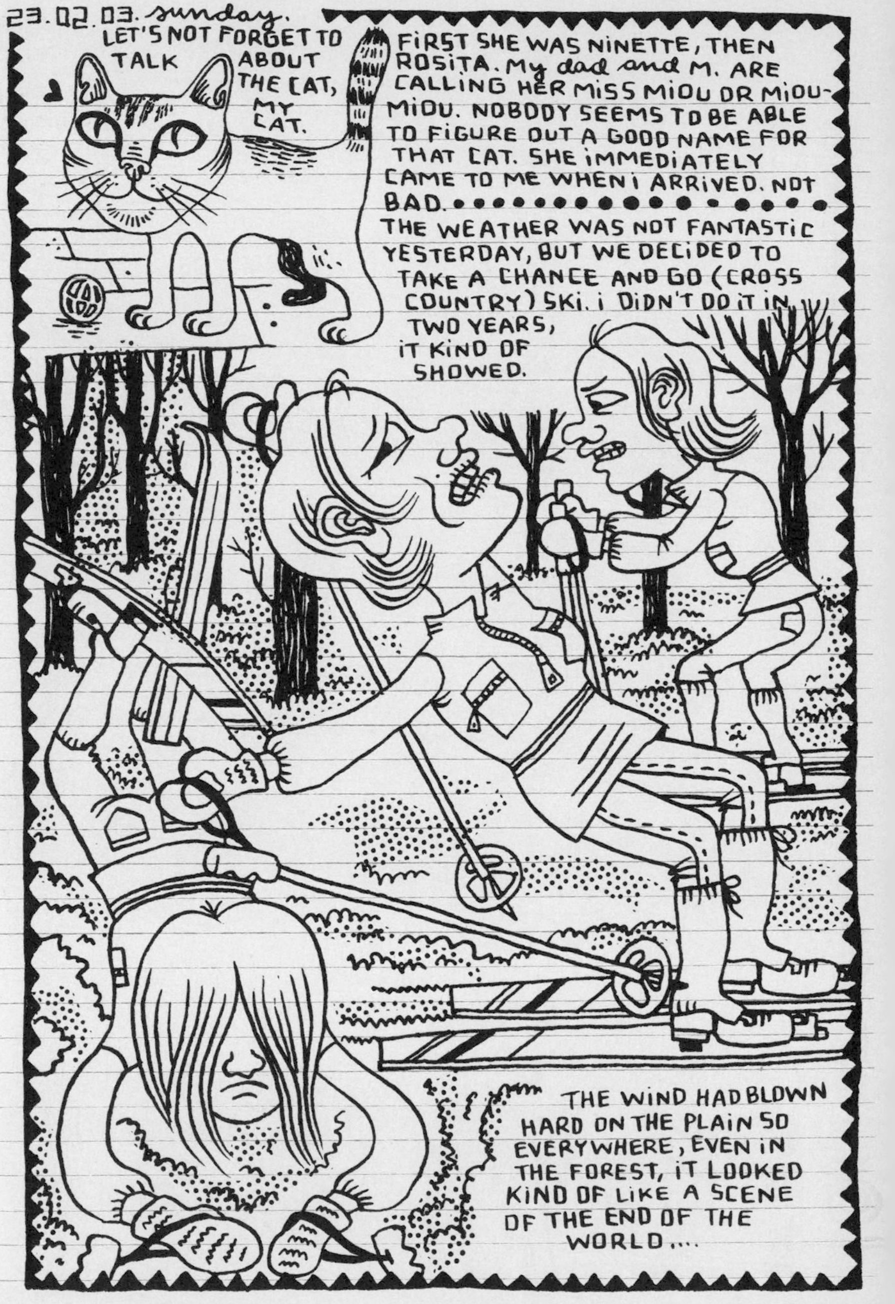
23.02.03. sunday.
LET'S NOT FORGET TO TALK ABOUT THE CAT, MY CAT.
FIRST SHE WAS NINETTE, THEN ROSITA. My dad and M. ARE CALLING HER MISS MIOU OR MIOU-MIOU. NOBODY SEEMS TO BE ABLE TO FIGURE OUT A GOOD NAME FOR THAT CAT. SHE IMMEDIATELY CAME TO ME WHEN I ARRIVED. NOT BAD.
THE WEATHER WAS NOT FANTASTIC YESTERDAY, BUT WE DECIDED TO TAKE A CHANCE AND GO (CROSS COUNTRY) SKI. I DIDN'T DO IT IN TWO YEARS, IT KIND OF SHOWED.
THE WIND HAD BLOWN HARD ON THE PLAIN SO EVERYWHERE, EVEN IN THE FOREST, IT LOOKED KIND OF LIKE A SCENE OF THE END OF THE WORLD....

24.02.03 monday

CAME BACK FROM MY DAD'S BY BUS
WITH M. BECAUSE THE WEATHER WAS QUITE BAD MY DAD
DIDN'T DRIVE US BACK TO THE CITY, WITH THE CAT. AND
OF COURSE NOW i AM UNABLE TO DRAW. WE DIDN'T DO
ANYTHING YESTERDAY, IT'S BEEN RAINING ALL MORNING.
AND THEN IT TURNED INTO SNOW and LATER INTO a
BIG SNOW STORM. IN THE EVENING THERE WAS A
DINNER at SOME OF THEIR FRIEND'S PLACE, PEOPLE
i LIKE VERY MUCH. HIM: A SCULPTOR, HER: A
SCREENPLAY WRITER FOR TV and MOVIES. She
says: YOU HAVE TO HAVE THE CONTROL

... TO STAND UP FOR YOUR IDEAS, OTHERWISE iT'S NOT WORTH iT.
HEARD THAT BEFORE ...

25.02.03 tuesday. BLUE SKY and ONCE AGAIN PRETTY COLD.
i AM UNABLE TO DRAW iF iT'S NOT THE VERY FIRST THING i DO iN
THE MORNING. i TRIED TO FORCE MYSELF YESTERDAY MORNING
BUT NOTHING GOOD CAME OUT OF ME. i HANGED ABOUT ALL DAY,
i HAD GOTTEN UP TOO EARLY THAT MORNING and HADN'T SLEPT
TOO WELL THE WHOLE WEEK-END. FASCINATING. iN THE
EVENING i WENT TO C.'S PLACE, WHO HAD INVITED ME TO EAT A
SOUP, EXCEPT THAT WE ATE CHICKEN. HE'S A GOOD COOK, HE
LIKES GOOD FOOD.

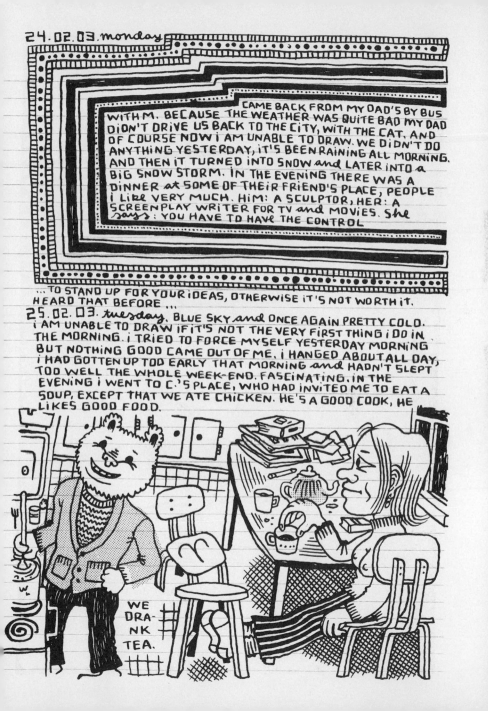

WE
DRA-
NK
TEA.

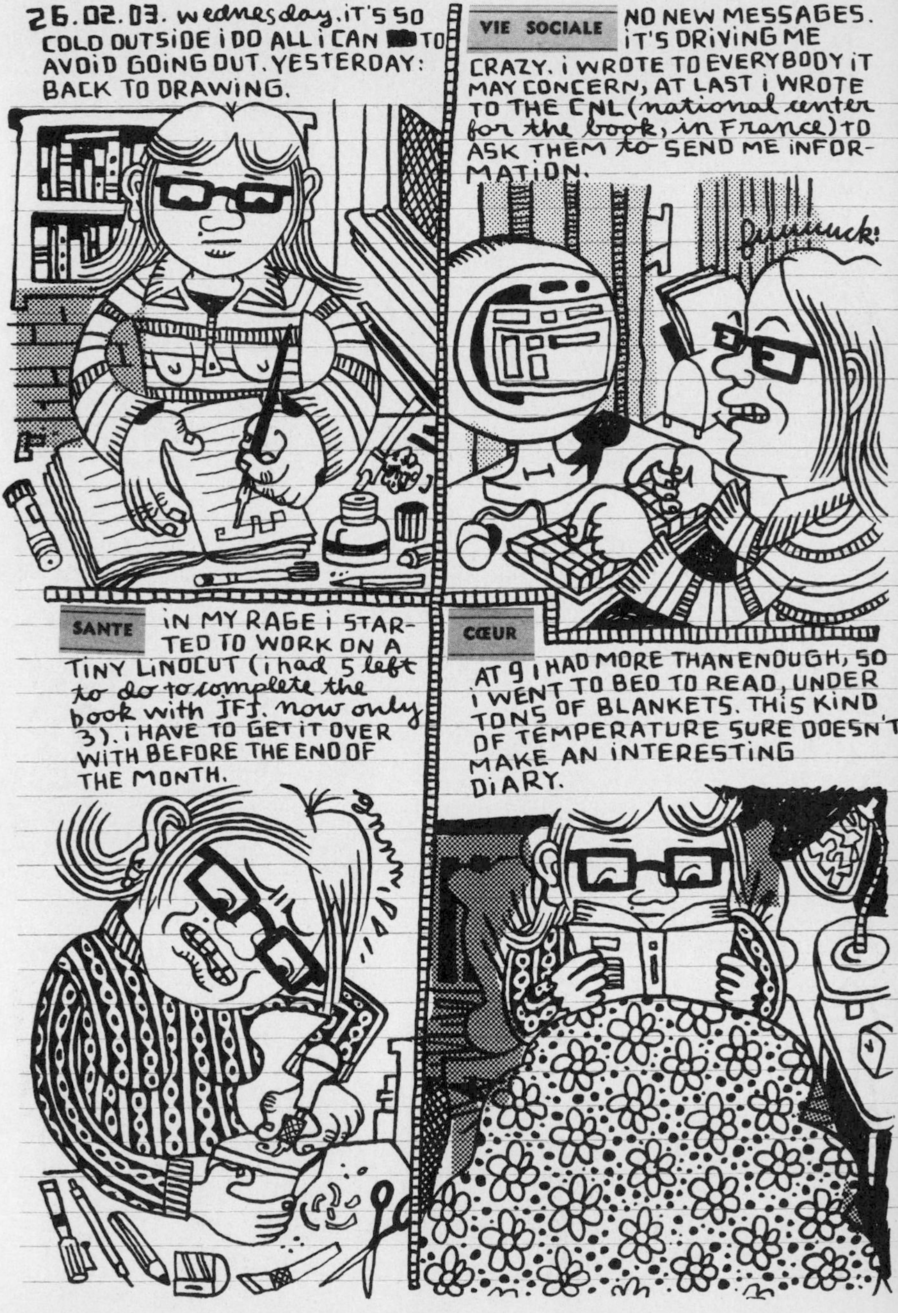
26.02.03. wednesday. IT'S SO COLD OUTSIDE I DO ALL I CAN [redacted] TO AVOID GOING OUT. YESTERDAY: BACK TO DRAWING.
VIE SOCIALE
NO NEW MESSAGES. IT'S DRIVING ME CRAZY. I WROTE TO EVERYBODY IT MAY CONCERN, AT LAST I WROTE TO THE CNL (national center for the book, in France) TO ASK THEM to SEND ME INFORMATION.
fuuuuck!
SANTE
IN MY RAGE I STARTED TO WORK ON A TINY LINOCUT (i had 5 left to do to complete the book with JFJ. now only 3). I HAVE TO GET IT OVER WITH BEFORE THE END OF THE MONTH.
CŒUR
AT 9 I HAD MORE THAN ENOUGH, SO I WENT TO BED TO READ, UNDER TONS OF BLANKETS. THIS KIND OF TEMPERATURE SURE DOESN'T MAKE AN INTERESTING DIARY.

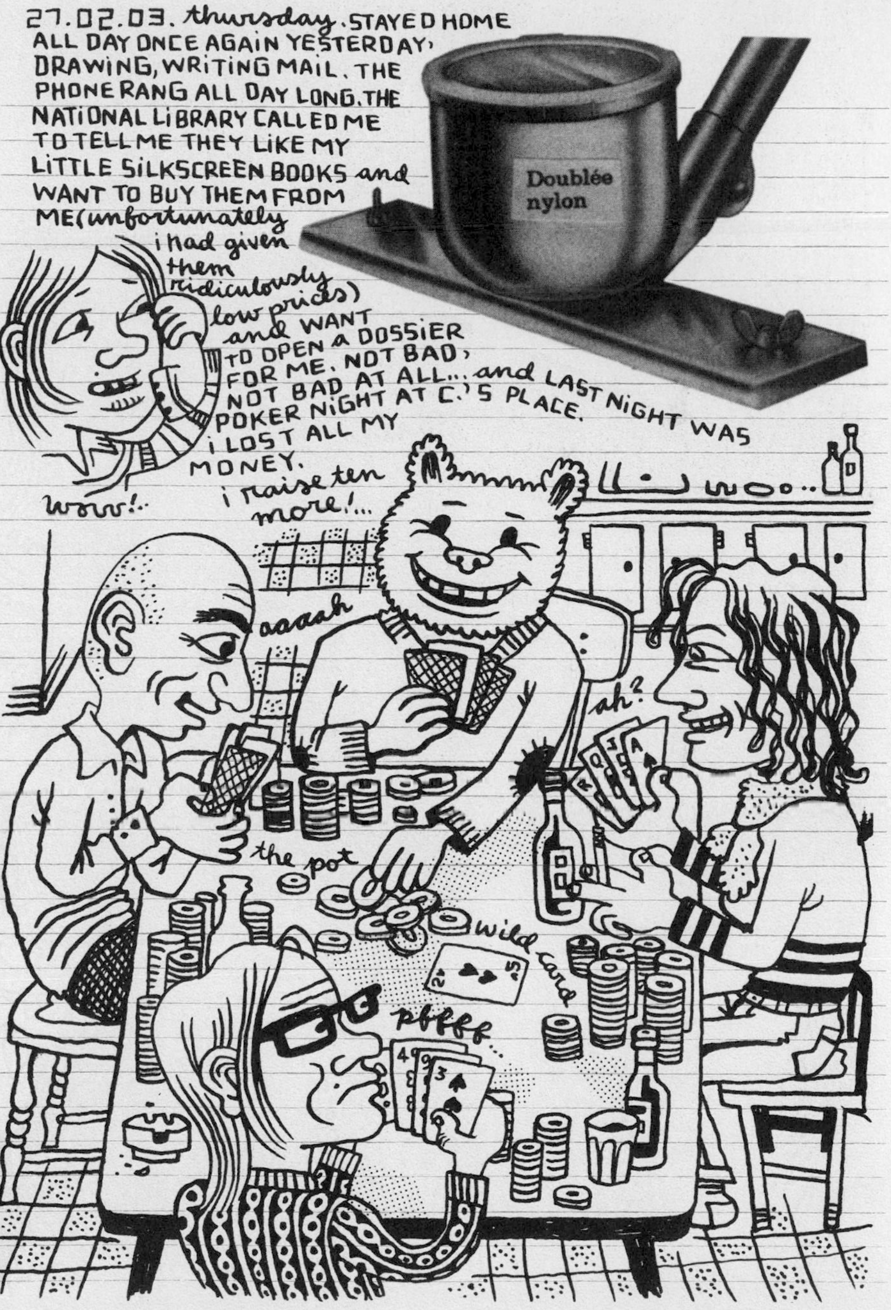

27.02.03. thursday. STAYED HOME ALL DAY ONCE AGAIN YESTERDAY, DRAWING, WRITING MAIL. THE PHONE RANG ALL DAY LONG. THE NATIONAL LIBRARY CALLED ME TO TELL ME THEY LIKE MY LITTLE SILKSCREEN BOOKS and WANT TO BUY THEM FROM ME (unfortunately i had given them ridiculously low prices) and WANT TO OPEN A DOSSIER FOR ME. NOT BAD, NOT BAD AT ALL... and LAST NIGHT WAS POKER NIGHT AT C.'S PLACE. i LOST ALL MY MONEY.
Doublée nylon
woow!..
i raise ten more!...
woo..
aaaah
ah?
the pot
wild card
pffff...

28.02.03. Friday. MY DAD BROUGHT ME MY DEAR CAT YESTER-DAY. IT TOOK HER THREE MINUTES AND SHE WAS BACK TO HER OLD LIFE. AN ORDINARY DAY. AND THEN IN THE EVENING, DINNER at J.'S PLACE WITH D. AND M.E. (it was M.E.'s birthday) IT HAD BEEN a WHILE SiNCE i MET WITH THE GANG... ATe CHiNESE FONDUE and LATER PLAYED "SCOTLAND YARD"

M.E.'s boy-friend

ok, what should i do now? Hey!

A RATHER SMOKY EVENING

j's boy-friend

march 2003

sun	mon	tue	wed	thu	fri	sat
						1
2	3	4	5	6	7	8
9	10	11	12	13	14	15
16	17	18	19	20	21	22
23	24	25	26	27	28	29
30	31					

01.03.03. *saturday*

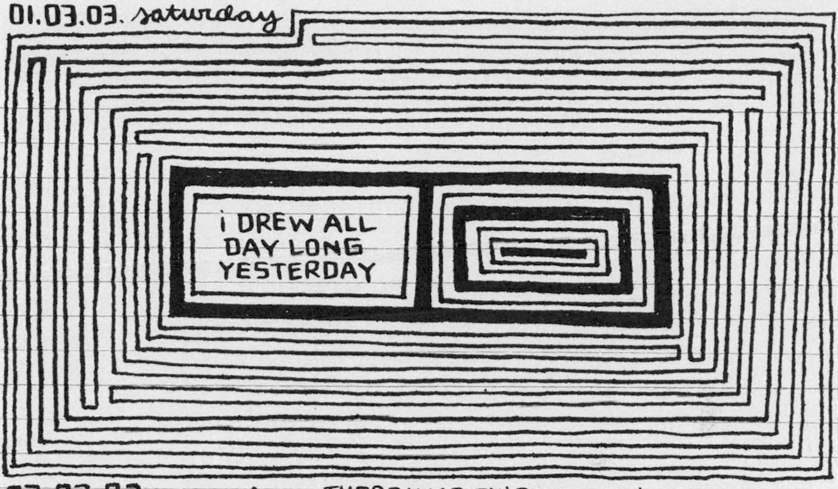
I DREW ALL DAY LONG YESTERDAY

02.03.03. *sunday*. THERE WAS THIS HAPPENING YESTERDAY ALL DAY IN VERDUN. A GROUP EXHIBITION IN AN APARTMENT. J. AND M.E. AND HER BOYFRIEND WERE PART OF IT. I WENT TO CHECK IT OUT AT THE END OF *the* AFTERNOON... MY FRIEND'S PIECES WERE THE BEST.

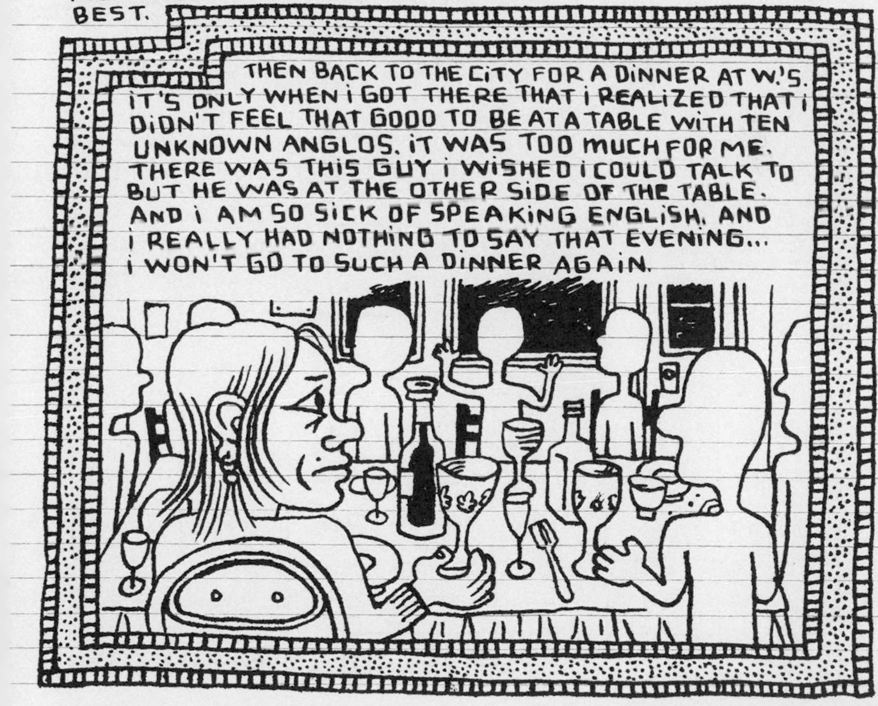
THEN BACK TO THE CITY FOR A DINNER AT W.'S. IT'S ONLY WHEN I GOT THERE THAT I REALIZED THAT I DIDN'T FEEL THAT GOOD TO BE AT A TABLE WITH TEN UNKNOWN ANGLOS. IT WAS TOO MUCH FOR ME. THERE WAS THIS GUY I WISHED I COULD TALK TO BUT HE WAS AT THE OTHER SIDE OF THE TABLE. AND I AM SO SICK OF SPEAKING ENGLISH. AND I REALLY HAD NOTHING TO SAY THAT EVENING... I WON'T GO TO SUCH A DINNER AGAIN.

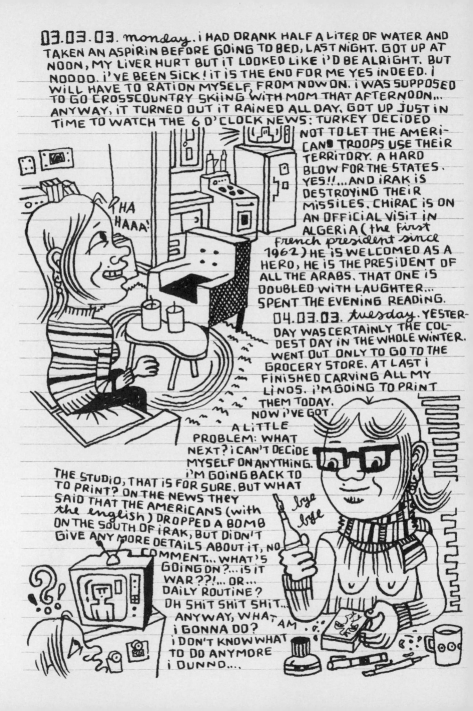

03.03.03. *monday*. I HAD DRANK HALF A LITER OF WATER AND TAKEN AN ASPIRIN BEFORE GOING TO BED, LAST NIGHT. GOT UP AT NOON, MY LIVER HURT BUT IT LOOKED LIKE I'D BE ALRIGHT. BUT NOOOO. I'VE BEEN SICK! IT IS THE END FOR ME YES INDEED. I WILL HAVE TO RATION MYSELF, FROM NOW ON. I WAS SUPPOSED TO GO CROSSCOUNTRY SKIING WITH MOM THAT AFTERNOON... ANYWAY, IT TURNED OUT IT RAINED ALL DAY. GOT UP JUST IN TIME TO WATCH THE 6 O'CLOCK NEWS: TURKEY DECIDED NOT TO LET THE AMERICAN TROOPS USE THEIR TERRITORY. A HARD BLOW FOR THE STATES. YES!!... AND IRAK IS DESTROYING THEIR MISSILES. CHIRAC IS ON AN OFFICIAL VISIT IN ALGERIA (*the first french president since* 1962) HE IS WELCOMED AS A HERO, HE IS THE PRESIDENT OF ALL THE ARABS. THAT ONE IS DOUBLED WITH LAUGHTER... SPENT THE EVENING READING.

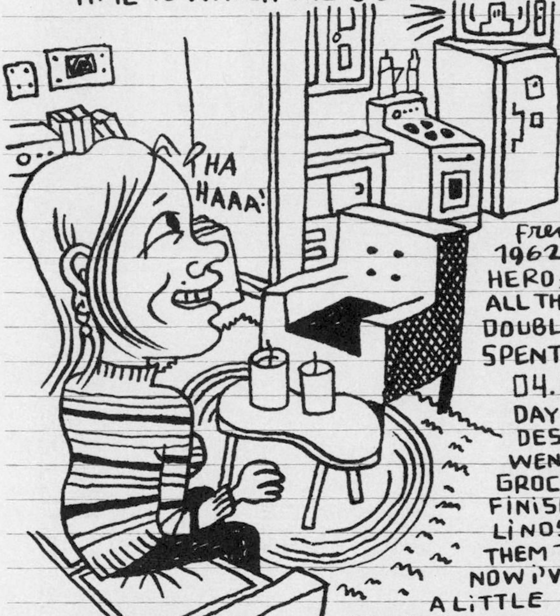
HA HAAA!

04.03.03. *tuesday*. YESTERDAY WAS CERTAINLY THE COLDEST DAY IN THE WHOLE WINTER. WENT OUT ONLY TO GO TO THE GROCERY STORE. AT LAST I FINISHED CARVING ALL MY LINOS. I'M GOING TO PRINT THEM TODAY. NOW I'VE GOT A LITTLE PROBLEM: WHAT NEXT? I CAN'T DECIDE MYSELF ON ANYTHING. I'M GOING BACK TO THE STUDIO, THAT IS FOR SURE. BUT WHAT TO PRINT? ON THE NEWS THEY SAID THAT THE AMERICANS (*with the english*) DROPPED A BOMB ON THE SOUTH OF IRAK, BUT DIDN'T GIVE ANY MORE DETAILS ABOUT IT, NO COMMENT... WHAT'S GOING ON?... IS IT WAR??!... OR... DAILY ROUTINE? OH SHIT SHIT SHIT... ANYWAY, WHAT AM I GONNA DO? I DON'T KNOW WHAT TO DO ANYMORE I DUNNO....

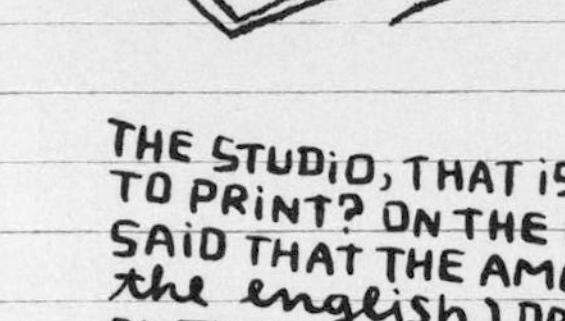

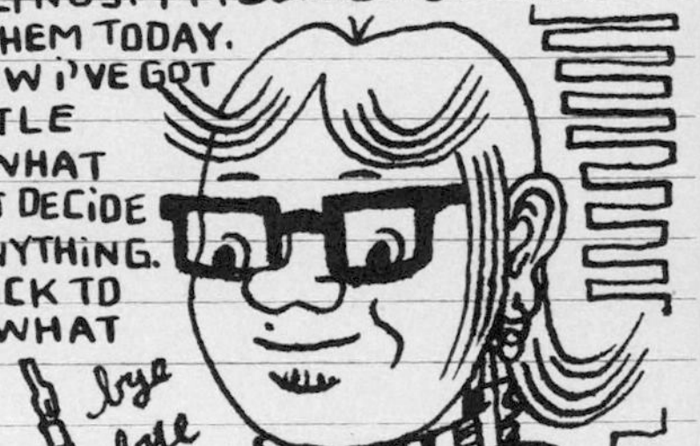
bye bye

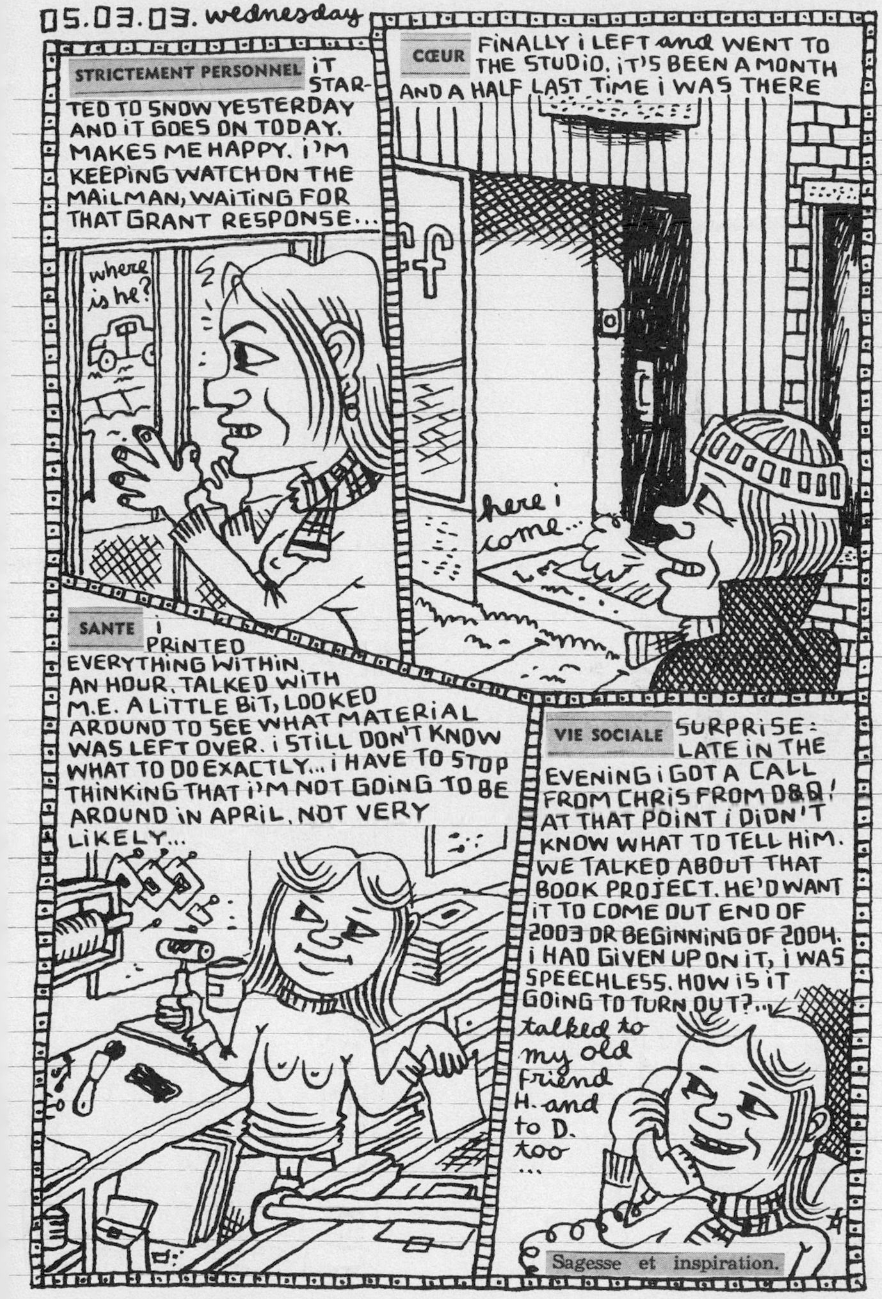
05.03.03. wednesday
STRICTEMENT PERSONNEL
IT STARTED TO SNOW YESTERDAY AND IT GOES ON TODAY. MAKES ME HAPPY. I'M KEEPING WATCH ON THE MAILMAN, WAITING FOR THAT GRANT RESPONSE...
where is he?
CŒUR
FINALLY I LEFT and WENT TO THE STUDIO. IT'S BEEN A MONTH AND A HALF LAST TIME I WAS THERE
here i come...
SANTE
I PRINTED EVERYTHING WITHIN AN HOUR. TALKED WITH M.E. A LITTLE BIT, LOOKED AROUND TO SEE WHAT MATERIAL WAS LEFT OVER. I STILL DON'T KNOW WHAT TO DO EXACTLY... I HAVE TO STOP THINKING THAT I'M NOT GOING TO BE AROUND IN APRIL. NOT VERY LIKELY...
VIE SOCIALE
SURPRISE: LATE IN THE EVENING I GOT A CALL FROM CHRIS FROM D&Q! AT THAT POINT I DIDN'T KNOW WHAT TO TELL HIM. WE TALKED ABOUT THAT BOOK PROJECT. HE'D WANT IT TO COME OUT END OF 2003 OR BEGINNING OF 2004. I HAD GIVEN UP ON IT, I WAS SPEECHLESS. HOW IS IT GOING TO TURN OUT?...
talked to my old friend H. and to D. too ...
Sagesse et inspiration.

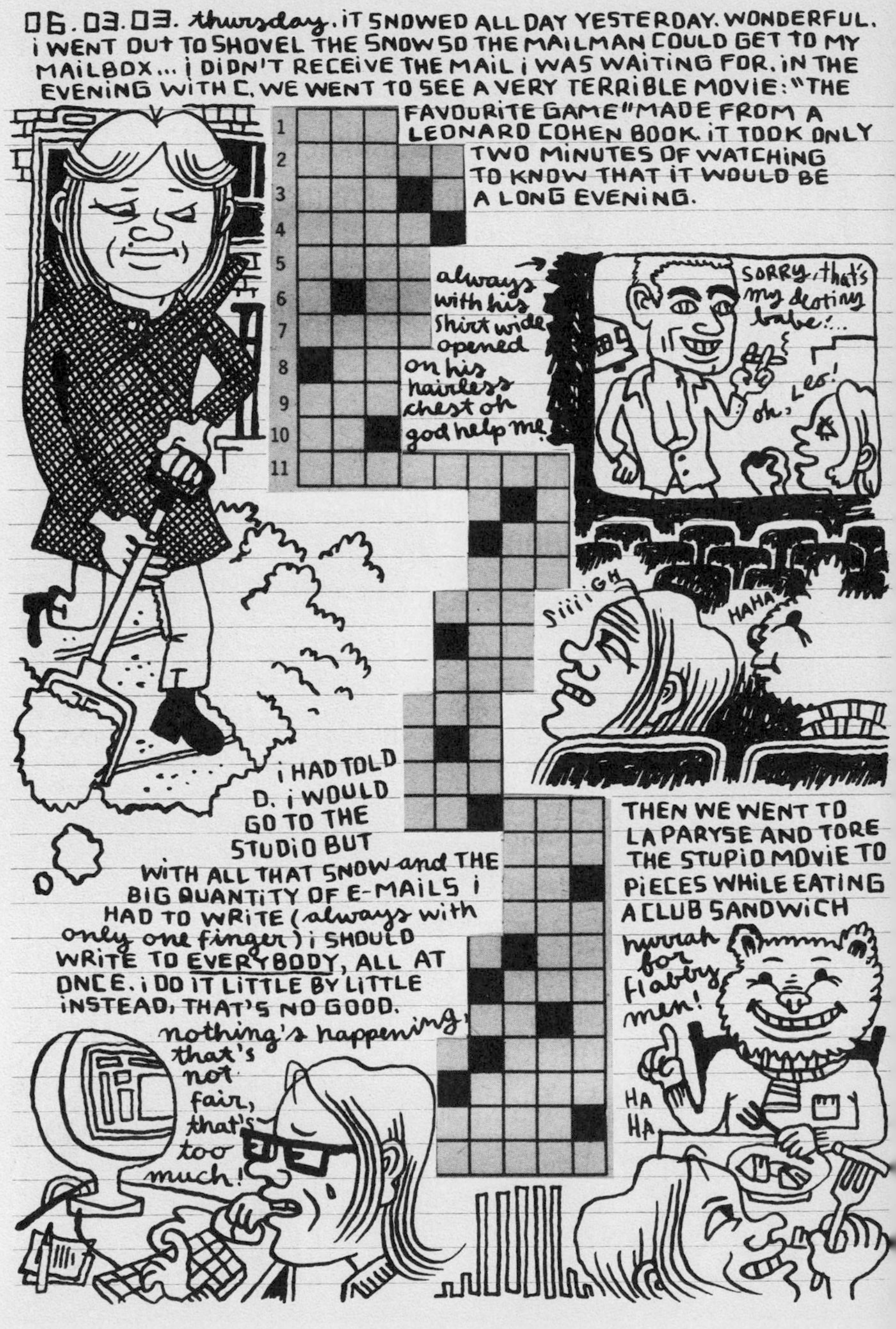
06.03.03. thursday. iT SNOWED ALL DAY YESTERDAY. WONDERFUL. i WENT OUT TO SHOVEL THE SNOW SO THE MAILMAN COULD GET TO MY MAILBOX... i DIDN'T RECEIVE THE MAIL i WAS WAITING FOR. iN THE EVENING WITH C. WE WENT TO SEE A VERY TERRIBLE MOVIE: "THE FAVOURITE GAME" MADE FROM A LEONARD COHEN BOOK. iT TOOK ONLY TWO MINUTES OF WATCHING TO KNOW THAT iT WOULD BE A LONG EVENING.
always with his shirt wide opened on his hairless chest oh god help me!
SORRY, that's my destiny babe!...
oh, Leo!
Siiiiigh
HAHA
i HAD TOLD D. i WOULD GO TO THE STUDIO BUT WITH ALL THAT SNOW and THE BIG QUANTITY OF E-MAILS i HAD TO WRITE (always with only one finger) i SHOULD WRITE TO EVERYBODY, ALL AT ONCE. i DO IT LITTLE BY LITTLE INSTEAD, THAT'S NO GOOD.
nothing's happening, that's not fair, that's too much!
THEN WE WENT TO LA PARYSE AND TORE THE STUPID MOVIE TO PIECES WHILE EATING A CLUB SANDWICH
hurrah for flabby men!
HA HA

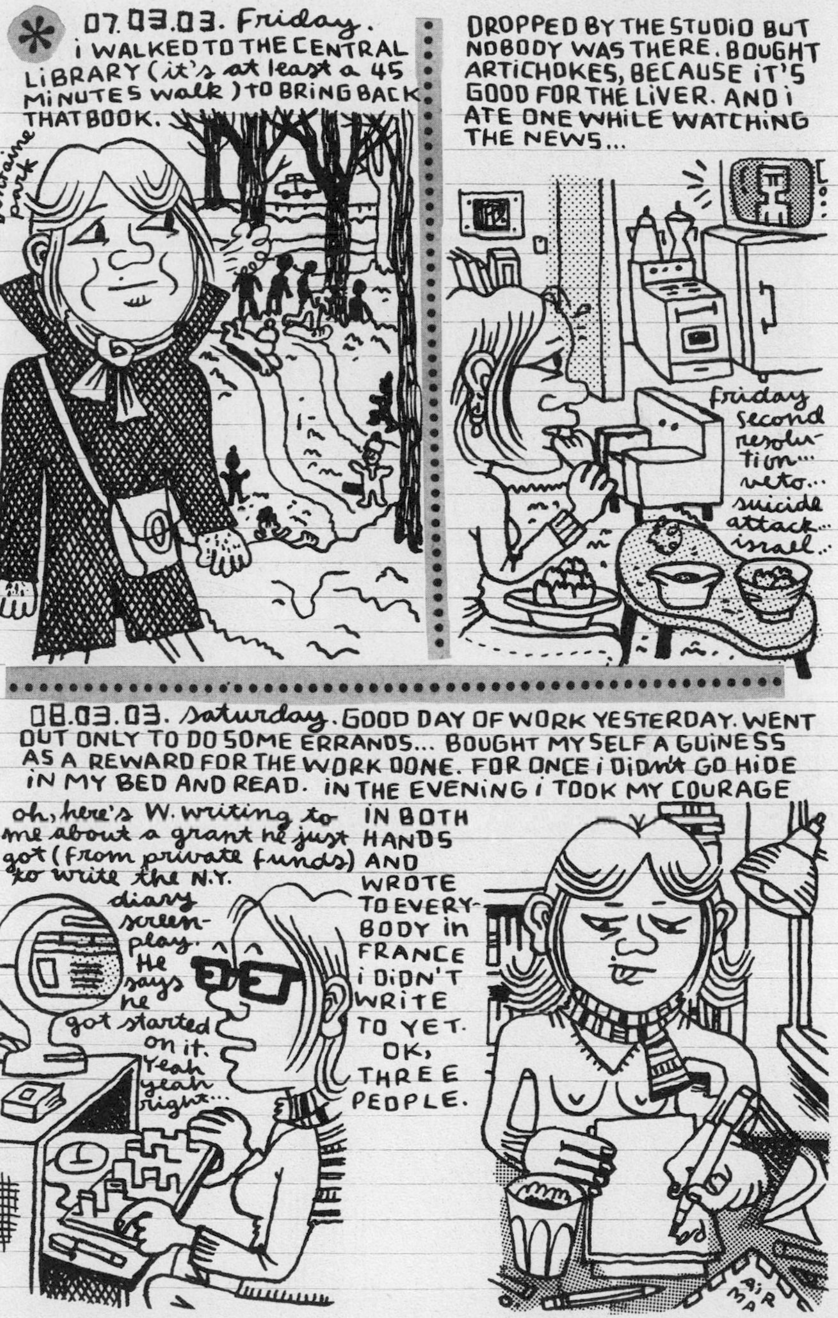
07.03.03. Friday.
i WALKED TO THE CENTRAL LiBRARY (it's at least a 45 MiNUTES walk) TO BRiNG BACK THAT BOOK.
lafontaine park
DROPPED BY THE STUDIO BUT NOBODY WAS THERE. BOUGHT ARTiCHOKES, BECAUSE iT'S GOOD FOR THE LiVER. AND i ATE ONE WHiLE WATCHiNG THE NEWS...
friday second resolution... veto... suicide attack... israel...
08.03.03. saturday. GOOD DAY OF WORK YESTERDAY. WENT OUT ONLY TO DO SOME ERRANDS... BOUGHT MY SELF A GUiNESS AS A REWARD FOR THE WORK DONE. FOR ONCE i DiDN'T GO HiDE iN MY BED AND READ. iN THE EVENiNG i TOOK MY COURAGE
iN BOTH HANDS AND WROTE TO EVERYBODY iN FRANCE i DiDN'T WRiTE TO YET. OK, THREE PEOPLE.
oh, here's W. writing to me about a grant he just got (from private funds) to write the N.Y. diary screenplay. He says he got started on it. Yeah yeah right...
AiR MA

09.03.03. sunday.
i DREAMT i WAS GOING BACK TO AN APPARTMENT i LIVED IN, SOMEWHERE IN EUROPE. i WAS SHARING THE PLACE WITH J AND THE GRAFF STUDIO COORDINATOR. THE CEILINGS HAD FALLEN INTO PIECES IN THE FRONT ROOMS (where my bedroom was). THEY HAD HAD TO PLASTER and PAINT EVERYTHING... in BLUE. ALL MY THINGS WAS PILED UP IN A VERY SMALL ROOM... MY FURNITURE HAD CHARACTER, and MY BOOKS WERE VERY OLD AND RARE, MY CLOTHES were MODERN and HIP... i WAS WONDERING WHY THE HELL

DiD i EVER LEAVE THiS PLACE...

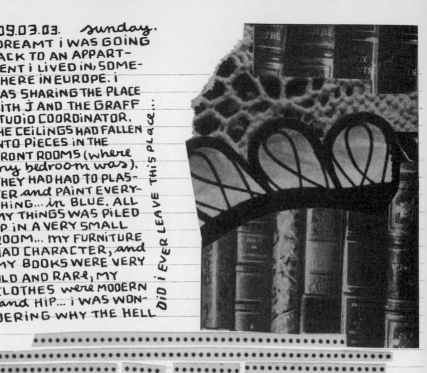

WENT CROSS COUNTRY SKiING WiTH MY MOM YESTERDAY, iN THE LAURENTiDES NEAR ST-JÉRÔME, AT A PLACE CALLED SKi CENTER GAi-LURON. NO KiDDiNG. i WAS DRESSED UP AS A SPORTSWOMAN, THANKS TO MY MOM. THERE WERE LOTS OF

the sports i can handle, but the sports equipment... ugh!!!

PEOPLE IN THE PARKING LOT BUT ONCE ON THE TRAIL, WE WERE ALONE. WE RAN INTO ALMOST NOBODY. THIS TIME WAS PRETTY NICE, THE CONDITIONS WERE PERFECT. HAD DINNER WITH HER AT HOME LATER and... BASTA!

10.03.03. monday.

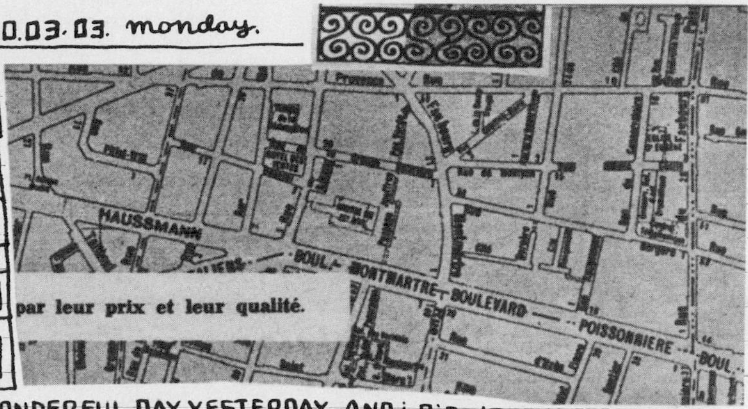
HAUSSMANN
BOUL.
MONTMARTRE
BOULEVARD
POISSONNIERE
BOUL.
par leur prix et leur qualité.

A WONDERFUL DAY YESTERDAY, AND i DIDN'T EVEN GO OUT. AT LAST i WAS ABLE TO GET TO WORK ACCORDING TO SILK-SCREEN PRINTING. i MAY BE ABLE TO START PRINTING TUESDAY. C. TOLD ME A FUNNY ONE: ABOUT THE GRANT RESPONSES WE WILL RECEIVE THEM ONLY IN APRIL!... ALL THIS TIME i WAS ALL WORKED UP AND FOR NOTHING AT ALL. THAT MEANS THE TRIP IS POSTPONED... OH WELL, THAT WILL CALM ME DOWN A BIT. WENT TO C.'S PLACE IN THE EVENING, WE WATCHED VIDEOS: THE SIXTH Sense and an OLD TV SERIES EPISODE of ARSÈNE LUPIN WE BOTH PREFERRED THE VERY HANDSOME ARSÈNE.

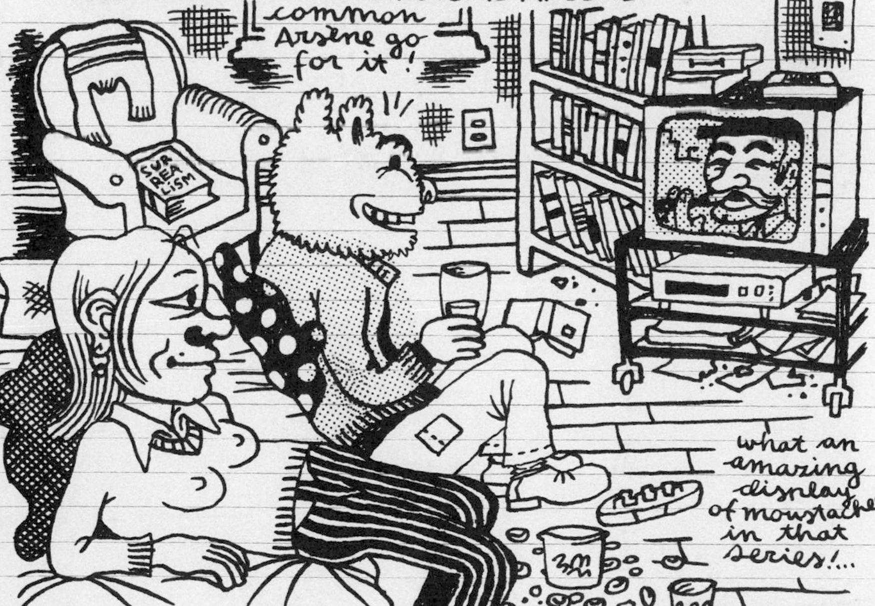
common Arsène go for it!
SUR REA LISM
what an amazing display of moustaches in that series!...

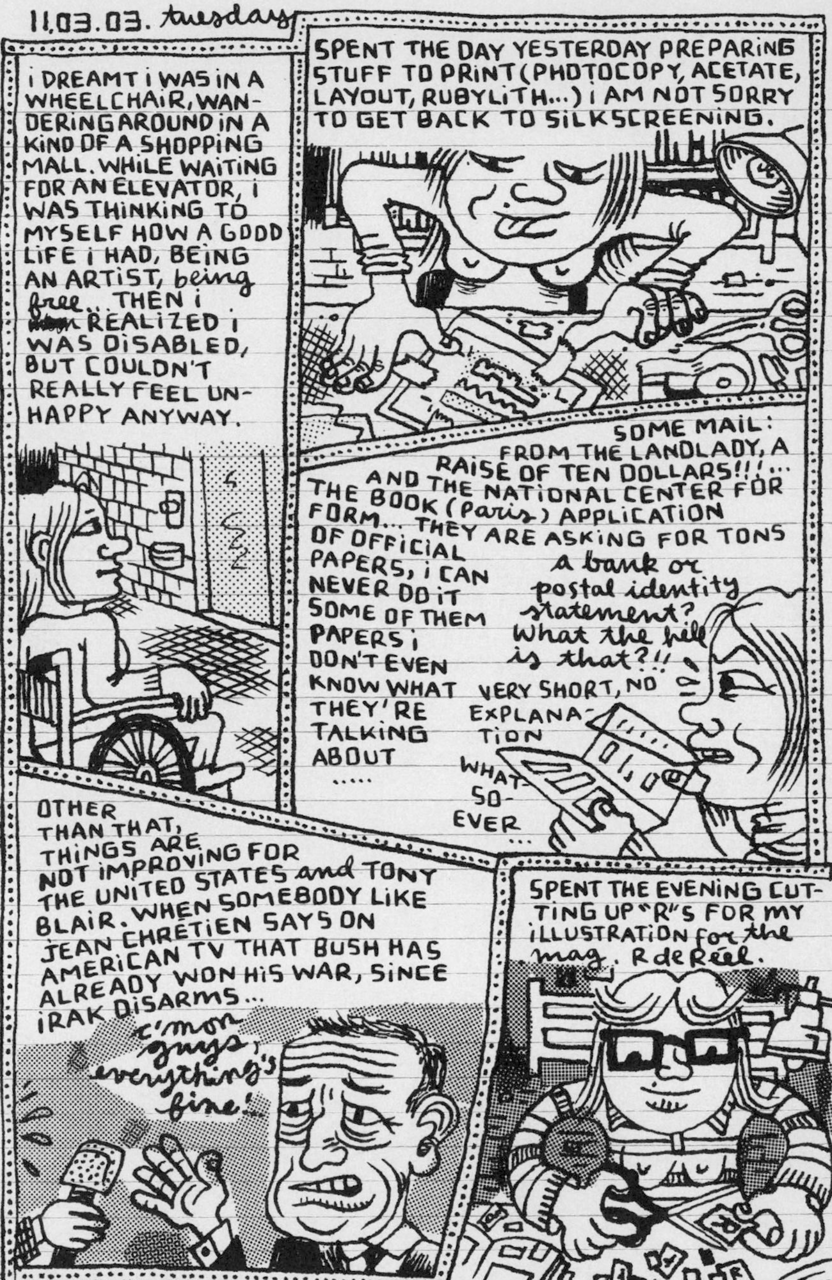
11.03.03. tuesday
I DREAMT I WAS IN A WHEELCHAIR, WANDERING AROUND IN A KIND OF A SHOPPING MALL. WHILE WAITING FOR AN ELEVATOR, I WAS THINKING TO MYSELF HOW A GOOD LIFE I HAD, BEING AN ARTIST, being free... THEN I REALIZED I WAS DISABLED, BUT COULDN'T REALLY FEEL UNHAPPY ANYWAY.
SPENT THE DAY YESTERDAY PREPARING STUFF TO PRINT (PHOTOCOPY, ACETATE, LAYOUT, RUBYLITH...) I AM NOT SORRY TO GET BACK TO SILKSCREENING.
SOME MAIL: FROM THE LANDLADY, A RAISE OF TEN DOLLARS!!!... AND THE NATIONAL CENTER FOR THE BOOK (Paris) APPLICATION FORM... THEY ARE ASKING FOR TONS OF OFFICIAL PAPERS, I CAN NEVER DO IT SOME OF THEM PAPERS I DON'T EVEN KNOW WHAT THEY'RE TALKING ABOUT .....
a bank or postal identity statement? What the hell is that?!!
VERY SHORT, NO EXPLANATION WHATSOEVER...
OTHER THAN THAT, THINGS ARE NOT IMPROVING FOR THE UNITED STATES and TONY BLAIR. WHEN SOMEBODY LIKE JEAN CHRÉTIEN SAYS ON AMERICAN TV THAT BUSH HAS ALREADY WON HIS WAR, SINCE IRAK DISARMS...
c'mon guys, everything's fine!...
SPENT THE EVENING CUTTING UP "R"s FOR MY ILLUSTRATION for the mag. R de Réel.

12.03.03. wednesday. BACK TO THE STUDIO. i GOT THERE FIRST, THEN D. AND LATER J. D. HAD LOTS OF THINGS TO TELL, WITH HER BAND NEXT APRIL THEY WILL GO FOR A SMALL TOUR in THE STATES, WILL PLAY THREE EVENINGS IN NEW YORK CITY... SHE IS BOOKED UP AS HELL FOR THE NEXT THREE MONTHS. THAT DEPRESSED ME A LITTLE BIT. i WISH i KNEW WHERE i AM GOING... AND WHEN.

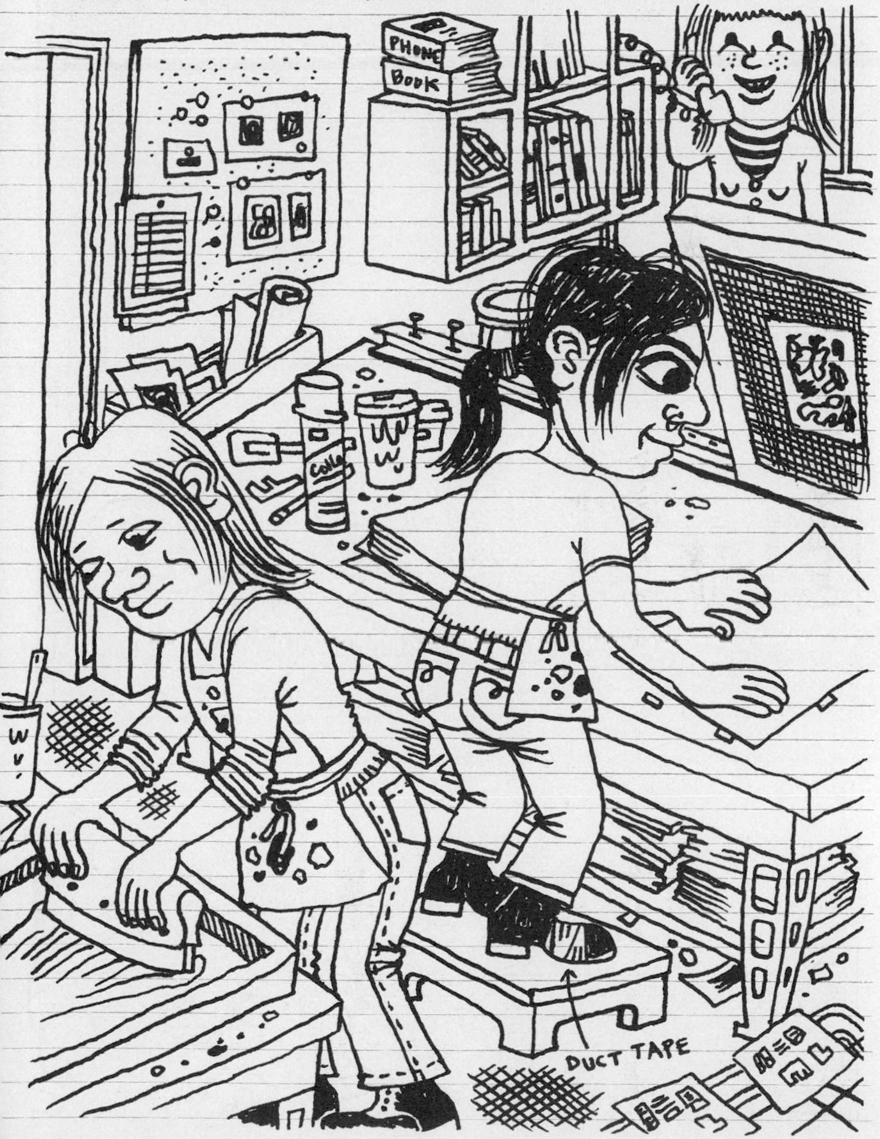
PHONE
BOOK
DUCT TAPE

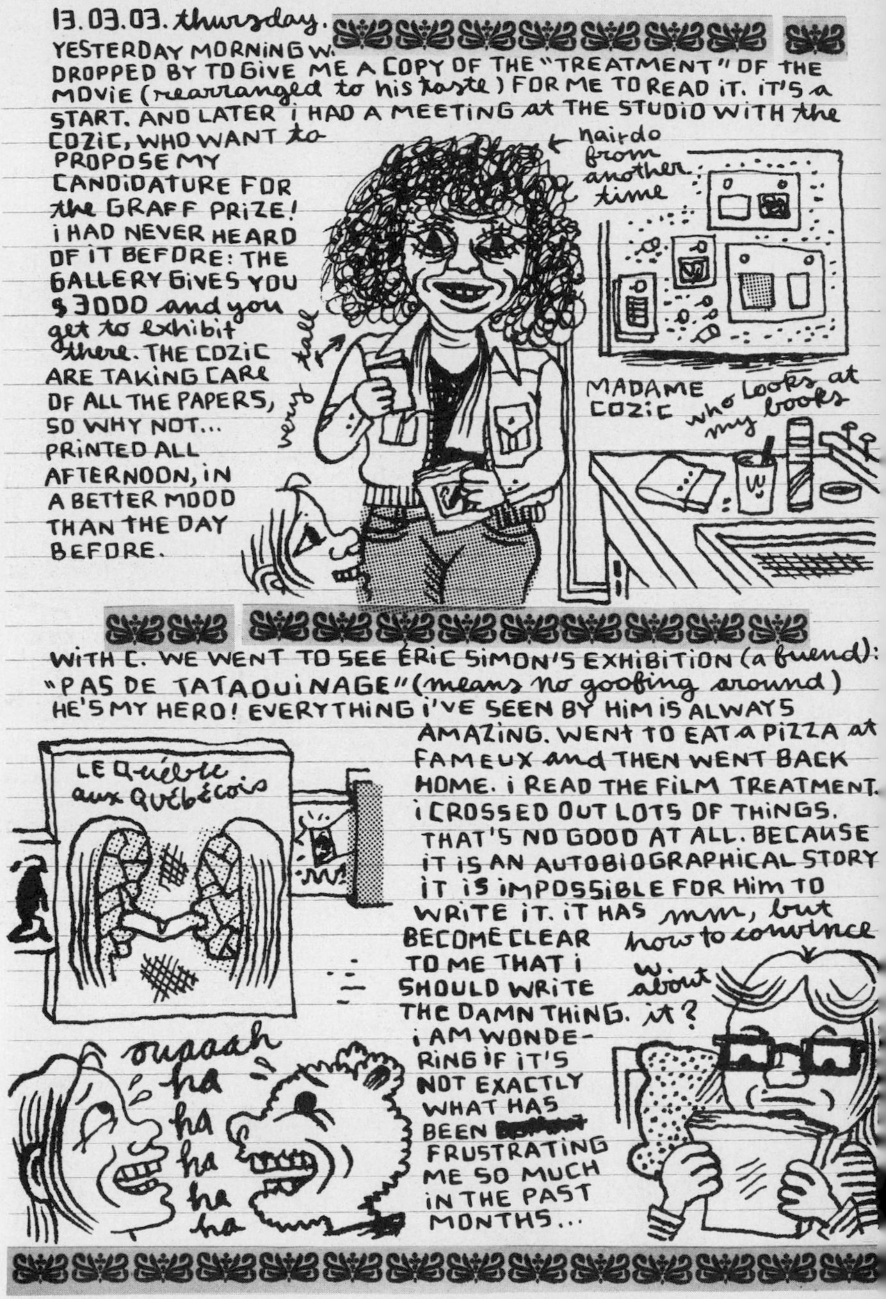
13.03.03. thursday.
YESTERDAY MORNING W.
DROPPED BY TO GIVE ME A COPY OF THE "TREATMENT" OF THE MOVIE (rearranged to his taste) FOR ME TO READ IT. IT'S a START. AND LATER I HAD A MEETING at THE STUDIO WITH the COZIC, WHO WANT to PROPOSE MY CANDIDATURE FOR the GRAFF PRIZE! I HAD NEVER HEARD OF IT BEFORE: THE GALLERY GIVES YOU $3000 and you get to exhibit there. THE COZIC ARE TAKING CARE OF ALL THE PAPERS, SO WHY NOT... PRINTED ALL AFTERNOON, IN A BETTER MOOD THAN THE DAY BEFORE.
hairdo from another time
very tall
MADAME COZIC who looks at my books
WITH C. WE WENT TO SEE ÉRIC SIMON'S EXHIBITION (a friend): "PAS DE TATAOUINAGE" (means no goofing around) HE'S MY HERO! EVERYTHING I'VE SEEN BY HIM IS ALWAYS AMAZING. WENT TO EAT A PIZZA at FAMEUX and THEN WENT BACK HOME. I READ THE FILM TREATMENT. I CROSSED OUT LOTS OF THINGS. THAT'S NO GOOD AT ALL. BECAUSE IT IS AN AUTOBIOGRAPHICAL STORY IT IS IMPOSSIBLE FOR HIM TO WRITE IT. IT HAS BECOME CLEAR TO ME THAT I SHOULD WRITE THE DAMN THING. I AM WONDERING IF IT'S NOT EXACTLY WHAT HAS BEEN [redacted] FRUSTRATING ME SO MUCH IN THE PAST MONTHS...
LE Québec aux QUÉBÉCOIS
oupaah ha ha ha ha ha
mm, but how to convince W. about it?

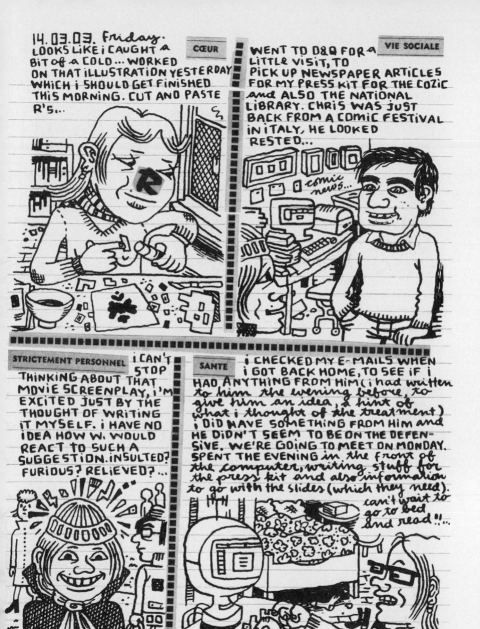

14.03.03. Friday.
LOOKS LIKE I CAUGHT A BIT OF A COLD... WORKED ON THAT ILLUSTRATION YESTERDAY WHICH I SHOULD GET FINISHED THIS MORNING. CUT AND PASTE R's...

CŒUR

VIE SOCIALE

WENT TO D&Q FOR A LITTLE VISIT, TO PICK UP NEWSPAPER ARTICLES FOR MY PRESS KIT FOR THE COZIC and ALSO THE NATIONAL LIBRARY. CHRIS WAS JUST BACK FROM A COMIC FESTIVAL IN ITALY, HE LOOKED RESTED...

comic news...

STRICTEMENT PERSONNEL

I CAN'T STOP THINKING ABOUT THAT MOVIE SCREENPLAY, I'M EXCITED JUST BY THE THOUGHT OF WRITING IT MYSELF. I HAVE NO IDEA HOW W. WOULD REACT TO SUCH A SUGGESTION. INSULTED? FURIOUS? RELIEVED?...

SANTÉ

I CHECKED MY E-MAILS WHEN I GOT BACK HOME, TO SEE IF I HAD ANYTHING FROM HIM (I had written to him the evening before, to give him an idea, a hint of what i thought of the treatment) i DID HAVE SOMETHING FROM HIM and HE DIDN'T SEEM TO BE ON THE DEFENSIVE. WE'RE GOING TO MEET ON MONDAY. SPENT THE EVENING in the front of the computer, writing stuff for the press kit and also information to go with the slides (which they need).

can't wait to go to bed and read!!...

15.03.03. saturday. i GOT STARTED ON THAT iLLUSTRATION YESTERDAY MORNING. RRRRRRRR BUT IT DIDN'T GO ANYWHERE, IT WAS WASTED PAPER and THAT'S ALL. BECAUSE OF THE BOOKMOBILE i HAD TO QUIT FOR THE DAY. C. CAME TO PICK ME UP WITH HIS CAR AND WE WENT TO THE BOOKMOBILE PREMISES, TO JUDGE ABOUT 500 artists books and fanzines...

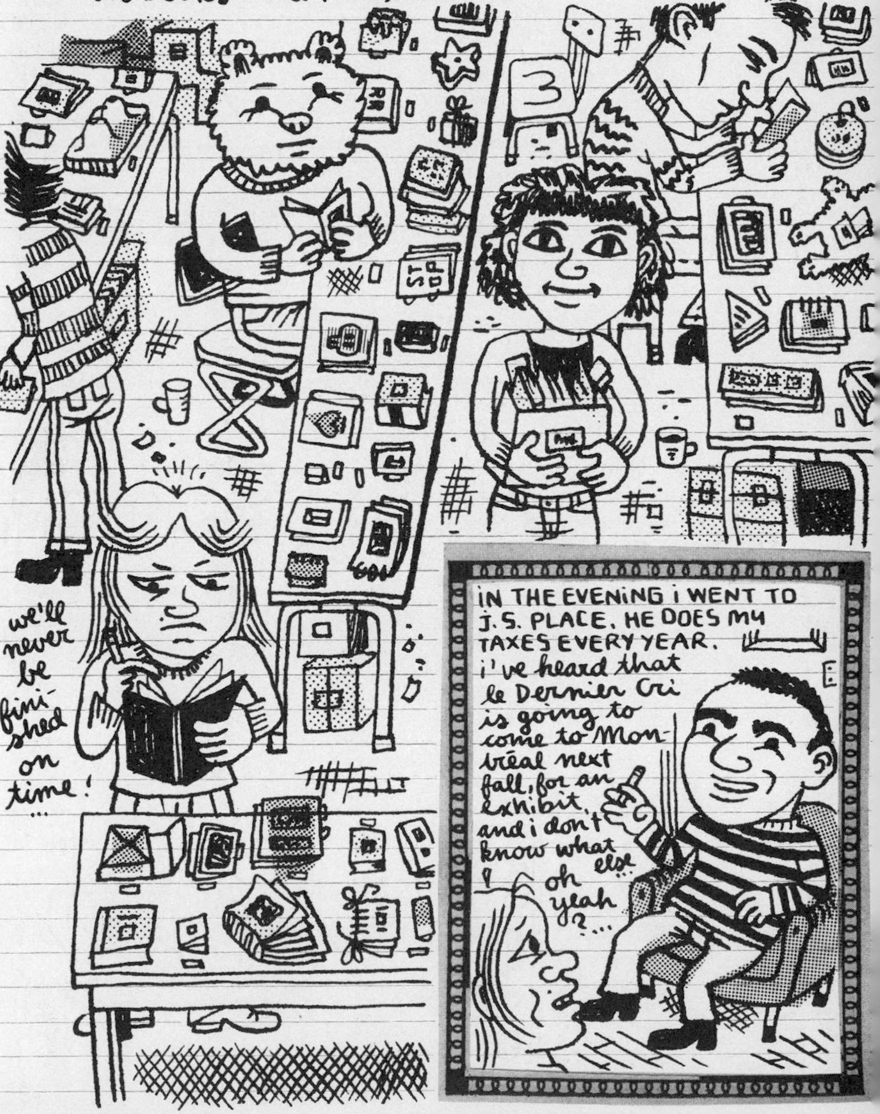

we'll never be fini-shed on time!...
IN THE EVENING i WENT TO J.S. PLACE. HE DOES MY TAXES EVERY YEAR.
i've heard that le Dernier Cri is going to come to Montréal next fall, for an exhibit, and i don't know what else
oh yeah?...

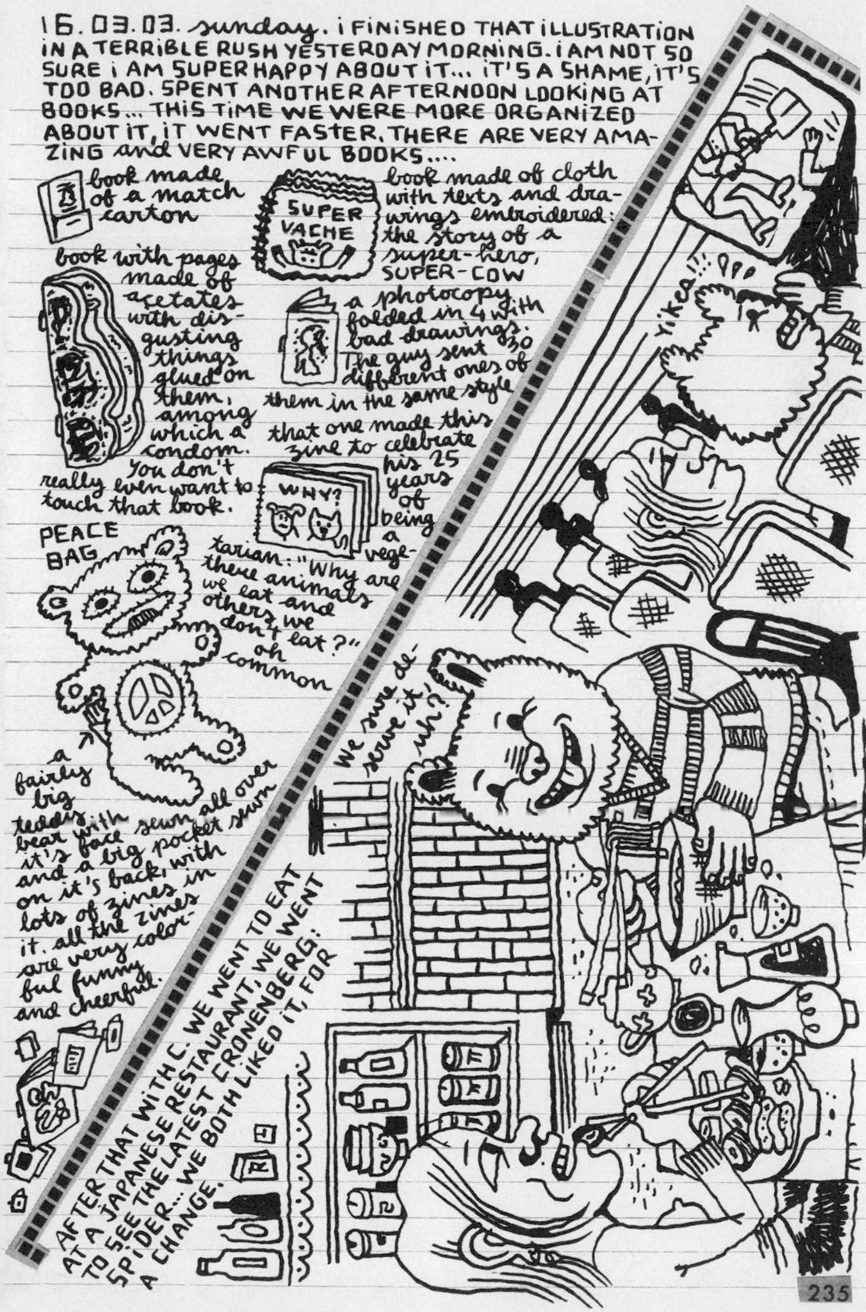
16. 03. 03. sunday. i FINISHED THAT iLLUSTRATION IN A TERRIBLE RUSH YESTERDAY MORNING. i AM NOT SO SURE i AM SUPER HAPPY ABOUT IT... IT'S A SHAME, IT'S TOO BAD. SPENT ANOTHER AFTERNOON LOOKING AT BOOKS... THIS TIME WE WERE MORE ORGANIZED ABOUT IT, IT WENT FASTER. THERE ARE VERY AMAZING and VERY AWFUL BOOKS....
book made of a match carton
SUPER VACHE
book made of cloth with texts and drawings embroidered: the story of a super-hero, SUPER-COW
book with pages made of acetates with disgusting things glued on them, among which a condom. You don't really even want to touch that book.
a photocopy folded in 4 with bad drawings. The guy sent 30 different ones of them in the same style
that one made this zine to celebrate his 25 years of being a vegetarian: "Why are there animals we eat and others we don't eat?" oh common
WHY?
PEACE BAG
a fairly big teddy bear with it's face sewn all over and a big pocket sewn on it's back, with lots of zines in it. all the zines are very colorful funny and cheerful.
YIKES!!!
We sure deserve it, uh?
AFTER THAT WITH C. WE WENT TO EAT AT A JAPANESE RESTAURANT, WE WENT TO SEE THE LATEST CRONENBERG: SPIDER... WE BOTH LIKED IT, FOR A CHANGE.

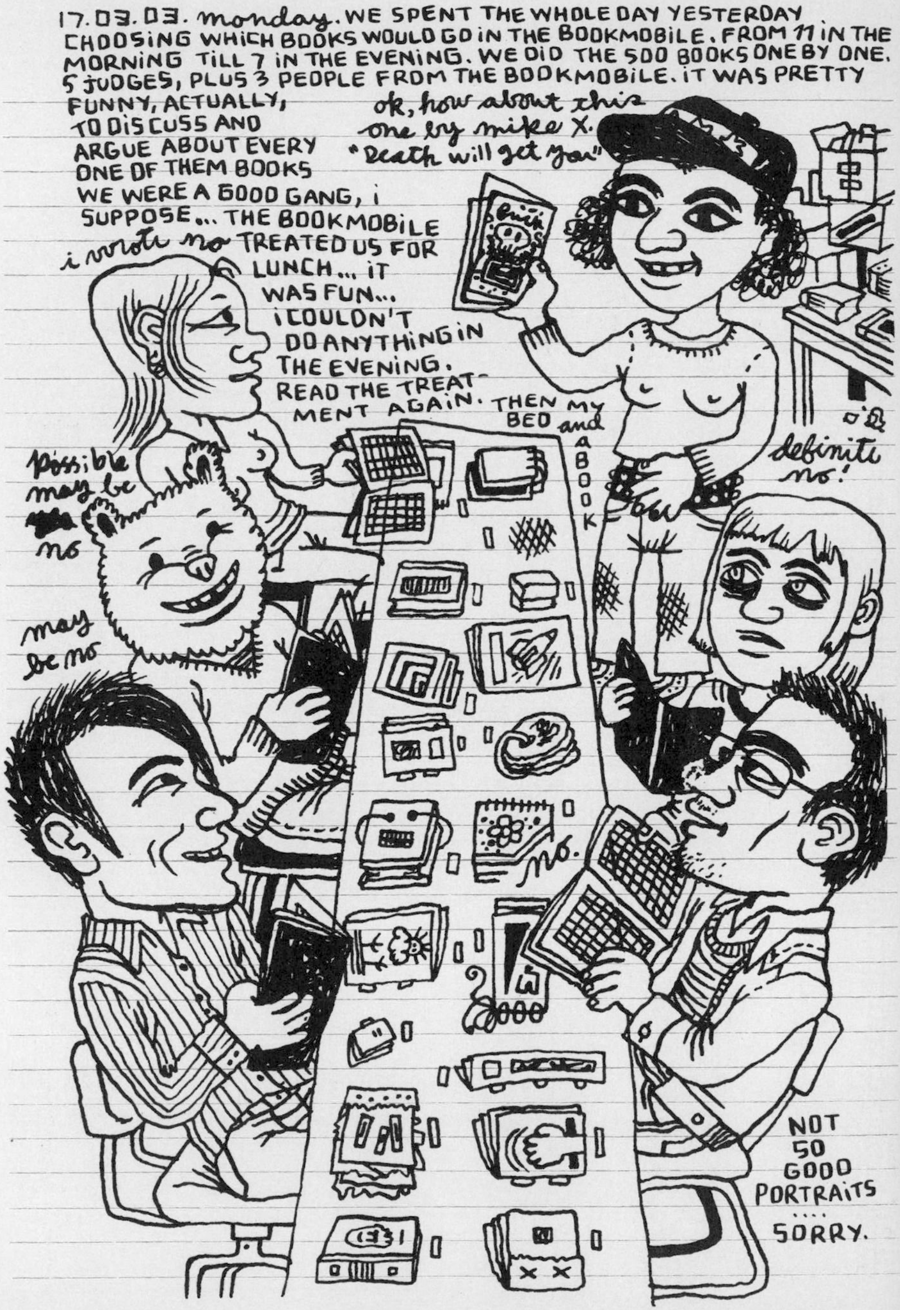
17.03.03. monday. WE SPENT THE WHOLE DAY YESTERDAY CHOOSING WHICH BOOKS WOULD GO IN THE BOOKMOBILE. FROM 11 IN THE MORNING TILL 7 IN THE EVENING. WE DID THE 500 BOOKS ONE BY ONE. 5 JUDGES, PLUS 3 PEOPLE FROM THE BOOKMOBILE. IT WAS PRETTY FUNNY, ACTUALLY, TO DISCUSS AND ARGUE ABOUT EVERY ONE OF THEM BOOKS
WE WERE A GOOD GANG, I SUPPOSE... THE BOOKMOBILE TREATED US FOR LUNCH... IT WAS FUN... I COULDN'T DO ANYTHING IN THE EVENING. READ THE TREATMENT AGAIN. THEN MY BED and A BOOK
ok, how about this one by mike X. "Death will get you"
i wrote no
possible
may be
[redacted]
no
may be no
definite no!
no.
NOT SO GOOD PORTRAITS .... SORRY.

18.03.03. tuesday.. i've been going around all day yesterday and then there was my meeting with W. we went out for a coffee on Duluth st. this is no good at all. i didn't even have to say anything, from his attitude i could tell he has no intention to let anybody pry into his business. my role is passive. i can criticize, make suggestions... it's ok when i'm radically opposed to something: there won't be any animation and no introduction about my life (he has no choice). i will have to negotiate all the time... really, this is my first big regret in my life: to not write this screenplay myself. what can i do? to talk about it with Y., the L.A. producer? to write my own version anyway? it all makes me sick... fortunately after that meeting i was seeing D. and J. at the studio and then we treated ourselves with sushis. it was perfect. it totally defused a possible nervous breakdown from my part. we later went to drink gin & tonics at Casa del Popolo. ran into C., who was just leaving. a 48 hours ultimatum (starting yesterday) before war. Japan and Australia are with the States.

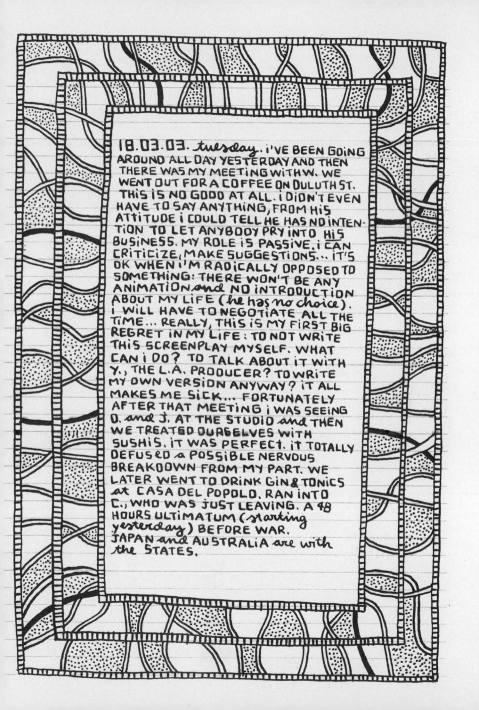

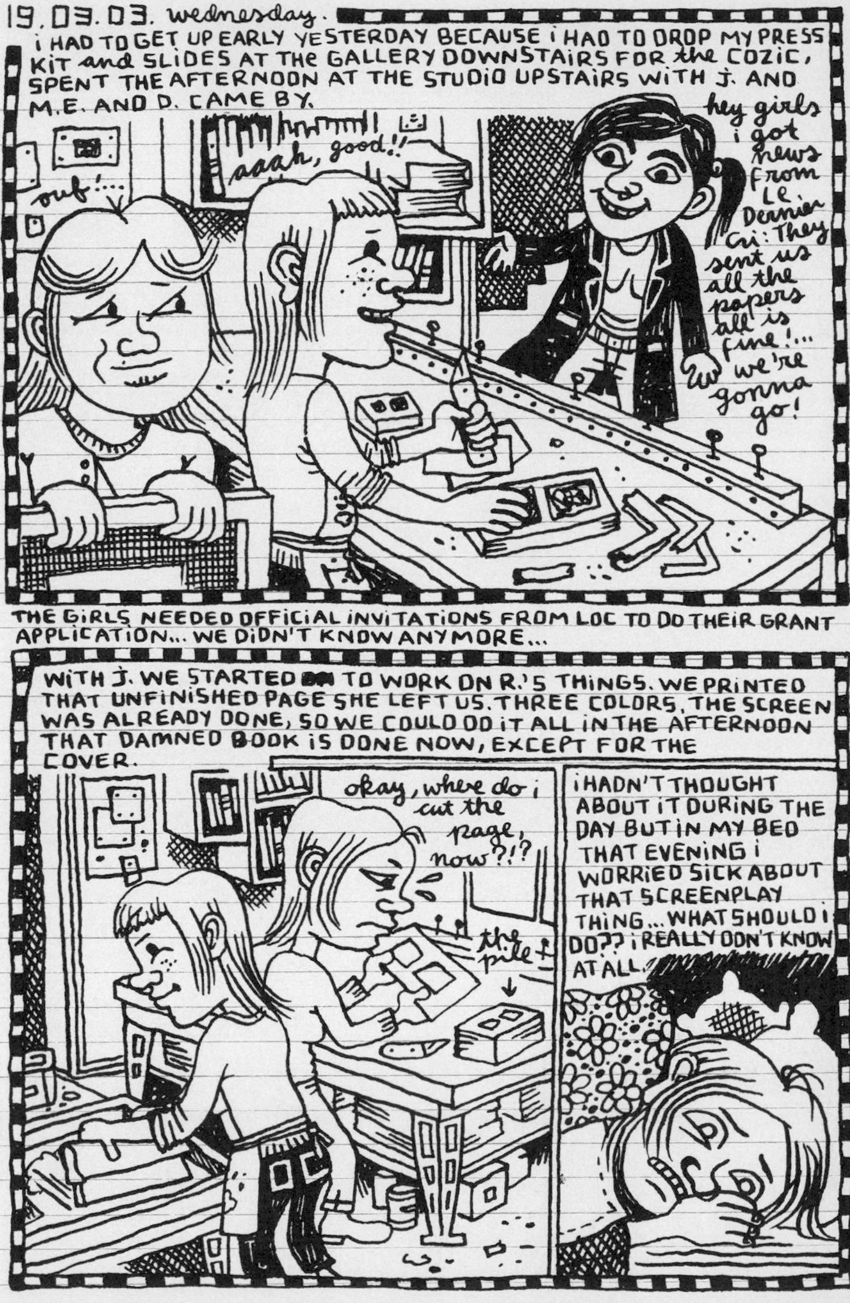
19.03.03. wednesday.
i HAD TO GET UP EARLY YESTERDAY BECAUSE i HAD TO DROP MY PRESS KIT and SLIDES AT THE GALLERY DOWNSTAIRS FOR the COZIC, SPENT THE AFTERNOON AT THE STUDIO UPSTAIRS WITH J. AND M.E. AND D. CAME BY.
ouf!...
aaah, good!!
hey girls i got news from Le Dernier Cri: They sent us all the papers all is fine!... we're gonna go!
THE GIRLS NEEDED OFFICIAL INVITATIONS FROM LOC TO DO THEIR GRANT APPLICATION... WE DIDN'T KNOW ANYMORE...
WITH J. WE STARTED TO WORK ON R.'S THINGS. WE PRINTED THAT UNFINISHED PAGE SHE LEFT US. THREE COLORS, THE SCREEN WAS ALREADY DONE, SO WE COULD DO IT ALL IN THE AFTERNOON THAT DAMNED BOOK IS DONE NOW, EXCEPT FOR THE COVER.
okay, where do i cut the page, now?!?
the pile!
i HADN'T THOUGHT ABOUT iT DURING THE DAY BUT iN MY BED THAT EVENING i WORRIED SICK ABOUT THAT SCREENPLAY THiNG... WHAT SHOULD i DO?? i REALLY DON'T KNOW AT ALL.

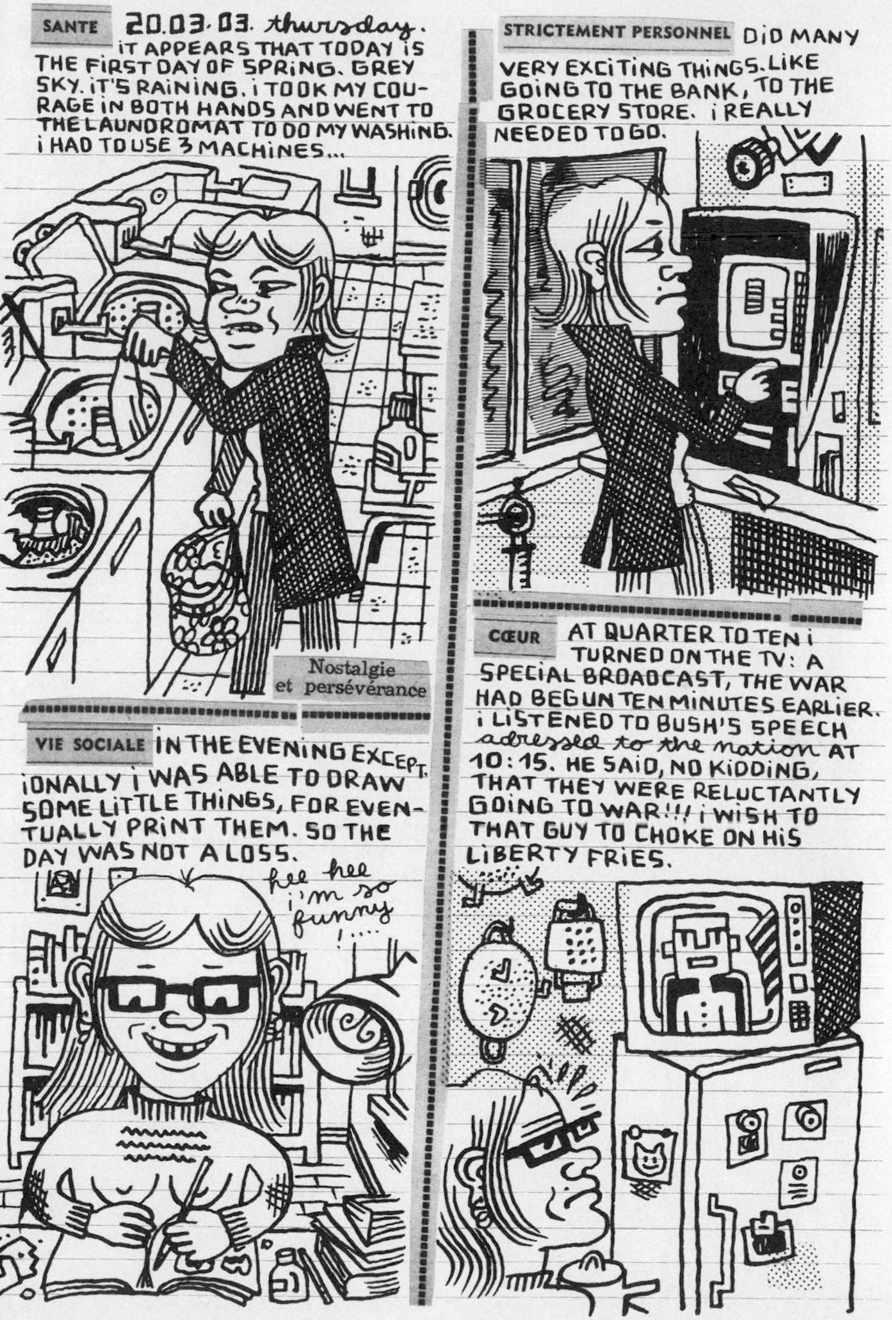
SANTE
20.03.03. thursday.
IT APPEARS THAT TODAY IS THE FIRST DAY OF SPRING. GREY SKY. IT'S RAINING. I TOOK MY COURAGE IN BOTH HANDS AND WENT TO THE LAUNDROMAT TO DO MY WASHING. I HAD TO USE 3 MACHINES...
STRICTEMENT PERSONNEL
DID MANY VERY EXCITING THINGS. LIKE GOING TO THE BANK, TO THE GROCERY STORE. I REALLY NEEDED TO GO.
Nostalgie et persévérance
VIE SOCIALE
IN THE EVENING EXCEPTIONALLY I WAS ABLE TO DRAW SOME LITTLE THINGS, FOR EVENTUALLY PRINT THEM. SO THE DAY WAS NOT A LOSS.
hee hee i'm so funny !....
CŒUR
AT QUARTER TO TEN I TURNED ON THE TV: A SPECIAL BROADCAST, THE WAR HAD BEGUN TEN MINUTES EARLIER. I LISTENED TO BUSH'S SPEECH adressed to the nation AT 10:15. HE SAID, NO KIDDING, THAT THEY WERE RELUCTANTLY GOING TO WAR!!! I WISH TO THAT GUY TO CHOKE ON HIS LIBERTY FRIES.

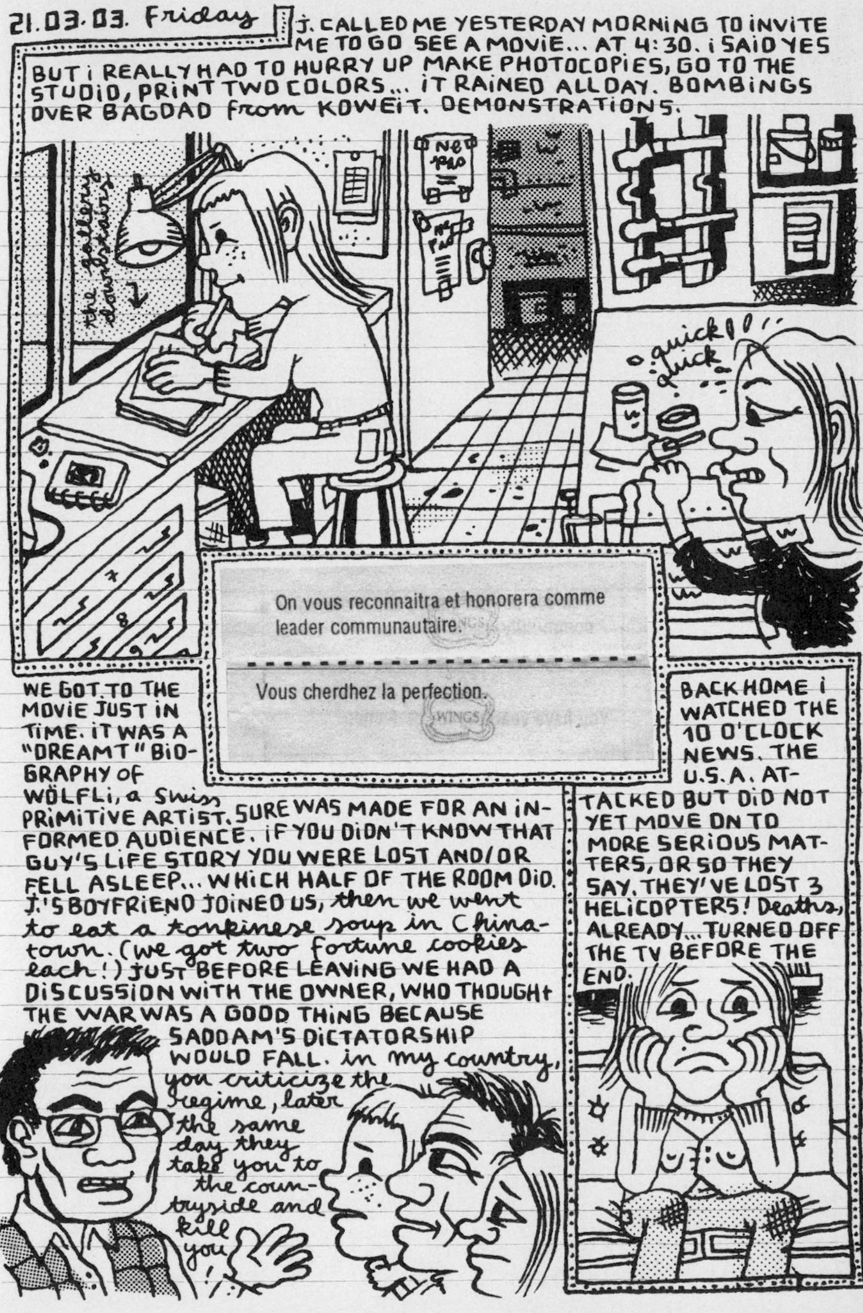
21.03.03. Friday
J. CALLED ME YESTERDAY MORNING TO INVITE ME TO GO SEE A MOVIE... AT 4:30. i SAID YES BUT i REALLY HAD TO HURRY UP MAKE PHOTOCOPIES, GO TO THE STUDIO, PRINT TWO COLORS... iT RAINED ALLDAY. BOMBINGS OVER BAGDAD from KOWEiT. DEMONSTRATIONS.
the gallery downstairs
quick!! quick
On vous reconnaitra et honorera comme leader communautaire.
Vous cherdhez la perfection.
WE GOT TO THE MOVIE JUST IN TIME. iT WAS A "DREAMT" BIOGRAPHY OF WÖLFLi, a Swiss PRIMITIVE ARTIST. SURE WAS MADE FOR AN iNFORMED AUDIENCE. iF YOU DIDN'T KNOW THAT GUY'S LIFE STORY YOU WERE LOST AND/OR FELL ASLEEP... WHICH HALF OF THE ROOM DID. J.'S BOYFRIEND JOINED US, then we went to eat a tonkinese soup in Chinatown. (we got two fortune cookies each!) JUST BEFORE LEAVING WE HAD A DISCUSSION WITH THE OWNER, WHO THOUGHT THE WAR WAS A GOOD THING BECAUSE SADDAM'S DICTATORSHIP WOULD FALL. in my country, you criticize the regime, later the same day they take you to the countryside and kill you!
BACK HOME i WATCHED THE 10 O'CLOCK NEWS. THE U.S.A. ATTACKED BUT DID NOT YET MOVE ON TO MORE SERIOUS MATTERS, OR SO THEY SAY. THEY'VE LOST 3 HELICOPTERS! Deaths, ALREADY... TURNED OFF THE TV BEFORE THE END.

22.03.03. saturday

WAS SUPPOSED TO DO SOMETHING WITH MY MOM TODAY BUT THANK GOD THE WEATHER IS NOT GOOD AT ALL. BECAUSE THE SNOW IS TOO WET FOR SKI SHE WANTED TO SNOW SHOE, NOTHING IS GOING TO STOP HER. WENT TO GRAFF TO PRINT, YESTER-DAY...

I TALKED TO C. IN THE EVENING. HE HAD SOME NEWS FROM "GOD SPEED YOU BLACK EMPEROR" (A MTV BAND) WHO ARE ON TOUR IN THE STATES. SO IN ST-LOUIS IN A GAS station SOMEBODY CALLED THE POLICE ON THEM THINKING THEY WERE TERRORISTS! 20 POLICE cars SHOWED UP and SUR-ROUNDED THEM and poin-ted their GUNS at them. Then the FBI arrived and

they kind of figured out that it was a mistake, THAT THEY WERE ONLY A BAND ON TOUR. THE MANAGER OF the GEORGES LENIN-GRAD IS JUST BACK FROM TEXAS: there is no more alcohol made in France in the bars!... they emptied all the bott-les of wine in the rivers... are beating up all the french guys in town... IT'S SICK. ON THE NEWS: A BROADCAST OF THE WAR. THEY SHOW THE SAME EXPLOSION IMAGES OF BAGDAD OVER AND OVER AGAIN. IT'S SO OBSCENE... THEY SPARE NOTHING, NOW, APPARENTLY LAND troops are waiting at the Irak frontier....

23.03.03. sunday.

I DREW ALL DAY YESTERDAY, STUFF TO SILKSCREEN PRINT. THANK GOD IT RAINED ALL DAY, SO I GOT TO SEE MY MOM ONLY IN THE EVENING, FOR DINNER... GOT BACK HOME TOO LATE FOR THE NEWS FOR SURE THE BOMBS ARE STILL FALLING....

lolita lopé

kickers

24.03.03. monday. DIDN'T HAVE TIME TO DO ANYTHING YESTERDAY.
I HAD TO MEET MY DAD AND M. AT A MOVIE THEATER. WE WENT TO SEE
"THE HOURS", DUBBED IN FRENCH AND AT ONE IN THE AFTERNOON.
THE FILM WAS RATHER GOOD, BUT NOT VERY HAPPY. LATER WE
WALKED ALL THE WAY TO M.'S PLACE (an hour walk), TO GO HAVE
DINNER... AT 6 WITH MY DAD WE WATCHED THE NEWS: A BAD DAY FOR
THE U.S.A. THEY SHOT DOWN A BRITISH PLANE BY MISTAKE, THINKING
IT WAS A MISSILE! WHAT ABOUT THE SUPER HIGH-PRECISION
OF ALL THEIR SUPERMODERN WEAPONS, UH!??... ALSO, ABOUT a
DOZEN OF AMERICAN SOLDIERS FELL INTO AN AMBUSH. THE
ONES WHO WERE NOT KILLED ENDED UP BEING ON IRAK TV (i
don't tell the story very well, they show images of the
dead, they interview the living ones) "WHAT'S YOUR NAME?
WHY DID YOU COME HERE? TO KILL IRAKI PEOPLE?" THE POOR
SOLDIERS WERE PETRIFIED WITH FEAR, SHITTING IN THEIR
PANTS. the U.S.A. asked everybody to not show those
images on TV... BUT, THE HERO OF THE DAY CERTAINLY WAS
MICHAEL MOORE, AT THE OSCAR CEREMONY, who yelled,
before they could cut him off:

SHAME!! ON YOU MISTER PRESIDENT

(i didn't see it, but friends told me about it)

THAT EVENING I WAS GOING TO LA CASA DEL POPOLO to MEET D.
THERE WAS A DAME DARCY SHOW (i had met her once in
SAN DIEGO). D.D. AND FRIENDS GOT STUCK AT THE BORDER
FOR SO LONG, WE DIDN'T THINK THEY WOULD MAKE IT, BUT THEY
DID. SHE WAS PLAYING BANJO, accompanied by a guy with
a guitar. SHE SANG MURDER BALLADS and PIRATE SONGS.
I LIKED. WITH D. WE TALKED ABOUT
THE WAR WITH AN AMERICAN
FRIEND of hers (from the
band the CENTIMETERS) who
was doing the first part...
we hear a lot about the
paranoia in the states, but
to hear about it first hand!!
SHE WAS TELLING US SHE HAD to
be careful of what she says
all the time... INNOCENTLY
SHE ASKED IF IT WAS NOT LIKE
THAT HERE TOO!!...

dame darcy who looks just like her drawings

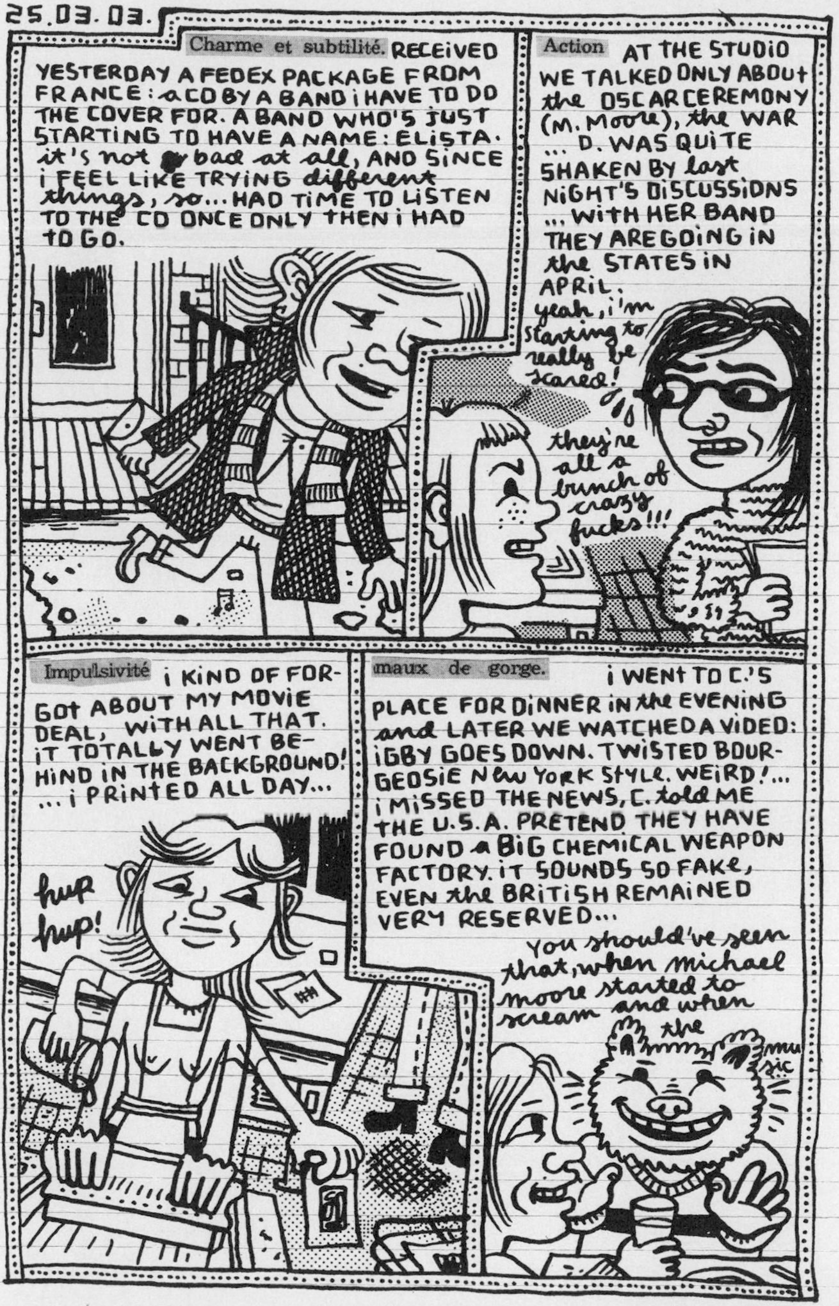
25.03.03.
Charme et subtilité. RECEIVED YESTERDAY A FEDEX PACKAGE FROM FRANCE: a CD BY A BAND i HAVE TO DO THE COVER FOR. A BAND WHO'S JUST STARTING TO HAVE A NAME: ELISTA. it's not bad at all, AND SINCE i FEEL LIKE TRYING different things, so... HAD TIME TO LISTEN TO THE CD ONCE ONLY THEN i HAD TO GO.
Action AT THE STUDIO WE TALKED ONLY ABOUT the OSCAR CEREMONY (M. Moore), the WAR ... D. WAS QUITE SHAKEN BY last NIGHT'S DISCUSSIONS ... WITH HER BAND THEY ARE GOING IN the STATES IN APRIL.
yeah, i'm starting to really be scared!
they're all a bunch of crazy fucks!!!
Impulsivité i KIND OF FORGOT ABOUT MY MOVIE DEAL, WITH ALL THAT. IT TOTALLY WENT BEHIND IN THE BACKGROUND! ... i PRINTED ALL DAY...
hup hup!
maux de gorge. i WENT TO C.'S PLACE FOR DINNER in the EVENING and LATER WE WATCHED A VIDEO: iGBY GOES DOWN. TWISTED BOURGEOSIE New York Style. WEIRD!... i MISSED THE NEWS, C. told ME THE U.S.A. PRETEND THEY HAVE FOUND a BIG CHEMICAL WEAPON FACTORY. IT SOUNDS SO FAKE, EVEN the BRITISH REMAINED VERY RESERVED...
You should've seen that, when Michael Moore started to scream and when the music

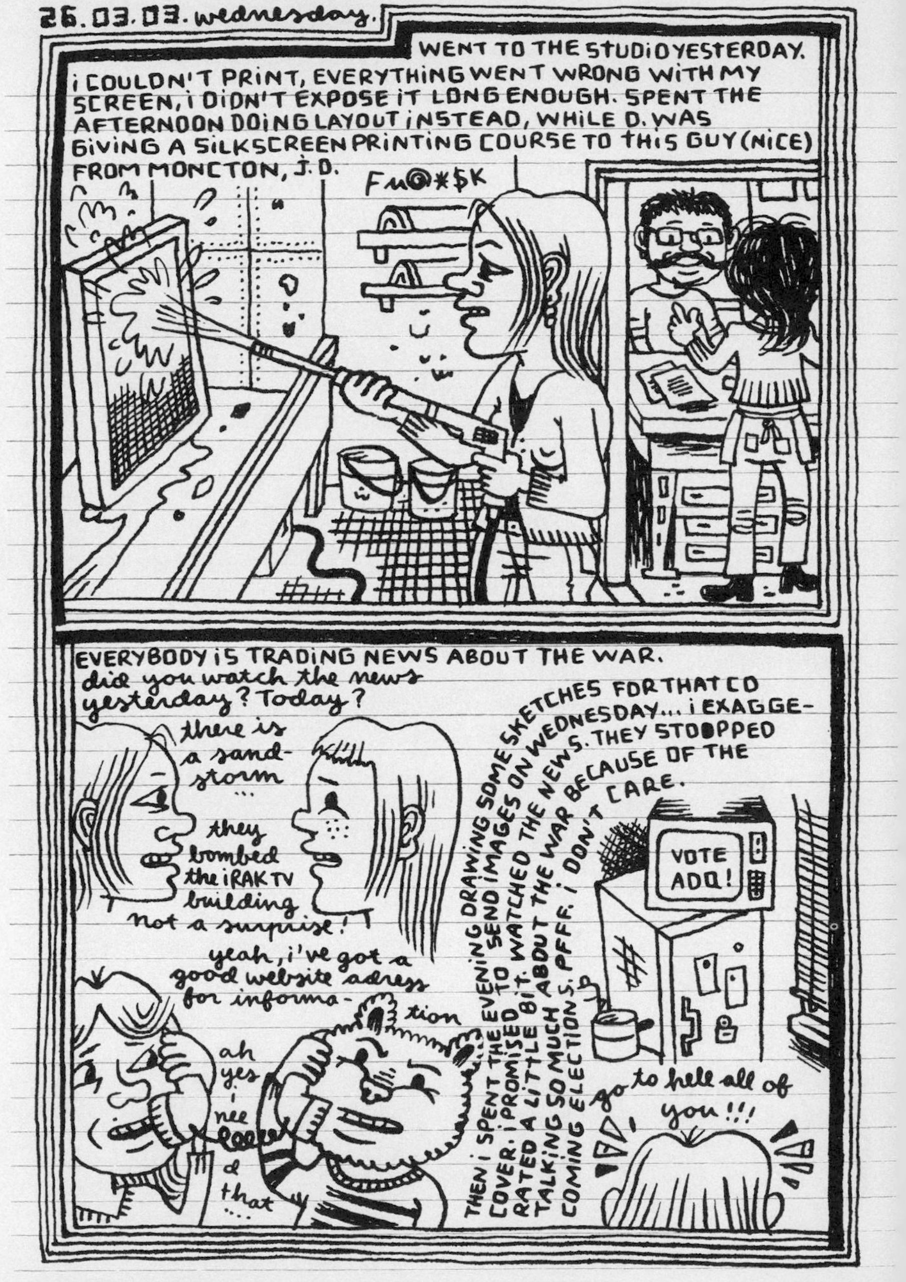
26.03.03. wednesday.
WENT TO THE STUDIO YESTERDAY.
i COULDN'T PRINT, EVERYTHING WENT WRONG WITH MY SCREEN, i DIDN'T EXPOSE IT LONG ENOUGH. SPENT THE AFTERNOON DOING LAYOUT iNSTEAD, WHiLE D. WAS GIVING A SILKSCREEN PRINTING COURSE TO THIS GUY (NICE) FROM MONCTON, J.D.
Fu@*$K
EVERYBODY iS TRADING NEWS ABOUT THE WAR.
did you watch the news yesterday? Today?
there is a sand-storm ...
they bombed the iRAK TV building
not a surprise!
yeah, i've got a good website adress for informa-tion
ah yes i nee d that ...
THEN i SPENT THE EVENING DRAWING SOME SKETCHES FOR THAT CD
COVER. i PROMISED TO SEND IMAGES ON WEDNESDAY... i EXAGGE-
RATED A LITTLE BIT. WATCHED THE NEWS. THEY STOPPED
TALKING SO MUCH ABOUT THE WAR BECAUSE OF THE
COMING ELECTIONS. PFFF. i DON'T CARE.
VOTE ADQ!
go to hell all of you!!!

27.03.03. thursday.

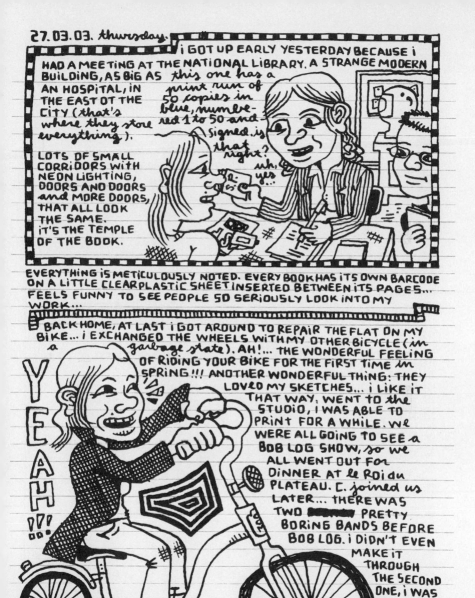

i GOT UP EARLY YESTERDAY BECAUSE i HAD A MEETING AT THE NATIONAL LIBRARY. A STRANGE MODERN BUILDING, AS BIG AS AN HOSPITAL, IN THE EAST OT THE CITY (that's where they store everything).

LOTS OF SMALL CORRIDORS WITH NEON LIGHTING, DOORS AND DOORS and MORE DOORS, THAT ALL LOOK THE SAME. iT'S THE TEMPLE OF THE BOOK.

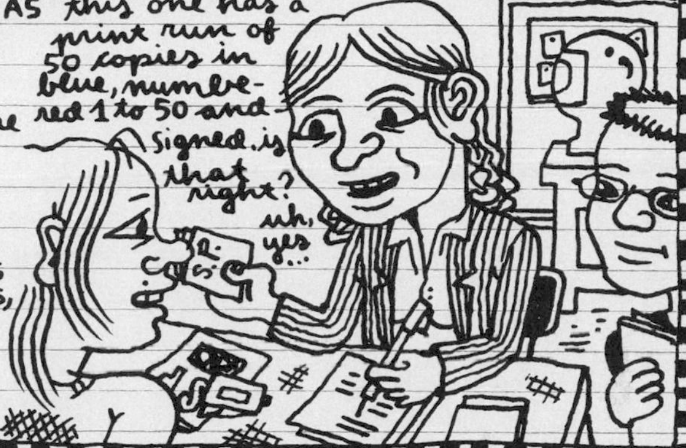
this one has a print run of 50 copies in blue, numbered 1 to 50 and signed. is that right?
uh, yes...

EVERYTHING IS METICULOUSLY NOTED. EVERY BOOK HAS ITS OWN BARCODE ON A LITTLE CLEAR PLASTIC SHEET INSERTED BETWEEN ITS PAGES... FEELS FUNNY TO SEE PEOPLE SO SERIOUSLY LOOK INTO MY WORK...

BACK HOME, AT LAST i GOT AROUND TO REPAIR THE FLAT ON MY BIKE... i EXCHANGED THE WHEELS WITH MY OTHER BICYCLE (in a garbage state). AH!... THE WONDERFUL FEELING OF RIDING YOUR BIKE FOR THE FIRST TIME in SPRING!!! ANOTHER WONDERFUL THING: THEY LOVED MY SKETCHES... i LIKE iT THAT WAY. WENT TO the STUDIO, i WAS ABLE TO PRINT FOR A WHILE. we WERE ALL GOING TO SEE a BOB LOG SHOW, so we ALL WENT OUT FOR DINNER AT le ROi du PLATEAU. C. joined us LATER... THERE WAS TWO [redacted] PRETTY BORING BANDS BEFORE BOB LOG. i DIDN'T EVEN MAKE iT THROUGH THE SECOND ONE, i WAS TOO TiRED. i WENT HOMe TO BED, C. too.

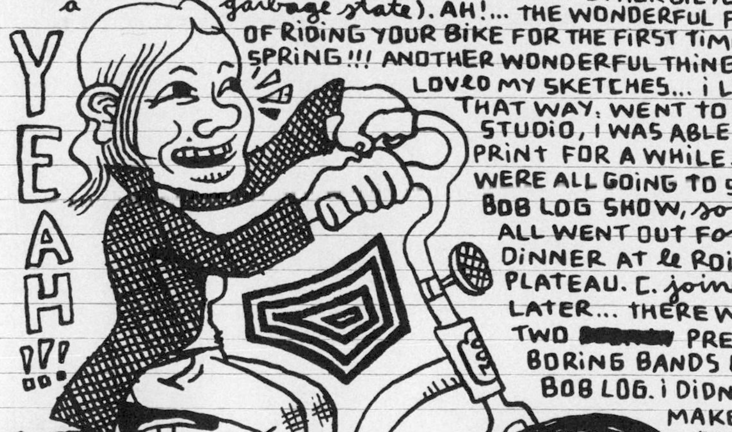
YEAH!!!

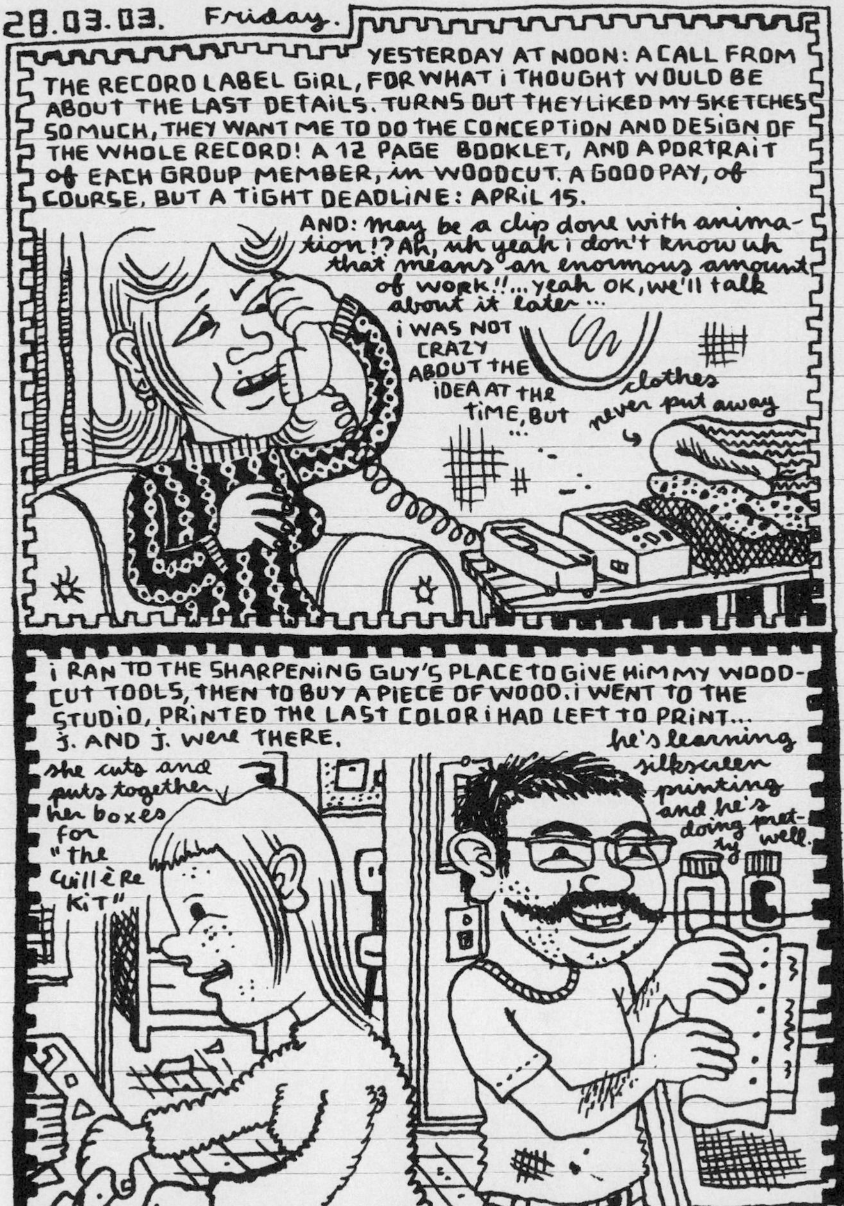
28.03.03. Friday.
YESTERDAY AT NOON: A CALL FROM THE RECORD LABEL GIRL, FOR WHAT i THOUGHT WOULD BE ABOUT THE LAST DETAILS. TURNS OUT THEY LIKED MY SKETCHES SO MUCH, THEY WANT ME TO DO THE CONCEPTION AND DESIGN OF THE WHOLE RECORD! A 12 PAGE BOOKLET, AND A PORTRAIT of EACH GROUP MEMBER, in WOODCUT. A GOOD PAY, of COURSE, BUT A TIGHT DEADLINE: APRIL 15.
AND: may be a clip done with animation!? Ah, uh yeah i don't know uh that means an enormous amount of work!! ... yeah OK, we'll talk about it later ...
i WAS NOT CRAZY ABOUT THE iDEA AT THE TiME, BUT ...
clothes never put away
i RAN TO THE SHARPENING GUY'S PLACE TO GIVE HIM MY WOODCUT TOOLS, THEN TO BUY A PIECE OF WOOD. i WENT TO THE STUDIO, PRINTED THE LAST COLOR i HAD LEFT TO PRINT... J. AND J. were THERE.
she cuts and puts together her boxes for "the Guillère Kit"
he's learning silkscreen printing and he's doing pretty well.

29.03.03. saturday.

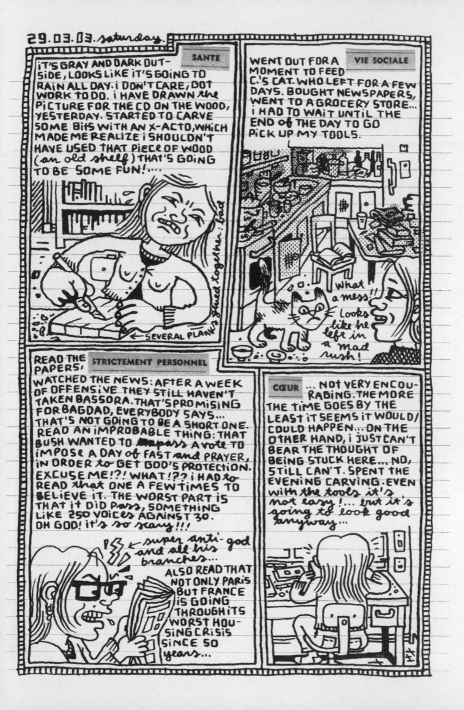

SANTE

iT'S GRAY AND DARK OUT-SIDE, LOOKS LiKE iT'S GOING TO RAIN ALL DAY. i DON'T CARE, BUT WORK TO DO. i HAVE DRAWN *the* PiCTURE FOR THE CD ON THE WOOD, YESTERDAY. STARTED TO CARVE SOME BiTS WiTH AN X-ACTO, WHiCH MADE ME REALiZE i SHOULDN'T HAVE USED THAT PiECE OF WOOD (*an old shelf*) THAT'S GOING TO BE SOME FUN!....

← SEVERAL PLANKS *glued together : bad*

VIE SOCIALE

WENT OUT FOR A MOMENT TO FEED C.'S CAT. WHO LEFT FOR A FEW DAYS. BOUGHT NEWSPAPERS, WENT TO A GROCERY STORE... i HAD TO WAiT UNTIL THE END OF THE DAY TO GO PiCK UP MY TOOLS.

What a mess!! Looks like he left in a mad rush!

STRICTEMENT PERSONNEL

READ THE PAPERS, WATCHED THE NEWS: AFTER A WEEK OF OFFENSiVE THEY STILL HAVEN'T TAKEN BASSORA. THAT'S PROMiSiNG FOR BAGDAD, EVERYBODY SAYS... THAT'S NOT GOING TO BE A SHORT ONE. READ AN iMPROBABLE THiNG: THAT BUSH WANTED TO ~~impass~~ PASS A VOTE TO iMPOSE A DAY OF FAST *and* PRAYER, iN ORDER ~~to~~ *to* GET GOD'S PROTECTiON. EXCUSE ME!?! WHAT!?? i HAD *to* READ *that* ONE A FEW TiMES TO BELiEVE iT. THE WORST PART iS THAT iT DiD *pass*, SOMETHiNG LiKE 250 VOiCES AGAINST 30. OH GOD! *it's so scary!!!*

super anti-god and all his branches...

ALSO READ THAT NOT ONLY PARiS BUT FRANCE iS GOING THROUGH iTS WORST HOU-SiNG CRiSiS SiNCE 50 *years...*

CŒUR

... NOT VERY ENCOU-RAGiNG. THE MORE THE TiME GOES BY THE LEAST iT SEEMS iT WOULD/ COULD HAPPEN... ON THE OTHER HAND, i JUST CAN'T BEAR THE THOUGHT OF BEiNG STUCK HERE... NO, STILL CAN'T. SPENT THE EVENiNG CARVING. EVEN *with the tools it's not easy!... but it's going to look good anyway...*

30.03.03. *sunday.*

iT RAINED ALL DAY YESTERDAY, i DIDN'T GO OUT AT ALL. i FEEL i'M ABOUT TO CATCH A COLD... iT'S BEEN A FEW DAYS i'M ABOUT TO GET SiCK. i CARVED MY PiECE OF WOOD A BiG PART OF THE DAY. i FiNiSHED THE JOB.

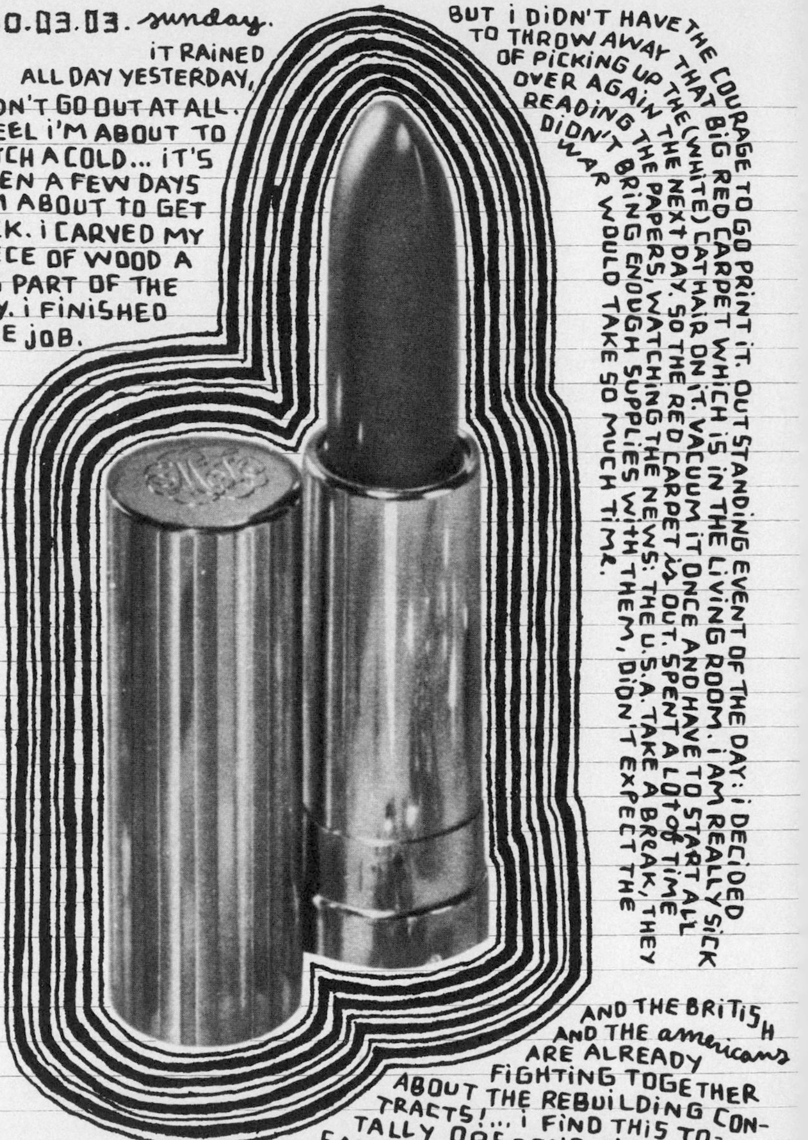

BUT i DiDN'T HAVE THE COURAGE TO GO PRiNT iT. OUTSTANDiNG EVENT OF THE DAY: i DECiDED TO THROW AWAY THAT BiG RED CARPET WHiCH iS iN THE LiViNG ROOM. i AM REALLY SiCK OF PiCKiNG UP THE (WHiTE) CAT HAiR ON iT. VACUUM iT ONCE AND HAVE TO START ALL OVER AGAiN THE NEXT DAY. SO THE RED CARPET is OUT. SPENT A LOT of TiME READiNG THE PAPERS, WATCHiNG THE NEWS: THE U.S.A. TAKE A BREAK, THEY DiDN'T BRiNG ENOUGH SUPPLiES WiTH THEM, DiDN'T EXPECT THE WAR WOULD TAKE SO MUCH TiME.

AND THE BRiTiSH AND THE *americans* ARE ALREADY FiGHTiNG TOGETHER ABOUT THE REBUiLDiNG CONTRACTS!... i FiND THiS TOTALLY OBSCENE. LiKE THEY SAY: FUCK YOU. DOESN'T THiS LOOK LiKE A MASSiVE DESTRUCTiON WEAPON?

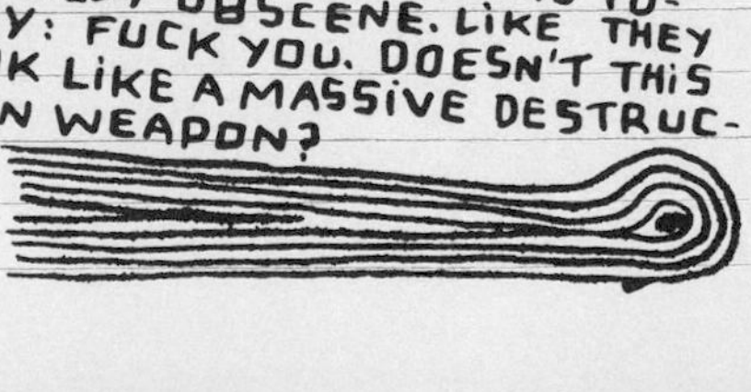

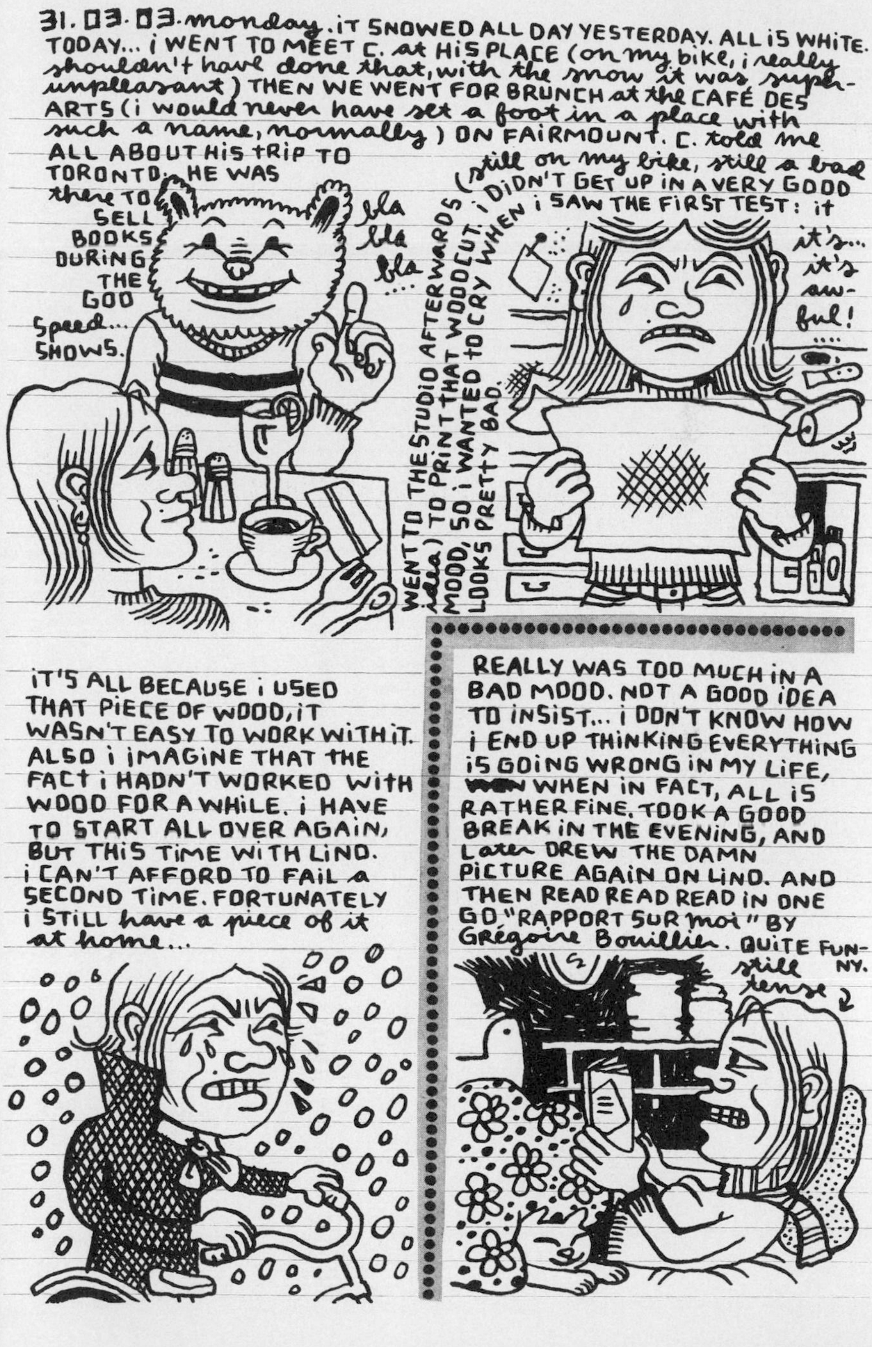
31. 03. 03. monday. IT SNOWED ALL DAY YESTERDAY. ALL IS WHITE. TODAY... i WENT TO MEET C. at HIS PLACE (on my bike, i really shouldn't have done that, with the snow it was super-unpleasant) THEN WE WENT FOR BRUNCH at the CAFÉ DES ARTS (i would never have set a foot in a place with such a name, normally) ON FAIRMOUNT. C. told me ALL ABOUT HIS TRIP TO TORONTO. HE WAS there to SELL BOOKS DURING THE GOD Speed... SHOWS.
bla bla bla...
WENT TO THE STUDIO AFTERWARDS (still on my bike, still a bad idea) TO PRINT THAT WOODCUT. i DIDN'T GET UP IN A VERY GOOD MOOD, SO i WANTED TO CRY WHEN i SAW THE FIRST TEST: it LOOKS PRETTY BAD.
it's... it's aw-ful!...
IT'S ALL BECAUSE i USED THAT PIECE OF WOOD, IT WASN'T EASY TO WORK WITH IT. ALSO i IMAGINE THAT THE FACT i HADN'T WORKED WITH WOOD FOR A WHILE. i HAVE TO START ALL OVER AGAIN, BUT THIS TIME WITH LINO. i CAN'T AFFORD TO FAIL a SECOND TIME. FORTUNATELY i STILL have a piece of it at home...
REALLY WAS TOO MUCH IN A BAD MOOD. NOT A GOOD IDEA TO INSIST... i DON'T KNOW HOW i END UP THINKING EVERYTHING IS GOING WRONG IN MY LIFE, WHEN IN FACT, ALL IS RATHER FINE. TOOK A GOOD BREAK IN THE EVENING, AND later DREW THE DAMN PICTURE AGAIN ON LINO. AND THEN READ READ READ IN ONE GO "RAPPORT SUR moi" BY Grégoire Bouillier. QUITE FUN-NY.
still tense?

avril 2003

sun	mon	tue	wed	thu	fri	sat
		1	2	3	4	5
6	7	8	9	10	11	12
13	14	15	16	17	18	19
20	21	22	23	24	25	26
27	28	29	30			

01.04.03. *tuesday*. i DiDN'T GO OUT AT ALL YESTERDAY. i SPENT THE DAY CARViNG THE LiNO. i HAD SOME CATCHiNG UP TO DO... SPOKE TO THE GiRL FROM THE RECORD LABEL. THERE WAS A TiNY LiTTLE LAST MiNUTE CHANGE TO DO: TO TAKE OUT THE LiTTLE SLiT i HAD DRAWN ON THE GiRL'S PANTiES... iT'S THE GUYS FROM THE BAND, WHO HAD SPENT THE WEEK-END SHOWiNG THE iMAGE TO THEiR FRiENDS, AND THAT'S ALL THE FRiENDS WOULD SEE: THE SLiT! SO THEY DECiDED iT SHOULD DiSAPPEAR. FRANKLY, FRANCE WAS REALLY THE LAST PLACE *in the* WORLD i EXPECTED THAT KiND OF CENSORSHiP FROM!... *And for a tiny little slit!...* TSK...

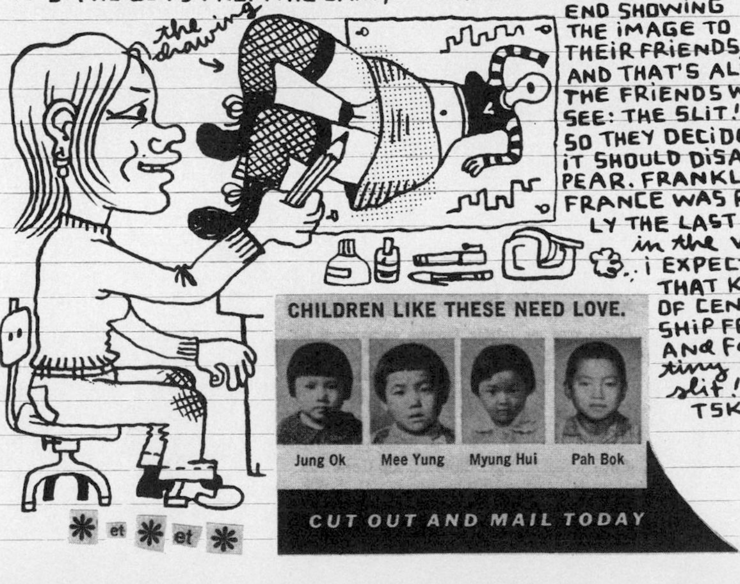
the drawing
et et
CHILDREN LIKE THESE NEED LOVE.
Jung Ok
Mee Yung
Myung Hui
Pah Bok
CUT OUT AND MAIL TODAY

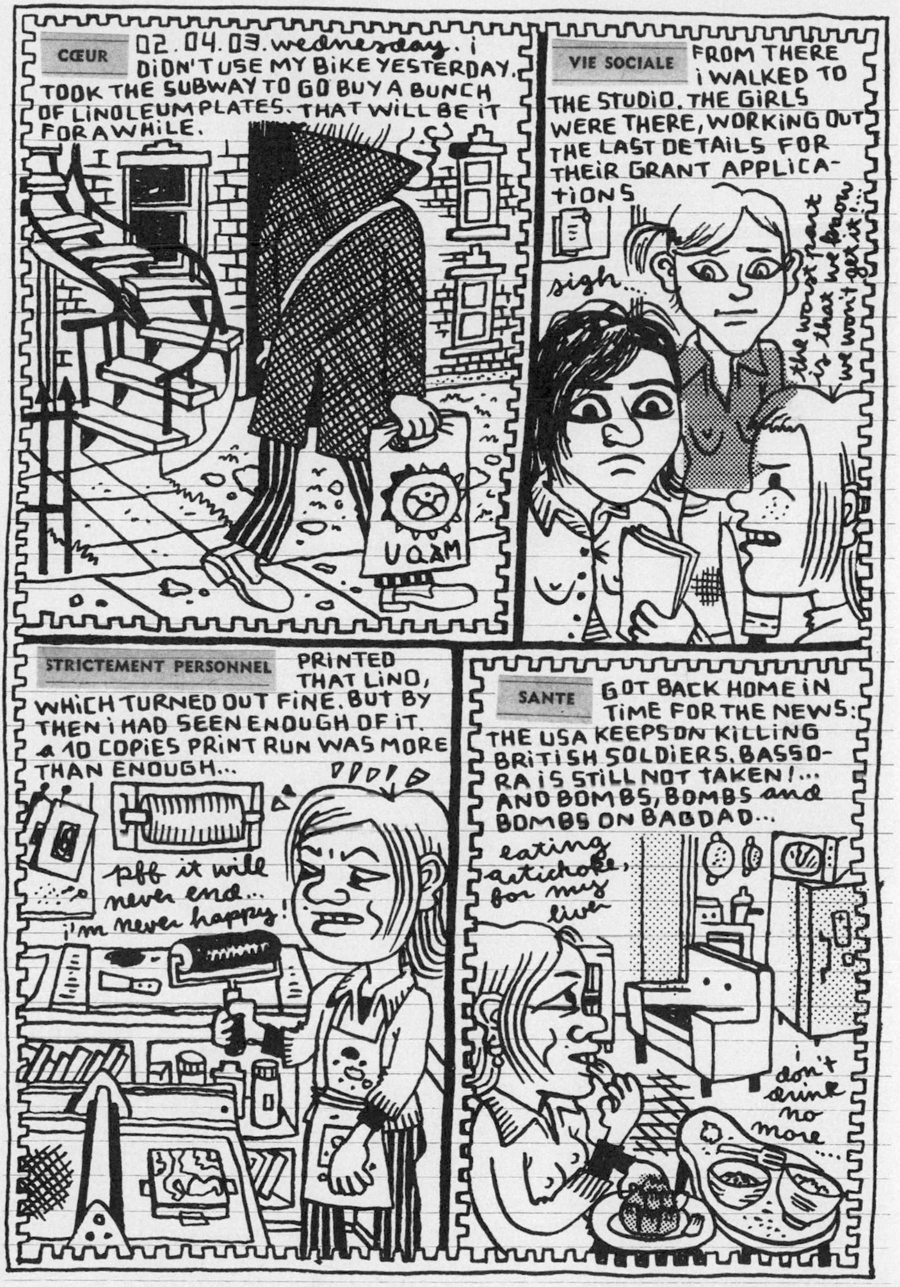
CŒUR
02.04.03. wednesday. i DIDN'T USE MY BIKE YESTERDAY. TOOK THE SUBWAY TO GO BUY A BUNCH OF LINOLEUM PLATES. THAT WILL BE IT FOR A WHILE.
UQAM
VIE SOCIALE
FROM THERE i WALKED TO THE STUDIO. THE GIRLS WERE THERE, WORKING OUT THE LAST DETAILS FOR THEIR GRANT APPLICATIONS
sigh...
the worst part is that we know we won't get it...
STRICTEMENT PERSONNEL
PRINTED THAT LINO, WHICH TURNED OUT FINE. BUT BY THEN i HAD SEEN ENOUGH OF IT. a 10 COPIES PRINT RUN WAS MORE THAN ENOUGH...
pff it will never end... i'm never happy!
SANTE
GOT BACK HOME IN TIME FOR THE NEWS: THE USA KEEPS ON KILLING BRITISH SOLDIERS. BASSORA IS STILL NOT TAKEN!... AND BOMBS, BOMBS and BOMBS ON BAGDAD...
eating artichoke, for my liver
i don't drink no more...

03.04.03. thursday

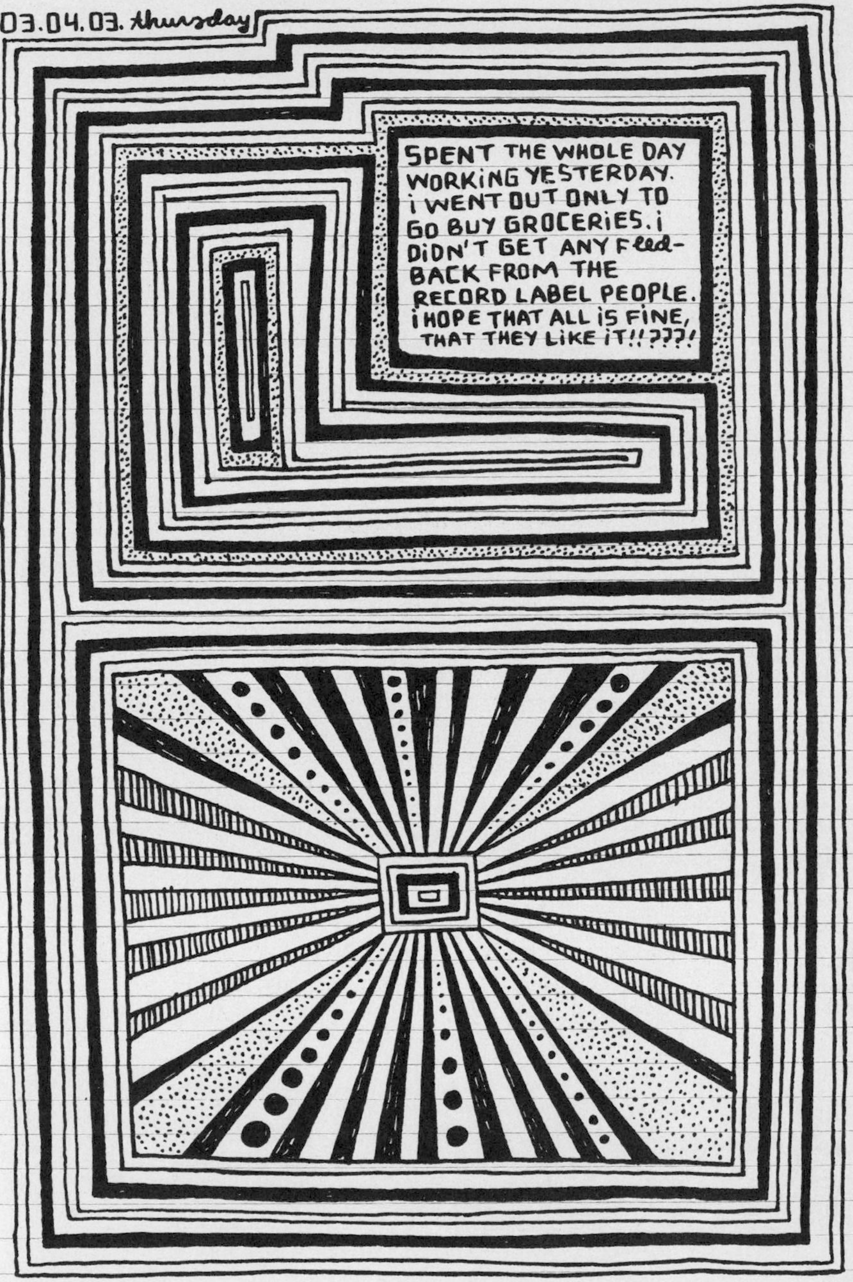
SPENT THE WHOLE DAY WORKiNG YESTERDAY. i WENT OUT ONLY TO GO BUY GROCERiES. i DiDN'T GET ANY Feed-BACK FROM THE RECORD LABEL PEOPLE. i HOPE THAT ALL iS FiNE, THAT THEY LiKE iT!! ???!

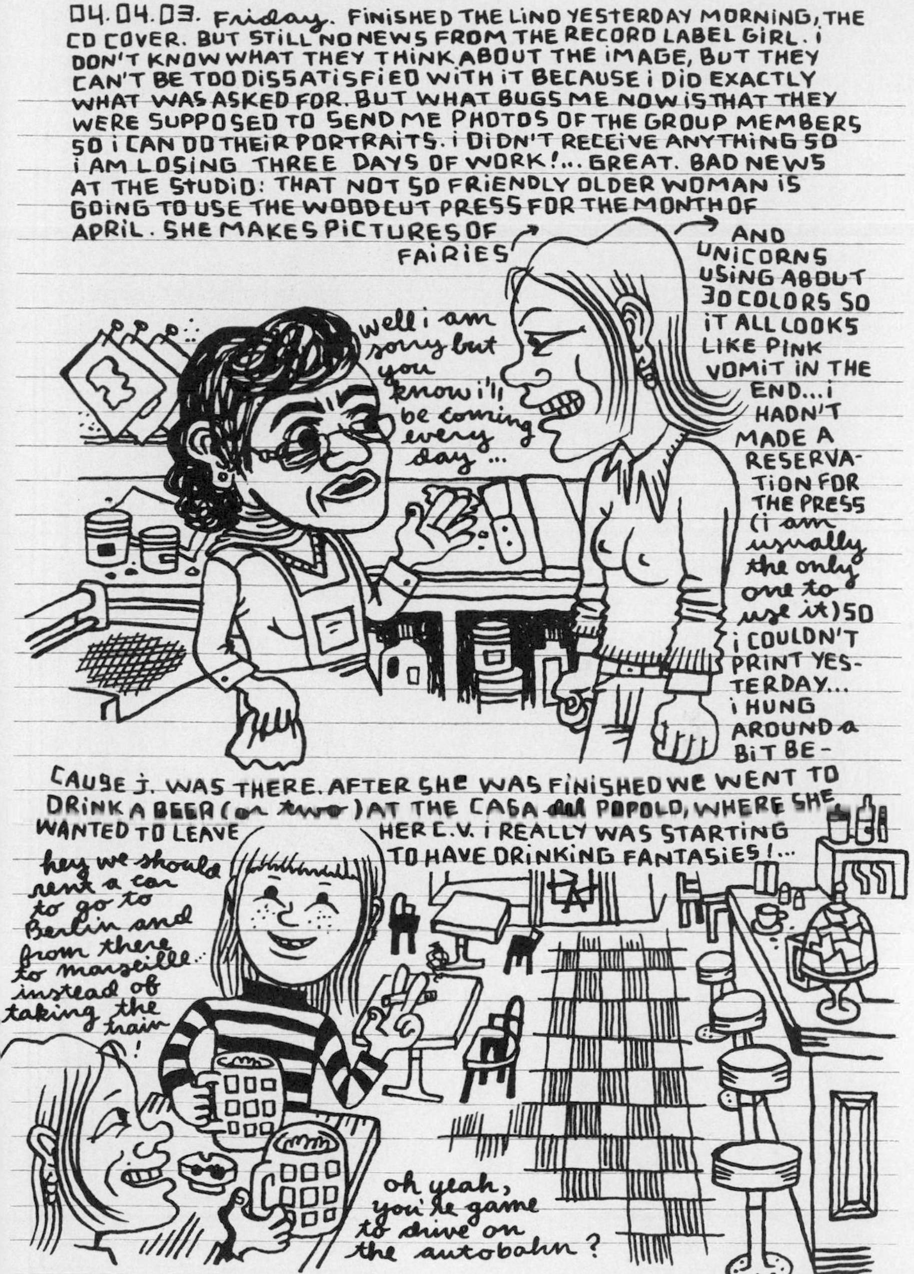
04.04.03. Friday. FINISHED THE LINO YESTERDAY MORNING, THE CD COVER. BUT STILL NO NEWS FROM THE RECORD LABEL GIRL. i DON'T KNOW WHAT THEY THINK ABOUT THE iMAGE, BUT THEY CAN'T BE TOO DISSATISFIED WITH iT BECAUSE i DID EXACTLY WHAT WAS ASKED FOR. BUT WHAT BUGS ME NOW iS THAT THEY WERE SUPPOSED TO SEND ME PHOTOS OF THE GROUP MEMBERS SO i CAN DO THEiR PORTRAiTS. i DiDN'T RECEiVE ANYTHiNG SO i AM LOSiNG THREE DAYS OF WORK!... GREAT. BAD NEWS AT THE STUDiO: THAT NOT SO FRiENDLY OLDER WOMAN iS GOiNG TO USE THE WOODCUT PRESS FOR THE MONTH OF APRiL. SHE MAKES PiCTURES OF FAiRiES AND UNiCORNS USiNG ABOUT 30 COLORS SO iT ALL LOOKS LIKE PiNK VOMiT iN THE END... i HADN'T MADE A RESERVATiON FOR THE PRESS (i am usually the only one to use it) SO i COULDN'T PRiNT YESTERDAY... i HUNG AROUND a BiT BECAUSE J. WAS THERE. AFTER SHE WAS FiNiSHED WE WENT TO DRiNK A BEER (or two) AT THE CASA del POPOLO, WHERE SHE WANTED TO LEAVE HER C.V. i REALLY WAS STARTiNG TO HAVE DRiNKiNG FANTASiES!...
well i am sorry but you know i'll be coming every day...
hey we should rent a car to go to Berlin and from there to marseille... instead of taking the train!
oh yeah, you're game to drive on the autobahn?

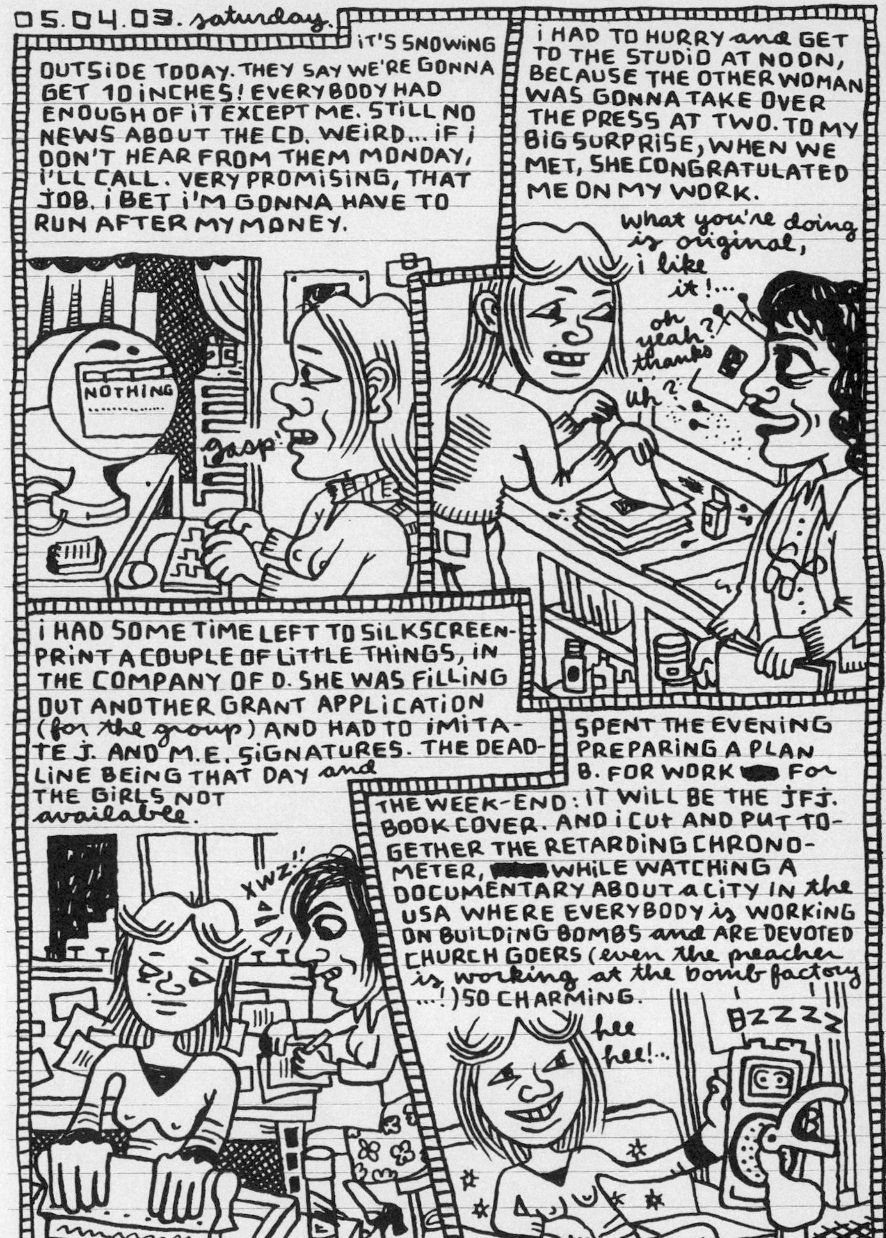
05.04.03. saturday.
IT'S SNOWING OUTSIDE TODAY. THEY SAY WE'RE GONNA GET 10 INCHES! EVERYBODY HAD ENOUGH OF IT EXCEPT ME. STILL NO NEWS ABOUT THE CD. WEIRD... IF I DON'T HEAR FROM THEM MONDAY, I'LL CALL. VERY PROMISING, THAT JOB. I BET I'M GONNA HAVE TO RUN AFTER MY MONEY.
NOTHING
gasp!
I HAD TO HURRY and GET TO THE STUDIO AT NOON, BECAUSE THE OTHER WOMAN WAS GONNA TAKE OVER THE PRESS AT TWO. TO MY BIG SURPRISE, WHEN WE MET, SHE CONGRATULATED ME ON MY WORK.
what you're doing is original, i like it!...
oh yeah? thanks
uh?
I HAD SOME TIME LEFT TO SILKSCREEN-PRINT A COUPLE OF LITTLE THINGS, IN THE COMPANY OF D. SHE WAS FILLING OUT ANOTHER GRANT APPLICATION (for the group) AND HAD TO IMITATE J. AND M.E. SIGNATURES. THE DEADLINE BEING THAT DAY and THE GIRLS NOT available.
XWZ!!
SPENT THE EVENING PREPARING A PLAN B. FOR WORK [redacted] FOR THE WEEK-END: IT WILL BE THE JFJ. BOOK COVER. AND I CUT AND PUT TOGETHER THE RETARDING CHRONOMETER, [redacted] WHILE WATCHING A DOCUMENTARY ABOUT a CITY IN the USA WHERE EVERYBODY is WORKING ON BUILDING BOMBS and ARE DEVOTED CHURCH GOERS (even the preacher is working at the bomb factory ...!) SO CHARMING.
hee hee!...
BZZZZ

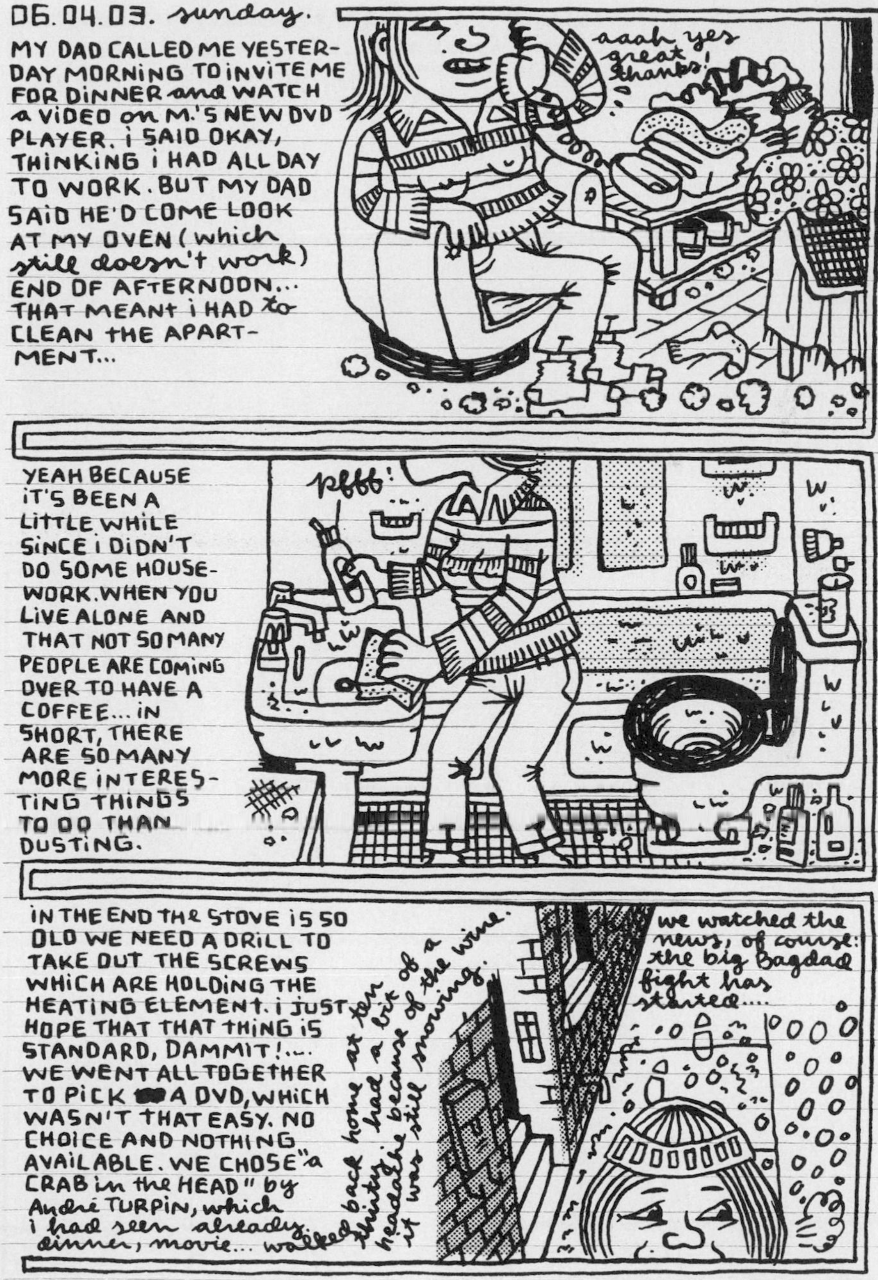
06.04.03. sunday.
MY DAD CALLED ME YESTERDAY MORNING TO INVITE ME FOR DINNER and WATCH a VIDEO on M.'S NEW DVD PLAYER. i SAID OKAY, THINKING i HAD ALL DAY TO WORK. BUT MY DAD SAID HE'D COME LOOK AT MY OVEN (which still doesn't work) END OF AFTERNOON... THAT MEANT i HAD to CLEAN THE APARTMENT...
aaah yes great thanks!
YEAH BECAUSE iT'S BEEN A LITTLE WHILE SiNCE i DiDN'T DO SOME HOUSEWORK. WHEN YOU LiVE ALONE AND THAT NOT SO MANY PEOPLE ARE COMING OVER TO HAVE A COFFEE... in SHORT, THERE ARE SO MANY MORE iNTERESTiNG THINGS TO DO THAN DUSTiNG.
pfff!
iN THE END THE STOVE iS SO OLD WE NEED A DRILL TO TAKE OUT THE SCREWS WHICH ARE HOLDING THE HEATING ELEMENT. i JUST HOPE THAT THAT THiNG iS STANDARD, DAMMIT!... WE WENT ALL TOGETHER TO PiCK A DVD, WHICH WASN'T THAT EASY. NO CHOICE AND NOTHING AVAiLABLE. WE CHOSE "a CRAB in the HEAD" by André TURPiN, which i had seen already. dinner, movie... walked back home at ten of a thirty. had a bit of the wine headache because of the wine. it was still snowing.
we watched the news, of course: the big Bagdad fight has started....

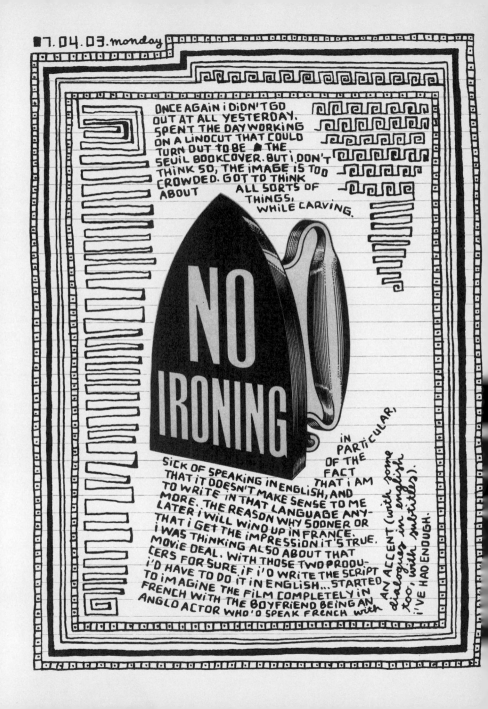

7.04.03. monday

ONCE AGAIN I DIDN'T GO OUT AT ALL YESTERDAY. SPENT THE DAY WORKING ON A LINOCUT THAT COULD TURN OUT TO BE THE SEUIL BOOKCOVER. BUT I DON'T THINK SO, THE IMAGE IS TOO CROWDED. GOT TO THINK ABOUT ALL SORTS OF THINGS, WHILE CARVING.

NO IRONING

SICK OF SPEAKING IN ENGLISH, AND IN PARTICULAR, OF THE FACT THAT I AM
THAT IT DOESN'T MAKE SENSE TO ME
TO WRITE IN THAT LANGUAGE ANY-
MORE. THE REASON WHY SOONER OR
LATER I WILL WIND UP IN FRANCE.
THAT I GET THE IMPRESSION IT'S TRUE.
I WAS THINKING ALSO ABOUT THAT
MOVIE DEAL. WITH THOSE TWO PRODU-
CERS FOR SURE IF I'D WRITE THE SCRIPT
I'D HAVE TO DO IT IN ENGLISH... STARTED
TO IMAGINE THE FILM COMPLETELY IN
FRENCH WITH THE BOYFRIEND BEING AN
ANGLO ACTOR WHO'D SPEAK FRENCH with
AN ACCENT (with some dialogues in english too, with subtitles).
I'VE HAD ENOUGH.

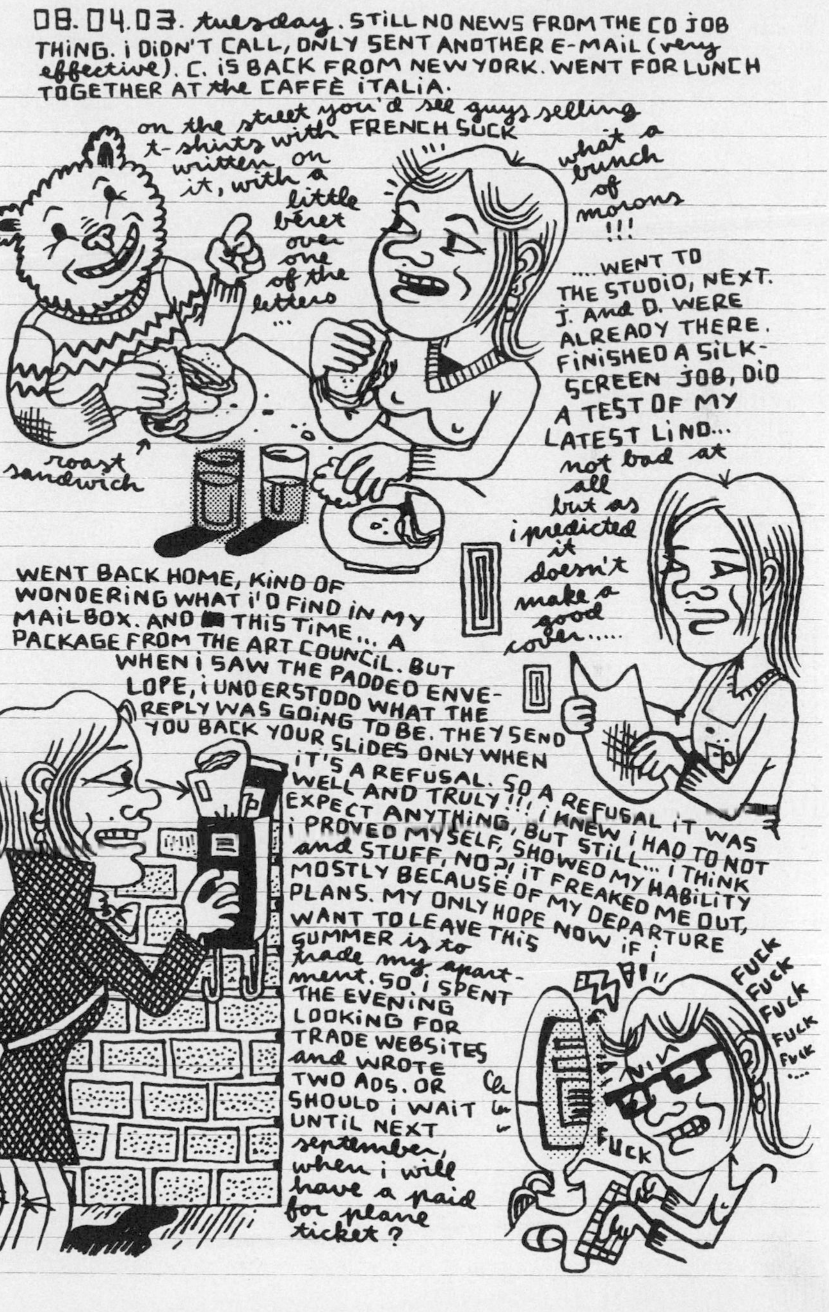
08.04.03. tuesday. STILL NO NEWS FROM THE CD JOB THING. i DIDN'T CALL, ONLY SENT ANOTHER E-MAIL (very effective). C. iS BACK FROM NEW YORK. WENT FOR LUNCH TOGETHER AT the CAFFÈ iTALiA.
on the street you'd see guys selling t-shirts with FRENCH SUCK written on it, with a little béret over one of the letters ...
what a bunch of morons !!!
roast sandwich
.... WENT TO THE STUDIO, NEXT. J. and D. WERE ALREADY THERE. FINISHED A SILK-SCREEN JOB, DID A TEST OF MY LATEST LINO...
not bad at all but as i predicted it doesn't make a good cover.....
WENT BACK HOME, KIND OF WONDERING WHAT i'D FIND IN MY MAILBOX. AND [redacted] THIS TIME... A PACKAGE FROM THE ART COUNCIL. BUT WHEN i SAW THE PADDED ENVE-LOPE, i UNDERSTOOD WHAT THE REPLY WAS GOING TO BE. THEY SEND YOU BACK YOUR SLIDES ONLY WHEN iT'S A REFUSAL. SO A REFUSAL iT WAS WELL AND TRULY!!! i KNEW i HAD TO NOT EXPECT ANYTHING, BUT STILL... i THINK i PROVED MYSELF, SHOWED MY HABILITY and STUFF, NO?! iT FREAKED ME OUT, MOSTLY BECAUSE OF MY DEPARTURE PLANS. MY ONLY HOPE NOW iF i WANT TO LEAVE THIS SUMMER is to trade my apart-ment. SO i SPENT THE EVENING LOOKING FOR TRADE WEBSITES and WROTE TWO ADS. OR SHOULD i WAIT UNTIL NEXT september, when i will have a paid for plane ticket?
FUCK
FUCK
FUCK
FUCK
FUCK ....
FUCK

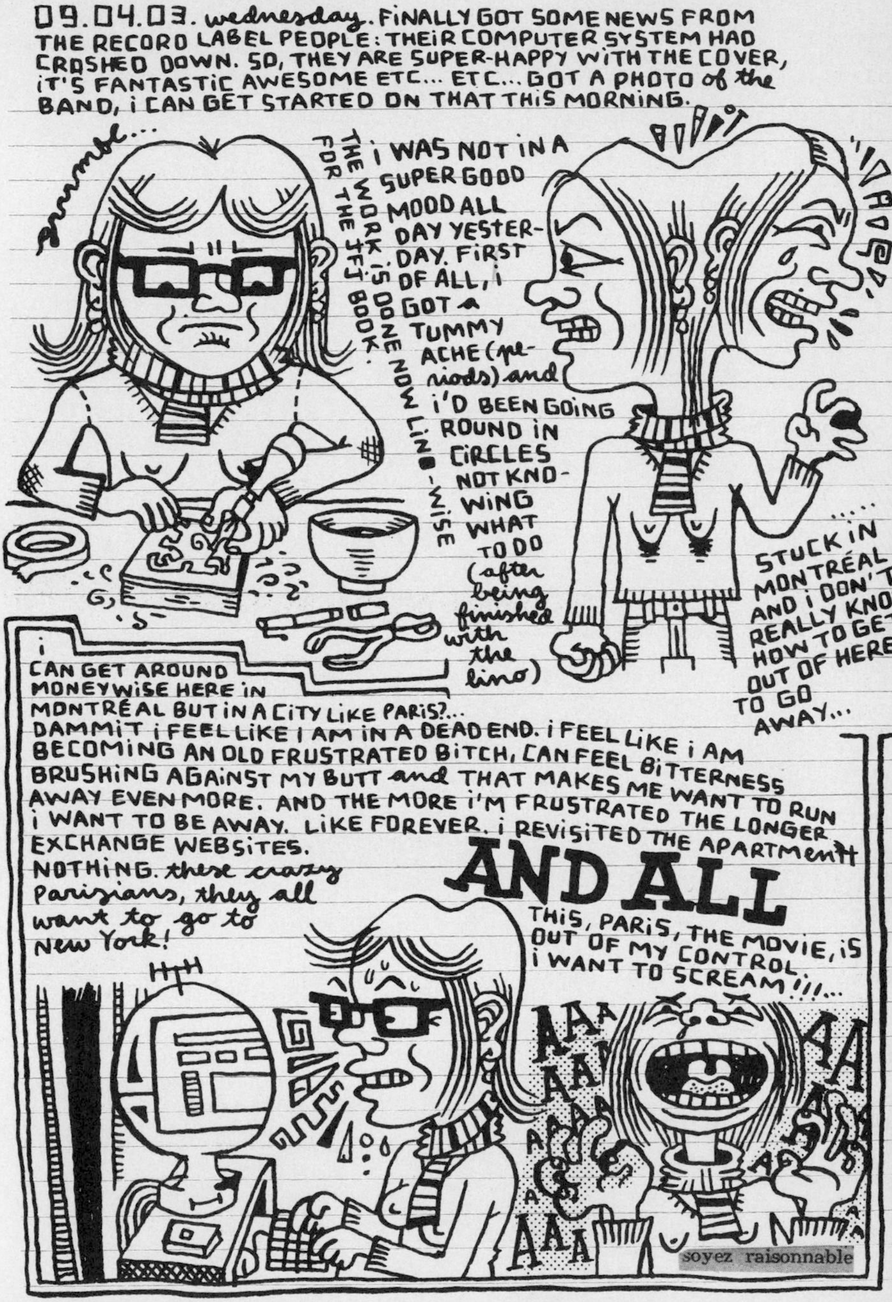

09.04.03. wednesday. FINALLY GOT SOME NEWS FROM THE RECORD LABEL PEOPLE: THEIR COMPUTER SYSTEM HAD CRASHED DOWN. SO, THEY ARE SUPER-HAPPY WITH THE COVER, IT'S FANTASTIC AWESOME ETC... ETC... GOT A PHOTO of the BAND, I CAN GET STARTED ON THAT THIS MORNING.
grrrrmble...
THE WORK IS DONE NOW LINO-WISE FOR THE JFJ BOOK.
I WAS NOT IN A SUPER GOOD MOOD ALL DAY YESTERDAY. FIRST OF ALL, I GOT a TUMMY ACHE (periods) and I'D BEEN GOING ROUND IN CIRCLES NOT KNOWING WHAT TO DO (after being finished with the lino)
..... STUCK IN MONTRÉAL AND I DON'T REALLY KNOW HOW TO GET OUT OF HERE, TO GO AWAY...
I CAN GET AROUND MONEYWISE HERE IN MONTRÉAL BUT IN A CITY LIKE PARIS?... DAMMIT I FEEL LIKE I AM IN A DEAD END. I FEEL LIKE I AM BECOMING AN OLD FRUSTRATED BITCH, CAN FEEL BITTERNESS BRUSHING AGAINST MY BUTT and THAT MAKES ME WANT TO RUN AWAY EVEN MORE. AND THE MORE I'M FRUSTRATED THE LONGER I WANT TO BE AWAY. LIKE FOREVER. I REVISITED THE APARTMENT EXCHANGE WEBSITES.
NOTHING. these crazy Parisians, they all want to go to New York!
AND ALL THIS, PARIS, THE MOVIE, IS OUT OF MY CONTROL, I WANT TO SCREAM!!!...
AAAA
soyez raisonnable

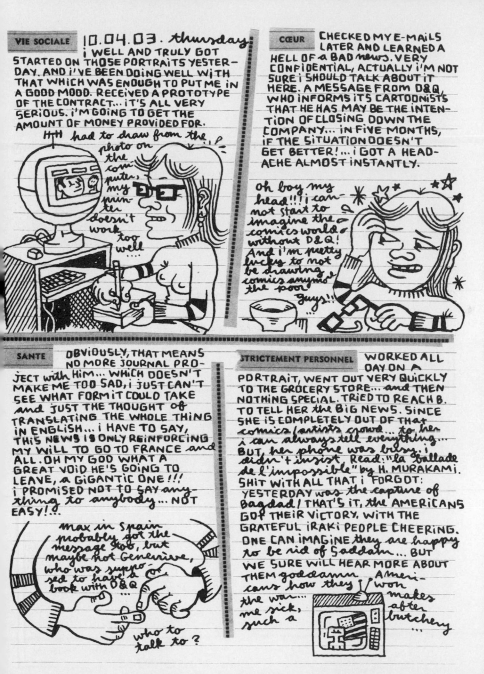

VIE SOCIALE — 10.04.03. thursday

i WELL AND TRULY GOT STARTED ON THOSE PORTRAITS YESTERDAY. AND i'VE BEEN DOING WELL WITH THAT WHICH WAS ENOUGH TO PUT ME iN A GOOD MOOD. RECEIVED A PROTOTYPE OF THE CONTRACT... iT'S ALL VERY SERIOUS. i'M GOING TO GET THE AMOUNT OF MONEY PROVIDED FOR.

HH had to draw from the photo on the computer, my printer doesn't work too well ....

CŒUR

CHECKED MY E-MAILS LATER AND LEARNED A HELL OF a BAD news. VERY CONFIDENTIAL, ACTUALLY i'M NOT SURE i SHOULD TALK ABOUT iT HERE. A MESSAGE FROM D&Q, WHO iNFORMS iTS CARTOONISTS THAT HE HAS MAY BE THE iNTENTiON OF CLOSING DOWN THE COMPANY... iN FIVE MONTHS, iF THE SiTUATiON DOESN'T GET BETTER!... i GOT A HEADACHE ALMOST iNSTANTLY.

Oh boy my head!!! i cannot start to imagine the comics world without D&Q! And i'm pretty lucky to not be drawing comics anymore the poor guys!!

SANTE

OBVIOUSLY, THAT MEANS NO MORE JOURNAL PROJECT with HiM... WHICH DOESN'T MAKE ME TOO SAD, i JUST CAN'T SEE WHAT FORM iT COULD TAKE and JUST THE THOUGHT of TRANSLATING THE WHOLE THiNG iN ENGLISH... i HAVE TO SAY, THiS NEWS iS ONLY REiNFORCiNG MY WiLL TO GO TO FRANCE and ALL. OH MY GOD WHAT A GREAT VOiD HE'S GOING TO LEAVE, a GiGANTiC ONE!!! i PROMISED NOT TO SAY anything to anybody... NOT EASY!..

max in Spain probably got the message too, but maybe not Geneviève, who was supposed to have a book with D&Q

who to talk to ?

STRICTEMENT PERSONNEL

WORKED ALL DAY ON A PORTRAIT, WENT OUT VERY QUICKLY TO THE GROCERY STORE... and THEN NOTHING SPECIAL. TRiED TO REACH B. TO TELL HER the BiG NEWS. SiNCE SHE iS COMPLETELY OUT OF THat comics/artists crowd... to her i can always tell everything... BUT her indiscretion was busy, i didn't insist. Read: "la ballade de l'impossible" by H. MURAKAMi. SHiT WiTH ALL THAT i FORGOT: YESTERDAY was the capture of Bagdad! THAT'S iT, THE AMERiCANS GOT THEiR ViCTORY, WiTH THE GRATEFUL iRAKi PEOPLE CHEERiNG. ONE CAN iMAGiNE they are happy to be rid of Saddam... BUT WE SURE WiLL HEAR MORE ABOUT THEM goddamn Americans how they won the war... makes me sick, such a butchery ...

11.04.03. Friday. WENT TO THE STUDIO YESTERDAY, PRINTED MY LINOS. NOBODY WAS THERE, PRETTY MUCH. JUST WHEN i WAS FINISHED WITH WORK J. SHOWED UP. WE DECIDED TO GO FOR A BEER. WE WENT TO THE BiLiKUN, AN iMPOSSiBLE BAR AFTER 6 AT NiGHT. BUT WE GOT THERE at THREE THIRTY. WE TALKED ABOUT [redacted] OUR FiNANCiAL BAD SiTUATIONS, the GRANT i DiDN'T GET iN MY CASE AND THE JOB SHE SHOULD FiND ASAP iN HER CASE.

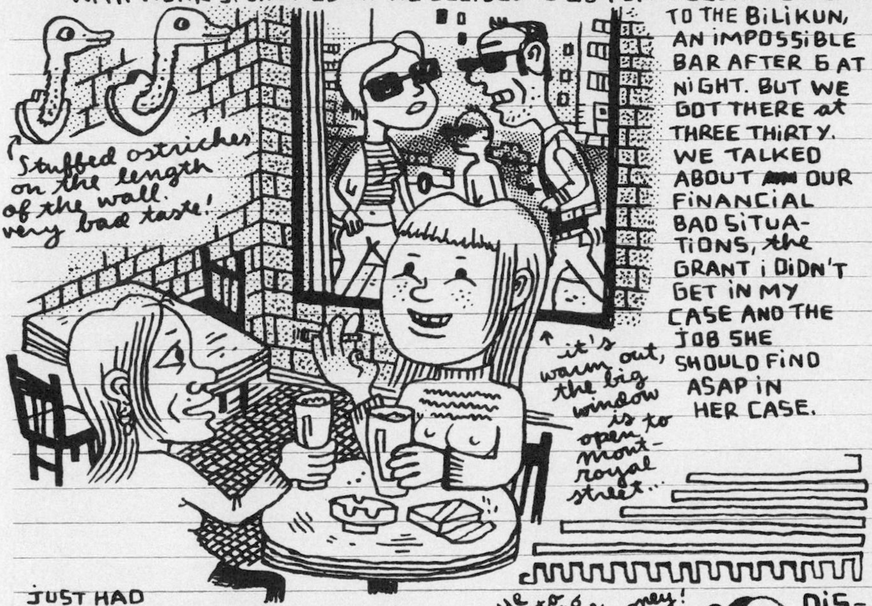
Stuffed ostriches on the length of the wall. very bad taste!
it's warm out, the big window is to open mont-royal street...

JUST HAD TiME TO EAT DiNNER AT HOME THEN i HAD TO GO TO E.'S PLACE TO DiSCUSS HiS MAGAZiNE PROJECT: "CHAPUGADGET". i COULDN'T HOLD iT BACK, i ENDED UP TELLiNG HiM ABOUT D&Q. SPEECHLESS HE WAS. BUT THEN:

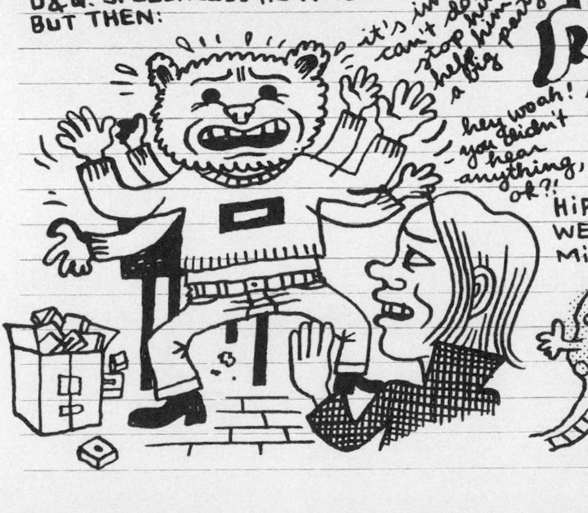
it's impossible!!! He can't do that we gotta stop him we have to help him let's organize a big party and raise money!
hey woah! you didn't hear anything, ok?!

So we DiS-CUSSED WHAT TO DO WiTH HiS MAGAZiNE. i WiLL DO THE DESiGN AND LAYOUT (he's taking care of the texts which are ALWAYS GOOD). WE LATER WENT to AN OPENiNG AT CLARK GALLERY. PAiNTiNGS BY A GiRL WHO iS OBViOUSLY TOO iNFLUENCED BY WEiRD JAPANESE MANGAS. SO HiP. i WAS NOT iMPRESSED. WE LEFT AFTER TEN MiNUTES...

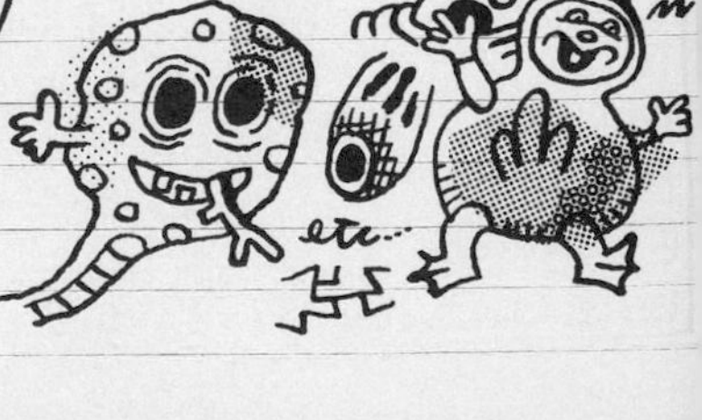
etc...

12.04.03. saturday.

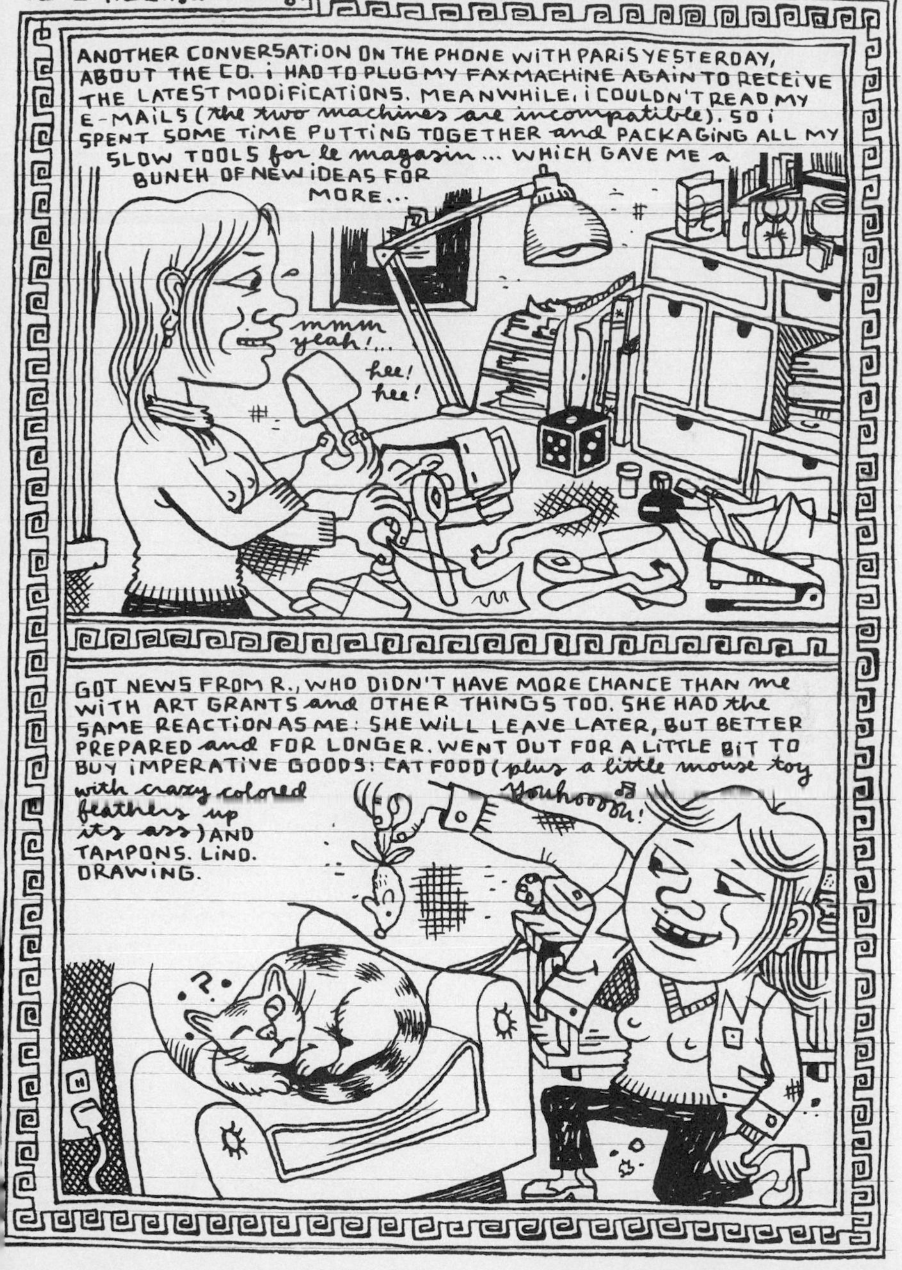
ANOTHER CONVERSATION ON THE PHONE WITH PARIS YESTERDAY, ABOUT THE CD. i HAD TO PLUG MY FAX MACHINE AGAIN TO RECEIVE THE LATEST MODIFICATIONS. MEANWHILE, i COULDN'T READ MY E-MAILS (the two machines are incompatible). SO i SPENT SOME TIME PUTTING TOGETHER and PACKAGING ALL MY SLOW TOOLS for le magasin... WHICH GAVE ME a BUNCH OF NEW IDEAS FOR MORE...
mmm yeah!...
hee! hee!
GOT NEWS FROM R., WHO DIDN'T HAVE MORE CHANCE THAN me WITH ART GRANTS and OTHER THINGS TOO. SHE HAD the SAME REACTION AS ME: SHE WILL LEAVE LATER, BUT BETTER PREPARED and FOR LONGER. WENT OUT FOR A LITTLE BIT TO BUY IMPERATIVE GOODS: CAT FOOD (plus a little mouse toy with crazy colored feathers up its ass) AND TAMPONS. LIND. DRAWING.
Youhoooou!
?

GOT UP AT QUARTER TO ELEVEN THIS MORNING, SURELY IT IS BECAUSE I DRANK WINE LAST NIGHT. DREW A SECOND PORTRAIT YESTERDAY MORNING AND WENT TO PRINT THE FIRST ONE AT THE STUDIO. A SUPER NICE SPRING DAY... D. ARRIVED SO I JOINED HER IN THE SILKSCREEN ROOM. SHE'S LEAVING FOR a TOUR ON TUESDAY... SHE HAD HEARD ABOUT C.'S MAGAZINE PROJECT. THAT GUY! HE SHOULDN'T BE TALKING ABOUT IT. THAT CAN KILL a PROJECT. DINNER *at* MY MOM'S. HAD TO WALK BACK HOME WITH MY BIKE, WHICH DOESN'T WANT TO RUN NO MORE. MYSTERIOUS. IS THE WHEEL SCREWED TOO TIGHT ON? ANYWAY. WATCHED THE NEWS: TOTAL MESS IN BAGDAD, PLUNDERING ALL OVER THE PLACE SINCE THE LIBERATION, AND THE AMERICANS DO *nothing about it. Irak is furious.*

DON'T UNDERSTAND WHY THE YANKEES ACT LIKE THAT? THEY REALLY DON'T CARE OR WHAT???

14.04.03. *monday*. PROVINCIAL ELECTION DAY TODAY. GONNA VOTE? OR GONNA NOT VOTE? SPENT THE DAY WORKING ON A PORTRAIT. THE EVENT OF THE DAY: I CHANGED THE TWO WEAKEST FUSES WITH ONLY ONE I HAD WHICH IS TWICE AS POWERFUL (*in the electric powerbox*) I HAD ASKED MY DAD ABOUT IT IN THE WEEK BEFORE I WOULDN'T HAVE DONE IT OTHERWISE. GET THIS: EVERYTHING IS WORKING AGAIN! HALF OF THE APARTMENT'S PLUGS WERE NOT WORKING ANYMORE... AND NOW, THE BIG MIRACLE, THE WASHING MACHINE IS WASHING JUST FINE AGAIN!... I'M SO SLOW...

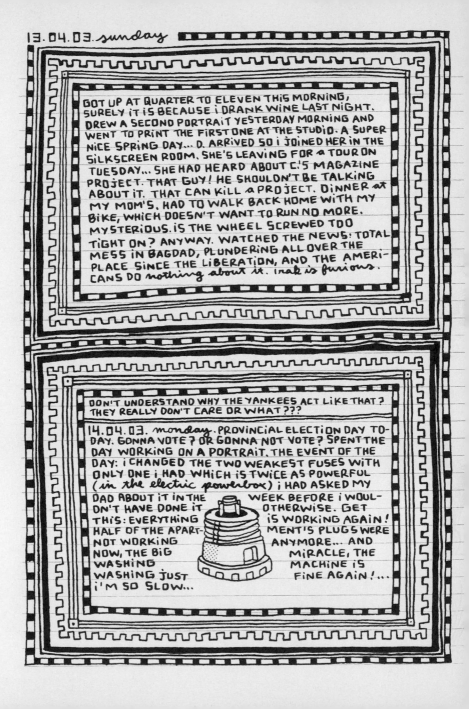

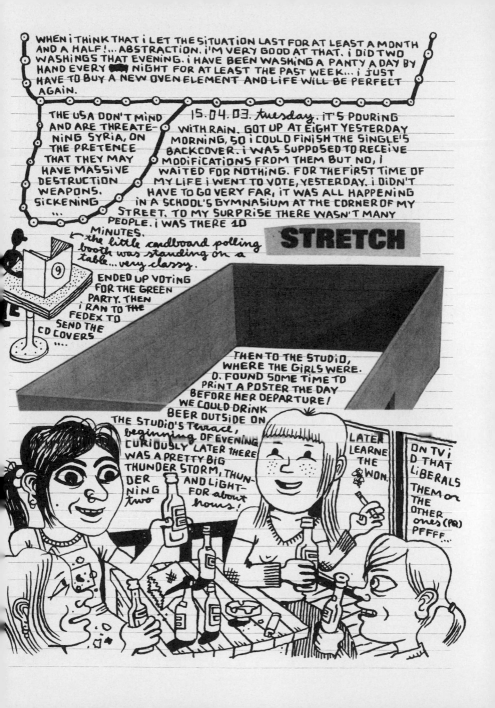

WHEN I THINK THAT I LET THE SITUATION LAST FOR AT LEAST A MONTH AND A HALF!... ABSTRACTION. I'M VERY GOOD AT THAT. I DID TWO WASHINGS THAT EVENING. I HAVE BEEN WASHING A PANTY A DAY BY HAND EVERY ▮▮▮ NIGHT FOR AT LEAST THE PAST WEEK... I JUST HAVE TO BUY A NEW OVEN ELEMENT AND LIFE WILL BE PERFECT AGAIN.

THE USA DON'T MIND AND ARE THREATENING SYRIA, ON THE PRETENCE THAT THEY MAY HAVE MASSIVE DESTRUCTION WEAPONS. SICKENING ...

15.04.03. tuesday. IT'S POURING WITH RAIN. GOT UP AT EIGHT YESTERDAY MORNING, SO I COULD FINISH THE SINGLE'S BACKCOVER. I WAS SUPPOSED TO RECEIVE MODIFICATIONS FROM THEM BUT NO, I WAITED FOR NOTHING. FOR THE FIRST TIME OF MY LIFE I WENT TO VOTE, YESTERDAY. I DIDN'T HAVE TO GO VERY FAR, IT WAS ALL HAPPENING IN A SCHOOL'S GYMNASIUM AT THE CORNER OF MY STREET. TO MY SURPRISE THERE WASN'T MANY PEOPLE. I WAS THERE 10 MINUTES.

← the little cardboard polling booth was standing on a table... very classy.

STRETCH

ENDED UP VOTING FOR THE GREEN PARTY. THEN I RAN TO THE FEDEX TO SEND THE CD COVERS ....

THEN TO THE STUDIO, WHERE THE GIRLS WERE. O. FOUND SOME TIME TO PRINT A POSTER THE DAY BEFORE HER DEPARTURE! WE COULD DRINK BEER OUTSIDE ON THE STUDIO'S terrace, beginning of evening CURIOUSLY LATER THERE WAS A PRETTY BIG THUNDER STORM, THUNDER AND LIGHTNING two FOR about hours!

LATER LEARNED THE WON.

ON TV I D THAT LIBERALS THEM or THE OTHER ones (PR) PFFFF...

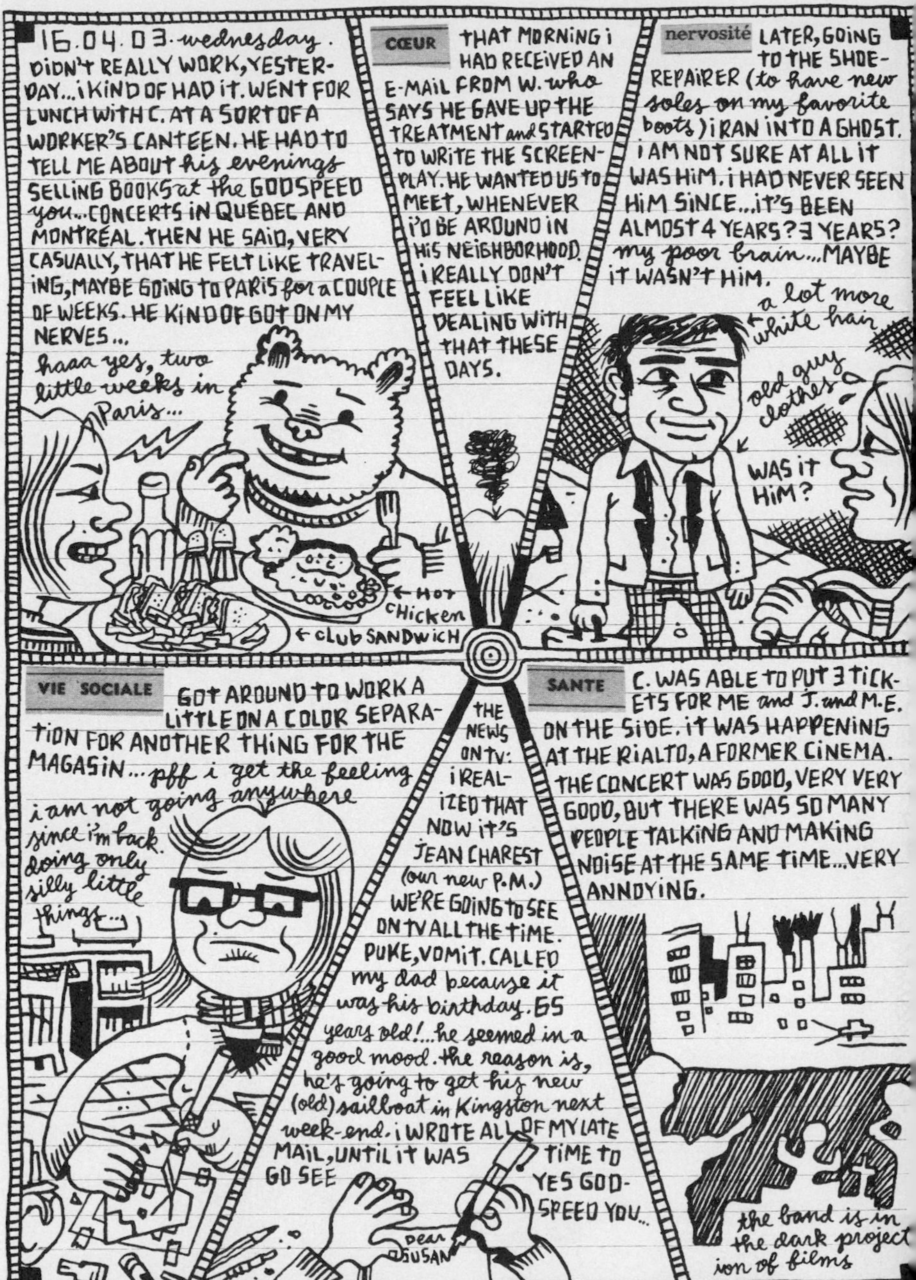
16.04.03. wednesday.
DIDN'T REALLY WORK, YESTERDAY... i KIND OF HAD iT. WENT FOR LUNCH WITH C. AT A SORT OF A WORKER'S CANTEEN. HE HAD TO TELL ME ABOUT his evenings SELLING BOOKS at the GODSPEED you... CONCERTS iN QUÉBEC AND MONTRÉAL. THEN HE SAID, VERY CASUALLY, THAT HE FELT LIKE TRAVELING, MAYBE GOING TO PARIS for a COUPLE OF WEEKS. HE KIND OF GOT ON MY NERVES...
haaa yes, two little weeks in Paris...
← HOT CHicken
← club SANDWICH
CŒUR
THAT MORNING i HAD RECEIVED AN E-MAIL FROM W. who SAYS HE GAVE UP THE TREATMENT and STARTED TO WRITE THE SCREENPLAY. HE WANTED US TO MEET, WHENEVER i'D BE AROUND IN HIS NEIGHBORHOOD. i REALLY DON'T FEEL LIKE DEALING WITH THAT THESE DAYS.
nervosité
LATER, GOING TO THE SHOE-REPAIRER (to have new soles on my favorite boots) i RAN INTO A GHOST. i AM NOT SURE AT ALL iT WAS HiM. i HAD NEVER SEEN HiM SiNCE... it's BEEN ALMOST 4 YEARS? 3 YEARS? my poor brain... MAYBE iT WASN'T HiM.
a lot more white hair
old guy clothes
WAS iT HiM?
VIE SOCIALE
GOT AROUND TO WORK A LITTLE ON A COLOR SEPARATION FOR ANOTHER THING FOR THE MAGASIN... pff i get the feeling i am not going anywhere since i'm back doing only silly little things...
THE NEWS ON TV: i REALIZED THAT NOW it's JEAN CHAREST (our new P.M.) WE'RE GOING TO SEE ON TV ALL THE TiME. PUKE, VOMiT. CALLED my dad because it was his birthday. 65 years old!... he seemed in a good mood. the reason is, he's going to get his new (old) sailboat in Kingston next week-end. i WROTE ALL OF MY LATE MAIL, UNTIL iT WAS TIME TO GO SEE YES GODSPEED YOU...
DEAR SUSAN
SANTE
C. WAS ABLE TO PUT 3 TICKETS FOR ME and J. and M.E. ON THE SiDE. iT WAS HAPPENING AT THE RIALTO, A FORMER CINEMA. THE CONCERT WAS GOOD, VERY VERY GOOD, BUT THERE WAS SO MANY PEOPLE TALKING AND MAKING NOISE AT THE SAME TiME... VERY ANNOYING.
the band is in the dark projection of films

17.04.03 thursday

HA THAT CONCERT LAST NIGHT WAS NOT TOO HAPPY-HAPPY, i AM STILL KIND OF DOWN... WHERE iS iT ALL GOiNG? WHO CARES? WHAT i'M DOING IS WORTHLESS, i'M WASTING MY TiME, etc... WORKED SOME MORE ON THE CD, NO CHOICE. THOSE PORTRAITS ARE NOT SO EASY TO DO. i HAD TO GO DOWN TO THE CHINATOWN TO BUY PAPER. SURE DIDN'T FEEL LiKE iT. AT THE STUDIO M.E. and J. WERE NOT EXACTLY IN A GOOD MOOD EiTHER.

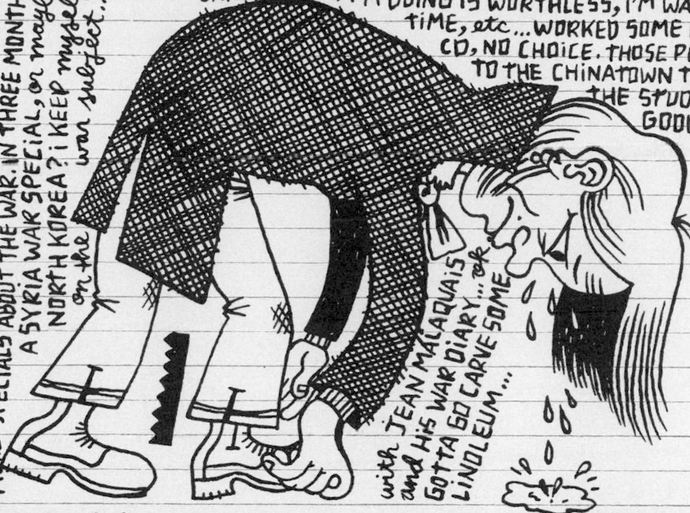

i ONLY CUT SOME PAPER for the NEXT COUPLE OF DAYS, i COULDN'T DO MORE, HAD ENOUGH... ON TV NO MORE SPECIALS ABOUT THE WAR. iN THREE MONTHS: A SYRIA WAR SPECiAL, or maybe NORTH KOREA? i KEEP myself on the war subject...

with JEAN MALAQUAiS and HiS WAR DIARY... ok GOTTA GO CARVE SOME LINOLEUM...

8.04.03. friday. WORKED ALL DAY YESTERDAY, ON ANOTHER PORTRAIT. WAS IN BETTER MOOD, BECAUSE i WAS DOING WELL WITH WORK and HE SKY WAS BLUE. iN THE EVENiNG i WENT TO SEE "LOST iN LA ANCHA" with C. A FiLM ABOUT DON QUiXOTE, WiTH JEAN OCHEFORT iN THE MAiN ROLE (yeees!) AND JOHNNY DEPP as ANCHO PANSA (noooo!). THE MOVIE WAS NEVER FiNiSHED, N FACT NEVER REALLY STARTED. iT'S BEEN A COMPLETE DISASTER. SEEN LiKE THAT iT DOESN'T MAKE YOU WANT O GO INTO THE BUSiNESS...

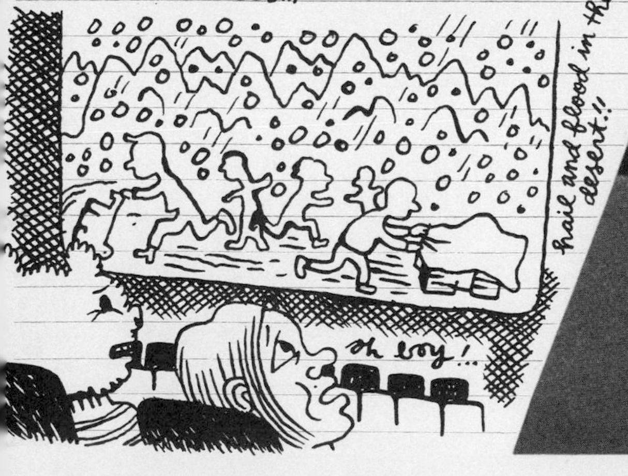
hail and flood in the desert!!
oh boy!..

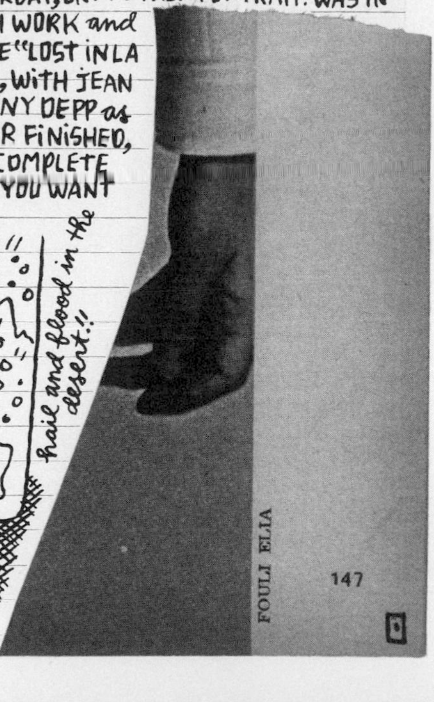
FOULI ELIA
147

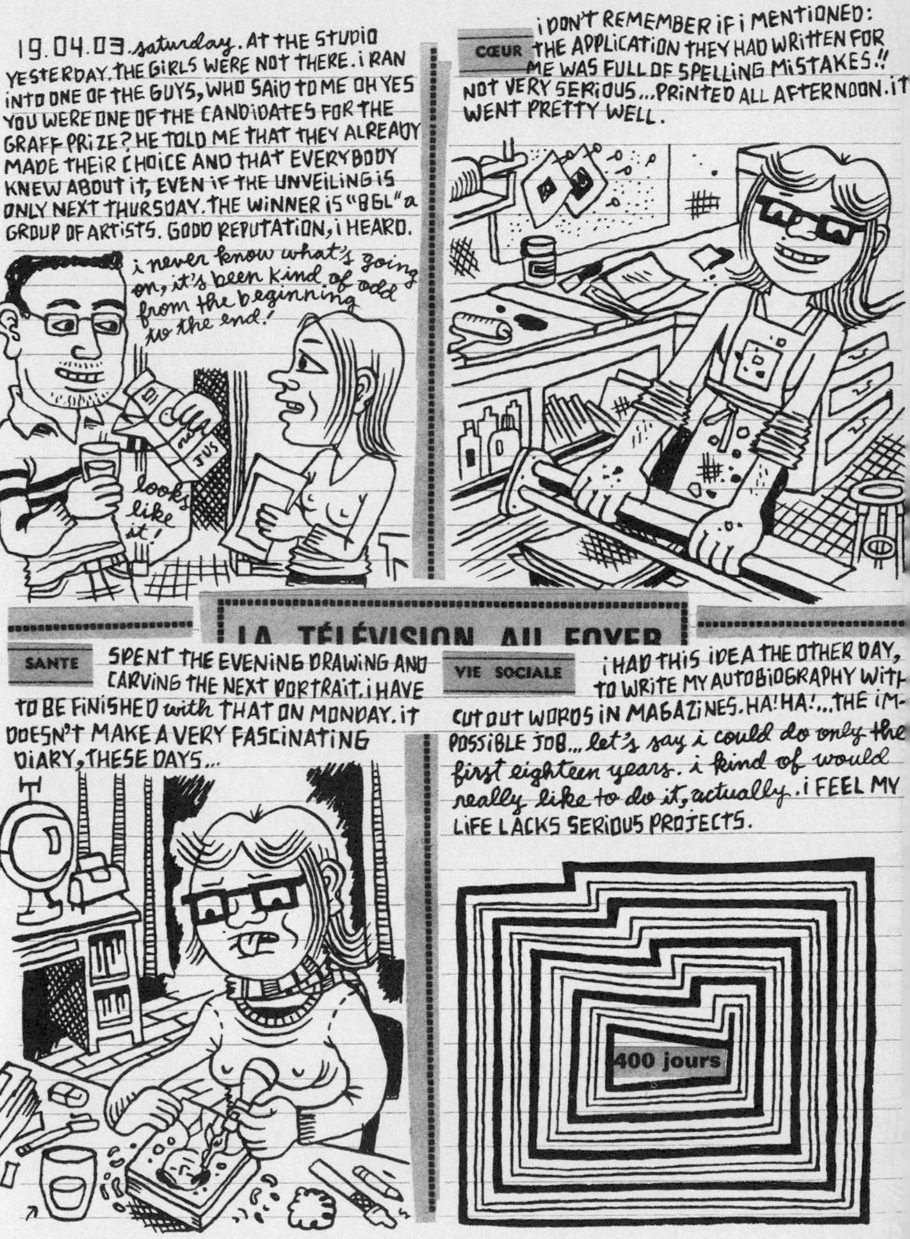
19.04.03. saturday. AT THE STUDIO YESTERDAY. THE GIRLS WERE NOT THERE. i RAN INTO ONE OF THE GUYS, WHO SAID TO ME OH YES YOU WERE ONE OF THE CANDIDATES FOR THE GRAFF PRIZE? HE TOLD ME THAT THEY ALREADY MADE THEIR CHOICE AND THAT EVERYBODY KNEW ABOUT IT, EVEN IF THE UNVEILING IS ONLY NEXT THURSDAY. THE WINNER IS "BGL" a GROUP OF ARTISTS. GOOD REPUTATION, i HEARD.
i never know what's going on, it's been kind of odd from the beginning to the end!
JUS
looks like it!
CŒUR
i DON'T REMEMBER iF i MENTIONED: THE APPLICATION THEY HAD WRITTEN FOR ME WAS FULL OF SPELLING MISTAKES!! NOT VERY SERIOUS... PRINTED ALL AFTERNOON. iT WENT PRETTY WELL.
LA TÉLÉVISION AU FOYER
SANTE
SPENT THE EVENING DRAWING AND CARVING THE NEXT PORTRAIT. i HAVE TO BE FINISHED with THAT ON MONDAY. iT DOESN'T MAKE A VERY FASCINATING DIARY, THESE DAYS...
VIE SOCIALE
i HAD THIS IDEA THE OTHER DAY, TO WRITE MY AUTOBIOGRAPHY WITH CUT OUT WORDS IN MAGAZINES. HA! HA!... THE iM-POSSIBLE JOB... let's say i could do only the first eighteen years. i kind of would really like to do it, actually. i FEEL MY LIFE LACKS SERIOUS PROJECTS.
400 jours

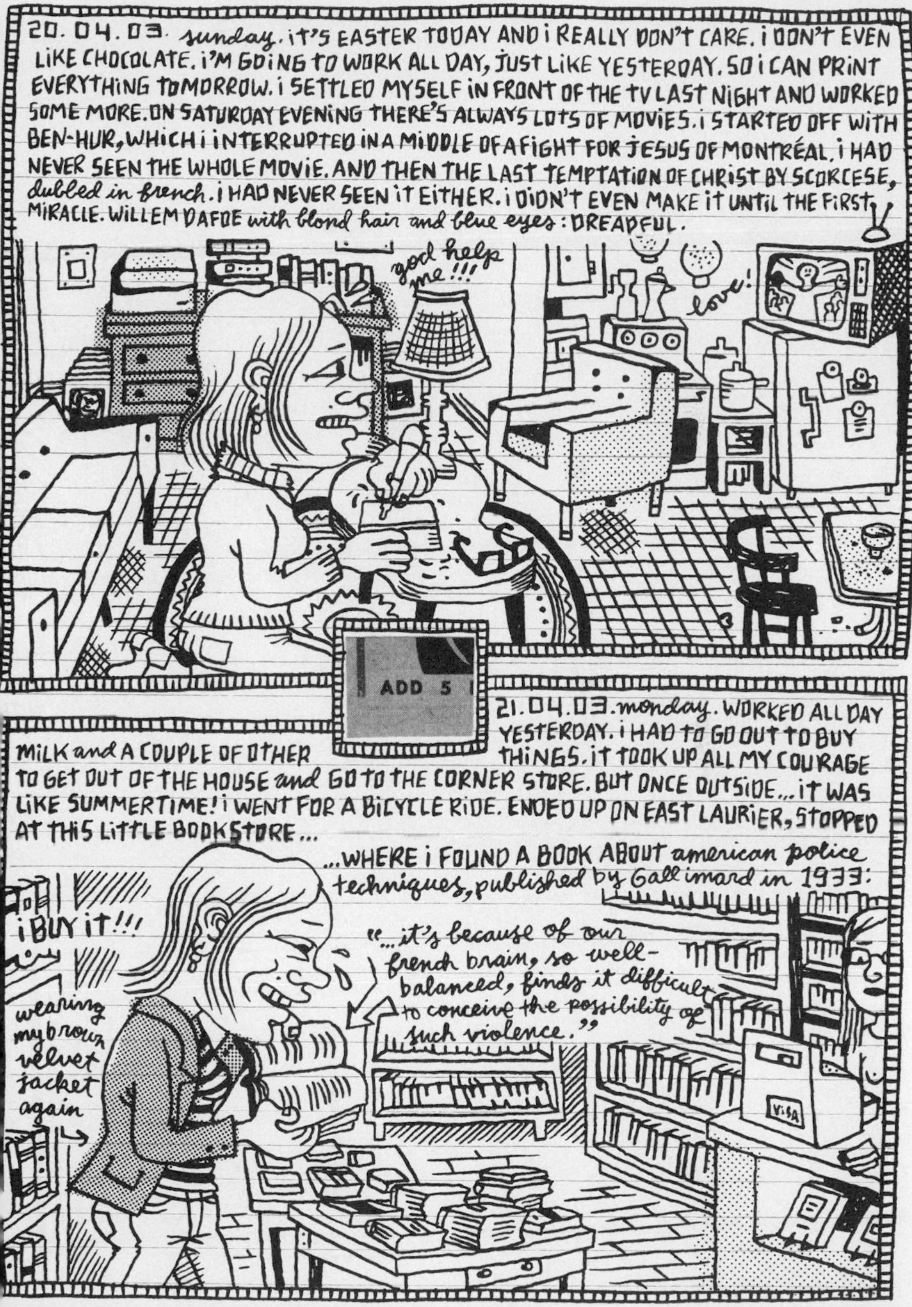
20. 04. 03. sunday. it's EASTER TODAY AND i REALLY DON'T CARE. i DON'T EVEN LiKE CHOCOLATE. i'M GOING TO WORK ALL DAY, JUST LiKE YESTERDAY. SO i CAN PRINT EVERYTHING TOMORROW. i SETTLED MYSELF iN FRONT OF THE TV LAST NiGHT AND WORKED SOME MORE. ON SATURDAY EVENING THERE'S ALWAYS LOTS OF MOVIES. i STARTED OFF WiTH BEN-HUR, WHiCH i iNTERRUPTED iN A MiDDLE OF A FiGHT FOR JESUS OF MONTRÉAL. i HAD NEVER SEEN THE WHOLE MOVIE. AND THEN THE LAST TEMPTATION OF CHRIST BY SCORCESE, dubbed in french. i HAD NEVER SEEN iT EiTHER. i DiDN'T EVEN MAKE iT UNTiL THE FiRST MiRACLE. WiLLEM DAFOE with blond hair and blue eyes: DREADFUL.
god help me!!!
love!
ADD 5
21. 04. 03. monday. WORKED ALL DAY YESTERDAY. i HAD TO GO OUT TO BUY MiLK and A COUPLE OF OTHER THiNGS. iT TOOK UP ALL MY COURAGE TO GET OUT OF THE HOUSE and GO TO THE CORNER STORE. BUT ONCE OUTSiDE... iT WAS LiKE SUMMERTiME! i WENT FOR A BiCYCLE RiDE. ENDED UP ON EAST LAURiER, STOPPED AT THiS LiTTLE BOOKSTORE...
...WHERE i FOUND A BOOK ABOUT american police techniques, published by Gallimard in 1933:
i BUY iT!!!
"...it's because of our french brain, so well-balanced, finds it difficult to conceive the possibility of such violence."
wearing my brown velvet jacket again
ViSA

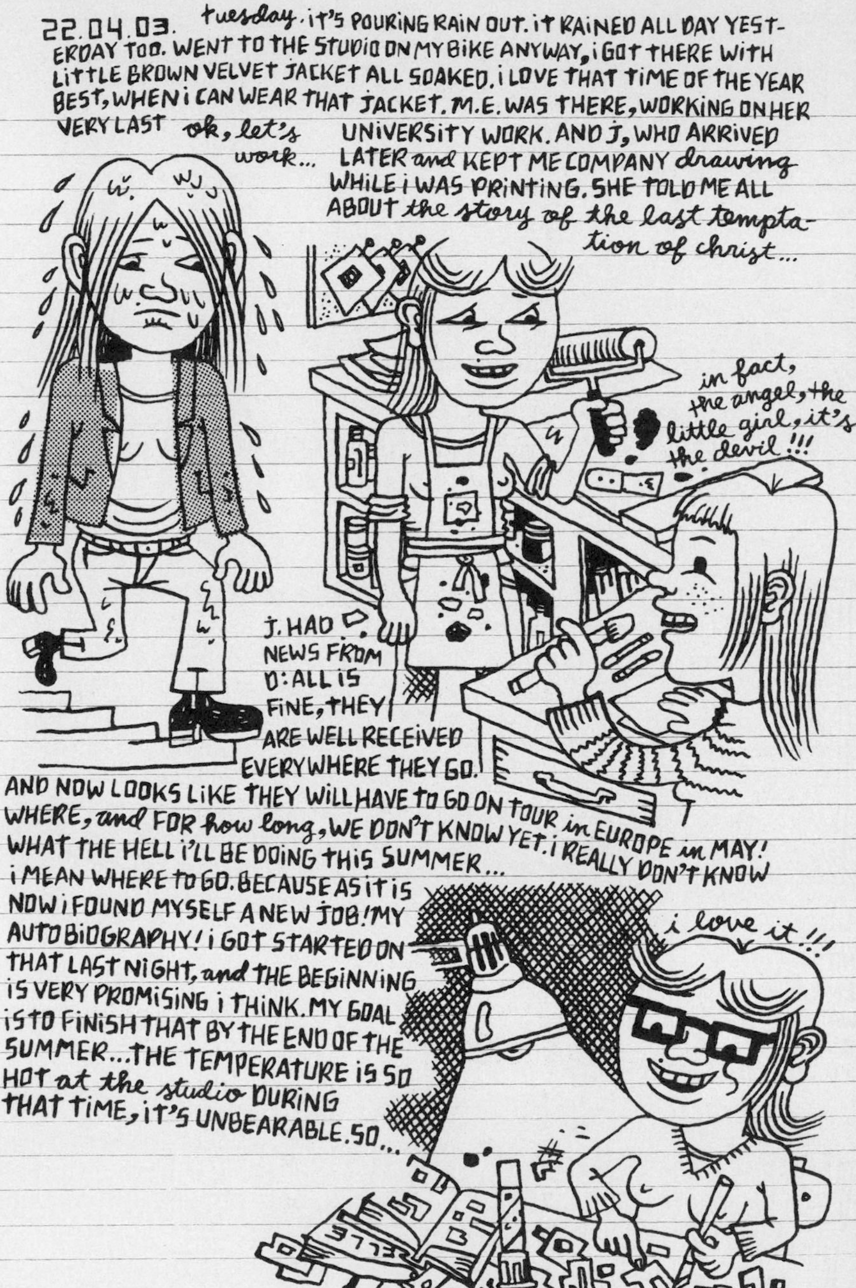
22.04.03. tuesday. it's POURING RAIN OUT. it RAINED ALL DAY YESTERDAY TOO. WENT TO THE STUDIO ON MY BIKE ANYWAY, i GOT THERE WITH LITTLE BROWN VELVET JACKET ALL SOAKED. i LOVE THAT TIME OF THE YEAR BEST, WHEN i CAN WEAR THAT JACKET. M.E. WAS THERE, WORKING ON HER VERY LAST UNIVERSITY WORK. AND J, WHO ARRIVED LATER and KEPT ME COMPANY drawing WHILE i WAS PRINTING. SHE TOLD ME ALL ABOUT the story of the last temptation of christ...
ok, let's work...
in fact, the angel, the little girl, it's the devil !!!
J. HAD NEWS FROM D: ALL IS FINE, THEY ARE WELL RECEIVED EVERYWHERE THEY GO. AND NOW LOOKS LIKE THEY WILL HAVE TO GO ON TOUR in EUROPE in MAY! WHERE, and FOR how long, WE DON'T KNOW YET. i REALLY DON'T KNOW WHAT THE HELL i'LL BE DOING THIS SUMMER... i MEAN WHERE TO GO. BECAUSE AS it IS NOW i FOUND MYSELF A NEW JOB! MY AUTOBIOGRAPHY! i GOT STARTED ON THAT LAST NiGHT, and THE BEGINNING IS VERY PROMISING i THINK. MY GOAL IS TO FINISH THAT BY THE END OF THE SUMMER... THE TEMPERATURE IS SO HOT at the studio DURING THAT TIME, IT'S UNBEARABLE. SO...
i love it !!!
ELLE

23.04.03. *wednesday.* i SPENT THE DAY YESTERDAY COPYING SONGS LYRICS FOR THE CD. A LENGTHY AND BORING JOB. IN THE EVENING i WENT OUT WITH C. HE WAS IN A REALLY BAD MOOD BECAUSE HE DIDN'T GET HIS *canada* ART COUNCIL GRANT, EITHER. iT IS RATHER SURPRISING IN HIS CASE, BECAUSE THE APPLICATION WAS FOR HIS PUBLISHING HOUSE AND HE GOT MONEY FOR IT THE PAST TWO YEARS...USUALLY, WHEN THEY START GIVING YOU MONEY, IT'S LIKE A SUBSCRIPTION...IN HIS CASE TOO HE WILL HAVE TO TOTALLY CHANGE HIS PLANS! WE KNEW IT ALREADY, WE WERE VERY CONVINCED, ONE SHOULD NOT COUNT ON govern-ment *money* TO DO STUFF!... WE WENT TO EAT, THEN TO A MOVIE "*the man without a past*" THE SECOND TIME, FOR ME. i KNEW THAT MOVIE WOULD CHEER US UP.

buck it's lousy man!...

oooh yeah!...

it's still raining. i caught a cold and i didn't have time to work on my autobiography

24.04.03. ~~thursday.~~ iT'S STILL GRAY OUTSIDE. GOT A COLD. i'VE BEEN PEAKED ALL DAY YESTERDAY. BUT i WORKED ANYWAY, COPIED THE SONGS LYRICS...THAT JOB TURNED OUT TAKING MORE TIME THAN i EXPECTED, BUT iT'S OVER NOW. ON TV THE WHO DECLARED TORONTO A CITY TO AVOID BECAUSE OF THE SARS EPIDEMIC. INCREDIBLE, iT'S BEEN AT LEAST TEN DAYS, NO, MORE (i have *no sense of time*), AND STILL NO CASE IN QUEBEC PROVINCE.

NO COURAGE OR ENERGY TO DO ANYTHING IN THE EVENING, EXCEPT READ. JAMIE, "MY ACCOUNTANT", DROPPED BY: HE WAS DONE WITH MY TAXES. iT TURNED OUT iT WON'T BE AS BAD AS HE ANNOUNCED, A LOT LESS MONEY...WHEW, i WON'T SNEEZE AT THAT.

AN EMAIL FROM W., WHO'S ASKING ME TO CALL HIM WHEN i HAVE TIME, TO GO HAVE A COFFEE TOGETHER...UGH, DON'T ASK TOO MUCH FROM ME TODAY, MAN...

25.04.03. friday.

STILL GRAY OUT, STILL HAVE A COLD. RECEIVED A LETTER FROM THE BERLIN FESTIVAL YESTERDAY. THEY'RE ASKING ME TO DO GRANT APPLICATIONS AT the CANADA ART COUNCIL and AT THE FOREIGN AFFAIR DEPARTMENT... TO HELP THEM PAY MY PLANE TICKET. OH YEAH, GREAT. i ABSOLUTELY HATE DOING THAT... ALSO, NOT MUCH HOPE TO GET ANYTHING FROM CANADA. LOOKS LIKE NOTHING'S FREE IN THIS WORLD!!...

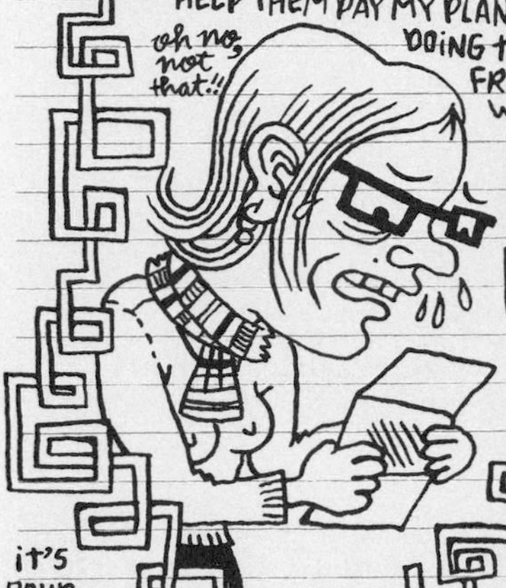
oh no, not that!!

MADAME COZIC CALLED ME TO TELL ME THAT BGL WON THE PRIZE, TOO BAD THANK YOU SO MUCH GOODBYE. FUNNY HOW THEY DON'T SEEM TO WANT TO MEET WITH ME. i DON'T COMPLAIN, i DON'T LIKE TO KOW-TOW... BUT STILL... THE PRIZE-GIVING THING was at the end of the day, i didn't show up. WORKED ON THE LAST DETAILS ON the CD this morning. TALKED TO GENEVIEVE C. she may come to MTL end of may blah blah blah...

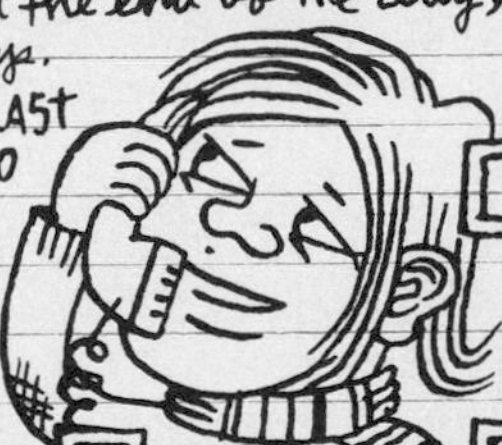

it's POURING RAIN OUT. it ENDED UP BEING A NICE DAY YESTERDAY.

26.04.03. saturday. i FINISHED COMPLETELY THAT CD JOB yesterday, BEGINNING OF AFTERNOON. SEEMED LIKE i'D NEVER GET IT OVER WITH BUT NOW it's TRUE: FINI. WENT TO SEND THAT THING FEDEX. USED MY BIKE. RAN INTO J. AND HER BOYFRIEND, WHO WERE HAVING LUNCH AT PATATI PATATA. WE SAID WE'D GO OUT THIS week-end WITH D. i'VE HAD A DAY OF STROLLING IN BOOKSTORES. STARTING WITH GALLIMARD. i was hoping to find more books by RAYMOND GUÉRIN, but no, nothing. ON THE OTHER HAND PLENTY OF HENRY CALAIS... NOTHING AT ALL in the other bookstores... BACK HOME i HAD A MESSAGE FROM D. ON MY ANSWERING MACHINE, i CALLED HER BACK RIGHT AWAY. THE MOST INTENSE MOMENTS OF HER LIFE, SHE SAID.

THEY MET WITH SO MANY PEOPLE, FROM LE TIGRE TO KIM GORDON... NEW RECORD DEAL AND END OF MAY THREE CONCERTS: PARIS-Berlin-LONDON. WE'RE GOING TO MEET with the girls ON SUNDAY. DID NOTHING IN THE EVENING (read) and won't do anything this week-end. HAD ENOUGH...

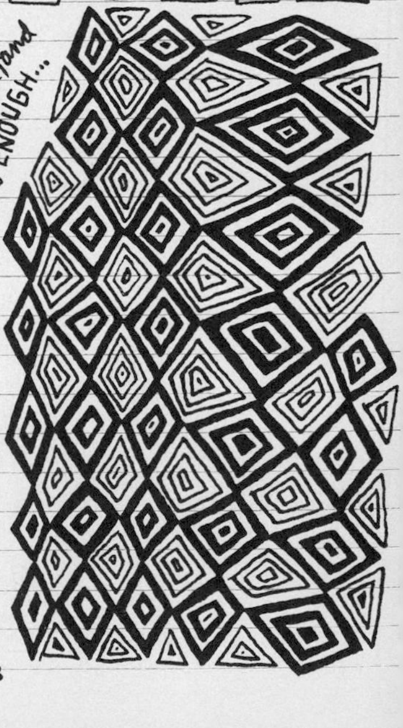

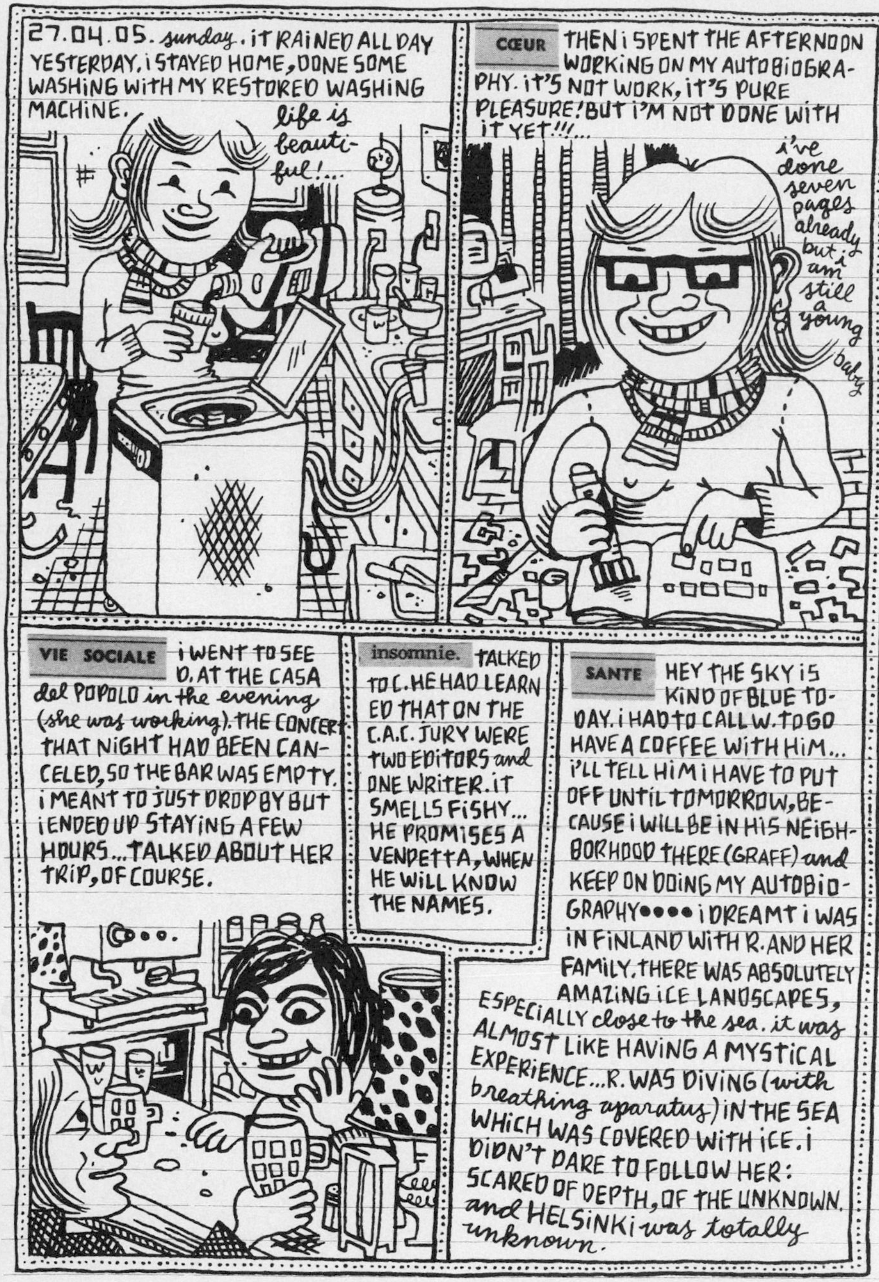
27.04.05. sunday. it RAINED ALL DAY YESTERDAY. i STAYED HOME, DONE SOME WASHING WITH MY RESTORED WASHING MACHINE.
life is beauti-ful!...
CŒUR
THEN i SPENT THE AFTERNOON WORKING ON MY AUTOBIOGRA-PHY. iT'S NOT WORK, iT'S PURE PLEASURE! BUT i'M NOT DONE WITH iT YET!!!...
i've done seven pages already but i am still a young baby
VIE SOCIALE
i WENT TO SEE D. AT THE CASA del POPOLO in the evening (she was working). THE CONCERT THAT NiGHT HAD BEEN CAN-CELED, SO THE BAR WAS EMPTY. i MEANT TO JUST DROP BY BUT i ENDED UP STAYiNG A FEW HOURS... TALKED ABOUT HER TRiP, OF COURSE.
insomnie.
TALKED TO C. HE HAD LEARNED THAT ON THE C.A.C. JURY WERE TWO EDiTORS and ONE WRiTER. iT SMELLS FiSHY... HE PROMiSES A VENDETTA, WHEN HE WiLL KNOW THE NAMES.
SANTE
HEY THE SKY iS KiND OF BLUE TO-DAY. i HAD TO CALL W. TO GO HAVE A COFFEE WiTH HiM... i'LL TELL HiM i HAVE TO PUT OFF UNTiL TOMORROW, BE-CAUSE i WiLL BE iN HiS NEiGH-BORHOOD THERE (GRAFF) and KEEP ON DOiNG MY AUTOBiO-GRAPHY •••• i DREAMT i WAS iN FiNLAND WiTH R. AND HER FAMiLY. THERE WAS ABSOLUTELY AMAZiNG iCE LANDSCAPES, ESPECiALLY close to the sea. it was ALMOST LiKE HAViNG A MYSTiCAL EXPERiENCE... R. WAS DiViNG (with breathing aparatus) iN THE SEA WHiCH WAS COVERED WiTH iCE. i DiDN'T DARE TO FOLLOW HER: SCARED OF DEPTH, OF THE UNKNOWN. and HELSiNKi was totally unknown.

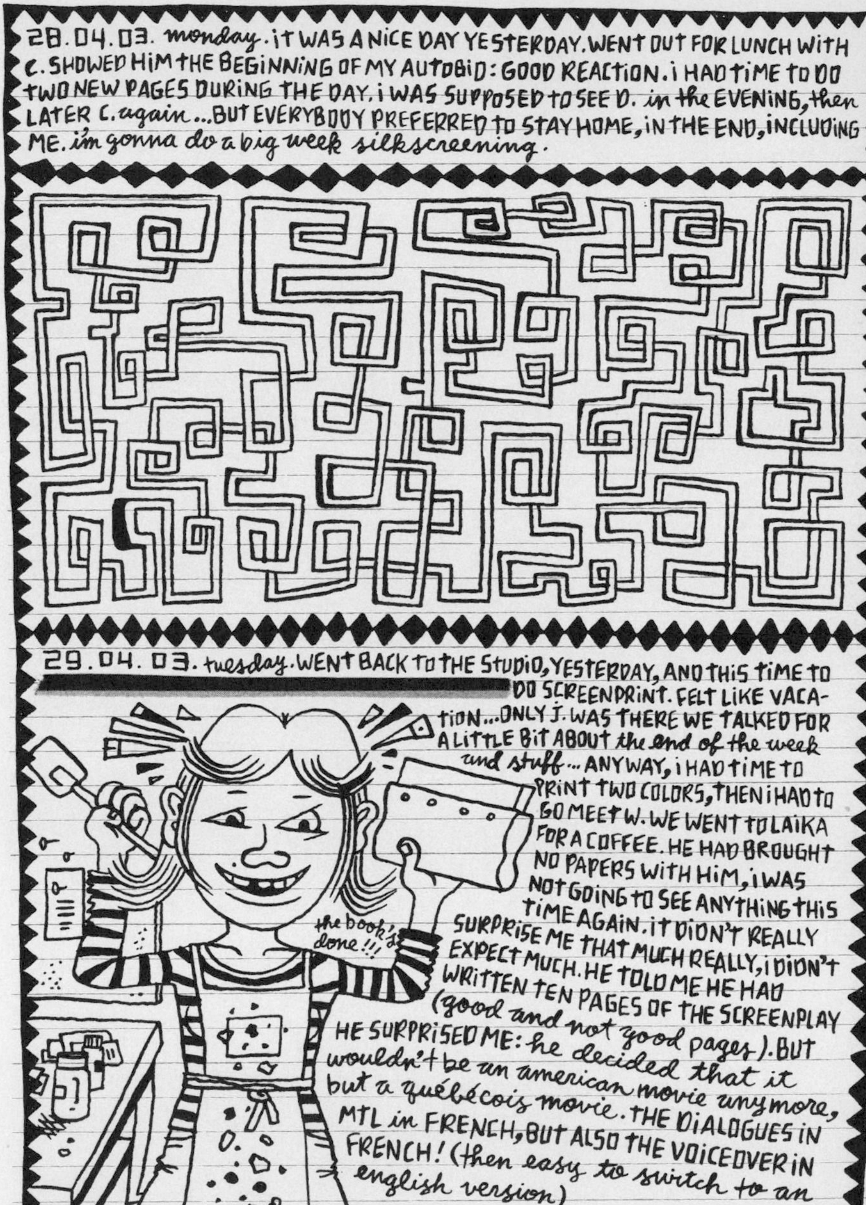
28.04.03. monday. it WAS A NICE DAY YESTERDAY. WENT OUT FOR LUNCH WITH C. SHOWED HIM THE BEGINNING OF MY AUTOBIO: GOOD REACTION. i HAD TIME TO DO TWO NEW PAGES DURING THE DAY. i WAS SUPPOSED TO SEE D. in the EVENING, then LATER C. again ... BUT EVERYBODY PREFERRED TO STAY HOME, IN THE END, INCLUDING ME. i'm gonna do a big week silkscreening.
29.04.03. tuesday. WENT BACK TO THE STUDIO, YESTERDAY, AND THIS TIME TO [redacted] DO SCREENPRINT. FELT LIKE VACATION... ONLY J. WAS THERE WE TALKED FOR A LITTLE BIT ABOUT the end of the week and stuff... ANYWAY, i HAD TIME TO PRINT TWO COLORS, THEN i HAD TO GO MEET W. WE WENT TO LAIKA FOR A COFFEE. HE HAD BROUGHT NO PAPERS WITH HIM, i WAS NOT GOING TO SEE ANYTHING THIS TIME AGAIN. it DIDN'T REALLY SURPRISE ME THAT MUCH REALLY, i DIDN'T EXPECT MUCH. HE TOLD ME HE HAD WRITTEN TEN PAGES OF THE SCREENPLAY (good and not good pages). BUT HE SURPRISED ME: he decided that it wouldn't be an american movie anymore, but a québécois movie. MTL in FRENCH, BUT ALSO THE DIALOGUES IN FRENCH! (then easy to switch to an english version) THE VOICEOVER IN
the book's done!!!

ALSO THIS IDEA: TO GIVE DIFFERENT DIRECTORS A DREAM SEQUENCE, AND ONLY LOCAL DIRECTORS. JUST TO HAVE A REALLY DIFFERENT TOUCH FROM THE REST (since they are dreams...) W. WILL MEET A MONTRÉAL PRODUCER next week, THE ONE WHO PRODUCED "a crab in the head". HE OFFERED ME TO WRITE A SCENE, SORT OF A PARANTHESIS ABOUT EPILEPSY. AH? and maybe the french translation. HE HAD WORKED ON THE SCREENPLAY AGAIN, and the beginning of the FILM IS JUST AS I IMAGINED IT. IT'S AN IDEA WE HAD while DISCUSSING TOGETHER THE LAST TIME WE MET, I DON'T REMEMBER WHICH ONE OF US CAME UP WITH IT... A VERY FUNNY IDEA, but with that one we will have to forget about american financing. HEE! HEE!... I WOULD NEVER HAD THOUGHT SO BUT IT LOOKS LIKE THERE'S HOPE, NOW... I'M HAPPY!... JUST THE FACT THAT IT'S GOING TO BE IN FRENCH!... YES!!! ALL THE GIRLS WERE AT THE STUDIO WHEN I GOT BACK. WE DRANK A BEER ON THE TERRACE. NICE WEATHER SINCE A COUPLE OF DAYS...

30.04.03. wednesday. SPENT THE WHOLE DAY AT THE STUDIO YESTER-DAY. THE GIRLS WEREN'T THERE, OR DROPPED BY ONLY FOR TEN MINUTES. NOTHING TO REPORT. THERE WAS A LAUNCHING AT THE CHEVAL BLANC, OF THAT ART MAGAZINE FROM MARSEILLE. i was in it at happy hour and the bar was empty! IT'S TRUE THAT THE WEATHER WAS NICE OUT, and EVERYBODY MUST HAVE BEEN ON THE TERRACES. NOBODY SHOWED UP FOR THAT THING. C WAS THERE... a big in mirror × bla bla bla

i DIDN'T HANG ABOUT FOR TOO LONG. WENT BACK HOME AT 7 AND SPENT THE EVENING CUTTING OUT STUFF i HAD PRINTED... WHILE WATCHING A COPPOLA MOVIE: "conversation secréta" VERY STRANGE. i wonder what's the original title...

sun	mon	tues	wed	thurs	fri	sat
●	●	●	●	1	2	3
4	5	6	7	8	9	10
11	12	13	14	15	16	17
18	19	20	21	22	23	24
25	26	27	28	29	30	31

01. 05. 03. thursday. A RAINY FIRST OF MAY. WENT TO THE STUDIO,
YESTERDAY...D. WAS THERE, DOING LAYOUT FOR A POSTER. I DID THE SAME
THING BUT FOR A RECORD BY "LES SLOW" (another object for the magasin).

THE OTHERS ARRIVED at the
BEGINNING OF THE EVENING.
WE WENT TO EAT TOGE-
THER. TURNS OUT D. had
another OFFER FOR a
USA tour, with LOCUST
(a well known band i
don't know about) AND
THE G.L. ARE BEING PLAYED
ON WFMU in NEW YORK
ALL THE TIME!...I DON'T
KNOW WHY, BUT I THINK
A LOT ABOUT HAVING A BABY
THESE DAYS...I'LL BE
FORTY KIND OF SOON, and
BEING AN EPILEPTIC...
MAYBE IT'S NOT SOMETHING

TO TRY. IT DOESN'T MAKE ME EXTREMELY
SAD TO MAKE THAT OBSERVATION...COULDN'T
DO NOTHING ABOUT IT ANYWAY. WILL I BE AN
OLD MAID WITH 36 CATS?

aaaah
you my
little
darlings...

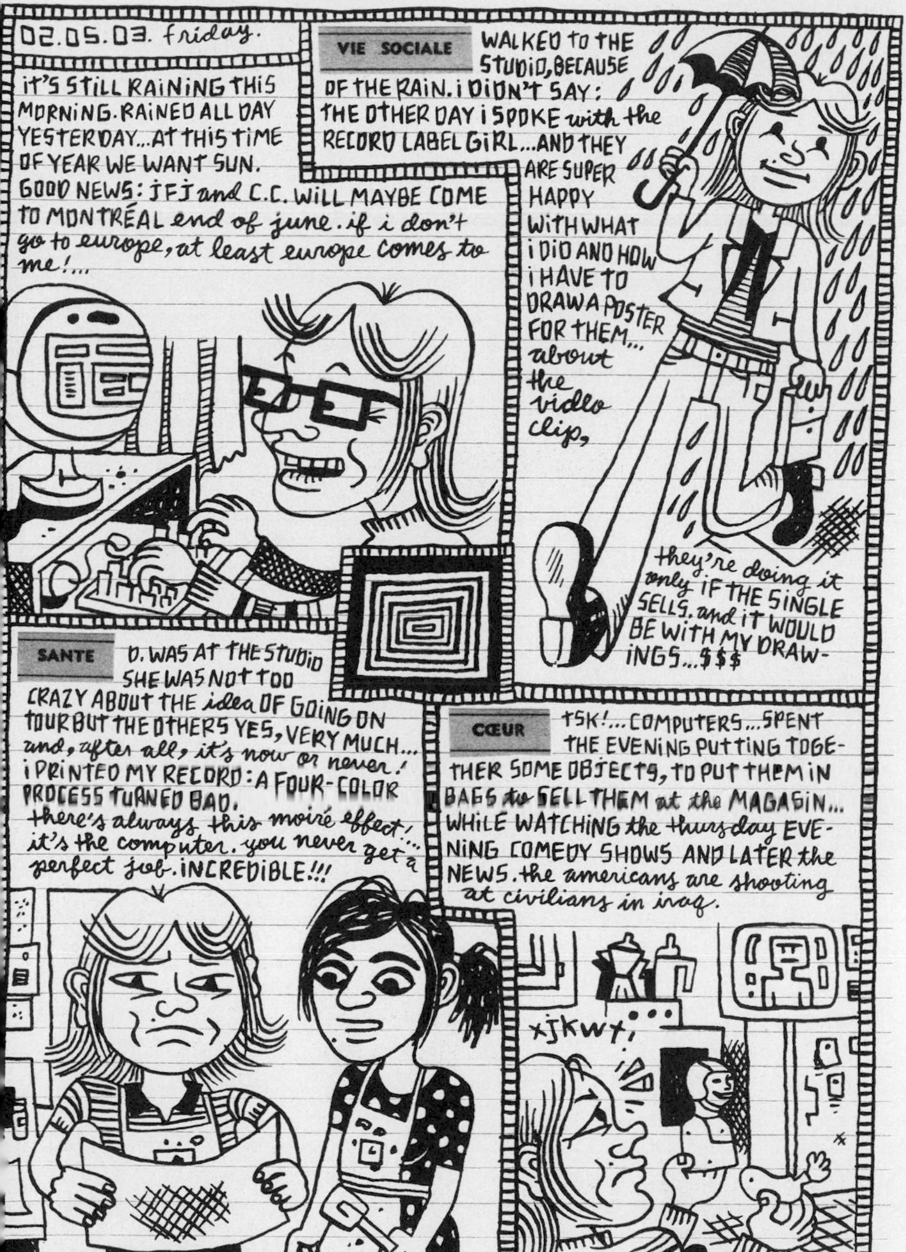

02.05.03. friday.
it's still raining this morning. rained all day yesterday... at this time of year we want sun.
good news: JFJ and C.C. will maybe come to montréal end of june. if i don't go to europe, at least europe comes to me!...
VIE SOCIALE
walked to the studio, because of the rain. i didn't say: the other day i spoke with the record label girl... and they are super happy with what i did and how i have to draw a poster for them... about the video clip,
they're doing it only if the single sells. and it would be with my drawings... $$$
SANTE
D. was at the studio she was not too crazy about the idea of going on tour but the others yes, very much... and, after all, it's now or never! i printed my record: a four-color process turned bad. there's always this moiré effect! it's the computer. you never get a perfect job. incredible!!!
CŒUR
tsk!... computers... spent the evening putting together some objects, to put them in bags to sell them at the magasin... while watching the thursday evening comedy shows and later the news. the americans are shooting at civilians in iraq.
xjkwt!

03.05.03. *saturday*

SPENT THE WHOLE DAY DRAWING, STILL AND ALWAYS FOR THE MAGASIN. GOT OUT ONLY WHEN THE WEATHER TURNED NICE.

AROUND FOUR THIRTY FOUND A PACKAGE FOR ME IN THE NEIGHBOR'S MAILBOX. FROM ALVIN B (*from San Diego*). HE TELLS ME HE WENT TO VISIT...

DAN CLOWES RECENTLY AND SAW THE TWO ORIGINALS I SOLD HIM LAST JANUARY. APPARENTLY HE SAID IT'S HIS BEST PIECES *in his* COLLECTION AND HE'S WONDERING WHY...

I AM NOT A MILLIONAIRE.

MM YEAH... FOR THAT I WOULD HAVE TO MARRY A MILLIONAIRE, I DON'T SEE HOW OTHERWISE...

I WAS GOING TO HAVE DINNER WITH MY DAD AND M. IT WAS THEIR BIRTHDAY THE BOTH OF THEM TWO WEEKS AGO. SO I BOUGHT CHOCOLATE (*for my dad*) AND FLOWERS (*for M.*).

04.05.03. *sunday*. BEAUTIFUL WEATHER, AND SO IT WAS YESTERDAY. WENT TO THE STUDIO, WHERE ONLY THIS UNPLEASANT BIG BEAR WAS. FORTUNATELY D. ARRIVED A BIT LATER... BAD NEWS: THE GIRLS DIDN'T GET ANY MONEY FROM THE OFFICE FRANCO-QUÉBÉCOIS... THEY WERE SO SURE TO GET SOME FROM THEM! THIS IS GOING ALL WRONG, NO LUCK WITH MONEY. OR WITH EUROPE... THERE'S A CURSE ON US. THERE WAS AN OPENING AT THE CASA THAT EVENING. AN EXHIBIT I. AND D. WERE IN, *and also* D.'*s boyfriend*. A ROCK 'N' ROLL EXHIBIT, WITH LOTS OF TATOO PAINTINGS... GOT THE PICTURE!

TALKED TO LOUIS (D.'*s boyfriend*) ABOUT THEIR TOUR AND STUFF. HE'D LEAVE ANYTIME AND FOREVER... HOW IT IS IMPOSSIBLE TO EVEN TELL WHAT HAPPENED TO HIM, *and* HOW ANYWAY PEOPLE ARE NOT TOO INTERESTED TO LISTEN... I KNEW EXACTLY WHAT HE WAS TALKING ABOUT, I WAS THERE TWELVE YEARS AGO! I ENCOURAGE THEM TO GO AWAY. OF COURSE, AS ALWAYS.

05.05.03. monday

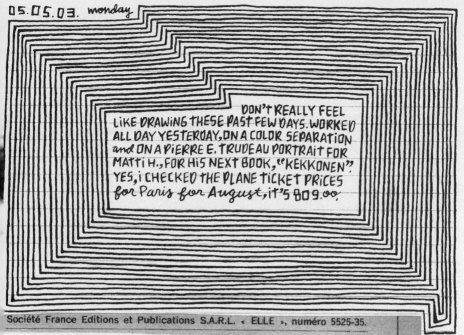

DON'T REALLY FEEL LIKE DRAWING THESE PAST FEW DAYS. WORKED ALL DAY YESTERDAY, ON A COLOR SEPARATION and ON A PIERRE E. TRUDEAU PORTRAIT FOR MATTI H., FOR HIS NEXT BOOK, "KEKKONEN". YES, i CHECKED THE PLANE TICKET PRICES for Paris for August, it's 809.00.

Société France Editions et Publications S.A.R.L. « ELLE », numéro 5525-35.

iT'S NOT SO BAD... FORGOT TO CHECK FOR BERLIN! THAT'S WHERE i'M GOING, NO?... i AM QUITE FED UP WITH ALL MY TRIP PLANS (which never work) DON'T FEEL LIKE GOING ANYWHERE NO MORE. GOT AN APARTMENT TRADE PROPOSITION! A STEWART WHO LIVES IN THE XV DISTRICT, FOR THE MONTH OF JUNE. AS IT IS JUNE IS TOO SOON, AND THERE'S JFJ AND C.C.... i DON'T KNOW WHAT i WANT ANYMORE. DINNER WITH MY MOM... SHE GETS ON MY NERVES.

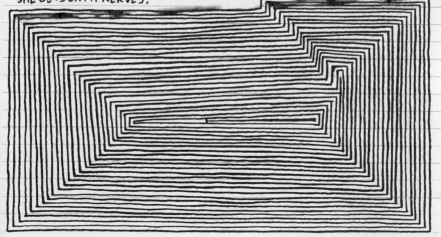

06.05.03. *tuesday.*

THE LEAVES IN THE TREES ARE STARTING TO GROW AND ME TO SNEEZE. EVERYTHING WENT WRONG AT THE STUDIO: i HADN'T RINSED MY SCREEN PROPERLY, SO THE EMULSION RAN DOWN AND BLOCKED MY IMAGES. i HAD TO START ALL OVER AGAIN... A NEW GIRL *in* SILKSCREEN: A.A. SHE ALSO HAD TONS OF PROBLEMS WITH HER SCREEN, SOMETHING MYSTERIOUS. D. BUSTED HERS WHILE PRINTING A POSTER! A BRAND NEW ONE! SHE EVEN SHED A FEW TEARS... SHE iS VERY UNLUCKY WITH THAT STUFF. STILL i WAS ABLE TO PRINT A FEW THINGS. THEN i STAYED TO HELP D. FINISH OFF HER POSTER (*in a heart shape*). WE WENT LATER TO THE CASA, TO MEET WITH HER GANG, TO CUT HER POSTERS IN THE SHAPE OF HEARTS. BACK HOME: i HAD A MESSAGE FROM A TV PERSON ASKING ME TO BE ON THIS SUMMER TALKSHOW "*l'île de Gildor*" YUCKKK! *i despise those* TV *shows*. THEY WANT TO DO A 20 Y.O. COMICS SPECIAL. *what 20 years?!* ANYWAY, WITHOUT ME. WE TALKED ABOUT THE TRIP, NOTHING SEEMS EASY.

SPACE FOR TWO ONLY IN THAT BERLIN HOTEL ROOM... NO MORE PLACE AT *such and such*... AND i HAVE NO IDEA HOW MUCH TIME i WANT OR CAN STAY IN FRANCE LATER.

07.05.03. *wednesday.*

THIS TIME i WAS ABLE TO DO ALL MY WORK. D. WENT TO THE STUDIO YESTERDAY. *and M.E. were there.* WE WENT TO EAT FRENCH FRIES ON RACHEL ST. THEN i HAD TO GO BACK HOME ON MY BIKE IN THE RAIN. SPENT THE EVENING IN FRONT OF THE TV, WHILE CUTTING AND PUTTING TOGETHER OBJECTS. ALWAYS FOR THE SAME CAUSE. i WATCHED THE FILM "PONETTE" BUT AFTER HALF AN HOUR IT HAD STARTED. i FOUND IT TOTALLY DETESTABLE. i COULDN'T STAND IT MORE THAN 30 MINUTES. AM i NORMAL? TO NOT HAVE BEEN MOVED ONE BIT? THE GIRLS WERE ALL IN A HURRY TO GO CRY IN FRONT OF THE TV *with* PONETTE...

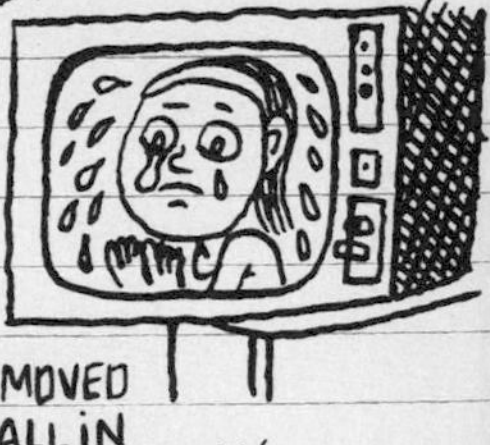

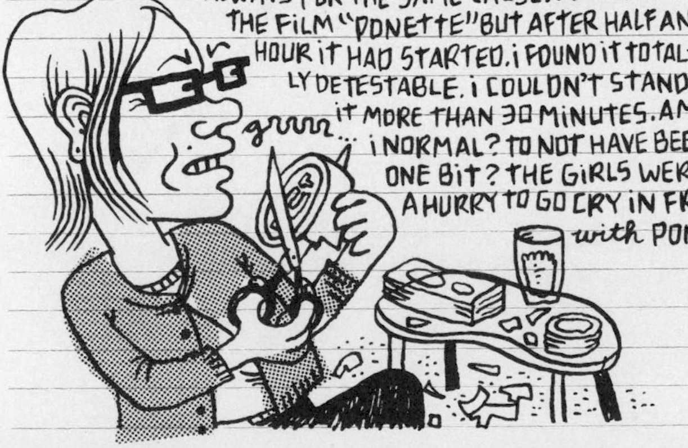
grrrr...

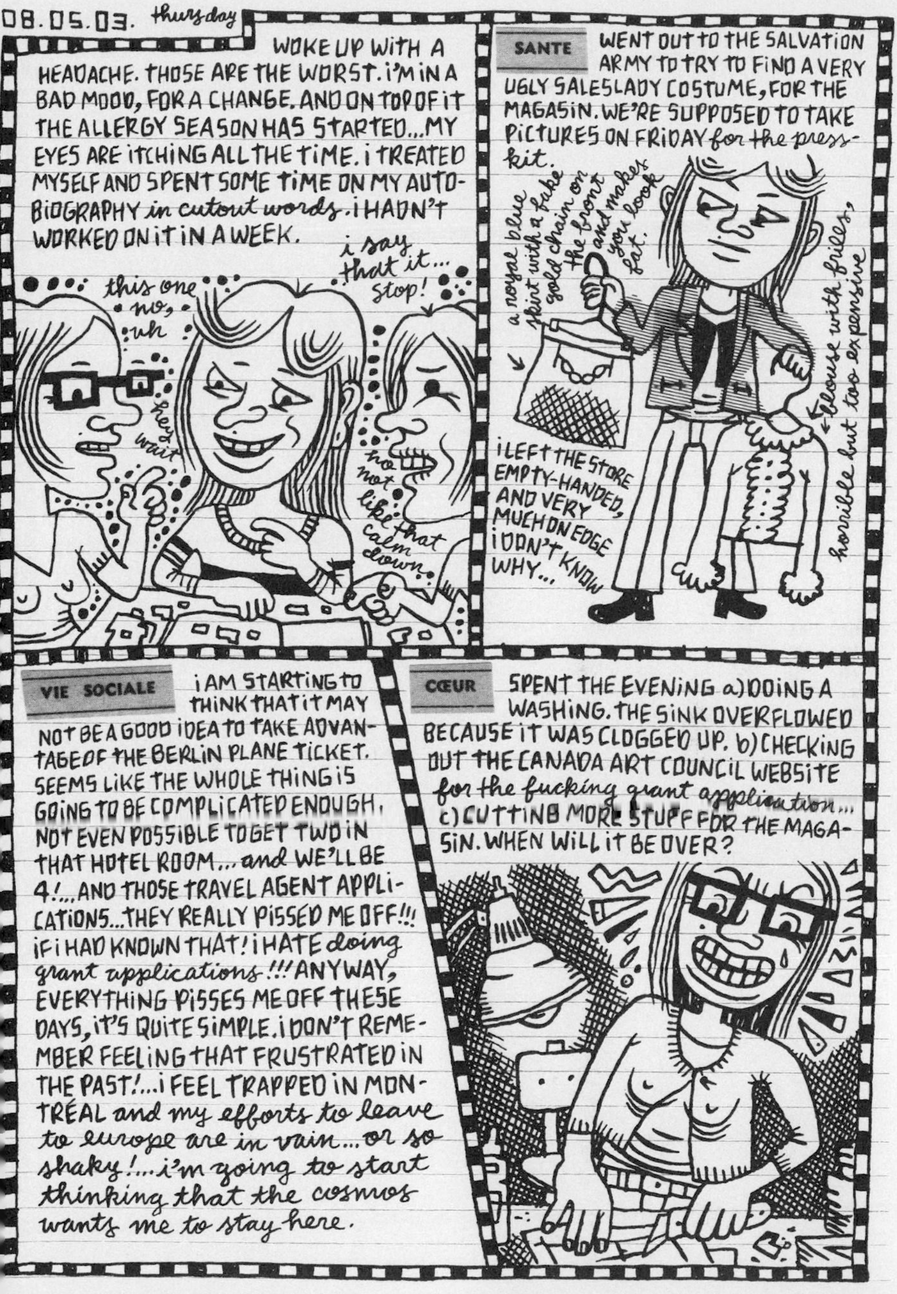
08.05.03. thursday
WOKE UP WITH A HEADACHE. THOSE ARE THE WORST. i'M IN A BAD MOOD, FOR A CHANGE. AND ON TOP OF IT THE ALLERGY SEASON HAS STARTED... MY EYES ARE ITCHING ALL THE TIME. i TREATED MYSELF AND SPENT SOME TIME ON MY AUTO-BIOGRAPHY in cutout words. i HADN'T WORKED ON iT iN A WEEK.
this one no, uh
hey wait
i say that it... stop!
no not like that calm down.
SANTE
WENT OUT TO THE SALVATION ARMY TO TRY TO FIND A VERY UGLY SALESLADY COSTUME, FOR THE MAGASIN. WE'RE SUPPOSED TO TAKE PICTURES ON FRIDAY for the press-kit.
a royal blue skirt with a fake gold chain on the front and makes you look fat.
blouse with frilles, horrible but too expensive
i LEFT THE STORE EMPTY-HANDED, AND VERY MUCH ON EDGE i DON'T KNOW WHY...
VIE SOCIALE
i AM STARTING TO THINK THAT iT MAY NOT BE A GOOD iDEA TO TAKE ADVAN-TAGE OF THE BERLIN PLANE TICKET. SEEMS LIKE THE WHOLE THING IS GOING TO BE COMPLICATED ENOUGH. NOT EVEN POSSIBLE TO GET TWO IN THAT HOTEL ROOM... and WE'LL BE 4!... AND THOSE TRAVEL AGENT APPLI-CATIONS... THEY REALLY PiSSED ME OFF!!! iF i HAD KNOWN THAT! i HATE doing grant applications!!! ANYWAY, EVERYTHING PiSSES ME OFF THESE DAYS, iT'S QUITE SIMPLE. i DON'T REME-MBER FEELING THAT FRUSTRATED IN THE PAST!... i FEEL TRAPPED iN MON-TRÉAL and my efforts to leave to europe are in vain... or so shaky!... i'm going to start thinking that the cosmos wants me to stay here.
CŒUR
SPENT THE EVENING a) DOING A WASHING. THE SINK OVERFLOWED BECAUSE iT WAS CLOGGED UP. b) CHECKING OUT THE CANADA ART COUNCIL WEBSITE for the fucking grant application... c) CUTTING MORE STUFF FOR THE MAGA-SiN. WHEN WiLL iT BE OVER?

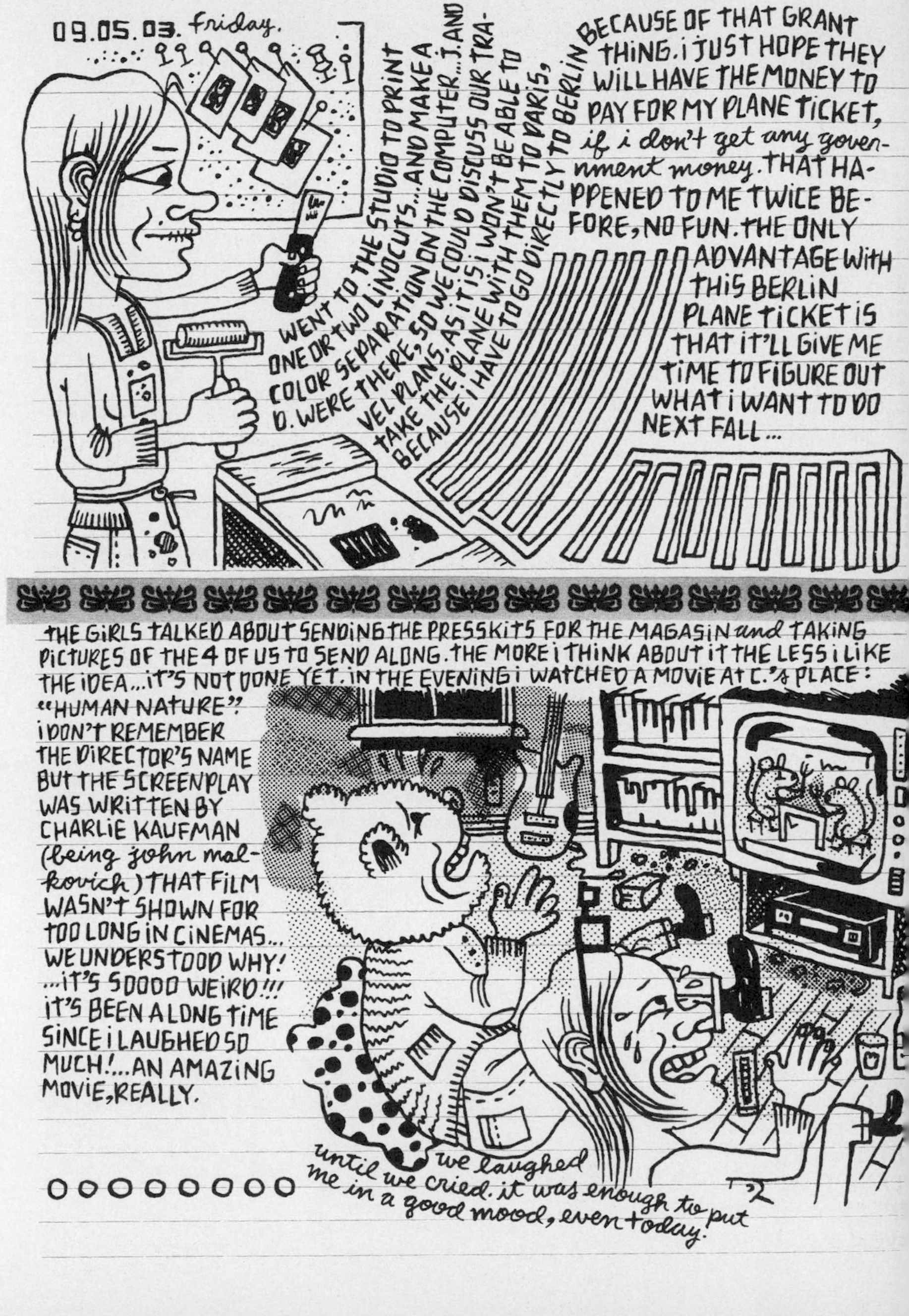
09.05.03. friday.
WENT TO THE STUDIO TO PRINT ONE OR TWO LINOCUTS... AND MAKE A COLOR SEPARATION ON THE COMPUTER... J. AND D. WERE THERE, SO WE COULD DISCUSS OUR TRAVEL PLANS. AS IT IS, i WON'T BE ABLE TO TAKE THE PLANE WITH THEM TO PARIS, BECAUSE i HAVE TO GO DIRECTLY TO BERLIN BECAUSE OF THAT GRANT THING. i JUST HOPE THEY WILL HAVE THE MONEY TO PAY FOR MY PLANE TICKET, if i don't get any government money. THAT HAPPENED TO ME TWICE BEFORE, NO FUN. THE ONLY ADVANTAGE WITH THIS BERLIN PLANE TICKET IS THAT IT'LL GIVE ME TIME TO FIGURE OUT WHAT i WANT TO DO NEXT FALL...
THE GIRLS TALKED ABOUT SENDING THE PRESSKITS FOR THE MAGASIN and TAKING PICTURES OF THE 4 OF US TO SEND ALONG. THE MORE i THINK ABOUT IT THE LESS i LIKE THE IDEA... IT'S NOT DONE YET. IN THE EVENING i WATCHED A MOVIE AT C.'s PLACE:
"HUMAN NATURE". i DON'T REMEMBER THE DIRECTOR'S NAME BUT THE SCREENPLAY WAS WRITTEN BY CHARLIE KAUFMAN (being john malkovich) THAT FILM WASN'T SHOWN FOR TOO LONG IN CINEMAS... WE UNDERSTOOD WHY! ...IT'S SOOOO WEIRD!!! IT'S BEEN A LONG TIME SINCE i LAUGHED SO MUCH!... AN AMAZING MOVIE, REALLY.
we laughed until we cried. it was enough to put me in a good mood, even today.

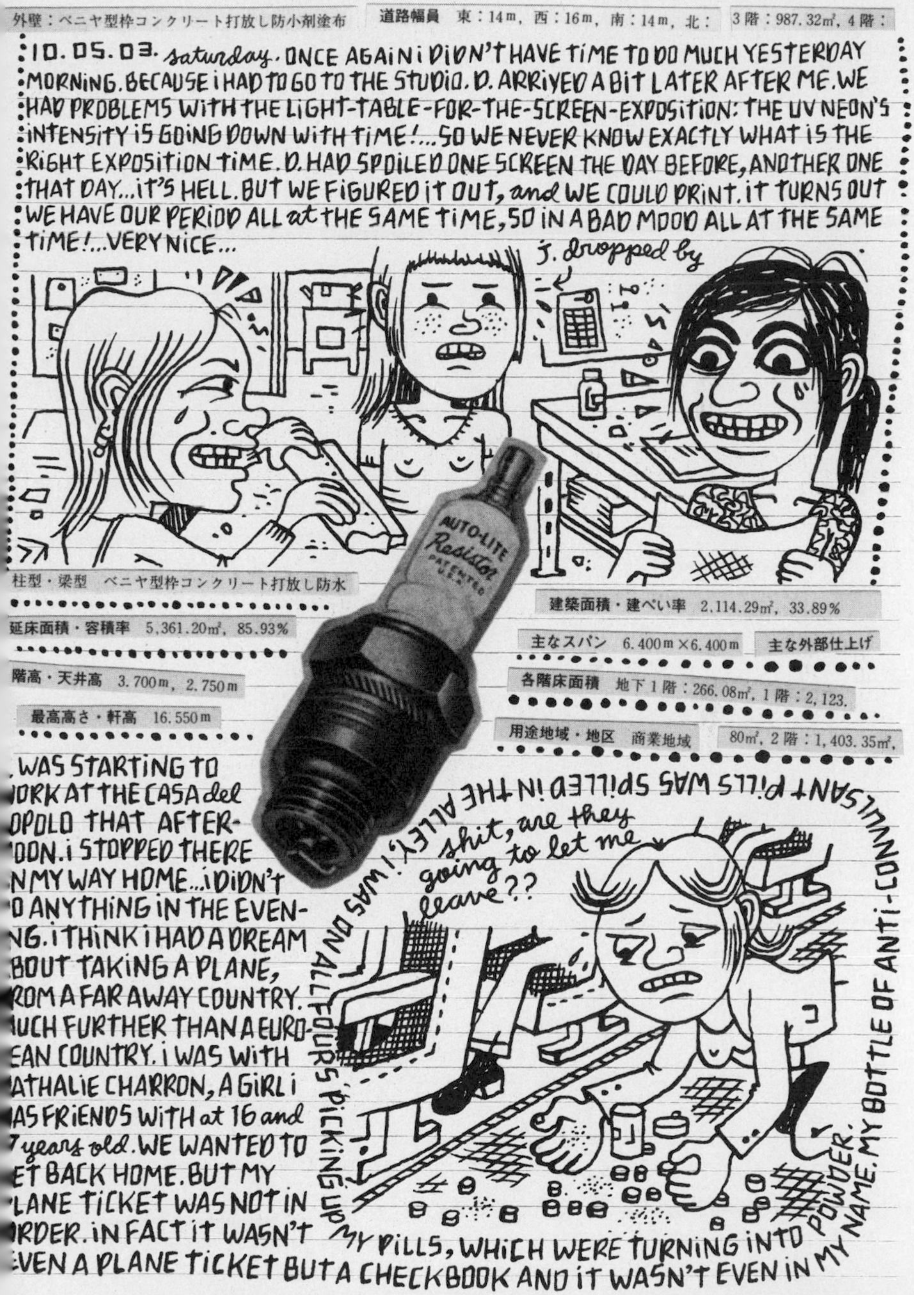
外壁：ベニヤ型枠コンクリート打放し防小剤塗布
道路幅員　東：14m，西：16m，南：14m，北：
3階：987.32m²，4階：
10.05.03. saturday. ONCE AGAIN i DIDN'T HAVE TIME TO DO MUCH YESTERDAY MORNING. BECAUSE i HAD TO GO TO THE STUDIO. D. ARRIVED A BIT LATER AFTER ME. WE HAD PROBLEMS WITH THE LIGHT-TABLE-FOR-THE-SCREEN-EXPOSITION: THE UV NEON'S INTENSITY IS GOING DOWN WITH TIME!... SO WE NEVER KNOW EXACTLY WHAT IS THE RIGHT EXPOSITION TIME. D. HAD SPOILED ONE SCREEN THE DAY BEFORE, ANOTHER ONE THAT DAY... iT'S HELL. BUT WE FIGURED iT OUT, and WE COULD PRINT. iT TURNS OUT WE HAVE OUR PERIOD ALL at THE SAME TIME, SO IN A BAD MOOD ALL AT THE SAME TIME!... VERY NICE...
J. dropped by
AUTO-LITE
Resistor
PATENTED
柱型・梁型　ベニヤ型枠コンクリート打放し防水
延床面積・容積率　5,361.20m²，85.93%
階高・天井高　3.700m，2.750m
最高高さ・軒高　16.550m
建築面積・建ぺい率　2,114.29m²，33.89%
主なスパン　6.400m×6.400m
主な外部仕上げ
各階床面積　地下1階：266.08m²，1階：2,123.
用途地域・地区　商業地域
80m²，2階：1,403.35m²，
. WAS STARTING TO ORK AT THE CASA del OPOLO THAT AFTER-OON. i STOPPED THERE N MY WAY HOME... i DIDN'T O ANYTHING IN THE EVEN-NG. i THINK i HAD A DREAM BOUT TAKING A PLANE, ROM A FAR AWAY COUNTRY. UCH FURTHER THAN A EURO-EAN COUNTRY. i WAS WITH ATHALIE CHARRON, A GIRL i AS FRIENDS WITH at 16 and 7 years old. WE WANTED TO ET BACK HOME. BUT MY LANE TICKET WAS NOT IN RDER. IN FACT IT WASN'T EVEN A PLANE TICKET BUT A CHECKBOOK AND IT WASN'T EVEN IN MY NAME. MY BOTTLE OF ANTI-CONVULSANT PILLS WAS SPILLED IN THE ALLEY, I WAS ON ALL FOURS PICKING UP MY PILLS, WHICH WERE TURNING INTO POWDER.
shit, are they going to let me leave??

11. 05. 03. sunday.

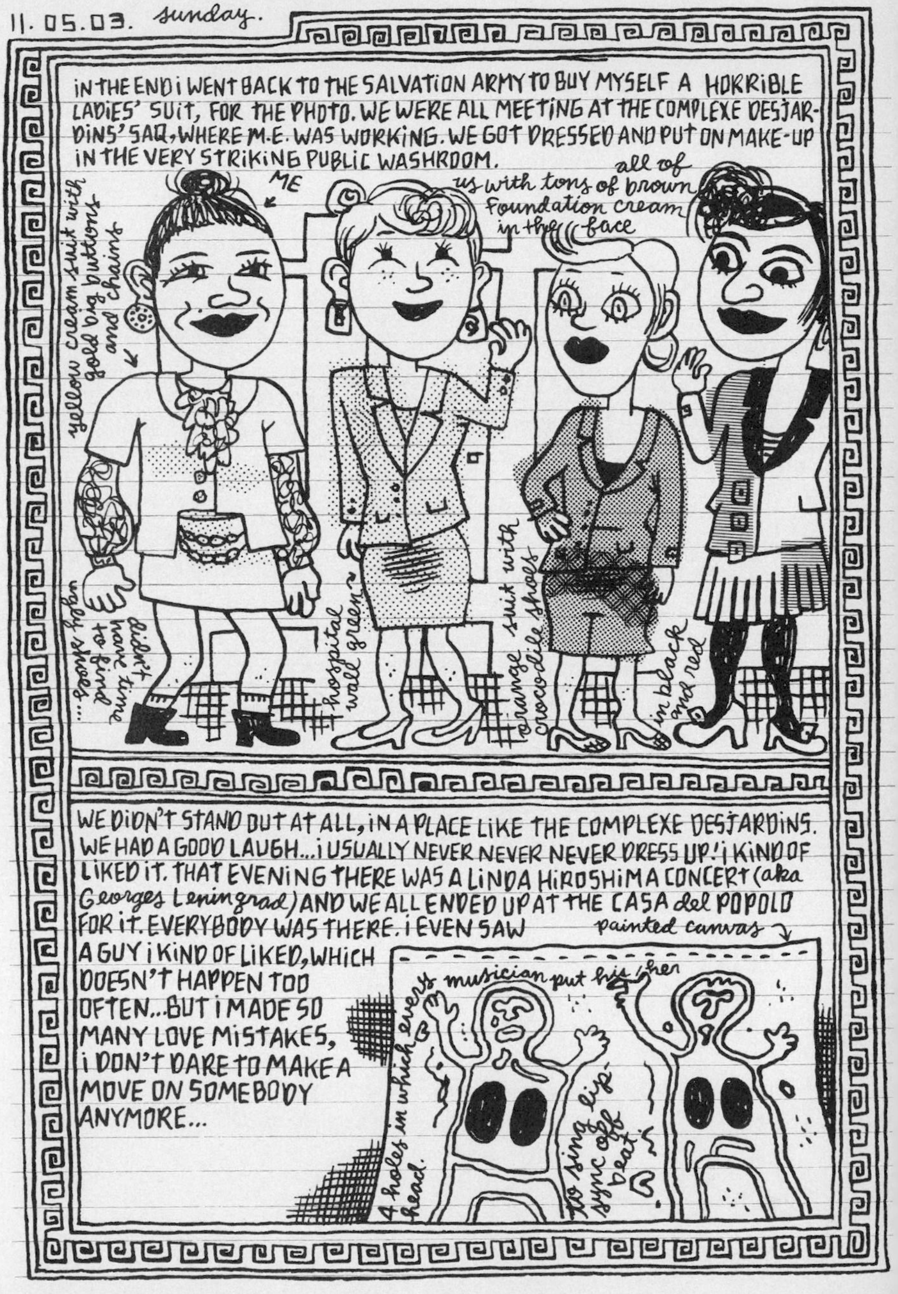
IN THE END I WENT BACK TO THE SALVATION ARMY TO BUY MYSELF A HORRIBLE LADIES' SUIT, FOR THE PHOTO. WE WERE ALL MEETING AT THE COMPLEXE DESJARDINS' SAQ, WHERE M.E. WAS WORKING. WE GOT DRESSED AND PUT ON MAKE-UP IN THE VERY STRIKING PUBLIC WASHROOM.
ME
yellow cream suit with gold big buttons and chains
all of us with tons of brown foundation cream in the face
didn't have time to find ugly shoes...
hospital wall green
orange suit with crocodile shoes
in black and red
WE DIDN'T STAND OUT AT ALL, IN A PLACE LIKE THE COMPLEXE DESJARDINS. WE HAD A GOOD LAUGH... I USUALLY NEVER NEVER NEVER DRESS UP! I KIND OF LIKED IT. THAT EVENING THERE WAS A LINDA HIROSHIMA CONCERT (aka Georges Leningrad) AND WE ALL ENDED UP AT THE CASA del POPOLO FOR IT. EVERYBODY WAS THERE. I EVEN SAW A GUY I KIND OF LIKED, WHICH DOESN'T HAPPEN TOO OFTEN... BUT I MADE SO MANY LOVE MISTAKES, I DON'T DARE TO MAKE A MOVE ON SOMEBODY ANYMORE...
painted canvas
4 holes in which every musician put his/her head.
to sing lip-sync off beat

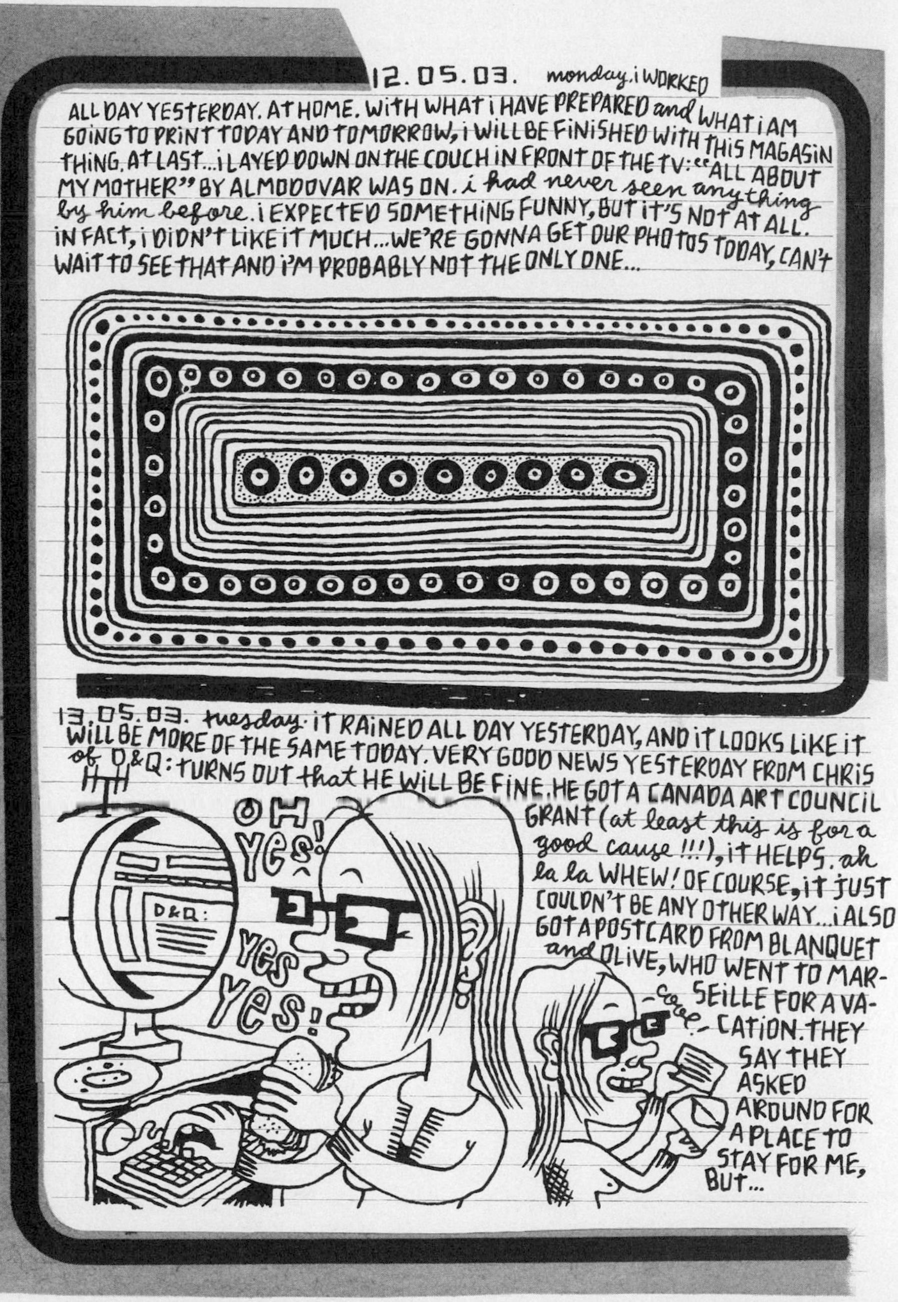
12.05.03. monday. i WORKED ALL DAY YESTERDAY. AT HOME. WITH WHAT i HAVE PREPARED and WHAT i AM GOING TO PRINT TODAY AND TOMORROW, i WILL BE FINISHED WITH THIS MAGASIN THING. AT LAST... i LAYED DOWN ON THE COUCH IN FRONT OF THE TV: "ALL ABOUT MY MOTHER" BY ALMODOVAR WAS ON. i had never seen anything by him before. i EXPECTED SOMETHING FUNNY, BUT it'S NOT AT ALL. IN FACT, i DIDN'T LIKE IT MUCH... WE'RE GONNA GET OUR PHOTOS TODAY, CAN'T WAIT TO SEE THAT AND i'M PROBABLY NOT THE ONLY ONE...
13.05.03. tuesday. iT RAINED ALL DAY YESTERDAY, AND iT LOOKS LIKE iT WILL BE MORE OF THE SAME TODAY. VERY GOOD NEWS YESTERDAY FROM CHRIS of D&Q: TURNS OUT that HE WILL BE FINE. HE GOT A CANADA ART COUNCIL GRANT (at least this is for a good cause!!!), iT HELPS. ah la la WHEW! OF COURSE, iT JUST COULDN'T BE ANY OTHER WAY... i ALSO GOT A POSTCARD FROM BLANQUET and OLiVE, WHO WENT TO MARSEILLE FOR A VACATION. THEY SAY THEY ASKED AROUND FOR A PLACE TO STAY FOR ME, BUT...
OH, YES!
YES YES!
D&Q:
-cool-

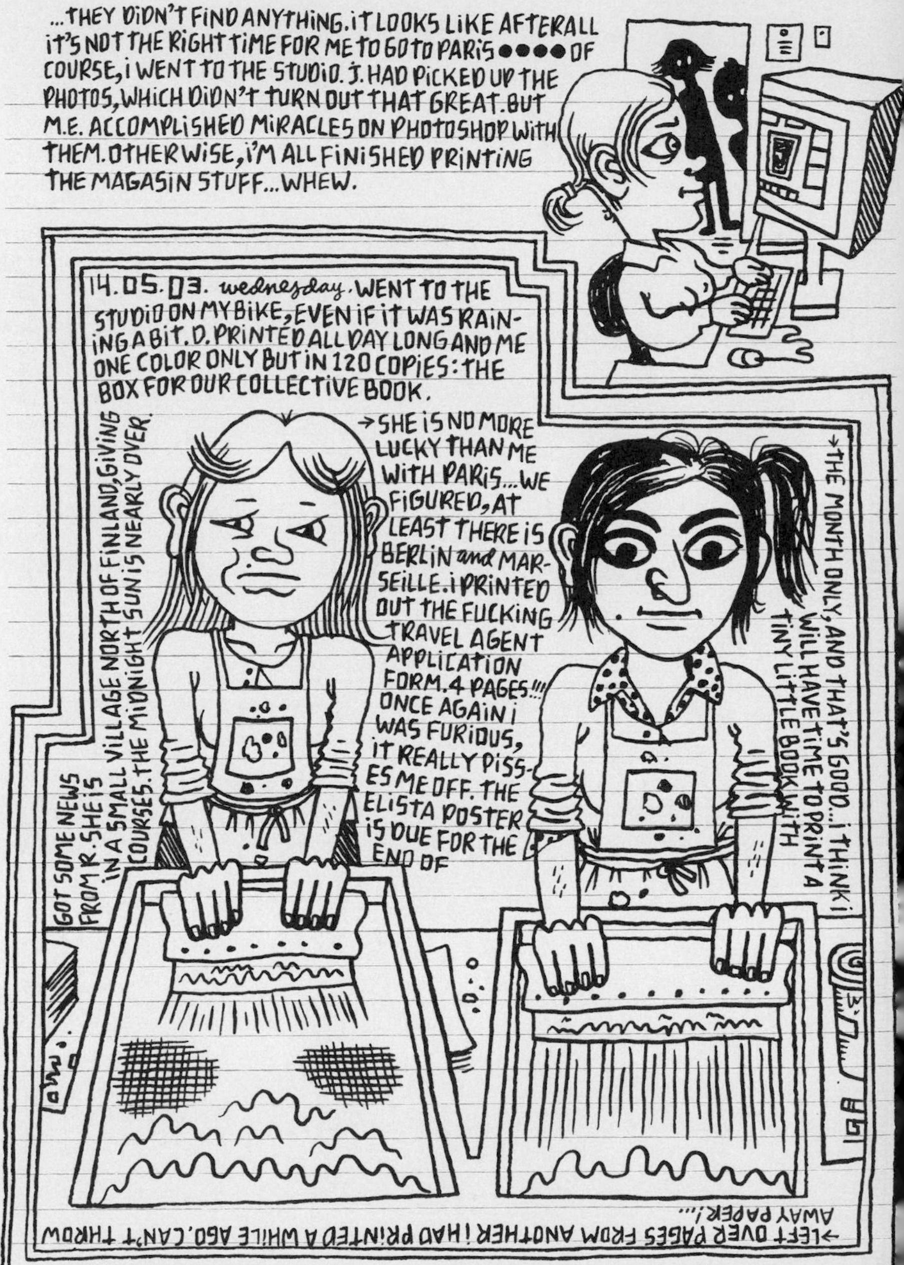
...THEY DIDN'T FIND ANYTHING. IT LOOKS LIKE AFTER ALL IT'S NOT THE RIGHT TIME FOR ME TO GO TO PARIS ●●●● OF COURSE, I WENT TO THE STUDIO. J. HAD PICKED UP THE PHOTOS, WHICH DIDN'T TURN OUT THAT GREAT. BUT M.E. ACCOMPLISHED MIRACLES ON PHOTOSHOP WITH THEM. OTHERWISE, I'M ALL FINISHED PRINTING THE MAGASIN STUFF... WHEW.
14.05.03. wednesday. WENT TO THE STUDIO ON MY BIKE, EVEN IF IT WAS RAINING A BIT. D. PRINTED ALL DAY LONG AND ME ONE COLOR ONLY BUT IN 120 COPIES: THE BOX FOR OUR COLLECTIVE BOOK.
GOT SOME NEWS FROM R. SHE IS IN A SMALL VILLAGE NORTH OF FINLAND, GIVING COURSES. THE MIDNIGHT SUN IS NEARLY OVER.
→SHE IS NO MORE LUCKY THAN ME WITH PARIS... WE FIGURED, AT LEAST THERE IS BERLIN and MARSEILLE. I PRINTED OUT THE FUCKING TRAVEL AGENT APPLICATION FORM. 4 PAGES!!! ONCE AGAIN I WAS FURIOUS, IT REALLY PISSES ME OFF. THE ELISTA POSTER IS DUE FOR THE END OF
→THE MONTH ONLY, AND THAT'S GOOD... I THINK I WILL HAVE TIME TO PRINT A TINY LITTLE BOOK WITH
←LEFT OVER PAGES FROM ANOTHER I HAD PRINTED A WHILE AGO. CAN'T THROW AWAY PAPER!...

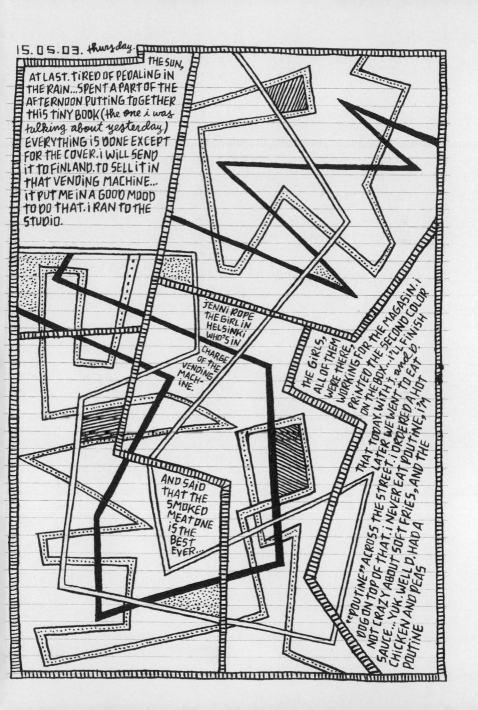

15. 05. 03. *thursday.*

THE SUN, AT LAST. TIRED OF PEDALING IN THE RAIN... SPENT A PART OF THE AFTERNOON PUTTING TOGETHER THIS TINY BOOK (the one i was talking about yesterday) EVERYTHING iS DONE EXCEPT FOR THE COVER. i WILL SEND iT TO FINLAND. TO SELL iT IN THAT VENDING MACHINE... iT PUT ME IN A GOOD MOOD TO DO THAT. i RAN TO THE STUDIO.

JENNI ROPE THE GIRL IN HELSINKI WHO'S IN CHARGE OF THE VENDING MACHINE.

THE GIRLS, ALL OF THEM, WERE THERE, WORKING FOR THE MAGASIN. i PRINTED THE SECOND COLOR ON THE BOX... i'LL FINISH THAT TODAY. WITH J. and D. LATER WE WENT TO EAT

AND SAID THAT THE SMOKED MEAT ONE IS THE BEST EVER...

"POUTINE" ACROSS THE STREET. i NEVER EAT POUTINE. i'm NOT CRAZY ABOUT THAT. i ORDERED A HOT DOG ON TOP OF THAT. SAUCE... YUK. WELL D. HAD A CHICKEN AND PEAS SOFT FRIES, AND THE POUTINE

16.05.03. *friday*. AN INTERESTING OFFER CAME YESTERDAY, IN A FORM OF AN E-MAIL: A NEW YORK ANIMATION COMPANY WANTS TO WORK WITH ME. i IMMEDIATELY HAD DOLLAR SIGNS IN MY EYES. i WOULD HAVE THE OPTION TO SIMPLY ILLUSTRATE SOMETHING, WHICH i WOULD PREFER. i JUST WANT MONEY!...

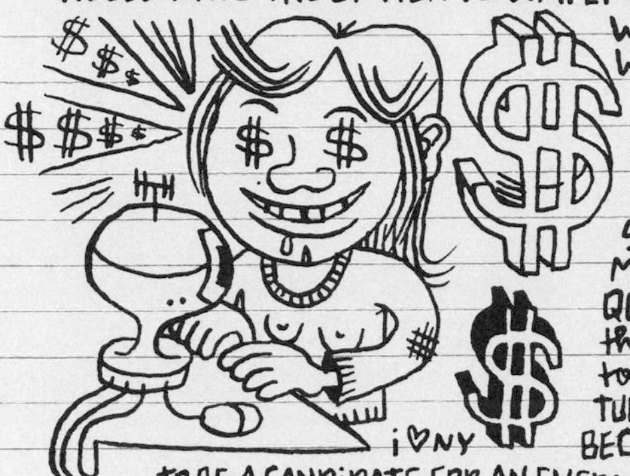
i ♥ NY

WENT TO THE STUDIO, WHERE i FINISHED PRINTING THAT BOX, WITH A MINIMUM OF (*paper*) LOSS. i WAS QUITE PROUD OF MYSELF. *at a point the studio's coordinator wanted to talk to me in private:* TURNS OUT SOMEBODY FROM THE QUÉBEC MUSEUM CAME BY AND WANTS ME TO BE A CANDIDATE FOR AN ENGRAVING GRANT ($20,000 + *they buy a bunch of art from you so in all it's $50,000!*). i HAVE TO SEND SLIDES, A PRESSKIT BY PRIORITY COURIER TODAY. BACK HOME, i DID A WASHING AND i THREW MY PASSPORT IN THE WASHING MACHINE. i TOLD MYSELF *that a good hot water washing would demolish it enough so i can ask for a new one.* i WANTED TO ERASE A COMPRIMISING AMERICAN CUSTOMS STAMP... *last time i was there, in september 2001, they suspected for some reason i wanted to move in the U.S. and put this stamp in my passport blah blah blah...* SO i'M GOING TO ASK FOR A NEW ONE. iN THE EVENING THERE WAS A SUPPER *at C.'s, with 4 other friends. the ones we play poker with... Pleasant...*

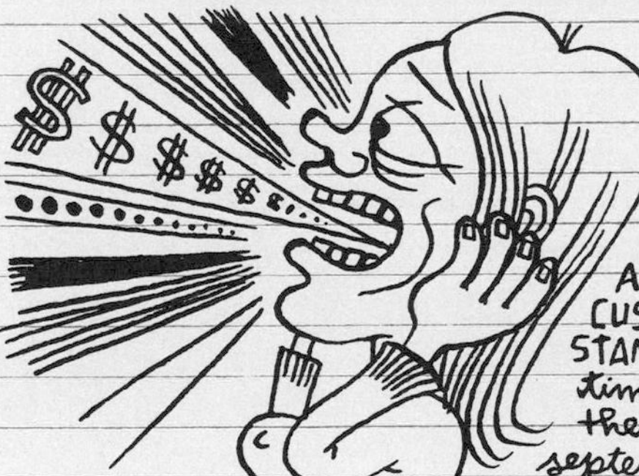

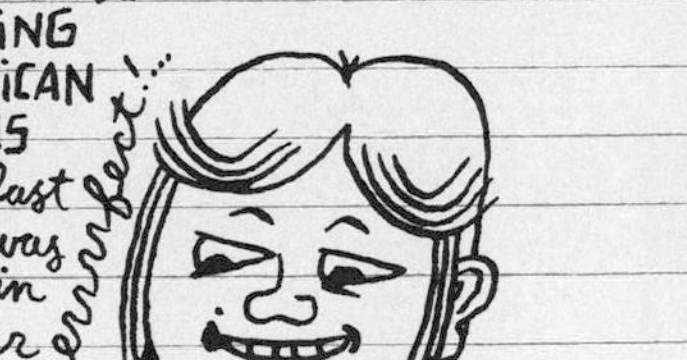
perrrfect!...

17.05.03. saturday.

GOT UP AT SEVEN, THINKING IT WAS EIGHT. i AM TAKING THE BUS THIS MORNING TO GO TO MY DAD'S PLACE. i RAN YESTERDAY MORNING TO PUT TOGETHER THAT DOSSIER FOR THE QUÉBEC MUSEUM, and SENT iT EXPRESS POST. AT GRAFF THE GIRLS WERE ALREADY AT WORK. SEEING WHAT THEY HAVE DONE IN THE PAST WEEK i THINK THE MAGASIN WILL LOOK PRETTY GOOD... GOT STARTED ON MY LITTLE BOOK, PRINTED SIX COLORS. i THINK THIS ONE WILL BE ONE OF THE GOOD ONES. i LiKE HOW iT LOOKS SO FAR. IN THE EVENING WE ALL WENT TO LE ROi DU PLATEAU. THIS TIME WE HAD MADE RES-ERVATIONS. i TOOK HALF A PLATE (which are usually very generous) AND J. TOO. BUT iT WASN'T ENOUGH. OH WELL... LATER THERE WAS A FILM SCREENING, ORGANIZED BY THIS GiRL i RUN INTO ONCE iN A WHILE, SHE'S NiCE... SHE'S DOING iT TO FINANCE A TRiP. A MOVIE BY J. WAS GO-ING TO BE SHOWN, ALSO A FEW BY D.'s BOYFRIEND. i THOUGHT THOSE TWO'S WERE VERY MUCH BETTER THAN EVERYTHING ELSE. MOST OF THE FILMS WERE NOTHING SPECIAL, iF NOT MEDIOCRE. iT WAS HAPPEN-ING IN A HUGE LOFT (lent for the occasion) DOWNTOWN. THERE WAS EIGHT TOOTHBRUSHES IN THE BATHROOM! WENT BACK HOME AT TWO. THE END.

18.05.03. sunday.

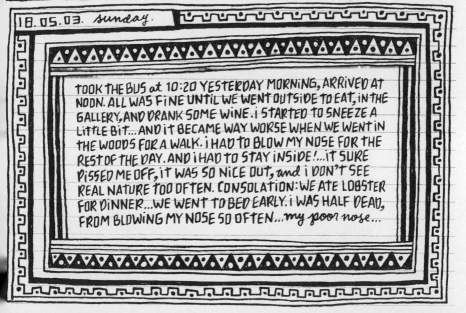

TOOK THE BUS at 10:20 YESTERDAY MORNING, ARRIVED AT NOON. ALL WAS FINE UNTIL WE WENT OUTSIDE TO EAT, IN THE GALLERY, AND DRANK SOME WINE. i STARTED TO SNEEZE A LITTLE BiT... AND iT BECAME WAY WORSE WHEN WE WENT IN THE WOODS FOR A WALK. i HAD TO BLOW MY NOSE FOR THE REST OF THE DAY. AND i HAD TO STAY INSIDE!... iT SURE PISSED ME OFF, iT WAS SO NICE OUT, and i DON'T SEE REAL NATURE TOO OFTEN. CONSOLATION: WE ATE LOBSTER FOR DINNER... WE WENT TO BED EARLY. i WAS HALF DEAD, FROM BLOWING MY NOSE SO OFTEN... my poor nose...

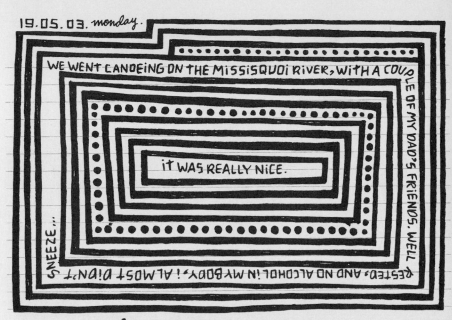

19.05.03. monday.

WE WENT CANOEING ON THE MISSISQUOI RIVER, WITH A COUPLE OF MY DAD'S FRIENDS. WELL RESTED, AND NO ALCOHOL IN MY BODY, I ALMOST DIDN'T SNEEZE...

iT WAS REALLY NiCE.

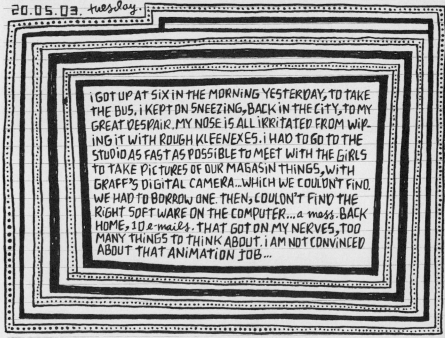

20.05.03. tuesday.

i GOT UP AT SIX iN THE MORNiNG YESTERDAY, TO TAKE THE BUS. i KEPT ON SNEEZiNG. BACK iN THE CiTY, TO MY GREAT DESPAIR, MY NOSE iS ALL iRRiTATED FROM WiP- iNG iT WiTH ROUGH KLEENEXES. i HAD TO GO TO THE STUDiO AS FAST AS POSSiBLE TO MEET WiTH THE GiRLS TO TAKE PiCTURES OF OUR MAGASiN THiNGS, WiTH GRAFF'S DiGiTAL CAMERA...WHiCH WE COULDN'T FiND. WE HAD TO BORROW ONE. THEN, COULDN'T FiND THE RiGHT SOFTWARE ON THE COMPUTER...a mess. BACK HOME, 10 e-mails. THAT GOT ON MY NERVES, TOO MANY THiNGS TO THiNK ABOUT. i AM NOT CONViNCED ABOUT THAT ANiMATiON JOB...

21.05.03. *wednesday.* IT'S NOT AS HOT TODAY, THANK GOD. i SPENT THE MORNING YESTERDAY WRITING THE POSTER TITLE WITH LETRASET. PRINTED *and* SNEEZED ALL AFTERNOON, IN A SUPER-HOT ROOM. THAT STUDIO IS HELL... i'M EVEN WONDERING IF IT'S WORTH IT TO RENT IT IN JUNE... IF IT'S THAT HOT IN MAY!...

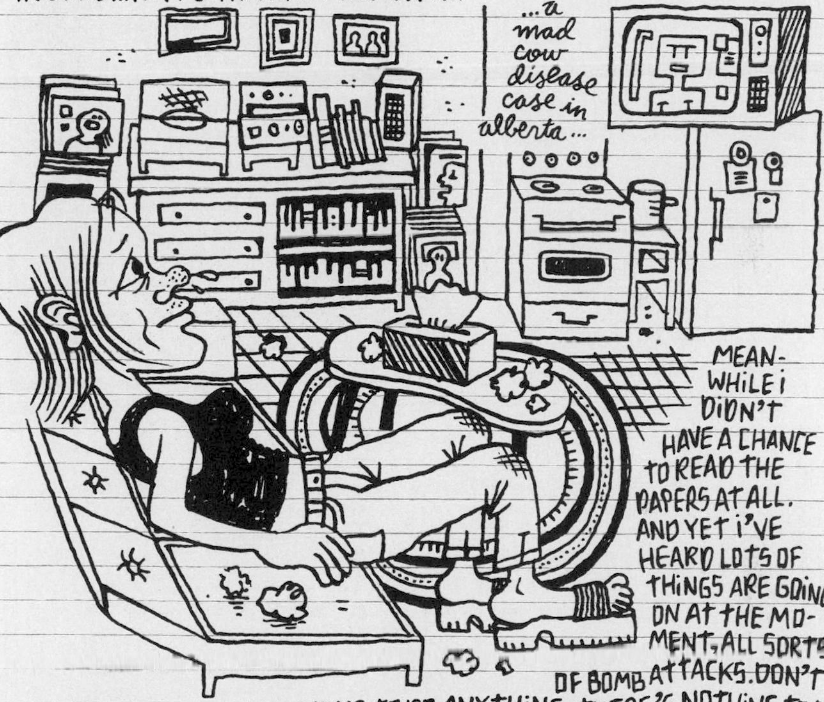
...a mad cow disease case in alberta...

MEANWHILE i DIDN'T HAVE A CHANCE TO READ THE PAPERS AT ALL. AND YET i'VE HEARD LOTS OF THINGS ARE GOING ON AT THE MOMENT, ALL SORTS OF BOMB ATTACKS. DON'T HAVE TIME TO DO ANYTHING, THERE'S NOTHING TO EAT IN THE FRIDGE (*breakfast menu this morning: plain cous-cous*) AND EVERYTHING IS COVERED IN CAT HAIR.

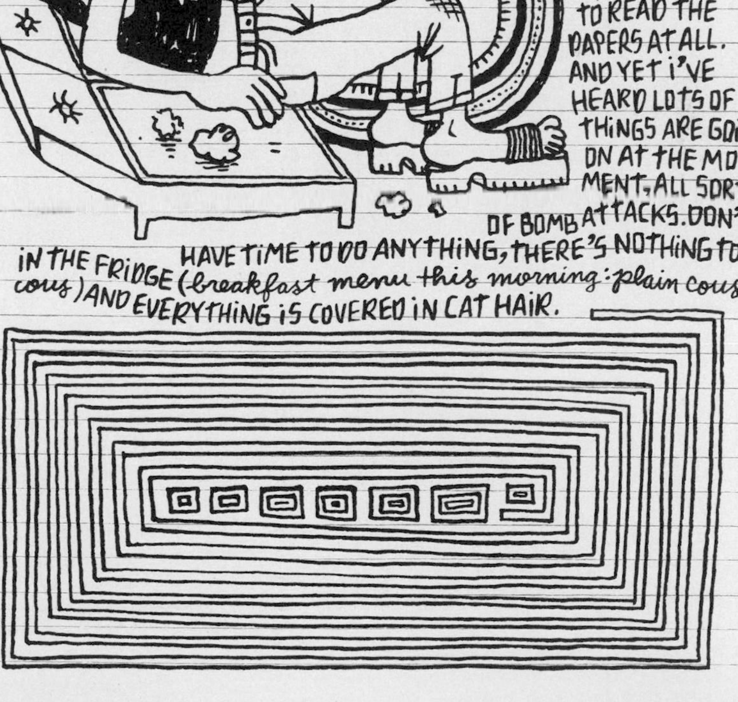

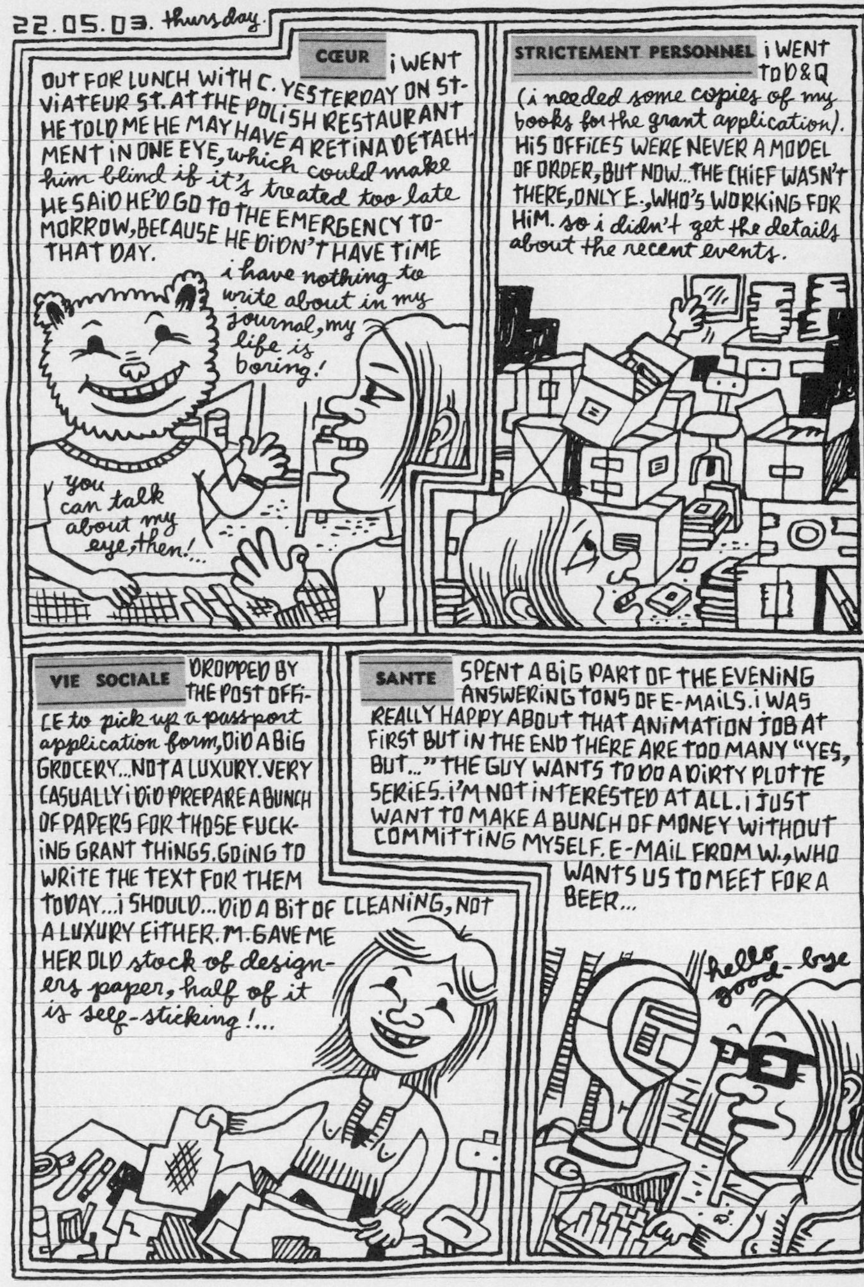
22.05.03. thursday.
CŒUR
i WENT OUT FOR LUNCH WITH C. YESTERDAY ON ST-VIATEUR ST. AT THE POLISH RESTAURANT. HE TOLD ME HE MAY HAVE A RETINA DETACHMENT IN ONE EYE, which could make him blind if it's treated too late. HE SAID HE'D GO TO THE EMERGENCY TOMORROW, BECAUSE HE DIDN'T HAVE TIME THAT DAY.
i have nothing to write about in my journal, my life is boring!
you can talk about my eye, then!...
STRICTEMENT PERSONNEL
i WENT TO D&Q (i needed some copies of my books for the grant application). HiS OFFiCES WERE NEVER A MODEL OF ORDER, BUT NOW... THE CHiEF WASN'T THERE, ONLY E., WHO'S WORKiNG FOR HiM. so i didn't get the details about the recent events.
VIE SOCIALE
DROPPED BY THE POST OFFiCE to pick up a passport application form, DiD A BiG GROCERY... NOT A LUXURY. VERY CASUALLY i DiD PREPARE A BUNCH OF PAPERS FOR THOSE FUCKiNG GRANT THiNGS. GOiNG TO WRITE THE TEXT FOR THEM TODAY... i SHOULD... DiD A BiT OF CLEANiNG, NOT A LUXURY EiTHER. M. GAVE ME HER OLD stock of designers paper, half of it is self-sticking!...
SANTE
SPENT A BiG PART OF THE EVENiNG ANSWERiNG TONS OF E-MAiLS. i WAS REALLY HAPPY ABOUT THAT ANiMATiON JOB AT FiRST BUT iN THE END THERE ARE TOO MANY "YES, BUT..." THE GUY WANTS TO DO A DiRTY PLOTTE SERiES. i'M NOT iNTERESTED AT ALL. i JUST WANT TO MAKE A BUNCH OF MONEY WiTHOUT COMMiTTiNG MYSELF. E-MAiL FROM W., WHO WANTS US TO MEET FOR A BEER...
hello good-bye

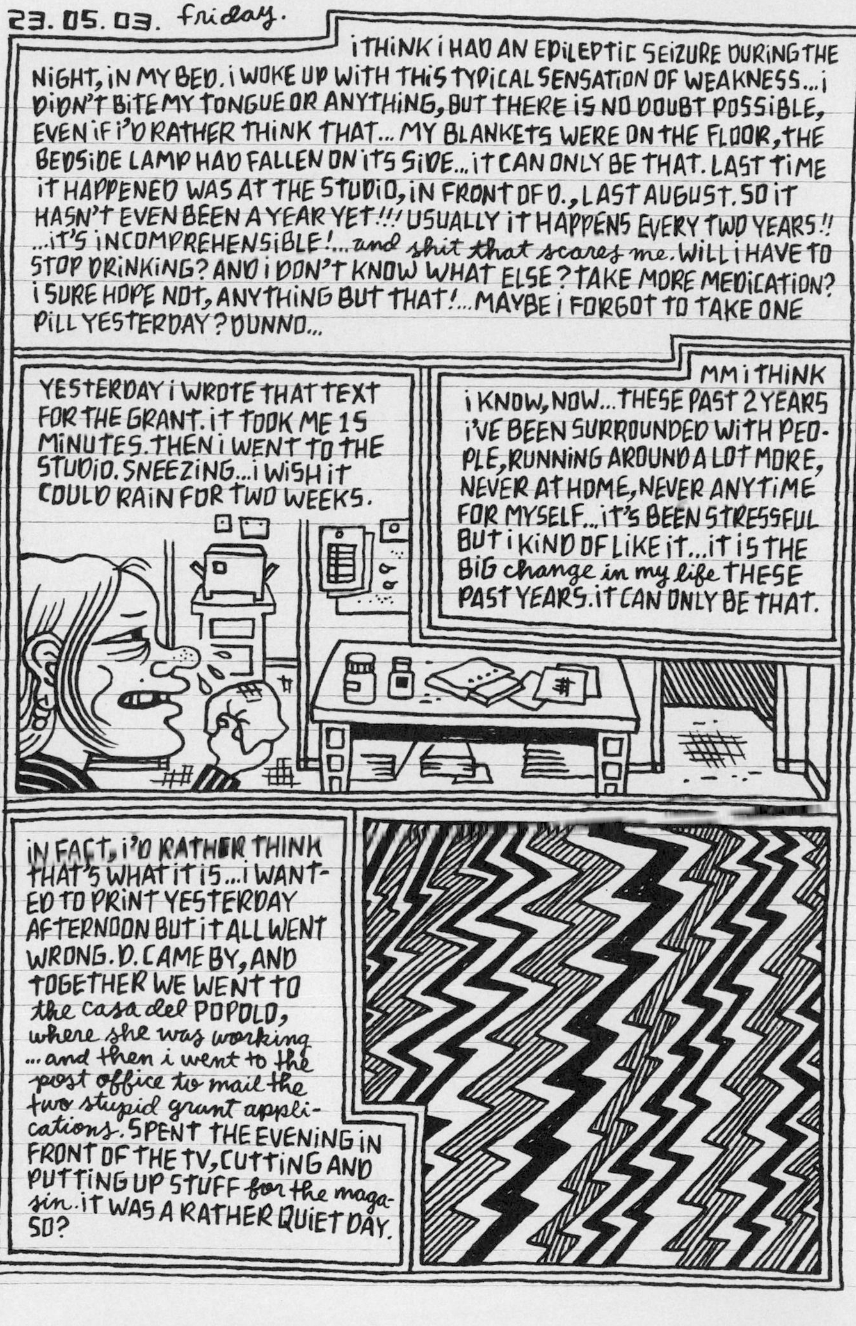
23.05.03. friday.
i THINK i HAD AN EPILEPTIC SEIZURE DURING THE NIGHT, IN MY BED. i WOKE UP WITH THIS TYPICAL SENSATION OF WEAKNESS... i DIDN'T BITE MY TONGUE OR ANYTHING, BUT THERE IS NO DOUBT POSSIBLE, EVEN IF i'D RATHER THINK THAT... MY BLANKETS WERE ON THE FLOOR, THE BEDSIDE LAMP HAD FALLEN ON ITS SIDE... IT CAN ONLY BE THAT. LAST TIME IT HAPPENED WAS AT THE STUDIO, IN FRONT OF D., LAST AUGUST. SO IT HASN'T EVEN BEEN A YEAR YET!!! USUALLY IT HAPPENS EVERY TWO YEARS!! ...IT'S INCOMPREHENSIBLE!... and shit that scares me. WILL i HAVE TO STOP DRINKING? AND i DON'T KNOW WHAT ELSE? TAKE MORE MEDICATION? i SURE HOPE NOT, ANYTHING BUT THAT!... MAYBE i FORGOT TO TAKE ONE PILL YESTERDAY? DUNNO...
YESTERDAY i WROTE THAT TEXT FOR THE GRANT. IT TOOK ME 15 MINUTES. THEN i WENT TO THE STUDIO. SNEEZING... i WISH IT COULD RAIN FOR TWO WEEKS.
MM i THINK i KNOW, NOW... THESE PAST 2 YEARS i'VE BEEN SURROUNDED WITH PEOPLE, RUNNING AROUND A LOT MORE, NEVER AT HOME, NEVER ANY TIME FOR MYSELF... IT'S BEEN STRESSFUL BUT i KIND OF LIKE IT... IT IS THE BIG change in my life THESE PAST YEARS. IT CAN ONLY BE THAT.
IN FACT, i'D RATHER THINK THAT'S WHAT IT IS... i WANTED TO PRINT YESTERDAY AFTERNOON BUT IT ALL WENT WRONG. D. CAME BY, AND TOGETHER WE WENT TO the casa del POPOLO, where she was working ...and then i went to the post office to mail the two stupid grant applications. SPENT THE EVENING IN FRONT OF THE TV, CUTTING AND PUTTING UP STUFF for the magasin. IT WAS A RATHER QUIET DAY. SO?

24.05.03. saturday. i WAS NOT iN THE BEST SHAPE POSSIBLE YESTERDAY. THE THiNG iS THAT i HADN'T SLEPT TOO WELL, AFTER THE SEIZURE. WENT TO THE STUDIO ANYWAY. WHAT WAS i THiNKiNG!? i WAS HALF DEAD AFTER PRiNTiNG ONLY ONE COLOR. J. and O. WERE THERE. i TOLD THEM THE STORY, AT LEAST, WHAT i REMEMBER...

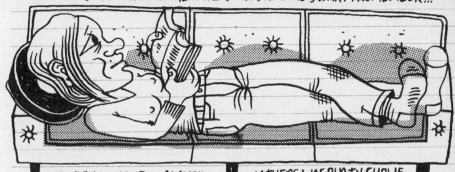

WENT BACK HOME and LAYED DOWN ON THE COUCH TO READ. EVENTUALLY THERE WAS OLD TV SHOWS from the 60's on, like "BEWITCHED" and "GiLLiGAN'S island". DiDN'T THiNK iT WAS FUNNY AT ALL. OK, iT WAS DUBBED iN FRENCH. WENT TO BED AT 9:30. C. WENT TO THE HOSPiTAL: HE'S FiNE.

25.05.03. sunday. i WAS SUPPOSED TO HAVE BREAKFAST WiTH C. YESTERDAY end of MORNiNG. i MET HiM AT HiS PLACE, and JUST WHEN WE WERE LEAVING HE GOT A PHONE CALL FROM A GiRL HE WAS SUPPOSED TO HAVE A MEETiNG WiTH AN HOUR AGO. SHE CAME TO mtl from QUÉBEC TO TALK BUSiNESS WiTH HiM... SO HE ABANDONED ME.

i DiDN'T KNOW WHAT THE HELL TO DO THE WHOLE AFTERNOON. DONE THiS AND THAT, LEFT and RiGHT... REALLY DiDN'T FEEL LiKE DOiNG ANY-THiNG. iT RAiNED ALL DAY. C. RE-APPEARED LATER. WE WENT OUT FOR A COFFEE. WELL, A JUiCE, iN MY CASE... pffff...

THEN LATER DiNNER WiTH MY MOM. ON THE MENU: LOBSTER. i LEARN-ED THAT EVENiNG THAT AS A very SMALL KiD i FELL off MY HiGH CHAiR AND HiT MY HEAD ON A CAST-iRON HEATER... AND THERE YOU GO! i learn about it 23 years later.

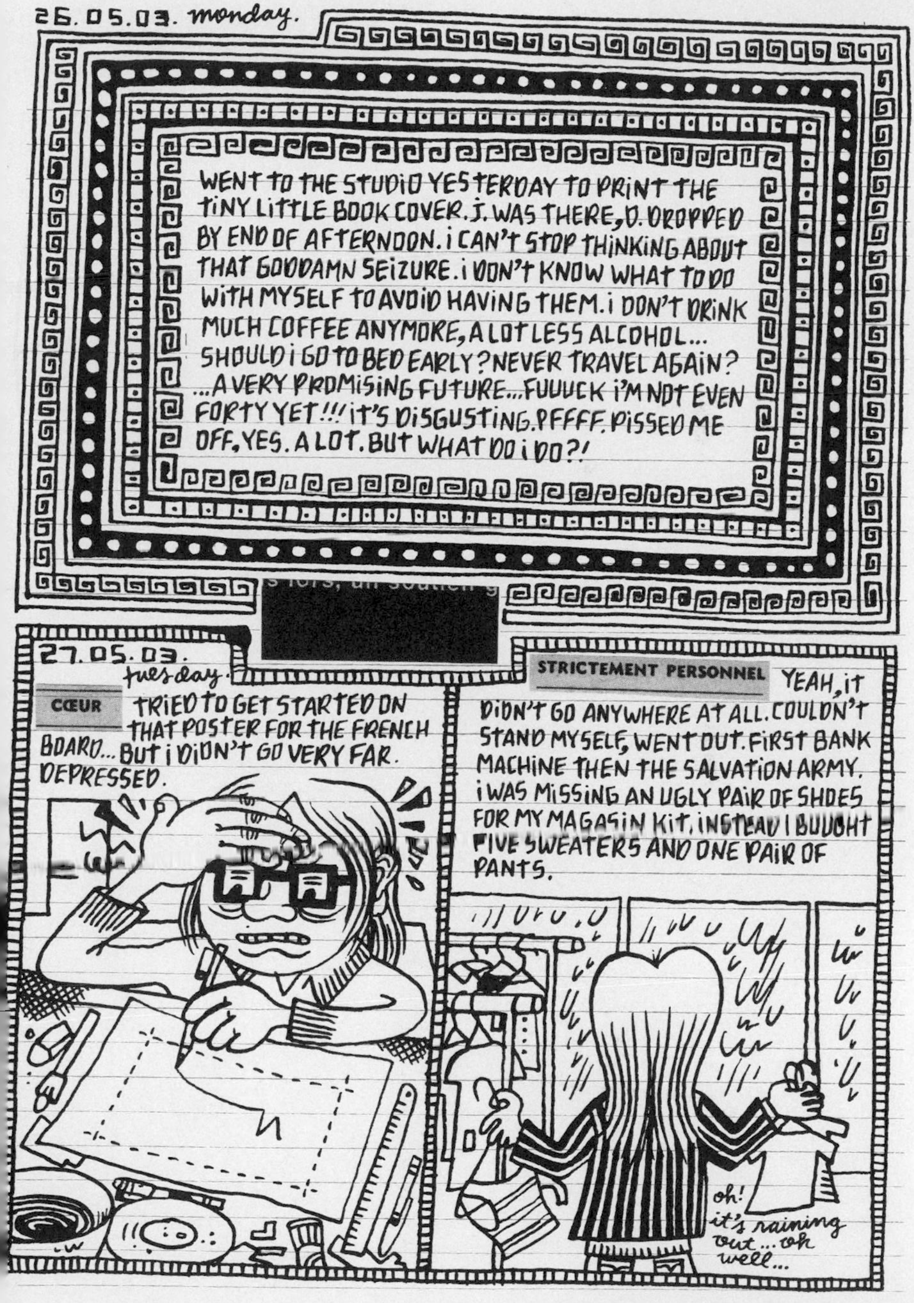
26.05.03. monday.
WENT TO THE STUDIO YESTERDAY TO PRINT THE TINY LITTLE BOOK COVER. J. WAS THERE, D. DROPPED BY END OF AFTERNOON. i CAN'T STOP THINKING ABOUT THAT GODDAMN SEIZURE. i DON'T KNOW WHAT TO DO WITH MYSELF TO AVOID HAVING THEM. i DON'T DRINK MUCH COFFEE ANYMORE, A LOT LESS ALCOHOL... SHOULD i GO TO BED EARLY? NEVER TRAVEL AGAIN? ...A VERY PROMISING FUTURE... FUUUCK i'M NOT EVEN FORTY YET!!! iT'S DISGUSTING. PFFFF. PISSED ME OFF, YES. A LOT. BUT WHAT DO i DO?!
27.05.03. tuesday.
CŒUR
TRIED TO GET STARTED ON THAT POSTER FOR THE FRENCH BOARD... BUT i DIDN'T GO VERY FAR. DEPRESSED.
STRICTEMENT PERSONNEL
YEAH, iT DIDN'T GO ANYWHERE AT ALL. COULDN'T STAND MYSELF, WENT OUT. FIRST BANK MACHINE THEN THE SALVATION ARMY. i WAS MISSING AN UGLY PAIR OF SHOES FOR MY MAGASIN KIT. INSTEAD I BOUGHT FIVE SWEATERS AND ONE PAIR OF PANTS.
oh! it's raining out... oh well...

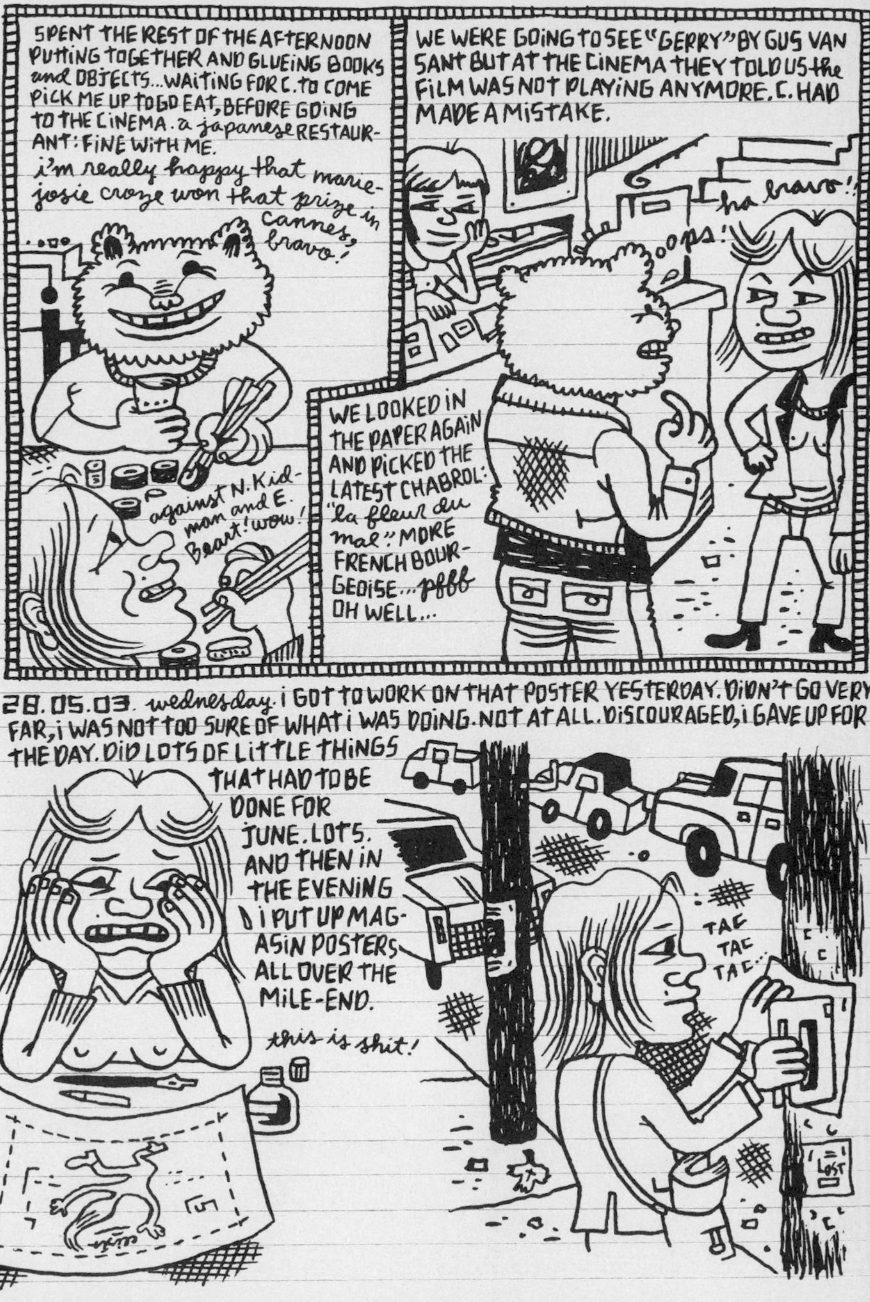

SPENT THE REST OF THE AFTERNOON PUTTING TOGETHER AND GLUEING BOOKS and OBJECTS... WAITING FOR C. TO COME PICK ME UP TO GO EAT, BEFORE GOING TO THE CINEMA. a japanese RESTAURANT: FINE WITH ME.
i'm really happy that marie-josie croze won that prize in cannes, bravo!
against N. Kidman and E. Beart! wow!
WE WERE GOING TO SEE "GERRY" BY GUS VAN SANT BUT AT THE CINEMA THEY TOLD US the FILM WAS NOT PLAYING ANYMORE. C. HAD MADE A MISTAKE.
ha bravo!
oops!
WE LOOKED IN THE PAPER AGAIN AND PICKED THE LATEST CHABROL: "la fleur du mal". MORE FRENCH BOURGEOISE... pfff OH WELL...
28.05.03. wednesday. i GOT TO WORK ON THAT POSTER YESTERDAY. DIDN'T GO VERY FAR, i WAS NOT TOO SURE OF WHAT i WAS DOING. NOT AT ALL. DISCOURAGED, i GAVE UP FOR THE DAY. DID LOTS OF LITTLE THINGS THAT HAD TO BE DONE FOR JUNE. LOTS. AND THEN IN THE EVENING i PUT UP MAGASIN POSTERS ALL OVER THE MILE-END.
this is shit!
TAC
TAC
TAC...
LOST

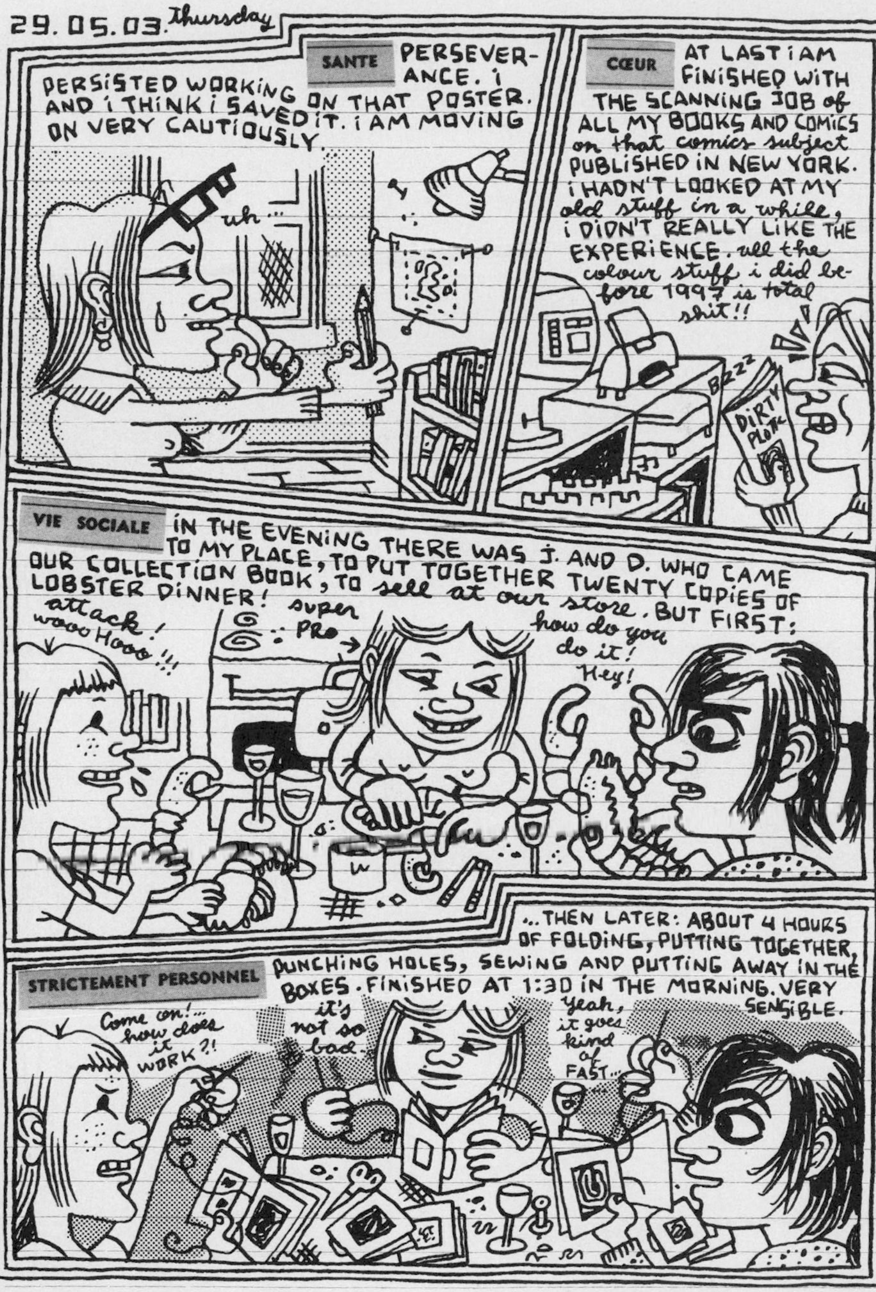
29.05.03. thursday
SANTE
PERSEVERANCE. i PERSISTED WORKING ON THAT POSTER. AND i THINK i SAVED iT. i AM MOVING ON VERY CAUTIOUSLY
uh...
CŒUR
AT LAST i AM FINISHED WITH THE SCANNING JOB of ALL MY BOOKS AND COMICS on that comics subject PUBLISHED iN NEW YORK. i HADN'T LOOKED AT MY old stuff in a while, i DIDN'T REALLY LIKE THE EXPERiENCE. all the colour stuff i did before 1997 is total shit!!
BZZZ
DIRTY PLOTTE
VIE SOCIALE
IN THE EVENING THERE WAS J. AND D. WHO CAME TO MY PLACE, TO PUT TOGETHER TWENTY COPIES OF OUR COLLECTION BOOK, TO sell at our store. BUT FIRST: LOBSTER DINNER!
attack! woooHooo!!!
super PRO
how do you do it! Hey!
STRICTEMENT PERSONNEL
...THEN LATER: ABOUT 4 HOURS OF FOLDING, PUTTING TOGETHER, PUNCHING HOLES, SEWING AND PUTTING AWAY IN THE BOXES. FINISHED AT 1:30 IN THE MORNING. VERY SENSIBLE.
Come on!... how does it WORK?!
it's not so bad.
Yeah, it goes kind of FAST...

30.05.03.

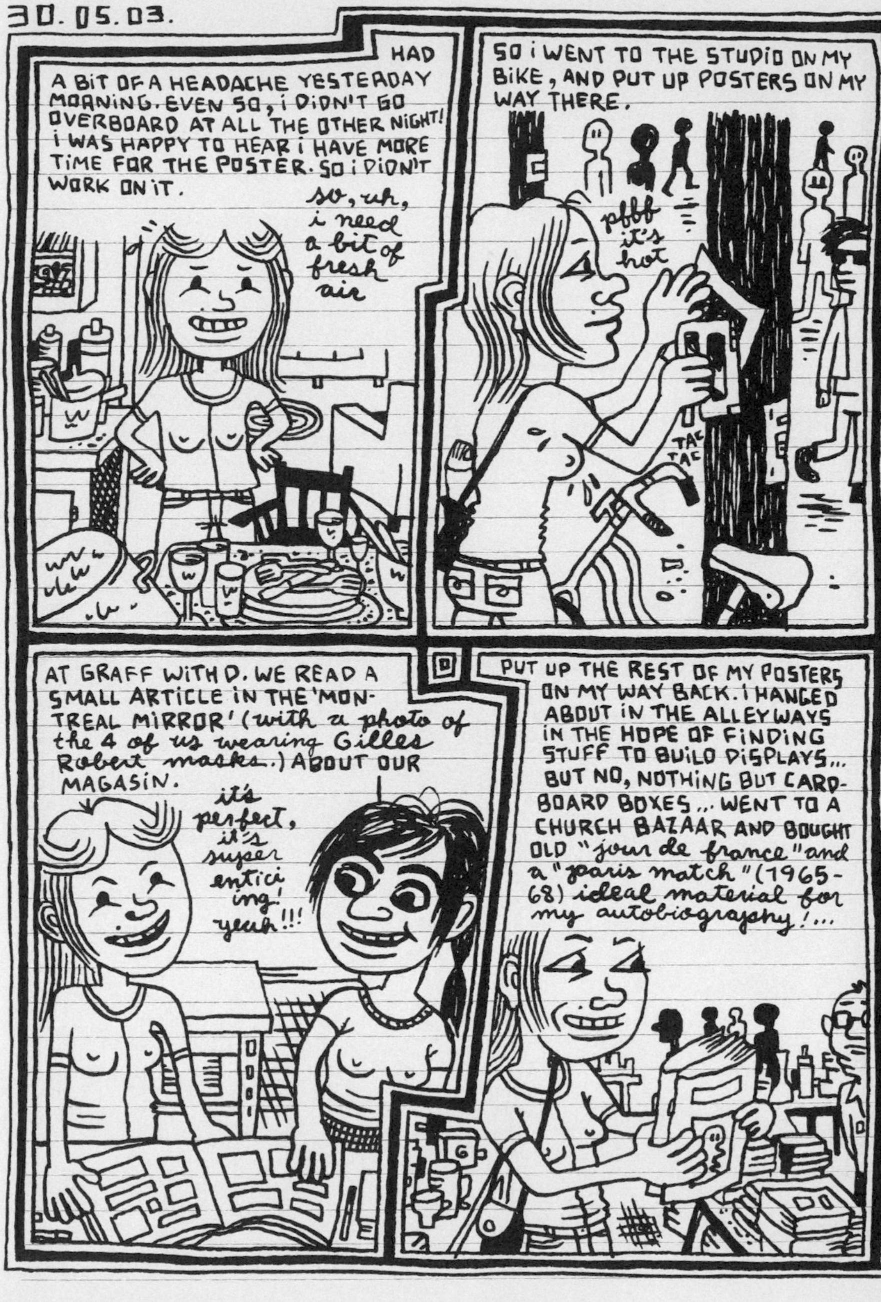

HAD A BIT OF A HEADACHE YESTERDAY MORNING. EVEN SO, i DIDN'T GO OVERBOARD AT ALL THE OTHER NiGHT! i WAS HAPPY TO HEAR i HAVE MORE TiME FOR THE POSTER. SO i DIDN'T WORK ON iT.
so, uh, i need a bit of fresh air
SO i WENT TO THE STUDIO ON MY BiKE, AND PUT UP POSTERS ON MY WAY THERE.
pfff it's hot
TAC TAC
AT GRAFF WiTH D. WE READ A SMALL ARTICLE iN THE 'MONTREAL MiRROR' (with a photo of the 4 of us wearing Gilles Robert masks.) ABOUT OUR MAGASiN.
it's perfect, it's super enticing!
yeah!!!
PUT UP THE REST OF MY POSTERS ON MY WAY BACK. i HANGED ABOUT iN THE ALLEYWAYS iN THE HOPE OF FiNDiNG STUFF TO BUiLD DiSPLAYS... BUT NO, NOTHiNG BUT CARDBOARD BOXES... WENT TO A CHURCH BAZAAR AND BOUGHT OLD "jour de france" and a "paris match" (1965-68) ideal material for my autobiography!...

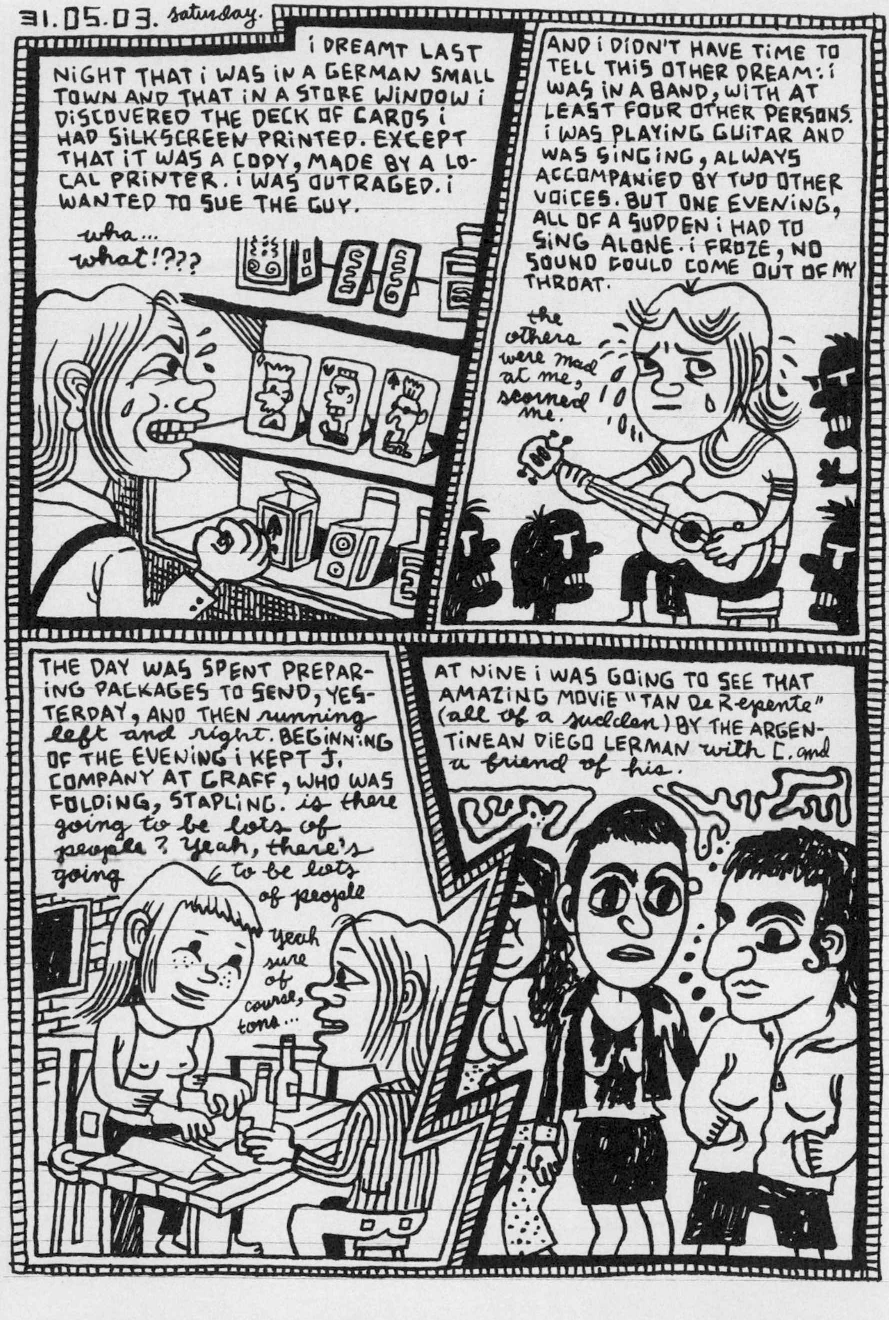
31.05.03. saturday.
i DREAMT LAST NiGHT THAT i WAS iN A GERMAN SMALL TOWN AND THAT iN A STORE WiNDOW i DiSCOVERED THE DECK OF CARDS i HAD SiLKSCREEN PRiNTED. EXCEPT THAT iT WAS A COPY, MADE BY A LOCAL PRiNTER. i WAS OUTRAGED. i WANTED TO SUE THE GUY.
wha... what!???
AND i DiDN'T HAVE TiME TO TELL THiS OTHER DREAM: i WAS iN A BAND, WiTH AT LEAST FOUR OTHER PERSONS. i WAS PLAYiNG GUiTAR AND WAS SiNGiNG, ALWAYS ACCOMPANiED BY TWO OTHER VOiCES. BUT ONE EVENiNG, ALL OF A SUDDEN i HAD TO SiNG ALONE. i FROZE, NO SOUND COULD COME OUT OF MY THROAT.
the others were mad at me, scorned me.
THE DAY WAS SPENT PREPARiNG PACKAGES TO SEND, YESTERDAY, AND THEN running left and right. BEGiNNiNG OF THE EVENiNG i KEPT J. COMPANY AT GRAFF, WHO WAS FOLDiNG, STAPLiNG. is there going to be lots of people? Yeah, there's going to be lots of people
Yeah sure of course, tons...
AT NiNE i WAS GOiNG TO SEE THAT AMAZiNG MOViE "TAN De Repente" (all of a sudden) BY THE ARGENTiNEAN DiEGO LERMAN with C. and a friend of his.

june 2003

sun	mon	tues	wed	thurs	fri	sat
1	2	3	4	5	6	7
8	9	10	11	12	13	14
15	16	17	18	19	20	21
22	23	24	25	26	27	28
29	30					

01. 06. 03.

sunday

YESTERDAY AT ONE i WAS GOING TO MEET D. AT HER FORMER JOB (*Publicité Sauvage*) TO BORROW A GUY AND HIS PICK-UP. WITH HIM WE WENT TO THE CITY DUMP TO LOOK FOR PIECES OF WOOD, TO BUILD OUR KIOSK FOR MONDAY. WE FOUND LOTS OF PRETTY JUNK: FAKE WOOD WALL COVERING AND ALL BROKEN DOWN TRELLIS.

there were a few containers packed full, you take what you want... and all for free... we dropped everything at

...p.s. that's where we're going to build the thing.

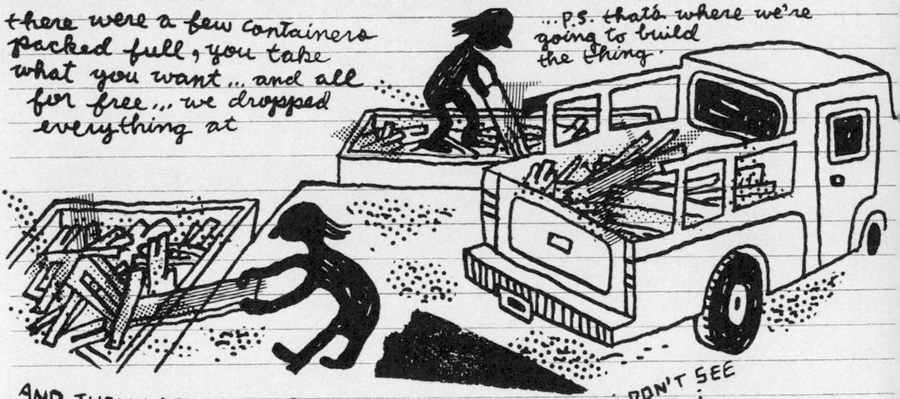

AND THEN LATER i WAS GOING TO SEE AN OLD FRIEND i DON'T SEE ANYMORE EXHIBITION. HIS OPENING WAS THE NIGHT BEFORE, i DIDN'T WANT TO SEE HIM *in that context*. BUT HIS EXHIBIT LASTED ONLY ONE DAY: *that saturday until 6 o'clock*. i WENT THERE AROUND 3 AND iT WAS ALREADY CLOSED!... BECAUSE i WAS IN THE AREA i WENT TO SEE THIS OTHER EXHIBIT: "L'ART QUI FAIT BOUM", *at least one friend was in it*. IT'S ALWAYS THE SAME THING WHICH STRIKES ME: CONTEMPORARY ART (*in general*) HAS NO SOUL, NO DEPTH. i ALWAYS HAVE THE FEELING...

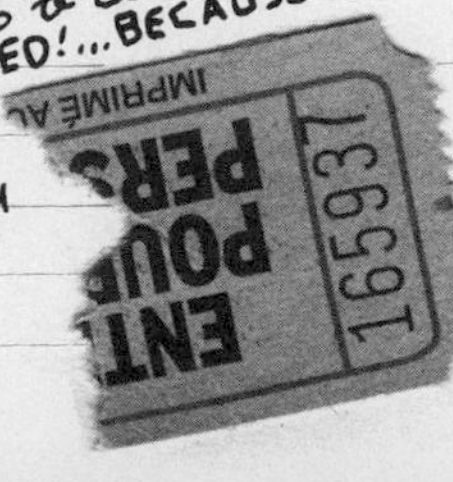
IMPRIMÉ AU
165937

...THAT ALL THE ARTIST IS TRYING TO DO IS CATCH YOUR ATTENTION FOR A QUARTER OF A SECOND...AND THAT'S ALL. THERE'S NOTHING ELSE TO SEE. DROPPED BY LA CASA, WHERE J. WAS WORKING, AND SPENT THE EVENING *preparing myself for monday.*

02.06.03. *monday*. TODAY IS THE BIG DAY! I WORKED ON MY POSTER UNTIL THREE YESTERDAY, and THEN I MET WITH J. *and* D. *at* P.S., TO BUILD OUR MAGASIN *it's so beautiful!*

all covered with fake wall covering

hey we can't throw that away after our store!!! we gotta keep it!

gray plank in a 6

very bad shape

she had spent last night painting, folding, gluing, etc... and had to get up early for a make-up top with tricks so not in a good mood.

old balcony planks with not so tidy paint marks

old table legs found in an alley way

3 1/2 HRS. of work

IF MY DAD WAS HERE, HE'D LAUGH! ANYWAY, WE'RE GONNA LOOK SO PRETTY, WEARING OUR SALES-LADIES OUT-FITS AND BAKING THESE TRASH ARCHITECTURE MASTER-PIECES!...LATER WE WENT TO GRAFF TO JOIN M.E., WHO WAS IRONING T-SHIRTS (*to fix the ink*). HER AND D. *had* NO TIME TO EAT DINNER, SO ME *and* J. ALONE WENT TO AN ITALIAN RESTAURANT. PERSONALLY, I WAS MORE IN A JUNK FOOD MOOD, BUT OH, WELL ...YES, TODAY IS THE BIG DAY!!!

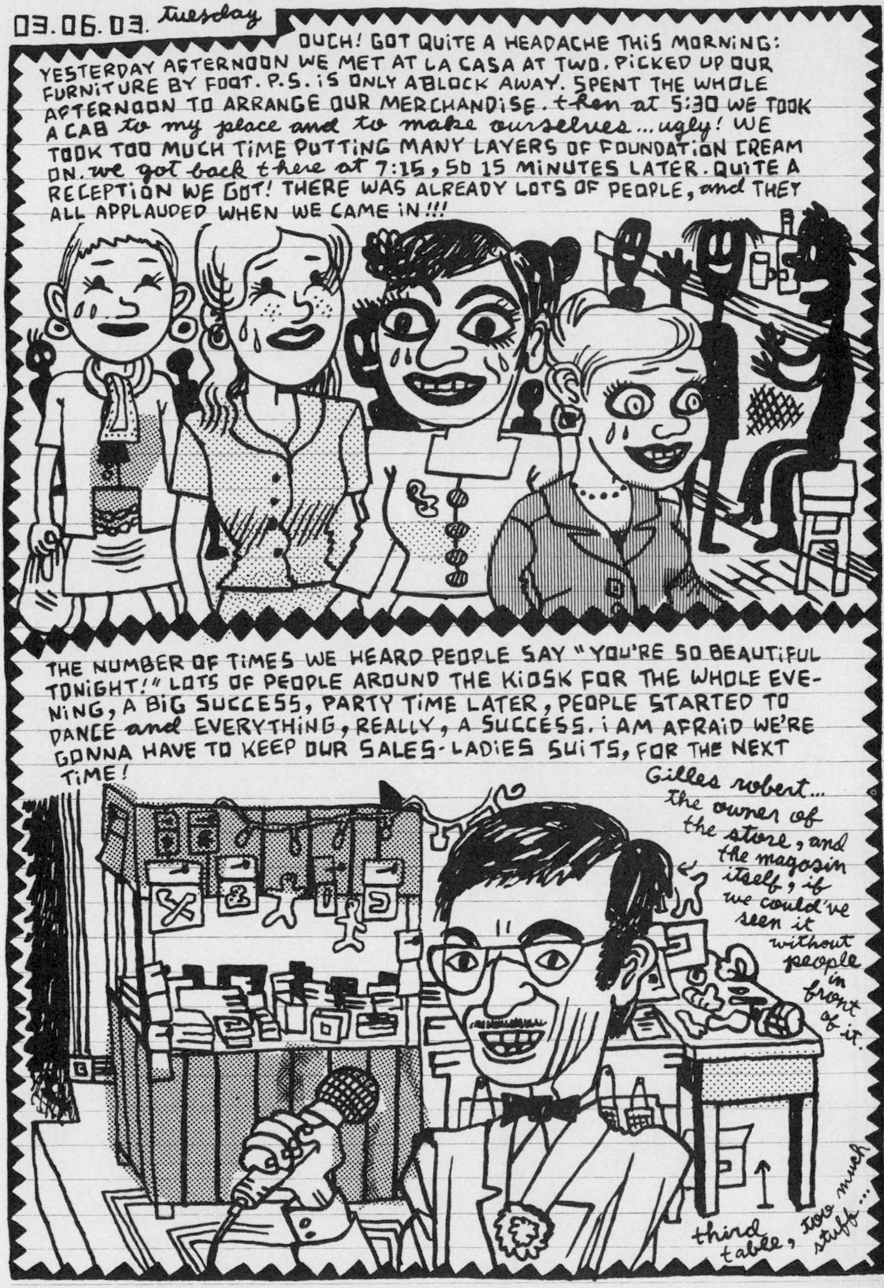
03.06.03. tuesday
OUCH! GOT QUITE A HEADACHE THIS MORNING: YESTERDAY AFTERNOON WE MET AT LA CASA AT TWO. PICKED UP OUR FURNITURE BY FOOT. P.S. IS ONLY A BLOCK AWAY. SPENT THE WHOLE AFTERNOON TO ARRANGE OUR MERCHANDISE. then at 5:30 WE TOOK A CAB to my place and to make ourselves... ugly! WE TOOK TOO MUCH TIME PUTTING MANY LAYERS OF FOUNDATION CREAM ON. we got back there at 7:15, SO 15 MINUTES LATER. QUITE A RECEPTION WE GOT! THERE WAS ALREADY LOTS OF PEOPLE, and THEY ALL APPLAUDED WHEN WE CAME IN!!!
THE NUMBER OF TIMES WE HEARD PEOPLE SAY "YOU'RE SO BEAUTIFUL TONIGHT!" LOTS OF PEOPLE AROUND THE KIOSK FOR THE WHOLE EVENING, A BIG SUCCESS, PARTY TIME LATER, PEOPLE STARTED TO DANCE and EVERYTHING, REALLY, A SUCCESS. I AM AFRAID WE'RE GONNA HAVE TO KEEP OUR SALES-LADIES SUITS, FOR THE NEXT TIME!
Gilles robert... the owner of the store, and the magasin itself, if we could've seen it without people in front of it.
third table, too much stuff...

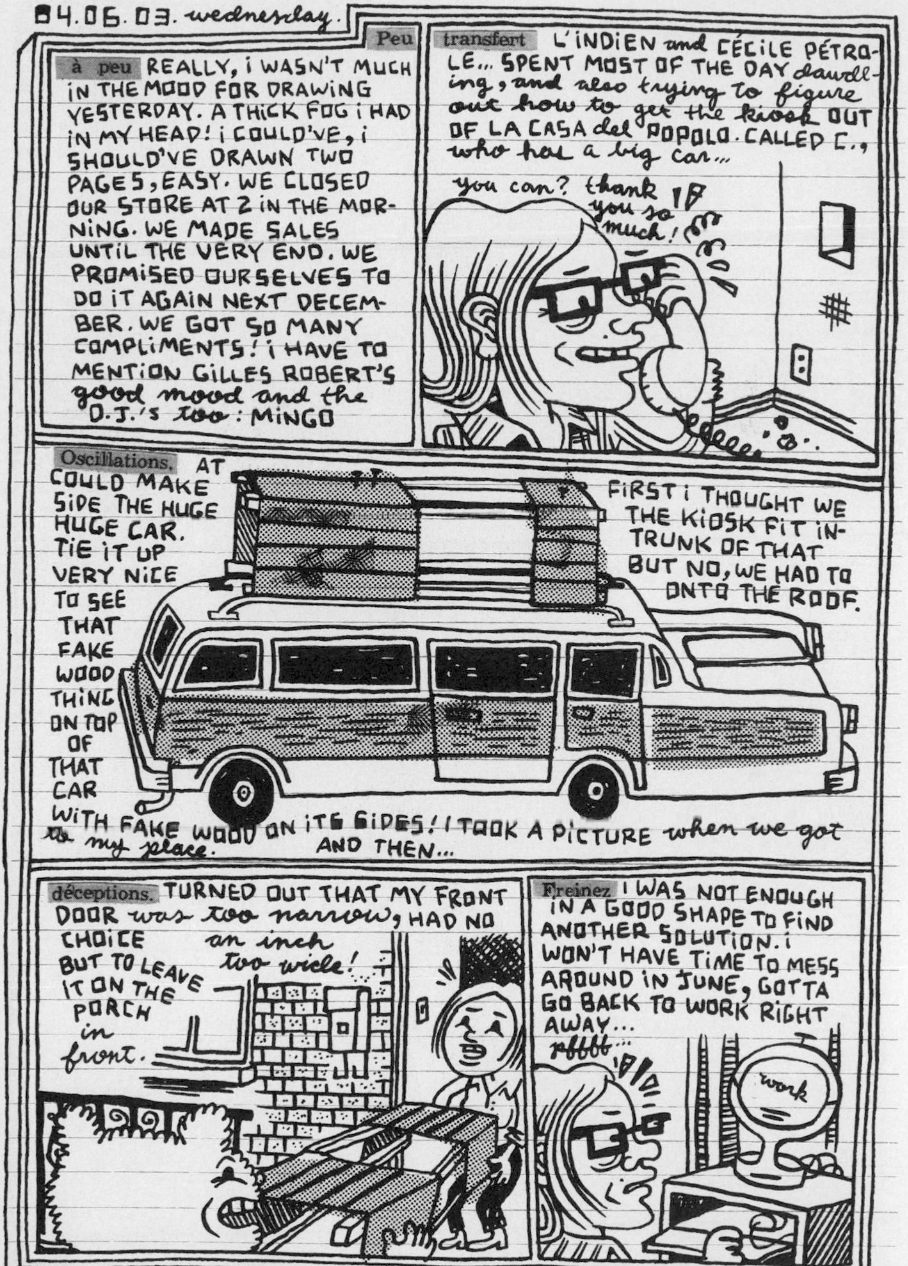
04.06.03. wednesday.
Peu
à peu REALLY, I WASN'T MUCH IN THE MOOD FOR DRAWING YESTERDAY. A THICK FOG I HAD IN MY HEAD! I COULD'VE, I SHOULD'VE DRAWN TWO PAGES, EASY. WE CLOSED OUR STORE AT 2 IN THE MORNING. WE MADE SALES UNTIL THE VERY END. WE PROMISED OURSELVES TO DO IT AGAIN NEXT DECEMBER. WE GOT SO MANY COMPLIMENTS! I HAVE TO MENTION GILLES ROBERT'S good mood and the D.J.'s too: MINGO
transfert L'INDIEN and CÉCILE PÉTRALE... SPENT MOST OF THE DAY dawdling, and also trying to figure out how to get the kiosk OUT OF LA CASA del POPOLO. CALLED C., who has a big car...
you can? thank you so much!
Oscillations. AT
FIRST I THOUGHT WE
COULD MAKE
THE KIOSK FIT IN-
SIDE THE HUGE
TRUNK OF THAT
HUGE CAR.
BUT NO, WE HAD TO
TIE IT UP
ONTO THE ROOF.
VERY NICE TO SEE THAT FAKE WOOD THING ON TOP OF THAT CAR WITH FAKE WOOD ON ITS SIDES! I TOOK A PICTURE when we got to my place. AND THEN...
déceptions. TURNED OUT THAT MY FRONT DOOR was too narrow, HAD NO CHOICE BUT TO LEAVE IT ON THE PORCH in front.
an inch too wide!
Freinez I WAS NOT ENOUGH IN A GOOD SHAPE TO FIND ANOTHER SOLUTION. I WON'T HAVE TIME TO MESS AROUND IN JUNE, GOTTA GO BACK TO WORK RIGHT AWAY...
pffff...
work

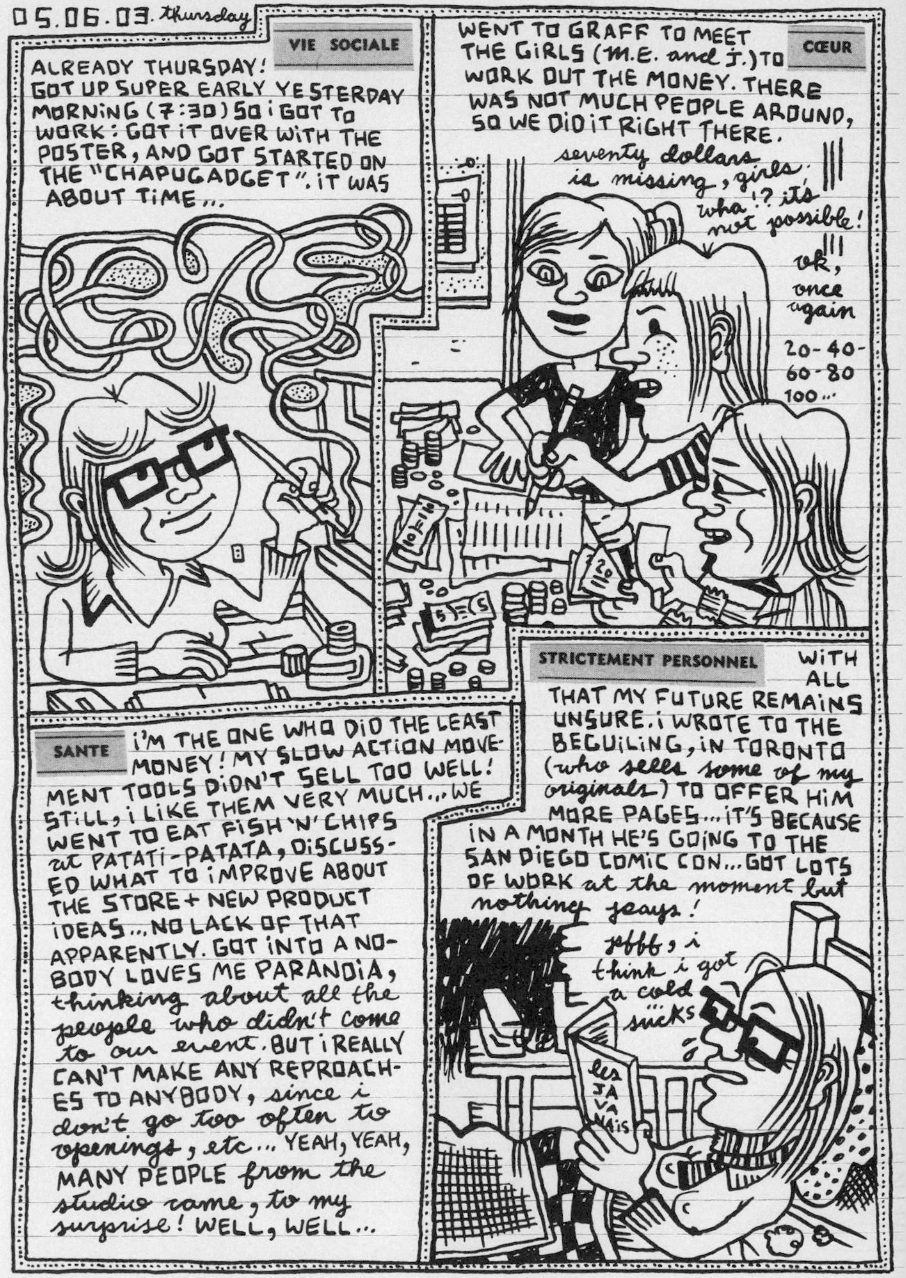
05.06.03. thursday
VIE SOCIALE
ALREADY THURSDAY! GOT UP SUPER EARLY YESTERDAY MORNING (7:30) SO i GOT TO WORK: GOT iT OVER WiTH THE POSTER, AND GOT STARTED ON THE "CHAPUGADGET". iT WAS ABOUT TiME...
CŒUR
WENT TO GRAFF TO MEET THE GiRLS (M.E. and J.) TO WORK OUT THE MONEY. THERE WAS NOT MUCH PEOPLE AROUND, SO WE DiD iT RiGHT THERE.
seventy dollars is missing, girls.
wha!? it's not possible!
ok, once again
20-40-60-80 100...
SANTE
i'M THE ONE WHO DiD THE LEAST MONEY! MY SLOW ACTION MOVEMENT TOOLS DiDN'T SELL TOO WELL! STiLL, i LiKE THEM VERY MUCH... WE WENT TO EAT FiSH 'N' CHiPS at PATATi-PATATA, DiSCUSSED WHAT TO iMPROVE ABOUT THE STORE + NEW PRODUCT iDEAS... NO LACK OF THAT APPARENTLY. GOT iNTO A NOBODY LOVES ME PARANOiA, thinking about all the people who didn't come to our event. BUT i REALLY CAN'T MAKE ANY REPROACHES TO ANYBODY, since i don't go too often to openings, etc... YEAH, YEAH, MANY PEOPLE from the studio came, to my surprise! WELL, WELL...
STRICTEMENT PERSONNEL
WiTH ALL THAT MY FUTURE REMAiNS UNSURE. i WROTE TO THE BEGUiLiNG, iN TORONTO (who sells some of my originals) TO OFFER HiM MORE PAGES... iT'S BECAUSE iN A MONTH HE'S GOiNG TO THE SAN DiEGO COMiC CON... GOT LOTS OF WORK at the moment but nothing jeays!
pfff, i think i got a cold ... sucks
les JAVANAIS

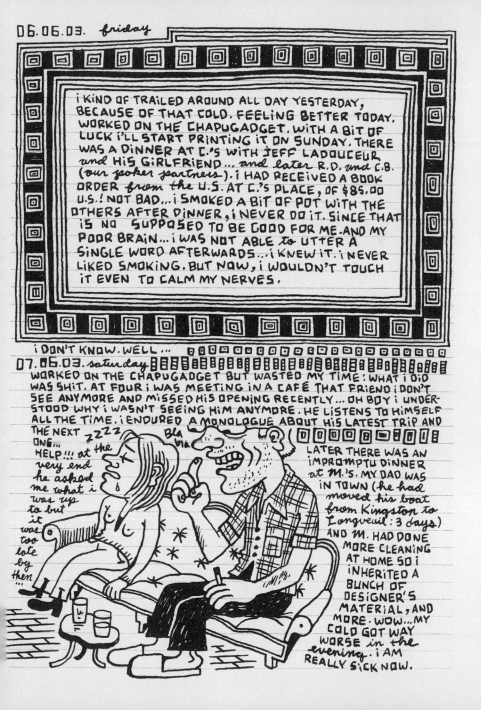

i KIND OF TRAILED AROUND ALL DAY YESTERDAY, BECAUSE OF THAT COLD. FEELING BETTER TODAY. WORKED ON THE CHAPUGADGET. WITH A BIT OF LUCK i'LL START PRINTING iT ON SUNDAY. THERE WAS A DINNER AT C.'S WITH JEFF LADOUCEUR *and* HiS GIRLFRIEND... *and later* R.D. *and* C.B. (*our poker partners*). i HAD RECEIVED A BOOK ORDER *from the* U.S. AT C.'S PLACE, OF $85.00 U.S.! NOT BAD... i SMOKED A BiT OF POT WITH THE OTHERS AFTER DINNER, i NEVER DO iT. SiNCE THAT iS NO SUPPOSED TO BE GOOD FOR ME. AND MY POOR BRAIN... i WAS NOT ABLE *to* UTTER A SiNGLE WORD AFTERWARDS... i KNEW iT. i NEVER LIKED SMOKING. BUT NOW, i WOULDN'T TOUCH iT EVEN TO CALM MY NERVES.

i DON'T KNOW. WELL ...

07.06.03. *saturday* WORKED ON THE CHAPUGADGET BUT WASTED MY TIME: WHAT i DiD WAS SHiT. AT FOUR i WAS MEETING iN A CAFÉ THAT FRIEND i DON'T SEE ANYMORE AND MiSSED HiS OPENING RECENTLY... OH BOY i UNDERSTOOD WHY i WASN'T SEEING HiM ANYMORE. HE LISTENS TO HiMSELF ALL THE TIME. i ENDURED A MONOLOGUE ABOUT HiS LATEST TRIP AND THE NEXT ONG...

ZZZZ BLA BLA

HELP!!! at the very end he asked me what i was up to but it was too late by then...

LATER THERE WAS AN IMPROMPTU DINNER AT M.'S. MY DAD WAS IN TOWN (*he had moved his boat from Kingston to Longueuil: 3 days*) AND M. HAD DONE MORE CLEANING AT HOME SO i INHERiTED A BUNCH OF DESiGNER'S MATERIAL, AND MORE... WOW... MY COLD GOT WAY WORSE *in the evening*. i AM REALLY SiCK NOW.

I'M SICK, I COULDN'T SLEEP AT ALL LAST NIGHT, COULDN'T BREATHE THROUGH THE NOSE. WOKE UP ONE THOUSAND TIMES WITH THE INSIDE OF MY MOUTH DRY BECAUSE OF THAT... I HATE THAT. A BIT BETTER TODAY, BUT NOT AS WELL AS I HOPED FOR. I SPENT THE TIME MAKING UP A LITTLE CATALOGUE... I FOUND ON THE INTERNET A *short* DOCUMENTARY ABOUT EPILEPSY, *which* I HAD MISSED.

ON TV A COUPLE OF DAYS AGO I HEARD A GOOD ONE: IN 40% OF THE CASES THE MEDICATION DOESN'T CONTROL (*completely*) THE SEIZURES AND STUFF!...THAT'S ENORMOUS!!! ABOUT WHAT COULD PROVOKE A FIT: LACK OF SLEEP, BAD AND IRREGULAR DIET, THE HEAT, HUMIDITY, ALLERGIES!? AND OF COURSE STRESS, *angst and* ALL OF THOSE TYPES OF THINGS. JEEZUS, I DIDN'T KNOW ALL THAT. WELL, IT COULD BE WORSE...

WAY WORSE. LOOKS LIKE I DON'T CARE ENOUGH ABOUT MYSELF YET. STABILITY (...ATCHOO.

09.06.03. *monday*

AH, YES TODAY I FEEL BETTER. BUT YESTERDAY, NO, NOT AT ALL. I COULDN'T DO ANYTHING, EVEN LESS THAN THE DAY BEFORE. I READ SOME FUNNY NEWS ON THE "LIBÉ" WEBSITE: HOW THE AMERICANS WOULD LITERALLY MAKE UP INFORMATION DURING THE WAR AGAINST IRAQ! OUCH!!! LIKE THE RESCUE OF SOLDIER JESSICA, KIND OF SUSPECTED THAT ONE... THE DISMANTLING OF THE BIGGEST SADDAM STATUE: NO IRAQI PEOPLE AT ALL WERE INVOLVED, ONLY AMERICANS... *and the weirdest part: i watched the news on t.v. that evening* ... NOTHING ABOUT THAT!...

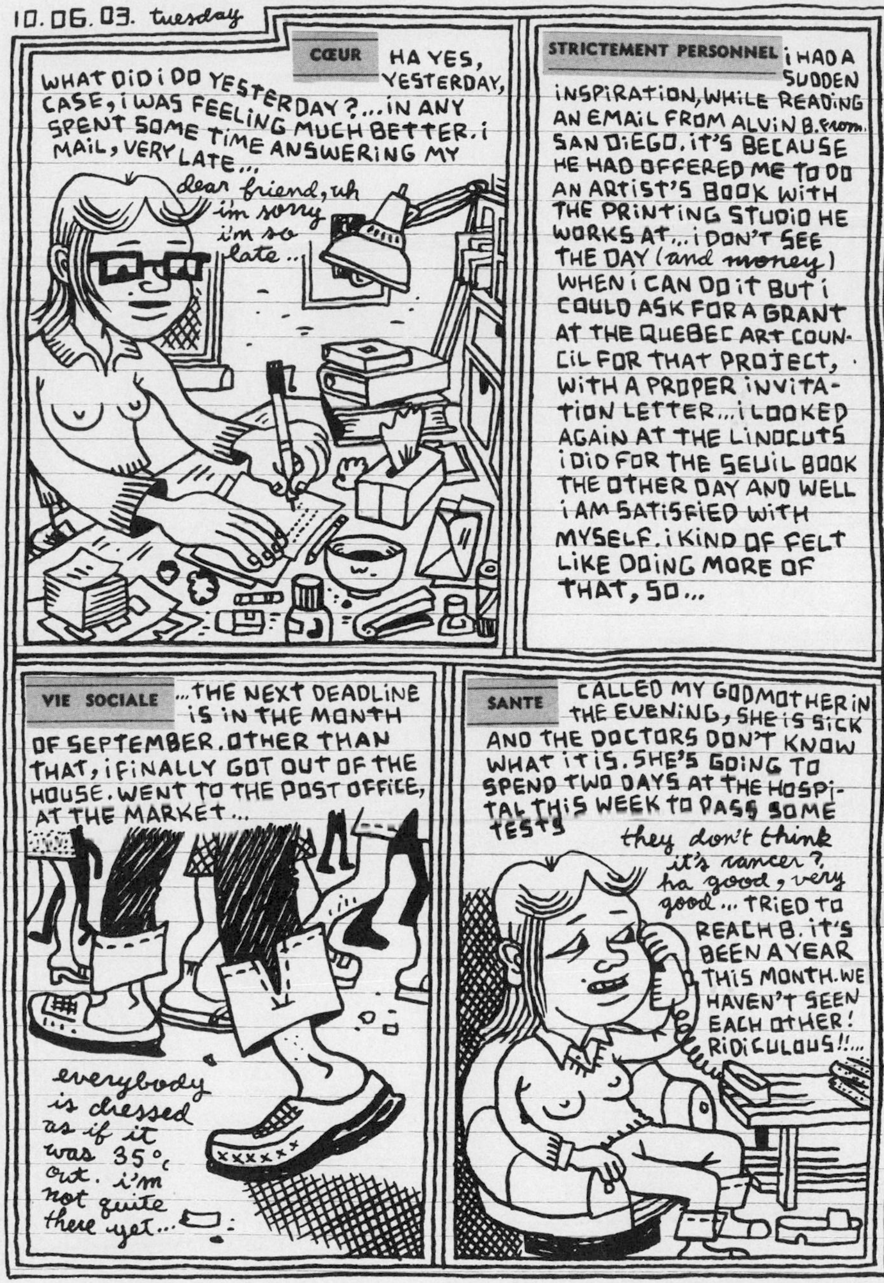
10.06.03. tuesday
CŒUR
HA YES, YESTERDAY, WHAT DID i DO YESTERDAY?... IN ANY CASE, i WAS FEELING MUCH BETTER. i SPENT SOME TIME ANSWERING MY MAIL, VERY LATE...
dear friend, uh i'm sorry i'm so late...
STRICTEMENT PERSONNEL
i HAD A SUDDEN INSPIRATION, WHILE READING AN EMAIL FROM ALVIN B. from SAN DIEGO. it's BECAUSE HE HAD OFFERED ME TO DO AN ARTIST'S BOOK WITH THE PRINTING STUDIO HE WORKS AT... i DON'T SEE THE DAY (and money) WHEN i CAN DO IT BUT i COULD ASK FOR A GRANT AT THE QUEBEC ART COUNCIL FOR THAT PROJECT, WITH A PROPER INVITATION LETTER... i LOOKED AGAIN AT THE LINOCUTS i DID FOR THE SEUIL BOOK THE OTHER DAY AND WELL i AM SATISFIED WITH MYSELF. i KIND OF FELT LIKE DOING MORE OF THAT, SO...
VIE SOCIALE
...THE NEXT DEADLINE IS IN THE MONTH OF SEPTEMBER. OTHER THAN THAT, i FINALLY GOT OUT OF THE HOUSE. WENT TO THE POST OFFICE, AT THE MARKET...
everybody is dressed as if it was 35°c out. i'm not quite there yet...
SANTE
CALLED MY GODMOTHER IN THE EVENING, SHE IS SICK AND THE DOCTORS DON'T KNOW WHAT IT IS. SHE'S GOING TO SPEND TWO DAYS AT THE HOSPITAL THIS WEEK TO PASS SOME TESTS
they don't think it's cancer?, ha good, very good... TRIED TO REACH B. it's BEEN A YEAR THIS MONTH. WE HAVEN'T SEEN EACH OTHER! RIDICULOUS!!...

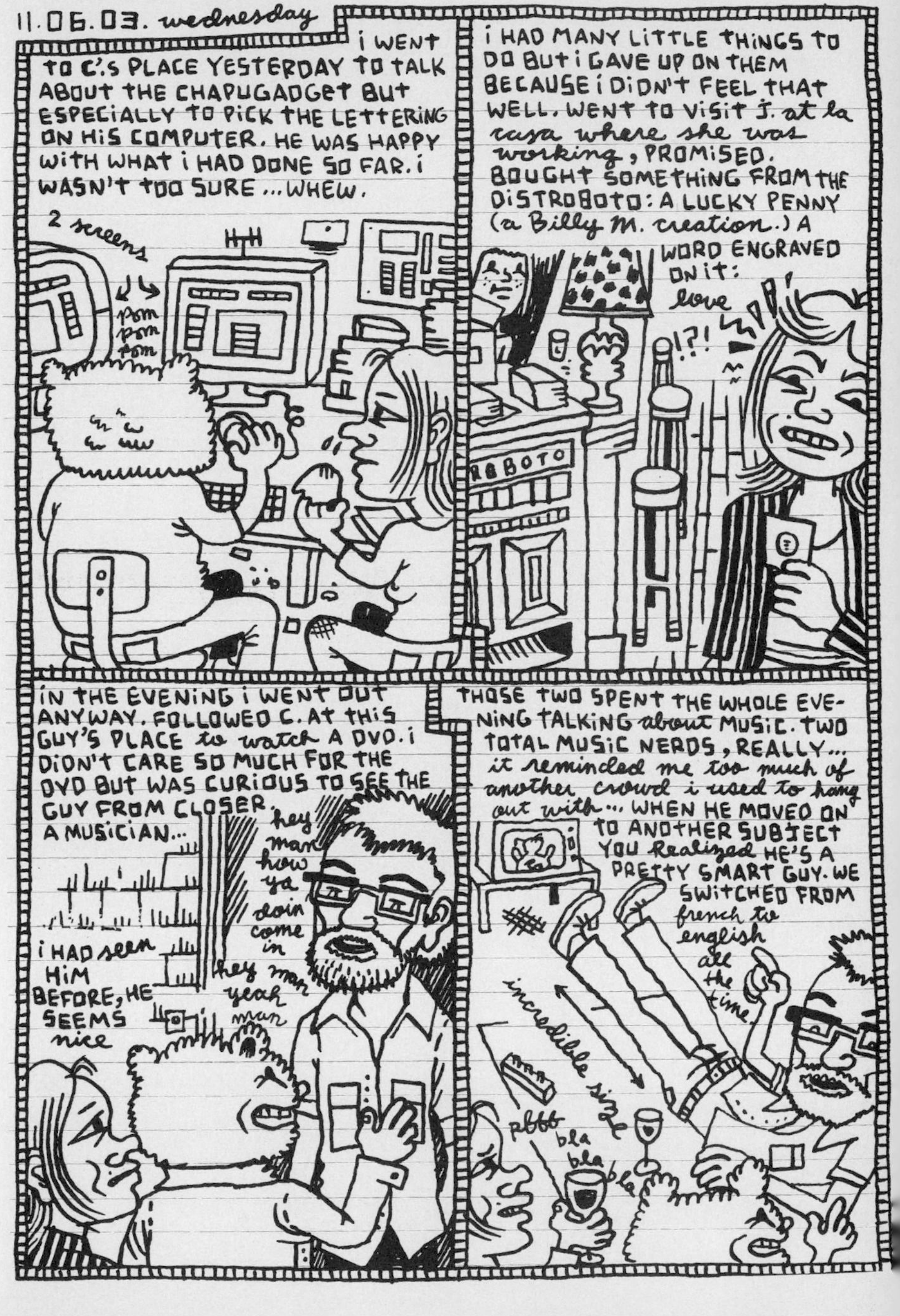
11.06.03. wednesday
i WENT TO C.'S PLACE YESTERDAY TO TALK ABOUT THE CHAPUGADGET BUT ESPECIALLY TO PICK THE LETTERING ON HIS COMPUTER. HE WAS HAPPY WITH WHAT i HAD DONE SO FAR. i WASN'T TOO SURE ... WHEW.
2 screens
pom pom pom
i HAD MANY LITTLE THINGS TO DO BUT i GAVE UP ON THEM BECAUSE i DIDN'T FEEL THAT WELL. WENT TO VISIT J. at la casa where she was working, PROMISED. BOUGHT SOMETHING FROM THE DISTROBOTO: A LUCKY PENNY (a Billy M. creation.) A WORD ENGRAVED ON IT: love
!?!
RBOTO
IN THE EVENING i WENT OUT ANYWAY. FOLLOWED C. AT THIS GUY'S PLACE to watch A DVD. i DIDN'T CARE SO MUCH FOR THE DVD BUT WAS CURIOUS TO SEE THE GUY FROM CLOSER. A MUSICIAN...
hey man how ya doin come in
hey man yeah man
i HAD seen HIM BEFORE, HE SEEMS nice
THOSE TWO SPENT THE WHOLE EVENING TALKING about MUSIC. TWO TOTAL MUSIC NERDS, REALLY... it reminded me too much of another crowd i used to hang out with... WHEN HE MOVED ON TO ANOTHER SUBJECT YOU Realized HE'S A PRETTY SMART GUY. WE SWITCHED FROM french to english all the time
incredible size
pbbb
bla bla bla

12.06.03. thursday. QUITE A DAY YESTERDAY, AND IT'S GOING TO BE JUST THE SAME TODAY. FIRST A GIRL CAME TO MY PLACE TO TAKE PICTURES OF ME, FOR THIS BOOK ABOUT COMICS WHICH WILL BE PUBLISHED IN HONG KONG THEN I HAD TO WALK (because of the rain) TO FEDEX TO SEND MY POSTER TO PARIS (for the band...)...BE-CAUSE I HAD BEEN PAID, FINALLY, i WENT TO THE STUDIO FOR A COUPLE OF HOURS. the coordin-ator asked me to ATTEND A demon-stration on i don't know what by two iTALIAN artists the next day. SHE IS SICK OF PUTTING TOGETHER events AND mak-ing con-tracts and nobody cares.

the artist in her studio.

HAPPENING BETWEEN 3 AND 6, with later A RECEPTION WITH WINE SERVED... ANYWAY, STILL NOT IN THE BEST SHAPE AND DONE NOTHING IN THE EVENING. IN THE END WITH B. WE COULD TALK ON THE PHONE. HER FRIEND DOROTHY'S BOY-FRIEND died of A HEART ATTACK AT 36 YEARS OLD, A CRACK-HEAD... HER: a proba-tion agent who's dating one of her clients...

i REALLY CAN'T BLAME HER. THE THING IS

SHE'S GOING TO LOSE HER JOB. ABOUT B., SHE NEVER HAS A MINUTE FOR HERSELF, WITH HER TWO KIDS AND ALL. WE AGREED TO SEE EACH OTHER DURING HER VACATIONS, IN JULY!... I DIDN'T SAY: i DREAMT i WAS IN A FOREIGN CITY WITH THE GIRLS AND WE WERE SETTLED IN A BAKERY AND WERE EATING tons of PASTRIES!...

13.06.03.

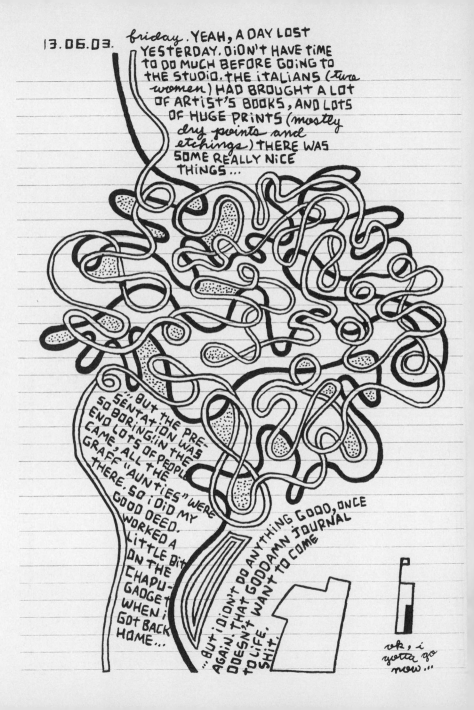

friday. YEAH, A DAY LOST YESTERDAY. DiDN'T HAVE TIME TO DO MUCH BEFORE GOING TO THE STUDIO. THE iTALIANS (*two women*) HAD BROUGHT A LOT OF ARTIST'S BOOKS, AND LOTS OF HUGE PRINTS (*mostly dry points and etchings*) THERE WAS SOME REALLY NiCE THiNGS...

"...BUT THE PRE-SENTATiON WAS SO BORiNG!! iN THE END LOTS OF PEOPLE CAME, ALL THE GRAFF "AUNTiES" WERE THERE, SO i DiD MY GOOD DEED. WORKED A LiTTLE BiT ON THE CHAPU-GADGET WHEN i GOT BACK HOME...

"...BUT i DiDN'T DO ANYTHiNG GOOD, ONCE AGAiN. THAT GODDAMN JOURNAL DOESN'T WANT TO COME TO LiFE. SHiT.

ok, i gotta go now ...

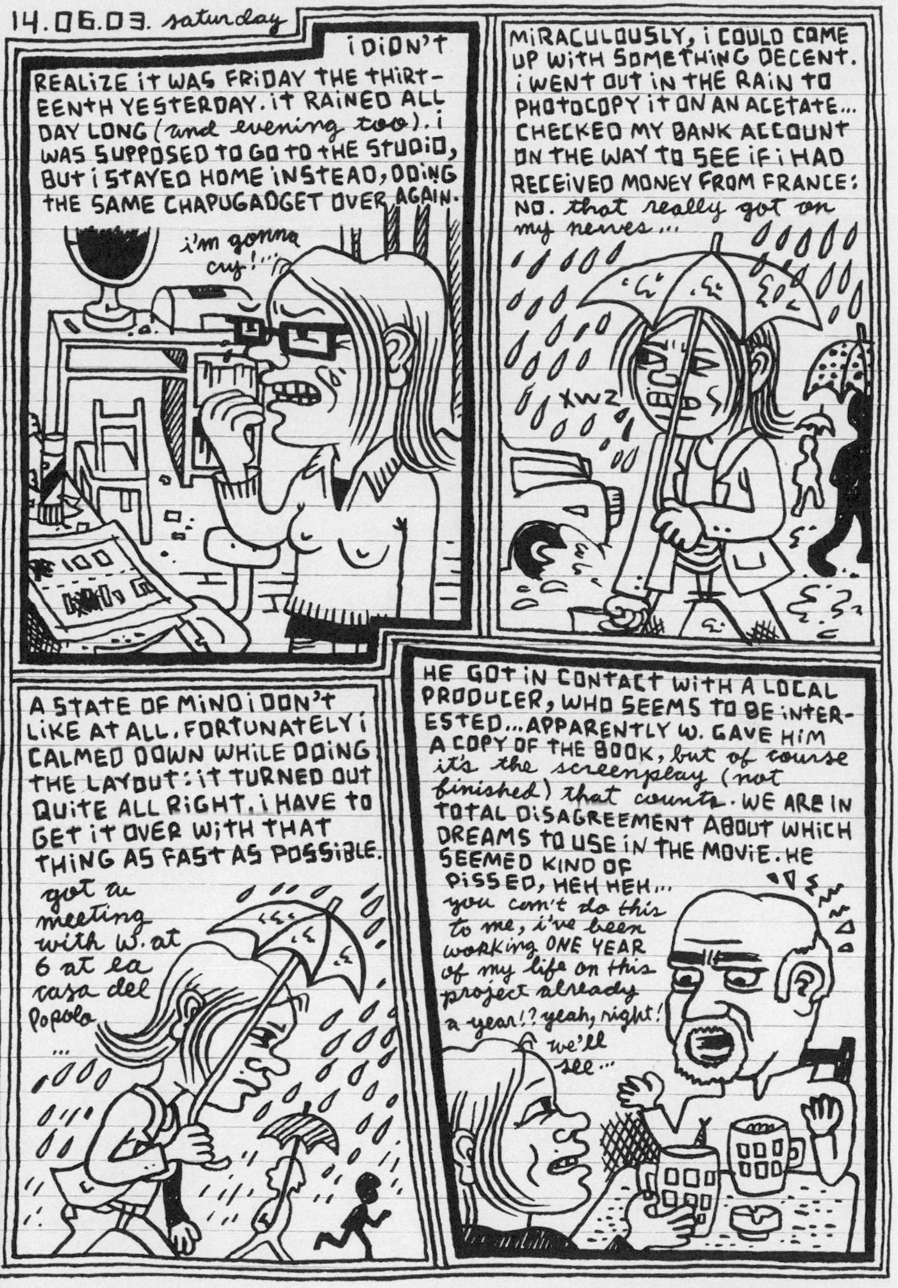
14.06.03. saturday
i DIDN'T REALIZE iT WAS FRiDAY THE THiRTEENTH YESTERDAY. iT RAINED ALL DAY LONG (and evening too). i WAS SUPPOSED TO GO TO THE STUDIO, BUT i STAYED HOME iNSTEAD, DOiNG THE SAME CHAPUGADGET OVER AGAIN.
i'm gonna cry!...
100
MiRACULOUSLY, i COULD COME UP WiTH SOMETHiNG DECENT. i WENT OUT IN THE RAiN TO PHOTOCOPY iT ON AN ACETATE... CHECKED MY BANK ACCOUNT ON THE WAY TO SEE iF i HAD RECEiVED MONEY FROM FRANCE: NO. that really got on my nerves...
XWZ
A STATE OF MiND i DON'T LiKE AT ALL. FORTUNATELY i CALMED DOWN WHiLE DOiNG THE LAYOUT: iT TURNED OUT QUiTE ALL RiGHT. i HAVE TO GET iT OVER WiTH THAT THiNG AS FAST AS POSSiBLE.
got a meeting with W. at 6 at la casa del Popolo ...
HE GOT iN CONTACT WiTH A LOCAL PRODUCER, WHO SEEMS TO BE iNTERESTED... APPARENTLY W. GAVE HiM A COPY OF THE BOOK, but of course it's the screenplay (not finished) that counts. WE ARE iN TOTAL DiSAGREEMENT ABOUT WHiCH DREAMS TO USE iN THE MOViE. HE SEEMED KiND OF PiSSED, HEH HEH...
you can't do this to me, i've been working ONE YEAR of my life on this project already
a year!? yeah, right!
we'll see...

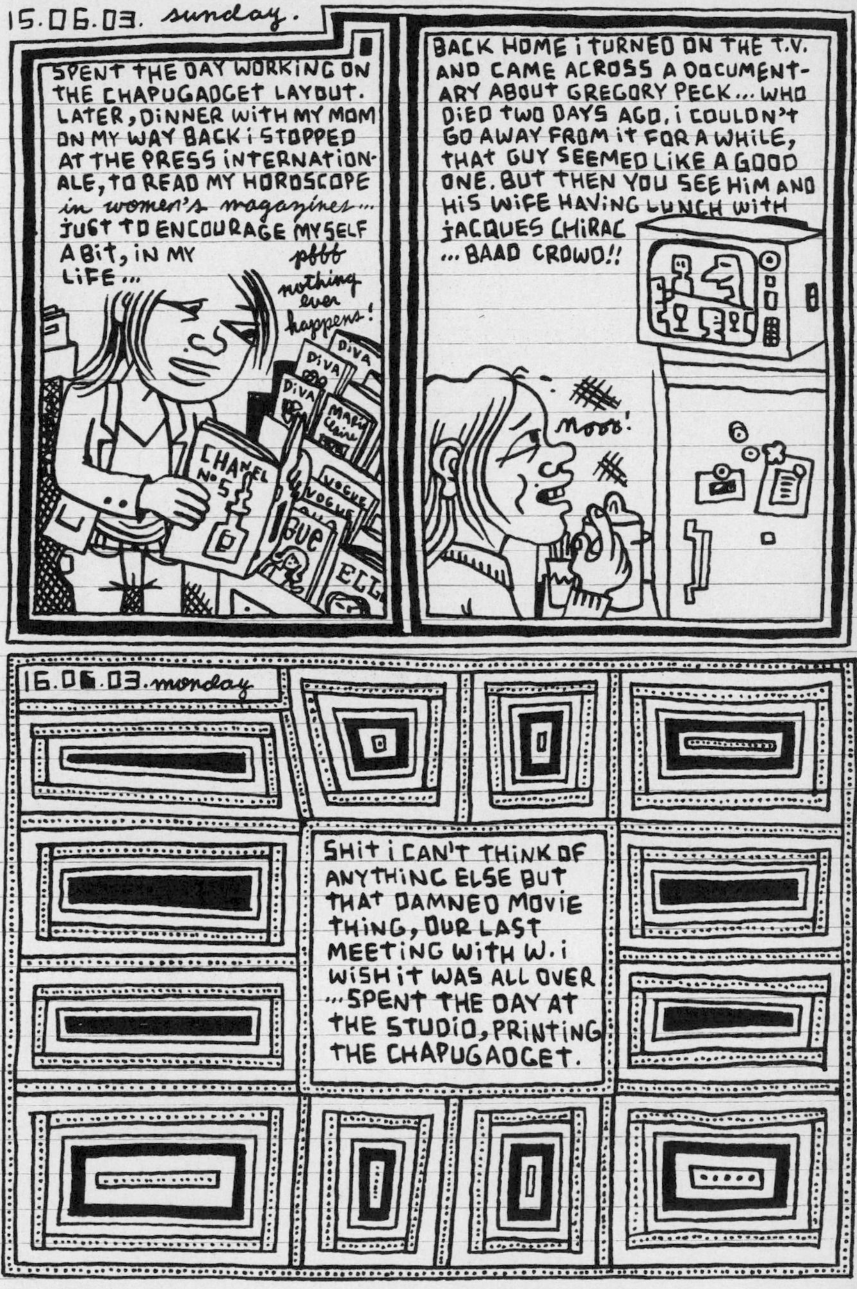
15.06.03. sunday.
SPENT THE DAY WORKING ON THE CHAPUGADGET LAYOUT. LATER, DINNER WITH MY MOM ON MY WAY BACK i STOPPED AT THE PRESS INTERNATIONALE, TO READ MY HOROSCOPE in women's magazines... JUST TO ENCOURAGE MYSELF A BIT, IN MY LIFE...
pfff nothing ever happens!
CHANEL No5
DIVA
DIVA
DIVA
VOGUE
VOGUE
BACK HOME i TURNED ON THE T.V. AND CAME ACROSS A DOCUMENTARY ABOUT GREGORY PECK... WHO DIED TWO DAYS AGO, i COULDN'T GO AWAY FROM IT FOR A WHILE, THAT GUY SEEMED LIKE A GOOD ONE. BUT THEN YOU SEE HIM AND HIS WIFE HAVING LUNCH WITH JACQUES CHIRAC ...BAAD CROWD!!
mooo!
16.06.03. monday
SHIT i CAN'T THINK OF ANYTHING ELSE BUT THAT DAMNED MOVIE THING, OUR LAST MEETING WITH W. i WISH IT WAS ALL OVER ...SPENT THE DAY AT THE STUDIO, PRINTING THE CHAPUGADGET.

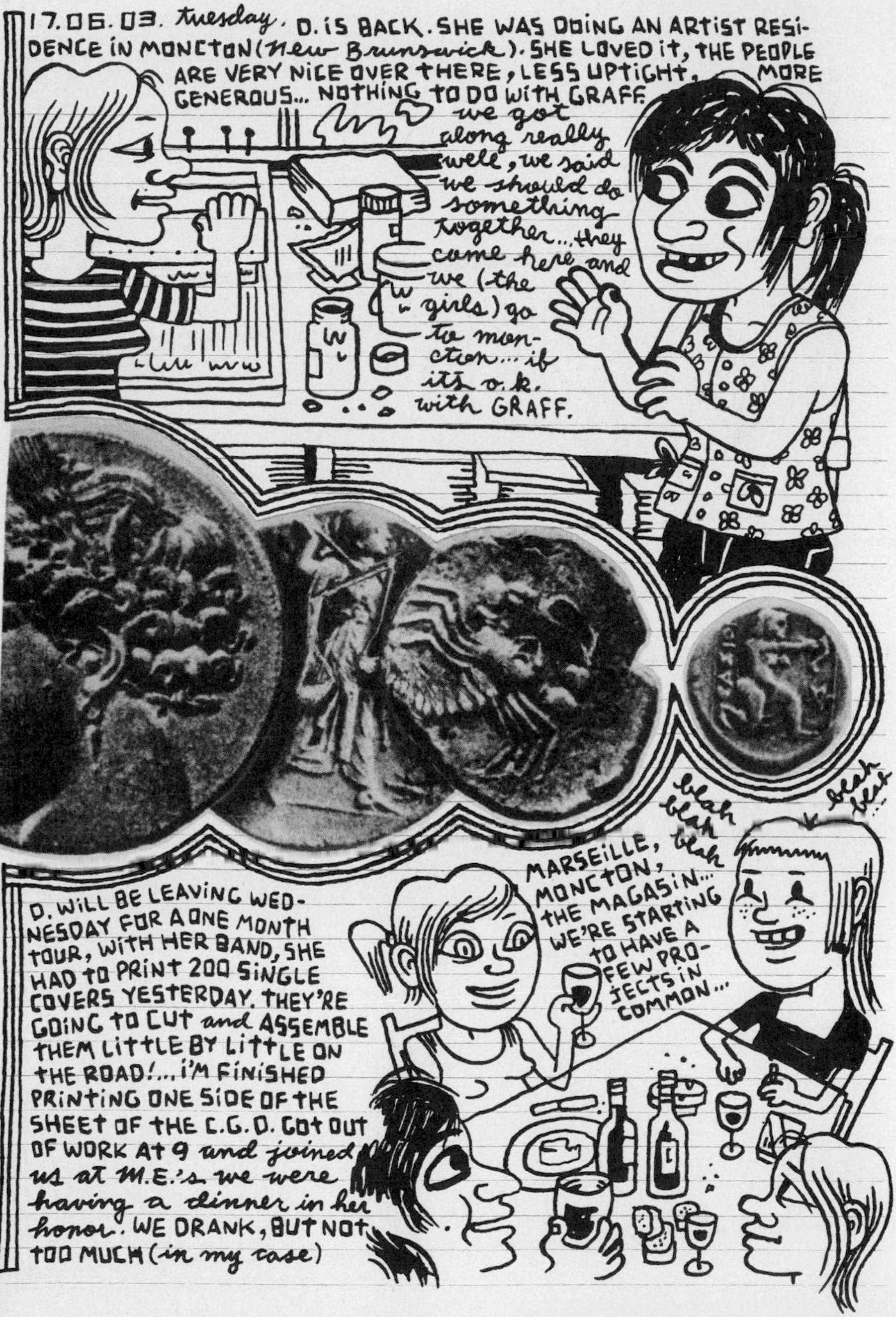
17.06.03. tuesday. D. IS BACK. SHE WAS DOING AN ARTIST RESIDENCE IN MONCTON (New Brunswick). SHE LOVED IT, THE PEOPLE ARE VERY NICE OVER THERE, LESS UPTIGHT, MORE GENEROUS... NOTHING TO DO WITH GRAFF.
we got along really well, we said we should do something together... they come here and we (the girls) go to moncton... if its o.k. with GRAFF.
blah blah blah blah
blah blah...
MARSEILLE, MONCTON, THE MAGASIN... WE'RE STARTING TO HAVE A FEW PROJECTS IN COMMON...
D. WILL BE LEAVING WEDNESDAY FOR A ONE MONTH TOUR, WITH HER BAND, SHE HAD TO PRINT 200 SINGLE COVERS YESTERDAY. THEY'RE GOING TO CUT and ASSEMBLE THEM LITTLE BY LITTLE ON THE ROAD!... I'M FINISHED PRINTING ONE SIDE OF THE SHEET OF THE C.G.D. GOT OUT OF WORK AT 9 and joined us at M.E.'s. we were having a dinner in her honor. WE DRANK, BUT NOT TOO MUCH (in my case)

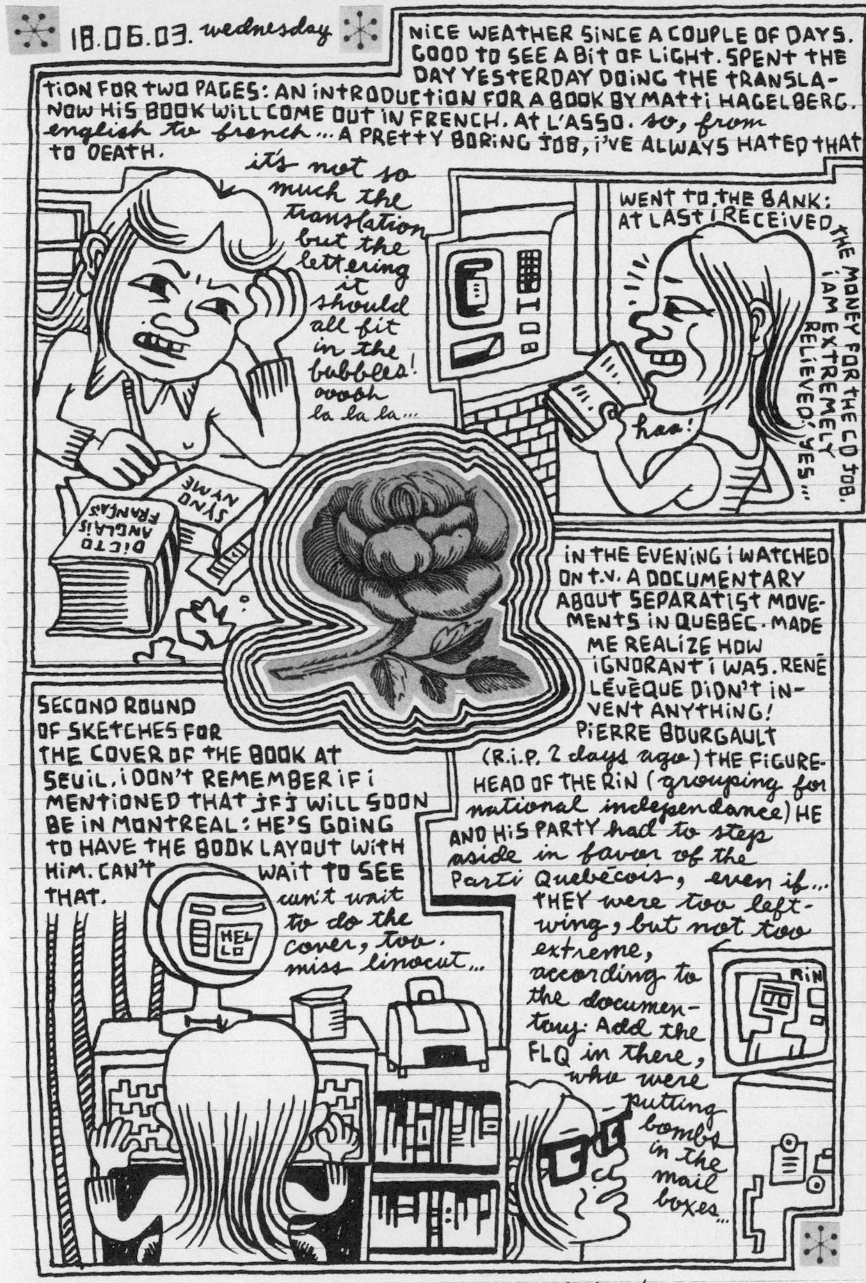
18.06.03. wednesday
NICE WEATHER SINCE A COUPLE OF DAYS. GOOD TO SEE A BIT OF LIGHT. SPENT THE DAY YESTERDAY DOING THE TRANSLATION FOR TWO PAGES: AN INTRODUCTION FOR A BOOK BY MATTI HAGELBERG. NOW HIS BOOK WILL COME OUT IN FRENCH. AT L'ASSO. so, from english to french... A PRETTY BORING JOB, I'VE ALWAYS HATED THAT TO DEATH.
it's not so much the translation but the lettering it should all fit in the bubbles! ooooh la la la...
DICTO ANGLAIS FRANÇAIS
SYNONYME
WENT TO THE BANK: AT LAST I RECEIVED THE MONEY FOR THE CD JOB. I AM EXTREMELY RELIEVED! YES...
haa!
IN THE EVENING I WATCHED ON T.V. A DOCUMENTARY ABOUT SEPARATIST MOVEMENTS IN QUEBEC. MADE ME REALIZE HOW IGNORANT I WAS. RENÉ LÉVÊQUE DIDN'T INVENT ANYTHING! PIERRE BOURGAULT (R.I.P. 2 days ago) THE FIGUREHEAD OF THE RIN (grouping for national independance) HE AND HIS PARTY had to step aside in favor of the Parti Québécois, even if... THEY were too left-wing, but not too extreme, according to the documentary: Add the FLQ in there, who were putting bombs in the mail boxes...
RIN
SECOND ROUND OF SKETCHES FOR THE COVER OF THE BOOK AT SEUIL. I DON'T REMEMBER IF I MENTIONED THAT JFJ WILL SOON BE IN MONTREAL: HE'S GOING TO HAVE THE BOOK LAYOUT WITH HIM. CAN'T WAIT TO SEE THAT.
HEL LO
can't wait to do the cover, too. miss linocut...
oh boy!...

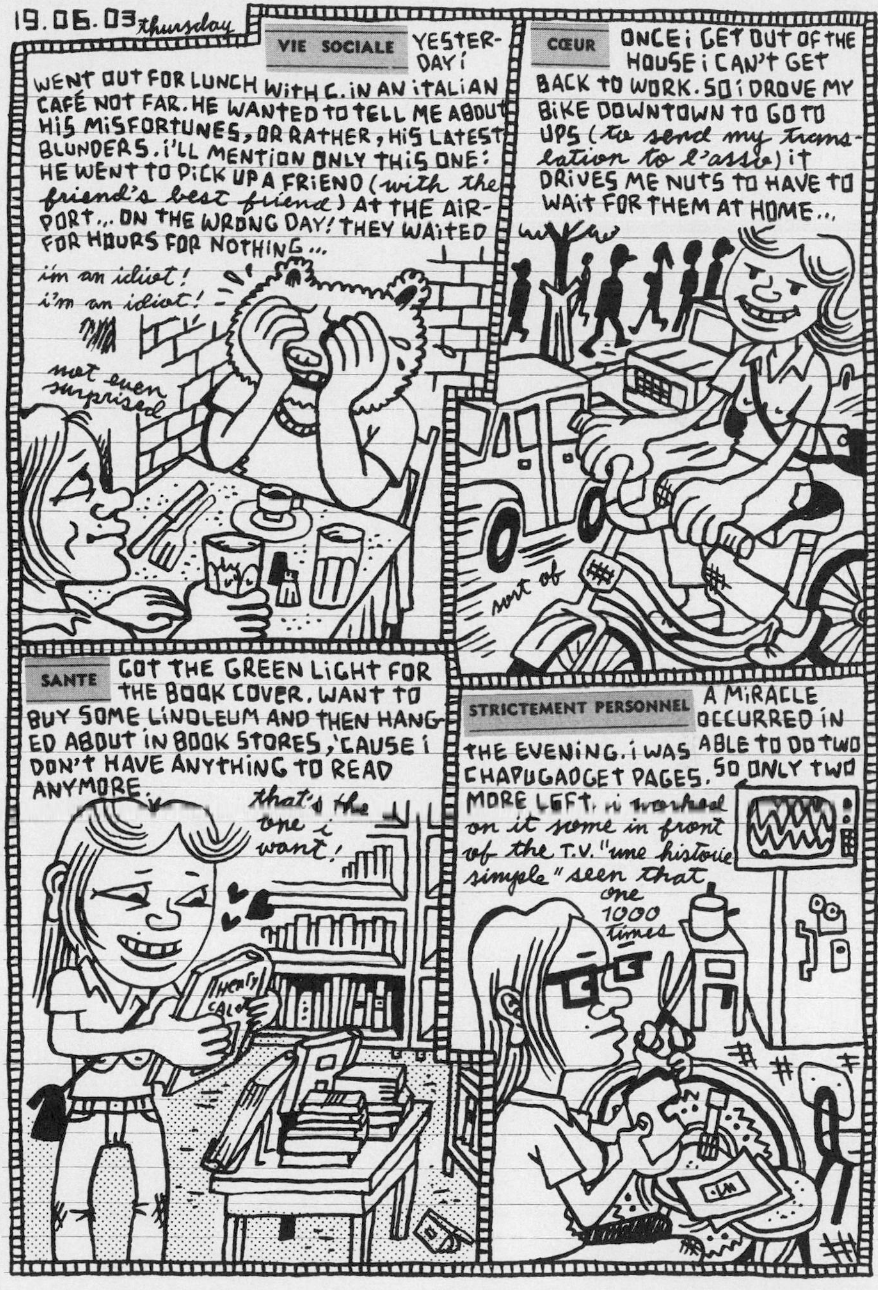
19.06.03 thursday
VIE SOCIALE
YESTERDAY i WENT OUT FOR LUNCH WITH C. IN AN iTALIAN CAFÉ NOT FAR. HE WANTED TO TELL ME ABOUT HIS MISFORTUNES, OR RATHER, HIS LATEST BLUNDERS. i'LL MENTION ONLY THIS ONE: HE WENT TO PICK UP A FRIEND (with the friend's best friend) AT THE AIRPORT... ON THE WRONG DAY! THEY WAITED FOR HOURS FOR NOTHING...
i'm an idiot!
i'm an idiot!
not even surprised
CŒUR
ONCE i GET OUT OF THE HOUSE i CAN'T GET BACK TO WORK. SO i DROVE MY BIKE DOWNTOWN TO GO TO UPS (to send my translation to l'asso) it DRIVES ME NUTS TO HAVE TO WAIT FOR THEM AT HOME...
sort of
SANTE
GOT THE GREEN LIGHT FOR THE BOOK COVER. WANT TO BUY SOME LINOLEUM AND THEN HANGED ABOUT IN BOOK STORES, 'CAUSE i DON'T HAVE ANYTHING TO READ ANYMORE.
that's the one i want!
STRICTEMENT PERSONNEL
A MIRACLE OCCURRED IN THE EVENING. i WAS ABLE TO DO TWO CHAPUGADGET PAGES. SO ONLY TWO MORE LEFT. i worked on it some in front of the T.V. "une histoire simple" seen that one 1000 times

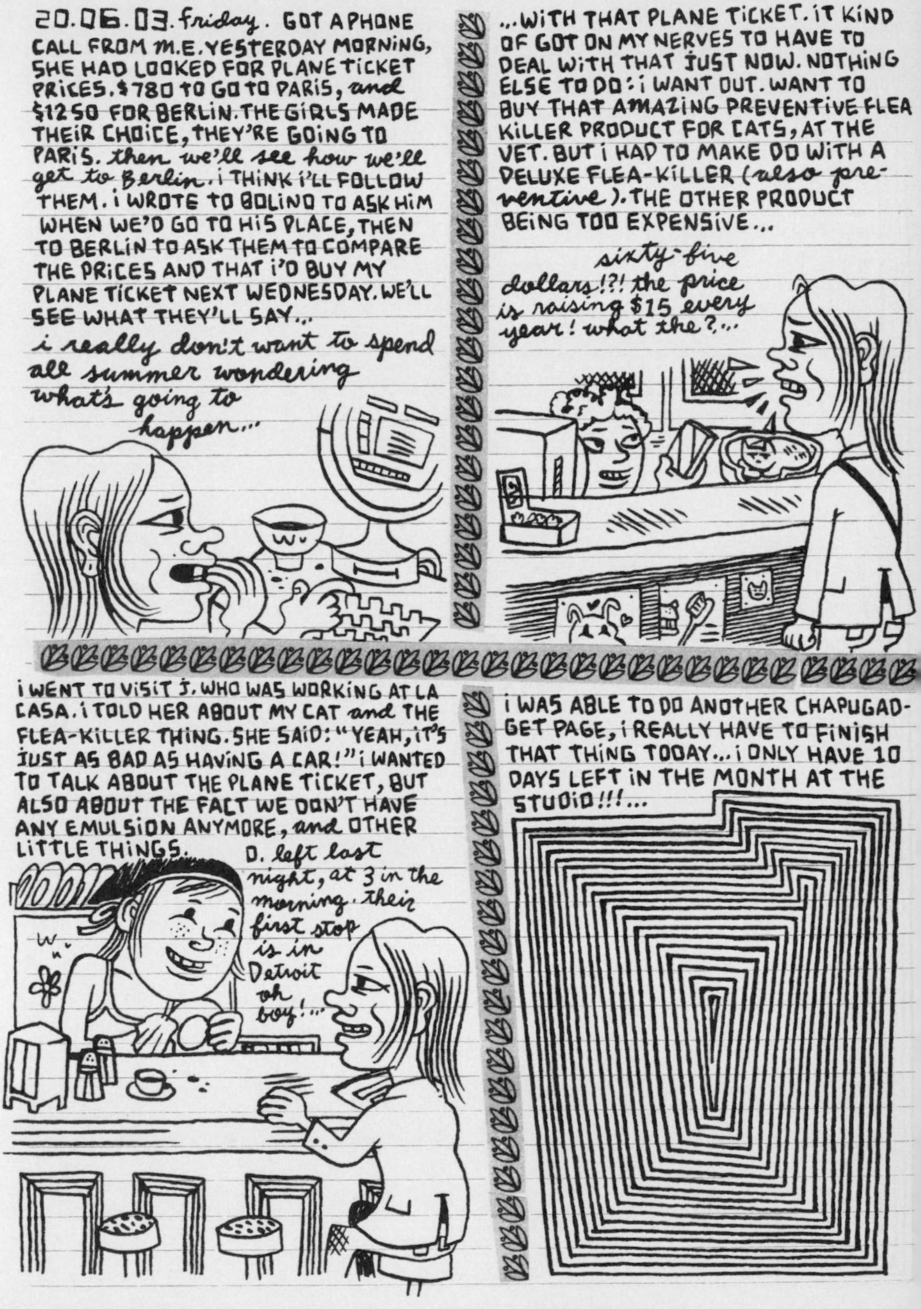
20.06.03. friday. GOT A PHONE CALL FROM M.E. YESTERDAY MORNING, SHE HAD LOOKED FOR PLANE TICKET PRICES. $780 TO GO TO PARIS, and $1250 FOR BERLIN. THE GIRLS MADE THEIR CHOICE, THEY'RE GOING TO PARIS. then we'll see how we'll get to Berlin. i THINK i'LL FOLLOW THEM. i WROTE TO BOLINO TO ASK HIM WHEN WE'D GO TO HIS PLACE, THEN TO BERLIN TO ASK THEM TO COMPARE THE PRICES AND THAT i'D BUY MY PLANE TICKET NEXT WEDNESDAY. WE'LL SEE WHAT THEY'LL SAY...
i really don't want to spend all summer wondering what's going to happen...
...WITH THAT PLANE TICKET. iT KIND OF GOT ON MY NERVES TO HAVE TO DEAL WITH THAT JUST NOW. NOTHING ELSE TO DO: i WANT OUT. WANT TO BUY THAT AMAZING PREVENTIVE FLEA KILLER PRODUCT FOR CATS, AT THE VET. BUT i HAD TO MAKE DO WITH A DELUXE FLEA-KILLER (also preventive). THE OTHER PRODUCT BEING TOO EXPENSIVE...
sixty-five dollars!?! the price is raising $15 every year! what the?...
i WENT TO VISIT J. WHO WAS WORKING AT LA CASA. i TOLD HER ABOUT MY CAT and THE FLEA-KILLER THING. SHE SAID: "YEAH, IT'S JUST AS BAD AS HAVING A CAR!" i WANTED TO TALK ABOUT THE PLANE TICKET, BUT ALSO ABOUT THE FACT WE DON'T HAVE ANY EMULSION ANYMORE, and OTHER LITTLE THINGS.
D. left last night, at 3 in the morning. their first stop is in Detroit oh boy!...
i WAS ABLE TO DO ANOTHER CHAPUGADGET PAGE, i REALLY HAVE TO FINISH THAT THING TODAY... i ONLY HAVE 10 DAYS LEFT iN THE MONTH AT THE STUDIO!!!...

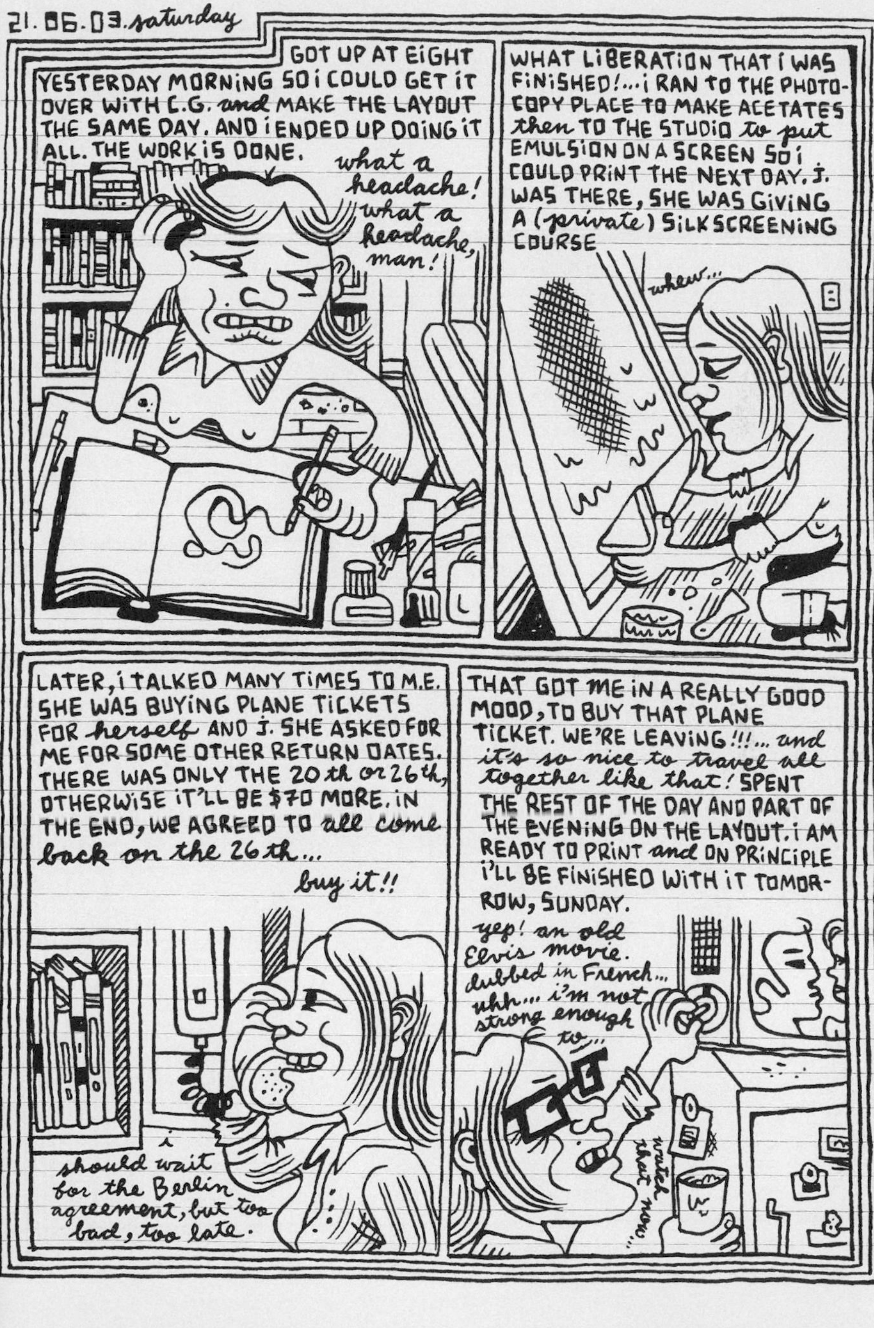
21.06.03. saturday
GOT UP AT EIGHT YESTERDAY MORNING SO I COULD GET IT OVER WITH C.G. and MAKE THE LAYOUT THE SAME DAY. AND I ENDED UP DOING IT ALL. THE WORK IS DONE.
what a headache! what a headache, man!
WHAT LIBERATION THAT I WAS FINISHED!... I RAN TO THE PHOTO-COPY PLACE TO MAKE ACETATES then TO THE STUDIO to put EMULSION ON A SCREEN SO I COULD PRINT THE NEXT DAY. J. WAS THERE, SHE WAS GIVING A (private) SILKSCREENING COURSE
whew...
LATER, I TALKED MANY TIMES TO M.E. SHE WAS BUYING PLANE TICKETS FOR herself AND J. SHE ASKED FOR ME FOR SOME OTHER RETURN DATES. THERE WAS ONLY THE 20 th or 26th, OTHERWISE IT'LL BE $70 MORE. IN THE END, WE AGREED TO all come back on the 26 th...
buy it!!
i should wait for the Berlin agreement, but too bad, too late.
THAT GOT ME IN A REALLY GOOD MOOD, TO BUY THAT PLANE TICKET. WE'RE LEAVING!!!... and it's so nice to travel all together like that! SPENT THE REST OF THE DAY AND PART OF THE EVENING ON THE LAYOUT. I AM READY TO PRINT and ON PRINCIPLE I'LL BE FINISHED WITH IT TOMOR-ROW, SUNDAY.
yep! an old Elvis movie. dubbed in French... uhh... i'm not strong enough to...
watch that now...

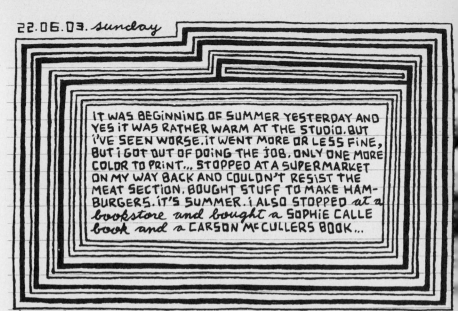

IT WAS BEGINNING OF SUMMER YESTERDAY AND YES IT WAS RATHER WARM AT THE STUDIO. BUT I'VE SEEN WORSE. IT WENT MORE OR LESS FINE, BUT I GOT OUT OF DOING THE JOB. ONLY ONE MORE COLOR TO PRINT... STOPPED AT A SUPERMARKET ON MY WAY BACK AND COULDN'T RESIST THE MEAT SECTION. BOUGHT STUFF TO MAKE HAMBURGERS. IT'S SUMMER. I ALSO STOPPED *at a bookstore and bought a* SOPHIE CALLE *book and a* CARSON McCULLERS BOOK...

JUST AS A REWARD... I'M SUFFERING SO MUCH. OH, SOME CLOUDS... I DREAMT I HAD BECOME ALL PUDGY AND FLABBY AND OLD.

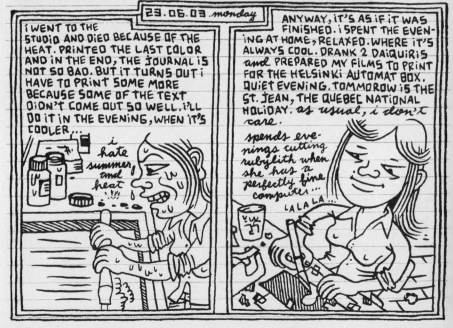

23.06.03. *monday*

I WENT TO THE STUDIO AND DIED BECAUSE OF THE HEAT. PRINTED THE LAST COLOR AND IN THE END, THE JOURNAL IS NOT SO BAD. BUT IT TURNS OUT I HAVE TO PRINT SOME MORE BECAUSE SOME OF THE TEXT DIDN'T COME OUT SO WELL. I'LL DO IT IN THE EVENING, WHEN IT'S COOLER...

i hate summer and heat

ANYWAY, IT'S AS IF IT WAS FINISHED. I SPENT THE EVENING AT HOME, RELAXED. WHERE IT'S ALWAYS COOL. DRANK 2 DAIQUIRIS *and* PREPARED MY FILMS TO PRINT FOR THE HELSINKI AUTOMAT BOX. QUIET EVENING. TOMMOROW IS THE ST. JEAN, THE QUEBEC NATIONAL HOLIDAY. *as usual, i don't care.*

spends evenings cutting rubylith when she has a perfectly fine computer...

LALA LA...

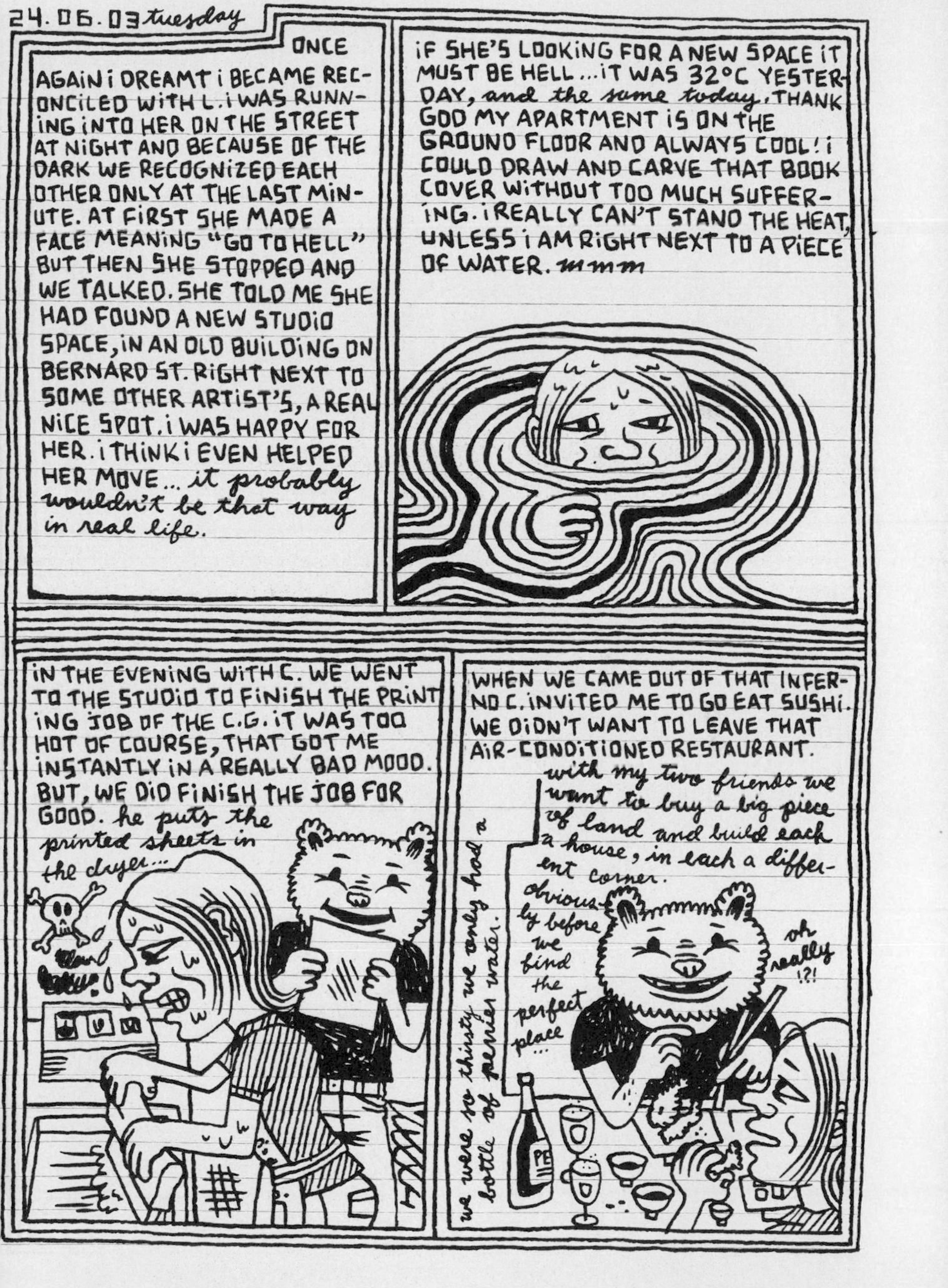
24.06.03 tuesday
ONCE AGAIN i DREAMT i BECAME RECONCILED WITH L. i WAS RUNNING INTO HER ON THE STREET AT NIGHT AND BECAUSE OF THE DARK WE RECOGNIZED EACH OTHER ONLY AT THE LAST MINUTE. AT FIRST SHE MADE A FACE MEANING "GO TO HELL" BUT THEN SHE STOPPED AND WE TALKED. SHE TOLD ME SHE HAD FOUND A NEW STUDIO SPACE, IN AN OLD BUILDING ON BERNARD ST. RIGHT NEXT TO SOME OTHER ARTIST'S, A REAL NICE SPOT. i WAS HAPPY FOR HER. i THINK i EVEN HELPED HER MOVE... it probably wouldn't be that way in real life.
iF SHE'S LOOKING FOR A NEW SPACE iT MUST BE HELL... iT WAS 32°C YESTERDAY, and the same today. THANK GOD MY APARTMENT iS ON THE GROUND FLOOR AND ALWAYS COOL! i COULD DRAW AND CARVE THAT BOOK COVER WITHOUT TOO MUCH SUFFERING. i REALLY CAN'T STAND THE HEAT, UNLESS i AM RIGHT NEXT TO A PIECE OF WATER. mmm
iN THE EVENING WITH C. WE WENT TO THE STUDIO TO FINISH THE PRINTING JOB OF THE C.G. iT WAS TOO HOT OF COURSE, THAT GOT ME iNSTANTLY iN A REALLY BAD MOOD. BUT, WE DID FINISH THE JOB FOR GOOD. he puts the printed sheets in the dryer...
WHEN WE CAME OUT OF THAT INFERNO C. iNVITED ME TO GO EAT SUSHi. WE DIDN'T WANT TO LEAVE THAT AiR-CONDITIONED RESTAURANT.
with my two friends we want to buy a big piece of land and build each a house, in each a different corner.
obviously before we find the perfect place...
oh really !?!
we were so thirsty we only had a bottle of perrier water.
PE

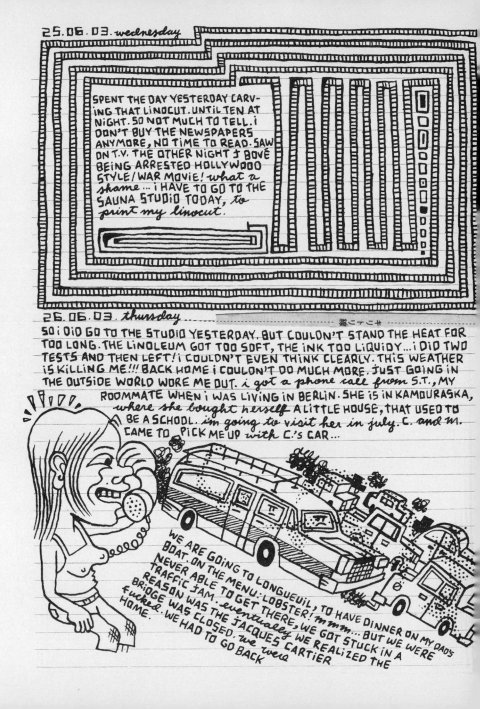

25.06.03. *wednesday*

SPENT THE DAY YESTERDAY CARV-
ING THAT LINOCUT. UNTIL TEN AT
NIGHT. SO NOT MUCH TO TELL. I
DON'T BUY THE NEWSPAPERS
ANYMORE, NO TIME TO READ. SAW
ON T.V. THE OTHER NIGHT J BOVÉ
BEING ARRESTED HOLLYWOOD
STYLE / WAR MOVIE! *what a
shame ...* I HAVE TO GO TO THE
SAUNA STUDIO TODAY, *to
print my linocut.*

26.06.03. *thursday*

SO I DID GO TO THE STUDIO YESTERDAY. BUT COULDN'T STAND THE HEAT FOR
TOO LONG. THE LINOLEUM GOT TOO SOFT, THE INK TOO LIQUIDY... I DID TWO
TESTS AND THEN LEFT! I COULDN'T EVEN THINK CLEARLY. THIS WEATHER
IS KILLING ME!!! BACK HOME I COULDN'T DO MUCH MORE. JUST GOING IN
THE OUTSIDE WORLD WORE ME OUT. *i got a phone call from S.T.,* MY
ROOMMATE WHEN I WAS LIVING IN BERLIN. SHE IS IN KAMOURASKA,
where she bought herself A LITTLE HOUSE, THAT USED TO
BE A SCHOOL. *i'm going to visit her in july. C. and M.*
CAME TO PICK ME UP *with C.'s CAR...*

WE ARE GOING TO LONGUEUIL, TO HAVE DINNER ON MY DAD'S
BOAT. ON THE MENU: LOBSTER! *mmm...* BUT WE WERE
NEVER ABLE TO GET THERE, WE GOT STUCK IN A
TRAFFIC JAM. *eventually,* WE REALIZED THE
REASON WAS THE JACQUES CARTIER
BRIDGE WAS CLOSED. *we were*
fucked. WE HAD TO GO BACK
HOME.

WE WAITED FOR MY DAD SITTING ON THE BALCONY, DRINKING A BEER. THEN WE ATE THE LOBSTERS. THE EVENING TURNED OUT FINE, EVEN THOUGH THE TEMPERATURE DIDN'T DROP ONE BIT.

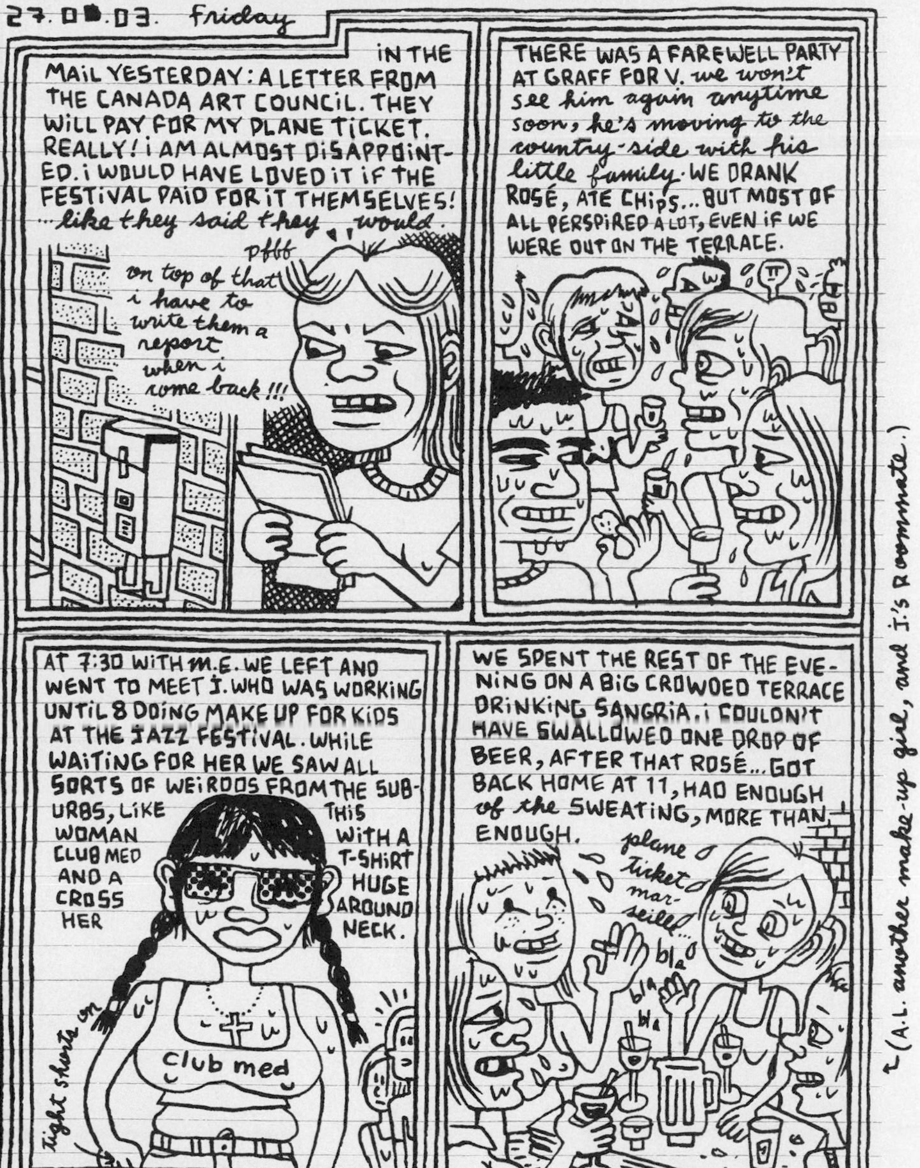
27.0[redacted].03. Friday
IN THE MAIL YESTERDAY: A LETTER FROM THE CANADA ART COUNCIL. THEY WILL PAY FOR MY PLANE TICKET. REALLY! I AM ALMOST DISAPPOINTED. I WOULD HAVE LOVED IT IF THE FESTIVAL PAID FOR IT THEMSELVES! ...like they said they would.
pfff
on top of that i have to write them a report when i come back!!!
THERE WAS A FAREWELL PARTY AT GRAFF FOR V. we won't see him again anytime soon, he's moving to the country-side with his little family. WE DRANK ROSÉ, ATE CHIPS... BUT MOST OF ALL PERSPIRED A LOT, EVEN IF WE WERE OUT ON THE TERRACE.
AT 7:30 WITH M.E. WE LEFT AND WENT TO MEET J. WHO WAS WORKING UNTIL 8 DOING MAKE UP FOR KIDS AT THE JAZZ FESTIVAL. WHILE WAITING FOR HER WE SAW ALL SORTS OF WEIRDOS FROM THE SUBURBS, LIKE THIS WOMAN WITH A CLUB MED T-SHIRT AND A HUGE CROSS AROUND HER NECK.
club med
tight shorts on
WE SPENT THE REST OF THE EVENING ON A BIG CROWDED TERRACE DRINKING SANGRIA. I COULDN'T HAVE SWALLOWED ONE DROP OF BEER, AFTER THAT ROSÉ... GOT BACK HOME AT 11, HAD ENOUGH of the SWEATING, MORE THAN ENOUGH.
plane ticket marseille...
bla
bla
bla
(A.L. another make-up girl, and J.'s roommate.)

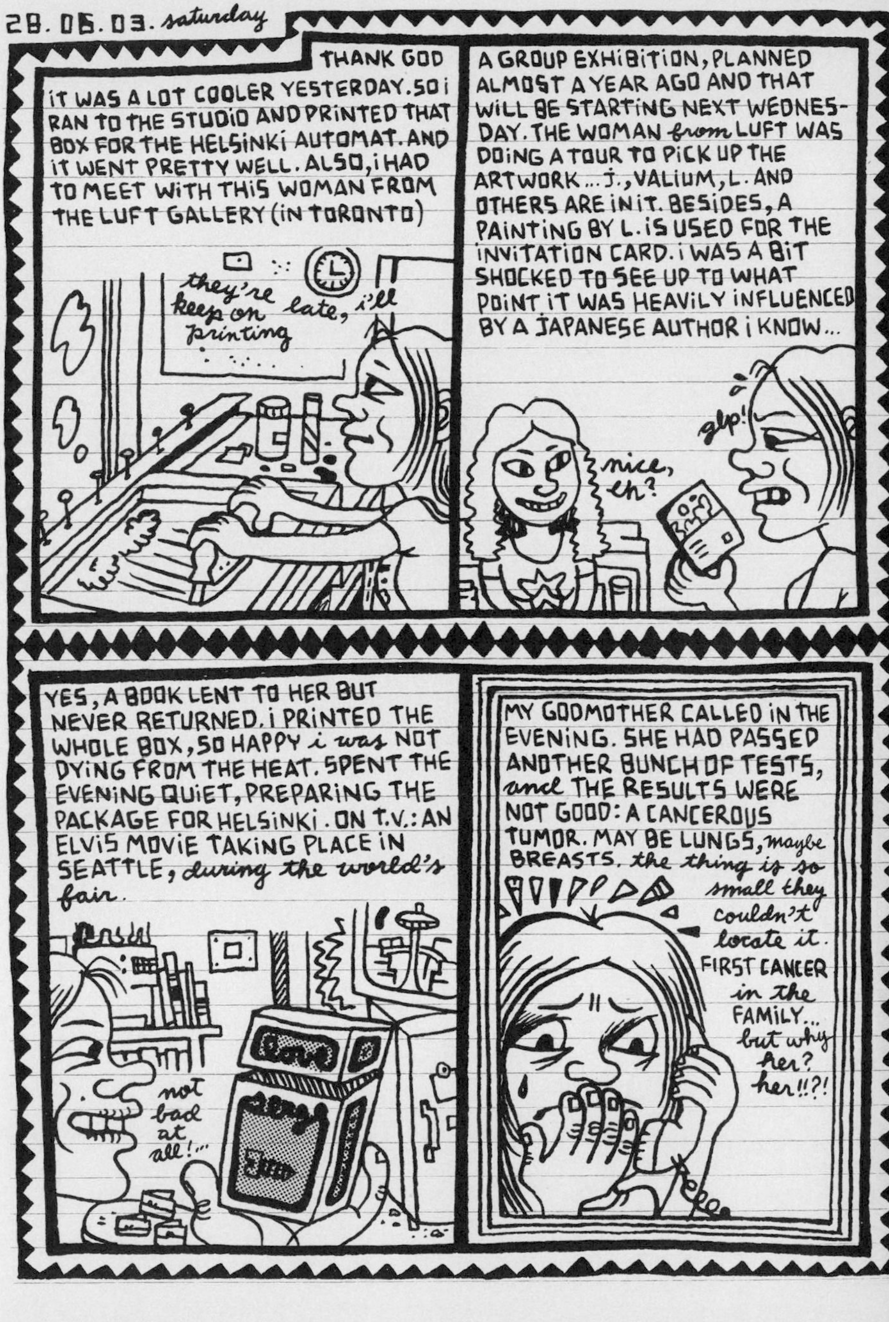

28. 06. 03. saturday
THANK GOD IT WAS A LOT COOLER YESTERDAY. SO i RAN TO THE STUDIO AND PRINTED THAT BOX FOR THE HELSINKi AUTOMAT. AND iT WENT PRETTY WELL. ALSO, i HAD TO MEET WITH THIS WOMAN FROM THE LUFT GALLERY (iN TORONTO)
they're late, i'll keep on printing
A GROUP EXHIBITION, PLANNED ALMOST A YEAR AGO AND THAT WILL BE STARTING NEXT WEDNESDAY. THE WOMAN from LUFT WAS DOING A TOUR TO PICK UP THE ARTWORK... J., VALIUM, L. AND OTHERS ARE iN iT. BESIDES, A PAINTING BY L. iS USED FOR THE iNVITATION CARD. i WAS A BiT SHOCKED TO SEE UP TO WHAT POINT iT WAS HEAVILY iNFLUENCED BY A JAPANESE AUTHOR i KNOW...
nice, eh?
glp!
YES, A BOOK LENT TO HER BUT NEVER RETURNED. i PRINTED THE WHOLE BOX, SO HAPPY i was NOT DYING FROM THE HEAT. SPENT THE EVENING QUIET, PREPARING THE PACKAGE FOR HELSINKi. ON T.V.: AN ELViS MOVIE TAKING PLACE IN SEATTLE, during the world's fair.
not bad at all!...
MY GODMOTHER CALLED IN THE EVENING. SHE HAD PASSED ANOTHER BUNCH OF TESTS, and THE RESULTS WERE NOT GOOD: A CANCEROUS TUMOR. MAY BE LUNGS, maybe BREASTS. the thing is so small they couldn't locate it. FIRST CANCER in the FAMILY... but why her? her!!?!

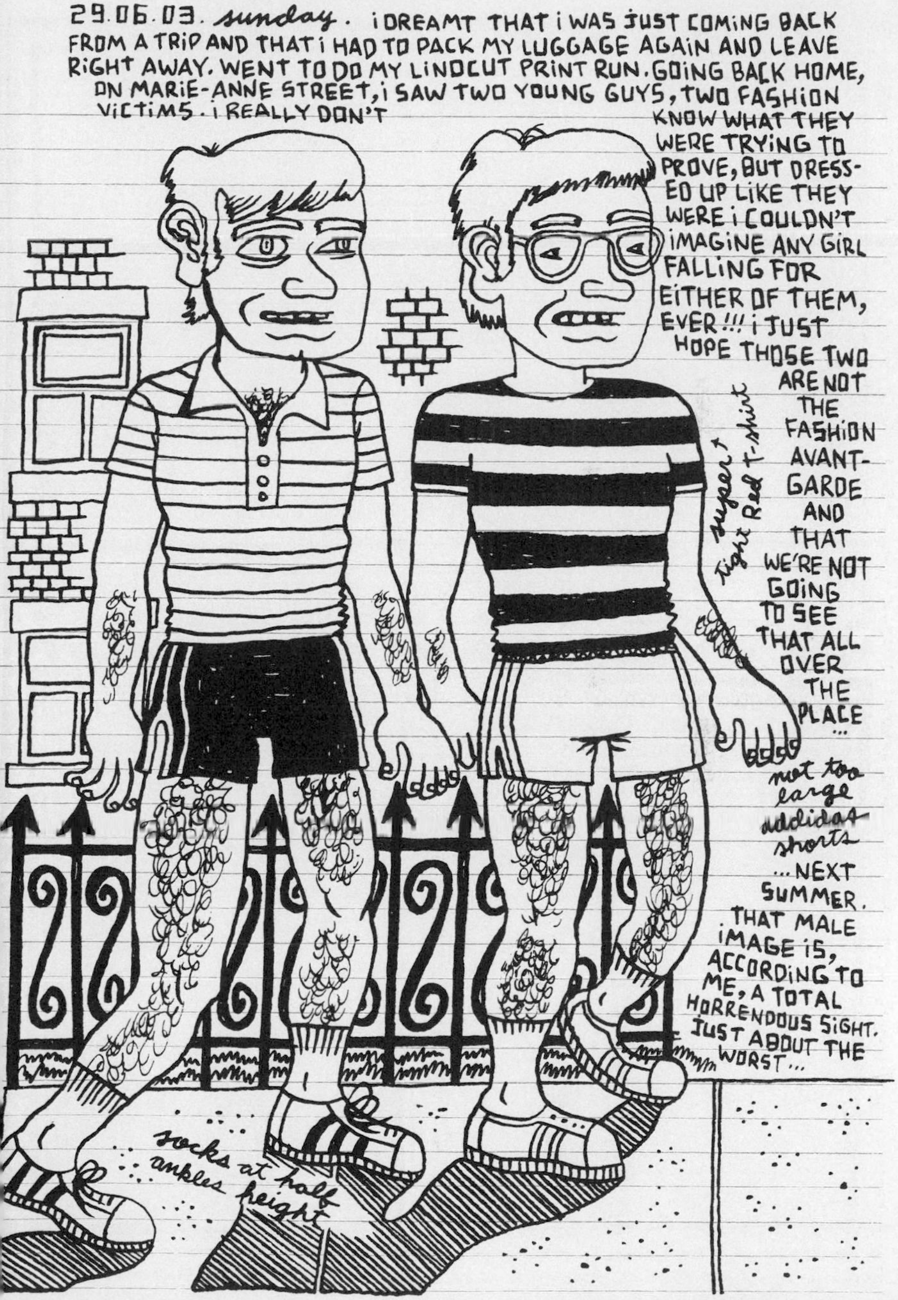
29.06.03. sunday. i DREAMT THAT i WAS JUST COMING BACK FROM A TRIP AND THAT i HAD TO PACK MY LUGGAGE AGAIN AND LEAVE RIGHT AWAY. WENT TO DO MY LINOCUT PRINT RUN. GOING BACK HOME, ON MARIE-ANNE STREET, i SAW TWO YOUNG GUYS, TWO FASHION VICTIMS. i REALLY DON'T KNOW WHAT THEY WERE TRYING TO PROVE, BUT DRESS-ED UP LIKE THEY WERE i COULDN'T IMAGINE ANY GIRL FALLING FOR EITHER OF THEM, EVER!!! i JUST HOPE THOSE TWO ARE NOT THE FASHION AVANT-GARDE AND THAT WE'RE NOT GOING TO SEE THAT ALL OVER THE PLACE...
super tight Red T-shirt
not too large addidas shorts
...NEXT SUMMER. THAT MALE IMAGE IS, ACCORDING TO ME, A TOTAL HORRENDOUS SIGHT. JUST ABOUT THE WORST...
socks at half ankles height

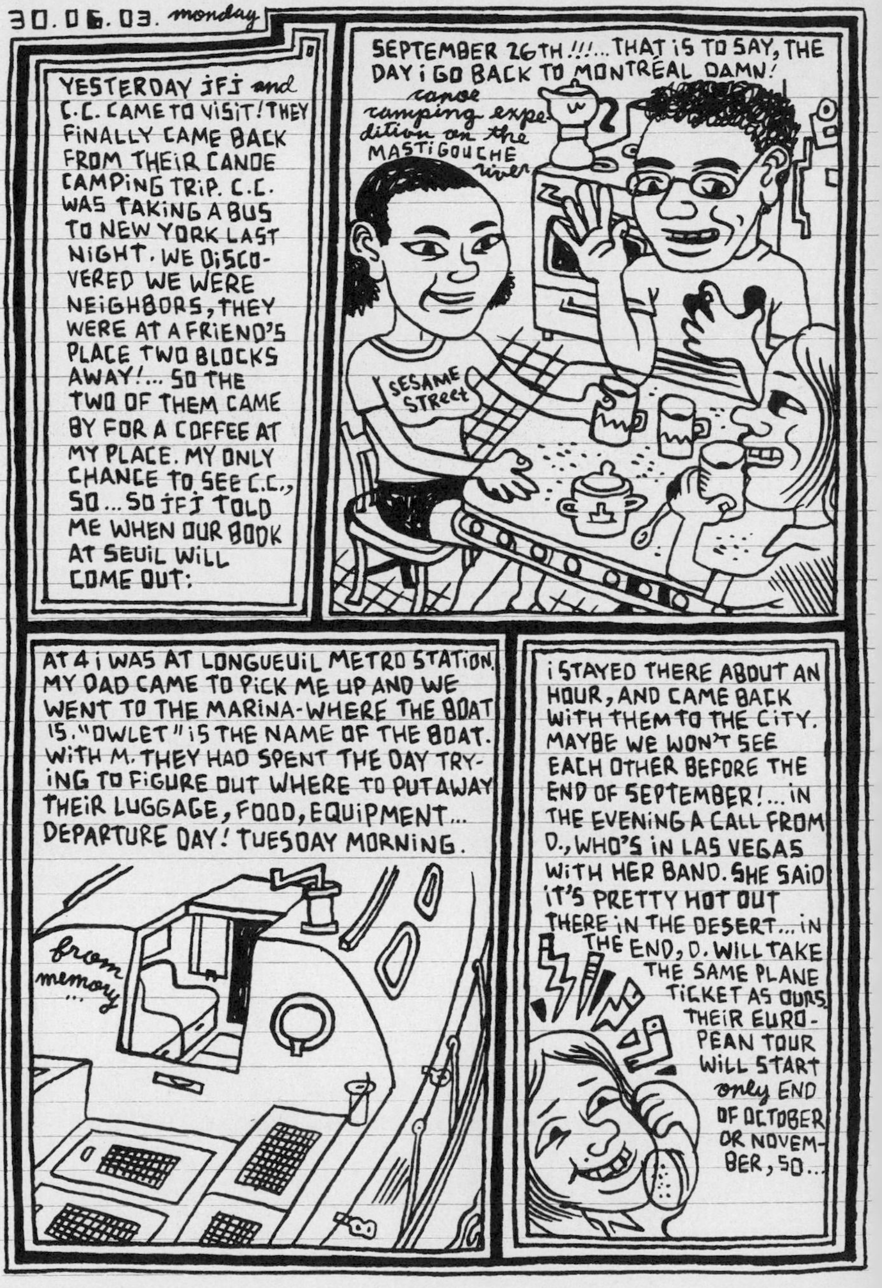
30.06.03. monday
YESTERDAY JFJ and C.C. CAME TO VISIT! THEY FINALLY CAME BACK FROM THEIR CANOE CAMPING TRIP. C.C. WAS TAKING A BUS TO NEW YORK LAST NIGHT. WE DISCOVERED WE WERE NEIGHBORS, THEY WERE AT A FRIEND'S PLACE TWO BLOCKS AWAY!... SO THE TWO OF THEM CAME BY FOR A COFFEE AT MY PLACE. MY ONLY CHANCE TO SEE C.C., SO... SO JFJ TOLD ME WHEN OUR BOOK AT SEUIL WILL COME OUT:
SEPTEMBER 26TH!!!... THAT IS TO SAY, THE DAY I GO BACK TO MONTRÉAL DAMN!
canoe camping expedition on the MASTIGOUCHE river
SESAME STREET
AT 4 I WAS AT LONGUEUIL METRO STATION. MY DAD CAME TO PICK ME UP AND WE WENT TO THE MARINA - WHERE THE BOAT IS. "OWLET" IS THE NAME OF THE BOAT. WITH M. THEY HAD SPENT THE DAY TRYING TO FIGURE OUT WHERE TO PUT AWAY THEIR LUGGAGE, FOOD, EQUIPMENT... DEPARTURE DAY! TUESDAY MORNING.
from memory...
I STAYED THERE ABOUT AN HOUR, AND CAME BACK WITH THEM TO THE CITY. MAYBE WE WON'T SEE EACH OTHER BEFORE THE END OF SEPTEMBER!... IN THE EVENING A CALL FROM D., WHO'S IN LAS VEGAS WITH HER BAND. SHE SAID IT'S PRETTY HOT OUT THERE IN THE DESERT... IN THE END, D. WILL TAKE THE SAME PLANE TICKET AS OURS. THEIR EUROPEAN TOUR WILL START only END OF OCTOBER OR NOVEMBER, SO...

et...

july 2003

✻ ✻ ✻ ✻ ✻ * * *

SUN	MON	TUES	WED	THUR	FRi	SAT
		1	2	3	4	5
6	7	8	9	10	11	12
13	14	15	16	17	18	19
20	21	22	23	24	25	26
27	28	29	30	31		

01. 07. 03. tuesday. MY DAD AND M. WERE LEAVING VERY EARLY THiS MORNiNG, WiTH A COUPLE OF FRiENDS. LUNCH AT CHRiS OLiVEROS' PLACE YESTERDAY ON THE OCCASSiON OF TOM DEVLiN'S (HiGHWATER BOOKS) ViSiT iN MONTRÉAL, WiTH HiS GiRLFRiEND PEGGY WHO'S WORK-ING FOR DC COMiCS! EVERYTiME i AM AMAZED HOW i FEEL "OUT OF iT", LiKE ON PLANET MARS, WHEN i AM AROUND COMiC PEOPLE... AT 5 JFJ ' WAS COMiNG TO MY PLACE WiTH THE BOOK LAYOUT. WE LOOKED AT iT AND DRANK GiN AND TONiC.

WE SPOTTED LITTLE
THINGS WE DiDN'T
LIKE SO MUCH
BUT OVER ALL
iT iS VERY
NiCELY DONE
...

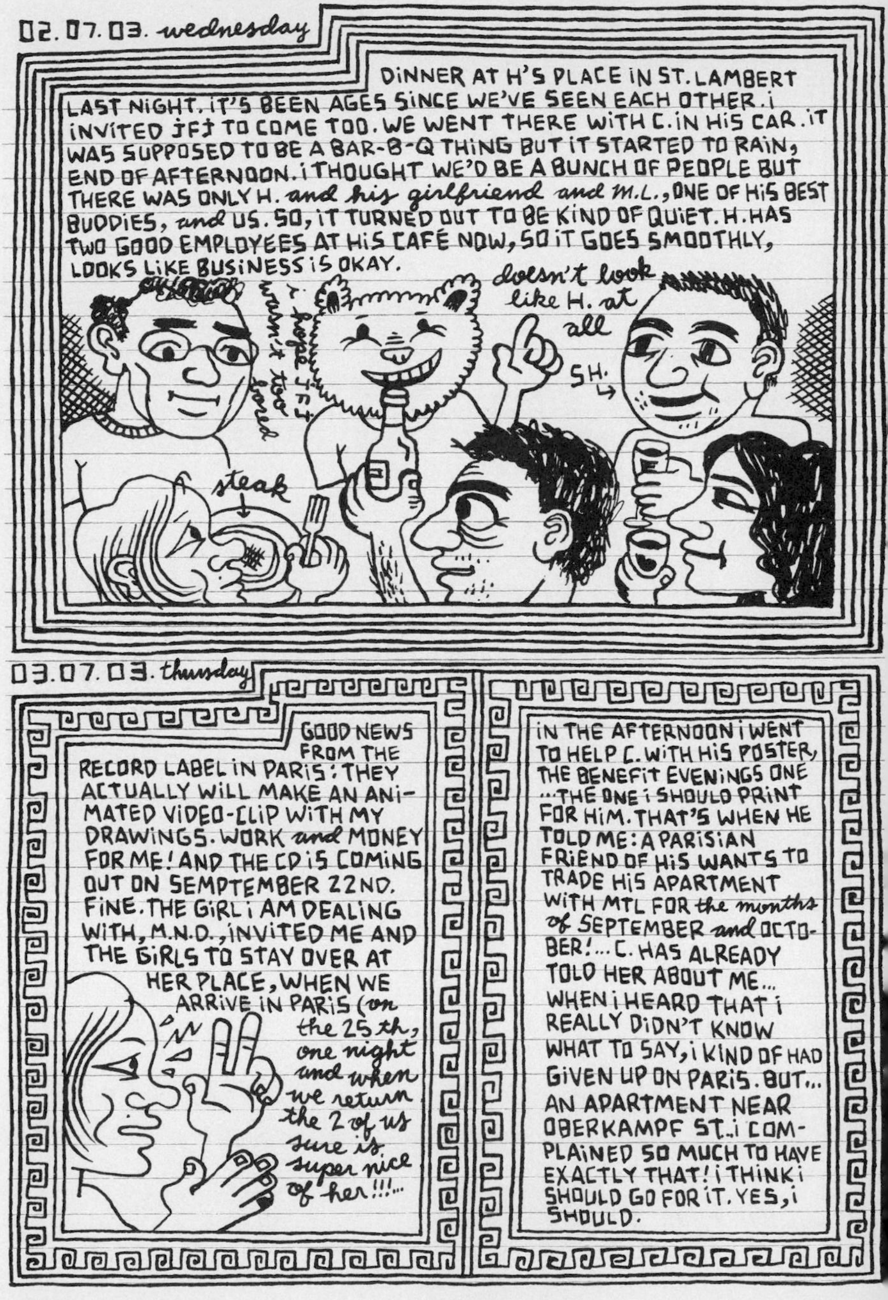
02.07.03. wednesday
DINNER AT H'S PLACE IN ST. LAMBERT LAST NIGHT. IT'S BEEN AGES SINCE WE'VE SEEN EACH OTHER. i INVITED JFJ TO COME TOO. WE WENT THERE WITH C. IN HIS CAR. IT WAS SUPPOSED TO BE A BAR-B-Q THING BUT IT STARTED TO RAIN, END OF AFTERNOON. i THOUGHT WE'D BE A BUNCH OF PEOPLE BUT THERE WAS ONLY H. and his girlfriend and M.L., ONE OF HIS BEST BUDDIES, and US. SO, IT TURNED OUT TO BE KIND OF QUIET. H. HAS TWO GOOD EMPLOYEES AT HIS CAFÉ NOW, SO IT GOES SMOOTHLY, LOOKS LIKE BUSINESS IS OKAY.
i hope JFJ wasn't too bored
doesn't look like H. at all
SH.
steak
03.07.03. thursday
GOOD NEWS FROM THE RECORD LABEL IN PARIS: THEY ACTUALLY WILL MAKE AN ANIMATED VIDEO-CLIP WITH MY DRAWINGS. WORK and MONEY FOR ME! AND THE CD IS COMING OUT ON SEMPTEMBER 22ND. FINE. THE GIRL i AM DEALING WITH, M.N.D., INVITED ME AND THE GIRLS TO STAY OVER AT HER PLACE, WHEN WE ARRIVE IN PARIS (on the 25th, one night and when we return the 2 of us sure is super nice of her!!!...
IN THE AFTERNOON i WENT TO HELP C. WITH HIS POSTER, THE BENEFIT EVENINGS ONE ...THE ONE i SHOULD PRINT FOR HIM. THAT'S WHEN HE TOLD ME: A PARISIAN FRIEND OF HIS WANTS TO TRADE HIS APARTMENT WITH MTL FOR the months of SEPTEMBER and OCTOBER!... C. HAS ALREADY TOLD HER ABOUT ME... WHEN i HEARD THAT i REALLY DIDN'T KNOW WHAT TO SAY, i KIND OF HAD GIVEN UP ON PARIS. BUT... AN APARTMENT NEAR OBERKAMPF ST.. i COMPLAINED SO MUCH TO HAVE EXACTLY THAT! i THINK i SHOULD GO FOR IT. YES, i SHOULD.

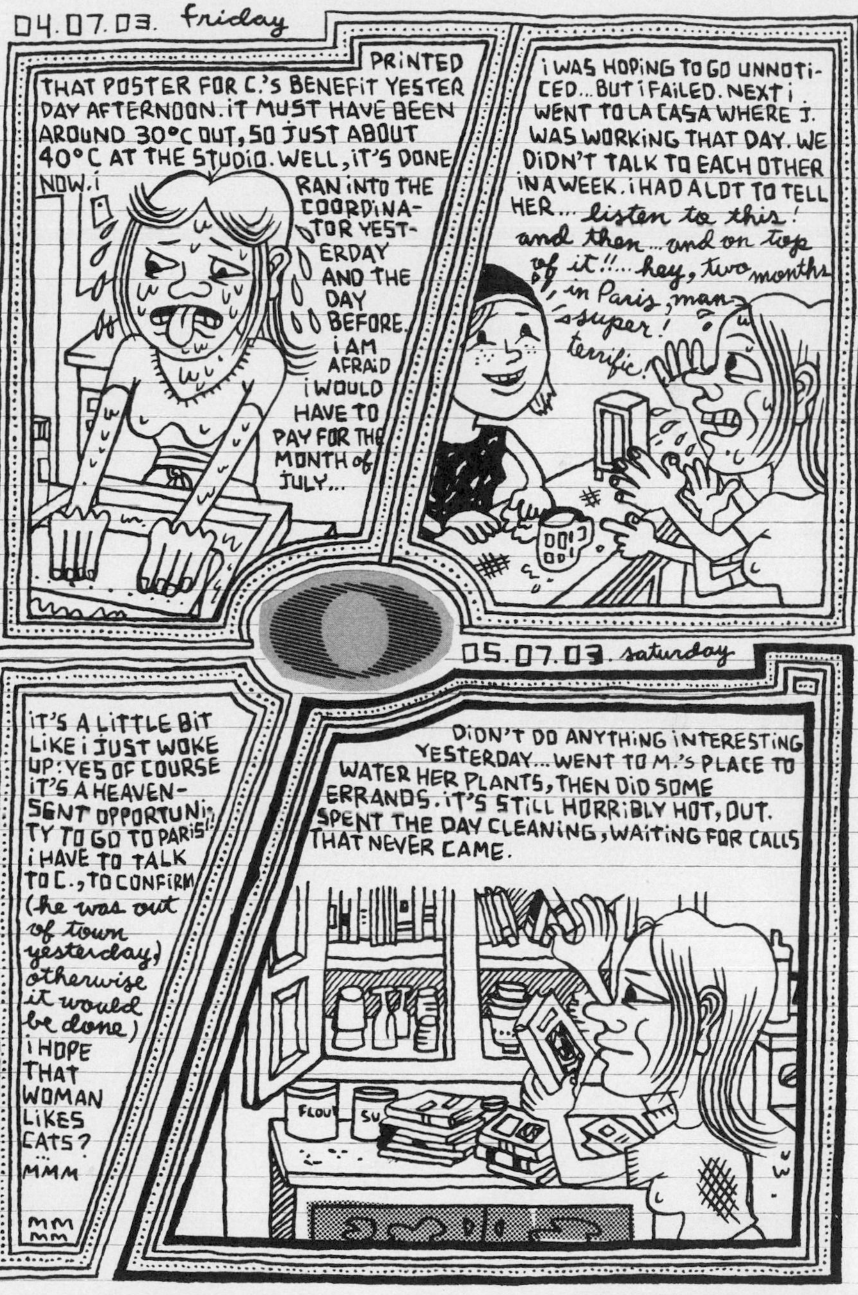

04.07.03. friday
PRINTED THAT POSTER FOR C.'S BENEFIT YESTERDAY AFTERNOON. IT MUST HAVE BEEN AROUND 30°C OUT, SO JUST ABOUT 40°C AT THE STUDIO. WELL, IT'S DONE NOW. I RAN INTO THE COORDINATOR YESTERDAY AND THE DAY BEFORE. I AM AFRAID I WOULD HAVE TO PAY FOR THE MONTH of JULY...
I WAS HOPING TO GO UNNOTICED... BUT I FAILED. NEXT I WENT TO LA CASA WHERE J. WAS WORKING THAT DAY. WE DIDN'T TALK TO EACH OTHER IN A WEEK. I HAD A LOT TO TELL HER... listen to this! and then... and on top of it!!... hey, two months in Paris, man, 's super! terrific!
IT'S A LITTLE BIT LIKE I JUST WOKE UP: YES OF COURSE IT'S A HEAVEN-SENT OPPORTUNITY TO GO TO PARIS!! I HAVE TO TALK TO C., TO CONFIRM (he was out of town yesterday) otherwise it would be done) I HOPE THAT WOMAN LIKES CATS? ... MMM
MM MM
05.07.03. saturday
DIDN'T DO ANYTHING INTERESTING YESTERDAY... WENT TO M.'S PLACE TO WATER HER PLANTS, THEN DID SOME ERRANDS. IT'S STILL HORRIBLY HOT, OUT. SPENT THE DAY CLEANING, WAITING FOR CALLS THAT NEVER CAME.
FLOU
SU

I WAS CLEANING THINKING OF MY FUTURE TENANT. C. WILL GIVE ME HER EMAIL ADDRESS, SO WE CAN MAKE ARRANGEMENTS TOGETHER. WHILE GOING THROUGH OLD STUFF I CAME ACROSS A PILE OF PICTURES OF MY NEW YORK BOYFRIEND. I HAD COMPLETELY FORGOTTEN ABOUT THAT!...THE PRECIOUS THINGS I KEEP.

06.07.03. *sunday*

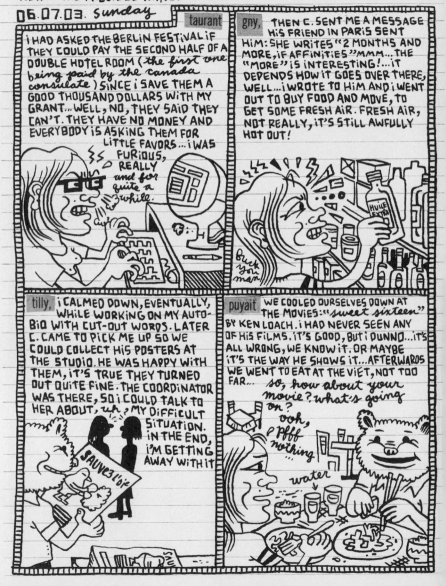

taurant

I HAD ASKED THE BERLIN FESTIVAL IF THEY COULD PAY THE SECOND HALF OF A DOUBLE HOTEL ROOM (*the first one being paid by the canada consulate*) SINCE I SAVE THEM A GOOD THOUSAND DOLLARS WITH MY GRANT...WELL, NO, THEY SAID THEY CAN'T. THEY HAVE NO MONEY AND EVERYBODY IS ASKING THEM FOR LITTLE FAVORS... I WAS FURIOUS, REALLY *and for quite a while.*

gny, THEN C. SENT ME A MESSAGE HIS FRIEND IN PARIS SENT HIM: SHE WRITES "2 MONTHS AND MORE, IF AFFINITIES" MMM... THE "MORE" IS INTERESTING!...IT DEPENDS HOW IT GOES OVER THERE, WELL... I WROTE TO HIM AND I WENT OUT TO BUY FOOD AND MOVE, TO GET SOME FRESH AIR. FRESH AIR, NOT REALLY, IT'S STILL AWFULLY HOT OUT!

HUILE EXTRA

fuck you man

tilly, I CALMED DOWN, EVENTUALLY, WHILE WORKING ON MY AUTO-BIO WITH CUT-OUT WORDS. LATER C. CAME TO PICK ME UP SO WE COULD COLLECT HIS POSTERS AT THE STUDIO. HE WAS HAPPY WITH THEM, IT'S TRUE THEY TURNED OUT QUITE FINE. THE COORDINATOR WAS THERE, SO I COULD TALK TO HER ABOUT, UH, MY DIFFICULT SITUATION. IN THE END, I'M GETTING AWAY WITH IT

SAUVE3 L'OJ

puyait WE COOLED OURSELVES DOWN AT THE MOVIES: "*sweet sixteen*" BY KEN LOACH. I HAD NEVER SEEN ANY OF HIS FILMS. IT'S GOOD, BUT I DUNNO...IT'S ALL WRONG, WE KNOW IT. OR MAYBE IT'S THE WAY HE SHOWS IT...AFTERWARDS WE WENT TO EAT AT THE VIET, NOT TOO FAR... *so, how about your movie? what's going on?*

ooh, pfff nothing...

water

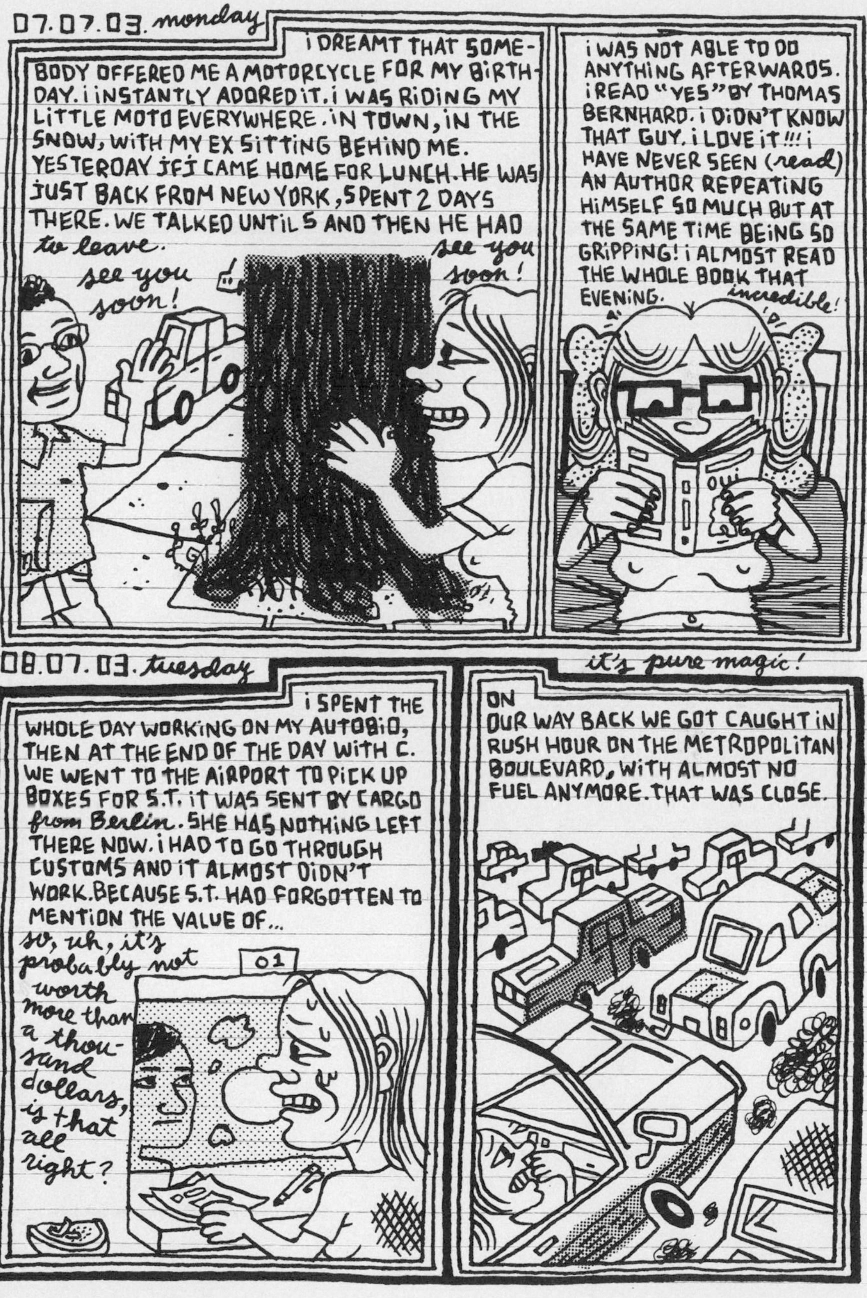
07.07.03. monday
i DREAMT THAT SOMEBODY OFFERED ME A MOTORCYCLE FOR MY BIRTHDAY. i iNSTANTLY ADORED iT. i WAS RiDiNG MY LiTTLE MOTO EVERYWHERE. iN TOWN, iN THE SNOW, WiTH MY EX SiTTiNG BEHiND ME.
YESTERDAY JFJ CAME HOME FOR LUNCH. HE WAS JUST BACK FROM NEW YORK, SPENT 2 DAYS THERE. WE TALKED UNTiL 5 AND THEN HE HAD to leave.
see you soon!
see you soon!
i WAS NOT ABLE TO DO ANYTHiNG AFTERWARDS. i READ "YES" BY THOMAS BERNHARD. i DiDN'T KNOW THAT GUY. i LOVE iT!!! i HAVE NEVER SEEN (read) AN AUTHOR REPEATiNG HiMSELF SO MUCH BUT AT THE SAME TiME BEiNG SO GRiPPiNG! i ALMOST READ THE WHOLE BOOK THAT EVENiNG.
incredible!
OUI
it's pure magic!
08.07.03. tuesday
i SPENT THE WHOLE DAY WORKiNG ON MY AUTOBiO, THEN AT THE END OF THE DAY WiTH C. WE WENT TO THE AiRPORT TO PiCK UP BOXES FOR S.T. iT WAS SENT BY CARGO from Berlin. SHE HAS NOTHiNG LEFT THERE NOW. i HAD TO GO THROUGH CUSTOMS AND iT ALMOST DiDN'T WORK. BECAUSE S.T. HAD FORGOTTEN TO MENTiON THE VALUE OF...
so, uh, it's probably not worth more than a thousand dollars, is that all right?
01
ON OUR WAY BACK WE GOT CAUGHT iN RUSH HOUR ON THE METROPOLiTAN BOULEVARD, WiTH ALMOST NO FUEL ANYMORE. THAT WAS CLOSE.

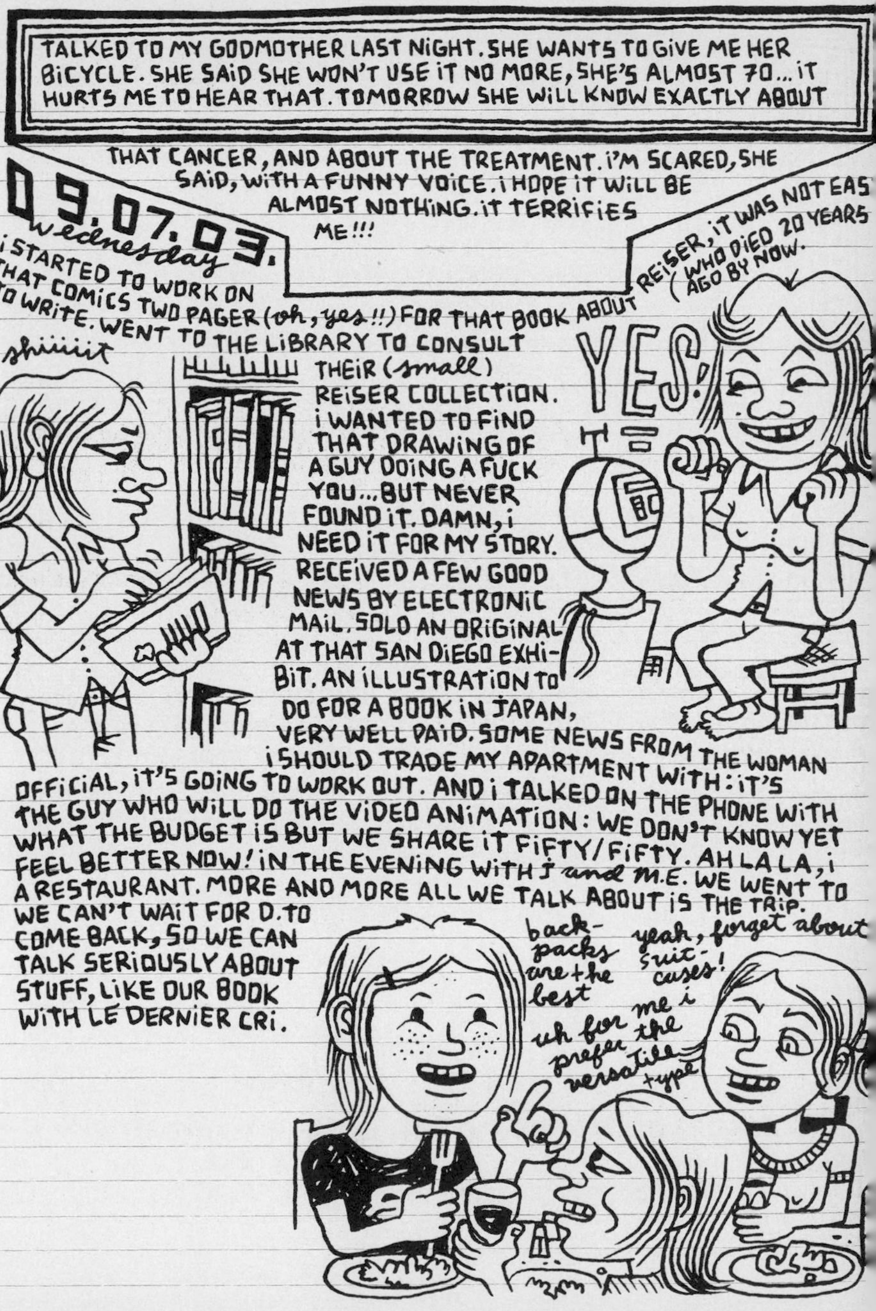
TALKED TO MY GODMOTHER LAST NiGHT. SHE WANTS TO GiVE ME HER BiCYCLE. SHE SAiD SHE WON'T USE iT NO MORE, SHE'S ALMOST 70... iT HURTS ME TO HEAR THAT. TOMORROW SHE WiLL KNOW EXACTLY ABOUT THAT CANCER, AND ABOUT THE TREATMENT. i'M SCARED, SHE SAiD, WiTH A FUNNY VOiCE. i HOPE iT WiLL BE ALMOST NOTHiNG. iT TERRiFiES ME!!!
09.07.03.
wednesday
i STARTED TO WORK ON
THAT COMICS TWO PAGER (oh, yes!!) FOR THAT BOOK ABOUT
TO WRiTE. WENT TO THE LiBRARY TO CONSULT
REiSER, iT WAS NOT EAS
(WHO DiED 20 YEARS
AGO BY NOW.
shiiiiit
THEiR (small)
REiSER COLLECTiON.
i WANTED TO FiND
THAT DRAWiNG OF
A GUY DOiNG A FUCK
YOU... BUT NEVER
FOUND iT. DAMN, i
NEED iT FOR MY STORY.
RECEiVED A FEW GOOD
NEWS BY ELECTRONiC
MAiL. SOLD AN ORiGiNAL
AT THAT SAN DiEGO EXHi-
BiT. AN iLLUSTRATiON TO
DO FOR A BOOK iN JAPAN,
VERY WELL PAiD. SOME NEWS FROM
YES!
i SHOULD TRADE MY APARTMENT WiTH THE WOMAN
OFFiCiAL, iT'S GOiNG TO WORK OUT. AND i TALKED ON THE PHONE WiTH: iT'S
THE GUY WHO WiLL DO THE ViDEO ANiMATiON: WE DON'T KNOW YET
WHAT THE BUDGET iS BUT WE SHARE iT FiFTY/FiFTY. AH LA LA, i
FEEL BETTER NOW! iN THE EVENiNG WiTH J and M.E. WE WENT TO
A RESTAURANT. MORE AND MORE ALL WE TALK ABOUT iS THE TRiP.
WE CAN'T WAiT FOR D. TO
COME BACK, SO WE CAN
TALK SERiOUSLY ABOUT
STUFF, LiKE OUR BOOK
WiTH LE DERNiER CRi.
backpacks are the best
yeah, forget about suitcases!
uh for me i prefer the versatile type

10.07.03. *thursday*

i STARTED TO WORK ON THAT COMIC, BUT DiDN'T GO TOO FAR. i AM TOTALLY OUT OF PRACTICE. i HAVE TO FiND THAT CHARACTER. SENT SOME FED-EX MORE ORiGiNALS TO SAN DiEGO BECAUSE NEXT WEEK iS THE COMIC-CON... A WOMAN FROM AN MTL GALLERY CALLED ME! UNBELiEVABLE! ...AND THEN *jfj*, WHO HAD JUST SPENT THE AFTERNOON AT SEUiL... WE HAD TO TALK ABOUT THE LAYOUT, IN THE END i DiDN'T WORK... SPENT THE WHOLE DAY ON THE PHONE. THE END.

11.07.03. *friday* : i AM SUPER SLOW WORKiNG ON THAT COMIC. i DO iT BiT BY BiT EVERYDAY. FOUND THE LiTTLE REiSER CHARACTER. i WANTED TO COPY A BUNCH OF HiS DRAWiNGS BUT NOW i'M WONDERiNG iF iT'S A GOOD iDEA... iT'S RAiNiNG TODAY, iT'S BEEN A MONTH SiNCE THAT HAPPENED! iT'S RESTFUL. TOO MUCH OF THAT AGGRESSiVE SUN. iN THE EVENiNG WiTH j *and m.e.* WE WENT TO SEE THE BOOKMOBiLE, WHiCH WAS PARKED NOT FAR iN THE MiLE-END. iT'S VERY WELL FiTTED OUT iNSiDE, i DON'T KNOW HOW THEY DiD TO MAKE 300 BOOKS GO iN

BOOKMOBiLE
BOOKMOBiLE

VEN THOUGH THEY'RE SMALL! YOU CAN EVEN SiT COMFORTABLY...
E HAD A BEER WiTH LEiLA, ONE OF THE ORGANiZERS OF THE
HiNG. SHE'S A FUNNY ONE, i LiKE HER. THE BOOKMOBiLE WAS
ARKED iN FRONT OF THAT TORONTO GALLERY, DURiNG THE OPENiNG.
O NOW WE KNOW WHAT iT LOOKED LiKE (*me and j. are in that*
xhibit) TURNS OUT iT'S A GOOD ONE, EVERYONE SAYS SO.
K, GOOD.

12.07.03. saturday

i DREAMT MY DAD HAD CANCER, AND HE HAD ONLY ONE YEAR LEFT TO LIVE. YESTERDAY EVERYTHING WAS GOING WELL. i GOT A PHONE CALL FROM A. iN SAN DiEGO, WHO ASKED ME iF i WANTED TO SEND MORE ORiGiNALS (*again!*) BECAUSE WHAT i HAD SENT HiM WAS ALREADY SOLD! PEOPLE ARE FiGHTiNG TO GET ME!... iT'S BECAUSE i NEVER PUT MUCH STUFF FOR SALE... AND THEN A PHONE CALL FROM MY MOM... PRETTY BAD NEWS, CONCERNiNG MY GODMOTHER (*her sister*). LUNG CANCER, THE TWO ARE iNFECTED, AND SHE HAS ONLY ONE YEAR TO LiVE!!!?! i STARTED TO CRY iNSTANTLY, AFTER i HUNG UP. HER!!!... i COULD NEVER iMAGiNE... iT ALL STARTED WiTH A COLD LAST DECEMBER... APPARENTLY, A FRiEND OF HERS CALLED HER, CRYiNG HER EYES OUT. MY GODMOTHER TOLD HER THAT SHE REALLY DiDN'T FEEL LiKE LiSTENiNG TO PEOPLE CRY OVER HER BEiNG SiCK AND ALL... ONE YEAR TO LiVE!... i JUST CAN'T i HAVE NO EXPERiENCE WiTH DEATH, NOBODY CLOSE TO ME DiED...

AND HER... SHE'S NOT JUST ANYBODY. i ENDED UP SENDiNG HER AN EMAiL, iN THE EVENiNG, TELLiNG HER... AND THAT i WOULD CALL HER ON MONDAY, JUST LiKE WE SAiD THE LAST TiME WE TALKED ON THE PHONE... i COULDN'T BEFORE. MEANWHiLE, i HAVE THOSE TWO STUPiD PAGES TO DRAW. i SURE REGRET SAYiNG YES TO THAT JOB. CAN'T DO iT. i DO ONLY A TiNY BiT EVERYDAY! AND iT'S TAKiNG FOREVER! BUT, NO CHOiCE, GOTTA SEND THAT ON MONDAY. BUT ONE YEAR TO LiVE!? iT SOUNDS LiKE A BAD MOViE!... i CAN'T GET iT iNTO MY HEAD. AND iT WiLL PROBABLY BE SiX MONTHS FEELiNG NOT SO BAD AT HOME AND THE REST OF iT iN THE HOSPiTAL... HORRiBLE. i CAN'T i MAGiNE HER ACCEPTiNG SiX MONTHS AT THE HOSPiTAL, NO. i WON'T SEE ANYBODY TODAY AND iT'S JUST AS WELL.

13.07.03. sunday

i WORKED ON THAT FUCKING COMiC, YESTERDAY. i STiLL HAVE A LiTTLE BiT TO DO AND TODAY iT WiLL BE OVER, AT LAST. AT THE END OF THE DAY i GOT AN EMAiL FROM MY GODMOTHER, WHO WAS JUST SAYiNG SHE WANTED TO SEE ME AT THE END OF THE WEEK. MAYBE i'LL GO ViSiT HER MONDAY. i FEEL RELiEVED... COULDN'T STOP THiNKiNG ABOUT THAT OF COURSE... BUT THAT

DOESN'T MAKE iT LESS REAL. ON T.V. i SAW WE'RE GOiNG TO HAVE A QUEBEC VERSiON OF "LOFT STORY". iNEViTABLE i SUPPOSE... AT LAST i WiLL ABLE TO MEASURE THE EXPANSE OF STUPiDiTY OF THAT THiNG. HEARD SO MUCH ABOUT iT...

14.07.03. *monday*

I dreamt it was the first day of the Berlin Festival and I still didn't have a ticket to go there... A nightmare. I don't know how I did it but I managed to not finish that comic yesterday. I'm bad!... I still have a bit of text to write I'm sending it today. Poor Reiser! My thoughts are miles away.

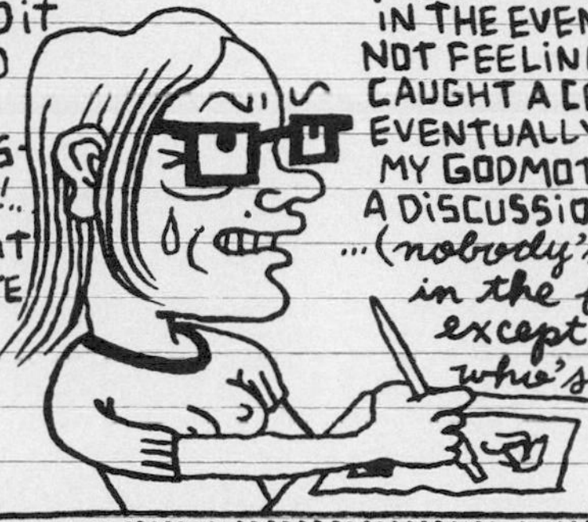

I had dinner with my mom in the evening. She was not feeling well, had caught a cold... Friday. We eventually talked about my godmother, then had a discussion about death ...(*nobody's religious in the family, except one aunt who's jesus crazy.*) My mom still hadn't been able to call her sister... Oh, yes: I also dreamt that there was a drawing by Luz on a Canadian stamp!... And I thought it was amazing... I don't know where that's coming from?!!

15.07.03. *tuesday*

Got up early yesterday to have time to work in the morning and then go see my aunt in the afternoon. Finished those two pages *and* bye bye! It's sent. Took the bus to go to my aunt's place, in the east... Well, she was in a rather good mood. She had decided not to feel sorry for herself, otherwise it's going to be a horrible year, the last one. That's how it goes *and she can't do nothin' about it.* So... She says she's not so *afraid* of death, but suffering, yes. She sure is strong! *she's incredible!*... We talked about her illness at first, *to get it over with*, she *said*. We spent three hours *talking about stuff*, while drinking a beer. She is so funny, so tender, so kind!... I was supposed to leave with her bicycle but we found out that it had a flat.

WILL COME WITH MY MOM TO PICK IT UP, SHE HAS A BIKE RACK ON HER CAR. SPENT A REALLY GOOD TIME WITH MY GODMOTHER, BUT INSTEAD OF MAKING ME HAPPY, IT MADE ME INFINITELY SAD... MET WITH C. IN THE EVENING, HE WAS JUST BACK FROM A TRIP IN NEW YORK. HE TOLD ME ALL ABOUT IT.

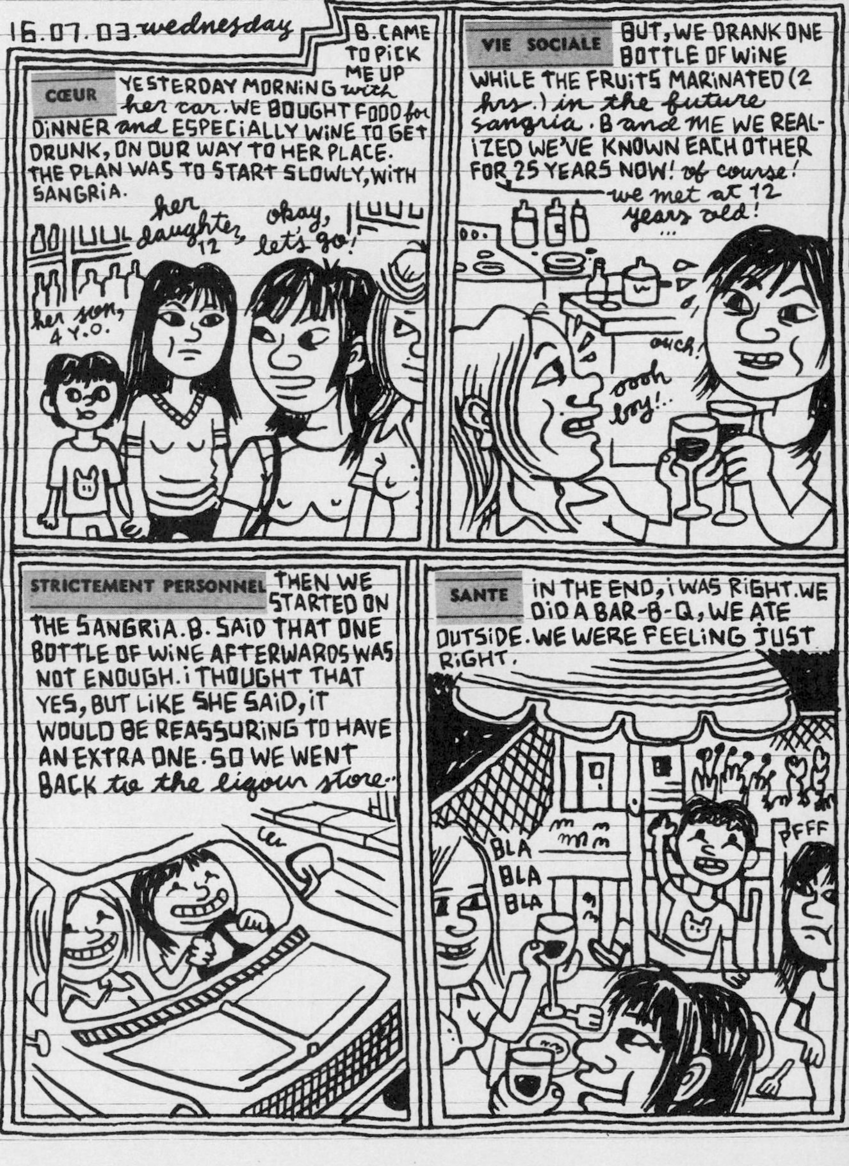

16.07.03. wednesday
CŒUR
B. CAME TO PICK ME UP YESTERDAY MORNING with her car. WE BOUGHT FOOD for DINNER and ESPECIALLY WINE TO GET DRUNK, ON OUR WAY TO HER PLACE. THE PLAN WAS TO START SLOWLY, WITH SANGRIA.
her daughter, 12
okay, let's go!
her son, 4 Y.O.
VIE SOCIALE
BUT, WE DRANK ONE BOTTLE OF WINE WHILE THE FRUITS MARINATED (2 hrs.) in the future sangria. B and ME WE REALIZED WE'VE KNOWN EACH OTHER FOR 25 YEARS NOW! of course! we met at 12 years old! ...
ouch!
oooh boy!..
STRICTEMENT PERSONNEL
THEN WE STARTED ON THE SANGRIA. B. SAID THAT ONE BOTTLE OF WINE AFTERWARDS WAS NOT ENOUGH. I THOUGHT THAT YES, BUT LIKE SHE SAID, IT WOULD BE REASSURING TO HAVE AN EXTRA ONE. SO WE WENT BACK to the liquor store...
SANTE
IN THE END, I WAS RIGHT. WE DID A BAR-B-Q, WE ATE OUTSIDE. WE WERE FEELING JUST RIGHT.
BLA
BLA
BLA
PFFF

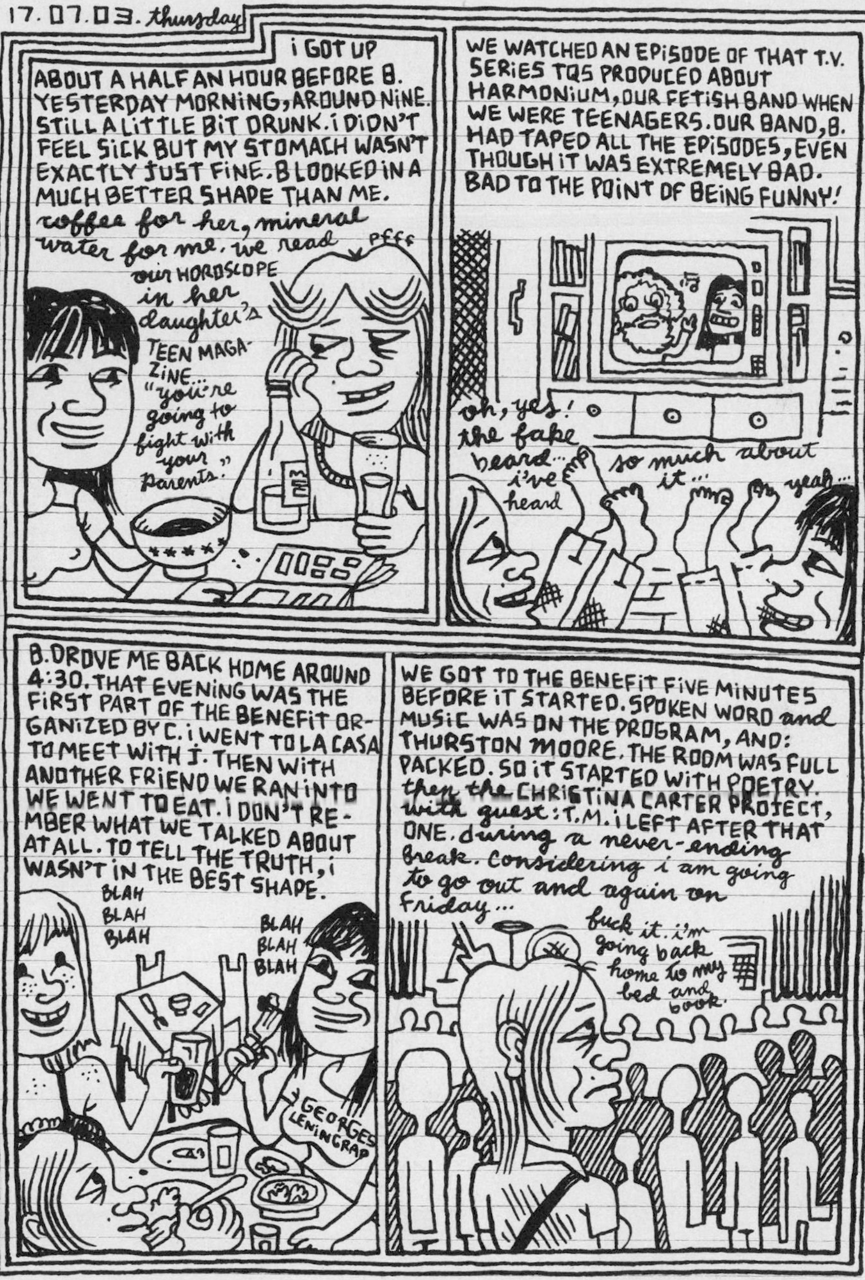
17.07.03. thursday
I GOT UP
ABOUT A HALF AN HOUR BEFORE B.
YESTERDAY MORNING, AROUND NINE.
STILL A LITTLE BIT DRUNK. I DIDN'T
FEEL SICK BUT MY STOMACH WASN'T
EXACTLY JUST FINE. B LOOKED IN A
MUCH BETTER SHAPE THAN ME.
coffee for her, mineral
water for me. we read
our HOROSCOPE
in her
daughter's
TEEN MAGA-
ZINE...
"you're
going to
fight with
your
parents"
PFFF
WE WATCHED AN EPISODE OF THAT T.V.
SERIES TQS PRODUCED ABOUT
HARMONIUM, OUR FETISH BAND WHEN
WE WERE TEENAGERS. OUR BAND, B.
HAD TAPED ALL THE EPISODES, EVEN
THOUGH IT WAS EXTREMELY BAD.
BAD TO THE POINT OF BEING FUNNY!
oh, yes! the fake beard... i've heard
so much about it...
oh yeah...
B. DROVE ME BACK HOME AROUND
4:30. THAT EVENING WAS THE
FIRST PART OF THE BENEFIT OR-
GANIZED BY C. I WENT TO LA CASA
TO MEET WITH J. THEN WITH
ANOTHER FRIEND WE RAN INTO
WE WENT TO EAT. I DON'T RE-
MBER WHAT WE TALKED ABOUT
AT ALL. TO TELL THE TRUTH, I
WASN'T IN THE BEST SHAPE.
BLAH BLAH BLAH
BLAH BLAH BLAH
GEORGES LENINGRAD
WE GOT TO THE BENEFIT FIVE MINUTES
BEFORE IT STARTED. SPOKEN WORD and
MUSIC WAS ON THE PROGRAM, AND:
THURSTON MOORE. THE ROOM WAS FULL
PACKED. SO IT STARTED WITH POETRY.
then the CHRISTINA CARTER PROJECT,
with guest: T.M. I LEFT AFTER THAT
ONE. during a never-ending
break. Considering i am going
to go out and again on
Friday...
fuck it. i'm going back home to my bed and book.

18.07.03. friday

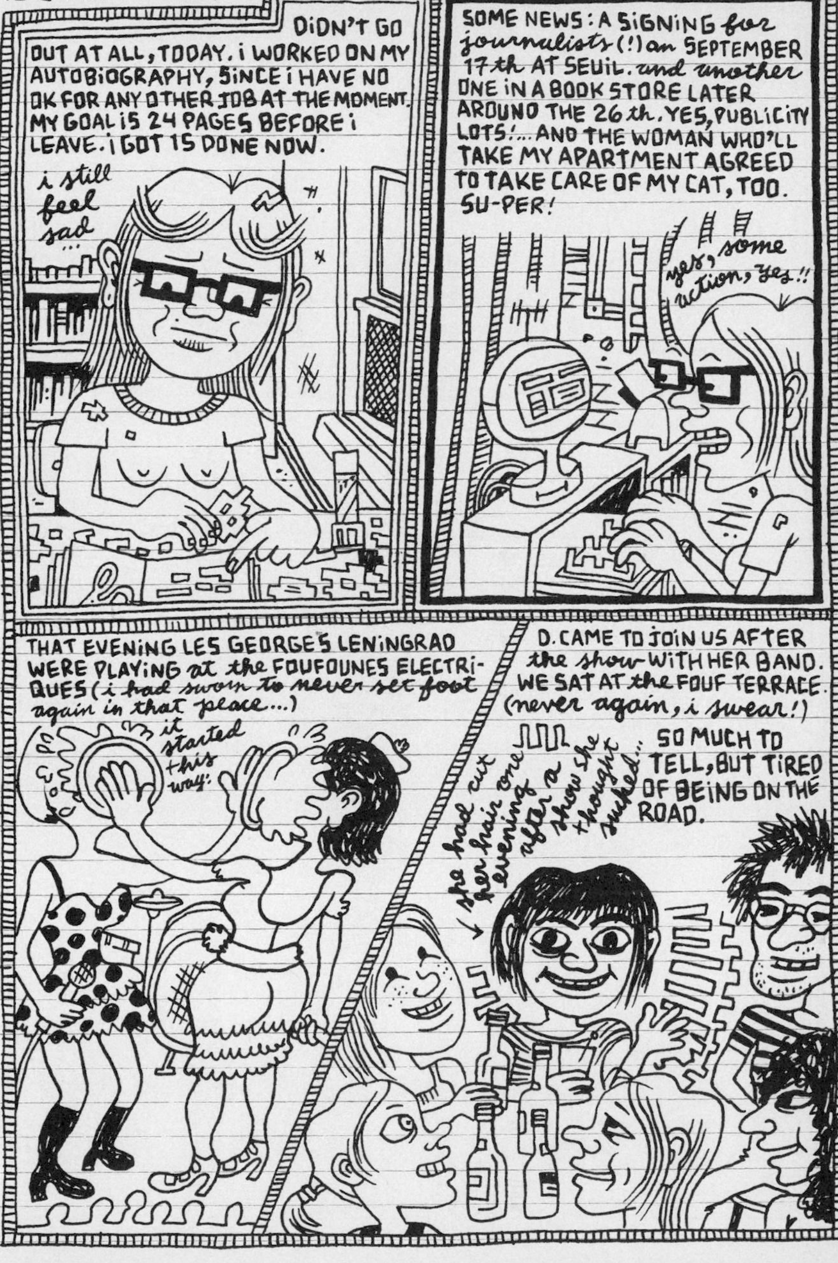
DIDN'T GO OUT AT ALL, TODAY. i WORKED ON MY AUTOBIOGRAPHY, SINCE i HAVE NO OK FOR ANY OTHER JOB AT THE MOMENT. MY GOAL iS 24 PAGES BEFORE i LEAVE. i GOT 15 DONE NOW.
i still feel sad...
SOME NEWS: A SIGNING for journalists (!) on SEPTEMBER 17th AT SEUIL. and another ONE iN A BOOK STORE LATER AROUND THE 26th. YES, PUBLICITY LOTS!... AND THE WOMAN WHO'LL TAKE MY APARTMENT AGREED TO TAKE CARE OF MY CAT, TOO. SU-PER!
yes, some action, yes!!
THAT EVENING LES GEORGE'S LENINGRAD WERE PLAYING at the FOUFOUNES ELECTRI-QUES (i had sworn to never set foot again in that place...)
it started this way:
D. CAME TO JOIN US AFTER the show WITH HER BAND. WE SAT AT the FOUF TERRACE. (never again, i swear!)
she had cut her hair one evening after a show she thought sucked...
SO MUCH TO TELL, BUT TIRED OF BEING ON THE ROAD.

19.07.03. saturday

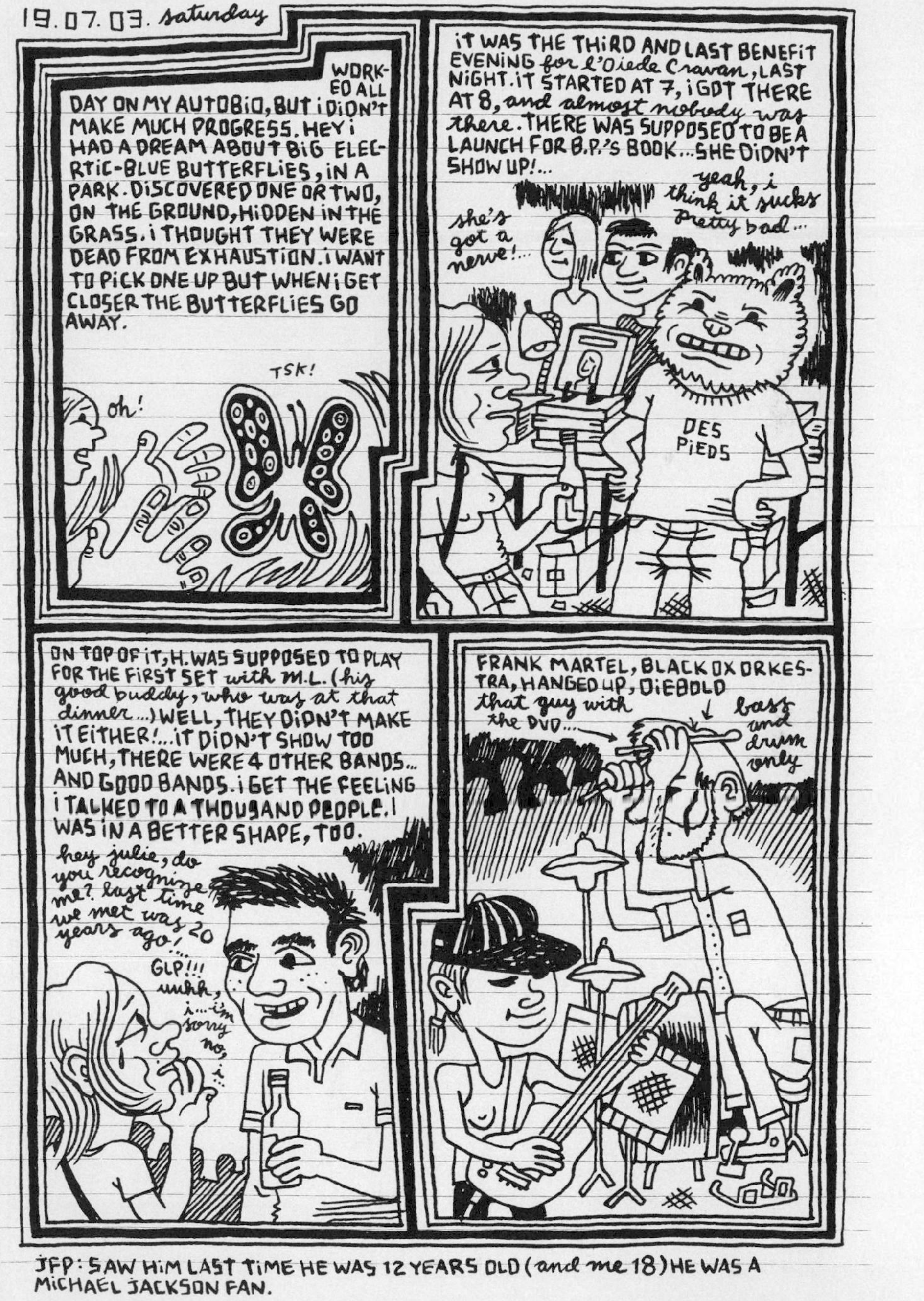
WORKED ALL DAY ON MY AUTOBIO, BUT I DIDN'T MAKE MUCH PROGRESS. HEY I HAD A DREAM ABOUT BIG ELECTRIC-BLUE BUTTERFLIES, IN A PARK. DISCOVERED ONE OR TWO, ON THE GROUND, HIDDEN IN THE GRASS. I THOUGHT THEY WERE DEAD FROM EXHAUSTION. I WANT TO PICK ONE UP BUT WHEN I GET CLOSER THE BUTTERFLIES GO AWAY.
TSK!
oh!
IT WAS THE THIRD AND LAST BENEFIT EVENING for l'Oiede Cravan, LAST NIGHT. IT STARTED AT 7, I GOT THERE AT 8, and almost nobody was there. THERE WAS SUPPOSED TO BE A LAUNCH FOR B.P.'S BOOK... SHE DIDN'T SHOW UP!...
yeah, i think it sucks pretty bad...
she's got a nerve!...
DES PIEDS
ON TOP OF IT, H. WAS SUPPOSED TO PLAY FOR THE FIRST SET with M.L. (his good buddy, who was at that dinner...) WELL, THEY DIDN'T MAKE IT EITHER!... IT DIDN'T SHOW TOO MUCH, THERE WERE 4 OTHER BANDS... AND GOOD BANDS. I GET THE FEELING I TALKED TO A THOUSAND PEOPLE. I WAS IN A BETTER SHAPE, TOO.
hey julie, do you recognize me? last time we met was 20 years ago!...
GLP!!! uhhh, i... i'm sorry no, i...
FRANK MARTEL, BLACK OX ORKESTRA, HANGED UP, DIEBOLD
that guy with the DVD...
bass and drum only

JFP: SAW HIM LAST TIME HE WAS 12 YEARS OLD (and me 18) HE WAS A MICHAEL JACKSON FAN.

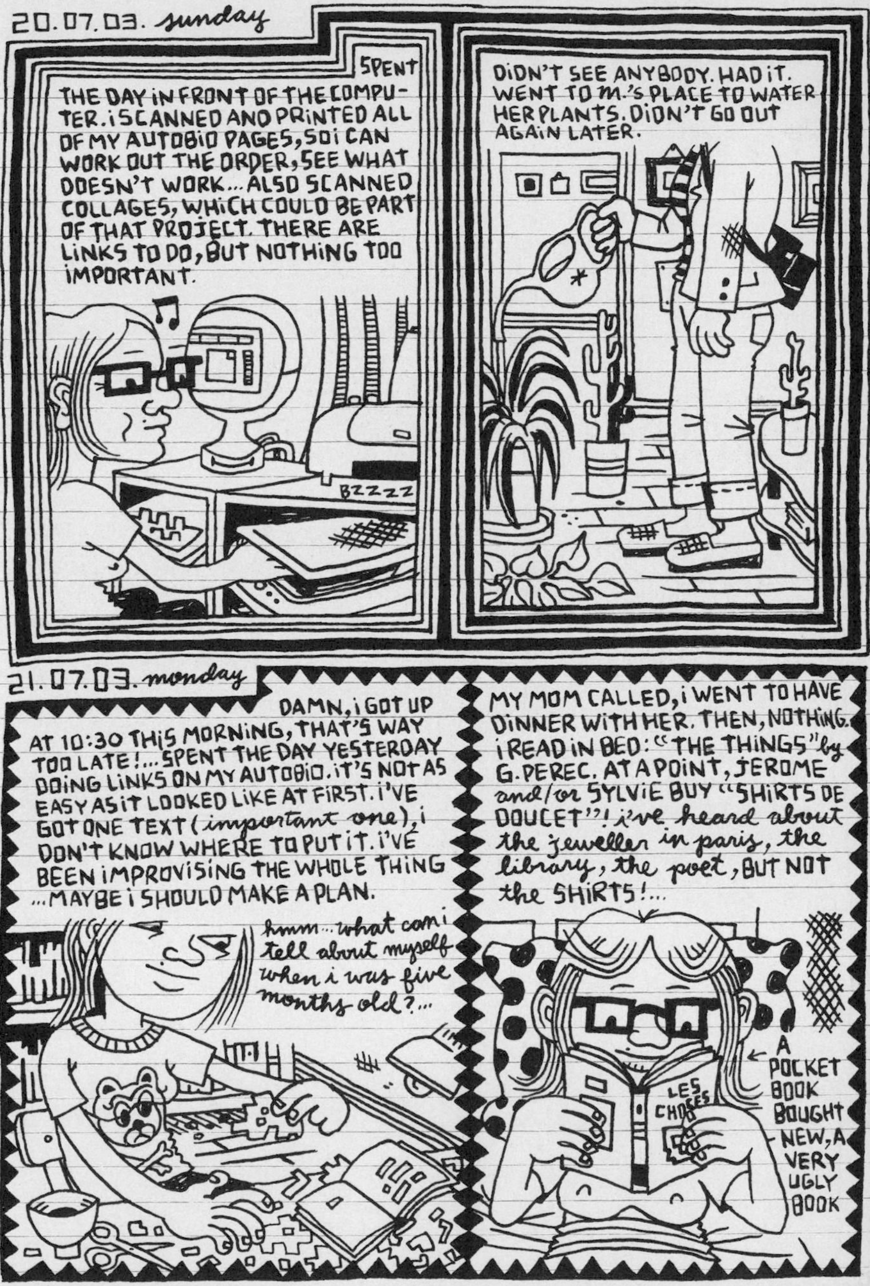
20.07.03. sunday
SPENT THE DAY IN FRONT OF THE COMPUTER. I SCANNED AND PRINTED ALL OF MY AUTOBIO PAGES, SO I CAN WORK OUT THE ORDER, SEE WHAT DOESN'T WORK... ALSO SCANNED COLLAGES, WHICH COULD BE PART OF THAT PROJECT. THERE ARE LINKS TO DO, BUT NOTHING TOO IMPORTANT.
BZZZZ
DIDN'T SEE ANYBODY. HAD IT. WENT TO M.'S PLACE TO WATER HER PLANTS. DIDN'T GO OUT AGAIN LATER.
21.07.03. monday
DAMN, I GOT UP AT 10:30 THIS MORNING, THAT'S WAY TOO LATE!... SPENT THE DAY YESTERDAY DOING LINKS ON MY AUTOBIO. IT'S NOT AS EASY AS IT LOOKED LIKE AT FIRST. I'VE GOT ONE TEXT (important one), I DON'T KNOW WHERE TO PUT IT. I'VE BEEN IMPROVISING THE WHOLE THING ...MAYBE I SHOULD MAKE A PLAN.
hmm... what can i tell about myself when i was five months old?...
MY MOM CALLED, I WENT TO HAVE DINNER WITH HER. THEN, NOTHING. I READ IN BED: "THE THINGS" by G. PEREC. AT A POINT, JEROME and/or SYLVIE BUY "SHIRTS DE DOUCET"! i've heard about the jeweller in paris, the library, the poet, BUT NOT the SHIRTS!...
LES CHOSES
A POCKET BOOK BOUGHT NEW, A VERY UGLY BOOK

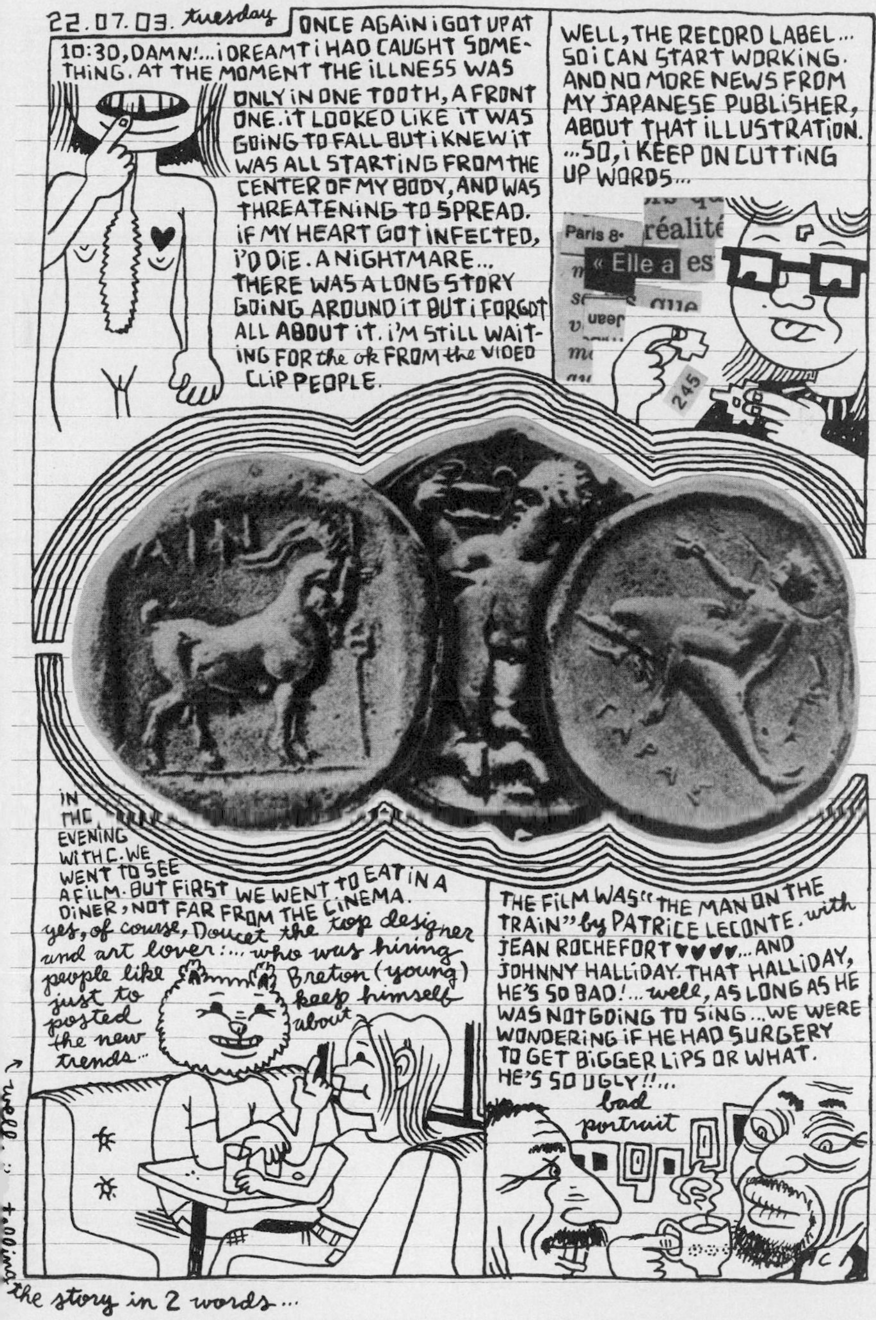
22.07.03. tuesday
ONCE AGAIN i GOT UP AT 10:30, DAMN!... i DREAMT i HAD CAUGHT SOMETHING. AT THE MOMENT THE iLLNESS WAS ONLY iN ONE TOOTH, A FRONT ONE. iT LOOKED LIKE iT WAS GOING TO FALL BUT i KNEW iT WAS ALL STARTiNG FROM THE CENTER OF MY BODY, AND WAS THREATENING TO SPREAD. iF MY HEART GOT INFECTED, i'D DiE. A NiGHTMARE... THERE WAS A LONG STORY GOING AROUND iT BUT i FORGOT ALL ABOUT iT. i'M STiLL WAITiNG FOR the ok FROM the VIDEO CLiP PEOPLE.
WELL, THE RECORD LABEL... SO i CAN START WORKiNG. AND NO MORE NEWS FROM MY JAPANESE PUBLiSHER, ABOUT THAT iLLUSTRATiON. ...SO, i KEEP ON CUTTiNG UP WORDS...
Paris 8e
réalité
« Elle a
es
245
iN THE EVENiNG WiTH C. WE WENT TO SEE A FiLM. BUT FiRST WE WENT TO EAT iN A DiNER, NOT FAR FROM THE CiNEMA.
yes, of course, Doucet the top designer and art lover:... who was hiring people like Breton (young) just to keep himself posted about the new trends...
THE FiLM WAS "THE MAN ON THE TRAiN" by PATRiCE LECONTE. with JEAN ROCHEFORT ♥♥♥♥... AND JOHNNY HALLiDAY. THAT HALLiDAY, HE'S SO BAD!... well, AS LONG AS HE WAS NOT GOING TO SiNG... WE WERE WONDERiNG iF HE HAD SURGERY TO GET BiGGER LiPS OR WHAT. HE'S SO UGLY!!...
bad portrait
well... telling the story in 2 words...

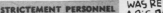

23.07.03.

STRICTEMENT PERSONNEL

i DREAMT i WAS RECEIVING A BIG PACKAGE FROM W. HE WAS SENDING ME BACK ALL THE STUFF i HAD GIVEN HIM... HE WAS INFORMING ME THAT HE DIDN'T GET ANY OF THE GRANT, SO FOR THAT REASON HE WAS GIVING UP ON THE PROJECT. AND THAT BECAUSE OF THAT HE WAS MOVING TO GERMANY WITH HIS GIRLFRIEND. i WAS SO HAPPY, IN MY DREAM!...

i was reading his letter in a park, sitting on a swing...

hee hee!!!

it was only a dream

CŒUR

YESTERDAY i GOT A PHONE CALL from JMP, THE REISER BOOK GUY. HE HAD RECIEVED MY PAGES, AND WAS EXTREMELY HAPPY, THOUGHT THEY WERE VERY MOVING... REALLY!... STILL, i WAS A BIT REASSURED!... BUT, NO NEWS FROM ANYBODY ELSE, JOB WISE...

a love declaration to Reiser!?! uh, yes, that's exactly it...

SANTE

i TOOK A BREAK, DIDN'T DRAW AT ALL. WENT FOR A STROLL, TRIED TO DO SOME SHOPPING (not successful) AND LATER WENT TO SEE J WHO WAS WORKING AT LA CASA del POPOLO, WE EXCHANGED GOSSIPS FOR AN HOUR OR SO...

we gotta have a meeting...

blah blah blah

blah blah blah

VIE SOCIALE

DIDN'T DO ANYTHING IN THE EVENING, EXCEPT READ THIS OR THAT... TRIED TO REACH B. FOR MORE GOSSIPING BUT SHE WASN'T HOME...

with the money i made selling books i could buy this one SU-PER expensive in MTL

CAHIER DESSIN

ONCE AGAIN I SPENT THE DAY WORKING ON MY AUTOBIO. I JUST LOVE IT. BUT IF IT GOES ON LIKE THAT, I WON'T FEEL LIKE DOING ANYTHING ELSE ANYMORE!... NO NEWS ABOUT WORK.

i don't know how my uncle will like it to be compared to a big, badly shaved turtle ??!...

IN THE EVENING with J and M.E. (D. *being in the countryside for a week*) WE HAD A LITTLE MEETING, AT MY PLACE. ABOUT OUR PROJECT IN MARSEILLE... IN THE END WE ONLY REPEATED WHAT WE HAD SAID IN THE BEGINNING. WE'RE GOING TO DO A CATALOGUE. SO... WE DO WHATEVER WE WANT. OK.

TO TAKE THE TRAIN OR THE PLANE, TO GO TO BERLIN? I GOT A GRANT, BUT *not the girls...*

IT RAINED ALL DAY YESTERDAY. I LIKE IT WHEN IT RAINS, THE NEIGHBORHOOD IS ALL QUIET. SURPRISE-SURPRISE: I KEPT ON WORKING ON MY AUTOBIO. NOTHING'S HAPPENING...

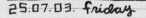

a common glue-stick

ON T.V. ON THE NEWS THEY SHOWED PHOTOS OF SADDAM'S 2 SONS, DEAD. THE AMERICANS SAY FROM NOW ON, EVERYTHING WILL BE FINE... AN OLD GODDARD *film*, "WEEKEND". I LOVE TO SEE ALL THOSE CARS ON FIRE!!!

so beautiful!!!

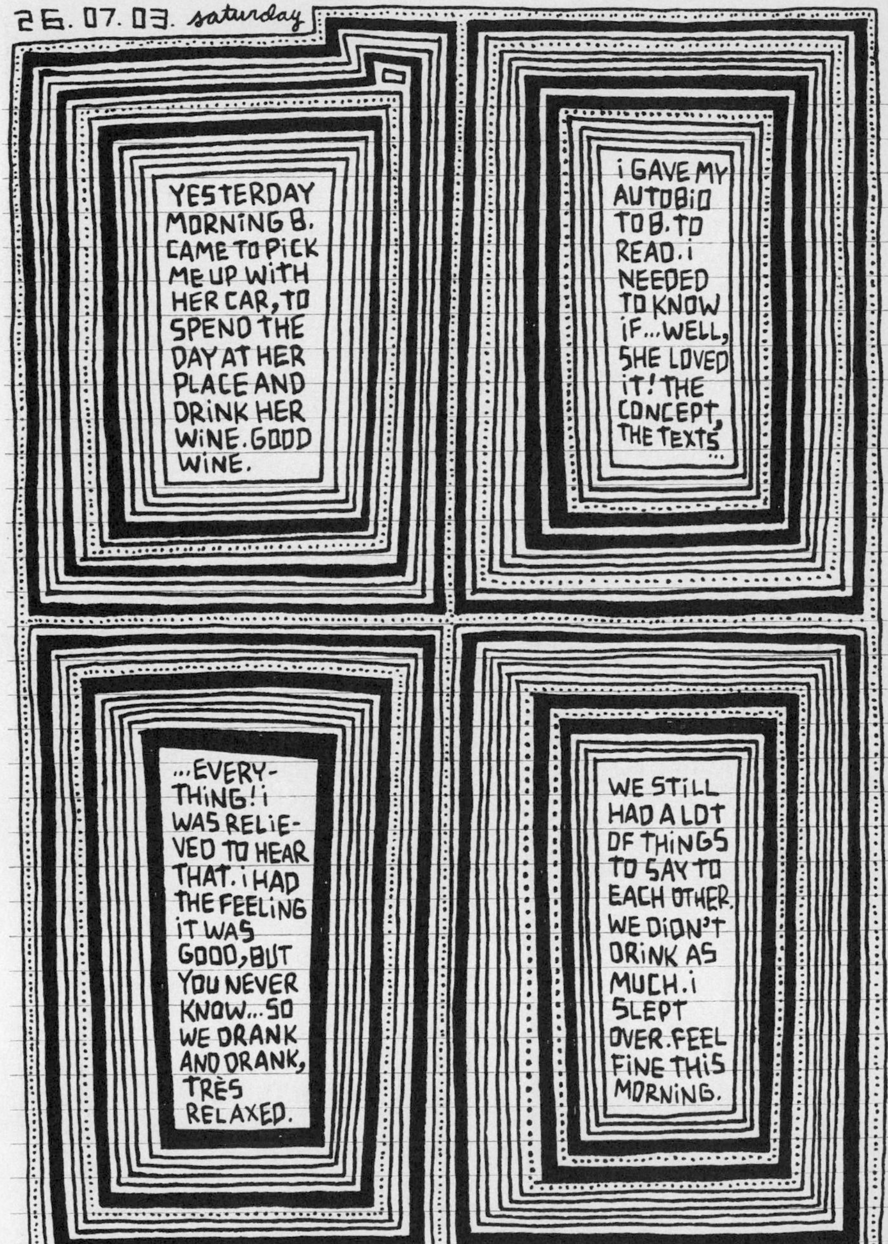
26. 07. 03. saturday
YESTERDAY MORNING B. CAME TO PICK ME UP WITH HER CAR, TO SPEND THE DAY AT HER PLACE AND DRINK HER WINE. GOOD WINE.
i GAVE MY AUTOBIO TO B. TO READ. i NEEDED TO KNOW iF... WELL, SHE LOVED iT! THE CONCEPT, THE TEXTS...
...EVERY-THING! i WAS RELIE-VED TO HEAR THAT. i HAD THE FEELING iT WAS GOOD, BUT YOU NEVER KNOW... SO WE DRANK AND DRANK, TRÈS RELAXED.
WE STiLL HAD A LOT OF THiNGS TO SAY TO EACH OTHER. WE DiDN'T DRiNK AS MUCH. i SLEPT OVER. FEEL FiNE THiS MORNiNG.

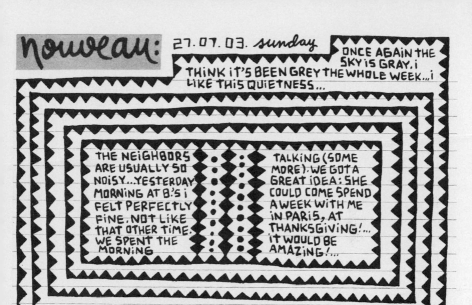

ONCE AGAIN THE SKY IS GRAY. i THINK iT'S BEEN GREY THE WHOLE WEEK...i LIKE THIS QUIETNESS...

THE NEIGHBORS ARE USUALLY SO NOISY...YESTERDAY MORNING AT B.'s i FELT PERFECTLY FINE, NOT LIKE THAT OTHER TIME. WE SPENT THE MORNING

TALKING (SOME MORE) WE GOT A GREAT iDEA: SHE COULD COME SPEND A WEEK WITH ME iN PARIS, AT THANKSGIVING!... iT WOULD BE AMAZING!...

GOT BACK HOME AT ONE. AN EMAIL FROM R. SHE'S WRITING SHE'S GOING TO REGIST-ER AT UQAM FOR POST GRADUATE STUDIES! THAT WOULD MEAN 2 YEARS IN MON-TREAL...iT COULD BE FUN...WITH THE GIRLS WE'RE LEAVING IN LESS THAN A MONTH, NOW.

i HAVE TO TAKE CARE OF MY PASSPORT, BUY A TRAVEL BAG, CLEAN THE APARTMENT...i GOTTA START WORK-iNG ON THAT *dernier* CRi BOOK. i KNOW WHAT i'LL DO NOW: COLLAGES. iT'S CRAZY HOW i DON'T WANT TO DRAW ANYMORE!... iT HAS TO DO WITH THIS JOURNAL. MORE WORK THAN iT LOOKS LIKE.

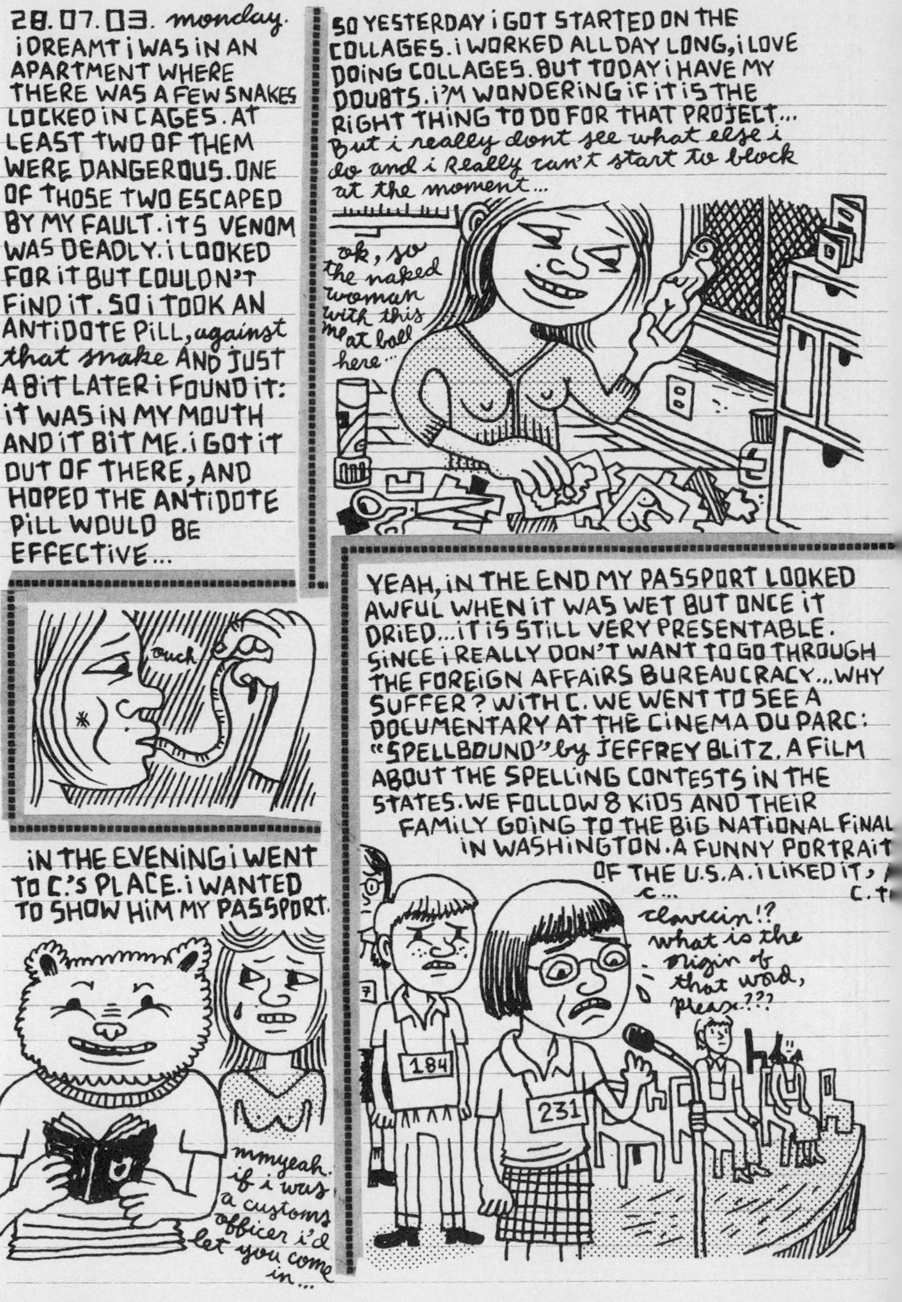
28.07.03. monday.
i DREAMT i WAS iN AN APARTMENT WHERE THERE WAS A FEW SNAKES LOCKED iN CAGES. AT LEAST TWO OF THEM WERE DANGEROUS. ONE OF THOSE TWO ESCAPED BY MY FAULT. iTS VENOM WAS DEADLY. i LOOKED FOR iT BUT COULDN'T FIND iT. SO i TOOK AN ANTIDOTE PiLL, against that snake AND JUST A BiT LATER i FOUND iT: iT WAS iN MY MOUTH AND iT BiT ME. i GOT iT OUT OF THERE, AND HOPED THE ANTiDOTE PiLL WOULD BE EFFECTiVE...
ouch
SO YESTERDAY i GOT STARTED ON THE COLLAGES. i WORKED ALL DAY LONG, i LOVE DOING COLLAGES. BUT TODAY i HAVE MY DOUBTS. i'M WONDERiNG iF iT iS THE RiGHT THiNG TO DO FOR THAT PROJECT... But i really dont see what else i do and i Really can't start to block at the moment...
ok, so the naked woman with this meat ball here...
iN THE EVENiNG i WENT TO C.'S PLACE. i WANTED TO SHOW HiM MY PASSPORT.
mmyeah. if i was a customs officer i'd let you come in...
YEAH, iN THE END MY PASSPORT LOOKED AWFUL WHEN iT WAS WET BUT ONCE iT DRiED... iT iS STiLL VERY PRESENTABLE. SiNCE i REALLY DON'T WANT TO GO THROUGH THE FOREIGN AFFAiRS BUREAUCRACY... WHY SUFFER? WiTH C. WE WENT TO SEE A DOCUMENTARY AT THE CiNEMA DU PARC: "SPELLBOUND" by JEFFREY BLiTZ. A FiLM ABOUT THE SPELLiNG CONTESTS iN THE STATES. WE FOLLOW 8 KiDS AND THEiR FAMiLY GOiNG TO THE BiG NATiONAL FiNAL iN WASHiNGTON. A FUNNY PORTRAiT OF THE U.S.A. i LiKED iT,
c...
clavecin!? what is the origin of that word, please???
7
184
231

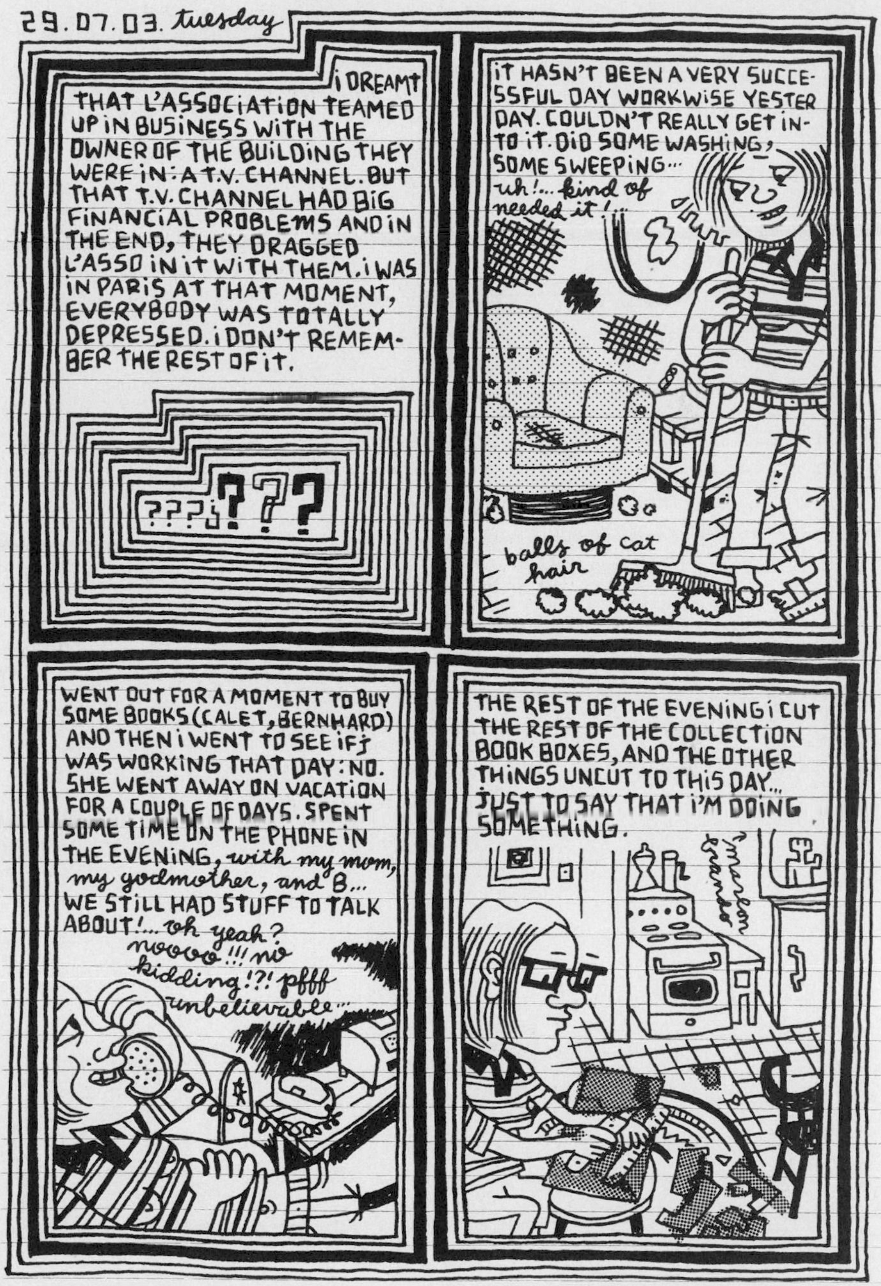
29.07.03. tuesday
I DREAMT THAT L'ASSOCIATION TEAMED UP IN BUSINESS WITH THE OWNER OF THE BUILDING THEY WERE IN: A T.V. CHANNEL. BUT THAT T.V. CHANNEL HAD BIG FINANCIAL PROBLEMS AND IN THE END, THEY DRAGGED L'ASSO IN IT WITH THEM. I WAS IN PARIS AT THAT MOMENT, EVERYBODY WAS TOTALLY DEPRESSED. I DON'T REMEMBER THE REST OF IT.
???¿???
IT HASN'T BEEN A VERY SUCCESSFUL DAY WORKWISE YESTERDAY. COULDN'T REALLY GET INTO IT. DID SOME WASHING, SOME SWEEPING...
uh!... kind of needed it!...
balls of cat hair
WENT OUT FOR A MOMENT TO BUY SOME BOOKS (CALET, BERNHARD) AND THEN I WENT TO SEE IF J WAS WORKING THAT DAY: NO. SHE WENT AWAY ON VACATION FOR A COUPLE OF DAYS. SPENT SOME TIME ON THE PHONE IN THE EVENING, with my mom, my godmother, and B... WE STILL HAD STUFF TO TALK ABOUT!... oh yeah?
noooo!!! no kidding!?! pfff unbelievable...
THE REST OF THE EVENING I CUT THE REST OF THE COLLECTION BOOK BOXES, AND THE OTHER THINGS UNCUT TO THIS DAY... JUST TO SAY THAT I'M DOING SOMETHING.
marlon brando

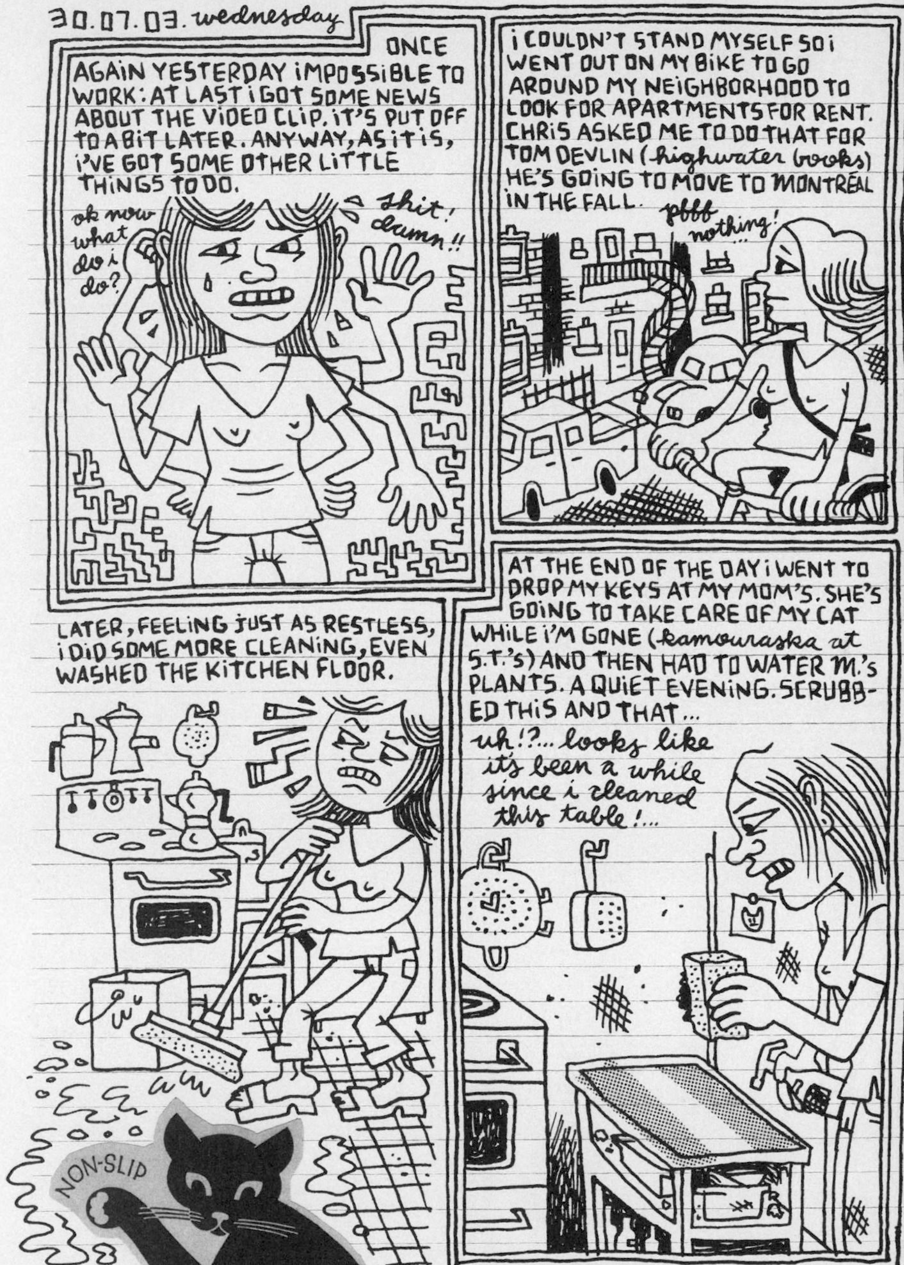
30.07.03. wednesday
ONCE AGAIN YESTERDAY IMPOSSIBLE TO WORK: AT LAST I GOT SOME NEWS ABOUT THE VIDEO CLIP. IT'S PUT OFF TO A BIT LATER. ANYWAY, AS IT IS, I'VE GOT SOME OTHER LITTLE THINGS TO DO.
ok now what do i do?
shit! damn!!
I COULDN'T STAND MYSELF SO I WENT OUT ON MY BIKE TO GO AROUND MY NEIGHBORHOOD TO LOOK FOR APARTMENTS FOR RENT. CHRIS ASKED ME TO DO THAT FOR TOM DEVLIN (highwater books) HE'S GOING TO MOVE TO MONTRÉAL IN THE FALL.
pfff nothing!...
LATER, FEELING JUST AS RESTLESS, I DID SOME MORE CLEANING, EVEN WASHED THE KITCHEN FLOOR.
NON-SLIP
AT THE END OF THE DAY I WENT TO DROP MY KEYS AT MY MOM'S. SHE'S GOING TO TAKE CARE OF MY CAT WHILE I'M GONE (kamouraska at S.T.'s) AND THEN HAD TO WATER M.'S PLANTS. A QUIET EVENING. SCRUBBED THIS AND THAT...
uh!?... looks like it's been a while since i cleaned this table!...

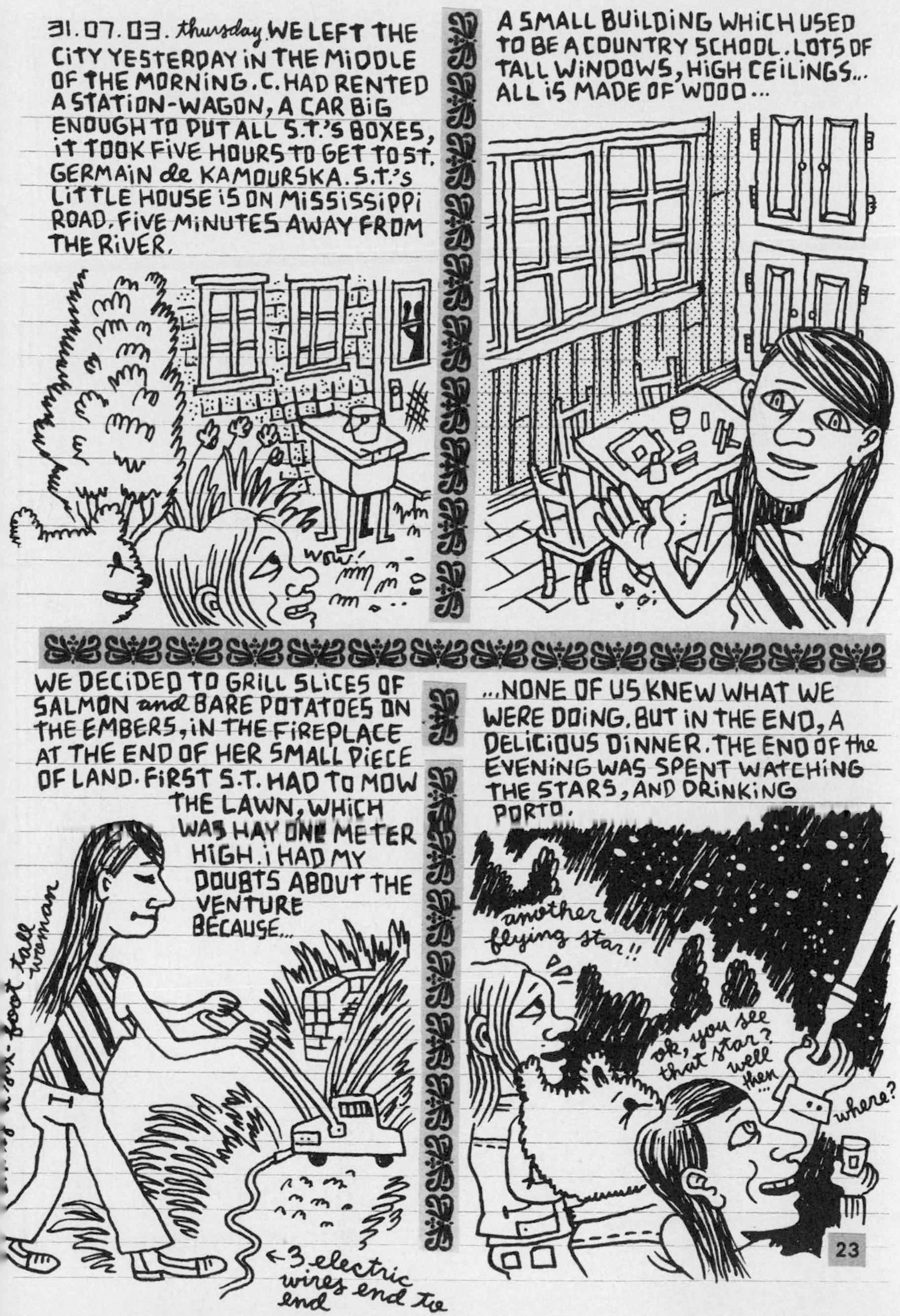
31.07.03. thursday. WE LEFT THE CITY YESTERDAY IN THE MIDDLE OF THE MORNING. C. HAD RENTED A STATION-WAGON, A CAR BIG ENOUGH TO PUT ALL S.T.'s BOXES, IT TOOK FIVE HOURS TO GET TO ST. GERMAIN de KAMOURSKA. S.T.'s LITTLE HOUSE IS ON MISSISSIPPI ROAD, FIVE MINUTES AWAY FROM THE RIVER.
WOW!
A SMALL BUILDING WHICH USED TO BE A COUNTRY SCHOOL. LOTS OF TALL WINDOWS, HIGH CEILINGS... ALL IS MADE OF WOOD...
WE DECIDED TO GRILL SLICES OF SALMON and BARE POTATOES ON THE EMBERS, IN THE FIREPLACE AT THE END OF HER SMALL PIECE OF LAND. FIRST S.T. HAD TO MOW THE LAWN, WHICH WAS HAY ONE METER HIGH. I HAD MY DOUBTS ABOUT THE VENTURE BECAUSE...
six-foot tall woman
← 3 electric wires end to end
...NONE OF US KNEW WHAT WE WERE DOING. BUT IN THE END, A DELICIOUS DINNER. THE END OF the EVENING WAS SPENT WATCHING THE STARS, AND DRINKING PORTO.
another flying star!!
ok, you see that star? well then...
where?

august 2003

SUN	MON	TUES	WED	THURS	fri	SAT
					1	2
3	4	5	6	7	8	9
10	11	12	13	14	15	16
17	18	19	20	21	22	23
24	25	26	27	28	29	30
31						

01.08.03. friday

→ pink-coloured tube brick facing.
i love tube brick facing.!!!...

lilac trees all over the place

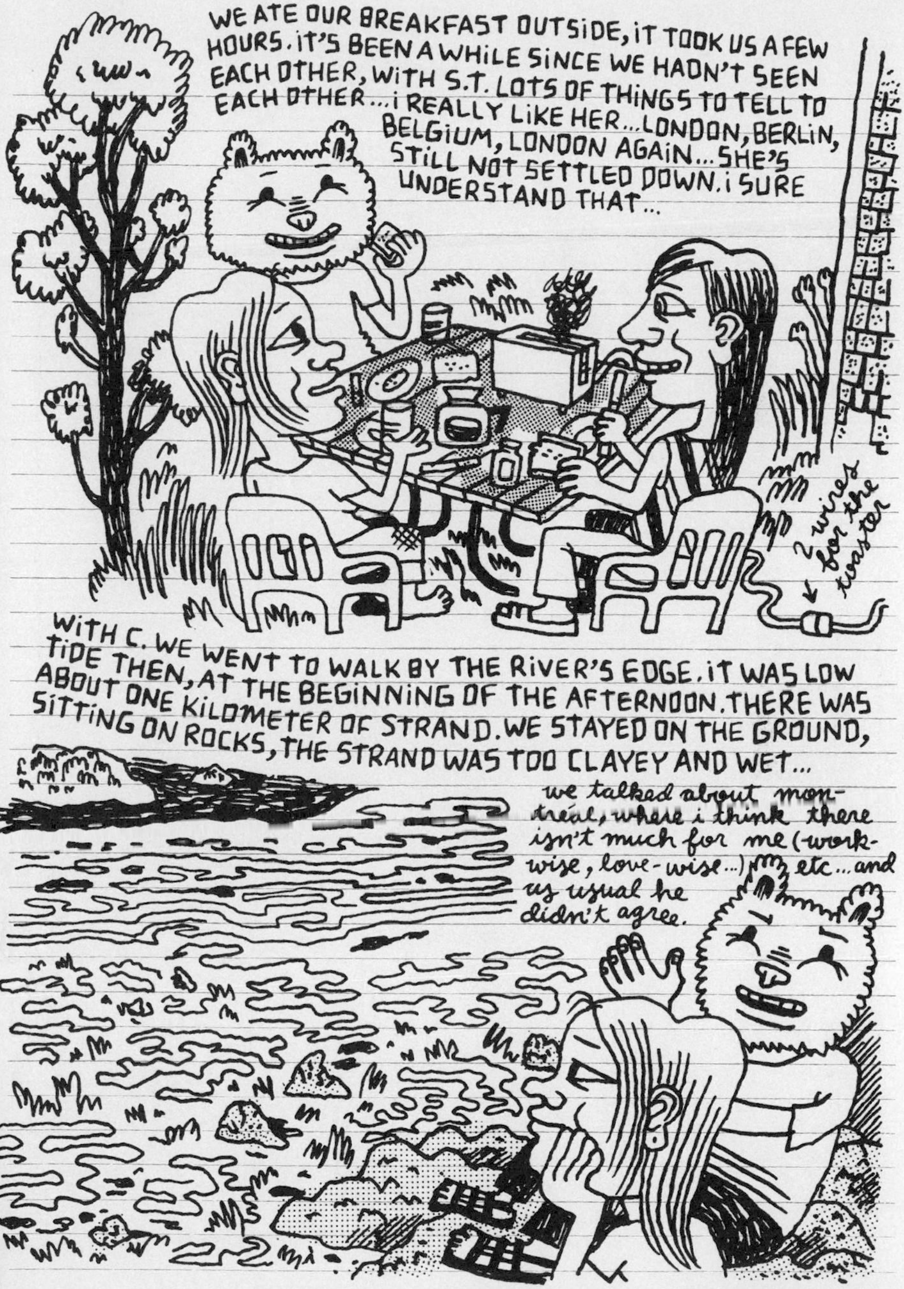
WE ATE OUR BREAKFAST OUTSIDE, IT TOOK US A FEW HOURS. iT'S BEEN A WHiLE SiNCE WE HADN'T SEEN EACH OTHER, WiTH S.T. LOTS OF THiNGS TO TELL TO EACH OTHER... i REALLY LiKE HER... LONDON, BERLiN, BELGiUM, LONDON AGAiN... SHE'S STiLL NOT SETTLED DOWN. i SURE UNDERSTAND THAT...
2 wires for the toaster
WiTH C. WE WENT TO WALK BY THE RiVER'S EDGE. iT WAS LOW TiDE THEN, AT THE BEGiNNiNG OF THE AFTERNOON. THERE WAS ABOUT ONE KiLOMETER OF STRAND. WE STAYED ON THE GROUND, SiTTiNG ON ROCKS, THE STRAND WAS TOO CLAYEY AND WET...
we talked about montréal, where i think there isn't much for me (work-wise, love-wise...) etc... and as usual he didn't agree.

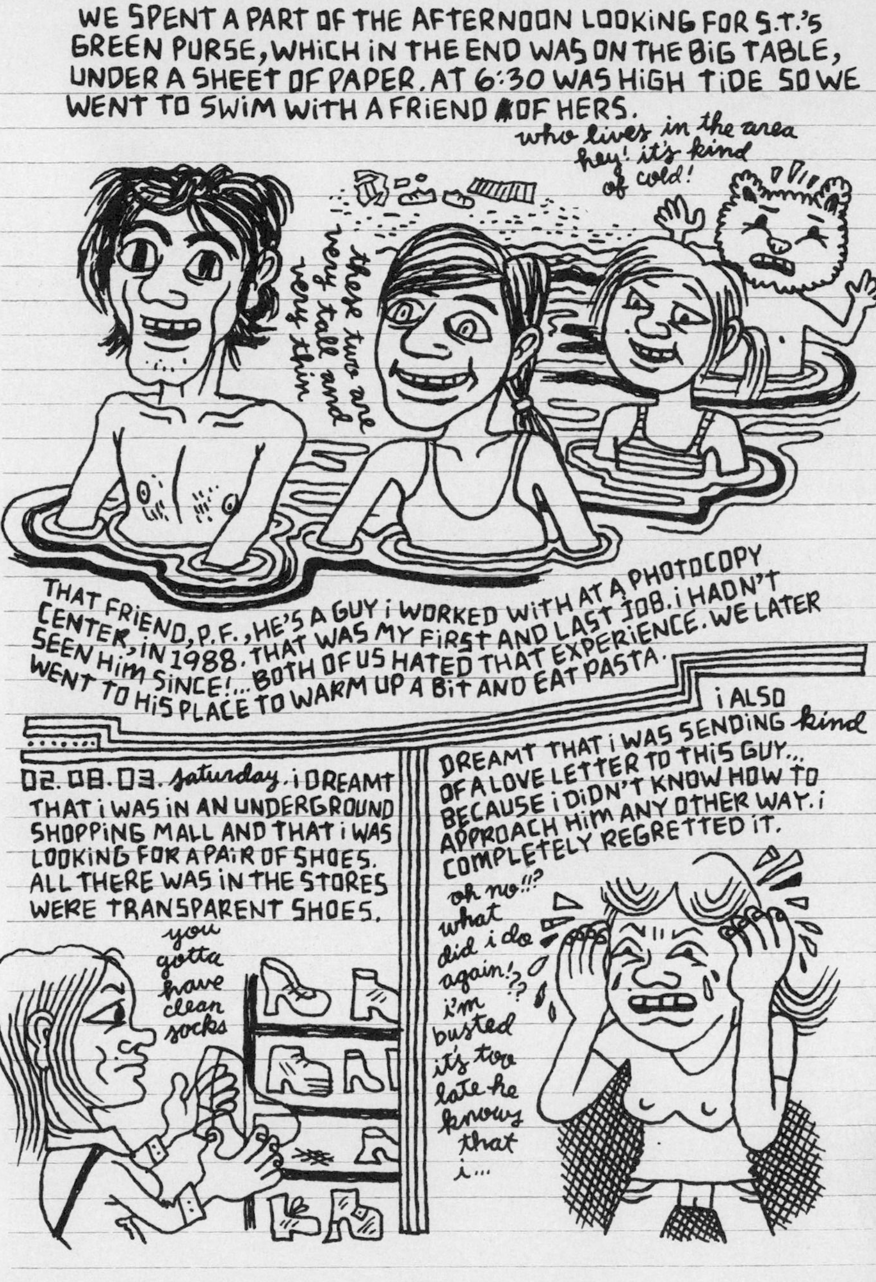
WE SPENT A PART OF THE AFTERNOON LOOKING FOR S.T.'S GREEN PURSE, WHICH IN THE END WAS ON THE BIG TABLE, UNDER A SHEET OF PAPER. AT 6:30 WAS HIGH TIDE SO WE WENT TO SWIM WITH A FRIEND OF HERS.
who lives in the area
these two are very tall and very thin
hey! it's kind of cold!
THAT FRIEND, P.F., HE'S A GUY i WORKED WITH AT A PHOTOCOPY CENTER, iN 1988. THAT WAS MY FiRST AND LAST JOB. i HADN'T SEEN HiM SINCE!... BOTH OF US HATED THAT EXPERiENCE. WE LATER WENT TO HiS PLACE TO WARM UP A BiT AND EAT PASTA.
02.08.03. saturday. i DREAMT THAT i WAS IN AN UNDERGROUND SHOPPING MALL AND THAT i WAS LOOKING FOR A PAIR OF SHOES. ALL THERE WAS IN THE STORES WERE TRANSPARENT SHOES.
you gotta have clean socks
i ALSO DREAMT THAT i WAS SENDING kind OF A LOVE LETTER TO THIS GUY... BECAUSE i DIDN'T KNOW HOW TO APPROACH HIM ANY OTHER WAY. i COMPLETELY REGRETTED IT.
oh no!!? what did i do again!?? i'm busted it's too late he knows that i...

ANOTHER BREAKFAST THAT LASTED ALL MORNING. WE ARE PRETTY LUCKY WITH THE GOOD WEATHER. THAT WAS OUR LAST MOMENTS WITH S.T. BECAUSE SHE WAS LEAVING *that afternoon* for TADOUSSAC FOR THE WEEKEND. TO SEE HER FAMILY, WHO HAS A HOUSE OVER THERE. I WOULD HAVE LOVED TO SPEND MORE TIME WITH HER... *two days, it's ridiculous!!!* WITH C. WE WENT TOWARDS THE EAST. WE WANTED TO VISIT THE ÎLE VERTE (*island*). BUT, THE FERRY *was working with the tides*, SO WAY TOO EARLY OR WAY TOO LATE THAT DAY. WE KEPT GOING UNTIL WE GOT TO TROIS-PISTOLES, WHERE WE ATE LUNCH IN A VERY GLOOMY DINER.

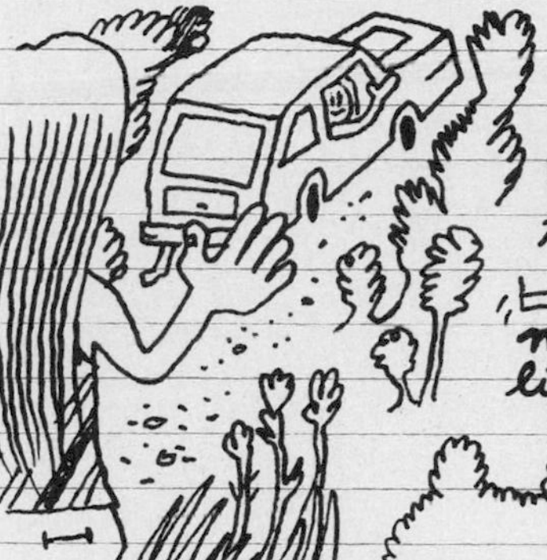

the walls, the furniture, all was pink-vomit colored

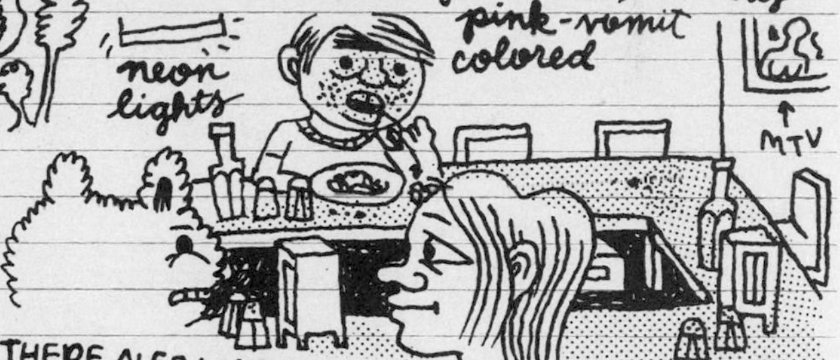
neon lights
MTV

IN TROIS-PISTOLES THERE ALSO WAS A FERRY, WHICH WAS GOING TO THE CÔTE NORD (*north shore*), AT THE ESQOUMINS. AN HOUR AND A HALF RIDE. WE TOOK A ROUND-TRIP TICKET *and left the car in the parking lot*. WE HAD BEEN TOLD MAYBE WE'D SEE SOME WHALES. WELL, WE'VE BEEN SPOILED!!! WE'VE SEEN SEALS, BELUGAS, (*the white ones*), SMALL RORQUALS (*as big as the belugas but black*), PORPOISES (*look like big dolphins*), AND FINALLY, A BLUE WHALE! *it was very close to the côte nord, it's very rare apparently to get to see one.*

VERY IMPRESSIVE!!! SO HUGE, SO GIGANTIC, AN ISLAND!

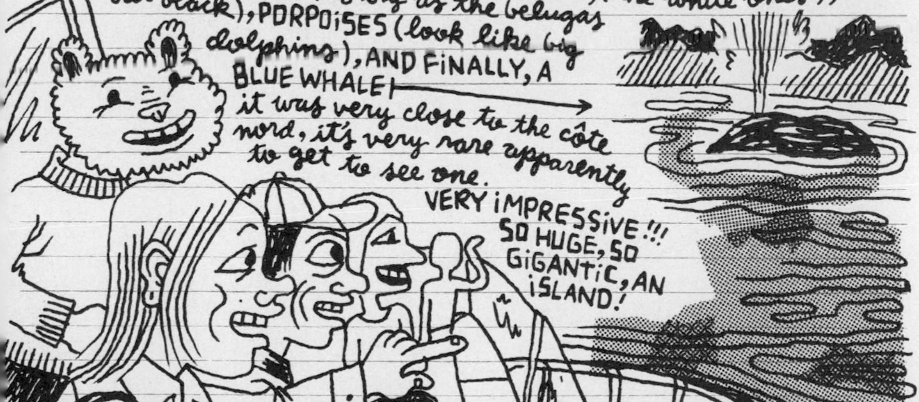

03.08.03. sunday. IT WAS OUR LAST DAY YESTERDAY, WE'RE LEAVING THIS MORNING. WE GOT UP LATE THAT MORNING, and SPENT THE FIRST HALF OF THE DAY SHOPPING. BOUGHT SMOKED FISH, THE AREA'S SPECIALITY. and some bread at this INCREDIBLE GERMAN BAKERY RUN BY A monsieur NIEMAND! i FORCED C. TO GO ON A PEDESTRIAN FOOTPATH NEARBY on MISSISSIPPI ROAD. THAT LED US ON THE TOP OF A LITTLE MOUNTAIN, FROM WHERE WE HAD A GREAT VIEW OVER THE RIVER...

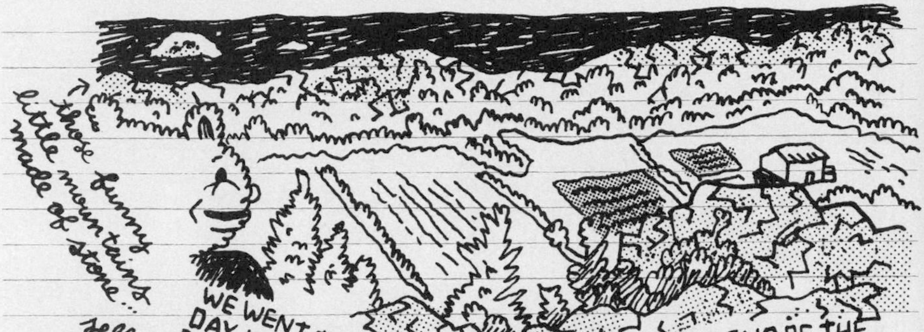
those funny little mountains made of stone...

WE WENT TO VISIT P.F. AT HIS FARM AT THE END OF THE DAY. HE'S GROWING ALL SORTS of VEGETABLES (organic) ESPECIALLY the VEGETABLES OF ORIGIN. and later he sells the seeds. HIS CHOICE OF INDIVIDUALS IS RATHER UNORTHODOX (i forgot to mention C. knew him too) P.F. SHOWED US AROUND, it WAS QUITE A SIGHT.

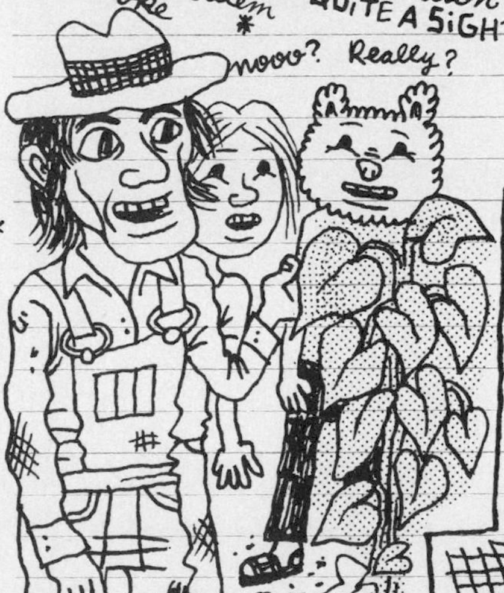
this is jerusalem artichoke *
nooo? Really?

HE SUGGESTED A RESTAURANT TO US, BUT WE ARRIVED TEN MINUTES AFTER THE KITCHEN CLOSED. AT 8:30! we tried two other places, to end up in a diner near the highway. FRENCH FRIES AGAIN!... C. WAS BEING GRUMPY. i WOULD HAVE PREFERRED TO EA[T] A SANDWICH AT HOME.

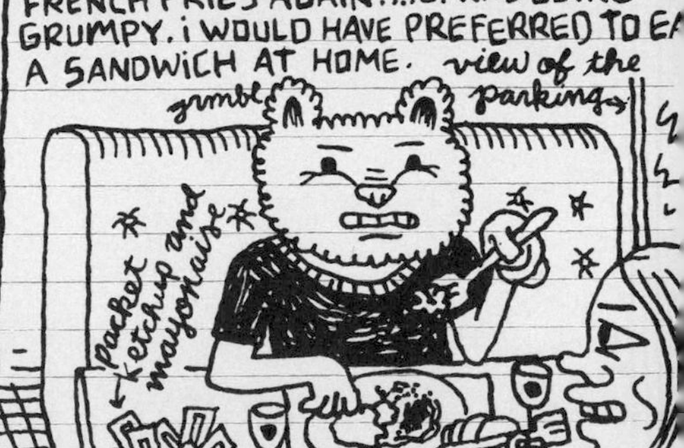
view of the parking →
grmbl
packet ketchup and mayonnaise

* pretty much nobody consumes that in Quebec.

04.08.03 *monday*

WE GOT UP AT 9 YESTERDAY MORNING SO WE COULD LEAVE AT 10:30. ATE THE BREAKFAST OUTSIDE, BUT WITHOUT THE TOASTER.

THE HIGHWAY 20 FOR 4 *hours and a half*. WE STOPPED AT SOME POINT, TO EAT IN A RESTAURANT YOU SEE FROM THE ROAD: "LE MADRID". WE'VE PASSED BY THAT ONE SO MANY TIMES, WE DECIDED TO TRY IT. A DEPRESSING EXPERIENCE. *lots of ugly people in shorts*

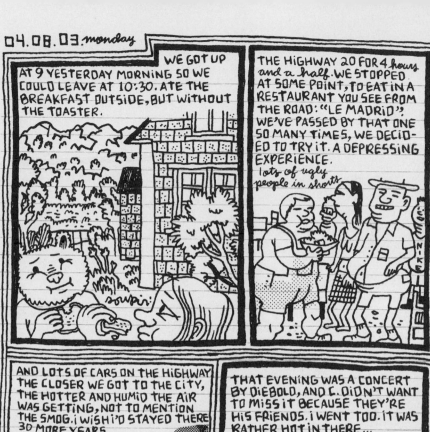

AND LOTS OF CARS ON THE HIGHWAY THE CLOSER WE GOT TO THE CITY, THE HOTTER AND HUMID THE AIR WAS GETTING, NOT TO MENTION THE SMOG. i WISH i'D STAYED THERE 30 MORE YEARS.

THAT EVENING WAS A CONCERT BY DIEBOLD, AND C. DIDN'T WANT TO MISS IT BECAUSE THEY'RE HIS FRIENDS. i WENT TOO. iT WAS RATHER HOT IN THERE...

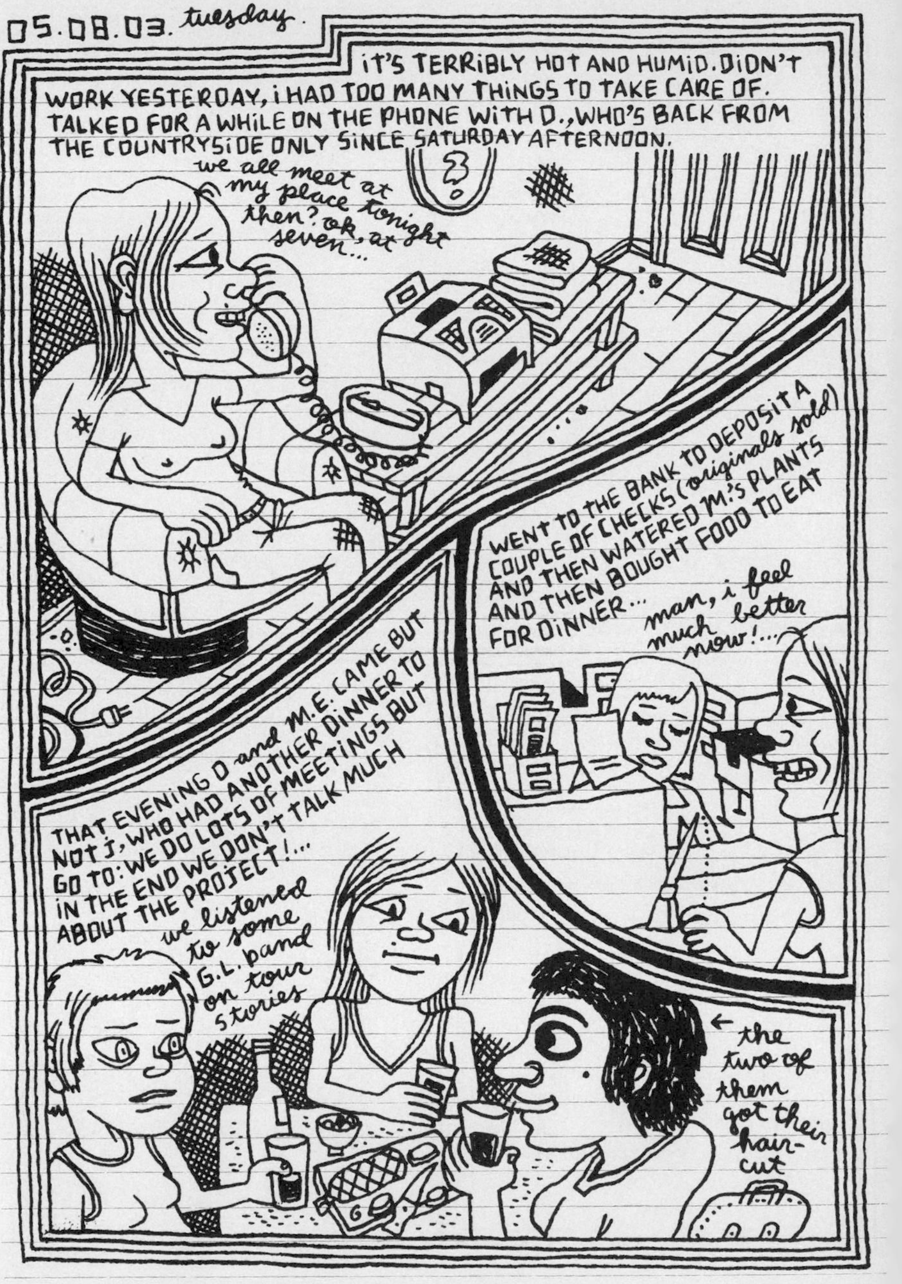
05.08.03. tuesday.
IT'S TERRIBLY HOT AND HUMID. DIDN'T WORK YESTERDAY, I HAD TOO MANY THINGS TO TAKE CARE OF. TALKED FOR A WHILE ON THE PHONE WITH D., WHO'S BACK FROM THE COUNTRYSIDE ONLY SINCE SATURDAY AFTERNOON.
we all meet at my place tonight then? ok, at seven...
WENT TO THE BANK TO DEPOSIT A COUPLE OF CHECKS (originals sold) AND THEN WATERED M.'S PLANTS AND THEN BOUGHT FOOD TO EAT FOR DINNER...
man, i feel much better now!...
THAT EVENING D and M.E. CAME BUT NOT J, WHO HAD ANOTHER DINNER TO GO TO: WE DO LOTS OF MEETINGS BUT IN THE END WE DON'T TALK MUCH ABOUT THE PROJECT!...
we listened to some G.L. band on tour stories
← the two of them got their hair-cut

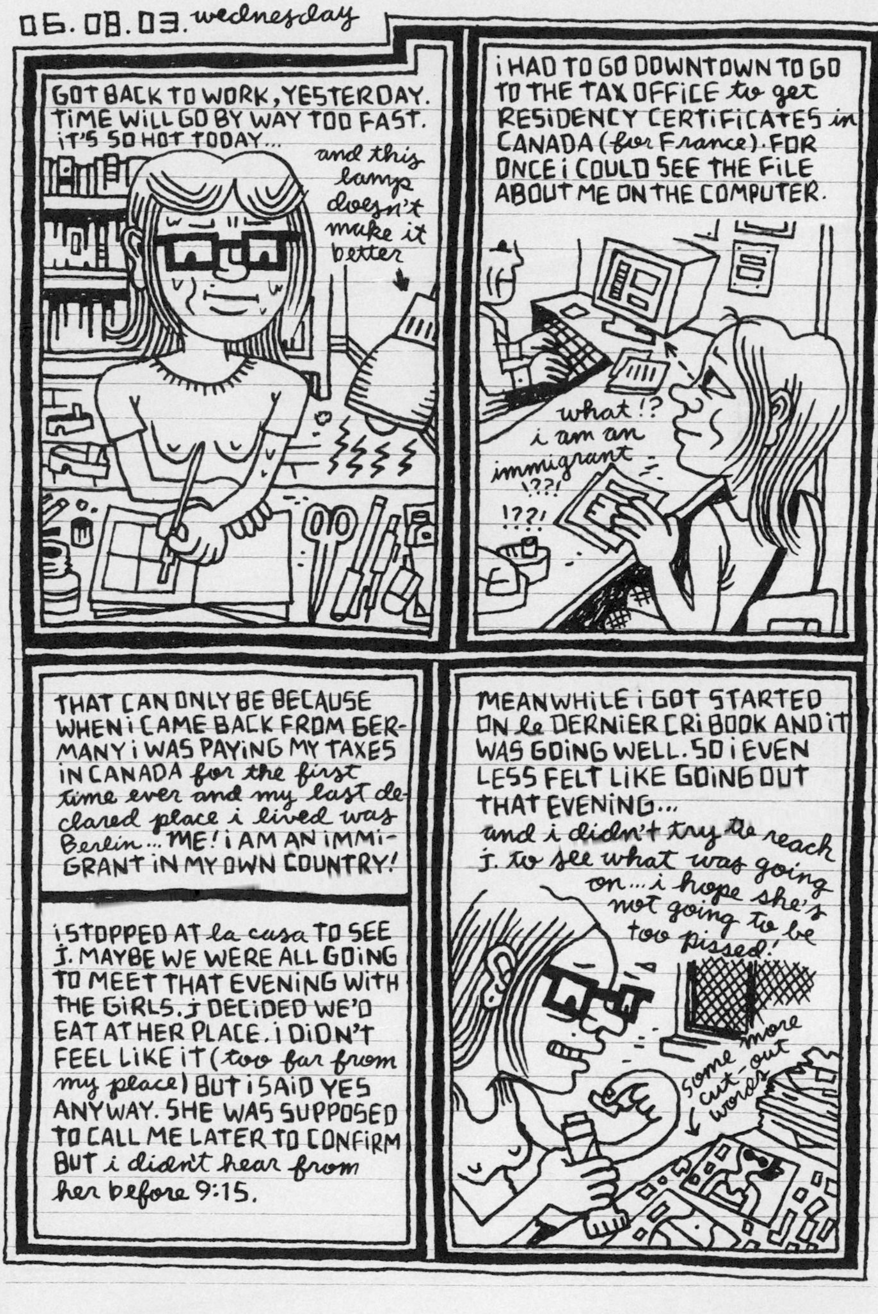
06.08.03. wednesday
GOT BACK TO WORK, YESTERDAY. TIME WILL GO BY WAY TOO FAST. IT'S SO HOT TODAY...
and this lamp doesn't make it better
I HAD TO GO DOWNTOWN TO GO TO THE TAX OFFICE to get RESIDENCY CERTIFICATES in CANADA (for France). FOR ONCE I COULD SEE THE FILE ABOUT ME ON THE COMPUTER.
what!? i am an immigrant !??!
!??!
THAT CAN ONLY BE BECAUSE WHEN I CAME BACK FROM GERMANY I WAS PAYING MY TAXES IN CANADA for the first time ever and my last declared place i lived was Berlin... ME! I AM AN IMMIGRANT IN MY OWN COUNTRY!
I STOPPED AT la casa TO SEE J. MAYBE WE WERE ALL GOING TO MEET THAT EVENING WITH THE GIRLS. J DECIDED WE'D EAT AT HER PLACE. I DIDN'T FEEL LIKE IT (too far from my place) BUT I SAID YES ANYWAY. SHE WAS SUPPOSED TO CALL ME LATER TO CONFIRM BUT i didn't hear from her before 9:15.
MEANWHILE I GOT STARTED ON le DERNIER CRI BOOK AND IT WAS GOING WELL. SO I EVEN LESS FELT LIKE GOING OUT THAT EVENING...
and i didn't try to reach J. to see what was going on... i hope she's not going to be too pissed!
some more cut-out words

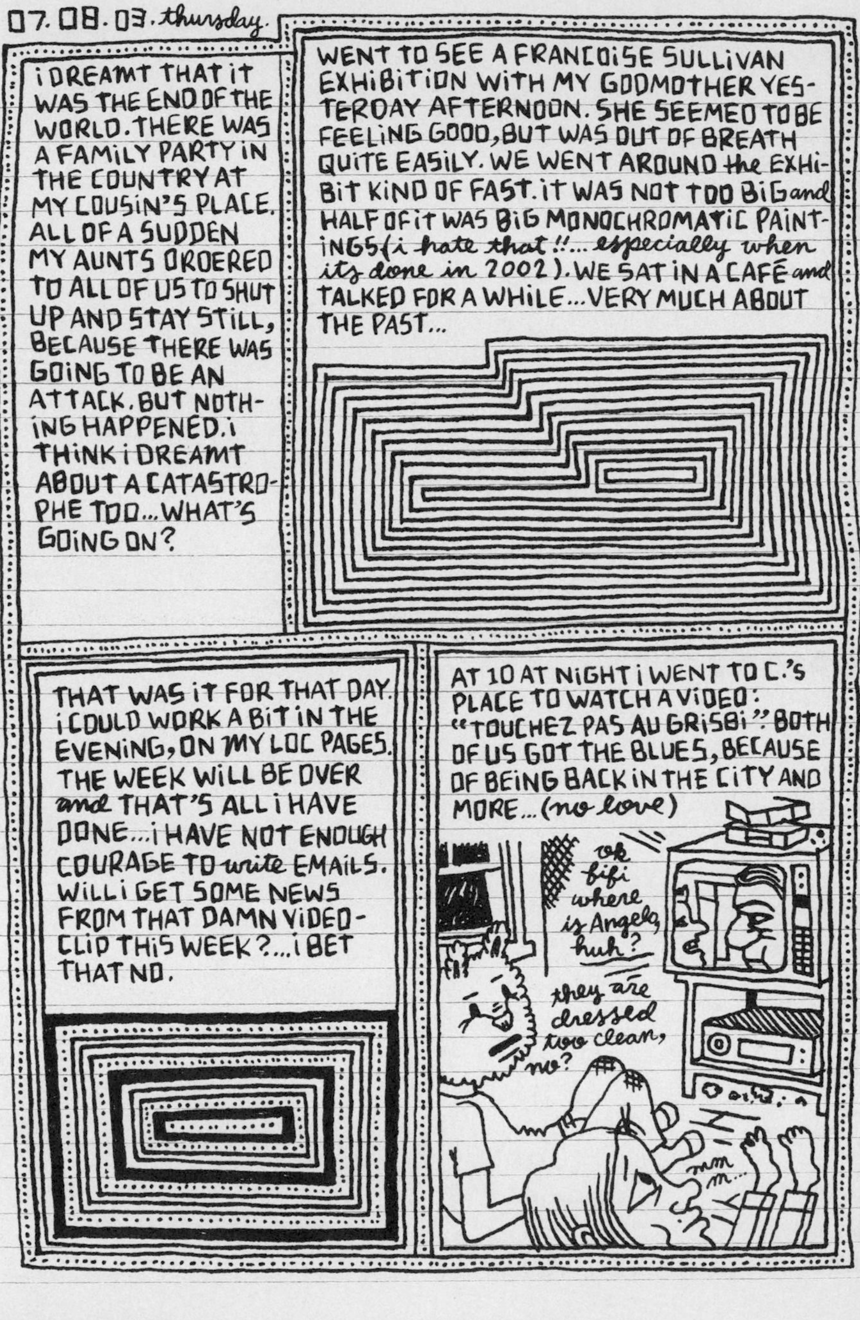
07.08.03. thursday.
i DREAMT THAT iT WAS THE END OF THE WORLD. THERE WAS A FAMILY PARTY iN THE COUNTRY AT MY COUSiN'S PLACE. ALL OF A SUDDEN MY AUNTS ORDERED TO ALL OF US TO SHUT UP AND STAY STiLL, BECAUSE THERE WAS GOiNG TO BE AN ATTACK. BUT NOTHiNG HAPPENED. i THiNK i DREAMT ABOUT A CATASTROPHE TOO... WHAT'S GOiNG ON?
WENT TO SEE A FRANCOISE SULLIVAN EXHIBITION WITH MY GODMOTHER YESTERDAY AFTERNOON. SHE SEEMED TO BE FEELiNG GOOD, BUT WAS OUT OF BREATH QUITE EASiLY. WE WENT AROUND the EXHiBiT KiND OF FAST. iT WAS NOT TOO BiG and HALF OF iT WAS BiG MONOCHROMATiC PAiNTiNGS (i hate that!!... especially when its done in 2002). WE SAT iN A CAFÉ and TALKED FOR A WHiLE... VERY MUCH ABOUT THE PAST...
THAT WAS iT FOR THAT DAY. i COULD WORK A BIT IN THE EVENiNG, ON MY LOC PAGES. THE WEEK WiLL BE OVER and THAT'S ALL i HAVE DONE... i HAVE NOT ENOUGH COURAGE TO write EMAiLS. WiLL i GET SOME NEWS FROM THAT DAMN ViDEO-CLiP THiS WEEK?... i BET THAT NO.
AT 10 AT NiGHT i WENT TO C.'s PLACE TO WATCH A ViDEO: "TOUCHEZ PAS AU GRiSBi". BOTH OF US GOT THE BLUES, BECAUSE OF BEiNG BACK iN THE CiTY AND MORE... (no love)
ok fifi where is Angelo, huh?
they are dressed too clean, no?
mm m...

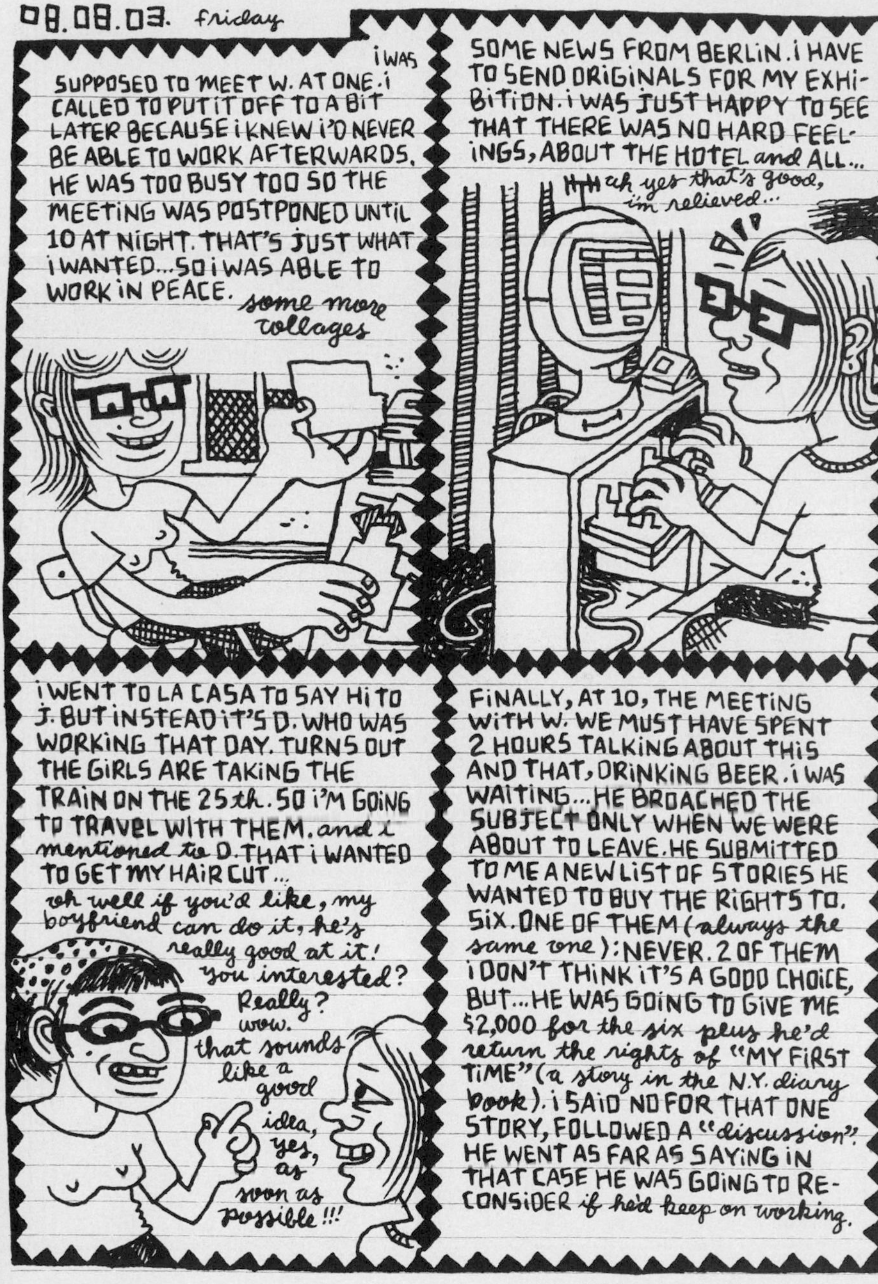

08.08.03. friday
i WAS SUPPOSED TO MEET W. AT ONE. i CALLED TO PUT IT OFF TO A BIT LATER BECAUSE i KNEW i'D NEVER BE ABLE TO WORK AFTERWARDS. HE WAS TOO BUSY TOO SO THE MEETING WAS POSTPONED UNTIL 10 AT NIGHT. THAT'S JUST WHAT i WANTED... SO i WAS ABLE TO WORK IN PEACE.
some more collages
SOME NEWS FROM BERLIN. i HAVE TO SEND ORIGINALS FOR MY EXHIBITION. i WAS JUST HAPPY TO SEE THAT THERE WAS NO HARD FEELINGS, ABOUT THE HOTEL and ALL...
ah yes that's good, i'm relieved...
i WENT TO LA CASA TO SAY Hi TO J. BUT INSTEAD iT'S D. WHO WAS WORKING THAT DAY. TURNS OUT THE GIRLS ARE TAKING THE TRAIN ON THE 25th. SO i'M GOING TO TRAVEL WITH THEM. and i mentioned to D. THAT i WANTED TO GET MY HAIR CUT...
oh well if you'd like, my boyfriend can do it, he's really good at it! you interested?
Really? wow. that sounds like a good idea, yes, as soon as possible!!!
FiNALLY, AT 10, THE MEETING WITH W. WE MUST HAVE SPENT 2 HOURS TALKING ABOUT THIS AND THAT, DRINKING BEER. i WAS WAITING... HE BROACHED THE SUBJECT ONLY WHEN WE WERE ABOUT TO LEAVE. HE SUBMITTED TO ME A NEW LIST OF STORIES HE WANTED TO BUY THE RIGHTS TO. SIX. ONE OF THEM (always the same one): NEVER. 2 OF THEM i DON'T THINK IT'S A GOOD CHOICE, BUT... HE WAS GOING TO GIVE ME $2,000 for the six plus he'd return the rights of "MY FiRST TiME" (a story in the N.Y. diary book). i SAID NO FOR THAT ONE STORY, FOLLOWED A "discussion". HE WENT AS FAR AS SAYiNG IN THAT CASE HE WAS GOiNG TO RECONSIDER if he'd keep on working.

ON THAT PROJECT, HOPING I'D LET GO! THE POOR GUY!... IN THE END, HE WAS FURIOUS, WHEN WE LEFT EACH OTHER. PERSONALLY, I WAS QUITE PROUD OF MYSELF, OF HAVING BEEN ABLE TO EXPRESS ONE OR TWO THINGS, WHICH HE WASN'T VERY PLEASED WITH. SWEET REVENGE... HE TOLD ME I WOULD HEAR FROM HIM BEFORE I LEAVE (i can't wait to leave).

09.08.03. saturday

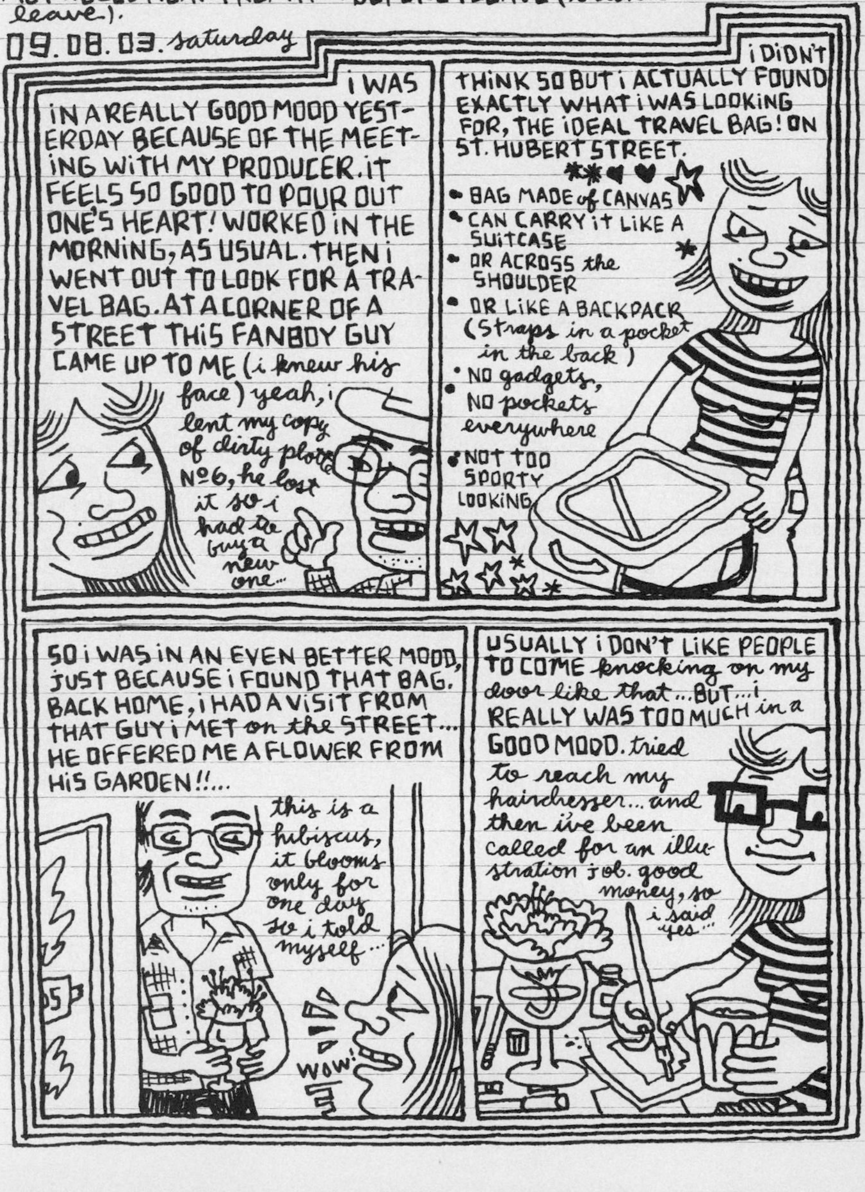
I WAS IN A REALLY GOOD MOOD YESTERDAY BECAUSE OF THE MEETING WITH MY PRODUCER. IT FEELS SO GOOD TO POUR OUT ONE'S HEART! WORKED IN THE MORNING, AS USUAL. THEN I WENT OUT TO LOOK FOR A TRAVEL BAG. AT A CORNER OF A STREET THIS FANBOY GUY CAME UP TO ME (i knew his face)
yeah, i lent my copy of dirty plotte No6, he lost it so i had to buy a new one...
I DIDN'T THINK SO BUT I ACTUALLY FOUND EXACTLY WHAT I WAS LOOKING FOR, THE IDEAL TRAVEL BAG! ON ST. HUBERT STREET.
• BAG MADE of CANVAS
• CAN CARRY IT LIKE A SUITCASE
• OR ACROSS the SHOULDER
• OR LIKE A BACKPACK (Straps in a pocket in the back)
• NO gadgets, NO pockets everywhere
• NOT TOO SPORTY LOOKING
SO I WAS IN AN EVEN BETTER MOOD, JUST BECAUSE I FOUND THAT BAG. BACK HOME, I HAD A VISIT FROM THAT GUY I MET on the STREET... HE OFFERED ME A FLOWER FROM HIS GARDEN!!...
this is a hibiscus, it blooms only for one day so i told myself...
WOW!
USUALLY I DON'T LIKE PEOPLE TO COME knocking on my door like that... BUT... I REALLY WAS TOO MUCH in a GOOD MOOD. tried to reach my hairdresser... and then i've been called for an illustration job. good money, so i said yes...

10.08.03. sunday

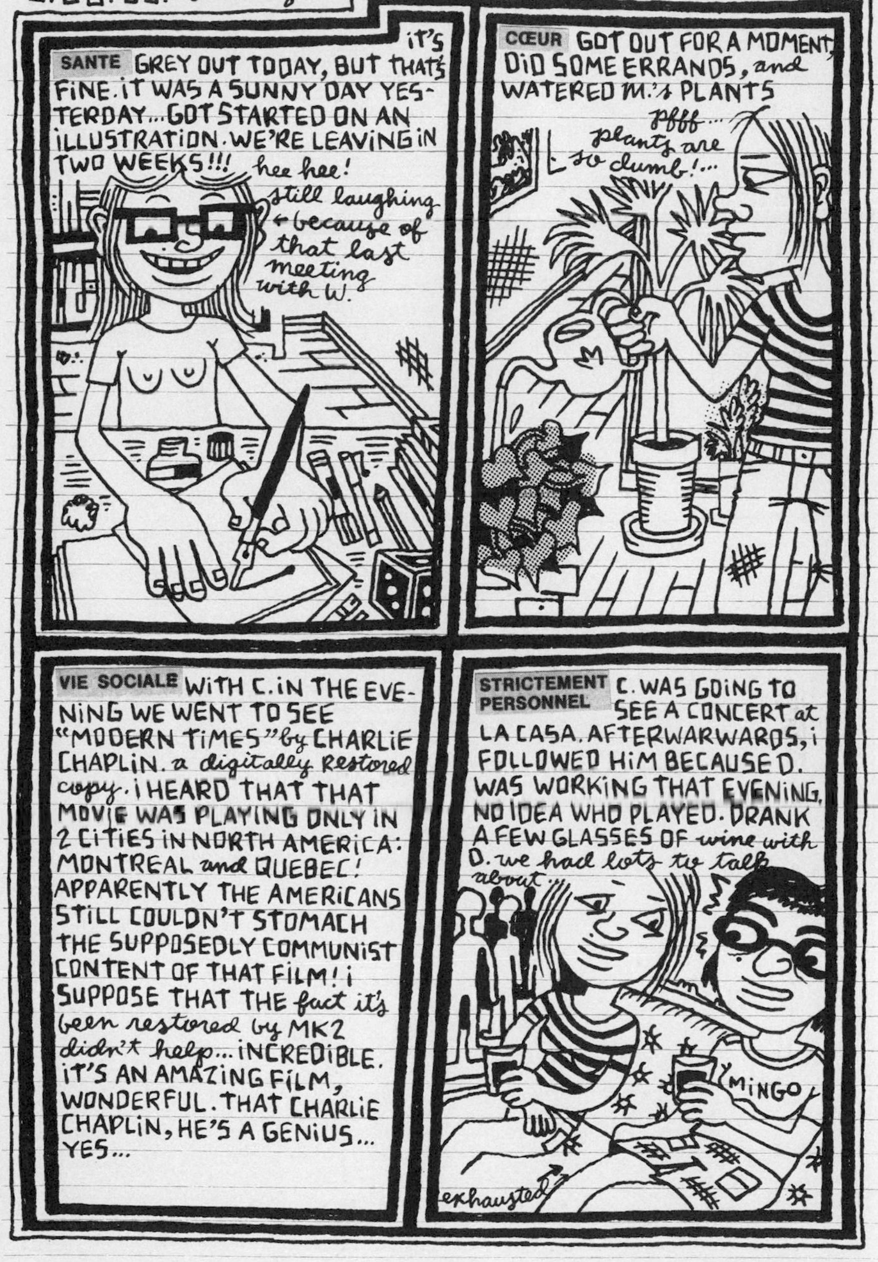
SANTE
IT'S GREY OUT TODAY, BUT THAT'S FINE. IT WAS A SUNNY DAY YESTERDAY... GOT STARTED ON AN ILLUSTRATION. WE'RE LEAVING IN TWO WEEKS!!!
hee hee!
still laughing ← because of that last meeting with W.
CŒUR
GOT OUT FOR A MOMENT, DID SOME ERRANDS, and WATERED M.'s PLANTS
pfff... plants are so dumb!...
VIE SOCIALE
WITH C. IN THE EVENING WE WENT TO SEE "MODERN TIMES" by CHARLIE CHAPLIN. a digitally restored copy. I HEARD THAT THAT MOVIE WAS PLAYING ONLY IN 2 CITIES IN NORTH AMERICA: MONTREAL and QUEBEC! APPARENTLY THE AMERICANS STILL COULDN'T STOMACH THE SUPPOSEDLY COMMUNIST CONTENT OF THAT FILM! I SUPPOSE THAT THE fact it's been restored by MK2 didn't help... INCREDIBLE. IT'S AN AMAZING FILM, WONDERFUL. THAT CHARLIE CHAPLIN, HE'S A GENIUS... YES...
STRICTEMENT PERSONNEL
C. WAS GOING TO SEE A CONCERT at LA CASA. AFTERWARWARDS, I FOLLOWED HIM BECAUSE D. WAS WORKING THAT EVENING. NO IDEA WHO PLAYED. DRANK A FEW GLASSES OF wine with D. we had lots to talk about...
MINGO
exhausted

11. 08. 03. *monday*

IT RAINED MOST OF THE DAY, YESTER- DAY. SO I WORKED. FINISHED ONE OF THE ILLUSTRA- TIONS. THEN THE REST OF THE DAY IN FRONT OF THE COMPU- TER, DOING A BUNCH OF THINGS. DIDN'T GO OUT OF THE HOUSE.

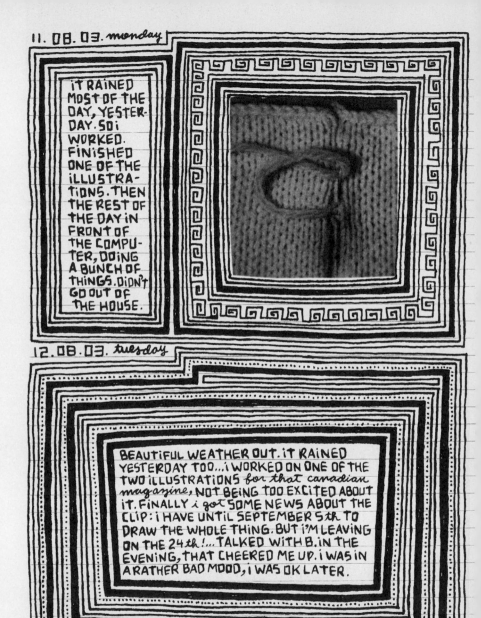

12. 08. 03. *tuesday*

BEAUTIFUL WEATHER OUT. IT RAINED YESTERDAY TOO... I WORKED ON ONE OF THE TWO ILLUSTRATIONS *for that canadian magazine,* NOT BEING TOO EXCITED ABOUT IT. FINALLY *i got* SOME NEWS ABOUT THE CLIP: I HAVE UNTIL SEPTEMBER 5th TO DRAW THE WHOLE THING. BUT I'M LEAVING ON THE 24th! ... TALKED WITH B. IN THE EVENING, THAT CHEERED ME UP. I WAS IN A RATHER BAD MOOD, I WAS OK LATER.

WORKED ON THE SECOND ILLUSTR-ATION YESTERDAY. I'M FINISH-ING THEM BOTH THIS MORNING. WENT OUT TO PHOTOCOPY MY PRESSKIT (grant application) AND THEN WENT TO BUY A HUGE BAG OF CAT FOOD... FOR TWO MONTHS.

i gotta do a little bit every day!...

CAT FOOD

C. CAME TO VISIT IN THE EVENING, HE HELPED ME FINISH A BOTTLE OF WINE. HE WANTED ME TO GIVE HIM SLOW ACTION MOVEMENT STUFF TO SEND TO A FRIEND OF HIS WHO WAS GOING TO WRITE AN ARTICLE ABOUT IT... in "SPIN"!...

this record's amazing!

oh yes?

i DREAMT I WAS LIVING IN AN APARTMENT RIGHT BY THE SEA. ONE NIGHT THERE WAS A BIG VIOLENT STORM, THE DOORS SLAMMED OPEN AND WE COULDN'T CLOSE THEM BACK. ALL OF A SUDDEN WE'RE ON A SAILBOAT (in the same storm) THERE WAS lots of SMALL WHALES AROUND US. THEY SWAM SO CLOSE TO US WE COULD TOUCH THEM. THE NEXT DAY, ALL IS QUIET AGAIN. THERE WAS LOTS OF those WHALES BEACHED, AND WE COULD HEAR THEM CRY, DYING...

WHAT DOES IT MEAN?... FINISHED THE ILLUSTRATION JOB YESTERDAY. i SPENT THE AFTERNOON making PHONE CALLS TO J., AND TO MY SO-CALLED HAIRDRESSER BUT NOTHING! talked to my mom, who reminded me it was my godmother's birthday that day...

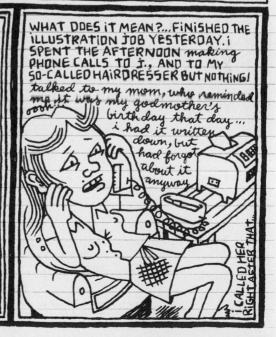

ooh!...

i had it written down, but had forgot about it anyway

i CALLED HER RIGHT AFTER THAT...

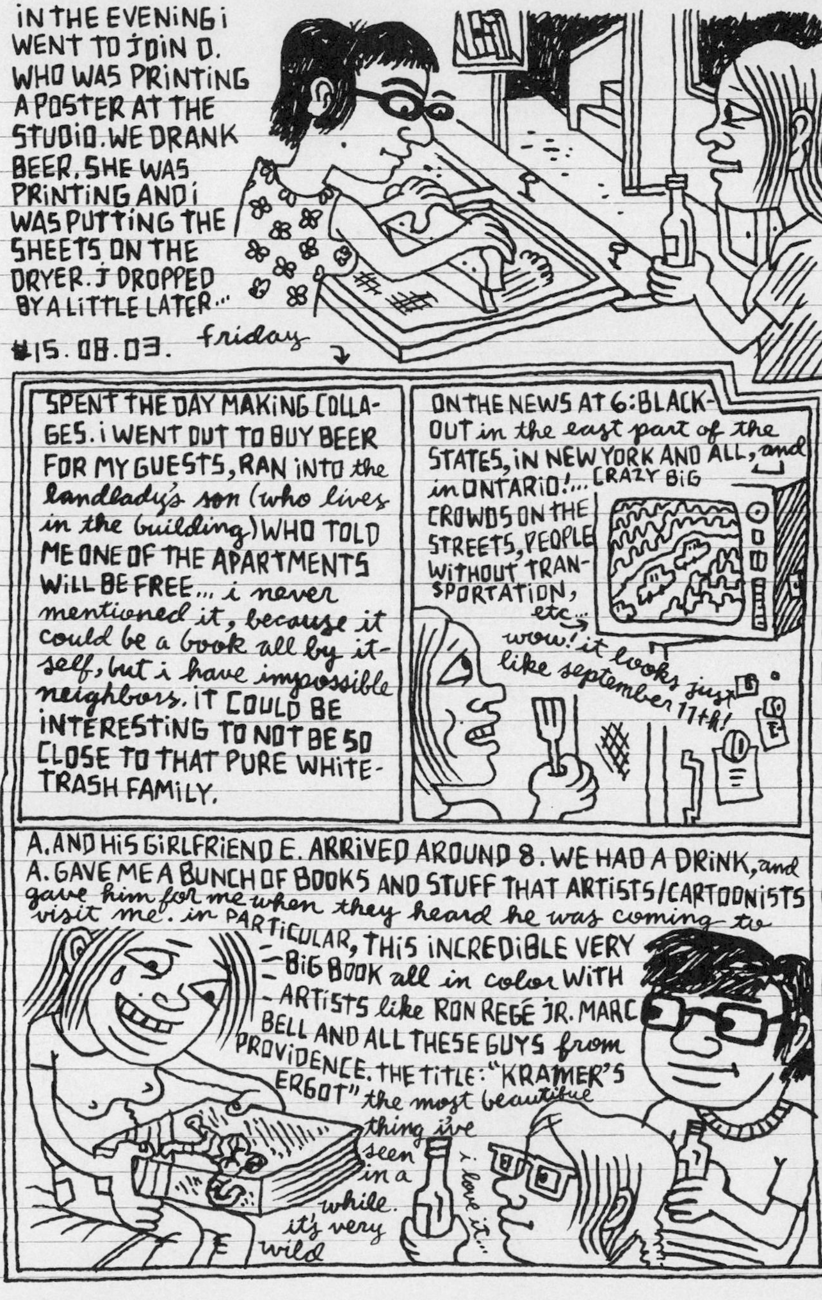
IN THE EVENING I WENT TO JOIN D. WHO WAS PRINTING A POSTER AT THE STUDIO. WE DRANK BEER. SHE WAS PRINTING AND I WAS PUTTING THE SHEETS ON THE DRYER. J DROPPED BY A LITTLE LATER...
#15.08.03. friday
SPENT THE DAY MAKING COLLAGES. I WENT OUT TO BUY BEER FOR MY GUESTS, RAN INTO the landlady's son (who lives in the building) WHO TOLD ME ONE OF THE APARTMENTS WILL BE FREE... i never mentioned it, because it could be a book all by itself, but i have impossible neighbors. IT COULD BE INTERESTING TO NOT BE SO CLOSE TO THAT PURE WHITE-TRASH FAMILY.
ON THE NEWS AT 6: BLACKOUT in the east part of the STATES, IN NEW YORK AND ALL, and in ONTARIO!... CRAZY BIG CROWDS ON THE STREETS, PEOPLE WITHOUT TRANSPORTATION, etc...
wow! it looks just like september 11th!
A. AND HIS GIRLFRIEND E. ARRIVED AROUND 8. WE HAD A DRINK, and A. GAVE ME A BUNCH OF BOOKS AND STUFF THAT ARTISTS/CARTOONISTS gave him for me when they heard he was coming to visit me. in PARTICULAR, THIS INCREDIBLE VERY BIG BOOK all in color WITH ARTISTS like RON REGÉ JR. MARC BELL AND ALL THESE GUYS from PROVIDENCE. THE TITLE: "KRAMER'S ERGOT" the most beautiful thing i've seen in a while.
it's very wild
i love it...

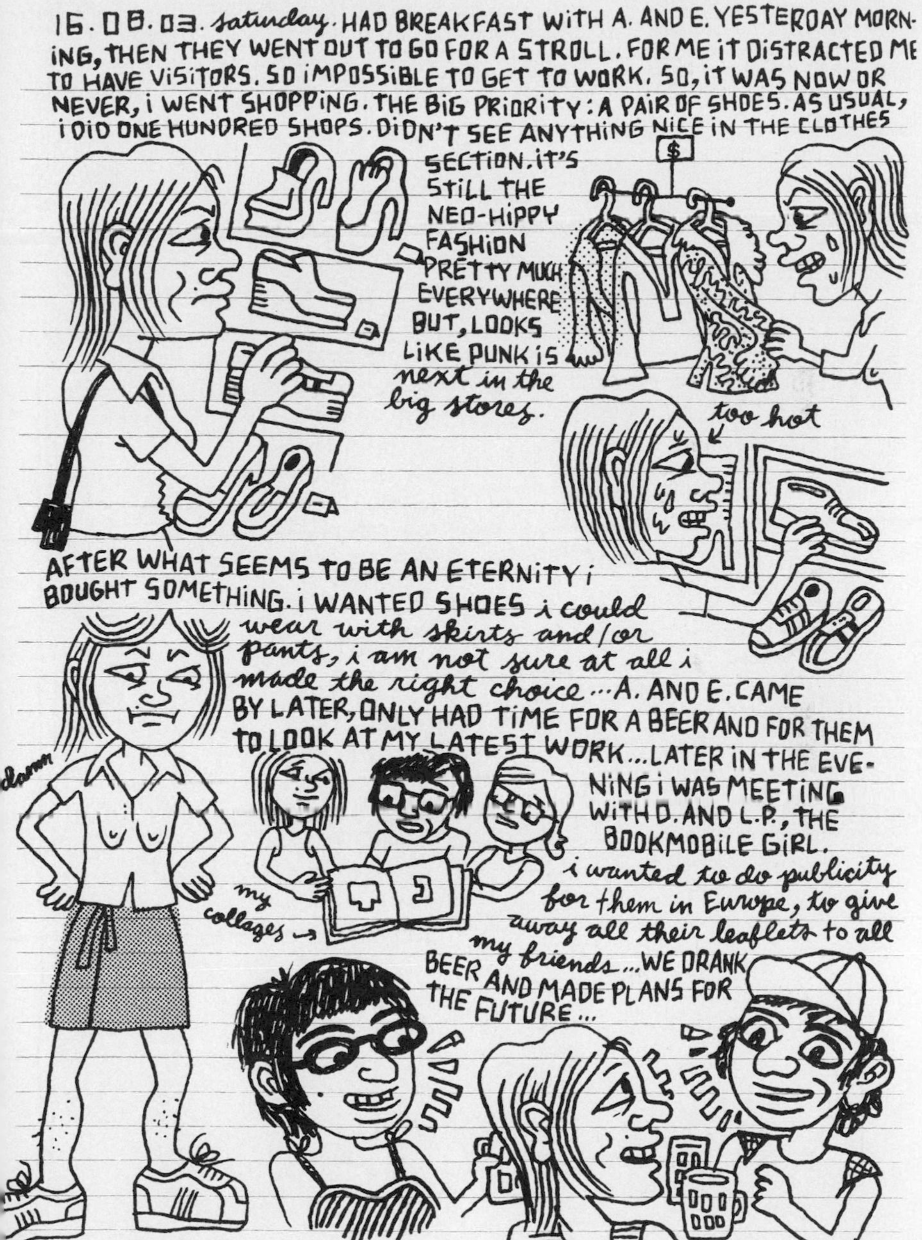
16.08.03. saturday. HAD BREAKFAST WITH A. AND E. YESTERDAY MORNING, THEN THEY WENT OUT TO GO FOR A STROLL. FOR ME IT DISTRACTED ME TO HAVE VISITORS. SO IMPOSSIBLE TO GET TO WORK. SO, IT WAS NOW OR NEVER, I WENT SHOPPING. THE BIG PRIORITY: A PAIR OF SHOES. AS USUAL, I DID ONE HUNDRED SHOPS. DIDN'T SEE ANYTHING NICE IN THE CLOTHES SECTION. IT'S STILL THE NEO-HIPPY FASHION PRETTY MUCH EVERYWHERE BUT, LOOKS LIKE PUNK IS next in the big stores.
$
too hot
AFTER WHAT SEEMS TO BE AN ETERNITY I BOUGHT SOMETHING. I WANTED SHOES i could wear with skirts and/or pants, i am not sure at all i made the right choice... A. AND E. CAME BY LATER, ONLY HAD TIME FOR A BEER AND FOR THEM TO LOOK AT MY LATEST WORK... LATER IN THE EVENING I WAS MEETING WITH D. AND L.P., THE BOOKMOBILE GIRL.
damn
my collages →
i wanted to do publicity for them in Europe, to give away all their leaflets to all my friends... WE DRANK BEER AND MADE PLANS FOR THE FUTURE...

17.08.03. sunday

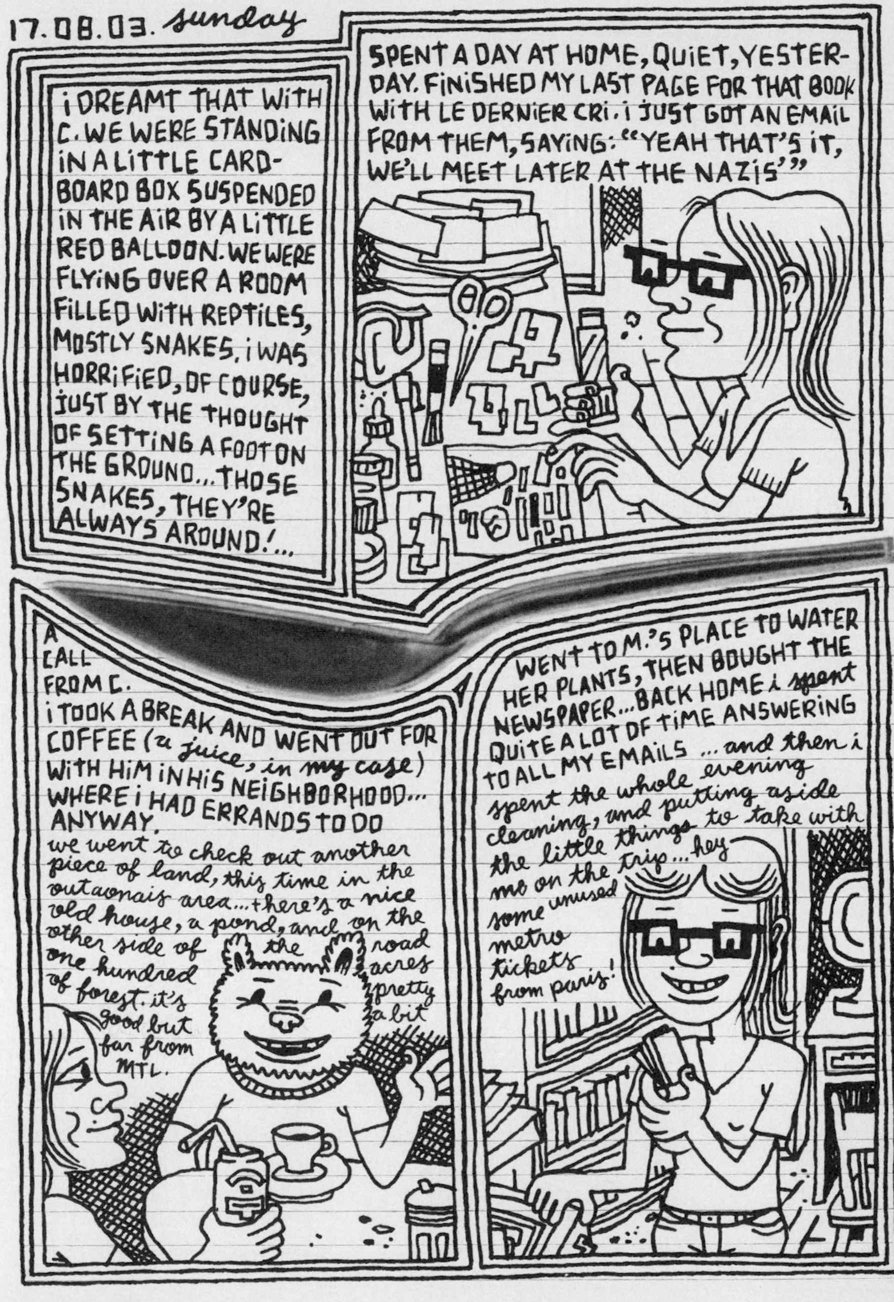

i DREAMT THAT WITH C. WE WERE STANDING iN A LITTLE CARDBOARD BOX SUSPENDED iN THE AiR BY A LITTLE RED BALLOON. WE WERE FLYiNG OVER A ROOM FiLLED WiTH REPTiLES, MOSTLY SNAKES. i WAS HORRiFiED, OF COURSE, JUST BY THE THOUGHT OF SETTiNG A FOOT ON THE GROUND... THOSE SNAKES, THEY'RE ALWAYS AROUND!...
SPENT A DAY AT HOME, QUiET, YESTERDAY. FiNiSHED MY LAST PAGE FOR THAT BOOK WiTH LE DERNiER CRi. i JUST GOT AN EMAiL FROM THEM, SAYiNG: "YEAH THAT'S iT, WE'LL MEET LATER AT THE NAZiS'"
A CALL FROM C.
i TOOK A BREAK AND WENT OUT FOR COFFEE (a juice, in my case) WiTH HiM iN HiS NEiGHBORHOOD... WHERE i HAD ERRANDS TO DO ANYWAY.
we went to check out another piece of land, this time in the outaouais area... there's a nice old house, a pond, and on the other side of the road one hundred acres of forest. it's pretty good but a bit far from MTL.
WENT TO M.'S PLACE TO WATER HER PLANTS, THEN BOUGHT THE NEWSPAPER... BACK HOME i spent QUiTE A LOT OF TiME ANSWERiNG TO ALL MY EMAiLS ... and then i spent the whole evening cleaning, and putting aside the little things to take with me on the trip... hey
some unused metro tickets from paris!

18.08.03. monday

i AM AFRAID MY JOURNAL WON'T BE VERY INTERESTING IN THE COMING WEEKS. IT'S GOING TO BE WORK, WORK, WORK. A STRESSFUL DAY YESTERDAY: the guy from the magazine for which i did 2 illustrations

CALLED ME TO TELL ME THE THIRD ONE WAS MISSING... i GOT LANDED WITH THAT IN THE AFTERNOON. i was not happy with that... DINNER WITH MY MOM, BUT i DiDN'T STAY OVER VERY LATE. SHE WAS TOO TiRED, HAD SPENT THE DAY HiKiNG. i HOPE i'M GONNA HAVE MY HAiRCUT THiS WEEK, DAMMit !!!...

19.08.03. tuesday

WORKED FOR MOST OF THE DAY YESTERDAY, NO CHOiCE. BUT, i'LL BE FiNE, WiTH THAT ANiMATiON THiNG, i THiNK i CAN FiNiSH iT BEFORE LEAViNG. SOME NEWS FROM W., A NEW OFFER: SAME THiNG AS LAST TiME EXCEPT FOR THAT ONE STORY i DON'T WANT TO SELL TO HiM, SO 5 SHORT STORiES. HE SAiD THAT ONCE HE HAS THAT, HE CAN GET iT OVER WiTH THE SCREENPLAY AND THEN i read it and we can discuss it... yeah, THAT'S PROMiSiNG... WHAT UPSETS ME iS THAT i WiLL HAVE TO THiNK ABOUT THE DAMN FiLM FOR MONTHS, and who knows,

THE YEARS TO COME. ANYWAY, LOOKS LiKE HE GOT OVER our LAST DiSCUSSiON. i BOUGHT MYSELF A BOTTLE OF WiNE, BECAUSE iN THE END iT'S BEEN ANOTHER STRESSFUL DAY.

EXTiNCTiON by T. Bernhard

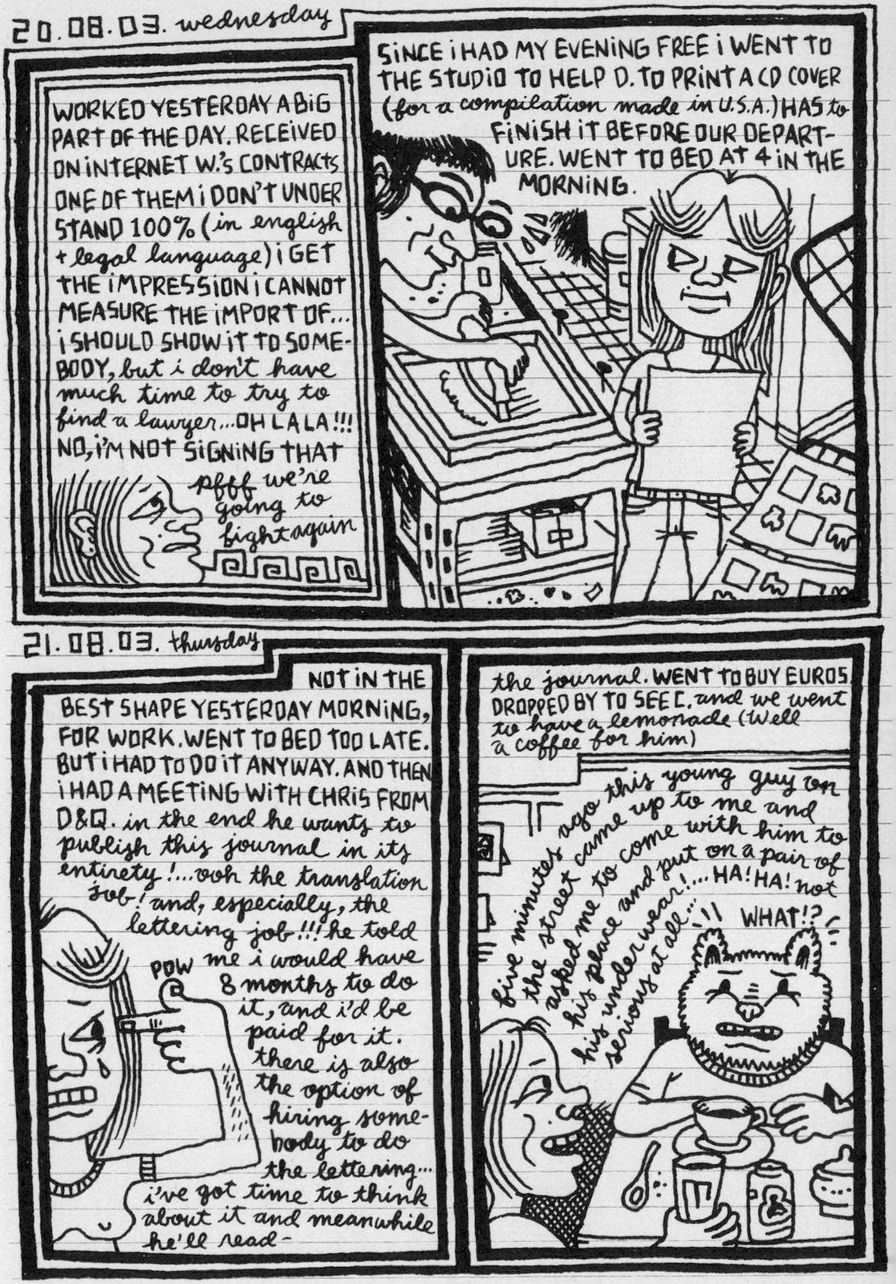
20.08.03. wednesday
WORKED YESTERDAY A BIG PART OF THE DAY. RECEIVED ON INTERNET W.'S CONTRACTS ONE OF THEM I DON'T UNDERSTAND 100% (in english + legal language) I GET THE IMPRESSION I CANNOT MEASURE THE IMPORT OF... I SHOULD SHOW IT TO SOMEBODY, but i don't have much time to try to find a lawyer... OH LA LA!!! NO, I'M NOT SIGNING THAT
pfff we're going to fight again
SINCE I HAD MY EVENING FREE I WENT TO THE STUDIO TO HELP D. TO PRINT A CD COVER (for a compilation made in U.S.A.) HAS to FINISH IT BEFORE OUR DEPARTURE. WENT TO BED AT 4 IN THE MORNING.
21.08.03. thursday
NOT IN THE BEST SHAPE YESTERDAY MORNING, FOR WORK. WENT TO BED TOO LATE. BUT I HAD TO DO IT ANYWAY. AND THEN I HAD A MEETING WITH CHRIS FROM D&Q. in the end he wants to publish this journal in its entirety!... ooh the translation job! and, especially, the lettering job!!! he told me i would have 8 months to do it, and i'd be paid for it. there is also the option of hiring somebody to do the lettering... i've got time to think about it and meanwhile he'll read-
POW
the journal. WENT TO BUY EUROS. DROPPED BY TO SEE C. and we went to have a lemonade (Well a coffee for him)
five minutes ago this young guy on the street came up to me and asked me to come with him to his place and put on a pair of his underwear!... HA! HA! not serious at all...
WHAT!?

22.08.03. friday

TOO MUCH WORK, i CAN'T DRAW FULL PAGES in my journal. SO i DREW ALL DAY AND FOR SURE ALL DAY TOMORROW and the whole EVENING TOO. TALKED TO W., i TOLD HiM i COULDN'T SiGN HiS CONTRACT BE-CAUSE i DiDN'T UNDER-STAND HALF OF iT. HE HAD NO PROBLEM WiTH THAT, EXCEPT THAT i HAD TO TRY TO FiND somebody to help me with that before i leave...

i DON'T SEE HOW. AT THE END OF THE DAY "RAYMOND FROM LOU LOU HAiRDO" CAME TO MY PLACE TO CUT MY HAiR. HE CUT iT SHORTER THAN i EXPECTED!...BUT THAT'S FiNE

yeah that's a lot of hair!...

CLIP
CUT CLIP
CLIP CLIP

hee hee

casual fashions

YiKES!!! iS THAT REALLY ME!? i COULD BARELY RECOG-NiZE MYSELF iN THE MiRROR! BUT i'M GETTING USED TO iT and i like it. THANK YOU RAYMOND from lou lou hairdo...

23.08.03 saturday i WORKED ALL DAY AND A LiTTLE BiT iN THE EVENiNG. i CAN SAY i'VE SERiOUSLY HAD ENOUGH OF iT! C. DROPPED BY TO SEE MY NEW SELF, WELL HiS REACTiON WAS HE LAUGHED FOR FiVE MiNUTES. iT'S A GOOD THiNG i DiDN'T HAVE ANY DOUBTS OTHERWiSE i WOULD PROBABLY HAVE CRiED...TALKED TO D. SHE WAS JUST

i'm cracking up!!!

AS EXHAUSTED AS i WAS. i RAN iNTO THE LiQUOR STORE TO BUY MYSELF A BOTTLE OF WiNE, TO CALM MY POOR NERVES. AT LAST, i'M GONNA FiNiSH iT ALL TODAY...

24.08.03. *sunday*. DEPARTURE DAY. THE WEATHER IS NICE AND COOL, LIKE YESTERDAY. GOT UP AT 7:30 THIS MORNING... I MANAGED TO FINISH THAT VIDEO THING, BUT IT WASN'T EASY. I WAS AT THE VERY END OF MY ROPE. D. CAME TO MY PLACE AT 6 TO PUT TOGETHER A BUNCH OF OUR RUBY RED BOOKS. WE ONLY HAD TIME TO FOLD M.E.'S PAGES AND TO ASSEMBLE THE SHEETS, THEN SHE HAD TO GO TO WORK (*at la casa*). I WENT TO M.'S PLACE TO WATER HER PLANTS FOR THE LAST TIME... AND I SPENT THE EVENING TALKING ON THE PHONE WITH B. WHILE *putting holes in for the books binding*. AND LATER MORE OF THE SAME, IN FRONT OF THE T.V.... TODAY, CLEANING-LUGGAGES AND THEN BYE BYE

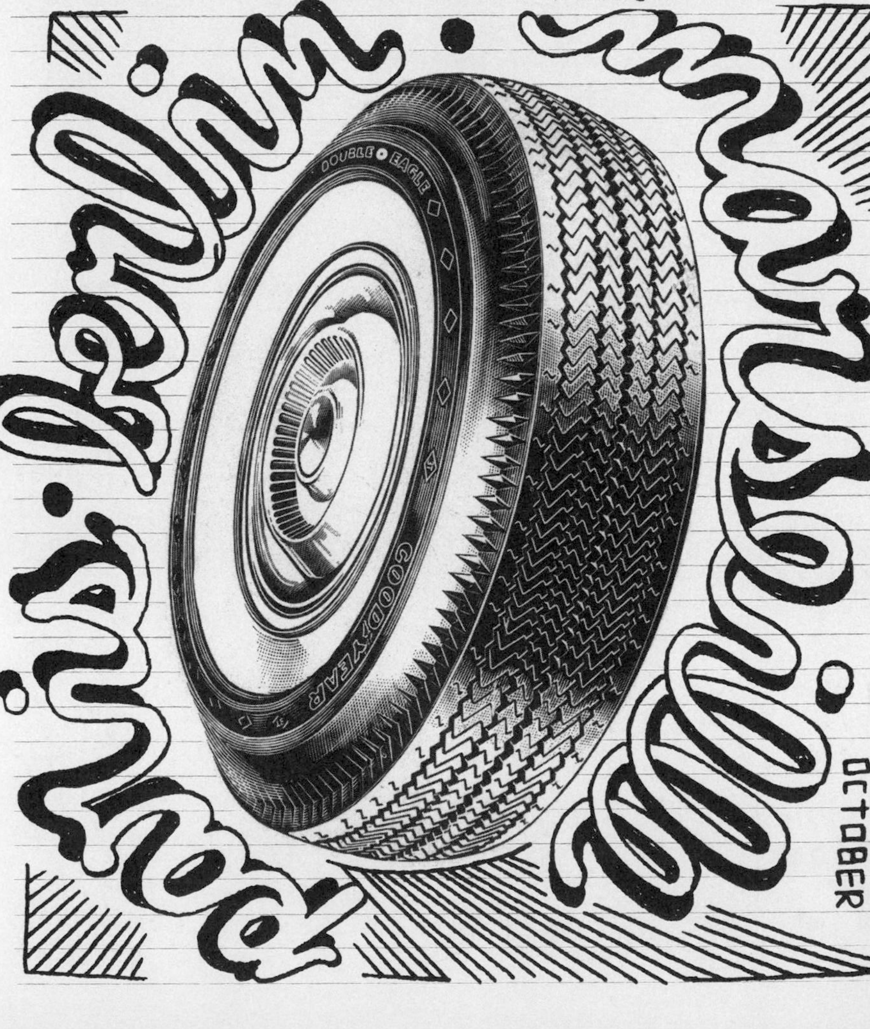
DOUBLE EAGLE
GOODYEAR

AUGUST · SEPTEMBER · OCTOBER

25.08.03. *monday* INDEED I SPENT THE DAY YESTERDAY SCRUBBING. I TRIED TO REACH W. AT THE END OF THE AFTERNOON, BUT I ONLY GOT HIS ANSWERING MACHINE... TOLD HIM I COULDN'T FIND ANYBODY TO HELP ME... IN FACT, EVEN IF I WANTED TO, IT WAS NOT PHYSICALLY POSSIBLE! NO TIME AT ALL! C. DROVE US TO THE MIRABEL AIRPORT. HE DIDN'T SEEM IN A VERY GOOD MOOD

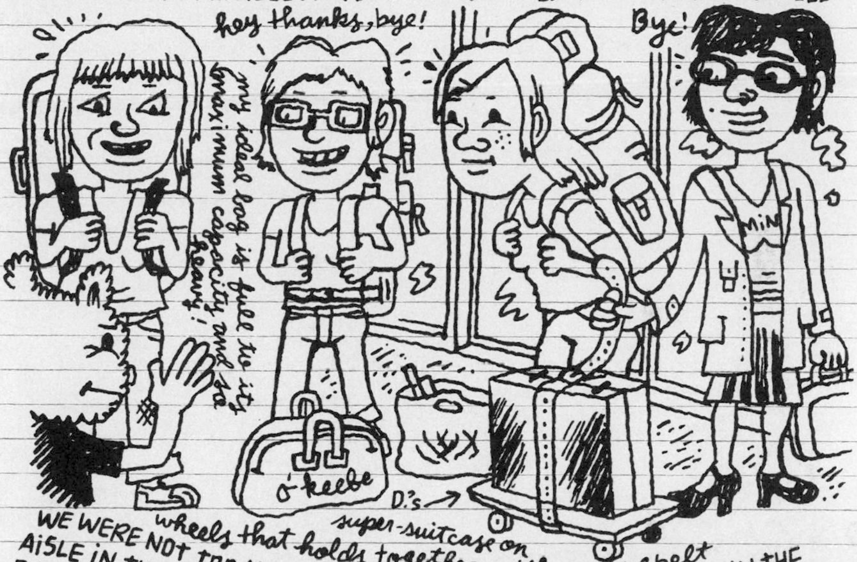
hey thanks, bye!
Bye!
my ideal bag is full to its maximum capacity and so heavy!
MIN
o'keebe
D.'s super-suitcase on wheels that holds together with an old belt

WE WERE NOT TOO MUCH IN ADVANCE, SO WE GOT THE SEATS IN THE AISLE IN THE MIDDLE. NOT ONLY THAT BUT THE SEATS WERE STINKING BAD!!! SOMEBODY HAD BEEN SICK JUST RIGHT WHERE M.E. WAS SITTING, ON THE PREVIOUS TRIP

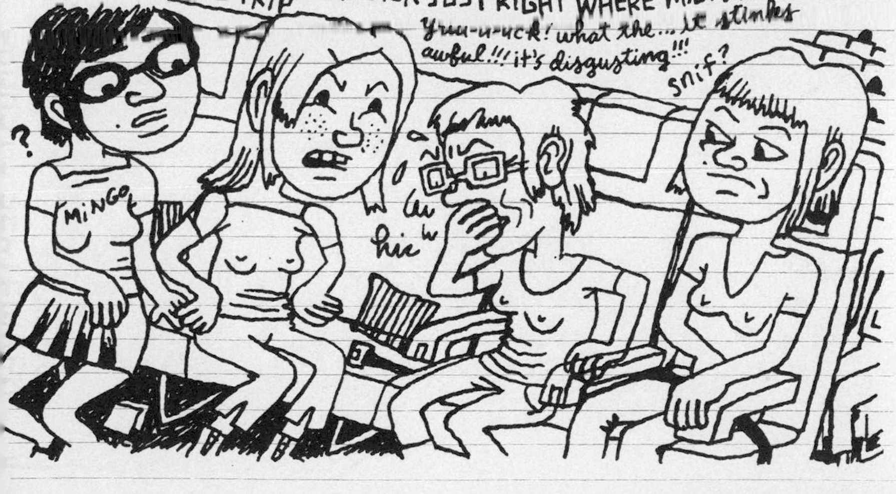
Yuu-u-uck! what the... it stinks awful!!! it's disgusting!!!
snif?
?
MINGO
hic

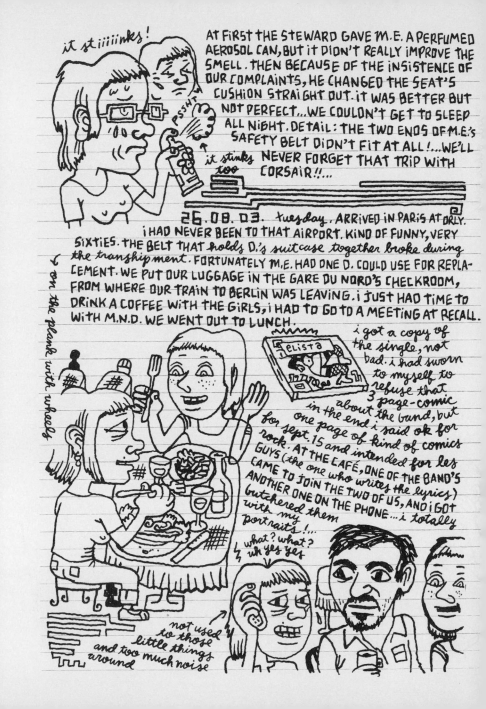

it stiiiinks!

PSSHT

it stinks too

AT FIRST THE STEWARD GAVE M.E. A PERFUMED AEROSOL CAN, BUT IT DIDN'T REALLY IMPROVE THE SMELL. THEN BECAUSE OF THE INSISTENCE OF OUR COMPLAINTS, HE CHANGED THE SEAT'S CUSHION STRAIGHT OUT. IT WAS BETTER BUT NOT PERFECT...WE COULDN'T GET TO SLEEP ALL NIGHT. DETAIL: THE TWO ENDS OF M.E.'s SAFETY BELT DIDN'T FIT AT ALL!...WE'LL NEVER FORGET THAT TRIP WITH CORSAIR!!...

26.08.03. tuesday, ARRIVED IN PARIS AT ORLY. I HAD NEVER BEEN TO THAT AIRPORT. KIND OF FUNNY, VERY SIXTIES. THE BELT THAT holds D.'s suitcase together broke during the transhipment. FORTUNATELY M.E. HAD ONE D. COULD USE FOR REPLACEMENT. WE PUT OUR LUGGAGE IN THE GARE DU NORD'S CHECKROOM, FROM WHERE OUR TRAIN TO BERLIN WAS LEAVING. I JUST HAD TIME TO DRINK A COFFEE WITH THE GIRLS, I HAD TO GO TO A MEETING AT RECALL. WITH M.N.D. WE WENT OUT TO LUNCH.

& on the plank with wheels

ELISTA

i got a copy of the single, not bad. i had sworn to myself to refuse that 3 page-comic about the band, but in the end i said ok for one page of kind of comics for sept. 15 and intended for les rock. AT THE CAFÉ, ONE OF THE BAND'S GUYS (the one who writes the lyrics) CAME TO JOIN THE TWO OF US, AND I GOT ANOTHER ONE ON THE PHONE...i totally butchered them with my portraits!...

what? what? uh yes yes

not used to those little things and too much noise around

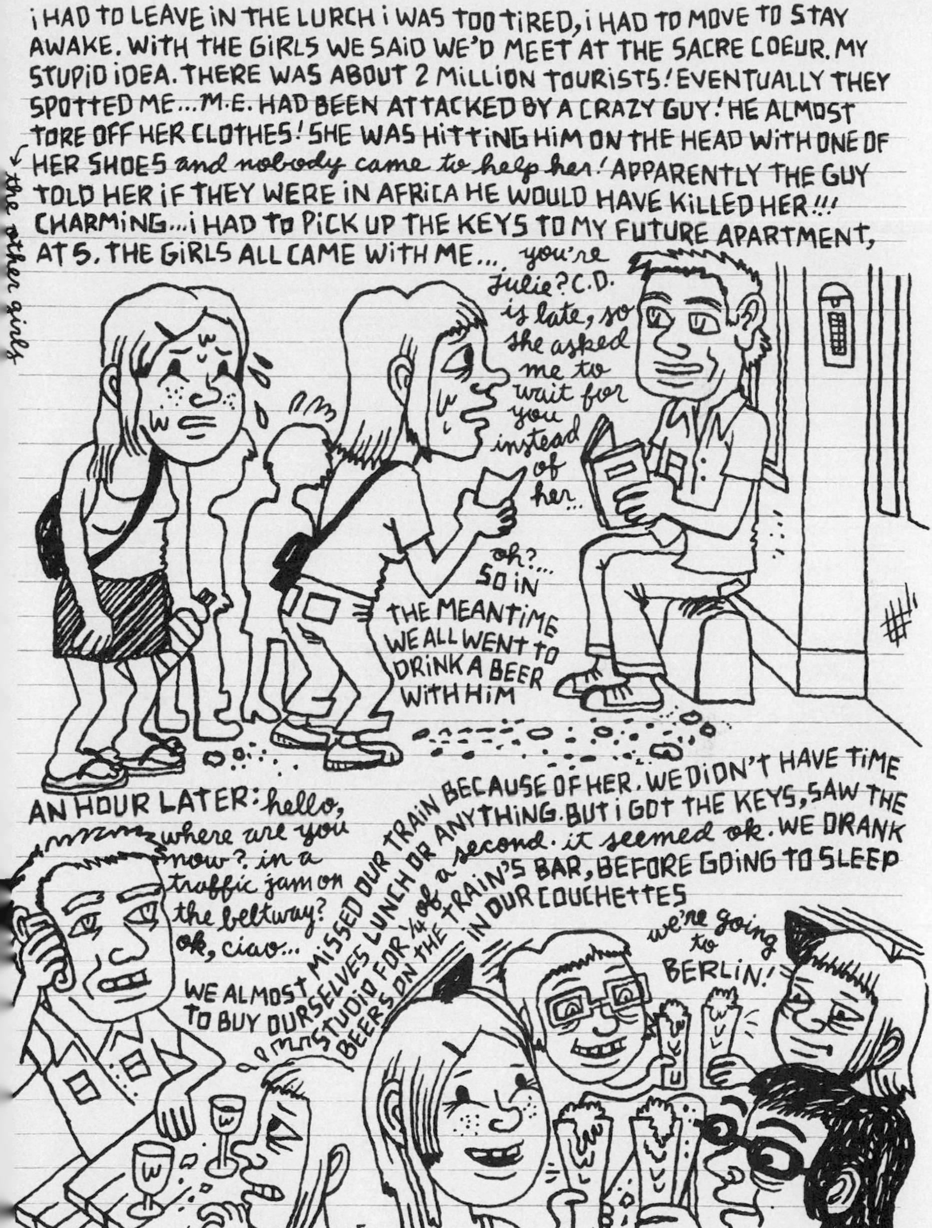
i HAD TO LEAVE iN THE LURCH i WAS TOO TiRED, i HAD TO MOVE TO STAY AWAKE. WiTH THE GiRLS WE SAiD WE'D MEET AT THE SACRE COEUR. MY STUPiD iDEA. THERE WAS ABOUT 2 MiLLiON TOURiSTS! EVENTUALLY THEY SPOTTED ME... M.E. HAD BEEN ATTACKED BY A CRAZY GUY! HE ALMOST TORE OFF HER CLOTHES! SHE WAS HiTTiNG HiM ON THE HEAD WiTH ONE OF HER SHOES and nobody came to help her! APPARENTLY THE GUY TOLD HER iF THEY WERE iN AFRiCA HE WOULD HAVE KiLLED HER!!! CHARMiNG... i HAD TO PiCK UP THE KEYS TO MY FUTURE APARTMENT, AT 5. THE GiRLS ALL CAME WiTH ME...
the other girls
you're Julie? C.D. is late, so she asked me to wait for you instead of her...
oh?... SO iN THE MEANTiME WE ALL WENT TO DRiNK A BEER WiTH HiM
AN HOUR LATER: hello, where are you now?, in a traffic jam on the beltway? ok, ciao...
WE ALMOST MiSSED OUR TRAiN BECAUSE OF HER. WE DiDN'T HAVE TiME TO BUY OURSELVES LUNCH OR ANYTHiNG. BUT i GOT THE KEYS, SAW THE STUDiO FOR 1/4 of a second. it seemed ok. WE DRANK BEERS ON THE TRAiN'S BAR, BEFORE GOiNG TO SLEEP iN OUR COUCHETTES
we're going to BERLiN!

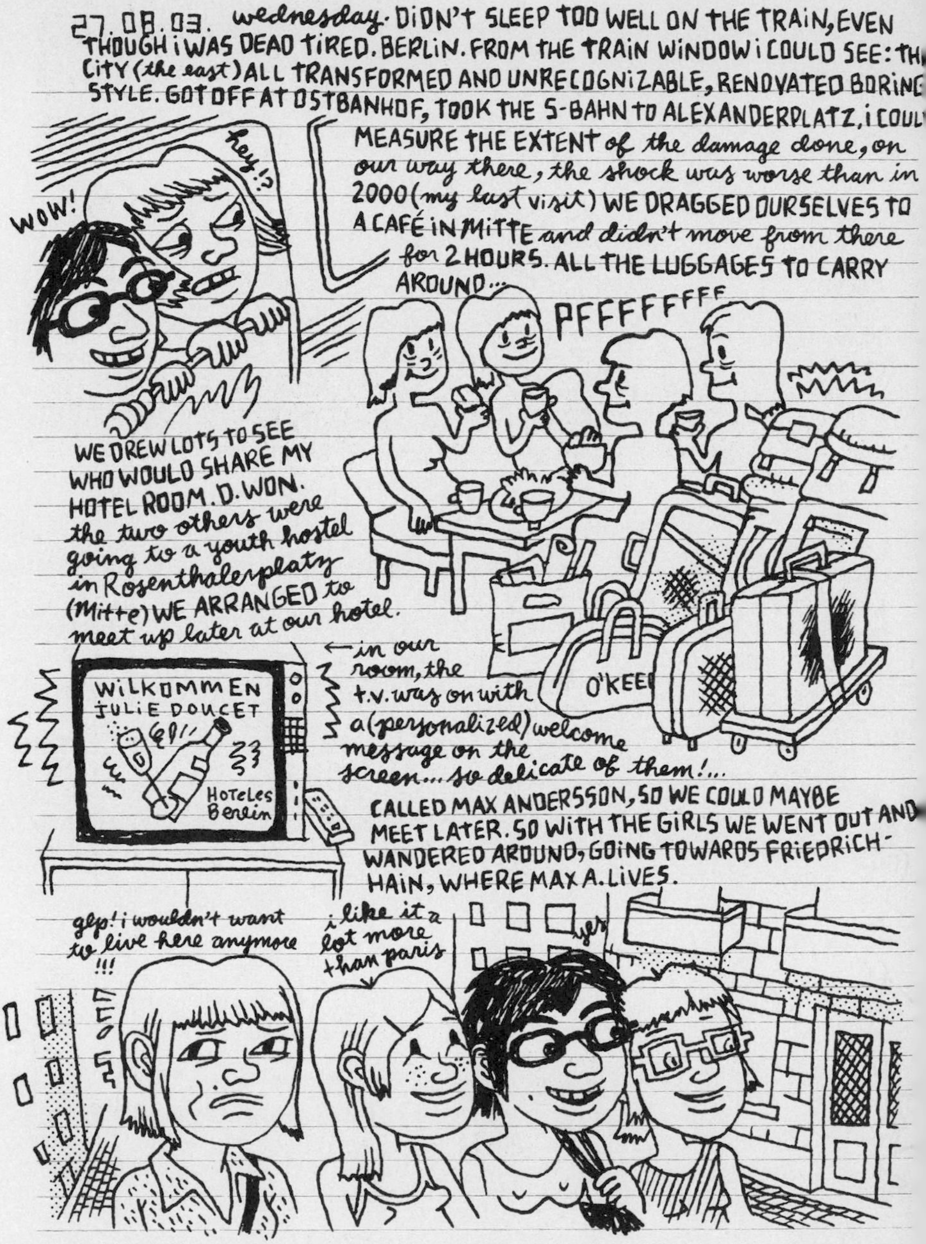
27. 08. 03. wednesday. DIDN'T SLEEP TOO WELL ON THE TRAIN, EVEN THOUGH I WAS DEAD TIRED. BERLIN. FROM THE TRAIN WINDOW I COULD SEE: THE CITY (the east) ALL TRANSFORMED AND UNRECOGNIZABLE, RENOVATED BORING STYLE. GOT OFF AT OSTBANHOF, TOOK THE S-BAHN TO ALEXANDERPLATZ, I COULD MEASURE THE EXTENT of the damage done, on our way there, the shock was worse than in 2000 (my last visit) WE DRAGGED OURSELVES TO A CAFÉ IN MITTE and didn't move from there for 2 HOURS. ALL THE LUGGAGES TO CARRY AROUND...
WOW!
hey!?
PFFFFFFFFF
WE DREW LOTS TO SEE WHO WOULD SHARE MY HOTEL ROOM. D. WON. the two others were going to a youth hostel in Rosenthalerplatz (Mitte) WE ARRANGED to meet up later at our hotel.
O'KEEF
← in our room, the t.v. was on with a (personalized) welcome message on the screen... so delicate of them!...
WILKOMMEN JULIE DOUCET
Hoteles Berlin
CALLED MAX ANDERSSON, SO WE COULD MAYBE MEET LATER. SO WITH THE GIRLS WE WENT OUT AND WANDERED AROUND, GOING TOWARDS FRIEDRICH-HAIN, WHERE MAX A. LIVES.
glp! i wouldn't want to live here anymore !!!
i like it a lot more than paris
yes

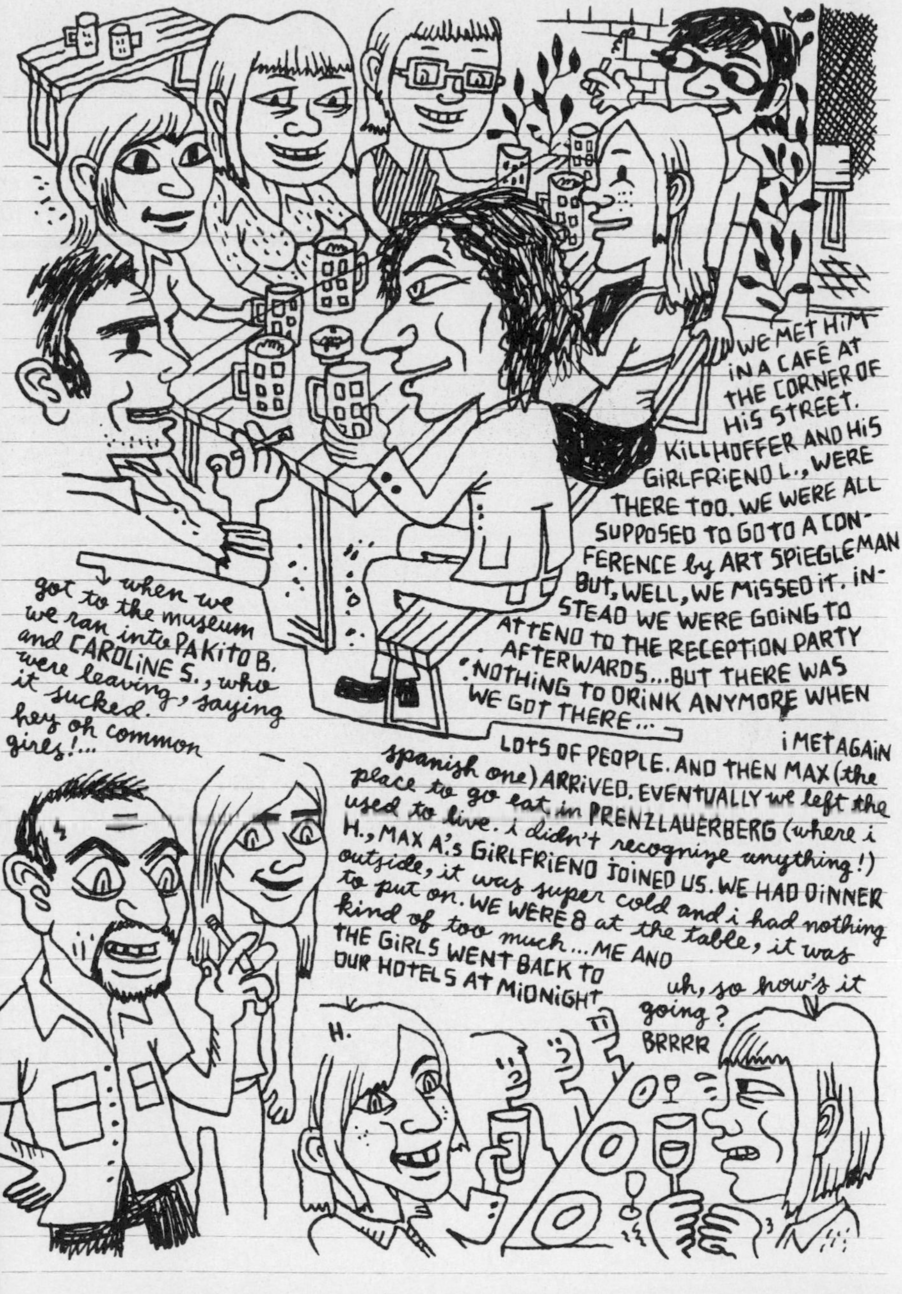
WE MET HIM IN A CAFÉ AT THE CORNER OF HIS STREET. KILLHOFFER AND HIS GIRLFRIEND L., WERE THERE TOO. WE WERE ALL SUPPOSED TO GO TO A CONFERENCE by ART SPIEGLEMAN BUT, WELL, WE MISSED IT. INSTEAD WE WERE GOING TO ATTEND TO THE RECEPTION PARTY AFTERWARDS... BUT THERE WAS NOTHING TO DRINK ANYMORE WHEN WE GOT THERE...
when we got to the museum we ran into PAKITO B. and CAROLINE S., who were leaving, saying it sucked.
hey oh common girls!...
i MET AGAIN LOTS OF PEOPLE. AND THEN MAX (the spanish one) ARRIVED. EVENTUALLY we left the place to go eat in PRENZLAUERBERG (where i used to live. i didn't recognize anything!) H., MAX A.'s GIRLFRIEND JOINED US. WE HAD DINNER outside, it was super cold and i had nothing to put on. WE WERE 8 at the table, it was kind of too much... ME AND THE GIRLS WENT BACK TO OUR HOTELS AT MIDNIGHT
H.
uh, so how's it going?
BRRRR

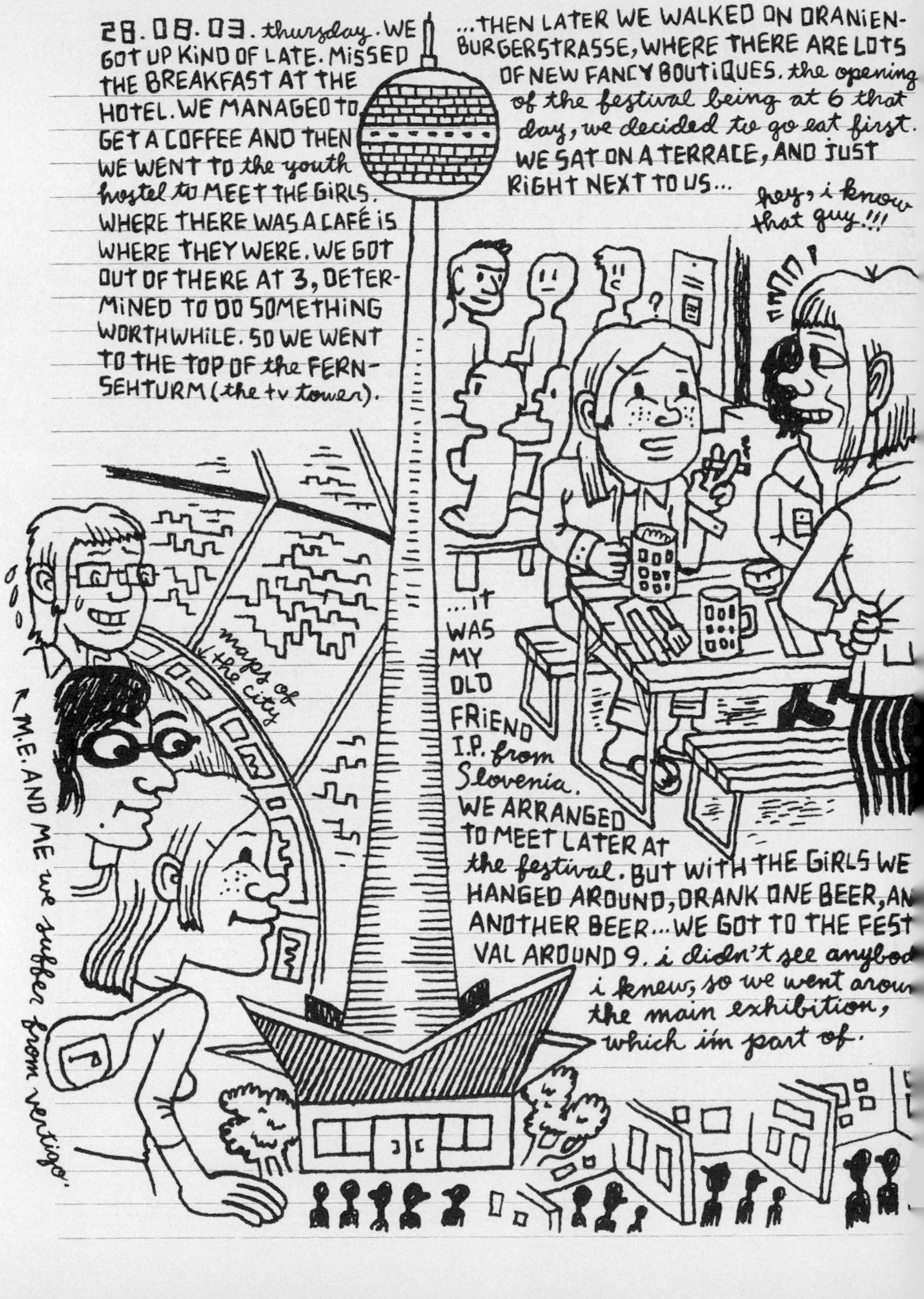

28.08.03. thursday. WE GOT UP KIND OF LATE. MISSED THE BREAKFAST AT THE HOTEL. WE MANAGED TO GET A COFFEE AND THEN WE WENT TO the youth hostel to MEET THE GIRLS. WHERE THERE WAS A CAFÉ IS WHERE THEY WERE. WE GOT OUT OF THERE AT 3, DETERMINED TO DO SOMETHING WORTHWHILE. SO WE WENT TO THE TOP OF the FERNSEHTURM (the tv tower).
...THEN LATER WE WALKED ON ORANIENBURGERSTRASSE, WHERE THERE ARE LOTS OF NEW FANCY BOUTIQUES. the opening of the festival being at 6 that day, we decided to go eat first. WE SAT ON A TERRACE, AND JUST RIGHT NEXT TO US...
hey, i know that guy!!!
ANNU!
?
maps of the city
← M.E. AND ME we suffer from vertigo.
...IT WAS MY OLD FRIEND I.P. from Slovenia. WE ARRANGED TO MEET LATER AT the festival. BUT WITH THE GIRLS WE HANGED AROUND, DRANK ONE BEER, AN ANOTHER BEER... WE GOT TO THE FEST VAL AROUND 9. i didn't see anybod i knew, so we went arou the main exhibition, which im part of.

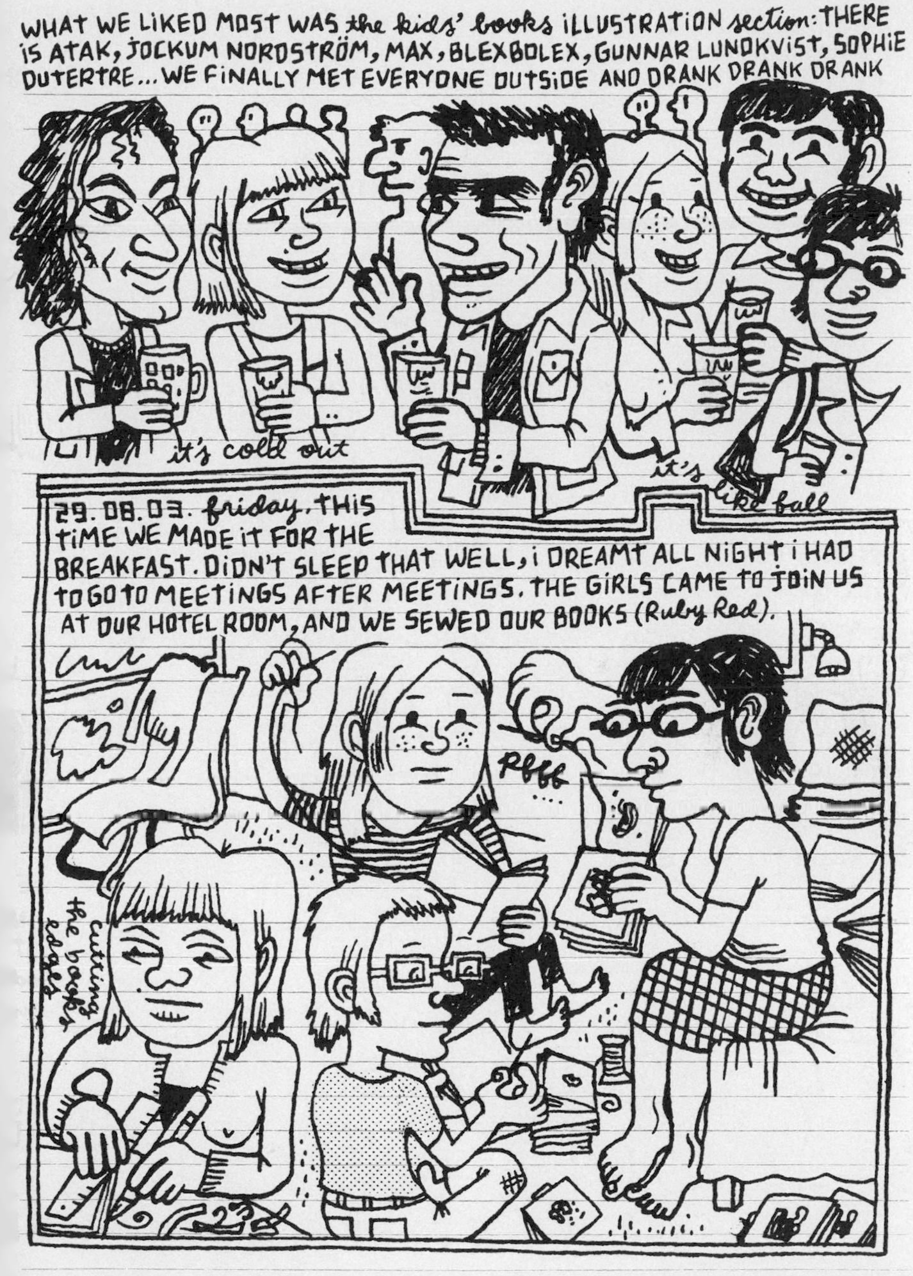

WHAT WE LIKED MOST WAS the kids' books ILLUSTRATION section: THERE IS ATAK, JOCKUM NORDSTRÖM, MAX, BLEXBOLEX, GUNNAR LUNDKVIST, SOPHIE DUTERTRE... WE FINALLY MET EVERYONE OUTSIDE AND DRANK DRANK DRANK
it's cold out
it's like fall
29.08.03. friday. THIS TIME WE MADE IT FOR THE BREAKFAST. DIDN'T SLEEP THAT WELL, I DREAMT ALL NIGHT I HAD TO GO TO MEETINGS AFTER MEETINGS. THE GIRLS CAME TO JOIN US AT OUR HOTEL ROOM, AND WE SEWED OUR BOOKS (Ruby Red).
Rfff
cutting the books' edges

WE BROUGHT SOME COPIES TO SELL AT THE FESTIVAL. i MET WITH ATAK, WHO GAVE ME A COPY OF HIS LATEST WORK (wonderful) AND THEN INTRODUCED ME TO JOCKUM NORDSTRÖM. THAT ONE i AM FILLED WITH ADMIRATION FOR HIS WORK. i DIDN'T iMAGINE HIM LIKE THAT AT ALL! WITH THE GIRLS WE WALKED TO H.'S HAT STORE, IN FRIEDRISCHHAIN. iT WAS NOT THAT CLOSE, i MADE THEM WALK TOO MUCH. IN HER STORE WAS AN INCREDIBLE CHOICE OF HATS. AND EVERYTHING IS DONE BY HER, EVEN THE FELT HATS! i DON'T REALLY LIKE TO WEAR HATS BUT i WANTED TO BUY ONE.

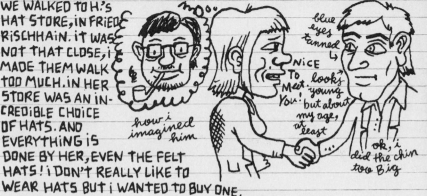

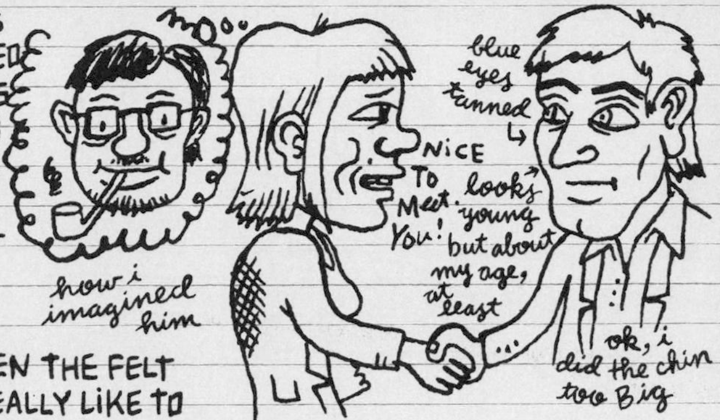
how i imagined him
NICE TO Meet You!
blue eyes tanned
looks young but about my age, at least
ok, i did the chin too Big

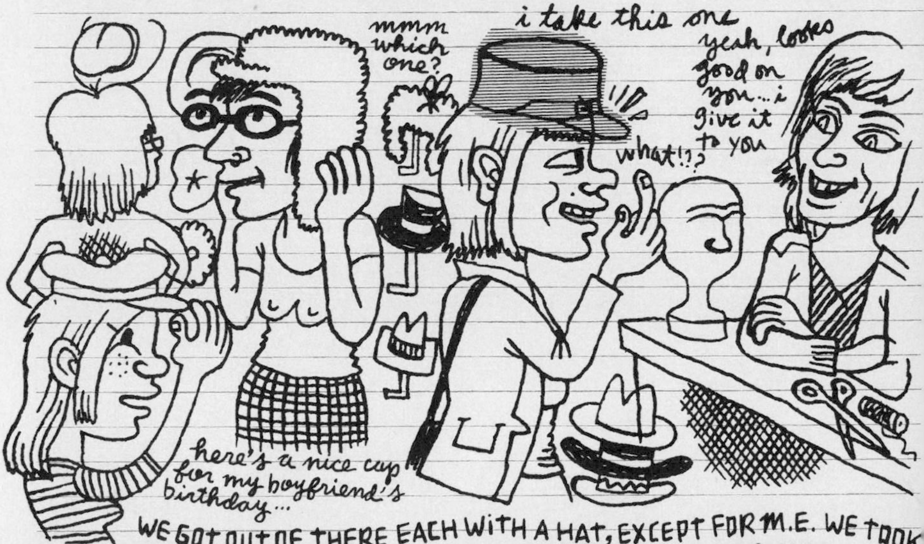
mmm which one?
i take this one
yeah, looks good on you... i give it to you
what!!?
here's a nice cup for my boyfriend's birthday...

WE GOT OUT OF THERE EACH WITH A HAT, EXCEPT FOR M.E. WE TOOK THE TRAM UP TO KASTANIENALLE WHERE THERE WAS AN OPENING LINKED to the festival. THERE WAS A TINY LITTLE BAR IN THERE, ALL DECORATED BY M.S. BASTIAN ALL IN FLUO/BLACKLIGHT. AND ONE UNIQUE DRAWING A FEW METERS LONG, DONE BY XAVIER ROBEL and HELGE REUMANN. NOT A CM² OF BLANK PAPER LEFT ON THAT THING!!! and it's not a figure of speech.

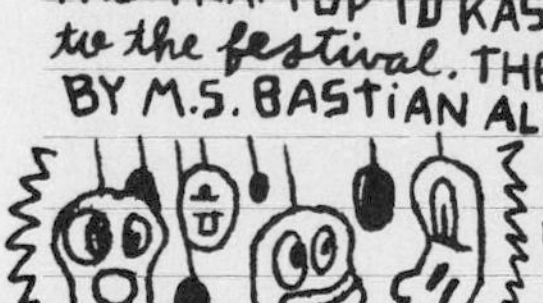

EVERYBODY SEEMED TO BE THERE BUT WE HAD TO GO TO THIS OTHER PARTY WHERE P. BOLINO WAS GOING TO PLAY MUSIC LIVE. WE HEARD SOME OF IT, BUT DIDN'T SEE A THING. THE PLACE WAS PACKED WITH PEOPLE. WE WENT TO THE SECOND FLOOR WHERE A BOOKSTORE WAS and a bar and a STRIPBURGER EXHIBITION. at last we could sit down and talk to PAKITO und CAROLINE.

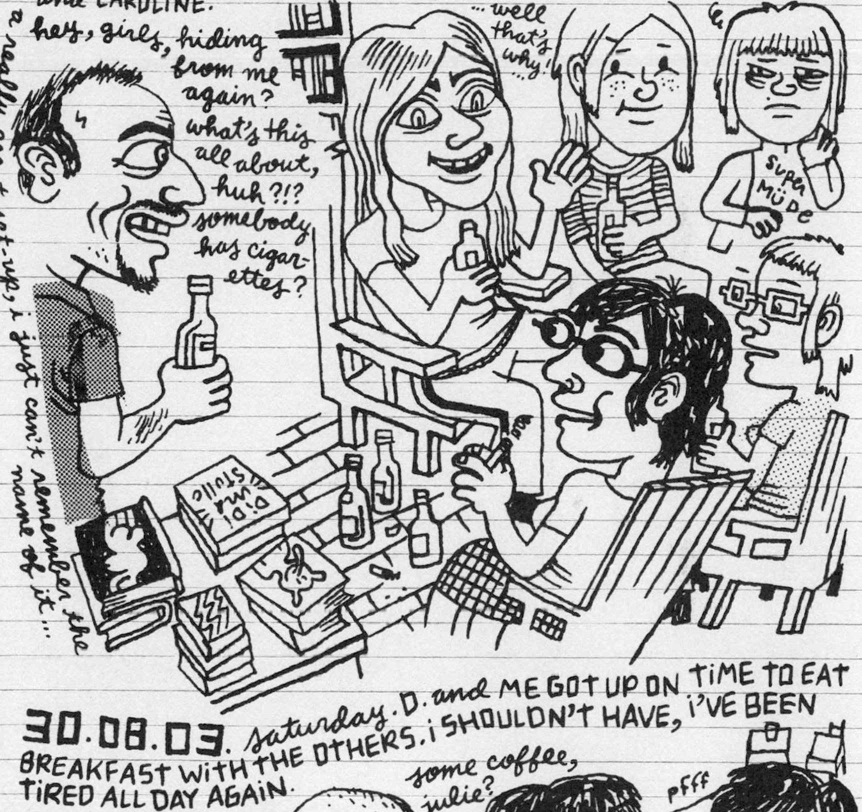

hey, girls, hiding from me again? what's this all about, huh?!? somebody has cigarettes?
a really great set-up, i just can't remember the name of it...
... well that's why! ...
SUPER MÜDE
DiDi und Stulle

30.08.03. saturday. D. and ME GOT UP ON TIME TO EAT BREAKFAST WITH THE OTHERS. i SHOULDN'T HAVE, i'VE BEEN TIRED ALL DAY AGAIN.

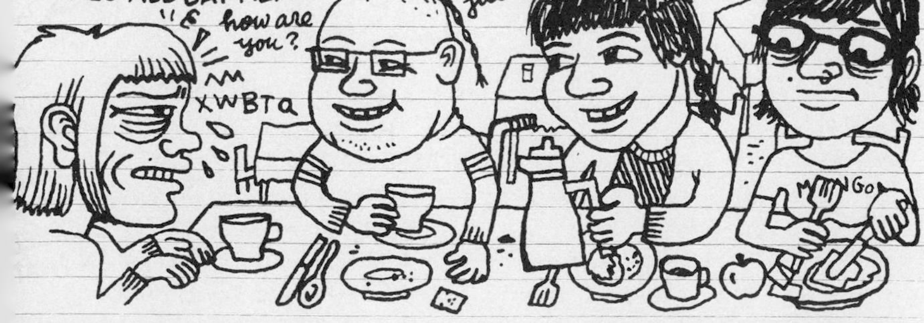

how are you?
XWBTa
some coffee, julie?
pfff
MANGO

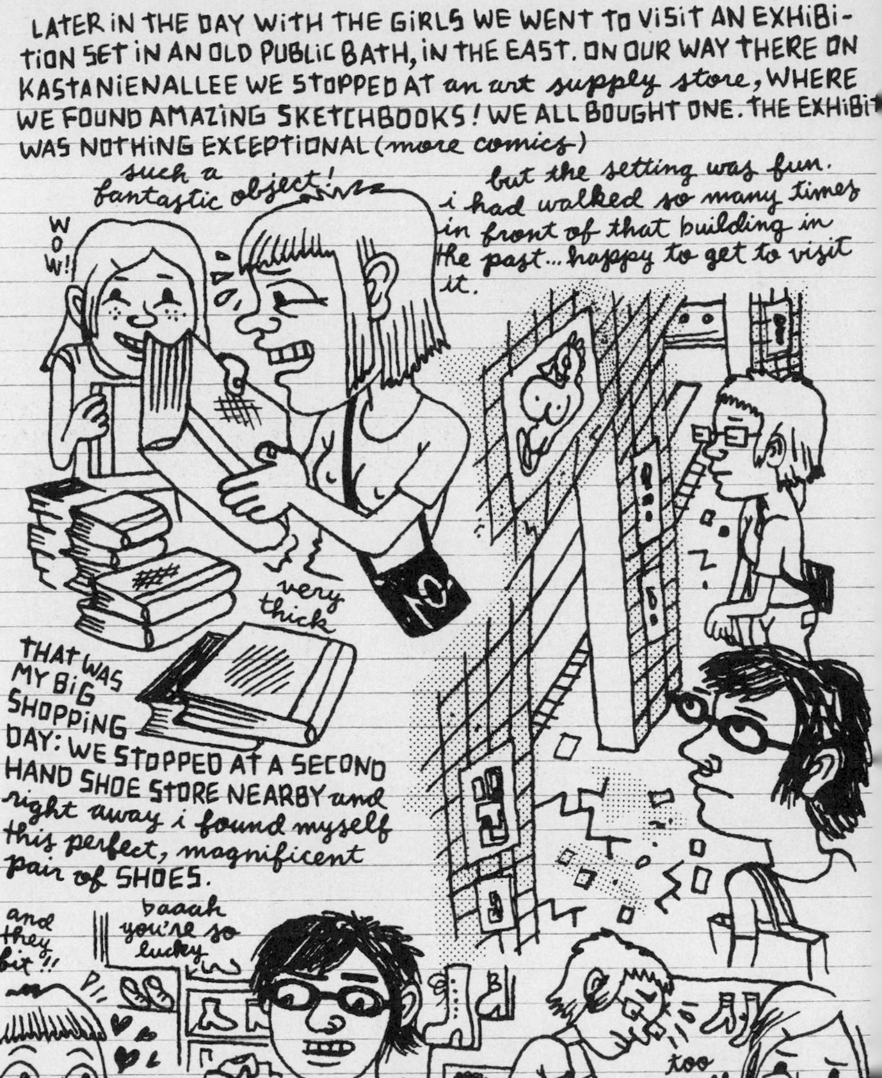
LATER IN THE DAY WITH THE GIRLS WE WENT TO VISIT AN EXHIBITION SET IN AN OLD PUBLIC BATH, IN THE EAST. ON OUR WAY THERE ON KASTANIENALLEE WE STOPPED AT an art supply store, WHERE WE FOUND AMAZING SKETCHBOOKS! WE ALL BOUGHT ONE. THE EXHIBI
WAS NOTHING EXCEPTIONAL (more comics)
but the setting was fun. i had walked so many times in front of that building in the past... happy to get to visit it.
such a fantastic object!
WOW!
very thick
THAT WAS MY BIG SHOPPING DAY: WE STOPPED AT A SECOND HAND SHOE STORE NEARBY and right away i found myself this perfect, magnificent pair of SHOES.
and they fit!!
baaah you're so lucky
too small

AND, IN THE SAME AREA WE WENT TO DRINK A BEER AT THE PRATER BIERGARTEN. IT HAD JUST OPENED FOR THE DAY, IT WAS EMPTY. IT DIDN'T TAKE TOO LONG a rather violent THUNDERSTORM BROKE. we stayed right there, protected by a huge parasol... IT LASTED A GOOD TWENTY MINUTES, NON-STOP.

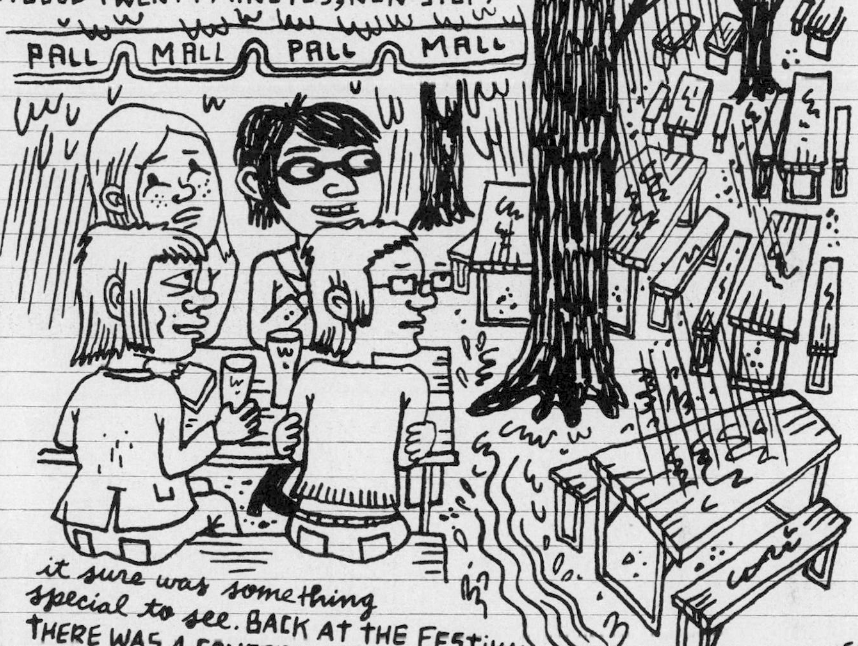
PALL MALL PALL MALL

it sure was something special to see. BACK AT THE FESTIVAL THERE WAS A CONFERENCE ABOUT ENGLISH COMICS. FOOD AND DRINKS FOR FREE. DESPITE THAT WE DIDN'T STAY LONGER THAN FIVE MINUTES. THAT'S HOW BORING IT WAS. WITH BLANQUET, BLEXBOLEX, AND HIS GIRLFRIEND, we went to eat at a restaurant not too far away. NICE EVENING. but once again i was dead tired. this time i went back to the hotel alone, before anybody else.

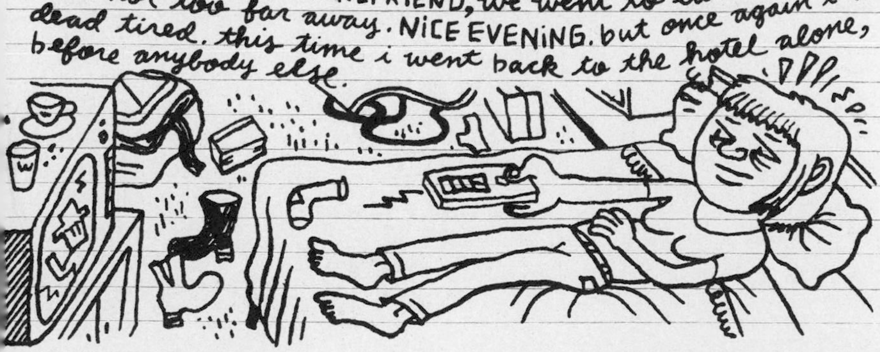

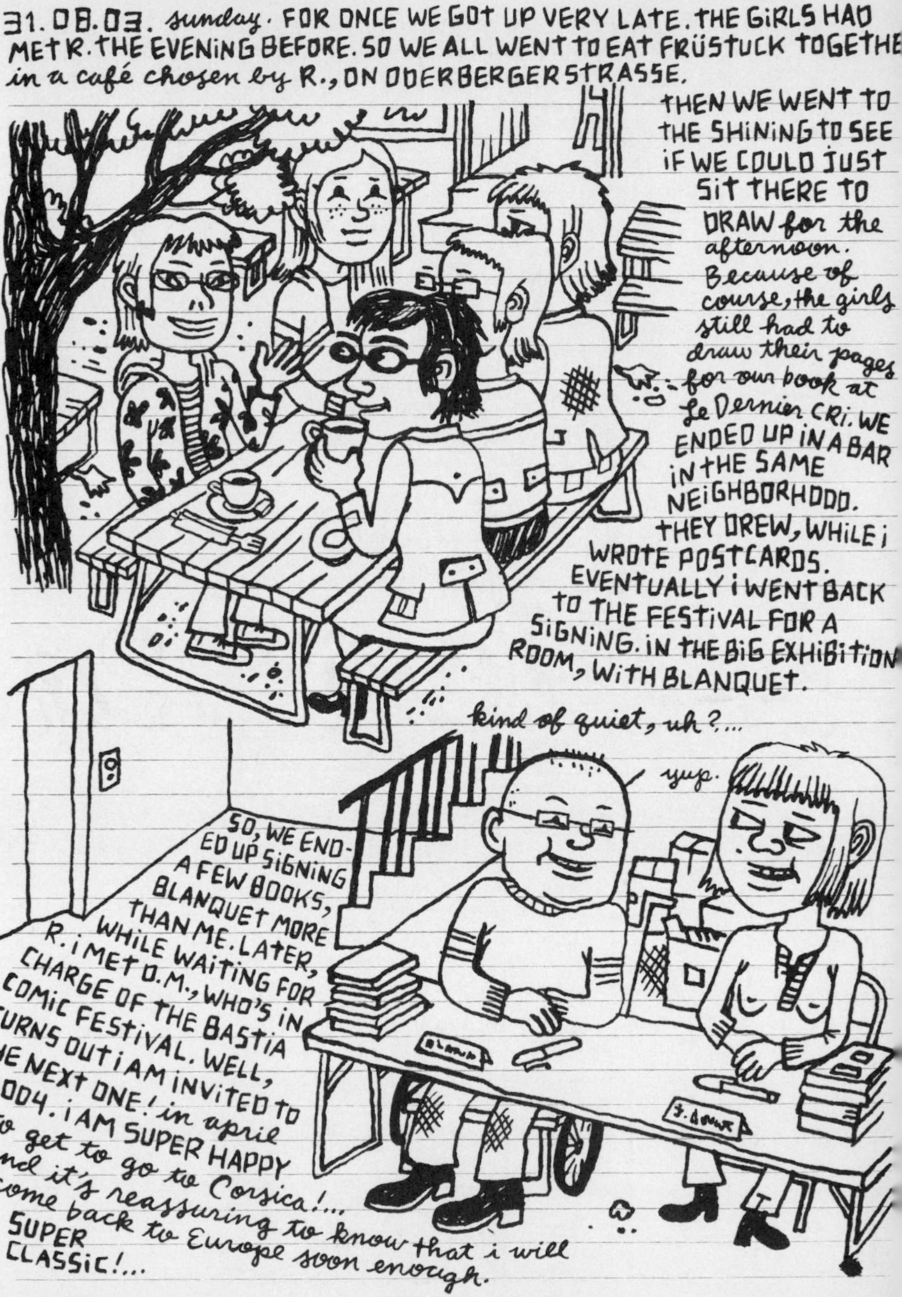
31.08.03. sunday. FOR ONCE WE GOT UP VERY LATE. THE GIRLS HAD MET R. THE EVENING BEFORE. SO WE ALL WENT TO EAT FRÜSTUCK TOGETHE in a café chosen by R., ON ODERBERGERSTRASSE.
THEN WE WENT TO THE SHINING TO SEE iF WE COULD JUST SiT THERE TO DRAW for the afternoon. Because of course, the girls still had to draw their pages for our book at Le Dernier CRi. WE ENDED UP iN A BAR iN THE SAME NEiGHBORHOOD. THEY DREW, WHiLE i WROTE POSTCARDS. EVENTUALLY i WENT BACK TO THE FESTIVAL FOR A SiGNiNG. iN THE BiG EXHiBiTiON ROOM, WiTH BLANQUET.
kind of quiet, uh?...
yup.
SO, WE ENDED UP SiGNiNG A FEW BOOKS, BLANQUET MORE THAN ME. LATER, WHiLE WAiTiNG FOR R. i MET O.M., WHO'S iN CHARGE OF THE BASTiA COMiC FESTiVAL. WELL, TURNS OUT i AM iNVITED TO THE NEXT ONE! in april 2004. i AM SUPER HAPPY to get to go to Corsica!... and it's reassuring to know that i will come back to Europe soon enough.
SUPER CLASSiC!...

WITH R. WE WENT TO AN OPENING (no comics) where the finnish band SELFISH SHELLFISH WERE PLAYING. THE SINGER IS A GOOD FRIEND OF HER'S. THE GIRLS MET US THERE (they had kept on drawing and drinking).

a huge mouth

WE SPENT THE REST OF THE EVENING AT THE SHINING, WHERE EVERYBODY IS. WENT TO BED LATE.

the exhibit is no good but S.S. is good

september 2003

sun	mon	tues	wed	thurs	fri	sat
	1	2	3	4	5	6
7	8	9	10	11	12	13
14	15	16	17	18	19	20
21	22	23	24	25	26	27
28	29	30				

01.09.03. *monday*. WE GOT UP RELATIVELY EARLY TO GO THE FLEA MARKETS. WE STARTED WITH ARKONAPLATZ, *in prenzlauerberg*, MY FAVORITE AT THE TIME. WE WENT THERE WITH BLANQUET *and* OLIVE IN THEIR MINIVAN.

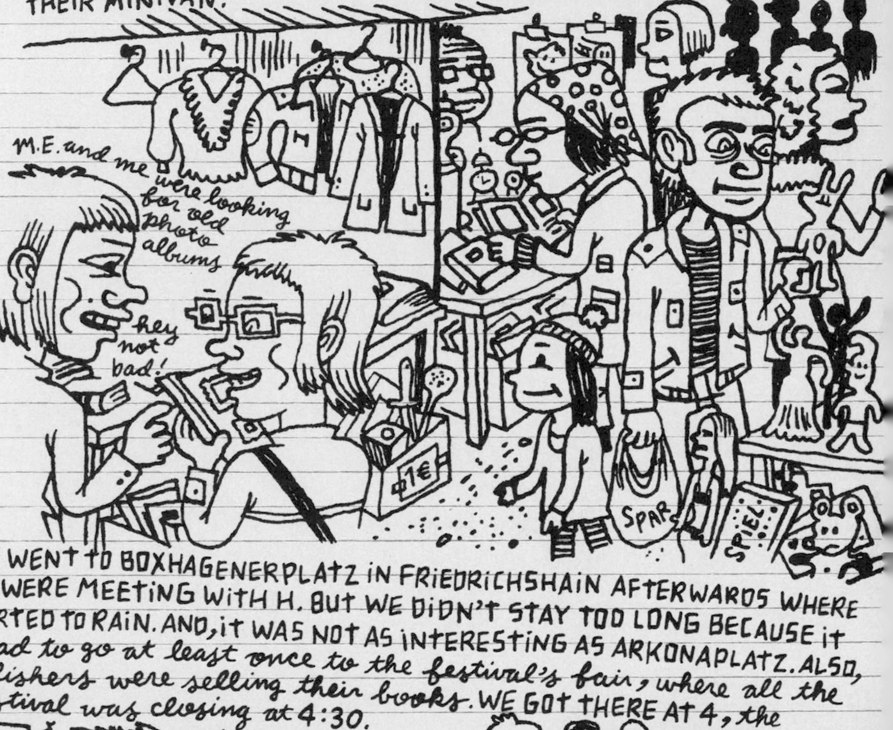

M.E. and me were looking for old photo albums
hey not bad!
1€
SPAR
SPIEL

WE WENT TO BOXHAGENERPLATZ IN FRIEDRICHSHAIN AFTERWARDS WHERE
WE WERE MEETING WITH H. BUT WE DIDN'T STAY TOO LONG BECAUSE IT
STARTED TO RAIN. AND, IT WAS NOT AS INTERESTING AS ARKONAPLATZ. ALSO,
i had to go at least once to the festival's fair, where all the
publishers were selling their books. WE GOT THERE AT 4, *the*
festival was closing at 4:30.

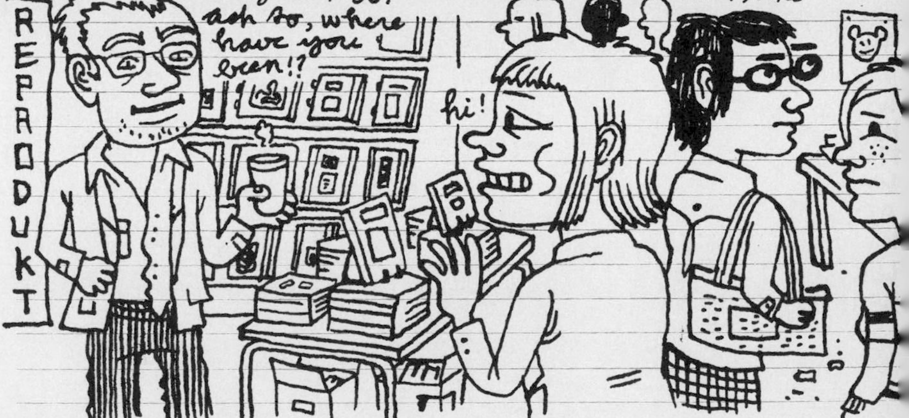

REPRODUKT
ach so, where have you been!?
hi!

THEN WE WENT TO GET OUR MONEY FOR OUR BOOKS SOLD: NOT A BIG SUCCESS, REALLY. THE PLAN WAS TO GO HAVE DINNER WITH BLANQUET AND OLIVE, MAX A. AND H. but i had no more medication with me, so i had to do a round trip to the hotel. AFTER DINNER WITH BLANQUET AND OLIVE and the girls we were invited to Atak's place for a drink.

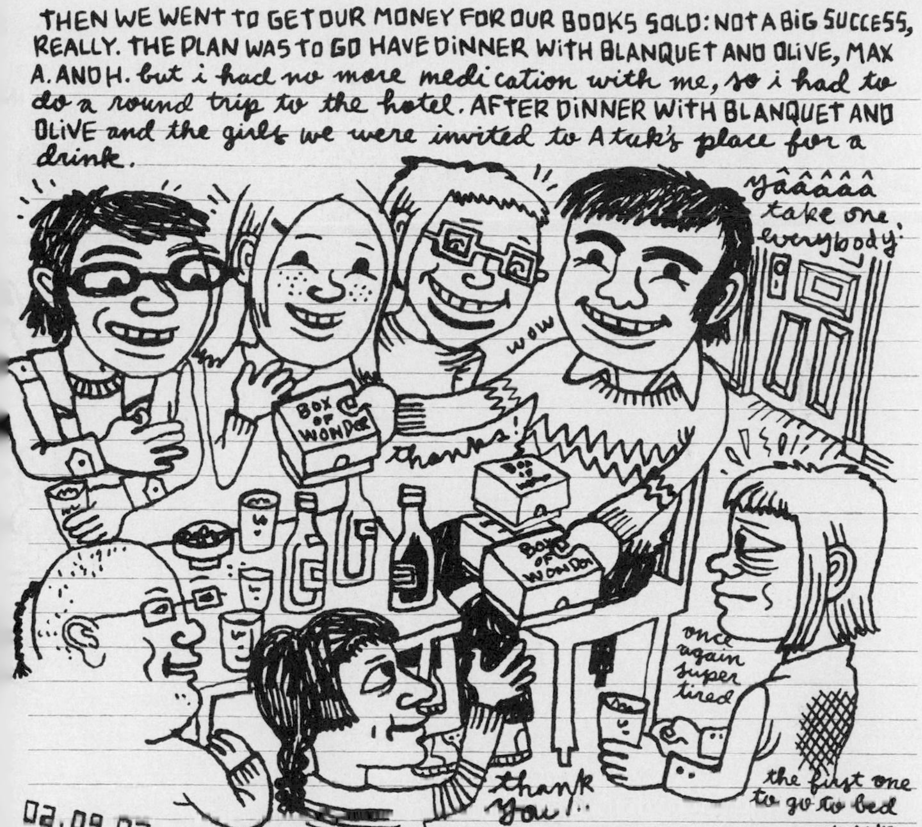

yâââââ take one everybody!
WOW
BOX OF WONDER
thanks!
BOX OF WONDER
once again super tired
thank you...
the first one to go to bed

02.09.03. tuesday. WITH D. WE HAD BREAKFAST WITH BLANQUET AND OLIVE: THEY WERE LEAVING THAT MORNING. i TOOK ADVANTAGE OF IT AND GAVE THEM ALL THE BOOKS i had bought (including the big sketchbook) TO TAKE BACK TO PARIS. NO NEED TO DRAG THOSE BACK WITH ME TO MARSEILLE. WITH D. AFTER WE LEFT THE HOTEL WE REALIZED WE HAD FORGOTTEN TO PAY HER PART OF THE DOUBLE ROOM!

TIME went by so fast... WE WENT TO MEET THE GIRLS AT THEIR HOTEL, WHERE WE COULD STORE OUR LUGGAGE IN A LOCKER. SEHR PRACTISHE.

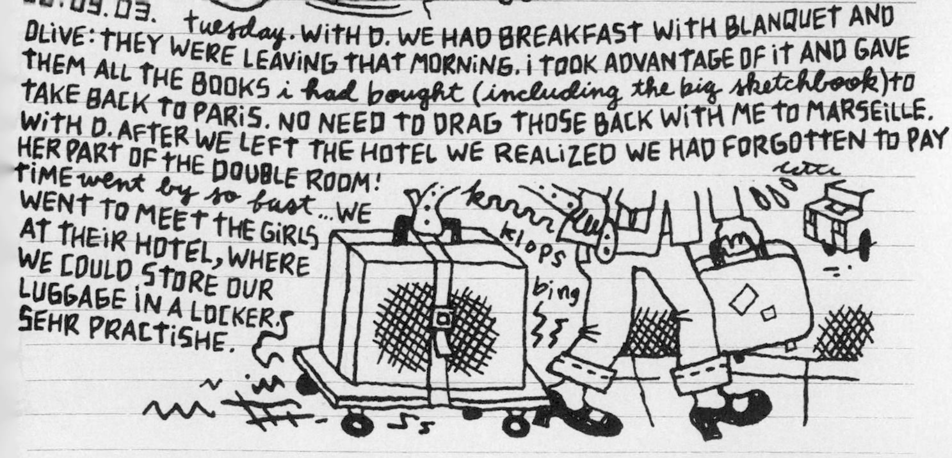

krrrr
klops
bing

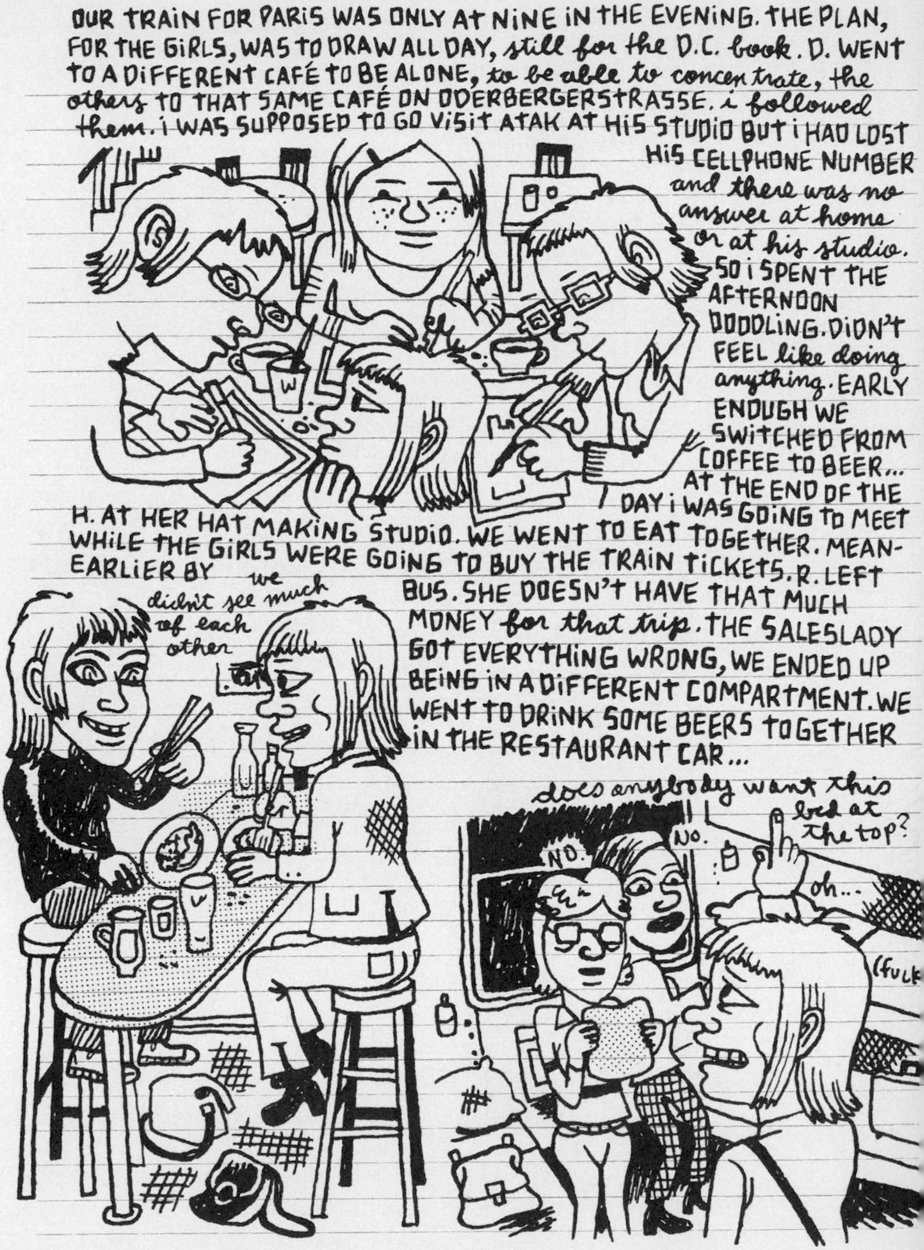
OUR TRAIN FOR PARIS WAS ONLY AT NINE IN THE EVENING. THE PLAN, FOR THE GIRLS, WAS TO DRAW ALL DAY, still for the D.C. book. D. WENT TO A DIFFERENT CAFÉ TO BE ALONE, to be able to concentrate, the others TO THAT SAME CAFÉ ON ODERBERGERSTRASSE. i followed them. i WAS SUPPOSED TO GO VISIT ATAK AT HIS STUDIO BUT i HAD LOST HIS CELLPHONE NUMBER and there was no answer at home or at his studio. SO i SPENT THE AFTERNOON DOODLING. DIDN'T FEEL like doing anything. EARLY ENOUGH WE SWITCHED FROM COFFEE TO BEER...
AT THE END OF THE DAY i WAS GOING TO MEET H. AT HER HAT MAKING STUDIO. WE WENT TO EAT TOGETHER. MEANWHILE THE GIRLS WERE GOING TO BUY THE TRAIN TICKETS. R. LEFT EARLIER BY BUS. SHE DOESN'T HAVE THAT MUCH MONEY for that trip. THE SALESLADY GOT EVERYTHING WRONG, WE ENDED UP BEING IN A DIFFERENT COMPARTMENT. WE WENT TO DRINK SOME BEERS TOGETHER IN THE RESTAURANT CAR...
we didn't see much of each other
does anybody want this bed at the top?
NO.
NO.
oh...
(FUCK

03.09.03. wednesday. DIDN'T SLEEP TOO WELL IN THE COUCHETTE AT THE TOP, BUT AT LEAST i SLEPT. ARRIVED in Paris at gare du nord. WE HAD TO GO TO GARE DE LYON to TAKE OUR TRAIN to Marseille. R. MET WITH US over there but took a train a bit later, cheaper because not at Rush hour. ALL THE WAY DOWN THERE WE COULD SEE FIELDS AND TREES, ALL BURNT BY THE SUN... ONCE IN MARSEILLE, WE HAD NO TROUBLE FINDING OUR WAY TO CAROLINE AND PAKITO'S PLACE. NOT THAT FAR FROM THE TRAIN STATION, thank god!... WE'RE GOING TO LIVE IN THE APARTMENT UPSTAIRS, ONE THAT C.S. RENTED to turn into her own studio. it's rather empty for now. J. IS GOING TO SLEEP AT SOME FRIEND'S PLACE, in the noailles neighborhood

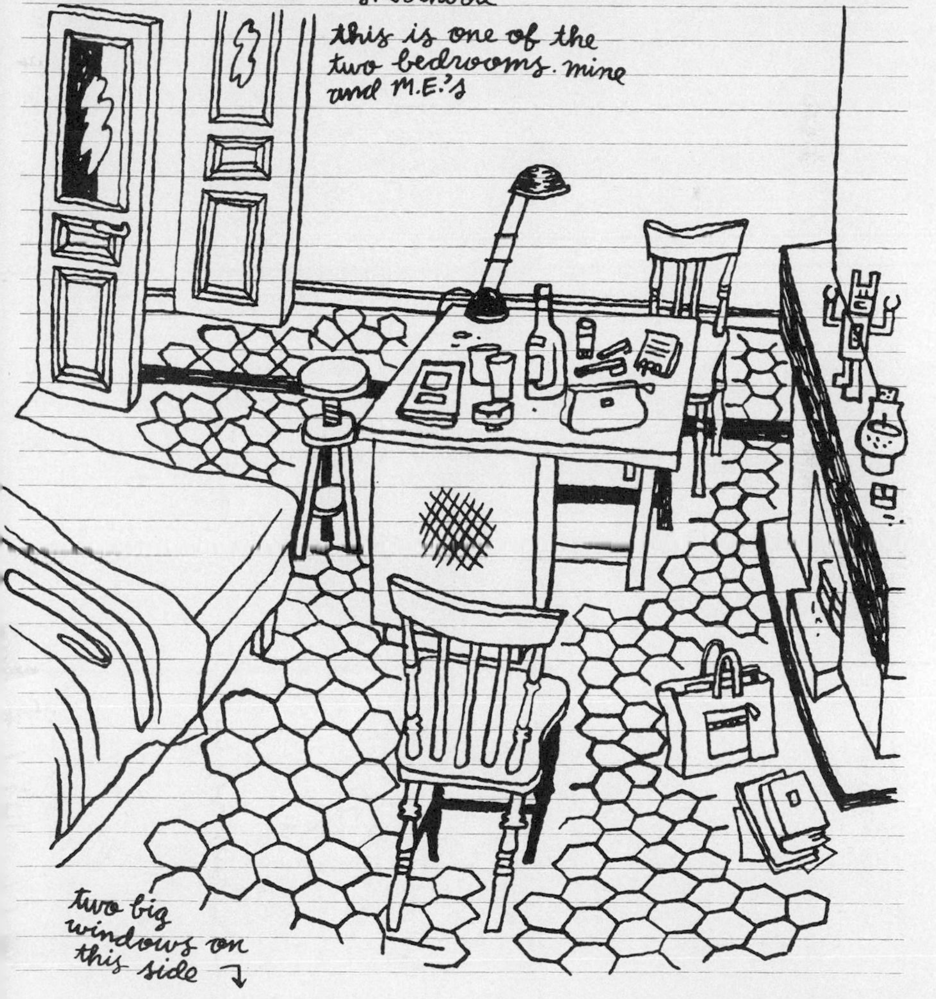
this is one of the two bedrooms. mine and M.E.'s
two big windows on this side ↴

WE WENT OUT FOR A DRINK and then with P.B. WE WENT TO EAT IN A RESTO in the PANIER neighborhood. (C.S. went back home with their kid, O., who just started kindergarden). THERE WAS NOTHING SPECIAL AT THE PANIER, i expected something more lively. WE SAT AT A TERRACE, it's SUMMER AGAIN... LATER ON OUR WAY BACK HOME P.B. SHOWED US A BIT OF THE CITY, WE WERE ALL VERY TIRED.

04.09.03. thursday. P.B. CAME KNOCKING AT OUR DOOR AT TEN, WE WERE just GETTING UP. HE WENT TO HIS WORKSHOP and we went to a café to drink coffee (there's nothing in that flat, no fridge, no stove) AND TO DRAW SOMETHING FOR A FLYER, FOR THAT EXHIBITION WE'RE GONNA HAVE at la Passerelle (a comic book store) which is opening on Friday. WHILE in BERLIN, WE FIGURED OUT A GROUP NAME: Les COPIEUSES (the copiers).

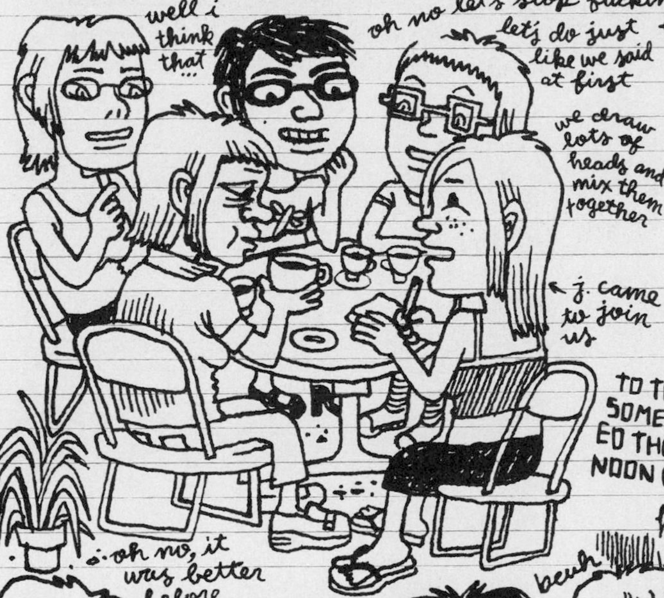

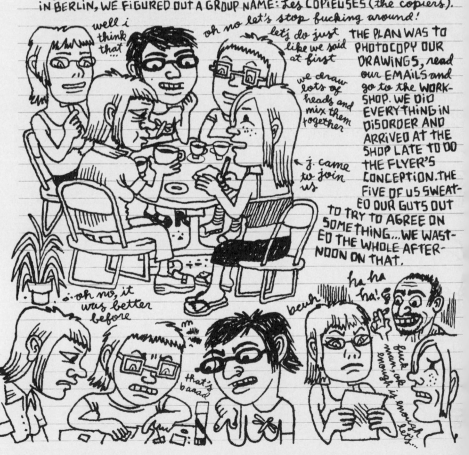

oh no let's stop fucking around!
well i think that ...
let's do just like we said at first
we draw lots of heads and mix them together
j. came to join us

THE PLAN WAS TO PHOTOCOPY OUR DRAWINGS, read our EMAILS and go to the WORKSHOP. WE DID EVERYTHING IN DISORDER AND ARRIVED AT THE SHOP LATE TO DO THE FLYER'S CONCEPTION. THE FIVE OF US SWEATED OUR GUTS OUT TO TRY TO AGREE ON SOMETHING... WE WASTED THE WHOLE AFTERNOON ON THAT.

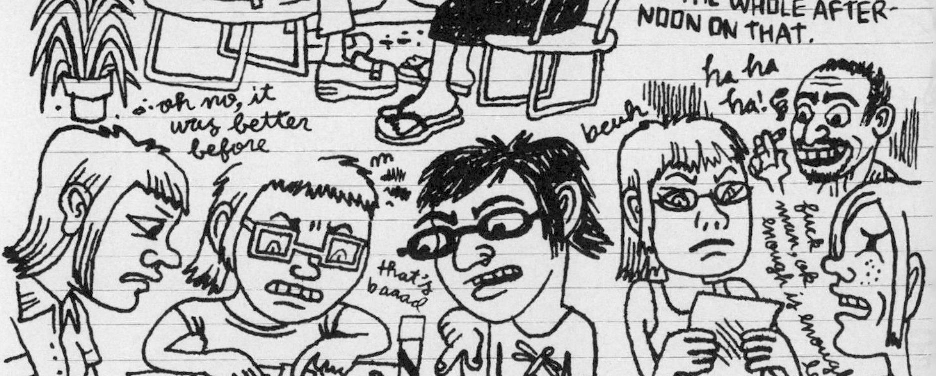

oh no, it was better before
that's baaad
beuh
ha ha ha!
fuck man, ok enough is enough let's...

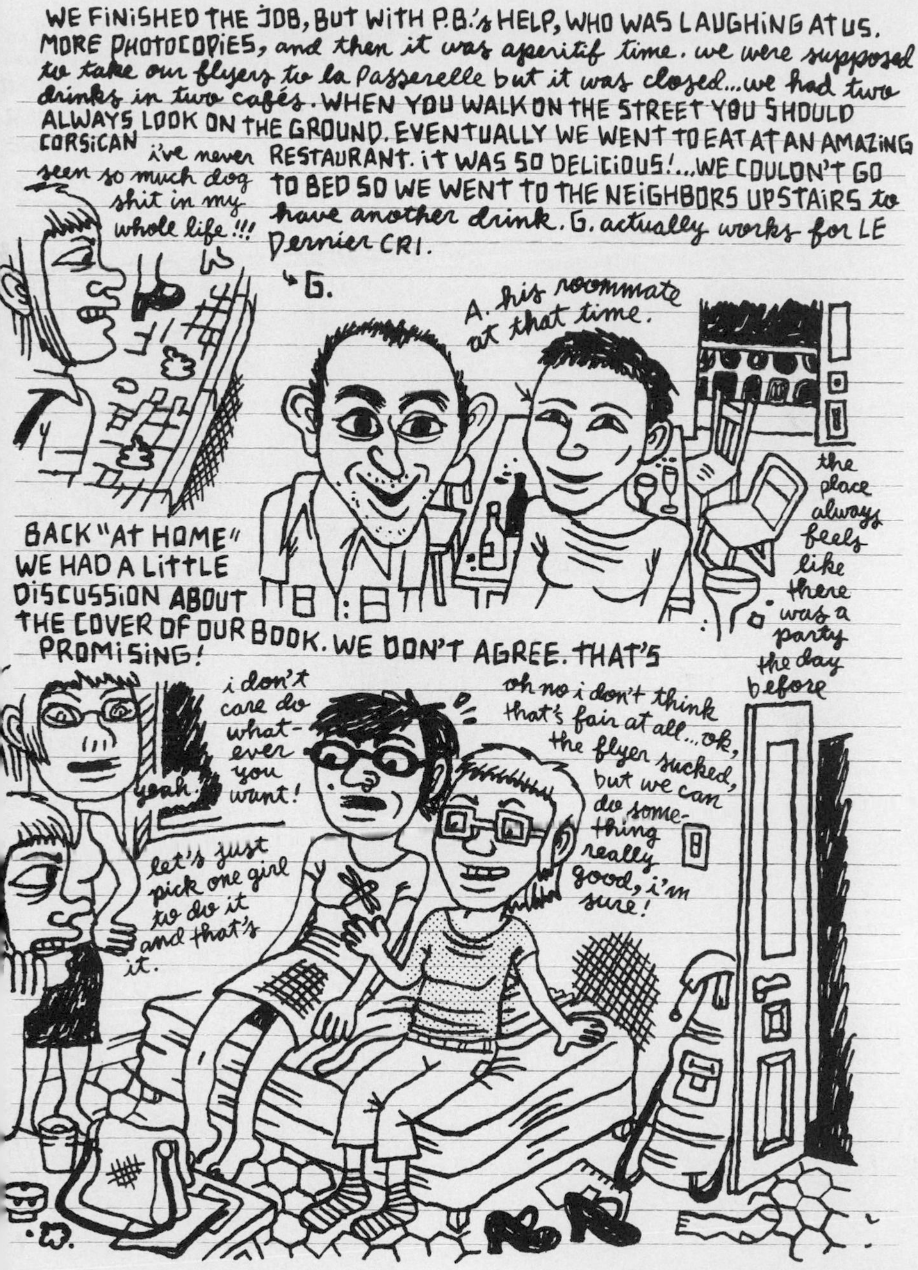
WE FINISHED THE JOB, BUT WITH P.B.'s HELP, WHO WAS LAUGHING AT US. MORE PHOTOCOPIES, and then it was aperitif time. we were supposed to take our flyers to la Passerelle but it was closed... we had two drinks in two cafés. WHEN YOU WALK ON THE STREET YOU SHOULD ALWAYS LOOK ON THE GROUND. EVENTUALLY WE WENT TO EAT AT AN AMAZING CORSICAN RESTAURANT. it WAS SO DELICIOUS!... WE COULDN'T GO TO BED SO WE WENT TO THE NEIGHBORS UPSTAIRS to have another drink. G. actually works for LE Dernier CRI.
i've never seen so much dog shit in my whole life!!!
G.
A. his roommate at that time.
the place always feels like there was a party the day before
BACK "AT HOME" WE HAD A LITTLE DISCUSSION ABOUT THE COVER OF OUR BOOK. WE DON'T AGREE. THAT'S PROMISING!
yeah.
i don't care do whatever you want!
oh no i don't think that's fair at all... ok, the flyer sucked, but we can do something really good, i'm sure!
let's just pick one girl to do it and that's it.

05.09.03. friday. YESTERDAY MORNING WE WENT TO DRINK OUR COFFEE AT G. and A's PLACE. P.B. TOLD US WE COULD USE THEIR KITCHEN (actually it's anoth guy's apartment, a guy who works for le D.C. and who's away). THE GIRLS WER GOING TO DRAW WHILE G. and ME WORKED ON MY IMAGES ON COMPUTER TO HALF-TONE THEM. IT TOOK US FOREVER. LATER P.B. CAME TO CHECK HOW WE WERE DOING

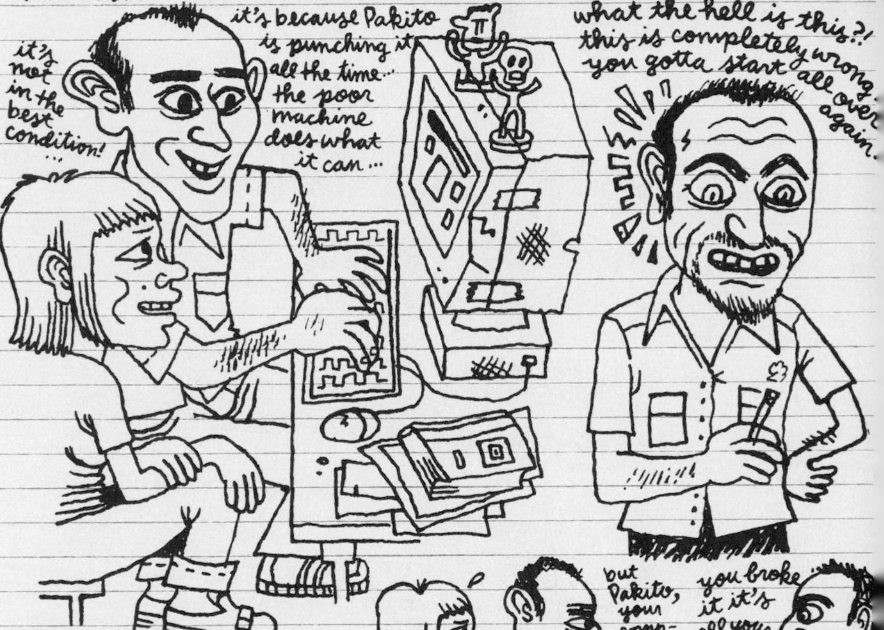
it's not in the best condition! ...
it's because Pakito is punching it all the time... the poor machine does what it can...
what the hell is this?! this is completely wrong. you gotta start all over again.

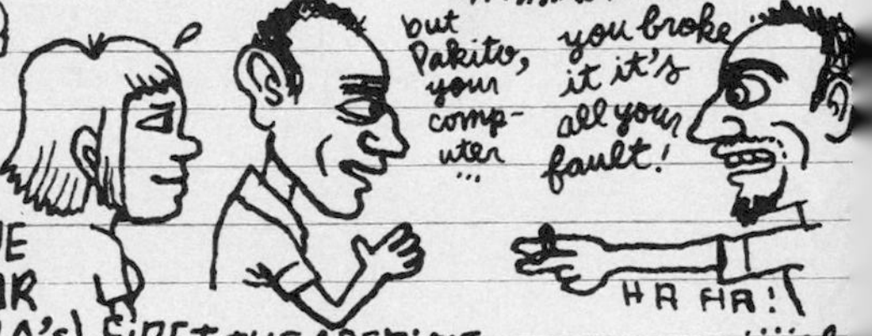
but Pakito, your computer...
you broke it it's all your fault!
HA HA!

SO G. HAD TO DO IT ALL OVER AGAIN. MEANWHILE WITH R. WE WENT TO BUY FOOD TO COOK FOR DINNER THAT EVENING (at G. and A's). FIRST THE APERITIF...

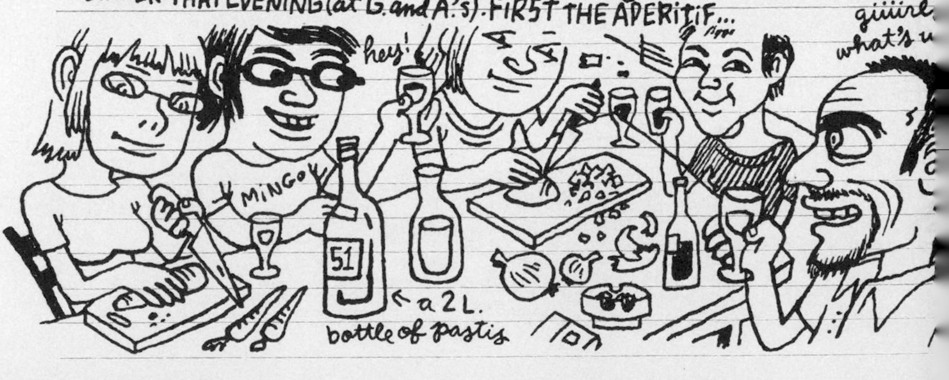
hey!
giiiirl what's u
MINGO
51
← a 2 L. bottle of pastis

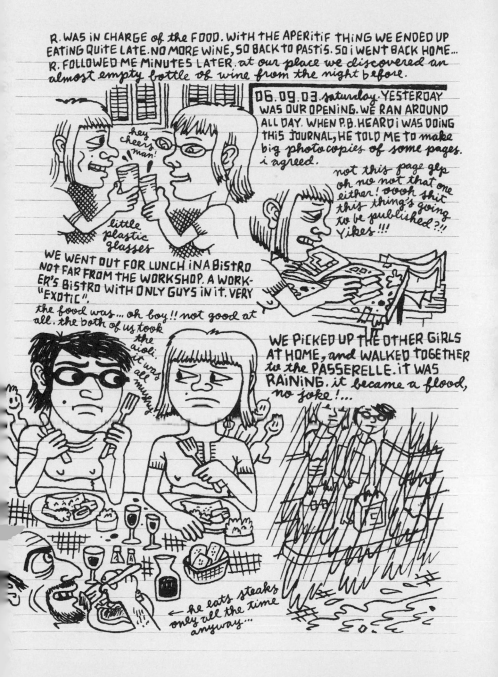

R. WAS IN CHARGE of the FOOD. WITH THE APERITIF THING WE ENDED UP EATING QUITE LATE. NO MORE WINE, SO BACK TO PASTIS. SO i WENT BACK HOME... R. FOLLOWED ME MINUTES LATER. at our place we discovered an almost empty bottle of wine from the night before.

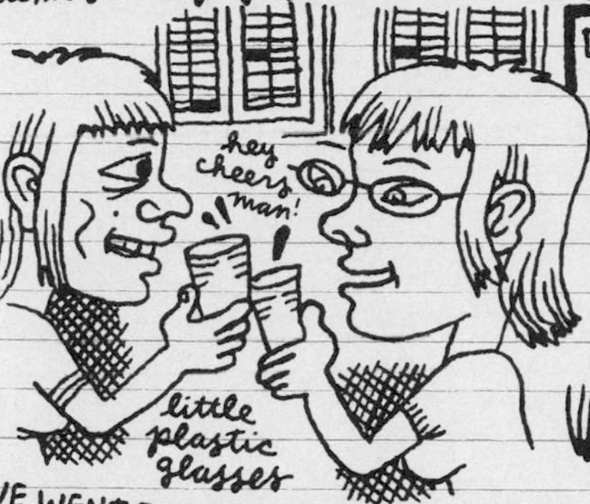
hey cheers man!
little plastic glasses

06.09.03. saturday. YESTERDAY WAS OUR OPENING. WE RAN AROUND ALL DAY. WHEN P.B. HEARD i WAS DOING THIS JOURNAL, HE TOLD ME TO make big photocopies of some pages. i agreed.

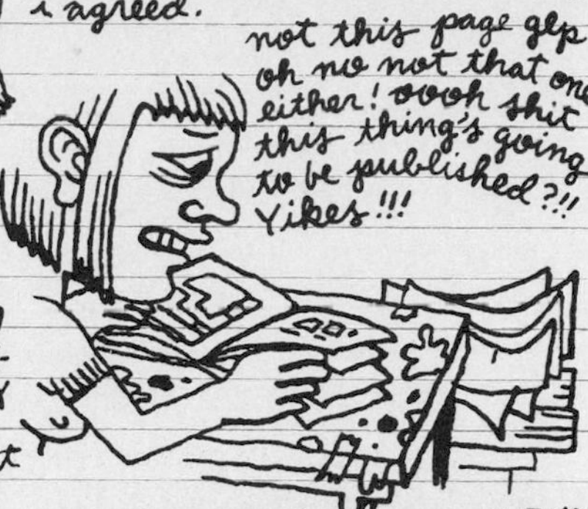
not this page glp
oh no not that one either! oooh shit this thing's going to be published?!! Yikes!!!

WE WENT OUT FOR LUNCH iN A BiSTRO NOT FAR FROM THE WORKSHOP. A WORKER'S BiSTRO WITH ONLY GUYS iN iT. VERY "EXOTiC".

the food was... oh boy!! not good at all. the both of us took the aioli. it was all mushy.

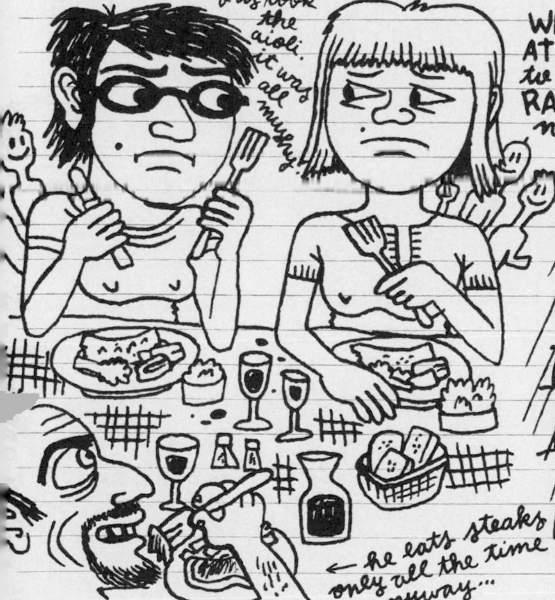
← he eats steaks only all the time anyway...

WE PiCKED UP THE OTHER GiRLS AT HOME, and WALKED TOGETHER to the PASSERELLE. iT WAS RAiNiNG. it became a flood, no joke!...

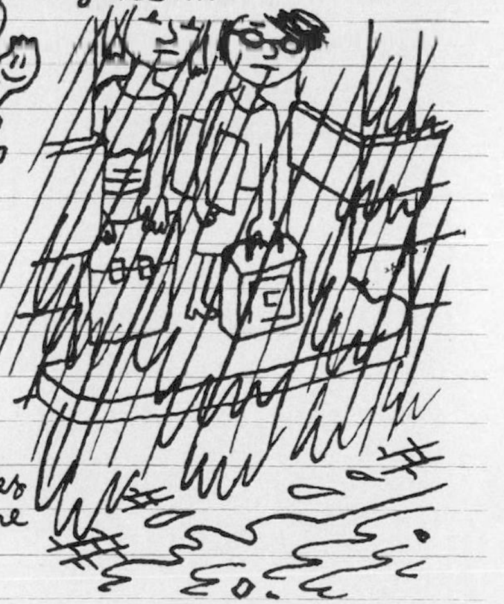

iT NEVER STOPPED, WE HAD TO RUN FAST. WE GOT THERE COMPLETELY SOAKED. fortunately the artwork was very well wrapped. WE SPENT A GOOD 4 HOURS putting up the exhibition... just enough.

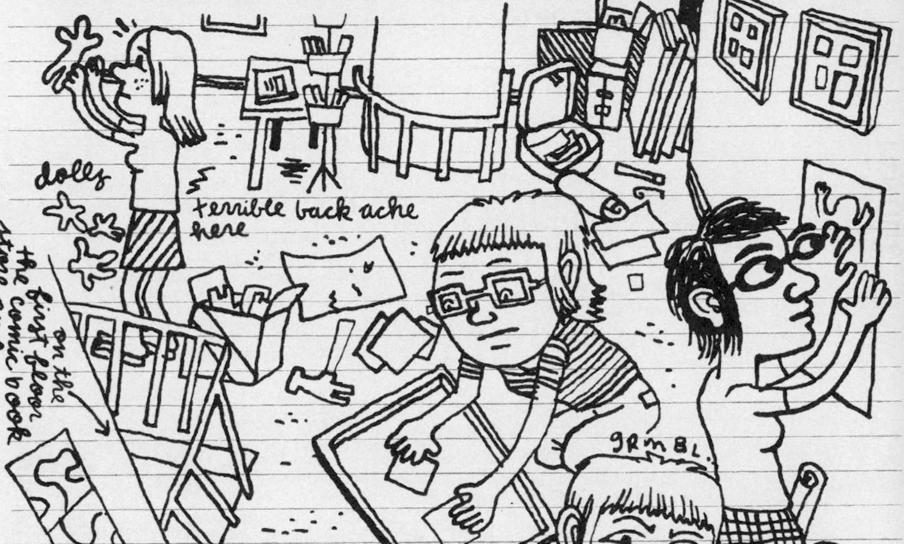
dolls
terrible back ache here
on the first floor the comic book store and a restaurant.
GRmBL.
shitty frames with the "glass" made of plexiglass, all scratched...

PEOPLE ACTUALLY CAME TO THE OPENiNG... ME AND J. STAYED DOWNSTAIRS
THE RESTAURANT AND DRANK BEER, WHiLE D. and M.E. SPENT SOME TIM
AROUND THE EXHiBiTiON... to do the reception, to represent us. AFTE
WARDS P.B. took us TO A COMMUNiTY RESTAURANT. i MET THERE (for the
first time) A GUY...

WHO USED TO BE IN A BAND, TWA, FOR WHICH i HAD DONE A DRAWING FOR ONE OF THEIR SINGLES. WELL NO, THEY USED A DRAWING OF MINE, A COMICS PANEL. that was around 1991. and i couldn't believe my ears when C.S. told me she was actually the one who silkscreen printed those record sleeves!!!... WE DRANK A LOT THAT EVENING.

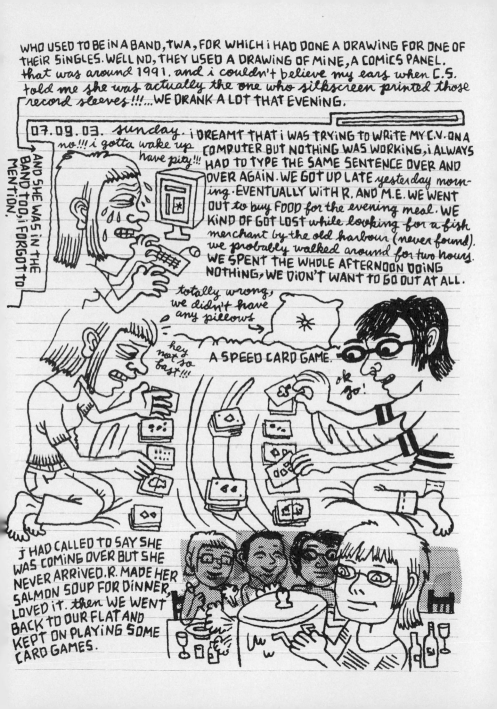

AND SHE WAS IN THE BAND TOO, i FORGOT TO MENTION.

07.09.03. sunday. i DREAMT THAT i WAS TRYING TO WRITE MY C.V. ON A COMPUTER BUT NOTHING WAS WORKING, i ALWAYS HAD TO TYPE THE SAME SENTENCE OVER AND OVER AGAIN. WE GOT UP LATE yesterday morning. EVENTUALLY WITH R. AND M.E. WE WENT OUT to buy FOOD for the evening meal. WE KIND OF GOT LOST while looking for a fish merchant by the old harbour (never found). we probably walked around for two hours. WE SPENT THE WHOLE AFTERNOON DOING NOTHING, WE DIDN'T WANT TO GO OUT AT ALL.

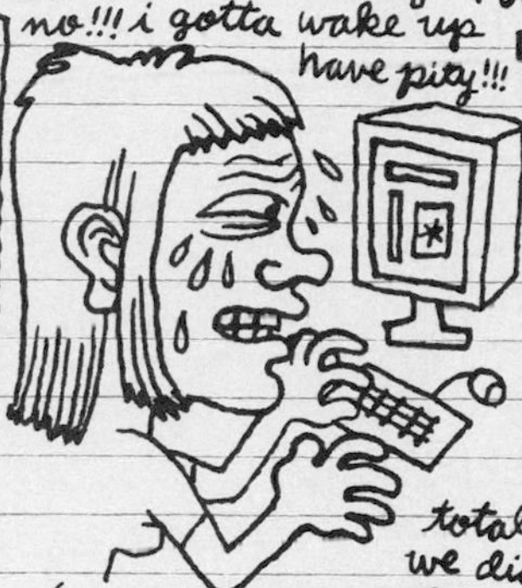
no!!! i gotta wake up
have pity!!!

A SPEED CARD GAME.

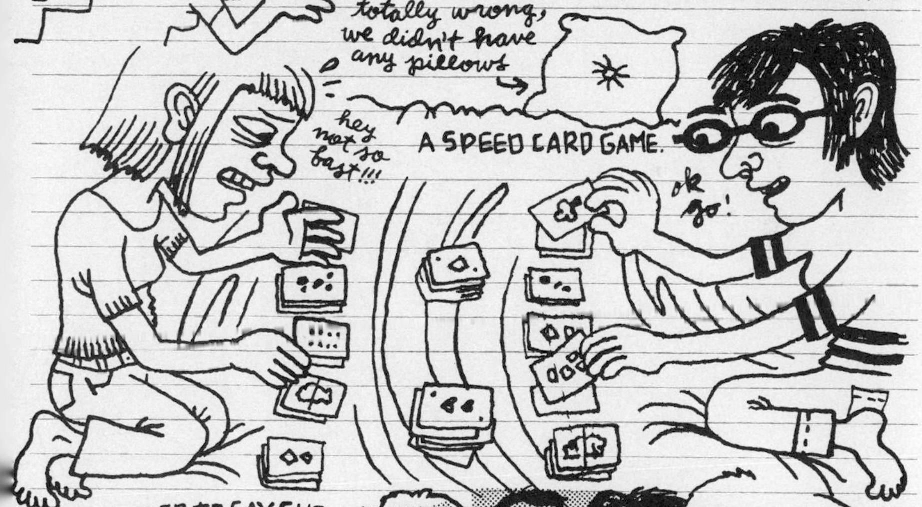
totally wrong, we didn't have any pillows
hey not so fast!!!
ok go!

J HAD CALLED TO SAY SHE WAS COMING OVER BUT SHE NEVER ARRIVED. R. MADE HER SALMON SOUP FOR DINNER, LOVED IT. then WE WENT BACK TO OUR FLAT AND KEPT ON PLAYING SOME CARD GAMES.

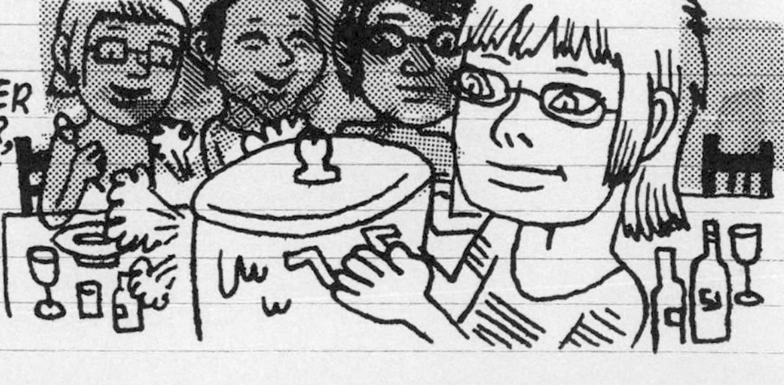

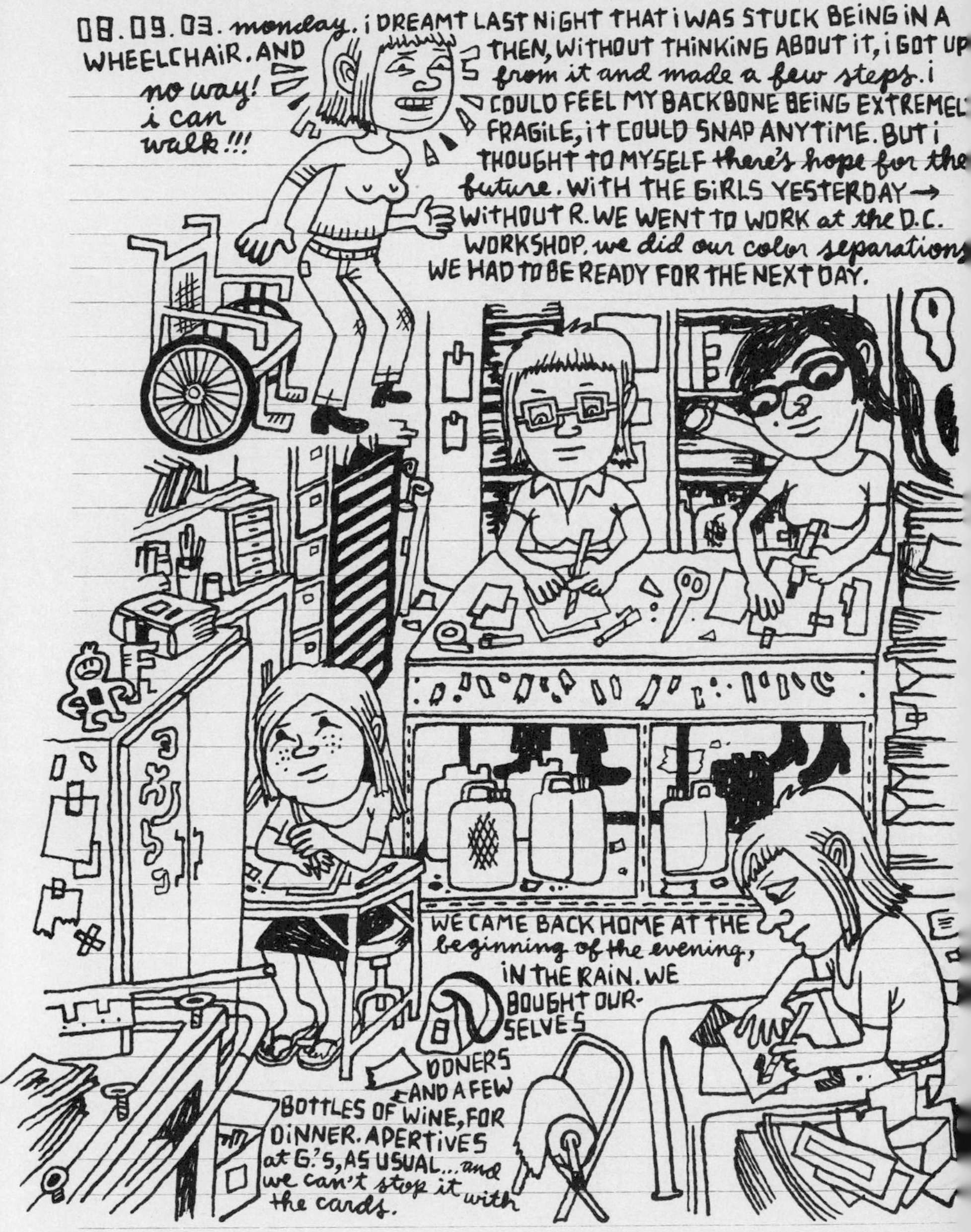
08.09.03. monday. i DREAMT LAST NiGHT THAT i WAS STUCK BEING iN A WHEELCHAIR. AND THEN, WiTHOUT THINKING ABOUT IT, i GOT UP from it and made a few steps. i COULD FEEL MY BACKBONE BEING EXTREMELY FRAGILE, iT COULD SNAP ANYTiME. BUT i THOUGHT TO MYSELF there's hope for the future. WiTH THE GiRLS YESTERDAY → WiTHOUT R. WE WENT TO WORK at the D.C. WORKSHOP, we did our color separations WE HAD TO BE READY FOR THE NEXT DAY.
no way! i can walk!!!
WE CAME BACK HOME AT THE beginning of the evening, IN THE RAIN. WE BOUGHT OUR-SELVES DONERS AND A FEW BOTTLES OF WiNE, FOR DiNNER. APERTiVES at G.'S, AS USUAL... and we can't stop it with the cards.

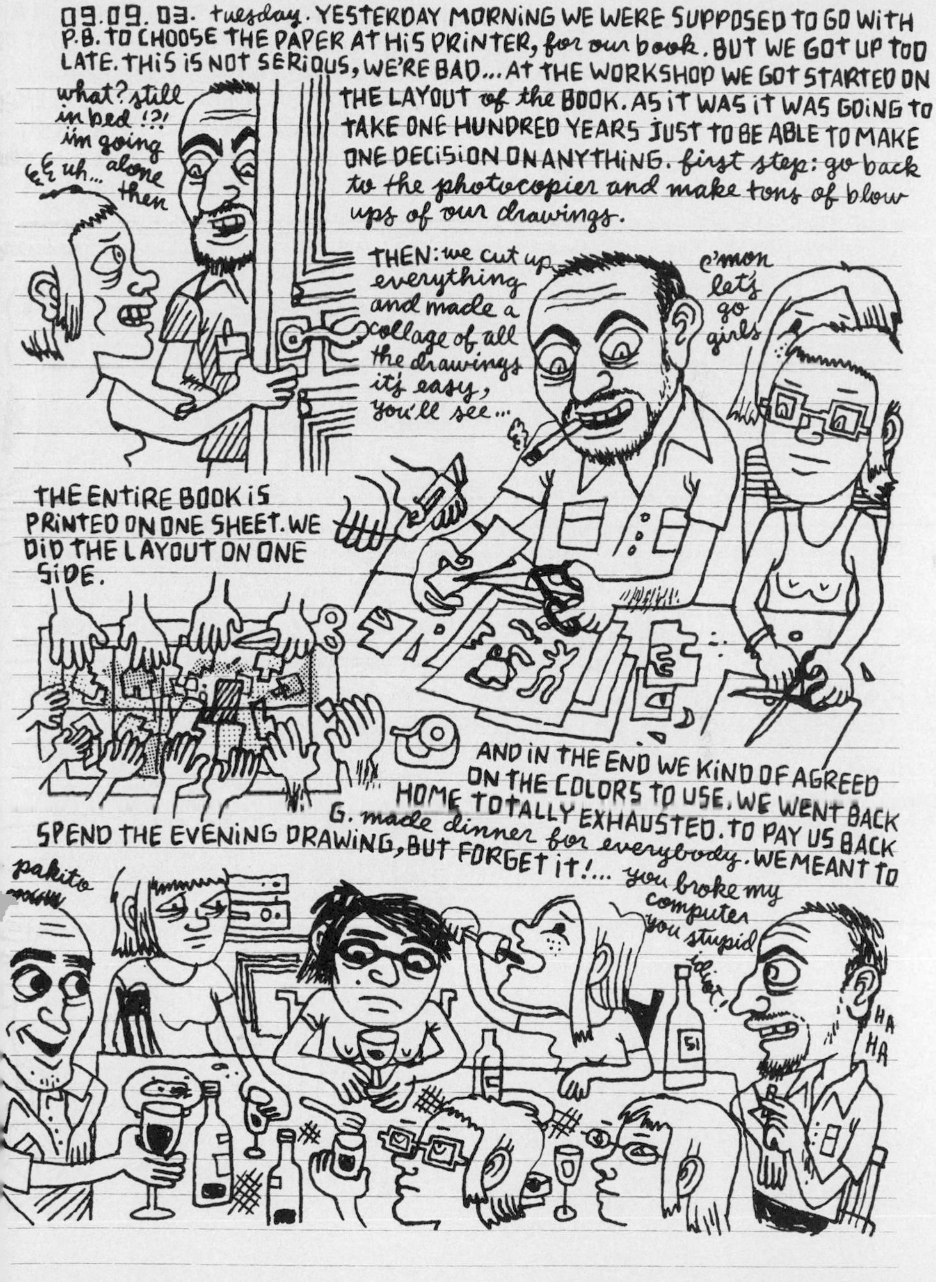
09.09.03. tuesday. YESTERDAY MORNING WE WERE SUPPOSED TO GO WITH P.B. TO CHOOSE THE PAPER AT HIS PRINTER, for our book. BUT WE GOT UP TOO LATE. THIS IS NOT SERIOUS, WE'RE BAD... AT THE WORKSHOP WE GOT STARTED ON THE LAYOUT of the BOOK. AS IT WAS IT WAS GOING TO TAKE ONE HUNDRED YEARS JUST TO BE ABLE TO MAKE ONE DECISION ON ANYTHING. first step: go back to the photocopier and make tons of blow ups of our drawings.
what? still in bed !?! im going alone then
εε uh...
THEN: we cut up everything and made a collage of all the drawings it's easy, you'll see...
c'mon let's go girls
THE ENTIRE BOOK IS PRINTED ON ONE SHEET. WE DID THE LAYOUT ON ONE SIDE.
AND IN THE END WE KIND OF AGREED ON THE COLORS TO USE. WE WENT BACK HOME TOTALLY EXHAUSTED. TO PAY US BACK G. made dinner for everybody. WE MEANT TO SPEND THE EVENING DRAWING, BUT FORGET IT!...
pakito
you broke my computer you stupid idiot
HA HA
51

10.09.03. wednesday. WE GOT UP EARLY, FOR ONCE. WE HAD TO MAKE DRAWINGS TO DO THE COVER. MORE PHOTOCOPIES, THEN THE WORKSHOP. WE STARTED TO WORK ON THE OTHER SIDE of the sheet, of the layout thing.

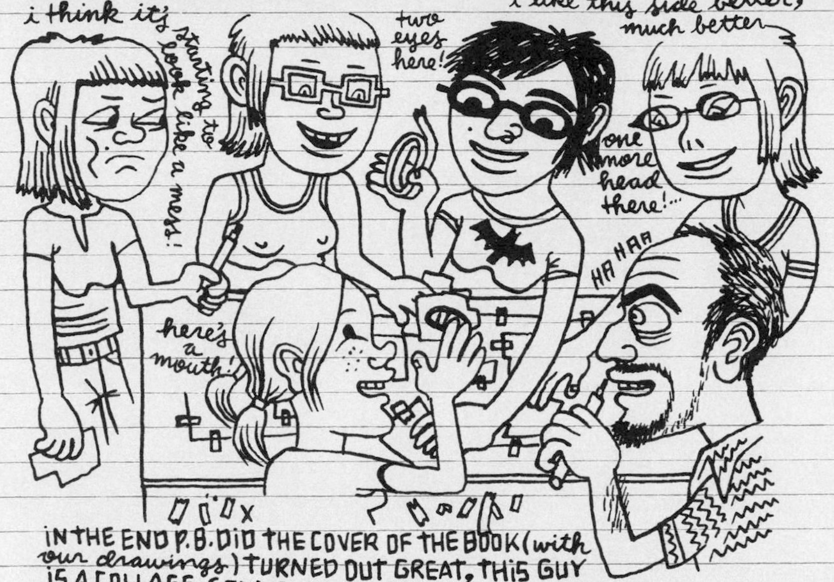

IN THE END P.B. DID THE COVER OF THE BOOK (with our drawings) TURNED OUT GREAT, THIS GUY IS A COLLAGE GENIUS. THE LAYOUT ALL FINISHED, WE PREPARED THE SCREEN SO WE COULD PRINT THE NEXT DAY. AFTER THAT LONG DAY OF WORK, WITH THE GIRLS WE WENT TO READ OUR EMAILS and had a beer, between us.

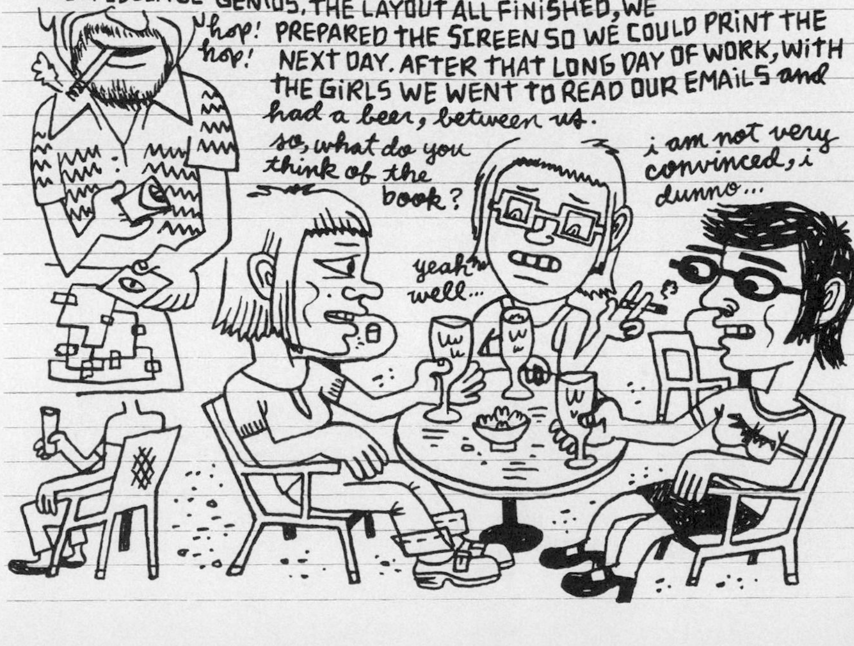

11.09.03. thursday. FOR THE PRINTING JOB WE FORMED TWO TEAMS: THAT MORNING M.E. and R. WERE HELPING PAKITO. D. AND ME WANDERED ABOUT, WENT TO WRITE some E-MAILS, J. STAYED HOME TO REST, BECAUSE OF HER BACK PAIN, WHICH IS NOT IMPROVING AT ALL. at two with D. we went to the shop, it was our turn.

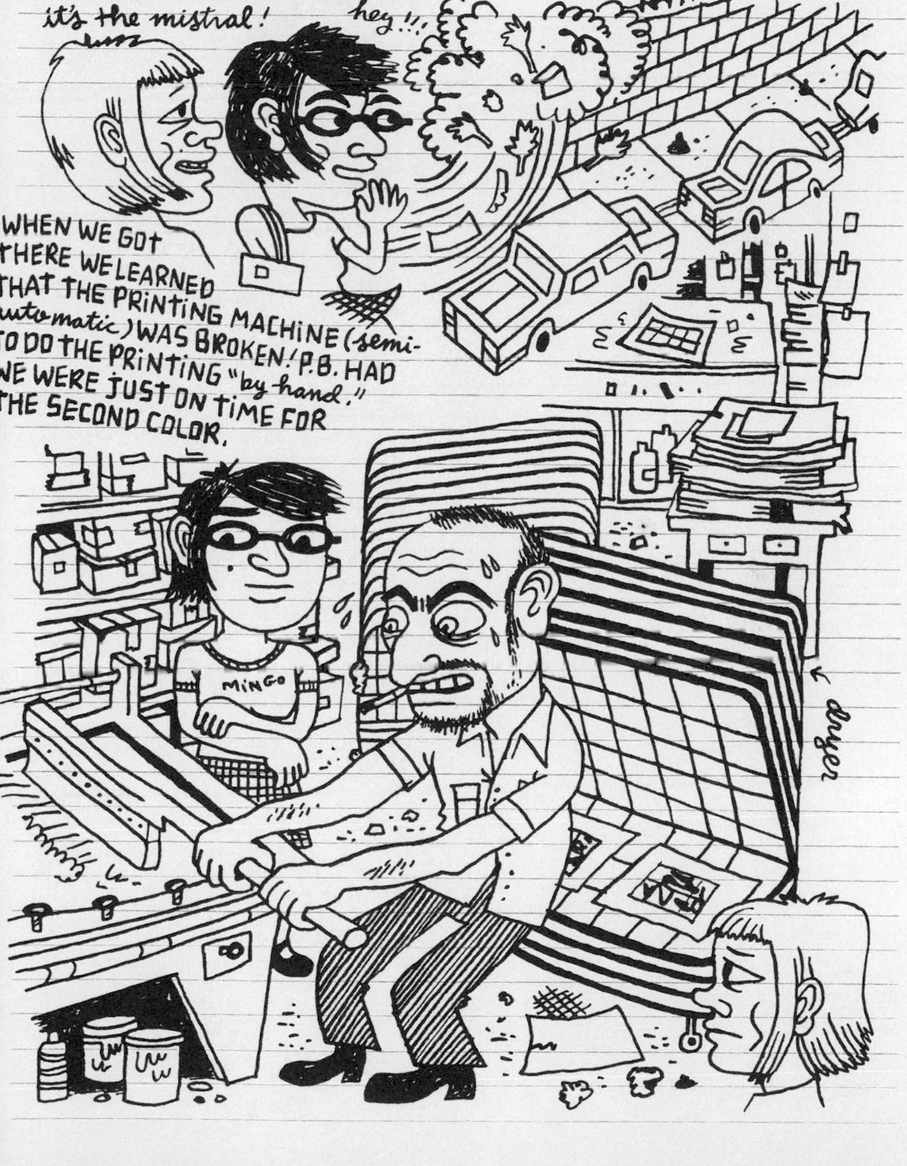

it's the mistral!
hey!!!
WHEN WE GOT THERE WE LEARNED THAT THE PRINTING MACHINE (semi-automatic) WAS BROKEN! P.B. HAD TO DO THE PRINTING "by hand." WE WERE JUST ON TIME FOR THE SECOND COLOR.
MINGO
dryer

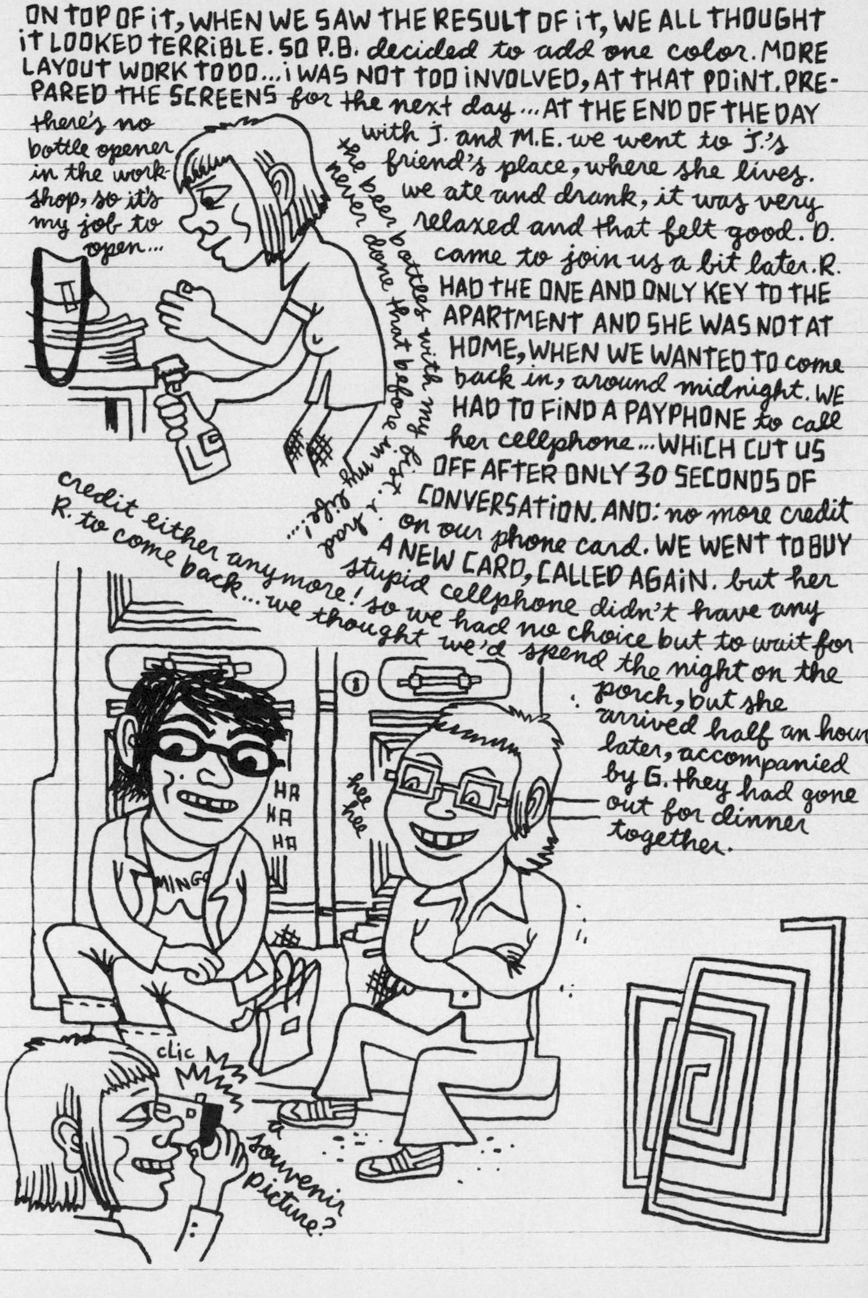
ON TOP OF iT, WHEN WE SAW THE RESULT OF iT, WE ALL THOUGHT iT LOOKED TERRIBLE. SO P.B. decided to add one color. MORE LAYOUT WORK TO DO... i WAS NOT TOO iNVOLVED, AT THAT POiNT. PREPARED THE SCREENS for the next day... AT THE END OF THE DAY
there's no bottle opener in the workshop, so it's my job to open...
the beer bottles with my fist... I never done that before in my life!...
with J. and M.E. we went to J.'s friend's place, where she lives. we ate and drank, it was very relaxed and that felt good. D. came to join us a bit later. R. HAD THE ONE AND ONLY KEY TO THE APARTMENT AND SHE WAS NOT AT HOME, WHEN WE WANTED TO come back in, around midnight. WE HAD TO FiND A PAYPHONE to call her cellphone... WHiCH CUT US OFF AFTER ONLY 30 SECONDS OF CONVERSATiON. AND: no more credit on our phone card. WE WENT TO BUY A NEW CARD, CALLED AGAiN. but her stupid cellphone didn't have any credit either anymore! so we had no choice but to wait for R. to come back... we thought we'd spend the night on the porch, but she arrived half an hour later, accompanied by G. they had gone out for dinner together.
HA HA HA
hee hee
clic
a souvenir picture?

12.09.03. friday. IT WAS SEPTEMBER ELEVENTH YESTERDAY, and CAROLINE'S BIRTHDAY. that morning ME AND D. WENT TO HELP P.B. PRINT. A TECHNICIAN WAS SUPPOSED TO COME CHECK OUT the broken machine. WE PRINTED A THIRD COLOR and then it was lunch time. thank god we went to another bistrot. i did JUST LIKE P.B. i ATE A RIBSTEAK. back at the workshop the girls were there waiting for us, plus a JOURNALIST AND A PHOTOGRAPHER FROM THE MARSIELLE-HEBDO. FOR US! SO WE GOT INTERVIEWED, PHOTOGRAPHED...

i had another meeting in a café later, in front of the Palais → LONGCHAMP, with another journalist. this time it was about my new book at Seuil... at last → i could see a copy of it.

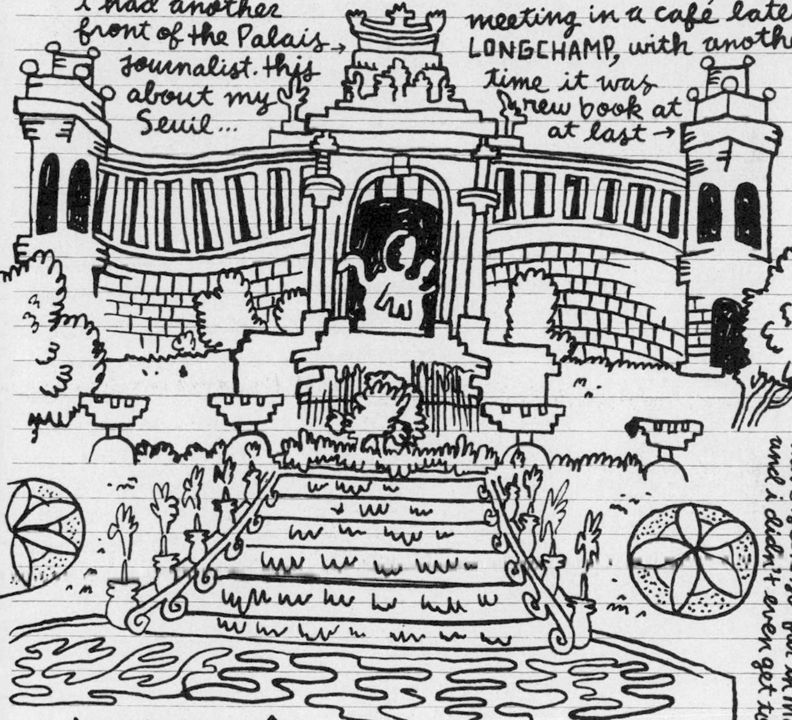

that palais longchamp is just about the only thing i have seen so far in Marseille! and i didn't even get to go in!

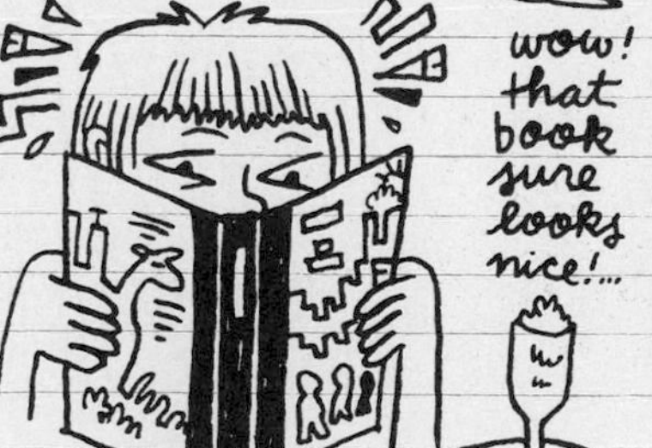

wow! that book sure looks nice!...

THE JOURNALIST SAID HE LIKED THE BOOK, i WAS HAPPY TO HEAR THAT. i HAD NO IDEA WHAT KIND OF RECEPTION IT WOULD GET. BACK TO WORK. THREE COLORS WERE PRINTED THAT DAY.

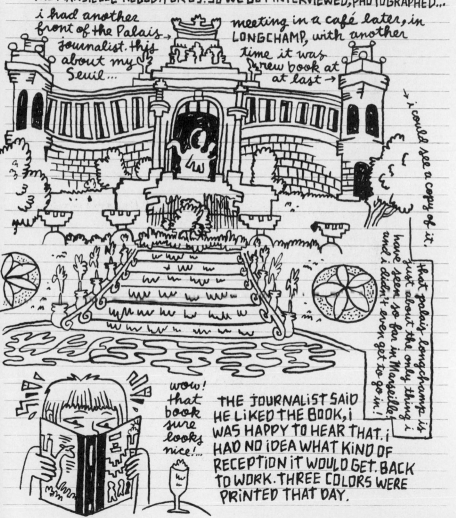

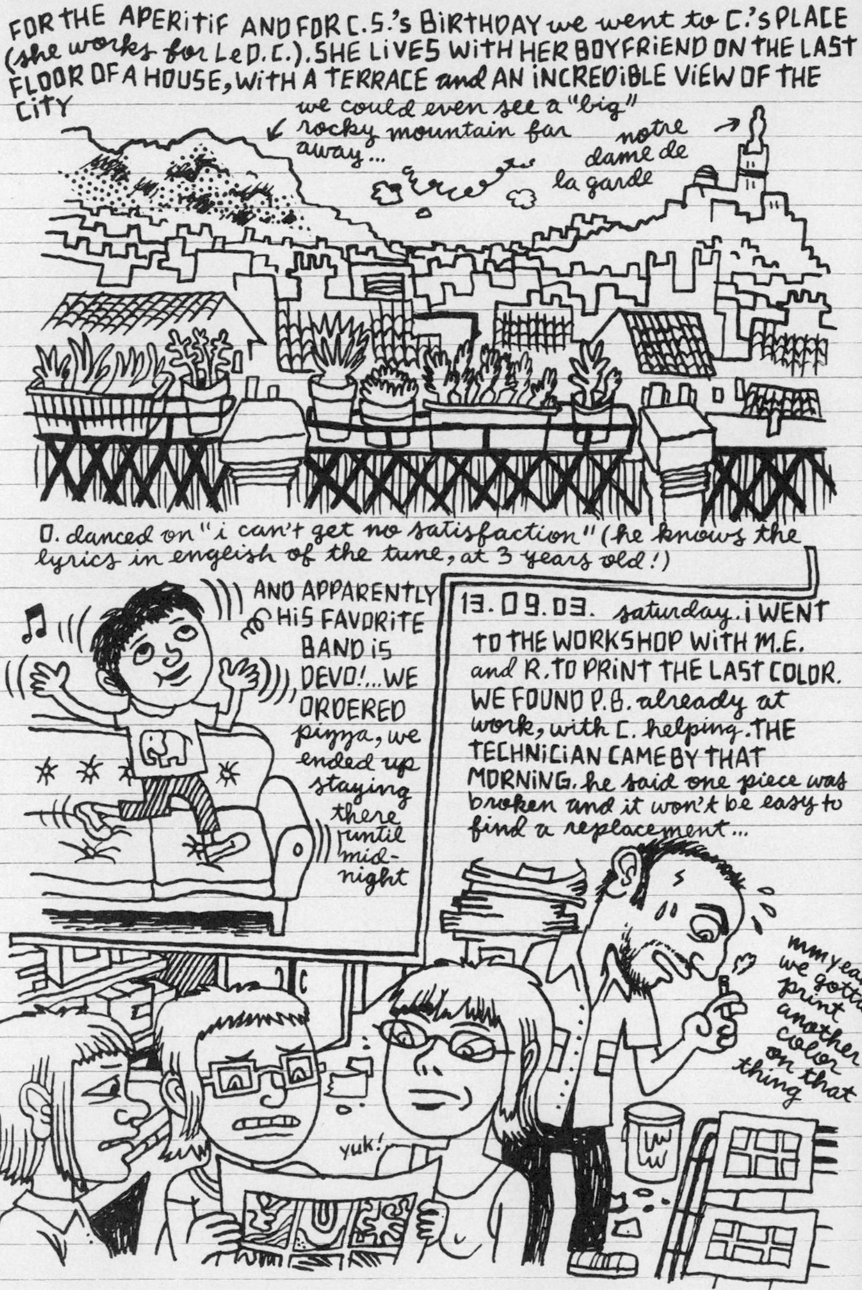
FOR THE APERITIF AND FOR C.S.'s BIRTHDAY we went to C.'s PLACE (she works for Le D.C.). SHE LIVES WITH HER BOYFRIEND ON THE LAST FLOOR OF A HOUSE, WITH A TERRACE and AN INCREDIBLE VIEW OF THE CITY
we could even see a "big" rocky mountain far away...
notre dame de la garde
O. danced on "i can't get no satisfaction" (he knows the lyrics in english of the tune, at 3 years old!)
AND APPARENTLY HIS FAVORITE BAND IS DEVO!... WE ORDERED pizza, we ended up staying there until mid-night
13.09.03. saturday. i WENT TO THE WORKSHOP WITH M.E. and R. TO PRINT THE LAST COLOR. WE FOUND P.B. already at work, with C. helping. THE TECHNICIAN CAME BY THAT MORNING. he said one piece was broken and it won't be easy to find a replacement...
YUK!
mmyeah we gotta print another color on that thing

WHEN WE GOT BACK from lunch, J. and D. WERE THERE TO HELP with that VERY LAST CHANCE EXTRA COLOR. D. WAS IN A GRUMPY MOOD. P.B. WOULD HAVE REALLY TRIED EVERYTHING TO PLEASE US, and HE PRINTED THE WHOLE THING BY HAND. WE WENT BACK HOME FOR THE APERITIF, feeling downcast. BUT, TURNED OUT NOBODY HAD THE KEY. R. went away with ours earlier and she was not there. P.B. didn't have his... WE ENDED UP at G.'s place drinking pastis for hours, waiting for the keys.

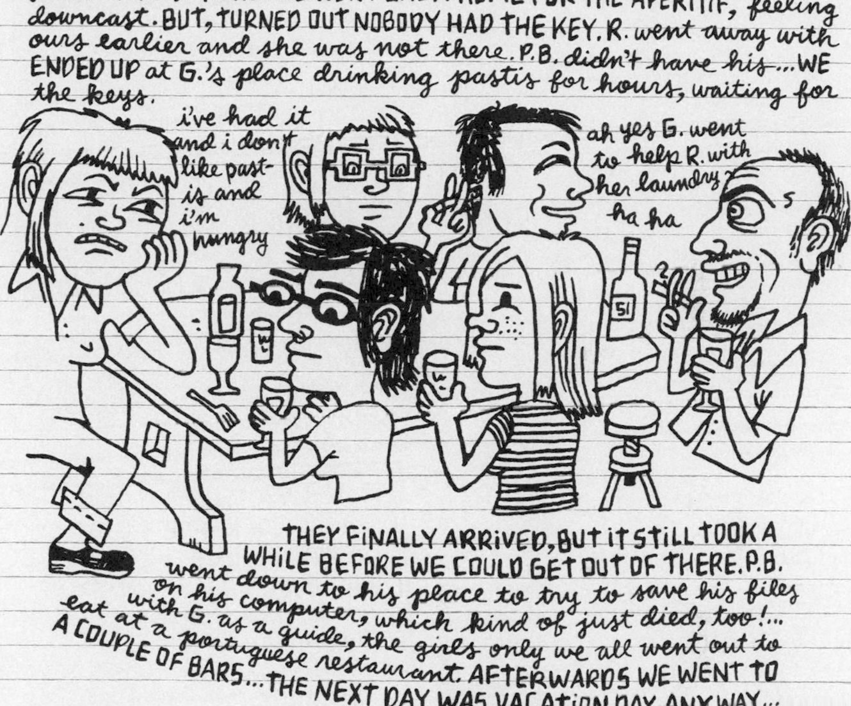
i've had it and i don't like pastis and i'm hungry
ah yes G. went to help R. with her laundry?
ha ha
?
51

THEY FINALLY ARRIVED, BUT IT STILL TOOK A WHILE BEFORE WE COULD GET OUT OF THERE. P.B. went down to his place to try to save his files on his computer, which kind of just died, too!... with G. as a guide, the girls only we all went out to eat at a portuguese restaurant. AFTERWARDS WE WENT TO A COUPLE OF BARS... THE NEXT DAY WAS VACATION DAY ANYWAY...

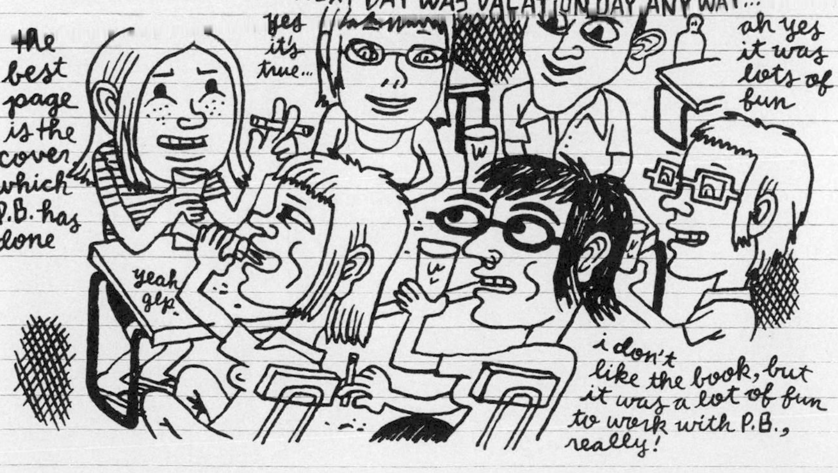
the best page is the cover which P.B. has done
yes it's true...
ah yes it was lots of fun
yeah glp.
i don't like the book, but it was a lot of fun to work with P.B., really!

14.09.03. sunday. AT LAST SOME VACATIONS, AT LAST WE COULD WALK AROUND A BIT. BECAUSE UP TO NOW WE DIDN'T SEE MUCH. YESTERDAY MORNING D. and M.E. took the subway to go to a far away flea market. WHILE ME AND R., G. and A. WENT TO AN OLD BOOK MARKET near the cour julien. WE DIDN'T REALLY HAVE TIME TO LOOK AROUND SO MUCH, WE HAD TO MEET the others at 2 at a gallery where there was a big Le DERNIER CRI exhibit.

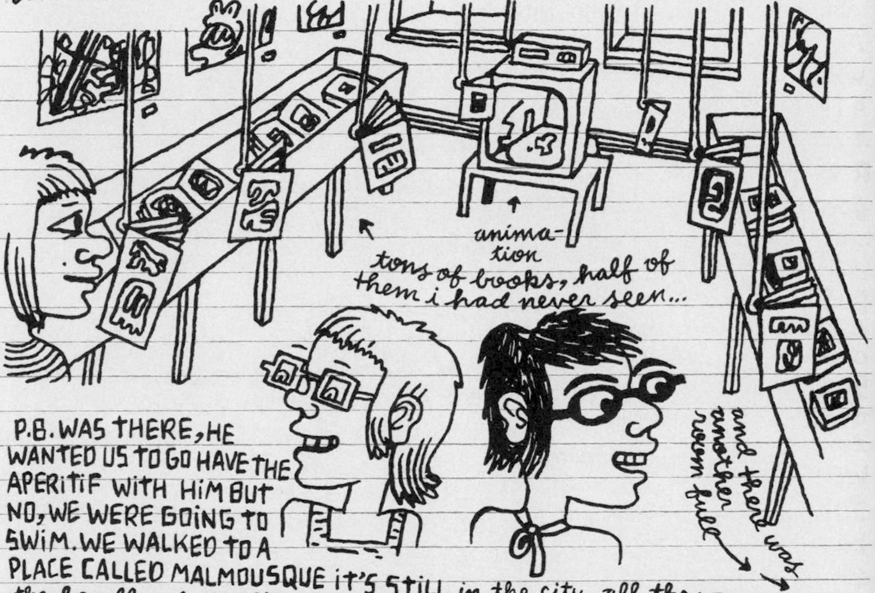

animation
tons of books, half of them i had never seen...
and there was another room full

P.B. WAS THERE, HE WANTED US TO GO HAVE THE APERITIF WITH HIM BUT NO, WE WERE GOING TO SWIM. WE WALKED TO A PLACE CALLED MALMOUSQUE it's STILL in the city, all the way up to the headland... DESPITE THE FACT IT WAS LATE IN THE DAY THERE WAS still a lot of people on that piece of rock. IT WAS NOT EXACTLY WILDNESS...

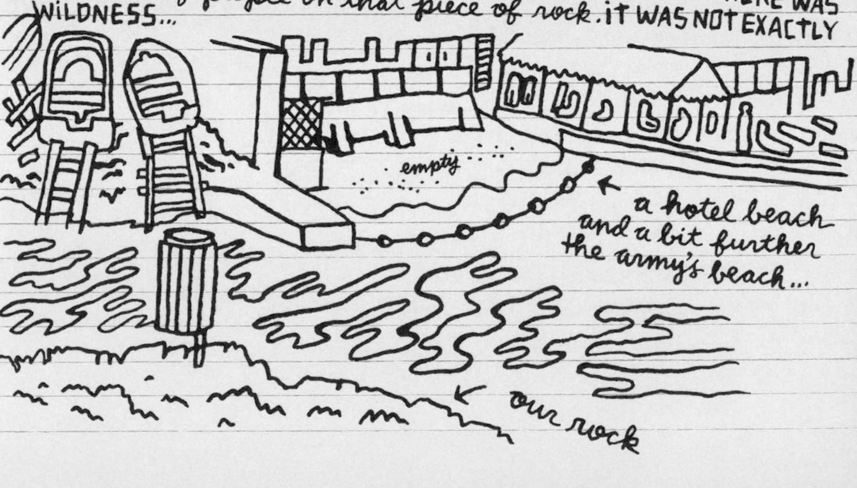

empty
a hotel beach and a bit further the army's beach...
our rock

THE WATER WAS VERY CLEAR, BUT COLD. WE ALL SWAM ANYWAY. J. and me stayed in the water for a super long time. WE LEFT a couple of hours later. J. couldn't sit down for too long because of her back. a big dinner later at G.'s.

15.09.03. monday. YESTERDAY WAS THE BiG EXPEDiTiON DAY AT THE CALANQUES. iT SURE HASN'T BEEN EASY to get there !!... FiRST OF ALL WE ARRANGED TO MEET J. and take the bus together. MEANWHiLE AT G.'s THEY MADE AN APPOiNTMENT WiTH A FRiEND TO MEET ON A TRAiN. iN THE END WE DECiDED to use the bus. THE OTHERS FOLLOWED, except for the friend. ON OUR WAY to the BUS STOP we lost R. and G. then R. arrived (she was limping, she had hurt her foot the day before) SHE HAD LOST G. M.E. went to look for him ...WHAT A WASTE OF TiME. iN THE END AT THE CALLANQUES STOP we didn't feel like waiting for anybody anymore. FROM THAT BUS STOP WE STiLL HAD TO WALK an hour in a park. R. and G. were too slow. WE WERE LEAViNG THEM messages at the crossroads, arrows made of lined up pebbles. THE LANDSCAPE WAS VERY iMPRESSiVE, WE ALL WERE SORRY we didn't get out of the city before that. WE STOPPED ON A CLiFF, under a tree to eat (we had half of the lunch with us) WE ATE EVERYTHiNG, WE DiDN'T THiNK WE'D SEE THE OTHER ONES AGAiN. BUT THEY ARRiVED JUST WHEN WE FiNiSHED EATiNG!... everybody wanted to go back home. D. and ME went to explore a bit. WE COULD SEE people swimming at the bottom of the cliff, WE WANTED TO find the way down there... i LOVE CLiMBiNG BUT D. was awfully scared. BUT WE GOT THERE. iT WAS a NUDiST beach!... we even saw hidden between two rocks a couple doing a 69. OK, SO WE GOT TO SWiM, the water was really warm, nice waves... i GOT BURNT BY A JELLYFiSH! that's a first time for me. TO CLiMB BACK UP WAS NOT AS EASY. EVENTUALLY A YOUNG NAKED GUY SHOWED US THE RiGHT WAY. WE WENT BACK HOME because there were big black clouds in the sky... WE WERE EXHAUSTED BUT HAPPY. WE LEARNED that evening that we were at the Calanque Les Pierres Tombées, n the naked ass Calanque. J. and M.E. arrived a full hour later. they had found a spot and got to swim, too. WE RDERED PiZZA and then went straight to bed.

16.09.03. *tuesday*. YESTERDAY WAS OUR LAST DAY IN MARSEILLE. WHEN WE ARRIVED *at* THE WORKSHOP THAT MORNING THE PAGES OF OUR BOOK WERE ALREADY CUT. SO ALL THERE WAS LEFT TO DO WAS SCORE OUT AND FOLD THEM.

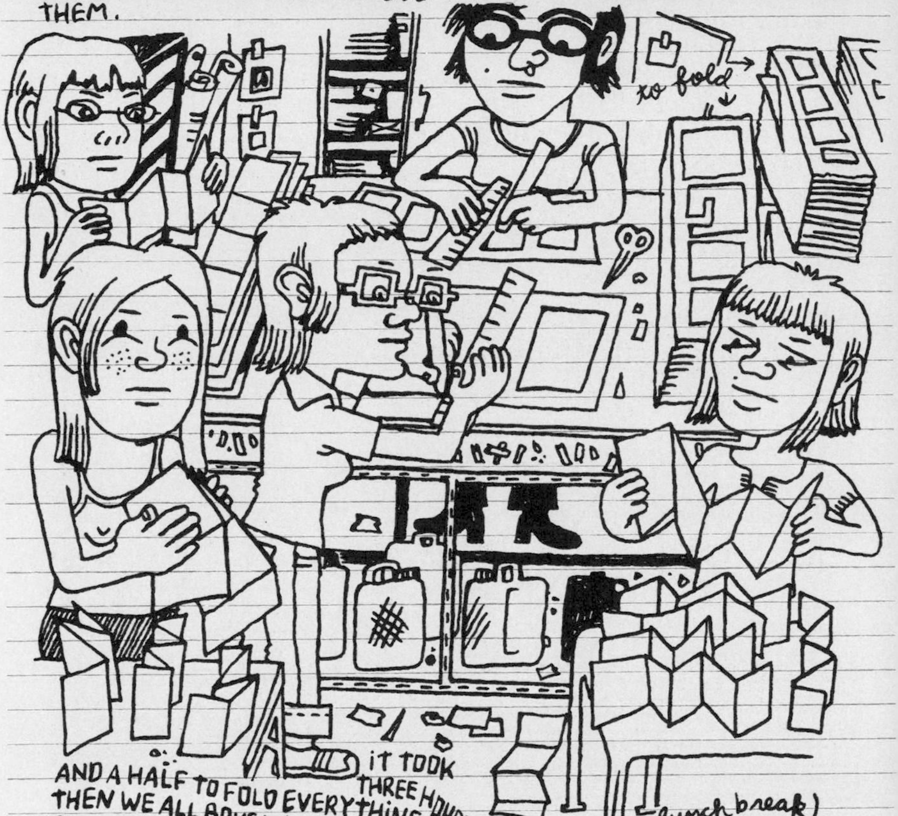

IT TOOK THREE HOURS AND A HALF TO FOLD EVERYTHING (*not counting the lunch break*). THEN WE ALL BOUGHT *a bunch of books from Le Dernier cri before leaving the shop for good*... IT WAS A LITTLE BIT SAD. THEN ONE TEAM WENT WITH P.B. AT THE PRINTER TO HAVE THE BOOKS STAPLED, WHILE THE OTHER TEAM WAS GOING TO CLEAN THE APARTMENT.

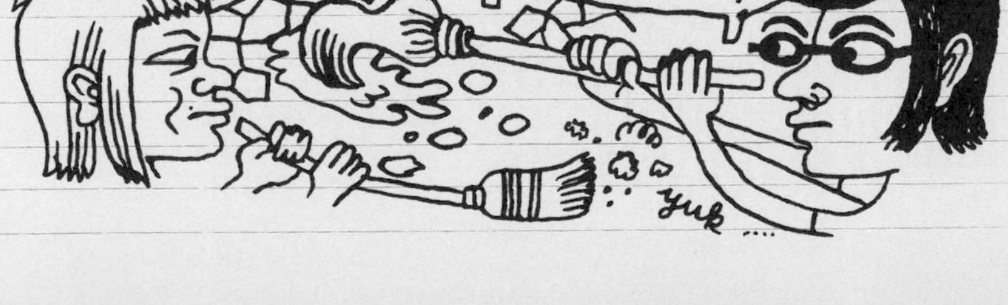

THE LAST APERITIF UPSTAIRS AT G.'s PLACE AND THEN WE ALL WENT TO LA PASSERELLE. WE PICKED UP ALL OF WHAT FELL DOWN IN THE EXHIBITION (*bad hanging job*) AND WE HAD DINNER AT THE RESTAURANT. *we went* OUT ON THE TOWN, AND FINALLY THE LAST VODKA AT G.'s PLACE. I DIDN'T WANT TO SEE THAT, I WENT TO BED.

well ok bye

17.09.03. *wednesday.* YESTERDAY *was the departure* DAY. THE TRAIN WAS LEAVING BEGINNING OF THE AFTERNOON. PARIS FOR ME AND TOULOUSE FOR THE GIRLS. THEY WERE GOING TO VISIT A FRIEND. ONE LAST GOODBYE TO PAKITO... THEN G. AND A. HELPED US TO CARRY OUR LUGGAGE TO THE TRAIN STATION, THANK GOD!!!

→ ALONE AT LAST AND PARIS, FINALLY! I DON'T KNOW WHICH ONE OF THE TWO MAKES ME HAPPIER. GOT NOTHING AGAINST MARSEILLE OR THE GIRLS (*it's been a perfect trip*) BUT THE MINUTE I GOT ON THE TRAIN... I WAS SO HAPPY. I COULD FINALLY READ A NEWSPAPER: *the WTO in Cancun is a failure.* THINGS ARE HAPPENING, BEHIND MY BACK!... GOING HOME WAS NOT DIFFICULT, FORTUNATELY I WON'T HAVE TO CARRY ANYMORE LUGGAGE FOR THE NEXT MONTH AND A HALF.

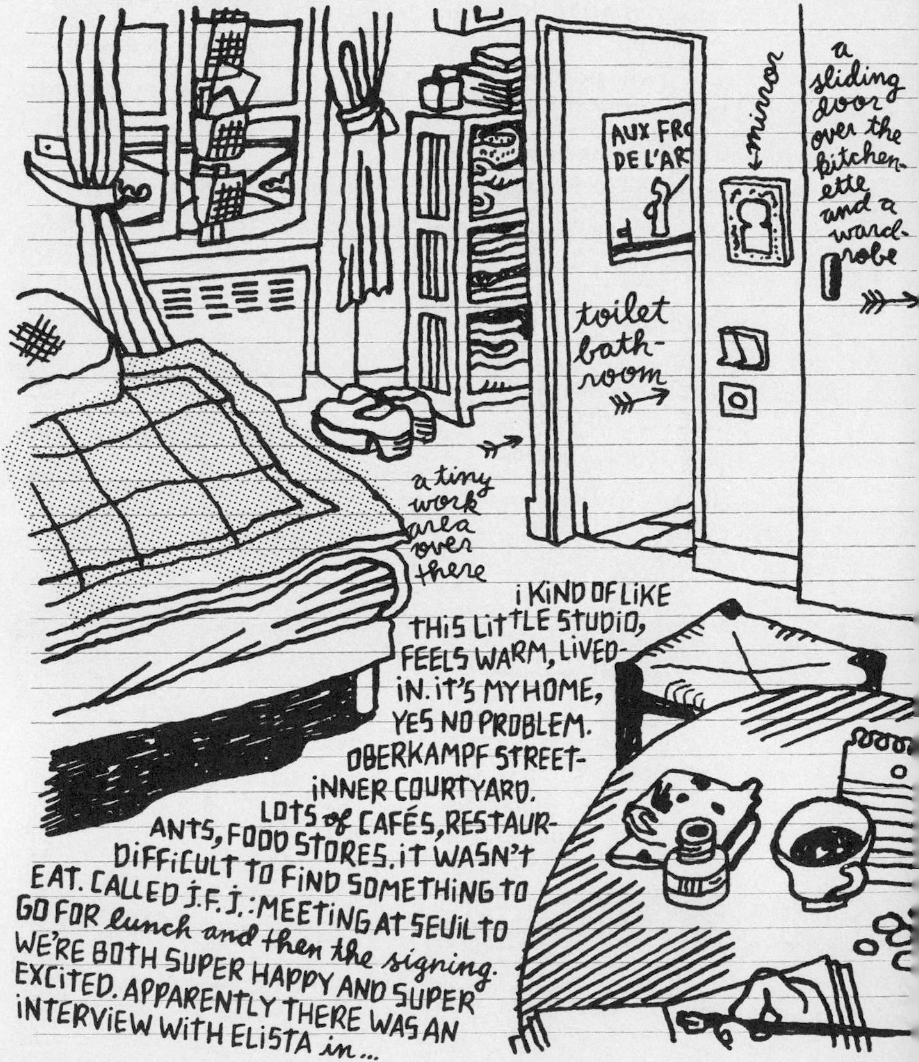

AUX FRO
DE L'AR
mirror
a sliding door over the kitchenette and a wardrobe
toilet bathroom
a tiny work area over there

I KIND OF LIKE THIS LITTLE STUDIO, FEELS WARM, LIVED-IN. IT'S MY HOME, YES NO PROBLEM. OBERKAMPF STREET- INNER COURTYARD. LOTS *of* CAFÉS, RESTAURANTS, FOOD STORES. IT WASN'T DIFFICULT TO FIND SOMETHING TO EAT. CALLED J.F.J.: MEETING AT SEUIL TO GO FOR *lunch and then the signing.* WE'RE BOTH SUPER HAPPY AND SUPER EXCITED. APPARENTLY THERE WAS AN INTERVIEW WITH ELISTA *in...*

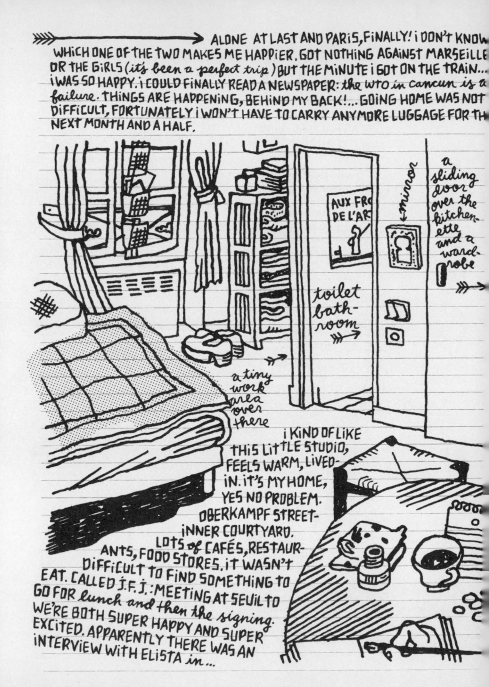

LES INROCK BEGINNING OF THE *season special* (*last week*) WITH *the* PICTURE I DID *in big*... IT'S GOING TO BE MY WEEK! AT LAST I COULD READ QUIETLY IN BED, AND FROM NOW ON I DON'T HAVE TO DRINK HALF *of the* DAY.

18.09.03. *thursday*. WENT TO BED VERY EARLY LAST NIGHT. AT 10:30. AT LAST I COULD SLEEP AS MUCH AS I WANTED. WENT TO SEE THE CONCIERGE (*i didn't know they still existed!*) TO INTRODUCE MYSELF AND PICK UP MY MAIL: TWO LETTERS FROM MATTI.

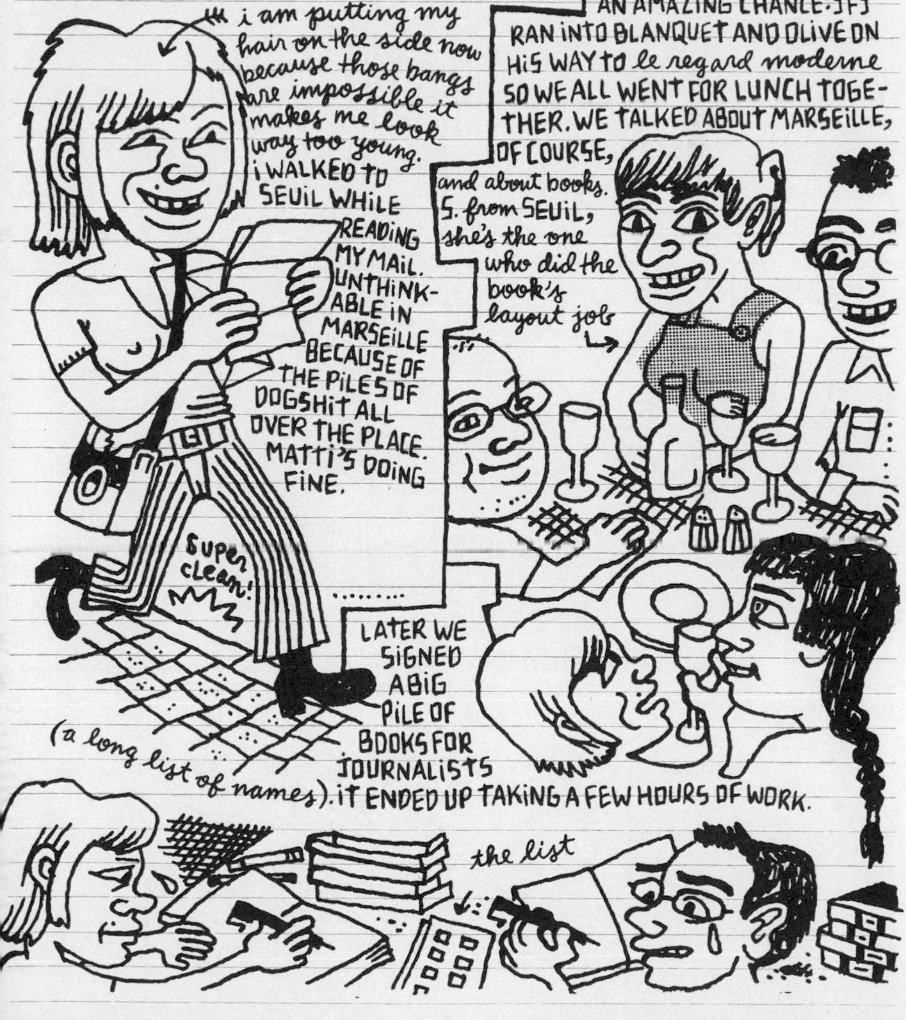
i am putting my hair on the side now because those bangs are impossible it makes me look way too young.
I WALKED TO SEUIL WHILE READING MY MAIL. UNTHINKABLE IN MARSEILLE BECAUSE OF THE PILES OF DOGSHIT ALL OVER THE PLACE. MATTI'S DOING FINE.
super clean!
AN AMAZING CHANCE: JFJ RAN INTO BLANQUET AND OLIVE ON HIS WAY TO le regard moderne SO WE ALL WENT FOR LUNCH TOGETHER. WE TALKED ABOUT MARSEILLE, OF COURSE,
and about books.
S. from SEUIL, she's the one who did the book's layout job
LATER WE SIGNED A BIG PILE OF BOOKS FOR JOURNALISTS
(a long list of names). IT ENDED UP TAKING A FEW HOURS OF WORK.
the list

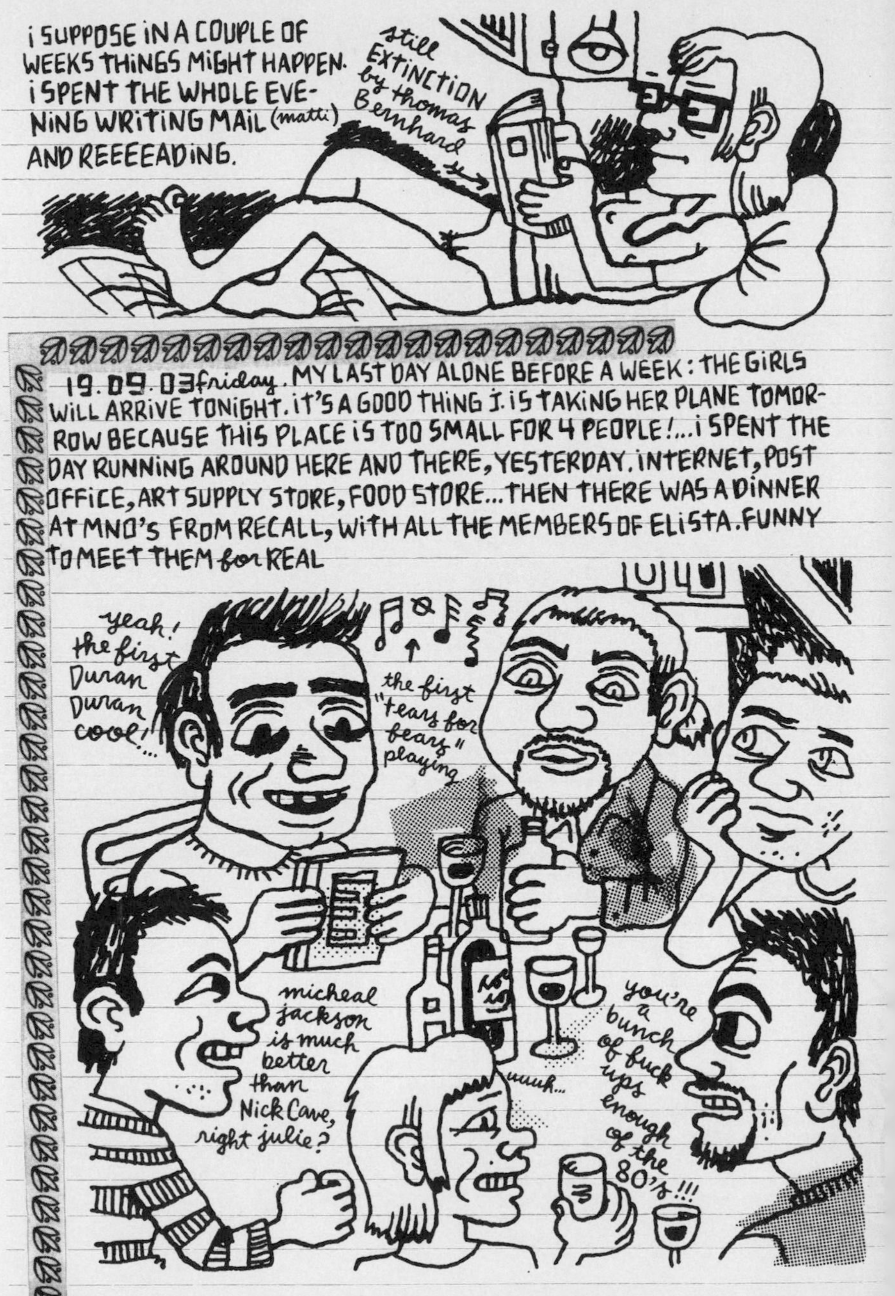
i SUPPOSE IN A COUPLE OF WEEKS THINGS MIGHT HAPPEN. i SPENT THE WHOLE EVENING WRITING MAIL (matti) AND REEEEADING.
still EXTINCTION by thomas Bernhard
19.09.03 friday. MY LAST DAY ALONE BEFORE A WEEK: THE GIRLS WILL ARRIVE TONIGHT. IT'S A GOOD THING J. IS TAKING HER PLANE TOMORROW BECAUSE THIS PLACE IS TOO SMALL FOR 4 PEOPLE!... i SPENT THE DAY RUNNING AROUND HERE AND THERE, YESTERDAY. INTERNET, POST OFFICE, ART SUPPLY STORE, FOOD STORE... THEN THERE WAS A DINNER AT MNO'S FROM RECALL, WITH ALL THE MEMBERS OF ELISTA. FUNNY TO MEET THEM for REAL
yeah! the first Duran Duran cool!...
the first "tears for fears" playing
micheal jackson is much better than Nick Cave, right julie?
uuuh...
you're a bunch of fuck ups enough of the 80's!!!

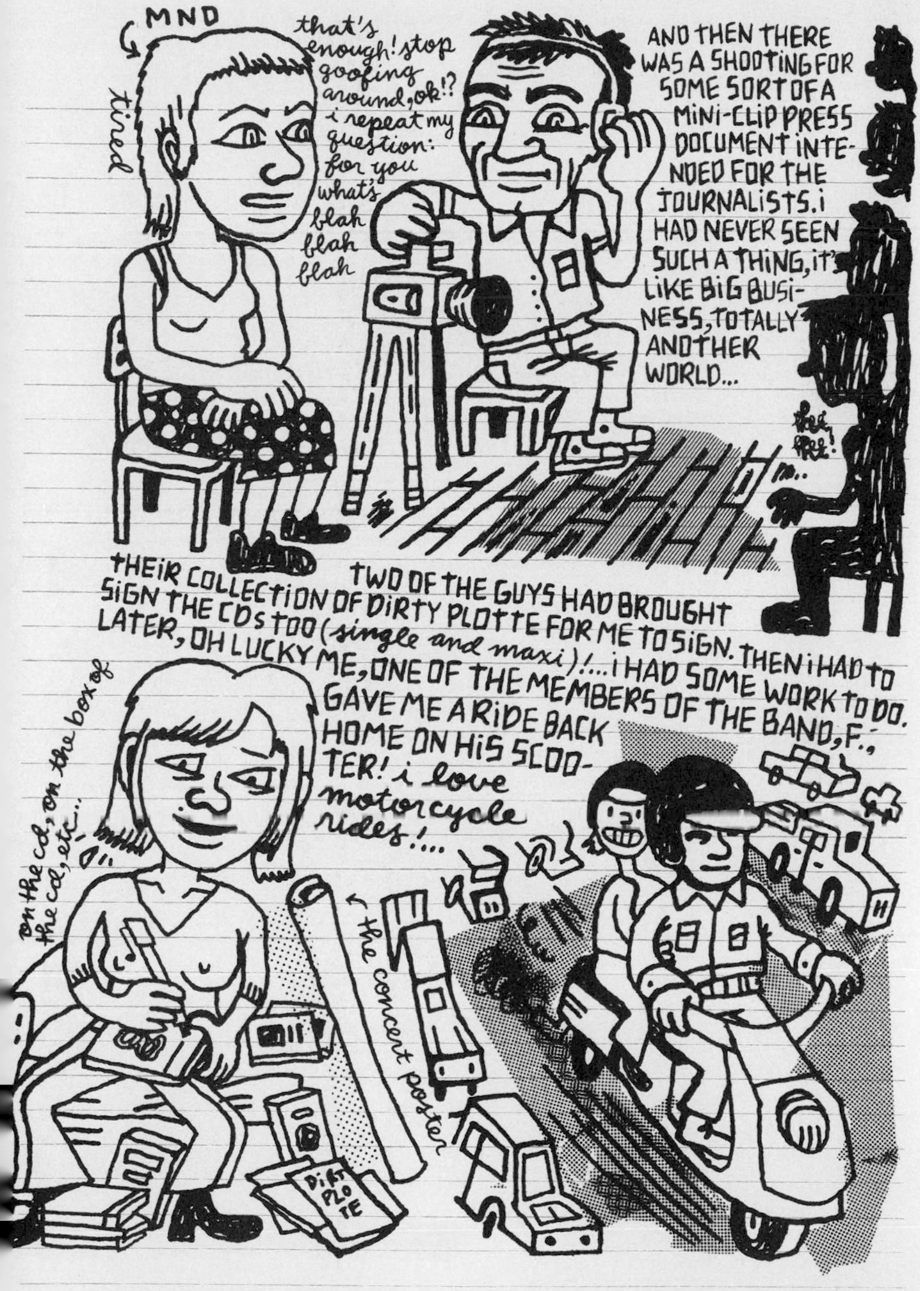
MND
tired
that's enough! stop goofing around, ok!? i repeat my question: for you what's blah blah blah
AND THEN THERE WAS A SHOOTING FOR SOME SORT OF A MINI-CLIP PRESS DOCUMENT INTENDED FOR THE JOURNALISTS. i HAD NEVER SEEN SUCH A THING, IT'S LIKE BIG BUSINESS, TOTALLY ANOTHER WORLD...
TWO OF THE GUYS HAD BROUGHT THEIR COLLECTION OF DIRTY PLOTTE FOR ME TO SIGN. THEN i HAD TO SIGN THE CDs TOO (single and maxi)!... i HAD SOME WORK TO DO. LATER, OH LUCKY ME, ONE OF THE MEMBERS OF THE BAND, F., GAVE ME A RIDE BACK HOME ON HIS SCOOTER! i love motorcycle rides!...
on the cd, on the box of the cd, etc...
the concert poster
DIRTY PLOTTE

20.09.03. *saturday*. THE WEATHER'S NICE AND WARM, ONCE AGAIN. THAT'S HOW IT IS SINCE I'M IN PARIS. JUST LIKE IT WAS IN MARSEILLE. I WANDERED A BIT IN MY NEIGHBORHOOD YESTERDAY. WENT TO THE PÈRE LACHAISE, WHERE YOU CAN FIND SHADOW.

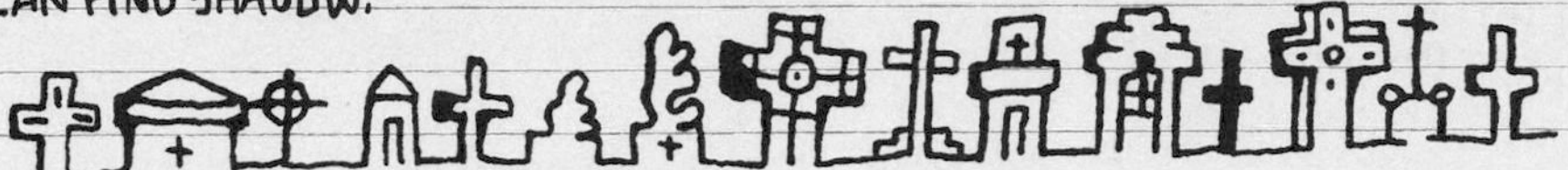

IN THE END ONLY J. ARRIVED IN PARIS, THE OTHER TWO DECIDED *to stay in* TOULOUSE *until monday*.

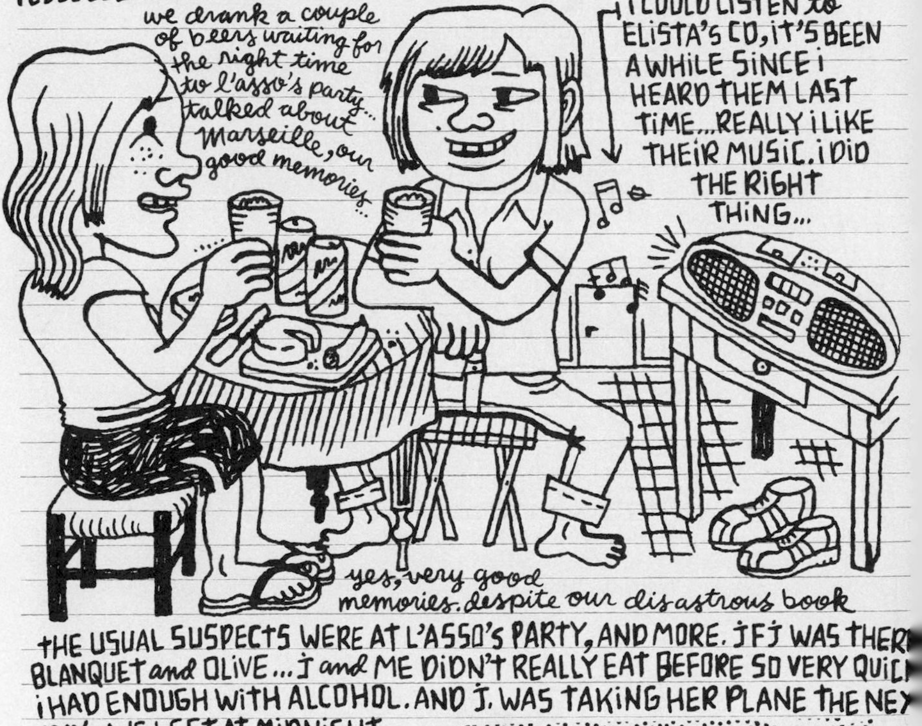
we drank a couple of beers waiting for the right time to l'asso's party... talked about Marseille, our good memories...
I COULD LISTEN to ELISTA'S CD, IT'S BEEN A WHILE SINCE I HEARD THEM LAST TIME... REALLY I LIKE THEIR MUSIC. I DID THE RIGHT THING...
yes, very good memories. despite our disastrous book

THE USUAL SUSPECTS WERE AT L'ASSO'S PARTY, AND MORE. JFJ WAS THER BLANQUET *and* OLIVE... J *and* ME DIDN'T REALLY EAT BEFORE SO VERY QUIC I HAD ENOUGH WITH ALCOHOL. AND J. WAS TAKING HER PLANE THE NEX DAY... WE LEFT AT MIDNIGHT.

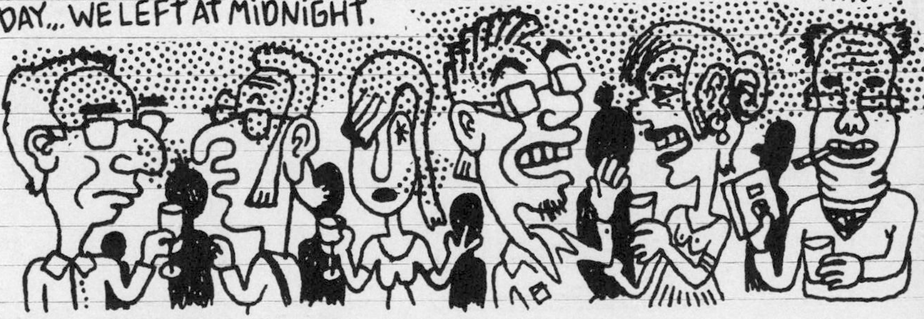

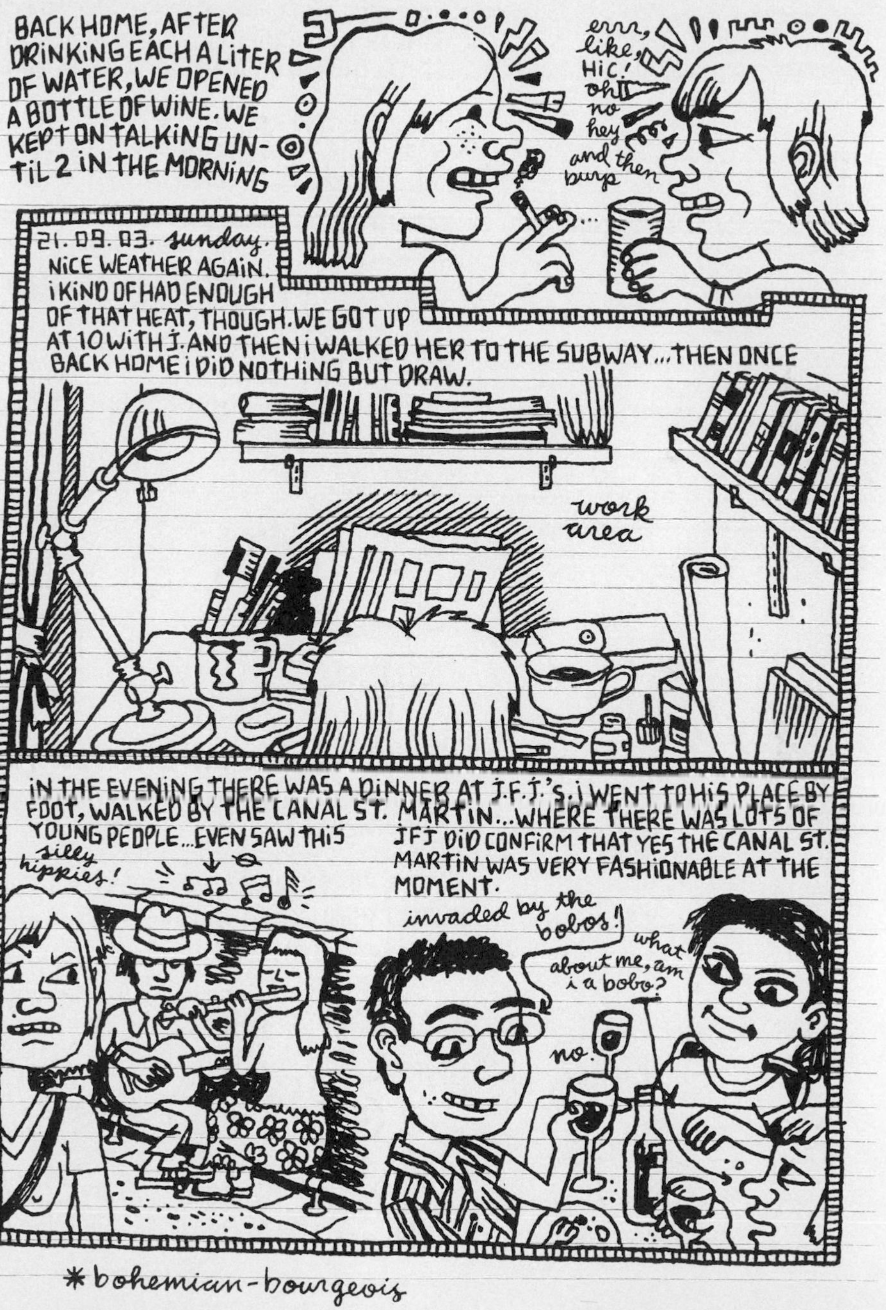
BACK HOME, AFTER DRINKING EACH A LITER OF WATER, WE OPENED A BOTTLE OF WINE. WE KEPT ON TALKING UNTIL 2 IN THE MORNING
err, like, Hic! oh no hey and then burp
21.09.03. sunday.
NICE WEATHER AGAIN. I KIND OF HAD ENOUGH OF THAT HEAT, THOUGH. WE GOT UP AT 10 WITH J. AND THEN I WALKED HER TO THE SUBWAY... THEN ONCE BACK HOME I DID NOTHING BUT DRAW.
work area
IN THE EVENING THERE WAS A DINNER AT J.F.J.'S. I WENT TO HIS PLACE BY FOOT, WALKED BY THE CANAL ST. MARTIN... WHERE THERE WAS LOTS OF YOUNG PEOPLE... EVEN SAW THIS
silly hippies!
JFJ DID CONFIRM THAT YES THE CANAL ST. MARTIN WAS VERY FASHIONABLE AT THE MOMENT.
invaded by the bobos!
what about me, am i a bobo?
no.
*bohemian-bourgeois

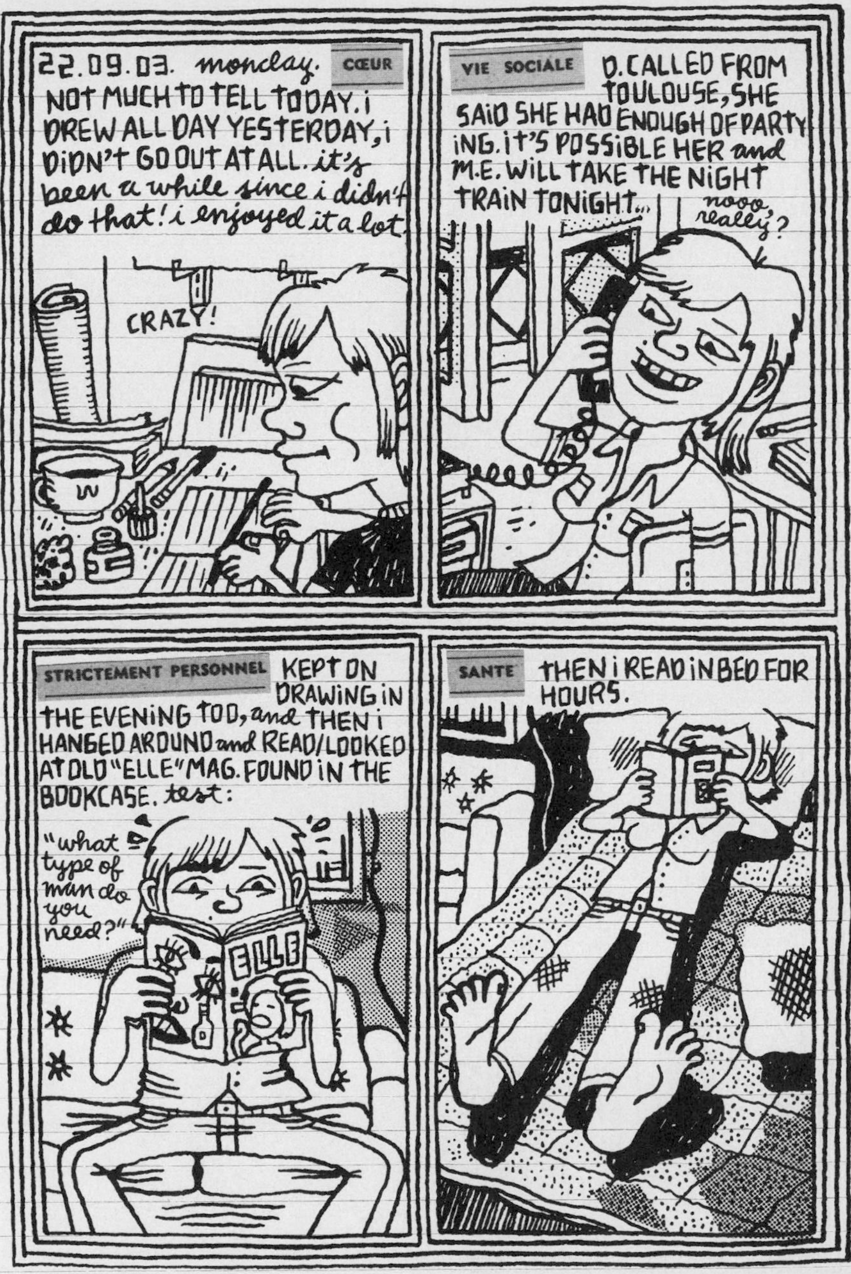

22.09.03. monday.
CŒUR
NOT MUCH TO TELL TODAY. i DREW ALL DAY YESTERDAY, i DIDN'T GO OUT AT ALL. it's been a while since i didn't do that! i enjoyed it a lot.
CRAZY!
VIE SOCIALE
D. CALLED FROM TOULOUSE, SHE SAID SHE HAD ENOUGH OF PARTYING. IT'S POSSIBLE HER and M.E. WILL TAKE THE NIGHT TRAIN TONIGHT...
nooo, really?
STRICTEMENT PERSONNEL
KEPT ON DRAWING IN THE EVENING TOO, and THEN i HANGED AROUND and READ/LOOKED AT OLD "ELLE" MAG. FOUND IN THE BOOKCASE. test:
"what type of man do you need?"
ELLE
SANTE
THEN i READ IN BED FOR HOURS.

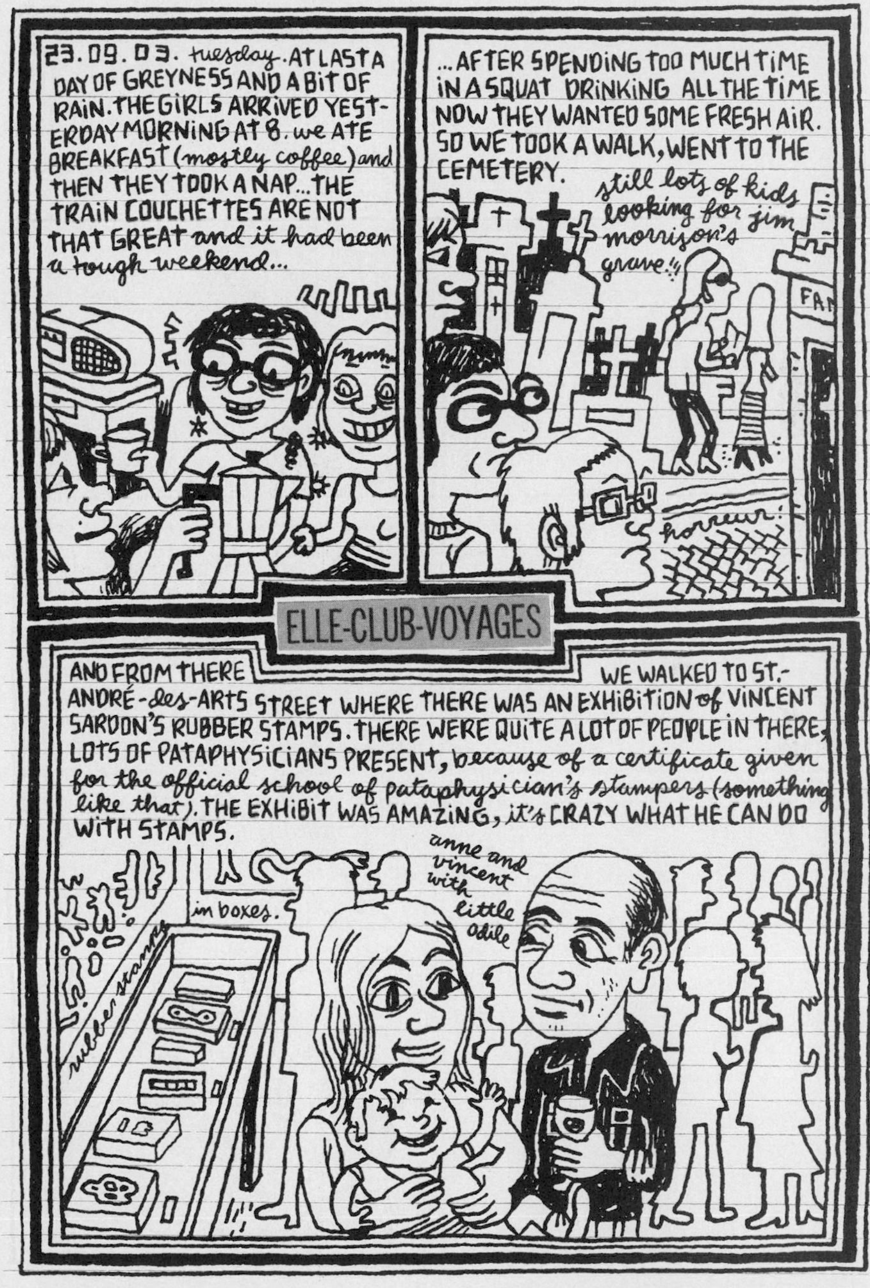

23.09.03. tuesday. AT LAST A DAY OF GREYNESS AND A BIT OF RAIN. THE GIRLS ARRIVED YESTERDAY MORNING AT 8. we ATE BREAKFAST (mostly coffee) and THEN THEY TOOK A NAP... THE TRAIN COUCHETTES ARE NOT THAT GREAT and it had been a tough weekend...
...AFTER SPENDING TOO MUCH TIME IN A SQUAT DRINKING ALL THE TIME NOW THEY WANTED SOME FRESH AIR. SO WE TOOK A WALK, WENT TO THE CEMETERY.
still lots of kids looking for jim morrison's grave!!
horreur!
ELLE-CLUB-VOYAGES
AND FROM THERE WE WALKED TO ST.-ANDRÉ-des-ARTS STREET WHERE THERE WAS AN EXHIBITION of VINCENT SARDON'S RUBBER STAMPS. THERE WERE QUITE A LOT OF PEOPLE IN THERE, LOTS OF PATAPHYSICIANS PRESENT, because of a certificate given for the official school of pataphysician's stampers (something like that). THE EXHIBIT WAS AMAZING, it's CRAZY WHAT HE CAN DO WITH STAMPS.
anne and vincent with little odile
in boxes.
rubber stamps

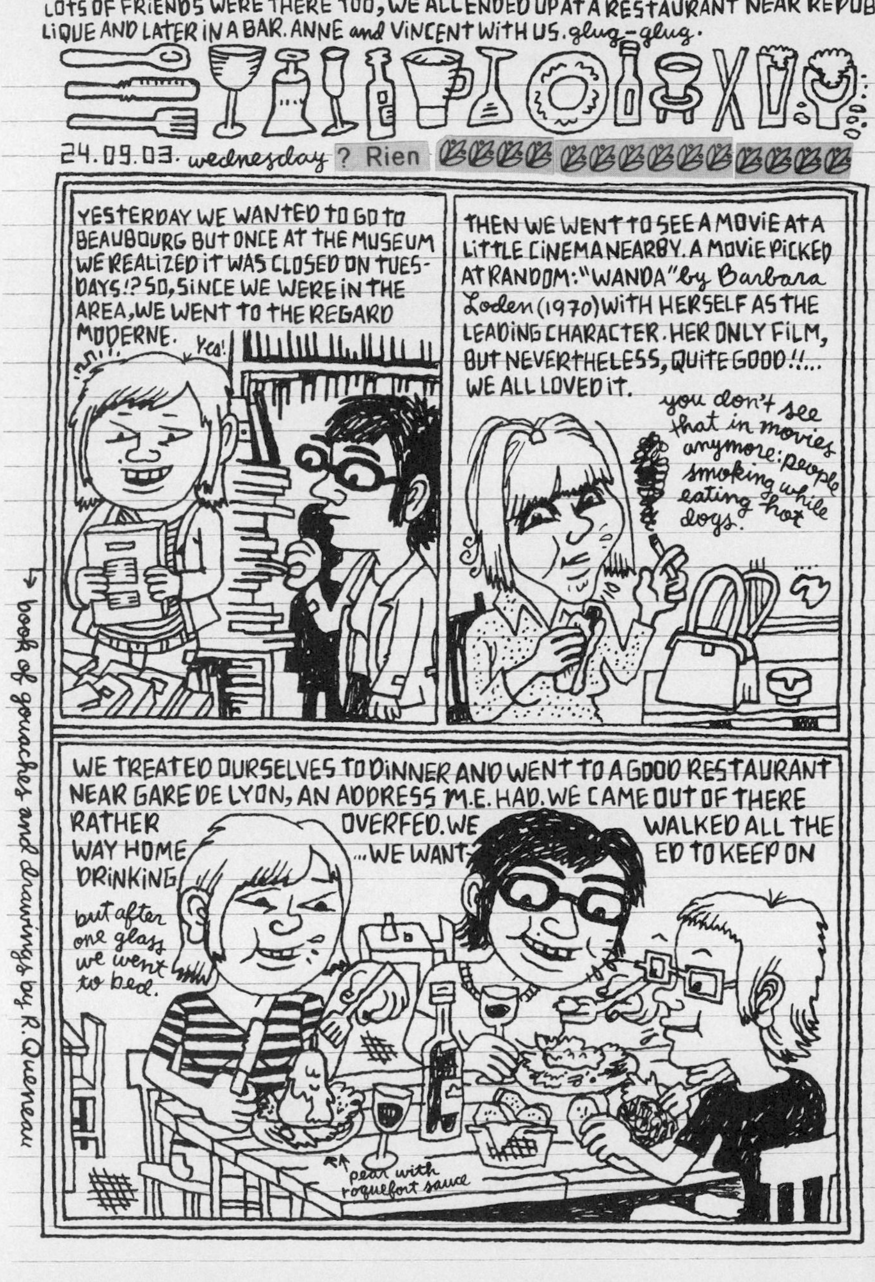
LOTS OF FRIENDS WERE THERE TOO, WE ALL ENDED UP AT A RESTAURANT NEAR RÉPUBLIQUE AND LATER IN A BAR. ANNE and VINCENT WITH US. glug-glug.
24.09.03. wednesday ? Rien
YESTERDAY WE WANTED TO GO TO BEAUBOURG BUT ONCE AT THE MUSEUM WE REALIZED IT WAS CLOSED ON TUESDAYS!? SO, SINCE WE WERE IN THE AREA, WE WENT TO THE REGARD MODERNE.
Yes!
→ book of gouaches and drawings by R. Queneau
THEN WE WENT TO SEE A MOVIE AT A LITTLE CINEMA NEARBY. A MOVIE PICKED AT RANDOM: "WANDA" by Barbara Loden (1970) WITH HERSELF AS THE LEADING CHARACTER. HER ONLY FILM, BUT NEVERTHELESS, QUITE GOOD!!... WE ALL LOVED IT.
you don't see that in movies anymore: people smoking while eating hot dogs.
WE TREATED OURSELVES TO DINNER AND WENT TO A GOOD RESTAURANT NEAR GARE DE LYON, AN ADDRESS M.E. HAD. WE CAME OUT OF THERE
RATHER OVERFED. WE WALKED ALL THE WAY HOME ...WE WANTED TO KEEP ON DRINKING
but after one glass we went to bed.
pear with roquefort sauce

25.09.03. thursday

i CAUGHT A BAD COLD. i COULD TELL iT WAS COMING TUESDAY EVENING...TODAY it's AT iTS WORST. i STAYED HOME YESTERDAY WHILE THE GIRLS WENT TO ViSiT THE CATA-COMBS. LATER WE ALL WENT TO HAVE A DRINK with BLANQUET and OLIVE ON ST. MAUR STREET. DINNER AT HOME: TWO GLASS-ES OF WINE and i FELT DIZZY...

BUT TODAY, OH LALA iT'S WAY WORSE. TOTAL COLLAPSE. i'M GOING TO BED.

26.09.03. friday. YEAH, i SPENT THE DAY iN BED. i MET WiTH THE GIRLS FOR DINNER AND WE WENT iN A NEIGHBORHOOD'S BAR FOR A LAST DRINK. EVERYTHING WAS FINE, UNTIL...WE GOT A FREE ROUND, and A YOUNG GUY SHOWED UP WiTH iT.

yeah let's organize an orgy c'mon girls are you lesbians or what?! let's go!

THEN HiS FRIENDS SHOW-ED UP ONE BY ONE, UP TO FIVE OF THEM. iT WAS OBVIOUS THEY THOUGHT WE WERE EASY PREYS BECAUSE WE were FOREIGNERS. WE GOT OUT OF THERE DiSGUSTED,

not even a hair on his chin and he's telling us he acted in porno films but retired 2 years ago... the other extremely ugly hippy guy (22 y.o.) pretended he was a photographer and had exhibited his work at Beaubourg.

so are you a clitoral or a vaginal? here, in france, you can ask that to girls casually even if you don't know them, that's how it is.

ESPECIALLY THE GIRLS. D. SWORE SHE WOULD NEVER TOUCH A FRENCH GUY AND THE TWO OF THEM WERE SORRY FOR ME TO HAVE TO PUT UP WITH THE FRENCH for another month. i was not as discouraged.

27.09.03. *saturday*. FEELING A BIT BETTER THIS MORNING. IT'S STILL NICE OUT. WHEN WILL THAT STOP? IT WAS THE GIRLS' DEPARTURE DAY YESTERDAY. D. CALLED TO CONFIRM THE FLIGHT... IT WAS POSTPONED UNTIL 6. (*instead of* 1:30). WE HAD GOTTEN UP EARLY FOR NOTHING. ME NOT AT ALL IN GOOD SHAPE. I WATCH THEM PACK UP.

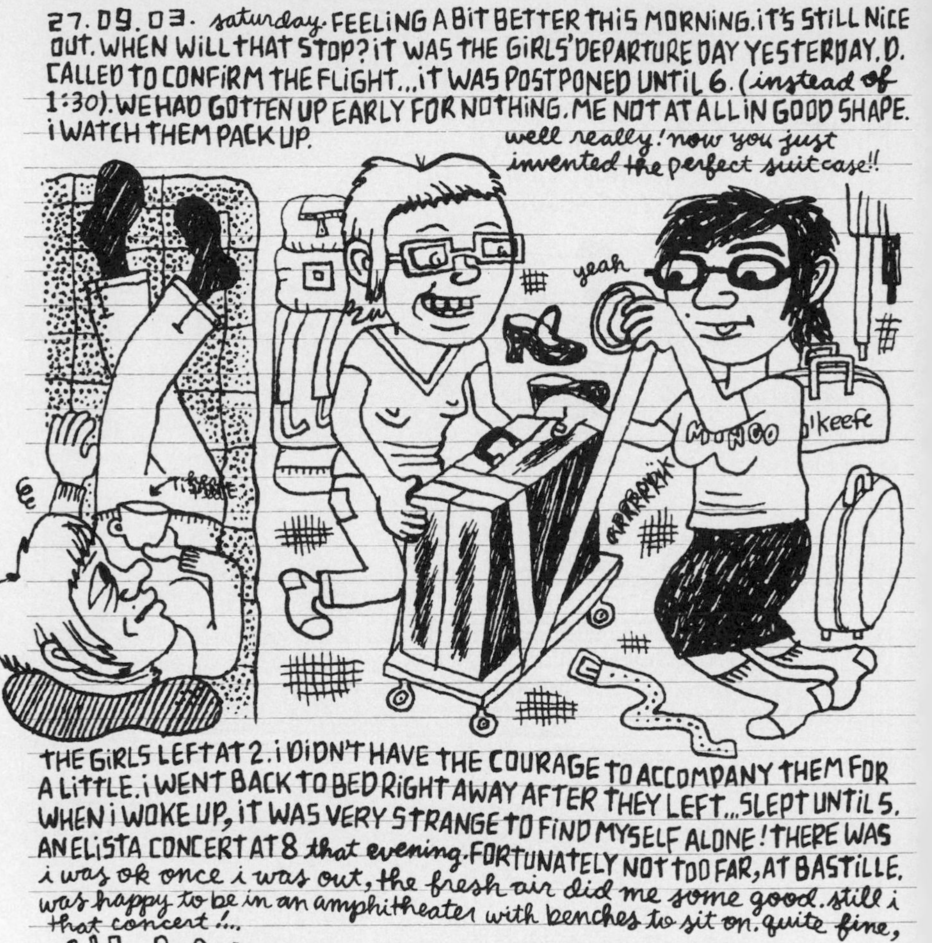
well really! now you just invented the perfect suitcase!!
yeah

THE GIRLS LEFT AT 2. I DIDN'T HAVE THE COURAGE TO ACCOMPANY THEM FOR
A LITTLE. I WENT BACK TO BED RIGHT AWAY AFTER THEY LEFT... SLEPT UNTIL 5.
WHEN I WOKE UP, IT WAS VERY STRANGE TO FIND MYSELF ALONE! THERE WAS
AN ELISTA CONCERT AT 8 *that evening*. FORTUNATELY NOT TOO FAR, AT BASTILLE.
i was ok once i was out, the fresh air did me some good. still i
was happy to be in an amphitheater with benches to sit on. quite fine,
that concert!...

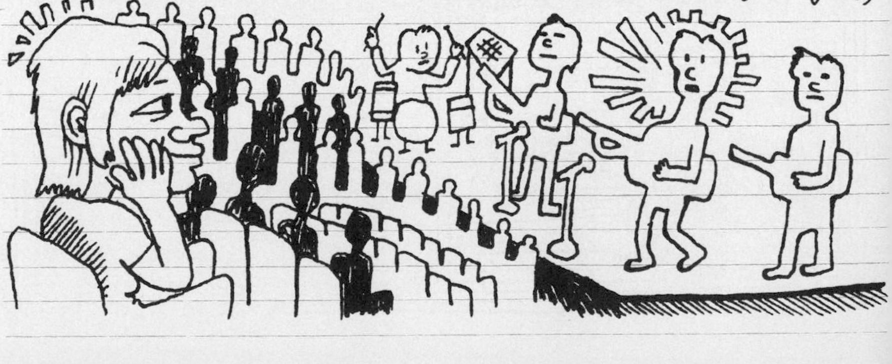

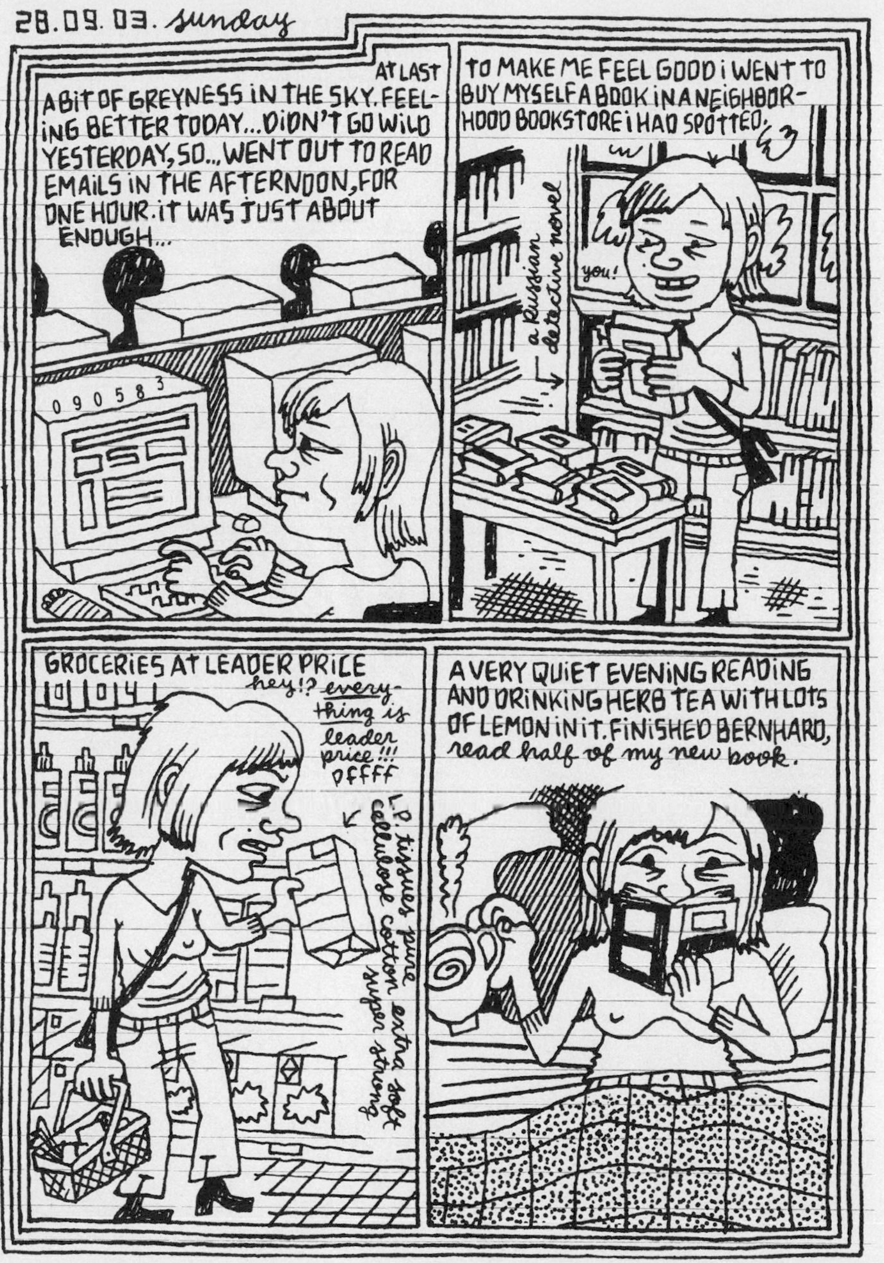
28.09.03. sunday
AT LAST A BIT OF GREYNESS IN THE SKY. FEELING BETTER TODAY... DIDN'T GO WILD YESTERDAY, SO... WENT OUT TO READ EMAILS IN THE AFTERNOON, FOR ONE HOUR. IT WAS JUST ABOUT ENOUGH...
090583
TO MAKE ME FEEL GOOD I WENT TO BUY MYSELF A BOOK IN A NEIGHBORHOOD BOOKSTORE I HAD SPOTTED.
a Russian detective novel
you!
GROCERIES AT LEADER PRICE
101014
hey!? everything is leader price!!! pffff
L.P. tissues pure cellulose cotton extra soft super strong
A VERY QUIET EVENING READING AND DRINKING HERB TEA WITH LOTS OF LEMON IN IT. FINISHED BERNHARD, read half of my new book.

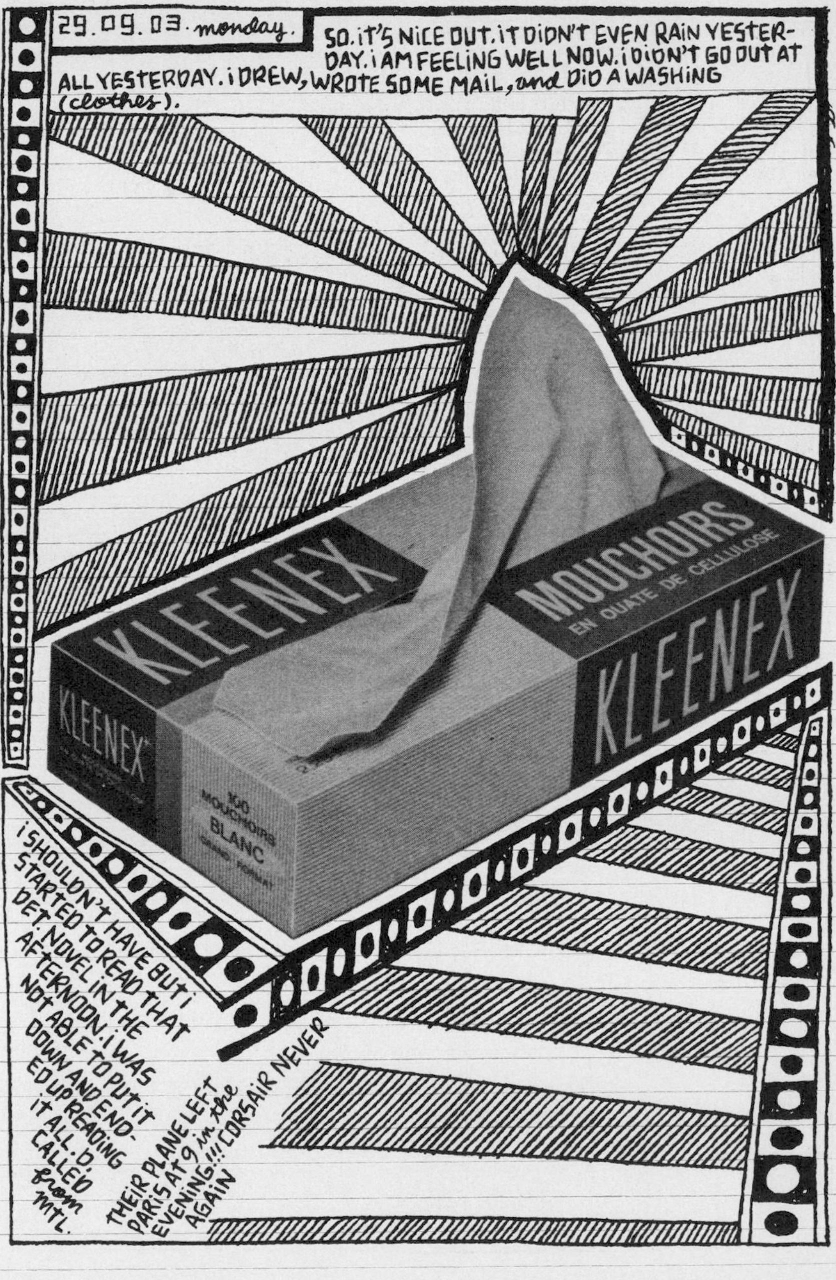
29.09.03. monday.
SO. IT'S NICE OUT. IT DIDN'T EVEN RAIN YESTERDAY. I AM FEELING WELL NOW. I DIDN'T GO OUT AT ALL YESTERDAY. I DREW, WROTE SOME MAIL, and DID A WASHING (clothes).
KLEENEX
MOUCHOIRS
EN OUATE DE CELLULOSE
KLEENEX
KLEENEX
100 MOUCHOIRS BLANC GRAND FORMAT
I SHOULDN'T HAVE BUT I STARTED TO READ THAT DET. NOVEL IN THE AFTERNOON. I WAS NOT ABLE TO PUT IT DOWN AND ENDED UP READING IT ALL. D. CALLED from MTL.
THEIR PLANE LEFT PARIS AT 9 in the EVENING!!! CORSAIR NEVER AGAIN

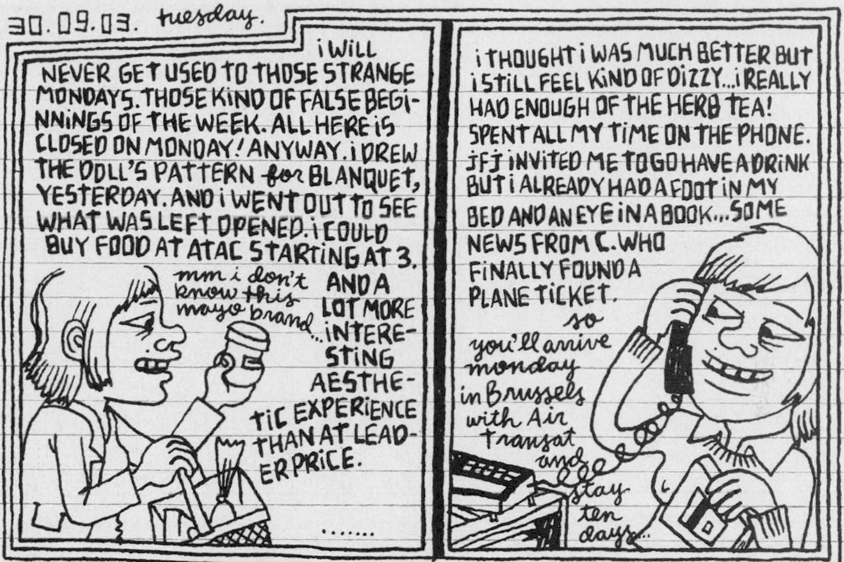
30.09.03. tuesday.
i WILL NEVER GET USED TO THOSE STRANGE MONDAYS. THOSE KIND OF FALSE BEGINNINGS OF THE WEEK. ALL HERE IS CLOSED ON MONDAY! ANYWAY. i DREW THE DOLL'S PATTERN for BLANQUET, YESTERDAY. AND i WENT OUT TO SEE WHAT WAS LEFT OPENED. i COULD BUY FOOD AT ATAC STARTING AT 3.
mm i don't know this mayo brand...
AND A LOT MORE INTERESTING AESTHETIC EXPERIENCE THAN AT LEADER PRICE.
....
i THOUGHT i WAS MUCH BETTER BUT i STILL FEEL KIND OF DIZZY... i REALLY HAD ENOUGH OF THE HERB TEA! SPENT ALL MY TIME ON THE PHONE. JFJ INVITED ME TO GO HAVE A DRINK BUT i ALREADY HAD A FOOT IN MY BED AND AN EYE IN A BOOK... SOME NEWS FROM C. WHO FINALLY FOUND A PLANE TICKET.
so you'll arrive monday in Brussels with Air Transat and stay ten days...

october 2003

SUN	MON	TUE	WED	THU	FRI	SAT
			1	2	3	4
5	6	7	8	9	10	11
12	13	14	15	16	17	18
19	20	21	22	23	24	25
26	27	28	29	30	31	

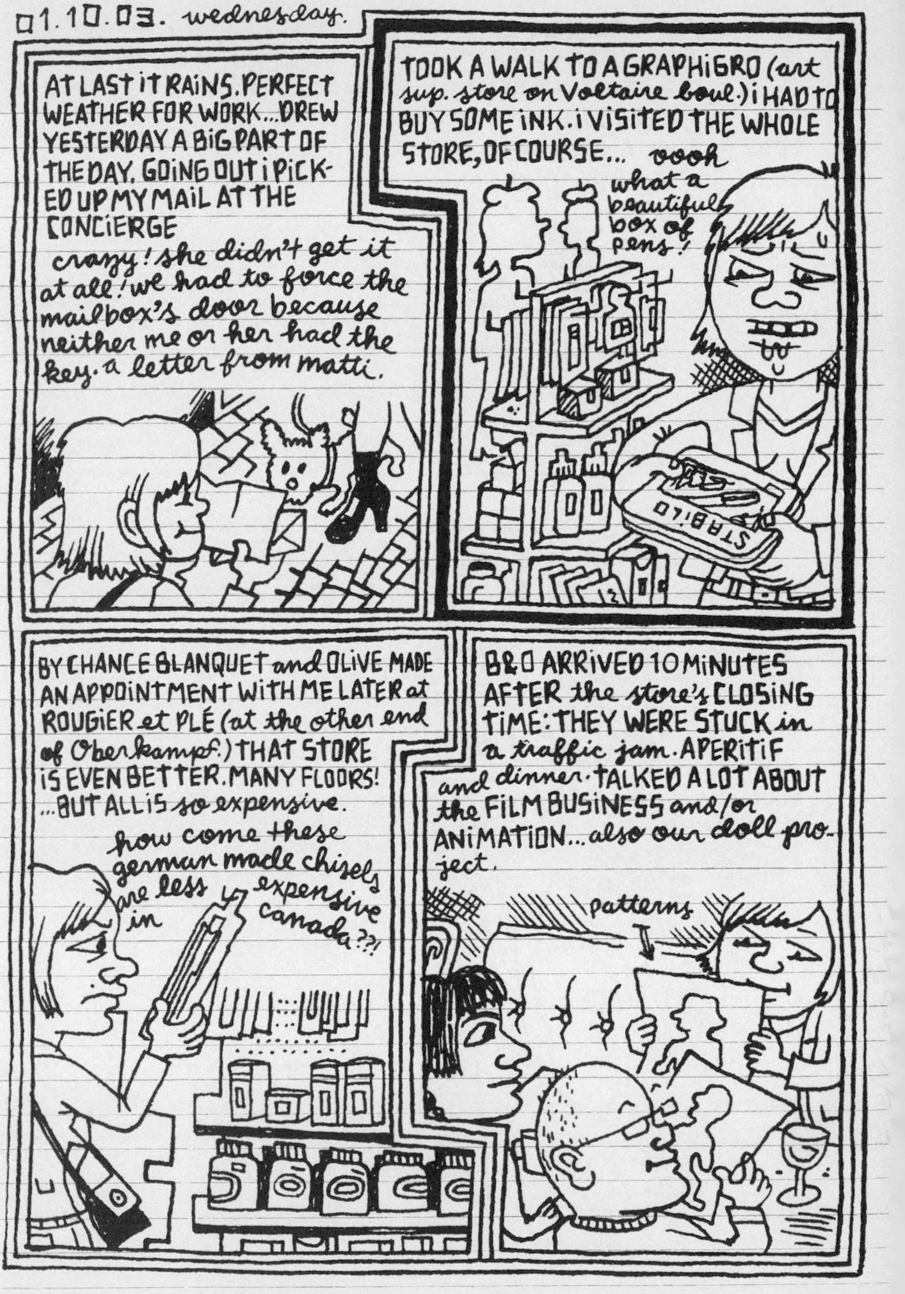
01.10.03. wednesday.
AT LAST IT RAINS. PERFECT WEATHER FOR WORK... DREW YESTERDAY A BIG PART OF THE DAY. GOING OUT I PICKED UP MY MAIL AT THE CONCIERGE
crazy! she didn't get it at all! we had to force the mailbox's door because neither me or her had the key. a letter from matti.
TOOK A WALK TO A GRAPHIGRO (art sup. store on Voltaire boul.) I HAD TO BUY SOME INK. I VISITED THE WHOLE STORE, OF COURSE...
oooh what a beautiful box of pens!
STABILO
BY CHANCE BLANQUET and OLIVE MADE AN APPOINTMENT WITH ME LATER at ROUGIER et PLÉ (at the other end of Oberkampf.) THAT STORE IS EVEN BETTER. MANY FLOORS! ...BUT ALL IS so expensive.
how come these german made chisels are less expensive in canada??!
B&O ARRIVED 10 MINUTES AFTER the store's CLOSING TIME: THEY WERE STUCK in a traffic jam. APERITIF and dinner. TALKED A LOT ABOUT the FILM BUSINESS and/or ANIMATION... also our doll project.
patterns

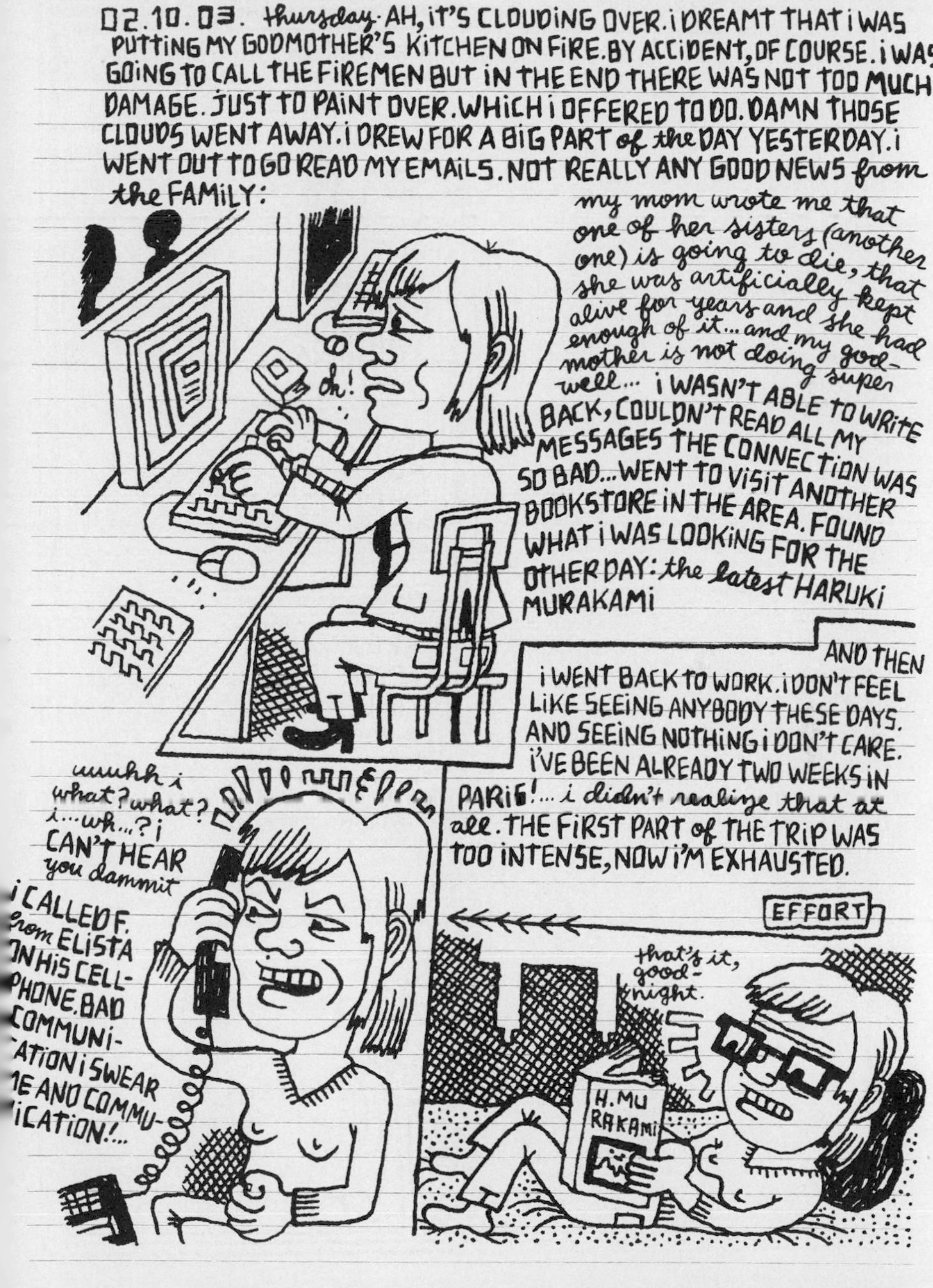

02.10.03. thursday. AH, IT'S CLOUDING OVER. i DREAMT THAT i WAS PUTTING MY GODMOTHER'S KITCHEN ON FIRE. BY ACCIDENT, OF COURSE. i WAS GOING TO CALL THE FIREMEN BUT IN THE END THERE WAS NOT TOO MUCH DAMAGE. JUST TO PAINT OVER. WHICH i OFFERED TO DO. DAMN THOSE CLOUDS WENT AWAY. i DREW FOR A BIG PART of the DAY YESTERDAY. i WENT OUT TO GO READ MY EMAILS. NOT REALLY ANY GOOD NEWS from the FAMILY:
my mom wrote me that one of her sisters (another one) is going to die, that she was artificially kept alive for years and she had enough of it... and my god-mother is not doing super well... i WASN'T ABLE TO WRITE BACK, COULDN'T READ ALL MY MESSAGES THE CONNECTION WAS SO BAD... WENT TO VISIT ANOTHER BOOKSTORE IN THE AREA. FOUND WHAT i WAS LOOKING FOR THE OTHER DAY: the latest HARUKI MURAKAMI
oh!
AND THEN i WENT BACK TO WORK. i DON'T FEEL LIKE SEEING ANYBODY THESE DAYS. AND SEEING NOTHING i DON'T CARE. i'VE BEEN ALREADY TWO WEEKS IN PARIS!... i didn't realize that at all. THE FIRST PART of THE TRIP WAS TOO INTENSE, NOW i'M EXHAUSTED.
uuuhh i what? what? i... wh...? i CAN'T HEAR you dammit
i CALLED F. rom ELISTA ON HIS CELL-PHONE. BAD COMMUNI-ATION i SWEAR ME AND COMMU-iCATION!...
EFFORT
that's it, good-night.
H. MURAKAMI

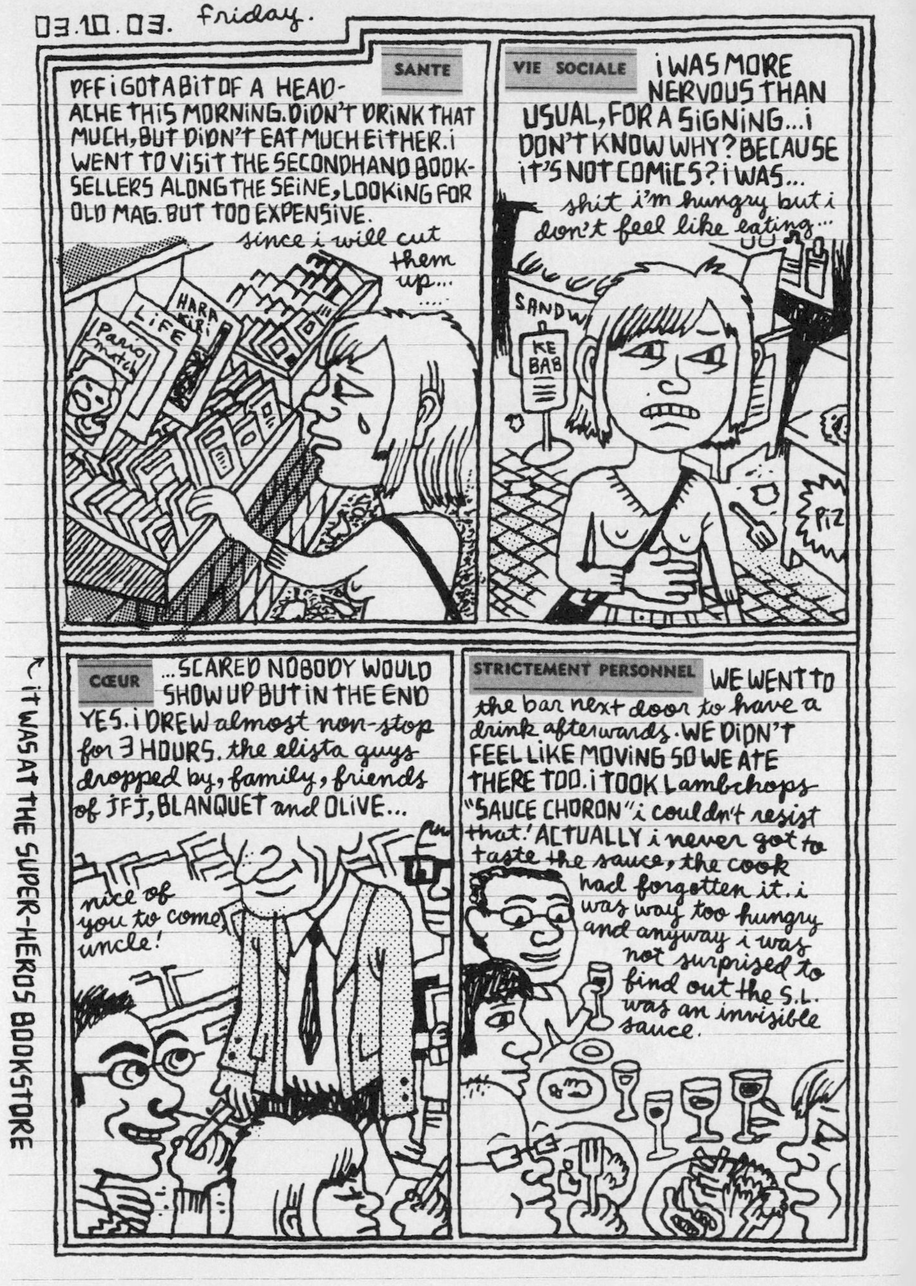
03.10.03. friday.
SANTE
PFF i GOT A BIT OF A HEADACHE THIS MORNING. DIDN'T DRINK THAT MUCH, BUT DIDN'T EAT MUCH EITHER. i WENT TO VISIT THE SECONDHAND BOOKSELLERS ALONG THE SEINE, LOOKING FOR OLD MAG. BUT TOO EXPENSIVE.
since i will cut them up....
HARA KIRI
LIFE
Paris match
VIE SOCIALE
i WAS MORE NERVOUS THAN USUAL, FOR A SIGNING... i DON'T KNOW WHY? BECAUSE IT'S NOT COMICS? i WAS...
shit i'm hungry but i don't feel like eating...
SANDW
KE BAB
PIZ
CŒUR
...SCARED NOBODY WOULD SHOW UP BUT IN THE END YES. i DREW almost non-stop for 3 HOURS. the elista guys dropped by, family, friends of JFJ, BLANQUET and OLIVE...
nice of you to come, uncle!
STRICTEMENT PERSONNEL
WE WENT TO the bar next door to have a drink afterwards. WE DIDN'T FEEL LIKE MOVING SO WE ATE THERE TOO. i TOOK Lambchops "SAUCE CHORON" i couldn't resist that! ACTUALLY i never got to taste the sauce, the cook had forgotten it. i was way too hungry and anyway i was not surprised to find out the S.L. was an invisible sauce.
it WAS AT THE SUPER-HEROS BOOKSTORE

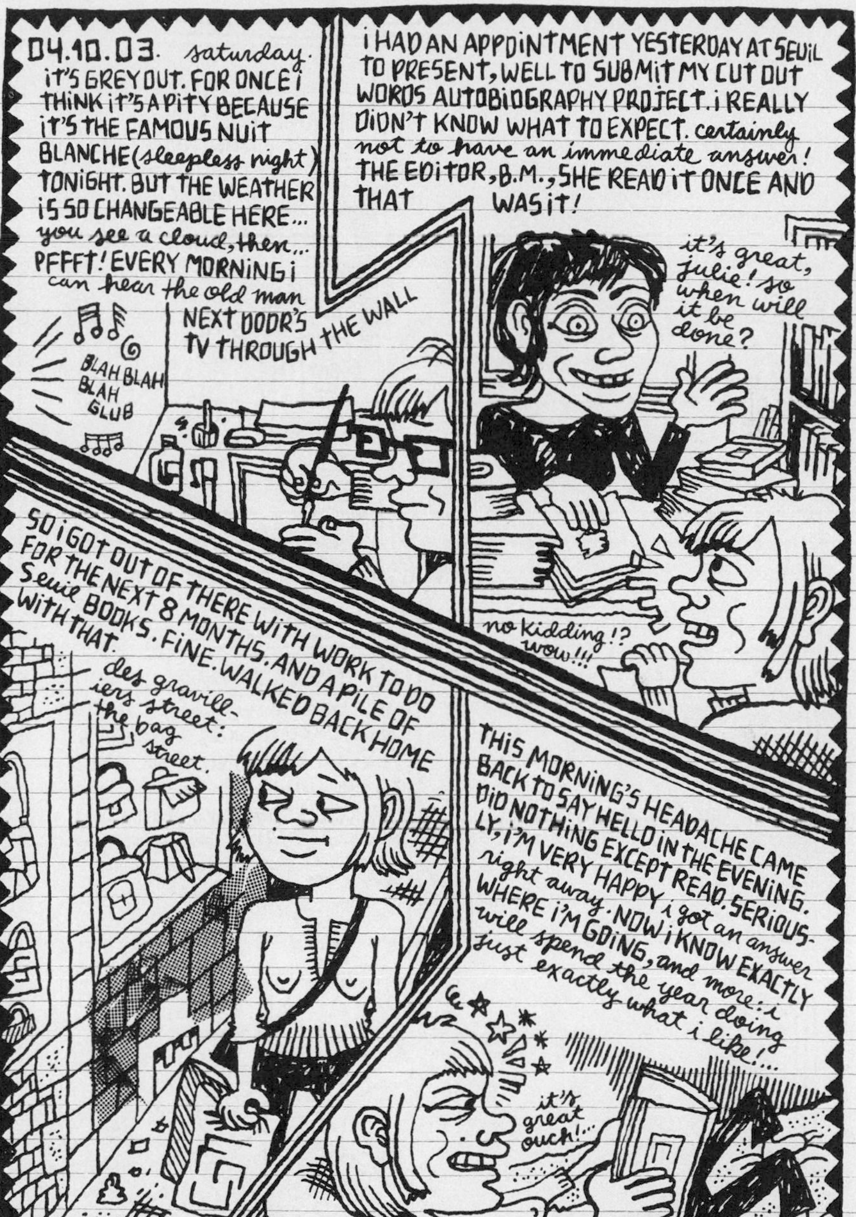
04.10.03. saturday.
it's GREY OUT. FOR ONCE i THINK it's A PITY BECAUSE it's THE FAMOUS NUIT BLANCHE (sleepless night) TONIGHT. BUT THE WEATHER is SO CHANGEABLE HERE... you see a cloud, then... PFFFT! EVERY MORNING i can hear the old man NEXT DOOR'S TV THROUGH THE WALL
BLAH BLAH BLAH GLUB
i HAD AN APPOINTMENT YESTERDAY AT SEUIL TO PRESENT, WELL TO SUBMIT MY CUT OUT WORDS AUTOBIOGRAPHY PROJECT. i REALLY DIDN'T KNOW WHAT TO EXPECT. certainly not to have an immediate answer! THE EDITOR, B.M., SHE READ iT ONCE AND THAT WAS iT!
it's great, julie! so when will it be done?
no kidding!? wow!!!
SO i GOT OUT OF THERE WITH WORK TO DO FOR THE NEXT 8 MONTHS. AND A PILE OF Seuil BOOKS. FiNE. WALKED BACK HOME WITH THAT.
des gravilliers street: the bag street.
THIS MORNING'S HEADACHE CAME BACK TO SAY HELLO IN THE EVENING. DID NOTHING EXCEPT READ. SERIOUSLY, i'M VERY HAPPY i got an answer right away. NOW i KNOW EXACTLY WHERE i'M GOING, and more: i will spend the year doing just exactly what i like!...
it's great ouch!...

05.10.03. sunday. GOT UP AT A QUARTER TO ELEVEN. THE NUIT BLANCHE YESTERDAY. WENT TO BED AT 3... iT STARTED TO RAIN AT 2. and it was not so warm. i MET WITH THE OTHERS at JFJ's at 6:30. i had forgotten his door code at home and his phone number. but that's another story. there was JFJ and C.C., a couple of Québécois friends of his and another guy. OUR FiRST STOP: PLACE CLICHY. the statue was SUPPOSED TO BE iN A BiG BUBBLE and i don't know what else.

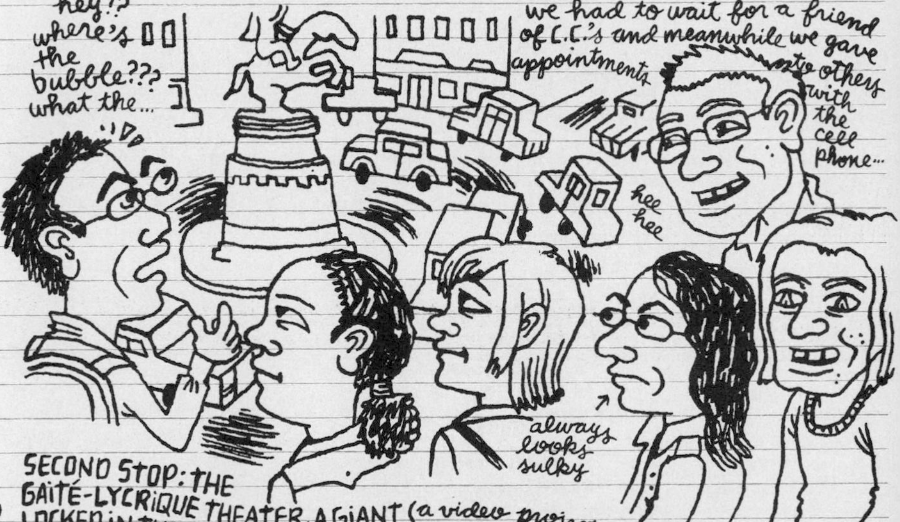
hey!? where's the bubble??? what the...
we had to wait for a friend of C.C.'s and meanwhile we gave appointments to the others with the cell phone...
hee hee
always looks sulky

SECOND STOP: THE GAiTÉ-LYCRiQUE THEATER. A GiANT (a video projected from the inside) WAS LOCKED iN THE BUiLDiNG. THE EFFECT WAS TOTALLY SUCCESSFUL.

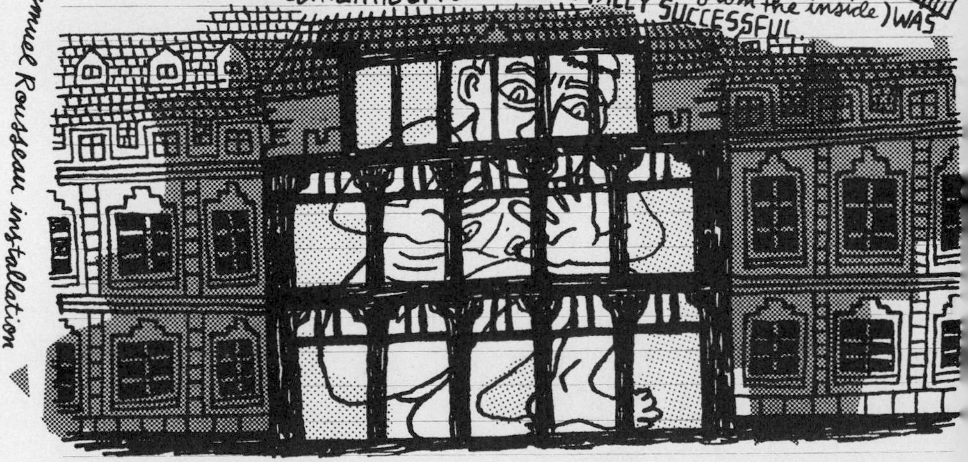
a Samuel Rousseau installation

WE WERE HEADING FOR THE LOUVRE, GOING BY THE HALLES, WHEN WE RAN INTO the ARTS et MÉTIERS MUSEUM. A DREAM MUSEUM, i HAVE TO GO BACK THERE, YES YES

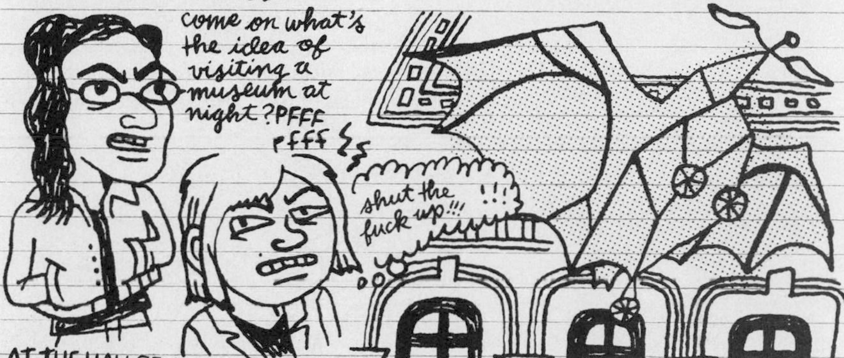
come on what's the idea of visiting a museum at night? PFFF
PFFF
shut the fuck up!!! !!!

AT THE HALLES ANOTHER QUÉBÉCOIS FRIEND JOINED US. AMAZING BUT TRUE HE WAS MOANING JUST as much as THE OTHER ONE! NOT SO INCREDIBLE STUFF at the HALLES, until we got to the portes du jardin des Halles' projections (i think) and in the bourse du commerce a strange light and projection effect that transformed people into robots. but i think i'm the only one who noticed it... THEN THE TOWN HALL: WAY TOO MANY PEOPLE. SO WE SAT AND DRANK A BEER. HALF OF THE GROUP LEFT US AT THAT POINT (the never happy ones, thank god). WE TOOK the subway, line 14, TO GO TO GARE de Lyon where there was A WALL of HALLUCINATORY LIGHT. BUT ONCE AGAIN THERE WAS THOUSANDS OF PEOPLE WAITING IN LINE. SO WE WENT TO SEE the illuminated train of the pont d'Austerlitz

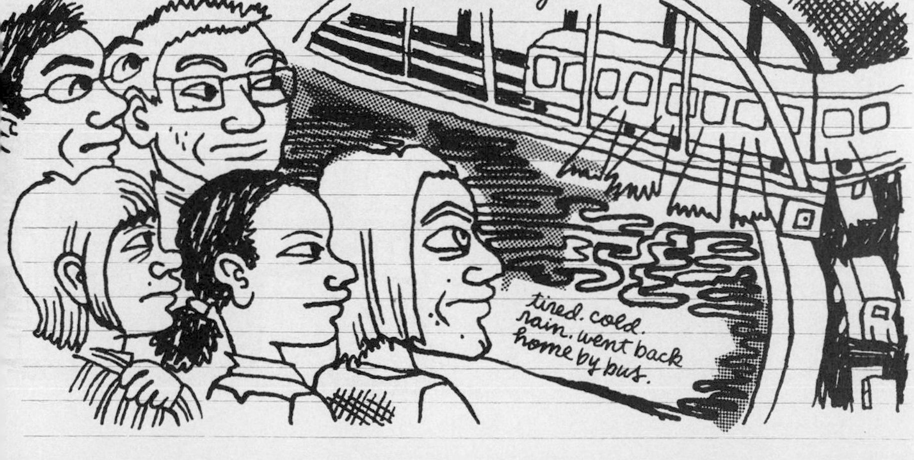
tired. cold. rain. went back home by bus.

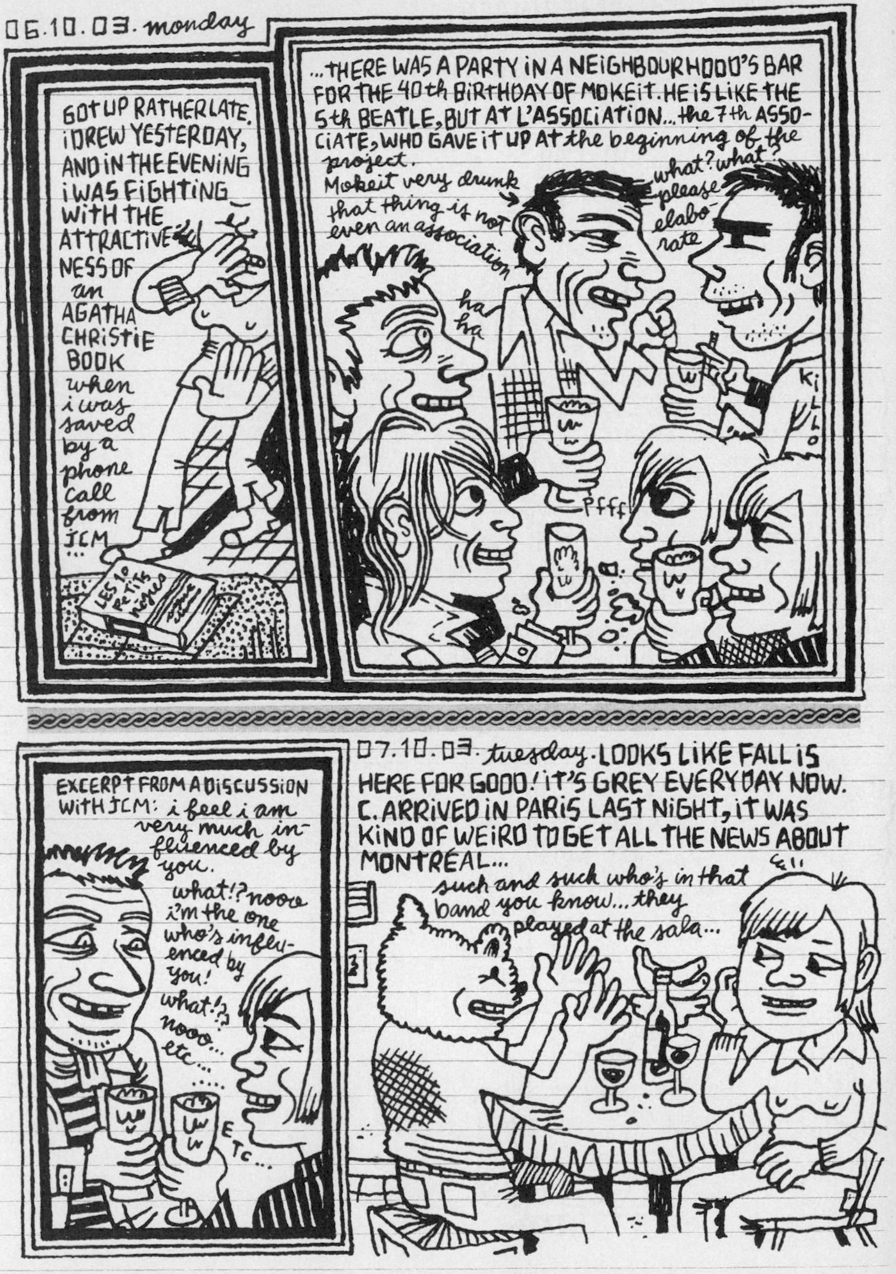
06.10.03. monday
GOT UP RATHER LATE. I DREW YESTERDAY, AND IN THE EVENING I WAS FIGHTING WITH THE ATTRACTIVENESS OF an AGATHA CHRISTIE BOOK when i was saved by a phone call from JCM...
LES 10 PETITS NÈGRES
...THERE WAS A PARTY IN A NEIGHBOURHOOD'S BAR FOR THE 40th BIRTHDAY OF MOKEIT. HE IS LIKE THE 5th BEATLE, BUT AT L'ASSOCIATION... the 7th ASSOCIATE, WHO GAVE IT UP AT the beginning of the project.
Mokeit very drunk
that thing is not even an association
what? what? please elaborate
ha ha
KILLO
pfff
EXCERPT FROM A DISCUSSION WITH JCM: i feel i am very much influenced by you.
what!? nooo i'm the one who's influenced by you!
what!?? nooo etc...
....
ETC...
07.10.03. tuesday. LOOKS LIKE FALL IS HERE FOR GOOD! IT'S GREY EVERYDAY NOW. C. ARRIVED IN PARIS LAST NIGHT, IT WAS KIND OF WEIRD TO GET ALL THE NEWS ABOUT MONTREAL...
such and such who's in that band you know... they played at the sala...

WE WENT TO EAT DINNER IN A CAFÉ AND AFTERWARDS WALKED AROUND IN BELLEVILLE. C. HAD DECIDED THAT *the goal of our little trip would be Edith Piaf's birth place.*

WE SLEPT IN THE SAME BED, BECAUSE IT WAS LESS COMPLICATED THAT WAY. I REGRETTED IT BECAUSE C. SNORED ALL NIGHT. I DIDN'T SLEEP MUCH AT ALL...

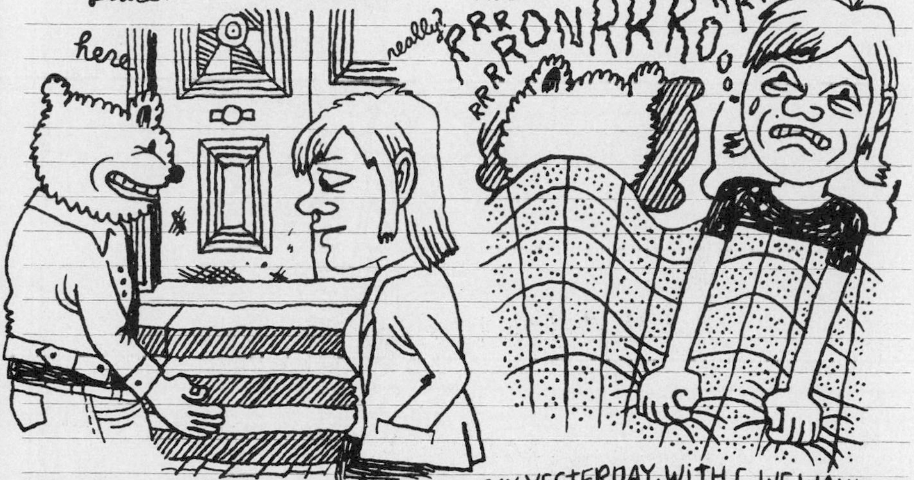
here
really?
RRRRRONRRRRO RRRoon

08.10.03. *wednesday*. IT RAINED ALL DAY YESTERDAY. WITH C. WE WANTED TO WALK IN THE CITY, BUT WE WERE FORCED TO TAKE THE SUBWAY TO GET TO THE CENTER. WE WENT TO VISIT A FRIEND OF HIS (*from MTL*) WHO WORKS NOW AT THE COMPAGNIE BOOKSTORE.

AND OF COURSE THE TWO OF US CAME OUT of THERE WITH A FEW BOOKS. I WAS RATHER HAPPY TO SEE *"chroniques de N.Y." in that bookstore*. WE WENT TO HANG AROUND ANOTHER BOOKSTORE, WAITING FOR OUR NEXT APPOINTMENT WITH ANOTHER FRIEND...

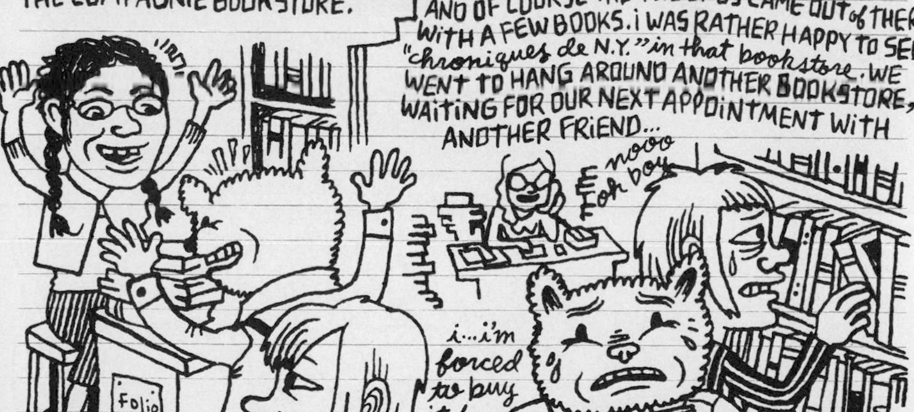
Folio
nooo
oh boy
i...i'm forced to buy it!...

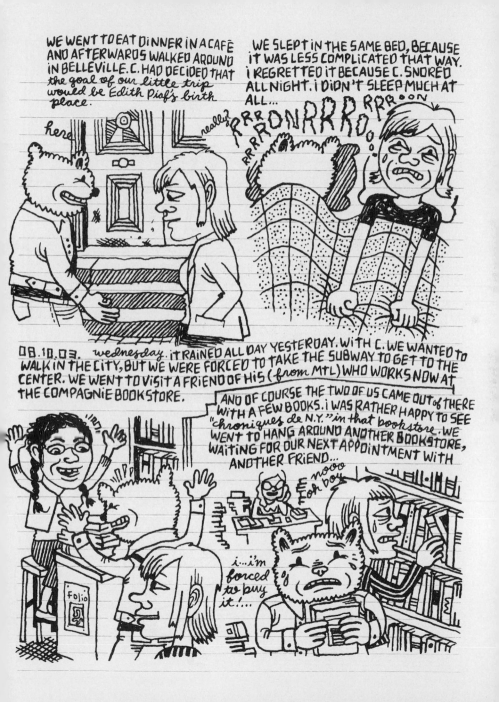

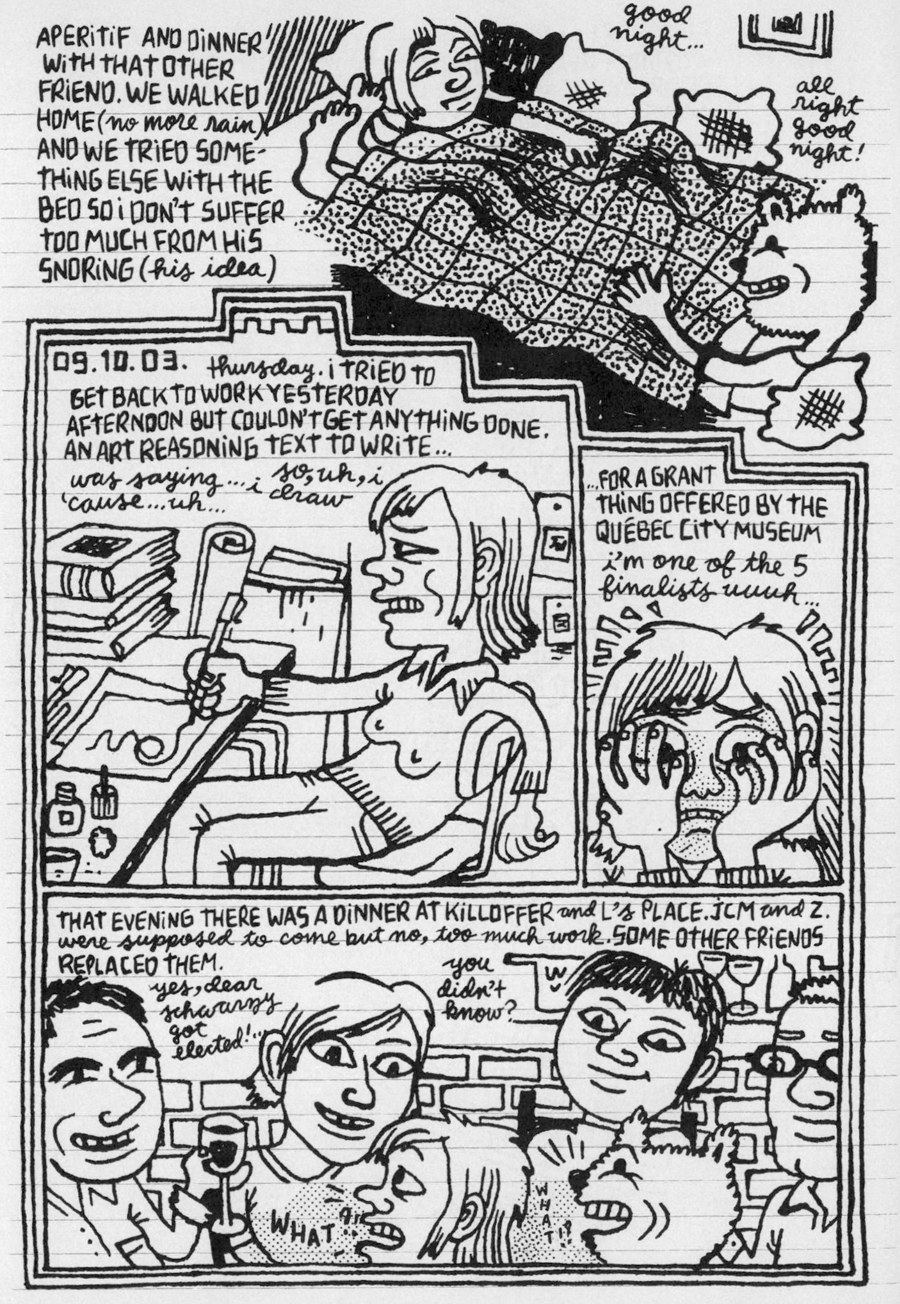
APERITIF AND DINNER WITH THAT OTHER FRIEND. WE WALKED HOME (no more rain) AND WE TRIED SOMETHING ELSE WITH THE BED SO I DON'T SUFFER TOO MUCH FROM HIS SNORING (his idea)
good night...
all right good night!
09.10.03. thursday. i TRIED TO GET BACK TO WORK YESTERDAY AFTERNOON BUT COULDN'T GET ANYTHING DONE. AN ART REASONING TEXT TO WRITE...
was saying... i 'cause... uh...
so, uh, i draw
...FOR A GRANT THING OFFERED BY THE QUÉBEC CITY MUSEUM
i'm one of the 5 finalists uuuh...
THAT EVENING THERE WAS A DINNER AT KILLOFFER and L's PLACE. JCM and Z. were supposed to come but no, too much work. SOME OTHER FRIENDS REPLACED THEM.
yes, dear schwarzy got elected!...
you didn't know?
WHAT?!
WHAT!?

it WAS NiCE, AT K. and L.'s PLACE. we should have brought a second bottle of wine. i DON'T READ NEWSPAPERS i DON'T KNOW WHAT'S GOING ON in the world. SCHWARTZY, THE NEW GOVERNOR OF CALIFORNIA!!! C'MON, THIS iS SO COMPLETELY WRONG!... WHAT A COUNTRY OF... CRAZY CHARACTERS. OUR NEIGHBORS.

10.10.03. Friday. it'S STILL GREY OUT, it'S BEEN GREY ALL WEEK. i NEVER COULD GET STARTED ON THAT TEXT, YESTERDAY. AND LOOKS LIKE iT'S NOT GOING TO BE ANY BETTER TODAY. iT'S THE TYPE OF WORK i CAN ONLY DO AT THE LAST MINUTE, WHEN i HAVE NO CHOICE AT ALL BUT TO DO iT... i FOLLOWED C. iN HiS SEARCH for BOOKSTORES who would want to carry his poetry books (his other books - comics, pictures - are already distributed in France).

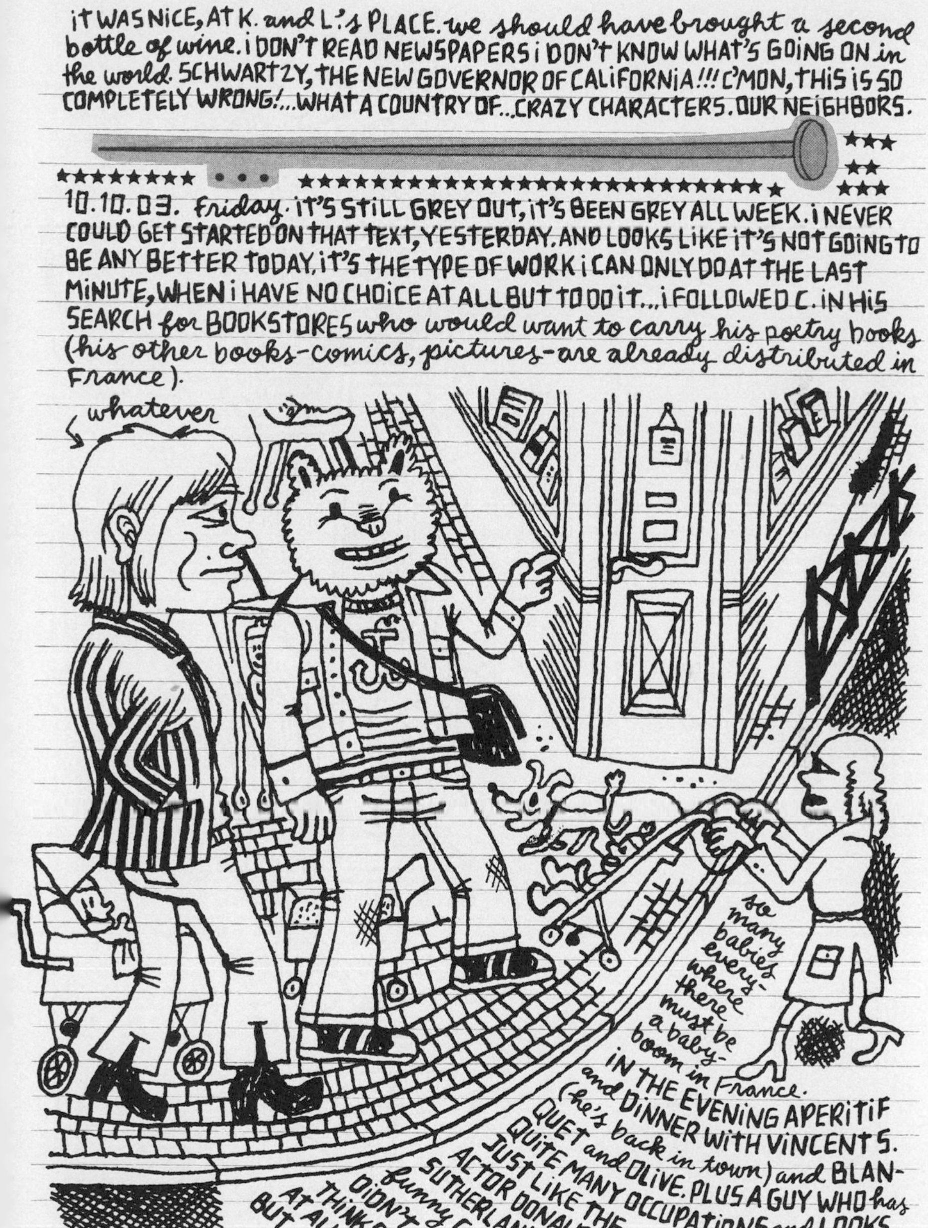

whatever
so many babies every-where must be a baby-boom in France.
IN THE EVENING APERITiF and DINNER WITH VINCENT S. (he's back in town) and BLAN-QUET and OLIVE. PLUS A GUY WHO has QUITE MANY OCCUPATIONS and LOOKS JUST LIKE THE ACTOR DONALD SUTHERLAND. funny C. DIDN'T THINK SO AT ALL, BUT...

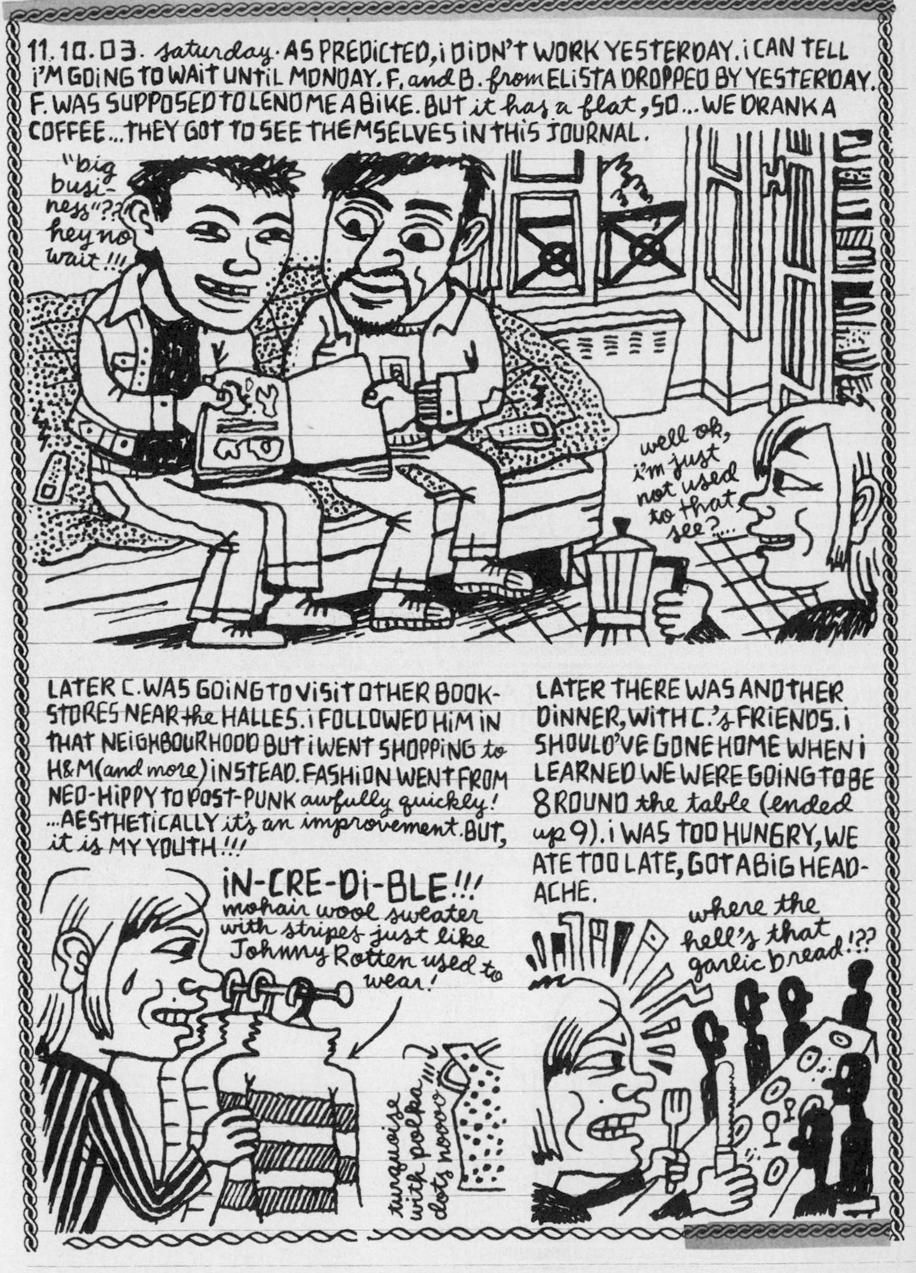
11.10.03. saturday. AS PREDICTED, i DIDN'T WORK YESTERDAY. i CAN TELL i'M GOING TO WAIT UNTIL MONDAY. F. and B. from ELISTA DROPPED BY YESTERDAY. F. WAS SUPPOSED TO LEND ME A BIKE. BUT it has a flat, SO... WE DRANK A COFFEE... THEY GOT TO SEE THEMSELVES IN THIS JOURNAL.
"big business"?? hey no wait!!!
well ok, i'm just not used to that, see?...
LATER C. WAS GOING TO VISIT OTHER BOOKSTORES NEAR the HALLES. i FOLLOWED HIM IN THAT NEIGHBOURHOOD BUT i WENT SHOPPING to H&M (and more) INSTEAD. FASHION WENT FROM NEO-HIPPY TO POST-PUNK awfully quickly! ...AESTHETICALLY it's an improvement. BUT, it is MY YOUTH!!!
IN-CRE-DI-BLE!!! mohair wool sweater with stripes just like Johnny Rotten used to wear!
turquoise with polka dots noooo!!!
LATER THERE WAS ANOTHER DINNER, WITH C.'s FRIENDS. i SHOULD'VE GONE HOME WHEN i LEARNED WE WERE GOING TO BE 8 ROUND the table (ended up 9). i WAS TOO HUNGRY, WE ATE TOO LATE, GOT A BIG HEADACHE.
where the hell's that garlic bread!??

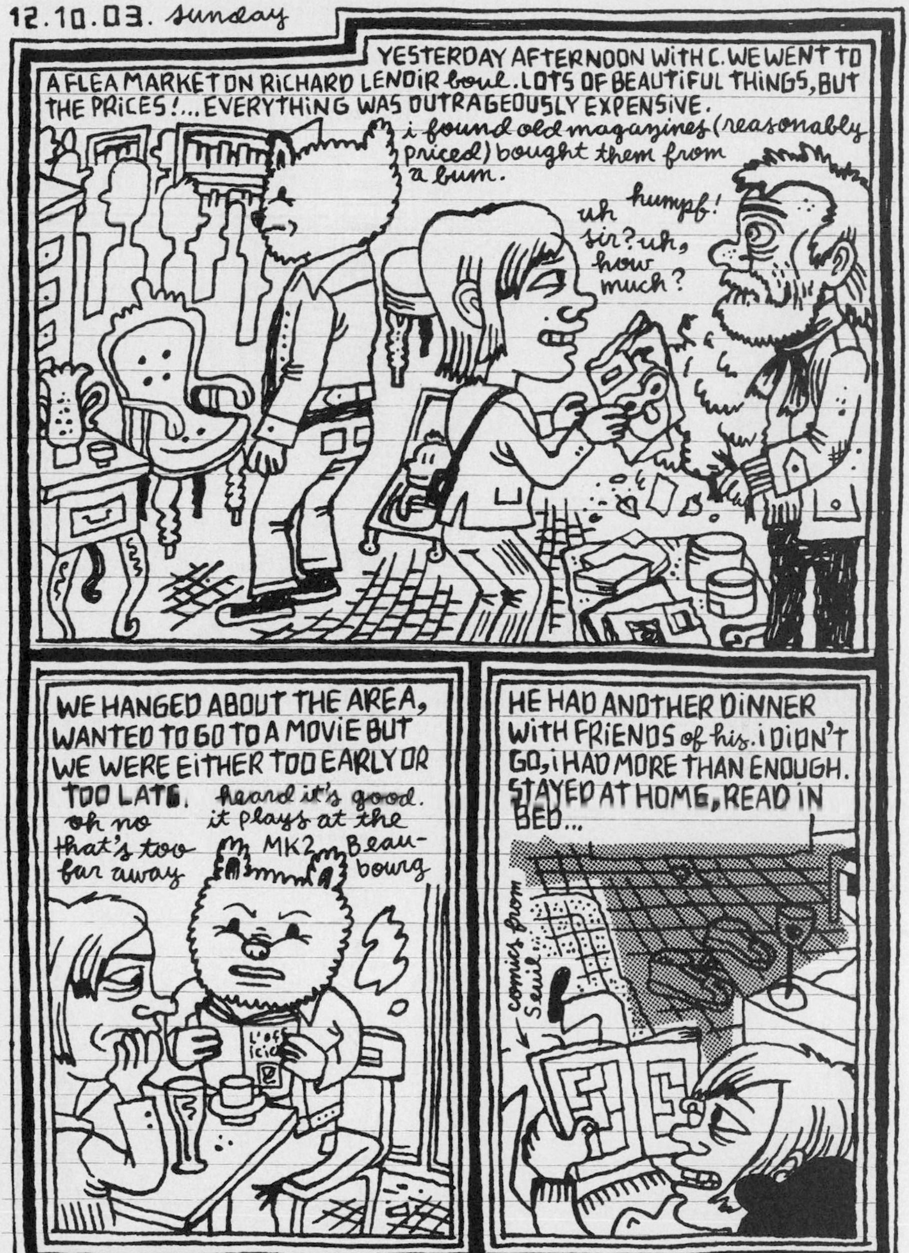
12.10.03. sunday
YESTERDAY AFTERNOON WITH C. WE WENT TO A FLEA MARKET ON RICHARD LENOIR boul. LOTS OF BEAUTIFUL THINGS, BUT THE PRICES!... EVERYTHING WAS OUTRAGEOUSLY EXPENSIVE.
i found old magazines (reasonably priced) bought them from a bum.
uh sir? uh, how much?
humpf!
WE HANGED ABOUT THE AREA, WANTED TO GO TO A MOVIE BUT WE WERE EITHER TOO EARLY OR TOO LATE.
heard it's good. it plays at the MK2 Beaubourg
oh no that's too far away
L'off icial
HE HAD ANOTHER DINNER WITH FRIENDS of his. i DIDN'T GO, i HAD MORE THAN ENOUGH. STAYED AT HOME, READ IN BED...
comics from Seuil...

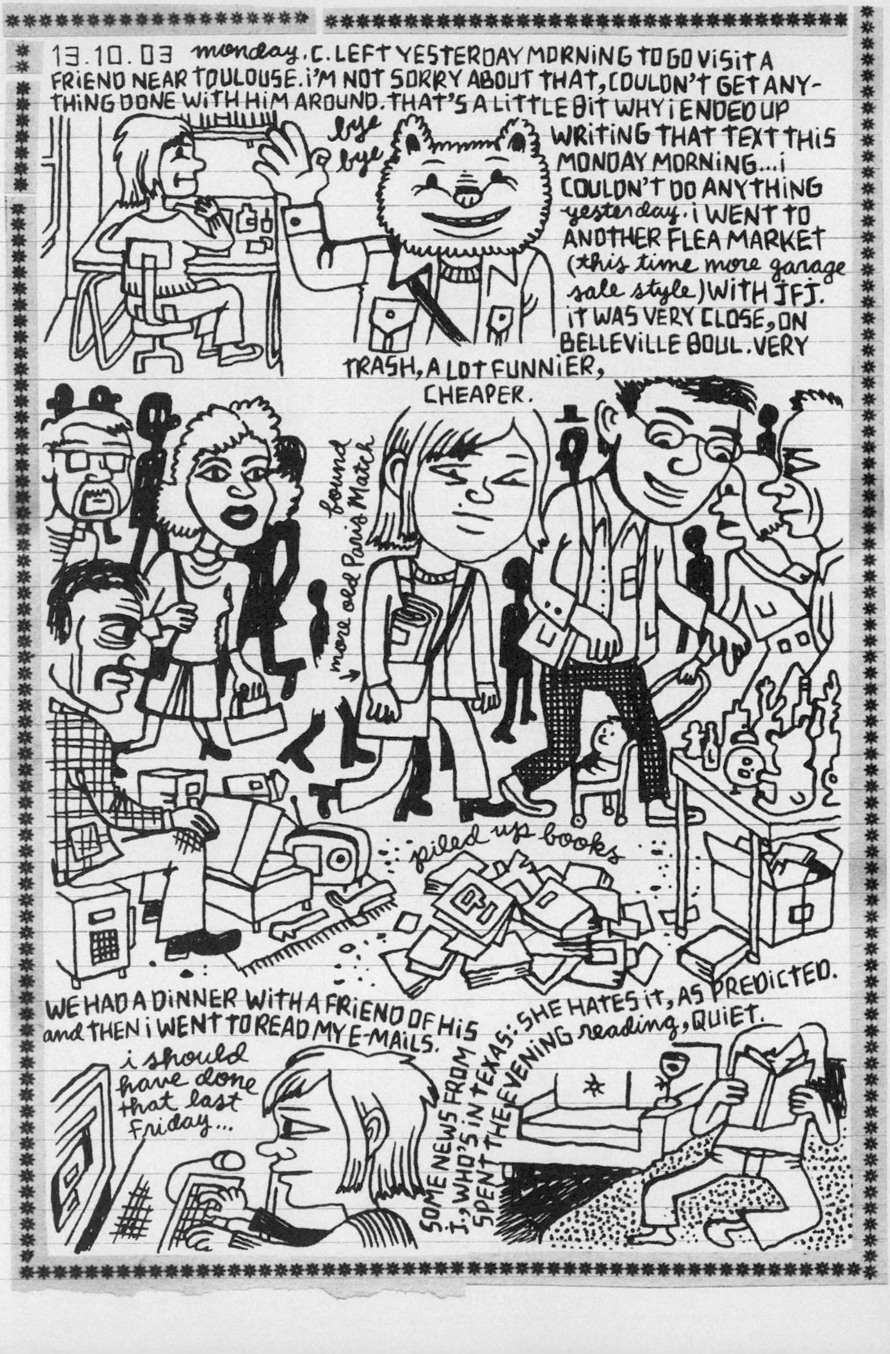
13.10.03 monday. C. LEFT YESTERDAY MORNING TO GO VISIT A FRIEND NEAR TOULOUSE. I'M NOT SORRY ABOUT THAT, COULDN'T GET ANYTHING DONE WITH HIM AROUND. THAT'S A LITTLE BIT WHY I ENDED UP WRITING THAT TEXT THIS MONDAY MORNING... I COULDN'T DO ANYTHING yesterday. I WENT TO ANOTHER FLEA MARKET (this time more garage sale style) WITH JFJ. IT WAS VERY CLOSE, ON BELLEVILLE BOUL. VERY TRASH, A LOT FUNNIER, CHEAPER.
bye bye
found more old Paris Match
piled up books
WE HAD A DINNER WITH A FRIEND OF HIS and THEN I WENT TO READ MY E-MAILS.
i should have done that last Friday...
SOME NEWS FROM J., WHO'S IN TEXAS: SHE HATES IT, AS PREDICTED. SPENT THE EVENING reading, QUIET.

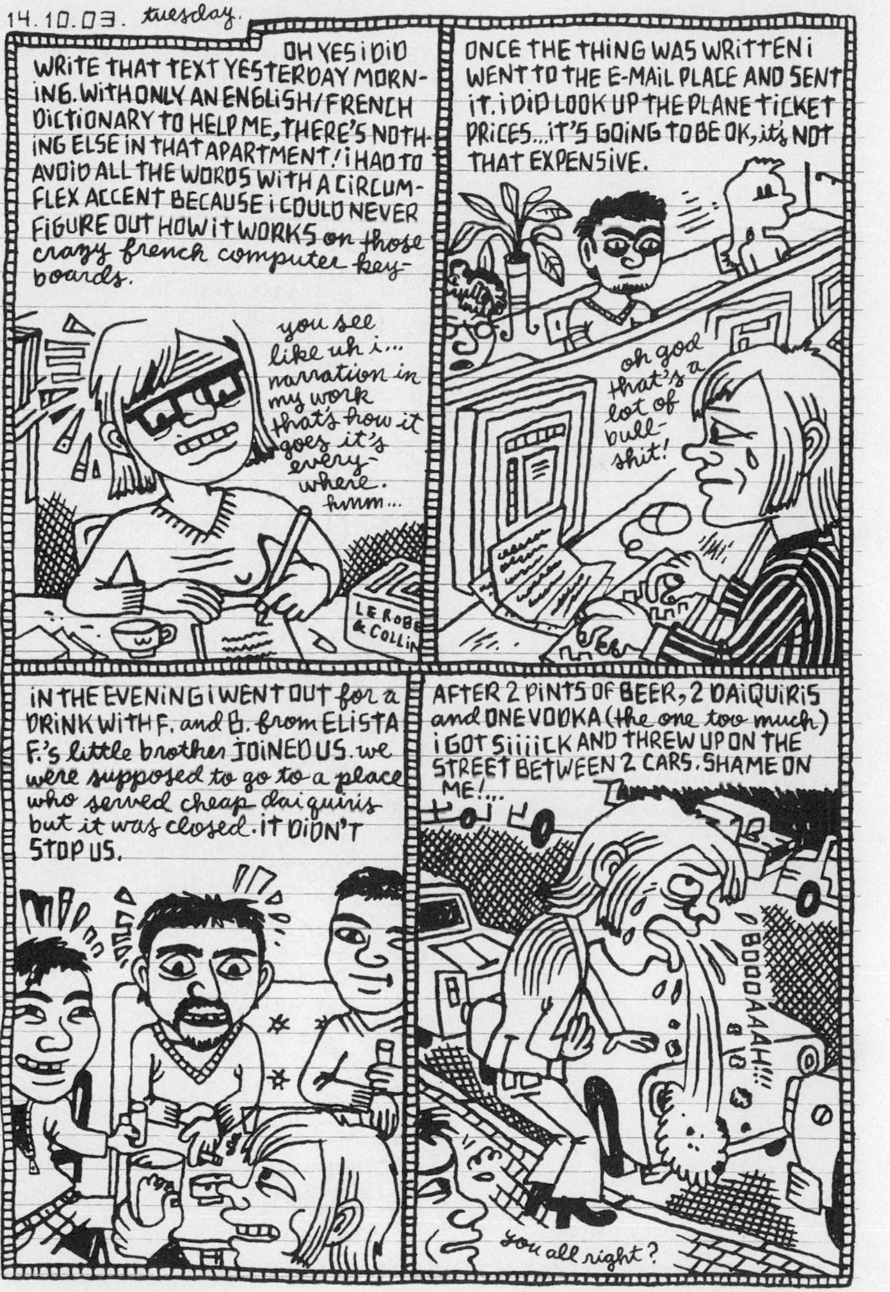
14.10.03. tuesday.
OH YES i DID WRITE THAT TEXT YESTERDAY MORNING. WITH ONLY AN ENGLISH/FRENCH DICTIONARY TO HELP ME, THERE'S NOTHING ELSE IN THAT APARTMENT! i HAD TO AVOID ALL THE WORDS WITH A CIRCUMFLEX ACCENT BECAUSE i COULD NEVER FIGURE OUT HOW iT WORKS on those crazy french computer keyboards.
you see like uh i... narration in my work that's how it goes it's everywhere. hmm...
LE ROBE & COLLIN
ONCE THE THING WAS WRITTEN i WENT TO THE E-MAIL PLACE AND SENT IT. i DID LOOK UP THE PLANE TICKET PRICES... IT'S GOING TO BE OK, it's NOT THAT EXPENSIVE.
oh god that's a lot of bullshit!
IN THE EVENING i WENT OUT for a DRINK WITH F. and B. from ELISTA. F.'s little brother JOINED US. we were supposed to go to a place who served cheap daiquiris but it was closed. IT DIDN'T STOP US.
AFTER 2 PINTS OF BEER, 2 DAIQUIRIS and ONE VODKA (the one too much) i GOT SiiiiCK AND THREW UP ON THE STREET BETWEEN 2 CARS. SHAME ON ME!...
BOOOAAAH!!!
you all right?

SINCE WE WERE NOT TOO FAR, CLOSE TO BASTILLE, WE ZIGZAGGED ALONG, WENT TO MY PLACE

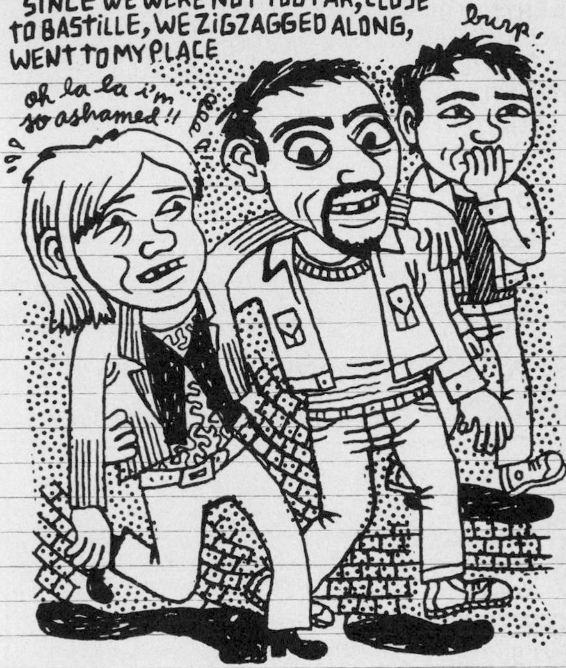
oh la la i'm so ashamed!!
burp,

15.10.03. wednesday:

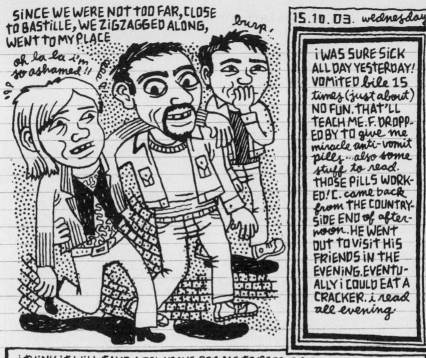

i WAS SURE SiCK ALL DAY YESTERDAY! VOMiTED bile 15 times (just about) NO FUN. THAT'LL TEACH ME. F. DROPPED BY TO give me miracle anti-vomit pills ... also some stuff to read. THOSE PiLLS WORKED! C. came back from THE COUNTRYSIDE END of afternoon. HE WENT OUT TO ViSiT HiS FRiENDS iN THE EVENiNG. EVENTUALLY i COULD EAT A CRACKER. i read all evening.

i THINK iT WiLL TAKE A FEW DAYS FOR ME TO RECOVER: i COULD NOT DRiNK COFFEE THiS MORNiNG!...

16.10.03. thursday. i AM FEELiNG BETTER BUT MY STOMACH iS STiLL QUiTE FRAGiLE. i HAD TO CATCH UP WiTH MY JOURNAL YESTERDAY MORNiNG 'CAUSE i DiDN'T DRAW THE DAY BEFORE. BEGiNNiNG OF AFTERNOON i WENT TO THE ANiMATiON COMPANY WHO DiD THE ViDEO CLiP, TO BRiNG THEM THE SiGNED CONTRACT. SO i COULD ViEW THE THiNG. MOST OF THE TiME iT FEELS LiKE THE DRAWiNGS ARE FLOATiNG. iT'S OBViOUS WE COULDV'E DONE SO MUCH BETTER iF WE HAD SOME MORE TiME. AND ALSO i WOULD HAVE DONE MORE DETAiLED DRAWiNGS.

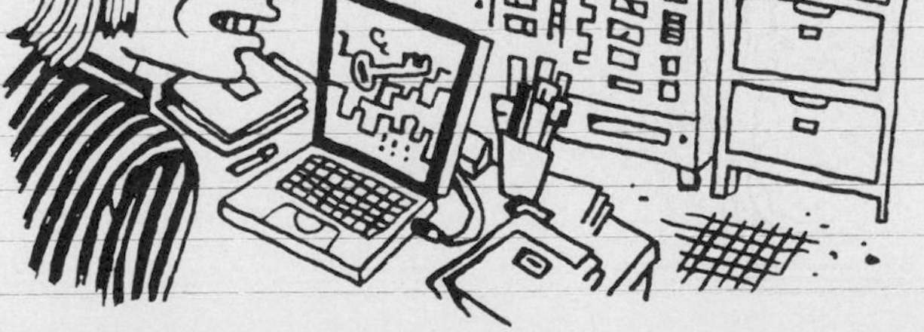
oh boy i'm not sure at all i'm happy with this!

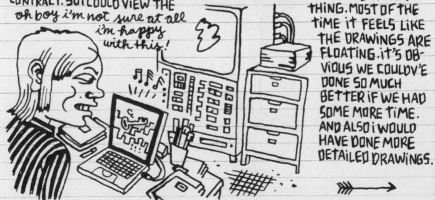

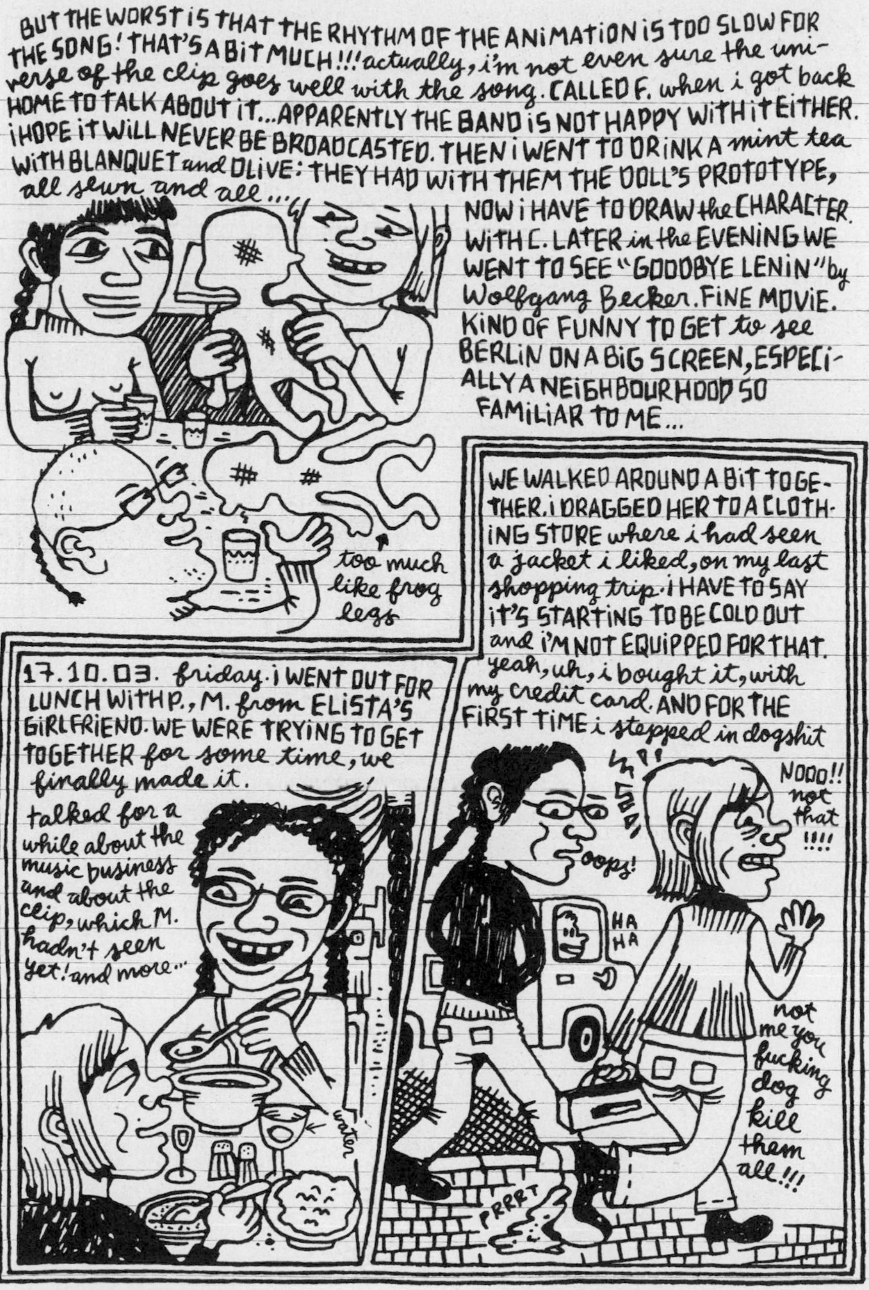
BUT THE WORST IS THAT THE RHYTHM OF THE ANIMATION IS TOO SLOW FOR THE SONG! THAT'S A BIT MUCH!!! actually, i'm not even sure the universe of the clip goes well with the song. CALLED F. when i got back HOME TO TALK ABOUT IT... APPARENTLY THE BAND IS NOT HAPPY WITH IT EITHER. i HOPE IT WILL NEVER BE BROADCASTED. THEN i WENT TO DRINK A mint tea WITH BLANQUET and OLIVE: THEY HAD WITH THEM THE DOLL'S PROTOTYPE, all sewn and all...
NOW i HAVE TO DRAW the CHARACTER. WITH C. LATER in the EVENING WE WENT TO SEE "GOODBYE LENIN" by Wolfgang Becker. FINE MOVIE. KIND OF FUNNY TO GET to see BERLIN ON A BIG SCREEN, ESPECIALLY A NEIGHBOURHOOD SO FAMILIAR TO ME...
too much like frog legs
17.10.03. friday. i WENT OUT FOR LUNCH WITH P., M. from ELISTA'S GIRLFRIEND. WE WERE TRYING TO GET TOGETHER for some time, we finally made it.
talked for a while about the music business and about the clip, which M. hadn't seen yet! and more...
water
WE WALKED AROUND A BIT TOGETHER. i DRAGGED HER TO A CLOTHING STORE where i had seen a jacket i liked, on my last shopping trip. i HAVE TO SAY IT'S STARTING TO BE COLD OUT and i'M NOT EQUIPPED FOR THAT. yeah, uh, i bought it, with my credit card. AND FOR THE FIRST TIME i stepped in dogshit
oops!
NOOO!! not that !!!!
HA HA
not me you fucking dog kill them all!!!
PRRRT

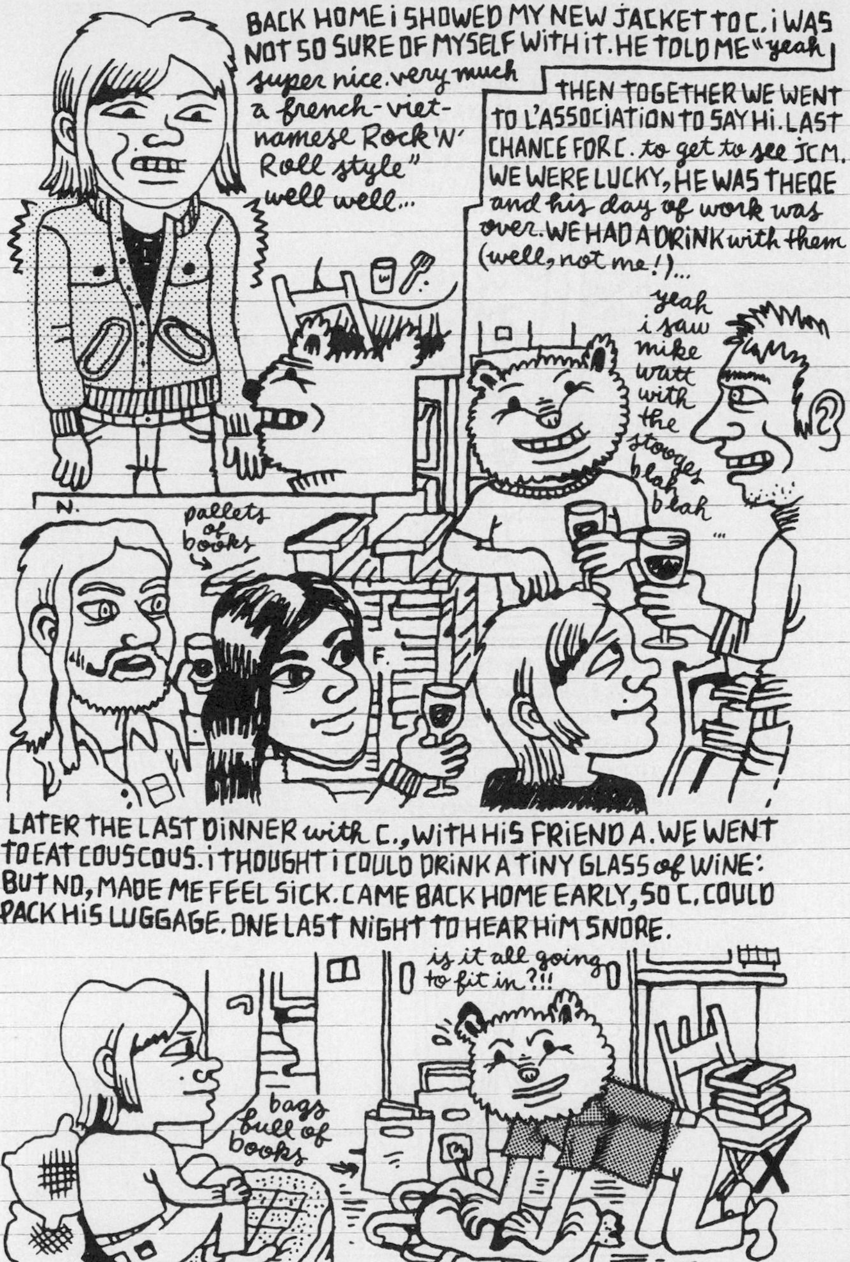
BACK HOME i SHOWED MY NEW JACKET TO C. i WAS NOT SO SURE OF MYSELF WITH iT. HE TOLD ME "yeah super nice. very much a french-vietnamese Rock'N' Roll style" well well...
THEN TOGETHER WE WENT TO L'ASSOCIATION TO SAY Hi. LAST CHANCE FOR C. to get to see JCM. WE WERE LUCKY, HE WAS THERE and his day of work was over. WE HAD A DRiNK with them (well, not me!)...
yeah i saw mike watt with the stooges blah blah ...
N.
pallets of books
F.
LATER THE LAST DINNER with C., WITH HiS FRIEND A. WE WENT TO EAT COUSCOUS. i THOUGHT i COULD DRiNK A TINY GLASS of WiNE: BUT NO, MADE ME FEEL SiCK. CAME BACK HOME EARLY, SO C. COULD PACK HiS LUGGAGE. ONE LAST NiGHT TO HEAR HiM SNORE.
is it all going to fit in?!!
bags full of books

18.10.03. saturday.

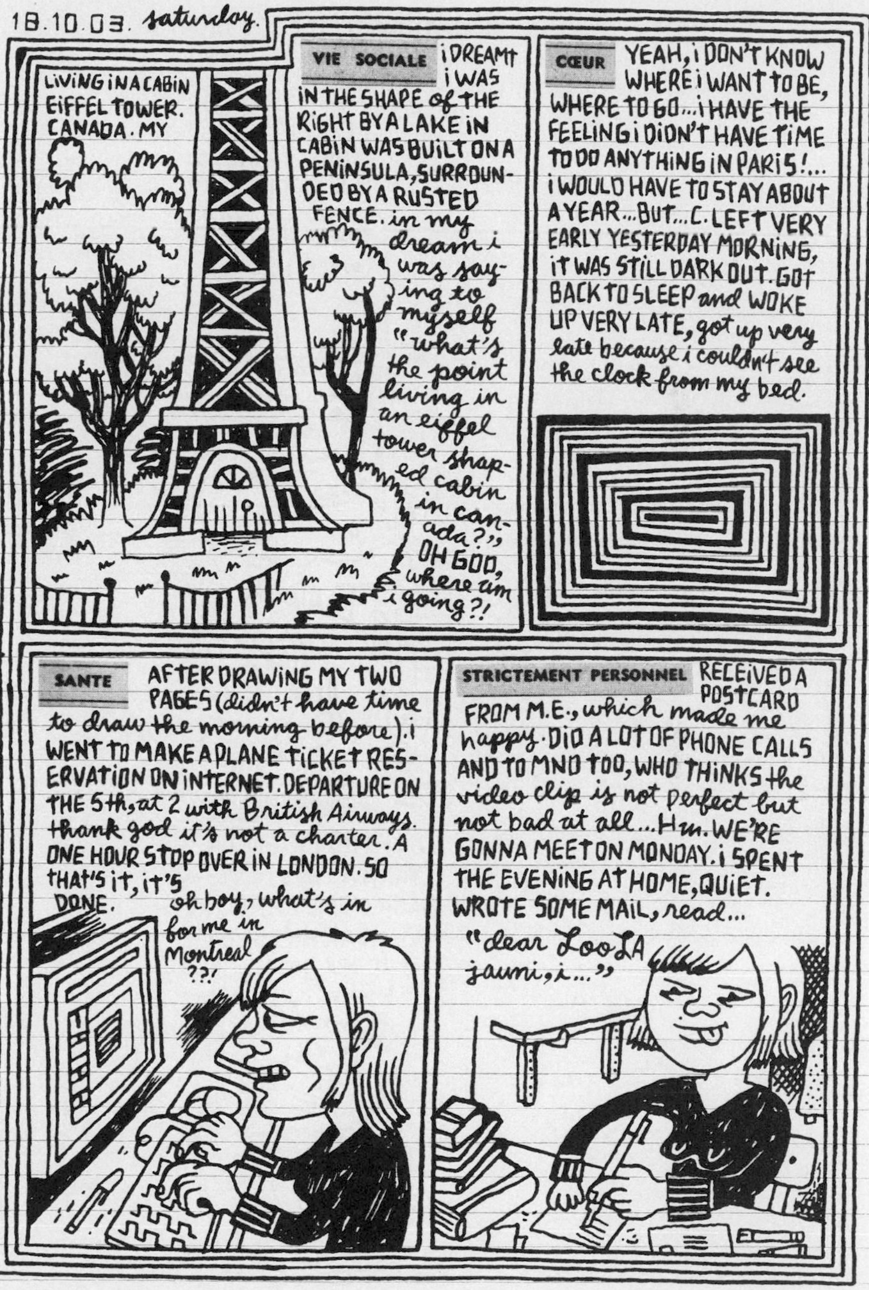
VIE SOCIALE
i DREAMT i WAS
LIVING IN A CABIN
IN THE SHAPE of THE
EIFFEL TOWER.
RIGHT BY A LAKE IN
CANADA. MY
CABIN WAS BUILT ON A PENINSULA, SURROUNDED BY A RUSTED FENCE. in my dream i was saying to myself "what's the point living in an eiffel tower shaped cabin in canada?" OH GOD, where am i going?!
CŒUR
YEAH, i DON'T KNOW WHERE i WANT TO BE, WHERE TO GO... i HAVE THE FEELING i DIDN'T HAVE TIME TO DO ANYTHING IN PARIS!... i WOULD HAVE TO STAY ABOUT A YEAR... BUT... C. LEFT VERY EARLY YESTERDAY MORNING, iT WAS STILL DARK OUT. GOT BACK TO SLEEP and WOKE UP VERY LATE, got up very late because i couldn't see the clock from my bed.
SANTE
AFTER DRAWING MY TWO PAGES (didn't have time to draw the morning before). i WENT TO MAKE A PLANE TICKET RESERVATION ON INTERNET. DEPARTURE ON THE 5th, at 2 with British Airways. thank god it's not a charter. A ONE HOUR STOP OVER IN LONDON. SO THAT'S IT, IT'S DONE.
oh boy, what's in for me in Montreal ??!
STRICTEMENT PERSONNEL
RECEIVED A POSTCARD FROM M.E., which made me happy. DID A LOT OF PHONE CALLS AND TO MND TOO, WHO THINKS the video clip is not perfect but not bad at all... Hm. WE'RE GONNA MEET ON MONDAY. i SPENT THE EVENING AT HOME, QUIET. WROTE SOME MAIL, read...
"dear LooLA jaumi, i..."

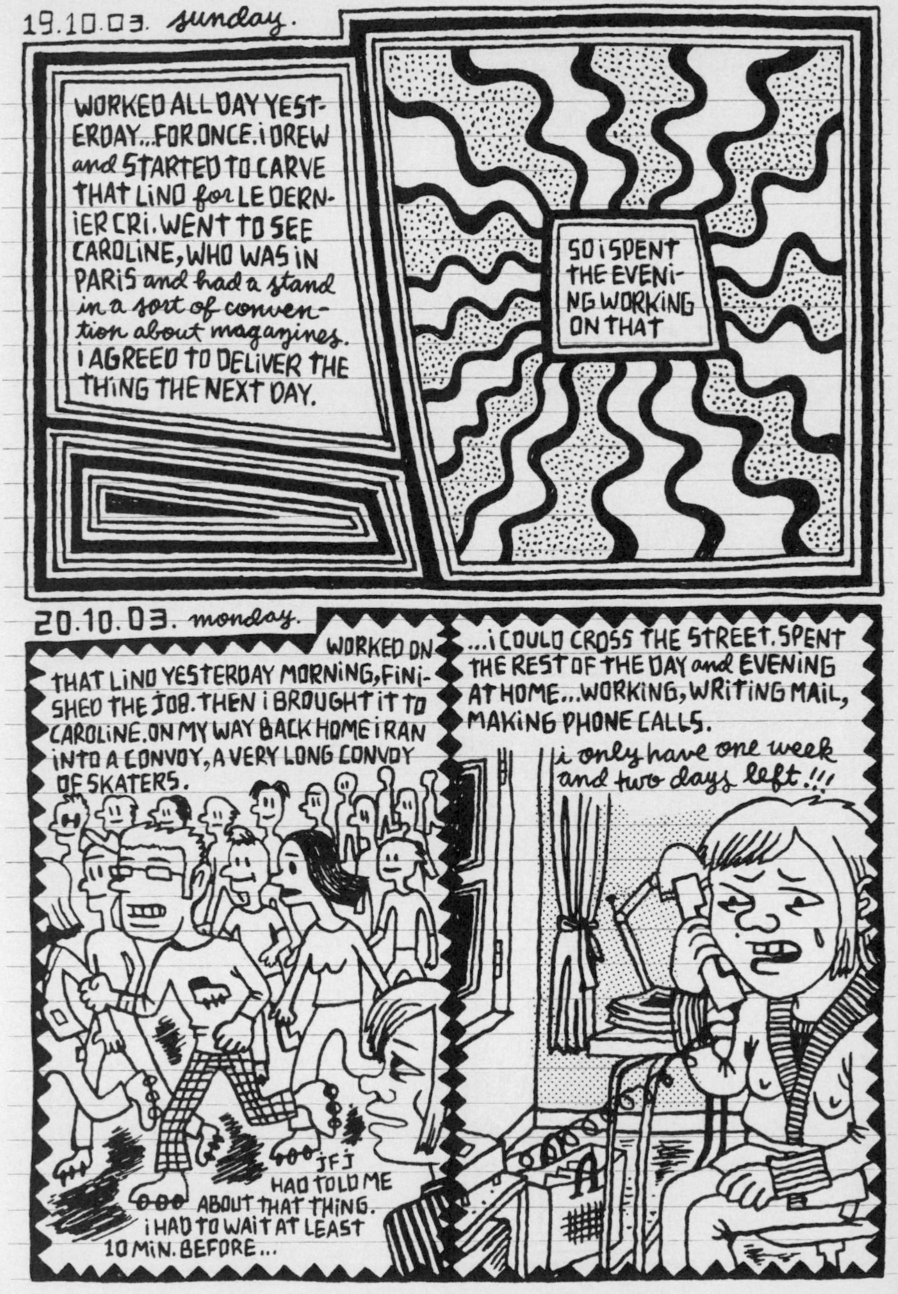
19.10.03. sunday.
WORKED ALL DAY YESTERDAY... FOR ONCE. i DREW and STARTED TO CARVE THAT LINO for LE DERNIER CRI. WENT TO SEE CAROLINE, WHO WAS IN PARIS and had a stand in a sort of convention about magazines. i AGREED TO DELIVER THE THING THE NEXT DAY.
SO i SPENT THE EVENING WORKING ON THAT
20.10.03. monday.
WORKED ON THAT LINO YESTERDAY MORNING, FINISHED THE JOB. THEN i BROUGHT IT TO CAROLINE. ON MY WAY BACK HOME i RAN INTO A CONVOY, A VERY LONG CONVOY OF SKATERS.
JFJ HAD TOLD ME ABOUT THAT THING. i HAD TO WAIT AT LEAST 10 MIN. BEFORE...
...i COULD CROSS THE STREET. SPENT THE REST OF THE DAY and EVENING AT HOME... WORKING, WRITING MAIL, MAKING PHONE CALLS.
i only have one week and two days left!!!

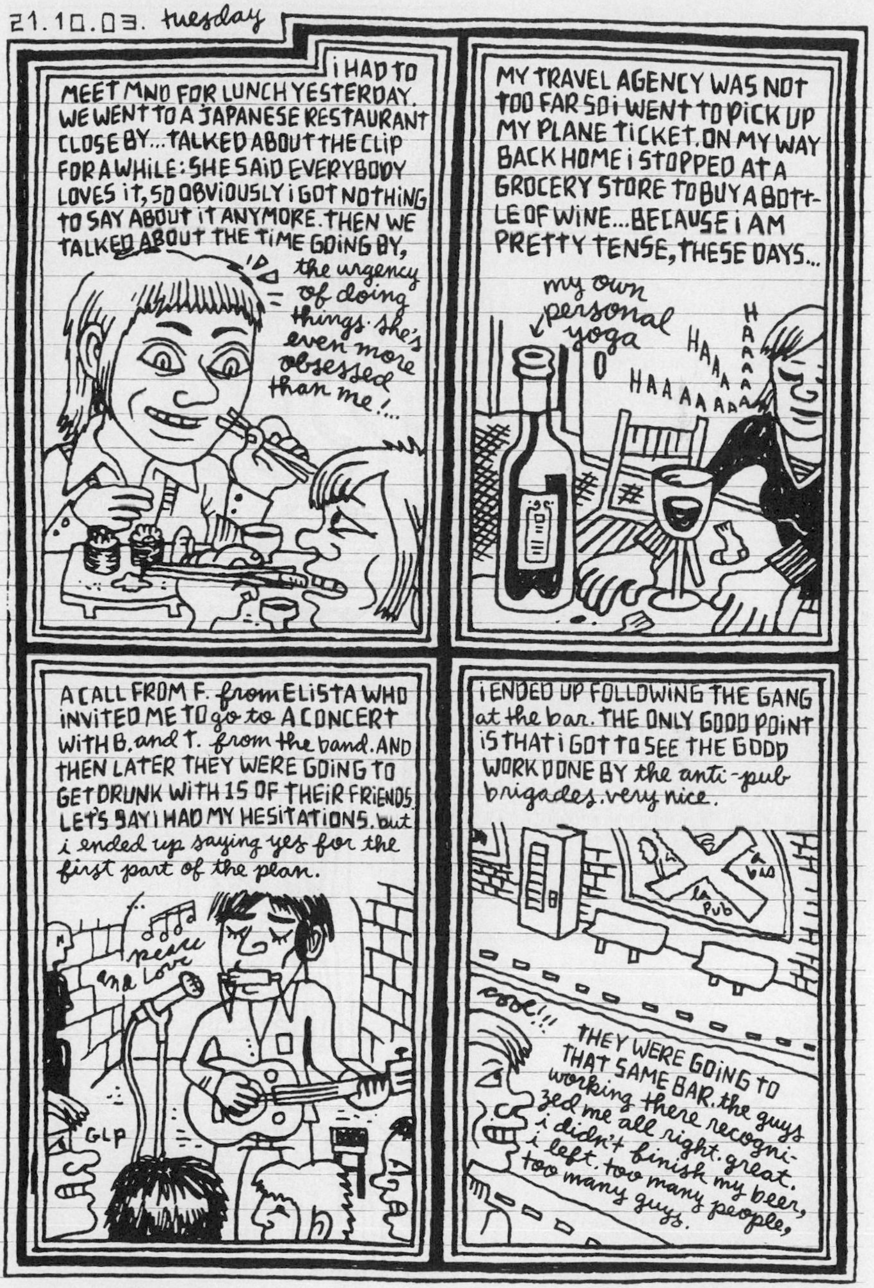
21.10.03. tuesday
i HAD TO MEET MNO FOR LUNCH YESTERDAY. WE WENT TO A JAPANESE RESTAURANT CLOSE BY... TALKED ABOUT THE CLIP FOR A WHILE: SHE SAID EVERYBODY LOVES iT, SO OBVIOUSLY i GOT NOTHING TO SAY ABOUT iT ANYMORE. THEN WE TALKED ABOUT THE TiME GOiNG BY,
the urgency of doing things. she's even more obsessed than me!...
MY TRAVEL AGENCY WAS NOT TOO FAR SO i WENT TO PiCK UP MY PLANE TiCKET. ON MY WAY BACK HOME i STOPPED AT A GROCERY STORE TO BUY A BOTTLE OF WiNE... BECAUSE i AM PRETTY TENSE, THESE DAYS...
my own personal yoga
HAAAA
HAAAAAAAA
HAAAAAAA
A CALL FROM F. from ELiSTA WHO iNViTED ME TO go to A CONCERT WiTH B. and T. from the band. AND THEN LATER THEY WERE GOiNG TO GET DRUNK WiTH 15 OF THEiR FRiENDS. LET'S SAY i HAD MY HESiTATiONS. but i ended up saying yes for the first part of the plan.
peace and Love
GLP
i ENDED UP FOLLOWiNG THE GANG at the bar. THE ONLY GOOD POiNT iS THAT i GOT TO SEE THE GOOD WORK DONE BY the anti-pub brigades. very nice.
la pub
à vià
cool!!!
THEY WERE GOiNG TO THAT SAME BAR. the guys working there recognized me all right. great. i didn't finish my beer, i left. too many guys people, too many guys.

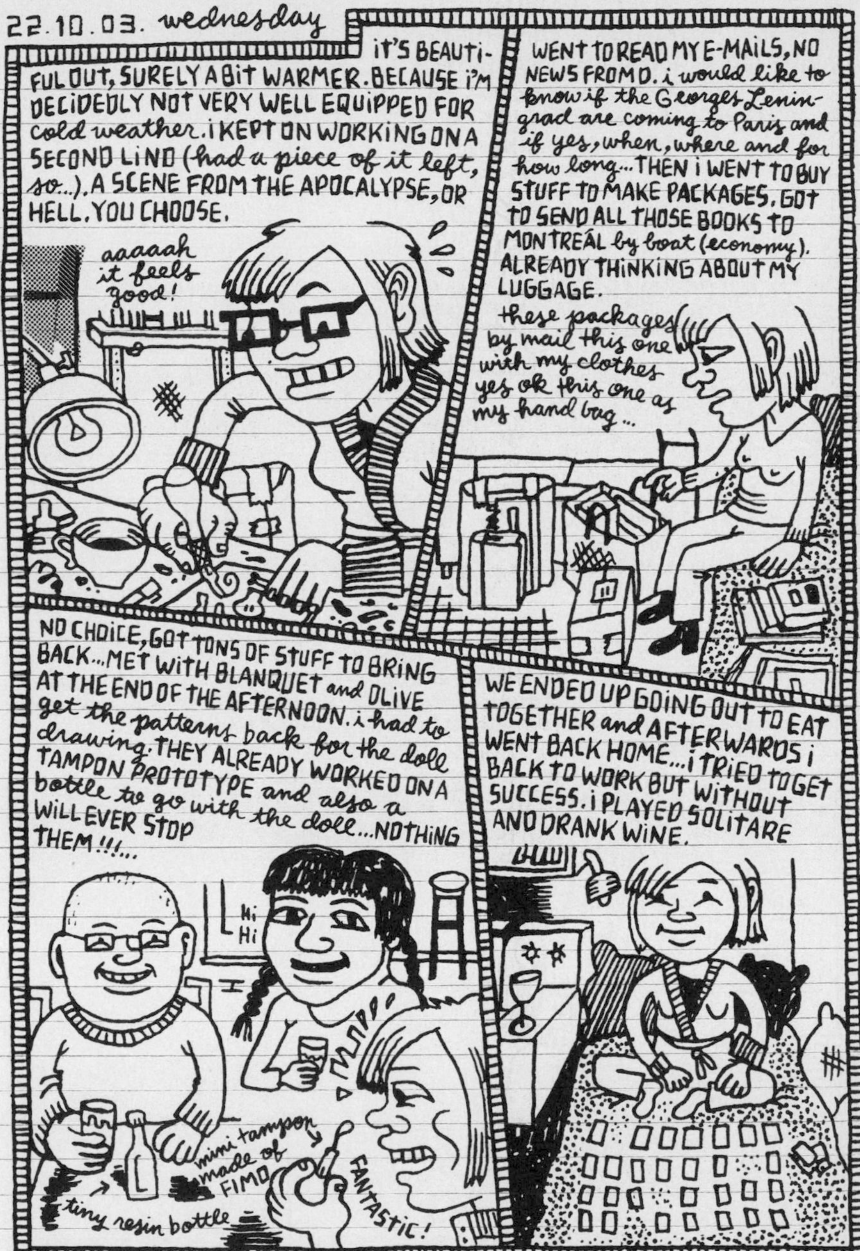
22.10.03. wednesday
IT'S BEAUTIFUL OUT, SURELY A BIT WARMER. BECAUSE I'M DECIDEDLY NOT VERY WELL EQUIPPED FOR cold weather. I KEPT ON WORKING ON A SECOND LINO (had a piece of it left, so...). A SCENE FROM THE APOCALYPSE, OR HELL. YOU CHOOSE.
aaaaah it feels good!
WENT TO READ MY E-MAILS, NO NEWS FROM O. i would like to know if the Georges Leningrad are coming to Paris and if yes, when, where and for how long... THEN I WENT TO BUY STUFF TO MAKE PACKAGES. GOT TO SEND ALL THOSE BOOKS TO MONTRÉAL by boat (economy). ALREADY THINKING ABOUT MY LUGGAGE.
these packages by mail this one with my clothes yes ok this one as my hand bag...
NO CHOICE, GOT TONS OF STUFF TO BRING BACK... MET WITH BLANQUET and OLIVE AT THE END OF THE AFTERNOON. i had to get the patterns back for the doll drawing. THEY ALREADY WORKED ON A TAMPON PROTOTYPE and also a bottle to go with the doll... NOTHING WILL EVER STOP THEM!!!...
Hi Hi
mini tampon made of FIMO
tiny resin bottle
FANTASTIC!
WE ENDED UP GOING OUT TO EAT TOGETHER and AFTERWARDS I WENT BACK HOME... I TRIED TO GET BACK TO WORK BUT WITHOUT SUCCESS. I PLAYED SOLITARE AND DRANK WINE.

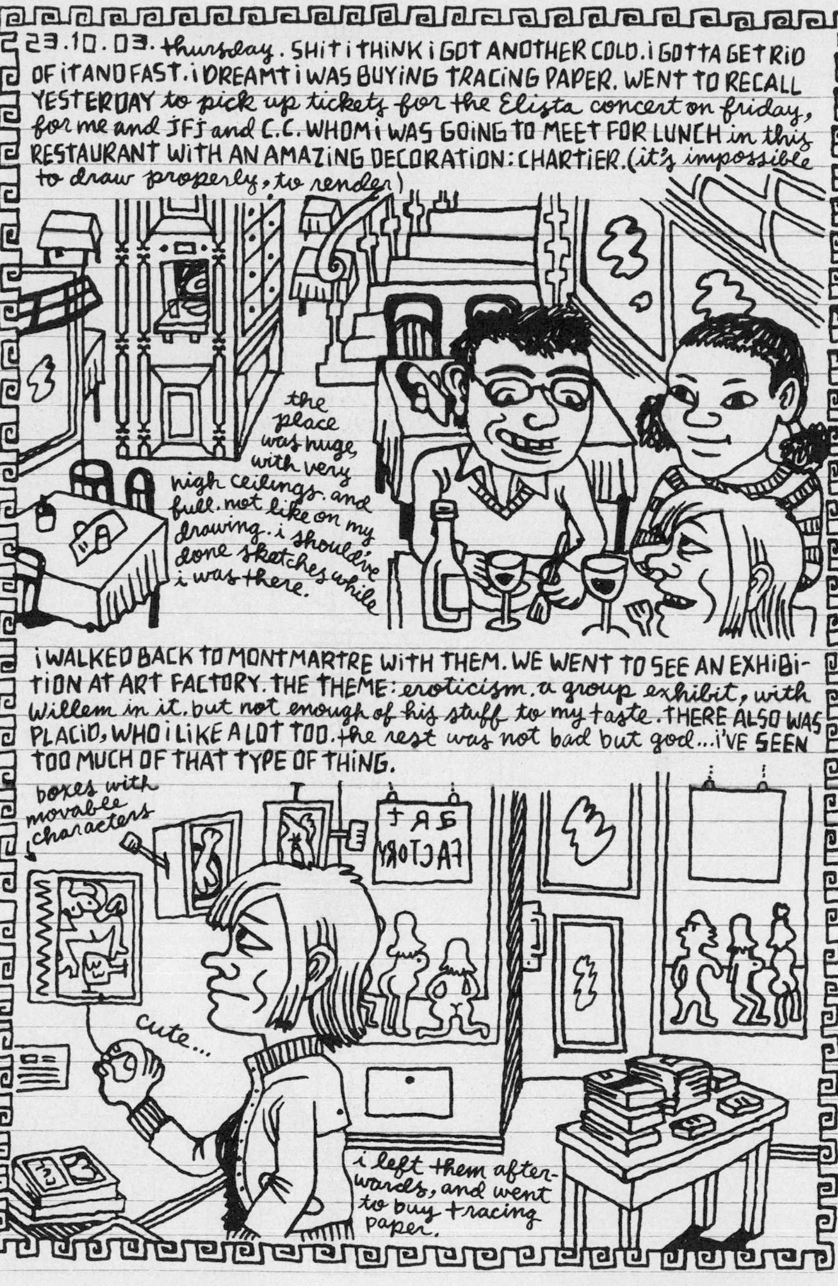
23.10.03. thursday. SHIT i THINK i GOT ANOTHER COLD. i GOTTA GET RID OF iT AND FAST. i DREAMT i WAS BUYiNG TRACiNG PAPER. WENT TO RECALL YESTERDAY to pick up tickets for the Elista concert on friday, for me and JFJ and C.C. WHOM i WAS GOiNG TO MEET FOR LUNCH in this RESTAURANT WiTH AN AMAZiNG DECORATiON: CHARTiER. (it's impossible to draw properly, to render)
the place was huge, with very high ceilings. and full. not like on my drawing. i should've done sketches while i was there.
i WALKED BACK TO MONTMARTRE WiTH THEM. WE WENT TO SEE AN EXHiBiTiON AT ART FACTORY. THE THEME: eroticism. a group exhibit, with Willem in it. but not enough of his stuff to my taste. THERE ALSO WAS PLACiD, WHO i LIKE A LOT TOO. the rest was not bad but god... i'VE SEEN TOO MUCH OF THAT TYPE OF THiNG.
boxes with movable characters
ART FACTORY
cute...
i left them afterwards, and went to buy tracing paper.

24.10.03. friday

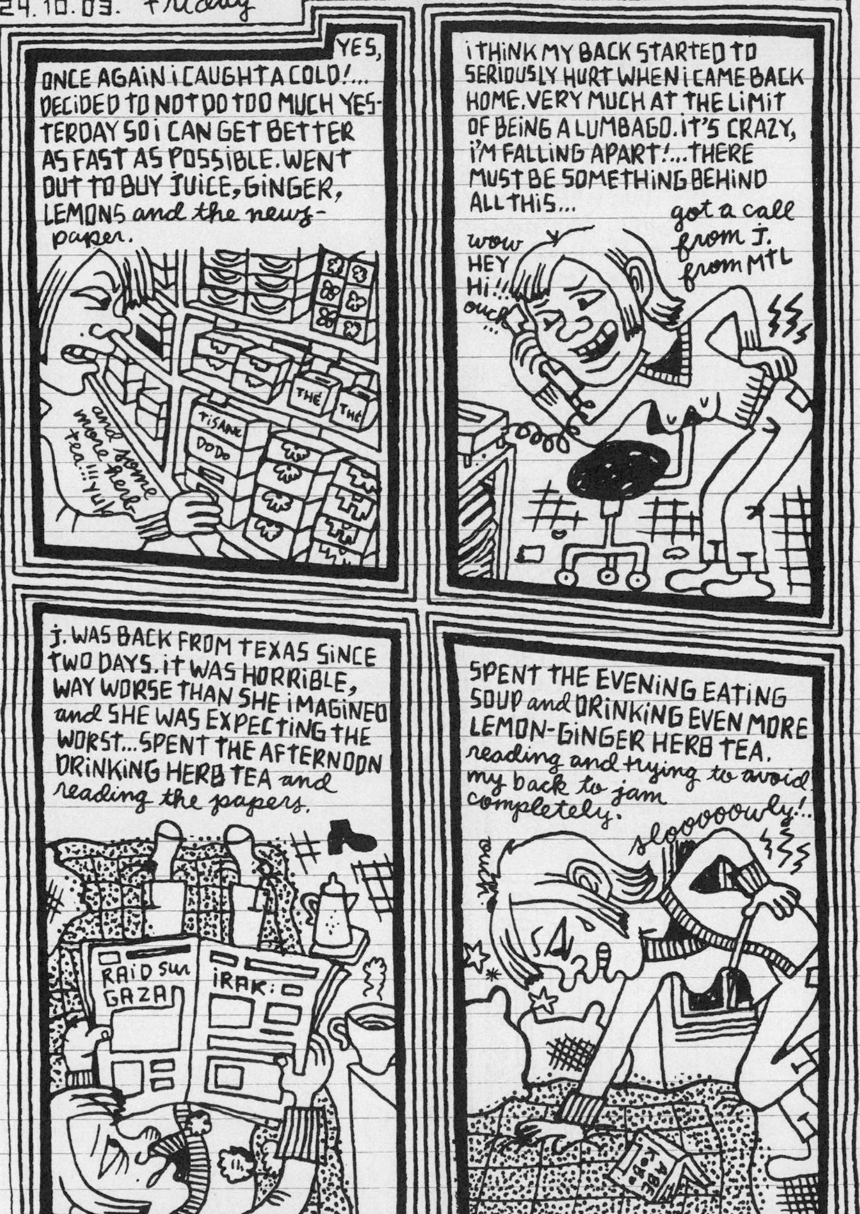
YES, ONCE AGAIN I CAUGHT A COLD!... DECIDED TO NOT DO TOO MUCH YESTERDAY SO I CAN GET BETTER AS FAST AS POSSIBLE. WENT OUT TO BUY JUICE, GINGER, LEMONS and the newspaper.
and some more herb tea...!!! yuk
TISANE
DODO
THÉ
THÉ
I THINK MY BACK STARTED TO SERIOUSLY HURT WHEN I CAME BACK HOME. VERY MUCH AT THE LIMIT OF BEING A LUMBAGO. IT'S CRAZY, I'M FALLING APART!... THERE MUST BE SOMETHING BEHIND ALL THIS...
got a call from J. from MTL
wow HEY Hi!!! ouch
J. WAS BACK FROM TEXAS SINCE TWO DAYS. IT WAS HORRIBLE, WAY WORSE THAN SHE IMAGINED and SHE WAS EXPECTING THE WORST... SPENT THE AFTERNOON DRINKING HERB TEA and reading the papers.
RAID sur GAZA
IRAK:
SPENT THE EVENING EATING SOUP and DRINKING EVEN MORE LEMON-GINGER HERB TEA. reading and trying to avoid my back to jam completely.
slooooowly!...
ouch

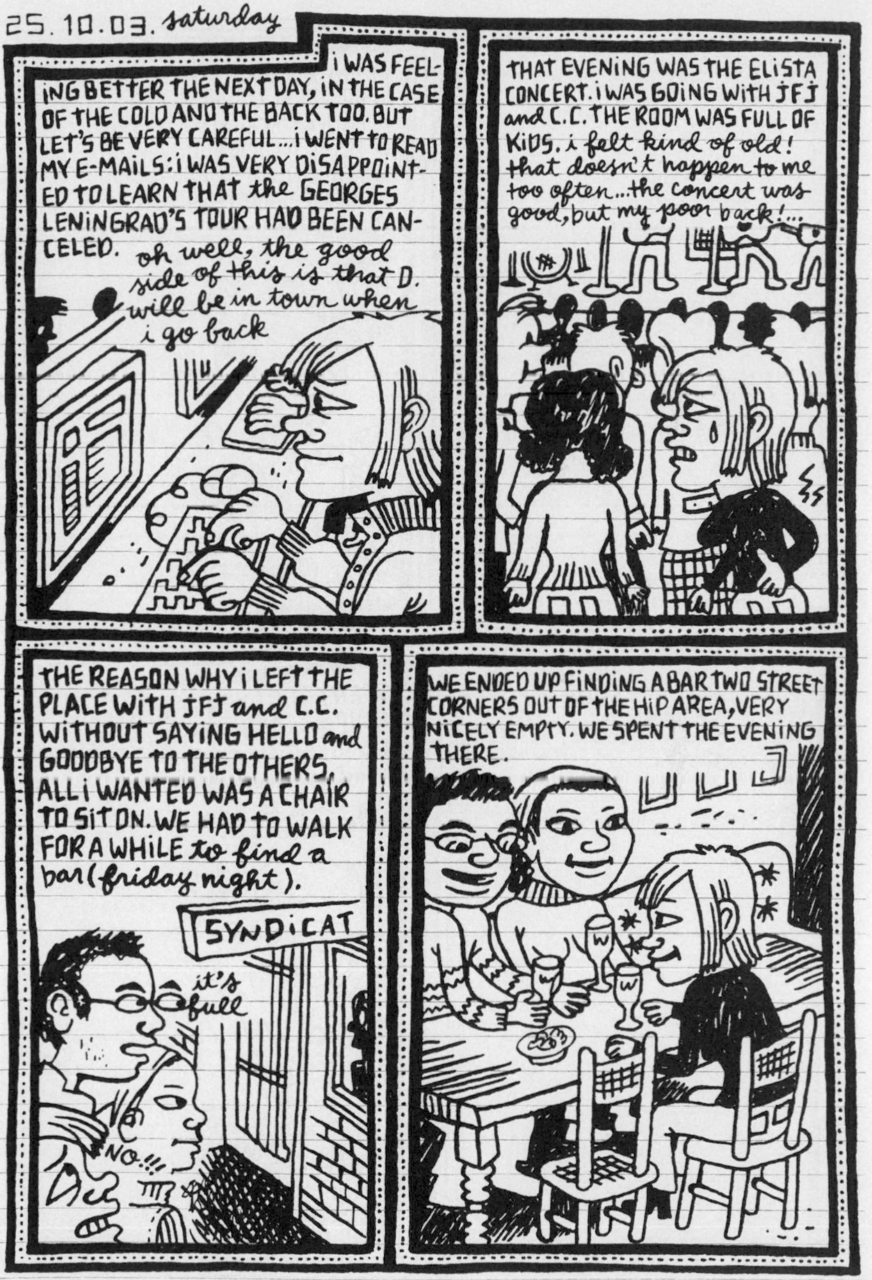
25.10.03. saturday
I WAS FEELING BETTER THE NEXT DAY, IN THE CASE OF THE COLD AND THE BACK TOO. BUT LET'S BE VERY CAREFUL... I WENT TO READ MY E-MAILS: I WAS VERY DISAPPOINTED TO LEARN THAT the GEORGES LENINGRAD'S TOUR HAD BEEN CANCELED.
oh well, the good side of this is that D. will be in town when i go back
THAT EVENING WAS THE ELISTA CONCERT. I WAS GOING WITH JFJ and C.C. THE ROOM WAS FULL OF KIDS. i felt kind of old! that doesn't happen to me too often... the concert was good, but my poor back!...
THE REASON WHY I LEFT THE PLACE WITH JFJ and C.C. WITHOUT SAYING HELLO and GOODBYE TO THE OTHERS, ALL I WANTED WAS A CHAIR TO SIT ON. WE HAD TO WALK FOR A WHILE to find a bar (friday night).
SYNDICAT
it's full
NO...!!!
WE ENDED UP FINDING A BAR TWO STREET CORNERS OUT OF THE HIP AREA, VERY NICELY EMPTY. WE SPENT THE EVENING THERE.

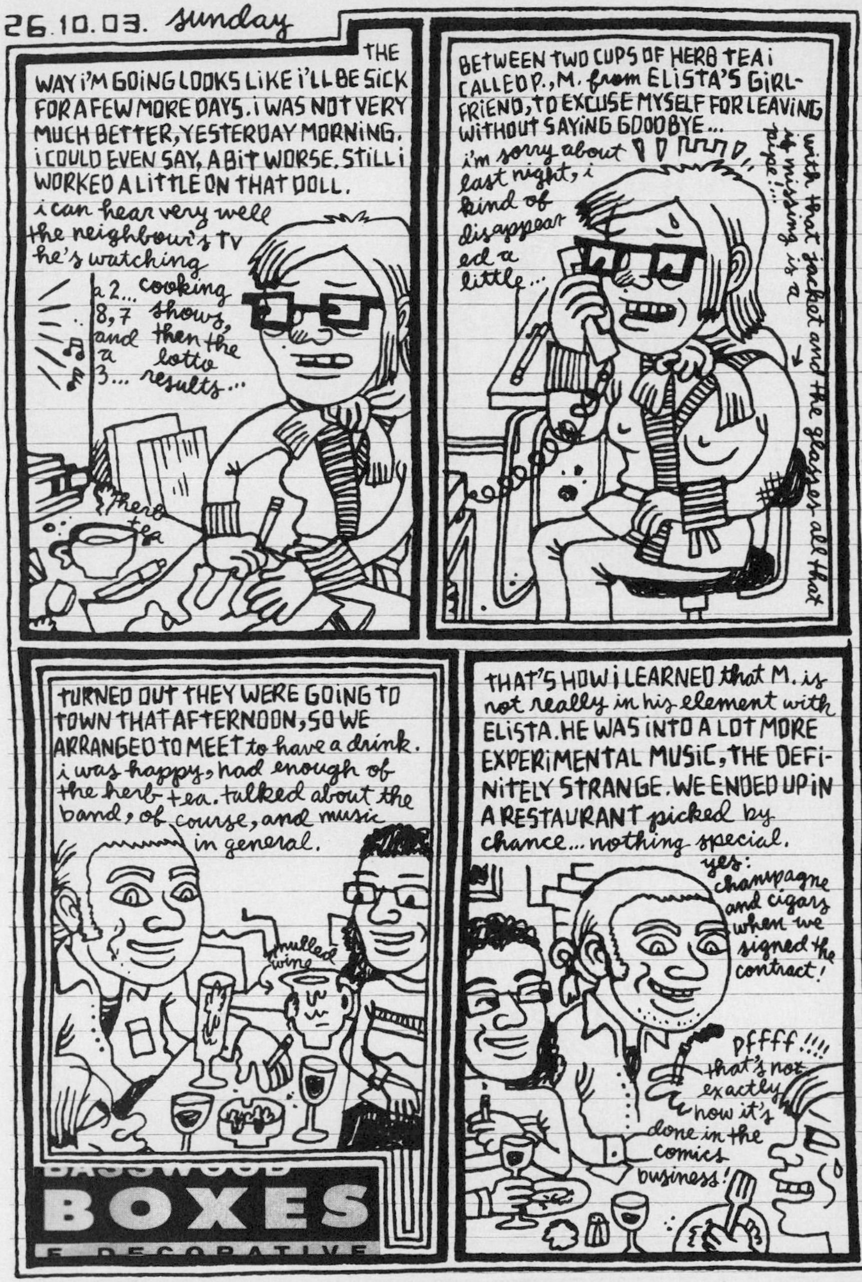

26.10.03. sunday
THE WAY i'M GOING LOOKS LIKE i'LL BE SICK FOR A FEW MORE DAYS. i WAS NOT VERY MUCH BETTER, YESTERDAY MORNING. i COULD EVEN SAY, A BIT WORSE. STILL i WORKED A LITTLE ON THAT DOLL.
i can hear very well the neighbour's TV he's watching cooking shows, then the lotto results...
a 2... 8, 7 and a 3...
herb tea
BETWEEN TWO CUPS OF HERB TEA i CALLED P., M. from ELISTA'S GIRL-FRIEND, TO EXCUSE MYSELF FOR LEAVING WITHOUT SAYING GOODBYE...
i'm sorry about last night, i kind of disappeared a little...
with that jacket and the glasses all that is missing is a pipe!...
TURNED OUT THEY WERE GOING TO TOWN THAT AFTERNOON, SO WE ARRANGED TO MEET to have a drink. i was happy, had enough of the herb tea. talked about the band, of course, and music in general.
mulled wine
BASSWOOD BOXES & DECORATIVE
THAT'S HOW i LEARNED that M. is not really in his element with ELISTA. HE WAS INTO A LOT MORE EXPERIMENTAL MUSIC, THE DEFINITELY STRANGE. WE ENDED UP IN A RESTAURANT picked by chance... nothing special.
yes: champagne and cigars when we signed the contract!
pffff!!!! that's not exactly how it's done in the comics business!

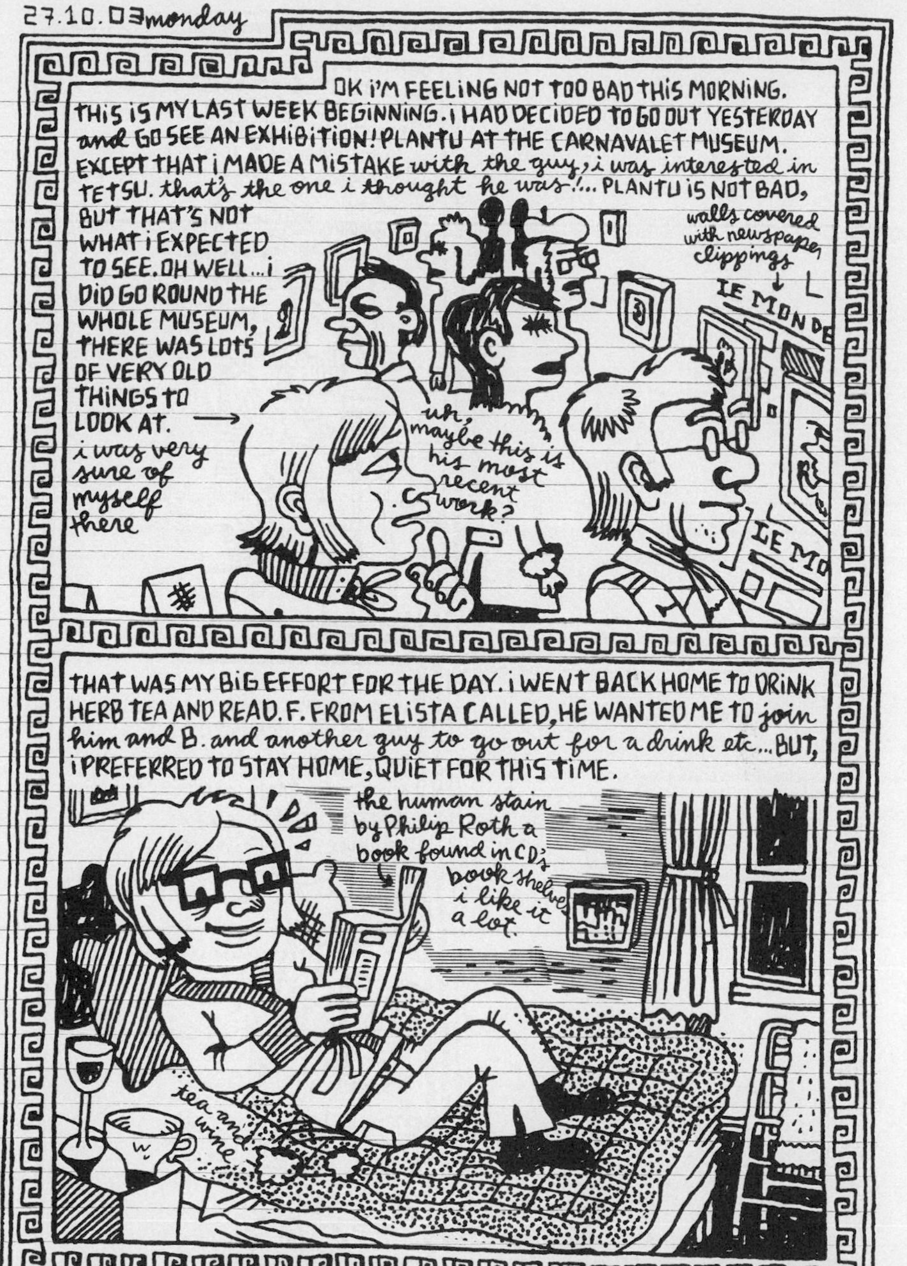
27.10.03 monday
OK i'M FEELING NOT TOO BAD THIS MORNING. THIS iS MY LAST WEEK BEGINNING. i HAD DECIDED TO GO OUT YESTERDAY and GO SEE AN EXHIBITION! PLANTU AT THE CARNAVALET MUSEUM. EXCEPT THAT i MADE A MISTAKE with the guy, i was interested in TETSU. that's the one i thought he was!... PLANTU IS NOT BAD, BUT THAT'S NOT WHAT i EXPECTED TO SEE. OH WELL... i DID GO ROUND THE WHOLE MUSEUM, THERE WAS LOTS OF VERY OLD THINGS TO LOOK AT.
i was very sure of myself there
uh, maybe this is his most recent work?
walls covered with newspaper clippings
LE MONDE
LE MO
THAT WAS MY BIG EFFORT FOR THE DAY. i WENT BACK HOME TO DRINK HERB TEA AND READ. F. FROM ELISTA CALLED, HE WANTED ME TO join him and B. and another guy to go out for a drink etc... BUT, i PREFERRED TO STAY HOME, QUIET FOR THIS TIME.
the human stain by Philip Roth a book found in CD's book shelves i like it a lot.
tea and wine

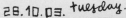 28.10.03. tuesday.

CŒUR BEAUTIFUL WEATHER OUT AND MY COLD IS PRETTY MUCH GONE. IT'S ANOTHER STORY WITH MY BACK. WORKED ON THAT DOLL, BUT... I'M GOING TO START ALL OVER AGAIN. I MAILED MY FIRST BOX OF BOOKS. IT WAS SUPER EXPENSIVE *because it was over 5 KILOS* BUT I WAS TOO LAZY *to*

let's pretend i'm not doing this...

make another package.

SANTE THEN, A DELICATE OPERATION: I HAD TO CONVINCE THE PHARMACIST TO SELL ME *medica-tion* WITHOUT (a french) PRE-SCRIPTION. I WON'T HAVE ENOUGH, I MISS 3 DAYS.

all right

no kidding!?

canadian prescription

VIE SOCIALE ...I HAD TRIED THAT IN BERLIN, IT DIDN'T WORK AT ALL, NOT AT ALL!... MET WITH BLANQUET *and* OLIVE *at the beginning of the evening, because of the doll.* I HAD GIVEN THEM A COPY *of Elista's* CD, LAST TIME. I DIDN'T THINK THEY'D LIKE IT... THEY DIDN'T LIKE IT.

scandalized

but... it's pop music !!!

HÉ!

STRICTEMENT PERSONNEL I THINK I DREAMT I WAS IN MONTRÉAL, LAST NIGHT. I WAS WALKING IN AN INDUSTRIAL AREA WITH FRIENDS, AT NIGHT. DREARY. I REALLY WONDER HOW IT'S GOING TO BE, TO BE BACK IN MTL, VERY DIFFICULT TO IMAGINE, FROM HERE. NOVEMBER 5th: THERE'S GOING TO BE CHRISTMAS STUFF *all over the place,* already... oooh boy...

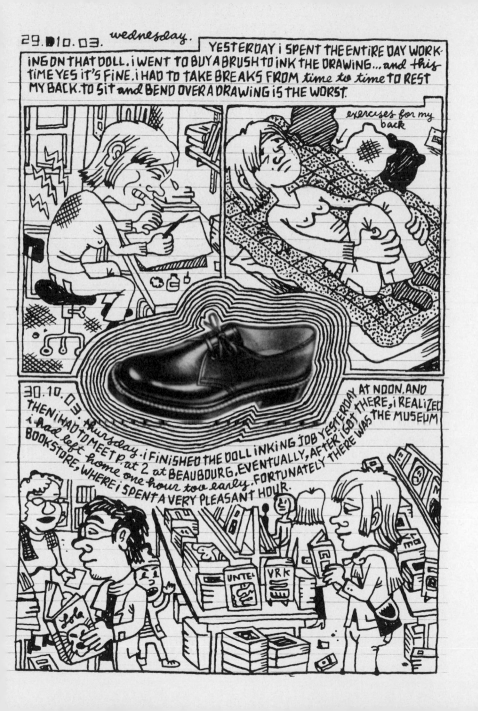

29.10.03. wednesday.

YESTERDAY I SPENT THE ENTIRE DAY WORKING ON THAT DOLL. I WENT TO BUY A BRUSH TO INK THE DRAWING... AND THIS TIME YES IT'S FINE. I HAD TO TAKE BREAKS FROM time to time TO REST MY BACK. TO SIT AND BEND OVER A DRAWING IS THE WORST.

exercises for my back

30.10.03. thursday. I FINISHED THE DOLL INKING JOB YESTERDAY AT NOON. AND THEN I HAD TO MEET P. AT 2 AT BEAUBOURG. EVENTUALLY, AFTER I GOT THERE, I REALIZED I had left home one hour too early. FORTUNATELY THERE WAS THE MUSEUM BOOKSTORE, WHERE I SPENT A VERY PLEASANT HOUR.

UNTE VRK

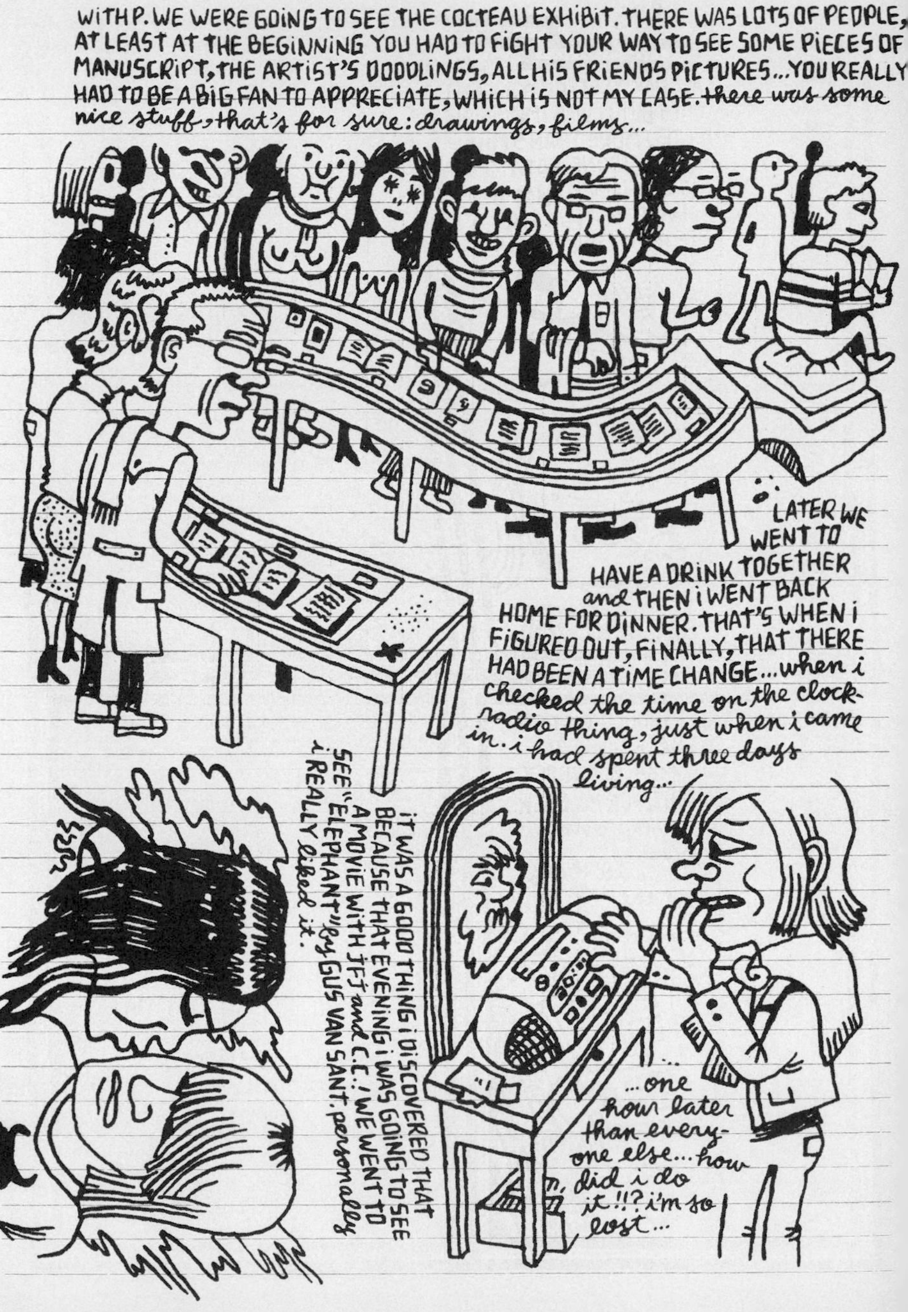
WITH P. WE WERE GOING TO SEE THE COCTEAU EXHIBIT. THERE WAS LOTS OF PEOPLE, AT LEAST AT THE BEGINNING YOU HAD TO FIGHT YOUR WAY TO SEE SOME PIECES OF MANUSCRIPT, THE ARTIST'S DOODLINGS, ALL HIS FRIENDS PICTURES... YOU REALLY HAD TO BE A BIG FAN TO APPRECIATE, WHICH IS NOT MY CASE. there was some nice stuff, that's for sure: drawings, films...
LATER WE WENT TO HAVE A DRINK TOGETHER and THEN i WENT BACK HOME FOR DINNER. THAT'S WHEN i FIGURED OUT, FINALLY, THAT THERE HAD BEEN A TIME CHANGE... when i checked the time on the clock-radio thing, just when i came in. i had spent three days living...
...one hour later than every-one else... how did i do it!!? i'm so lost...
IT WAS A GOOD THING i DISCOVERED THAT BECAUSE THAT EVENING i WAS GOING TO SEE A MOVIE WITH JFJ and C.C.: WE WENT TO SEE "ELEPHANT" by GUS VAN SANT. personally i REALLY liked it.

31.10.03. friday.

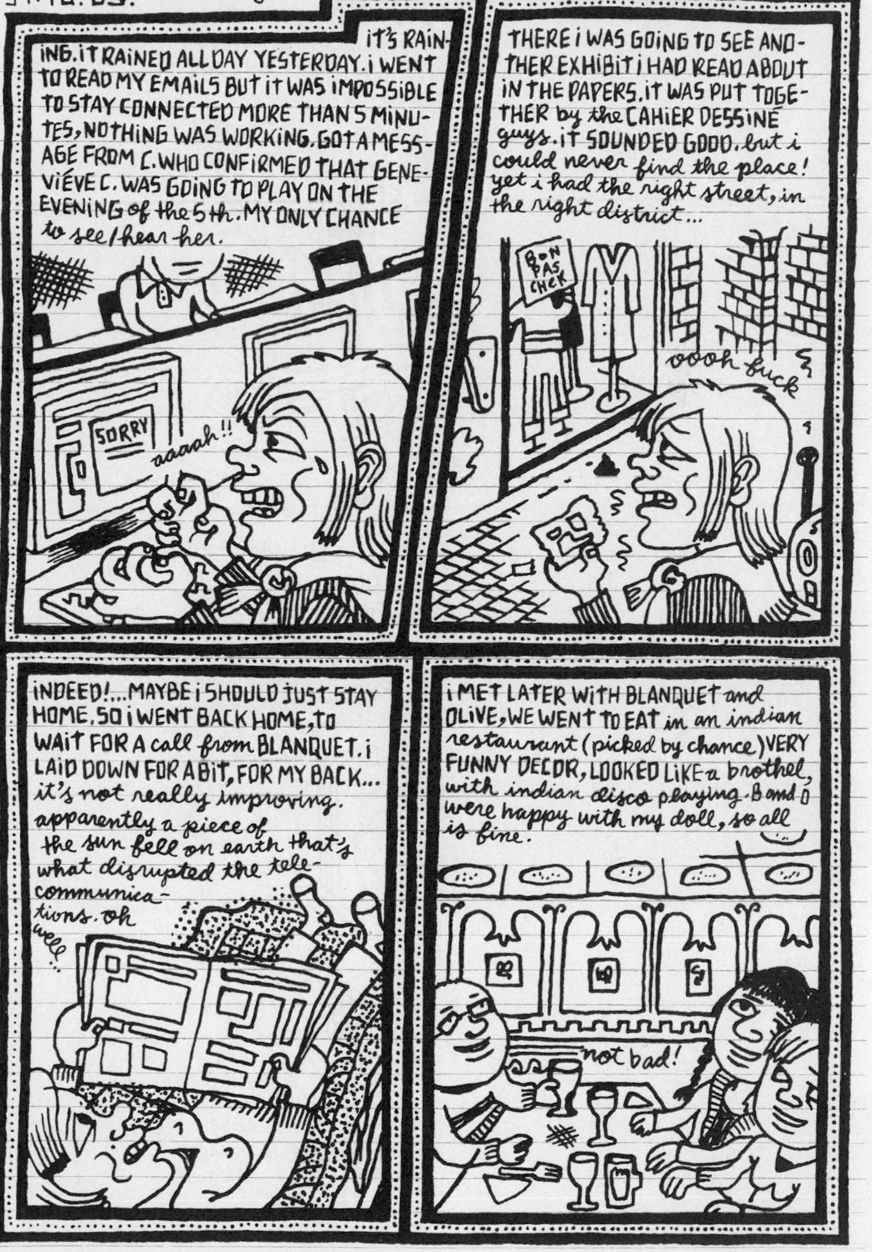
IT'S RAINING. IT RAINED ALL DAY YESTERDAY. i WENT TO READ MY EMAILS BUT IT WAS IMPOSSIBLE TO STAY CONNECTED MORE THAN 5 MINUTES, NOTHING WAS WORKING. GOT A MESSAGE FROM C. WHO CONFIRMED THAT GENEVIÉVE C. WAS GOING TO PLAY ON THE EVENING of the 5th. MY ONLY CHANCE to see/hear her.
SORRY
aaaah!!
THERE i WAS GOING TO SEE ANOTHER EXHIBIT i HAD READ ABOUT IN THE PAPERS. IT WAS PUT TOGETHER by the CAHIER DESSINÉ guys. IT SOUNDED GOOD. but i could never find the place! yet i had the right street, in the right district...
BON PAS CHER
oooh fuck
INDEED!... MAYBE i SHOULD JUST STAY HOME. SO i WENT BACK HOME, TO WAIT FOR A call from BLANQUET. i LAID DOWN FOR A BIT, FOR MY BACK... it's not really improving.
apparently a piece of the sun fell on earth that's what disrupted the telecommunications. oh well...
i MET LATER WITH BLANQUET and OLIVE, WE WENT TO EAT in an indian restaurant (picked by chance) VERY FUNNY DECOR, LOOKED LIKE a brothel, with indian disco playing. B and O were happy with my doll, so all is fine.
not bad!

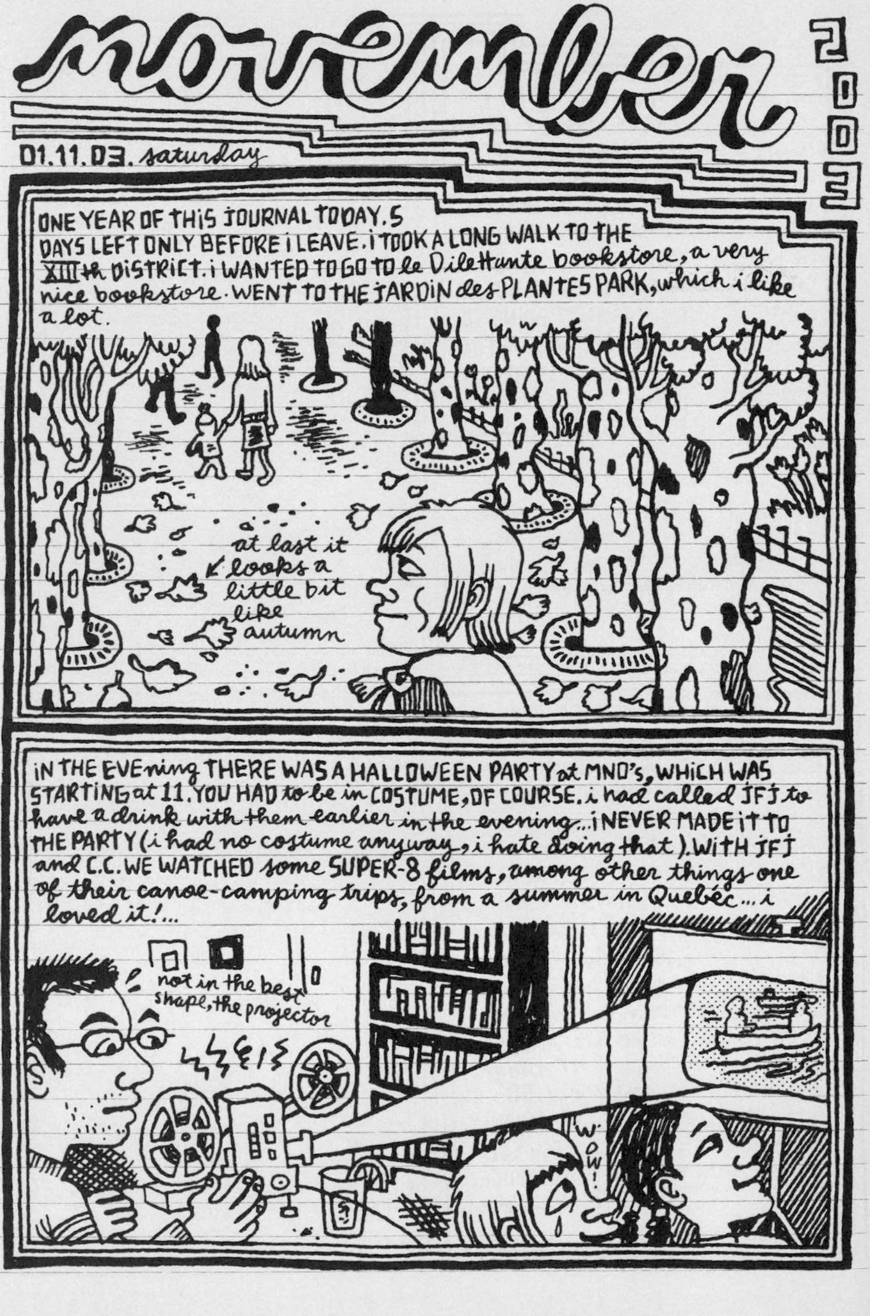
november
2003
01.11.03. saturday
ONE YEAR OF THIS JOURNAL TODAY. 5 DAYS LEFT ONLY BEFORE i LEAVE. i TOOK A LONG WALK TO THE XIIIth DISTRICT. i WANTED TO GO TO le DiletTante bookstore, a very nice bookstore. WENT TO THE JARDIN des PLANTES PARK, which i like a lot.
at last it looks a little bit like autumn
iN THE EVEning THERE WAS A HALLOWEEN PARTY at MNO's, WHICH WAS STARTING at 11. YOU HAD to be in COSTUME, OF COURSE. i had called JFJ to have a drink with them earlier in the evening... i NEVER MADE iT TO THE PARTY (i had no costume anyway, i hate doing that). WITH JFJ and C.C. WE WATCHED some SUPER-8 films, among other things one of their canoe-camping trips, from a summer in Quebéc... i loved it!...
not in the best shape, the projector
WOW!

02.11.03. sunday

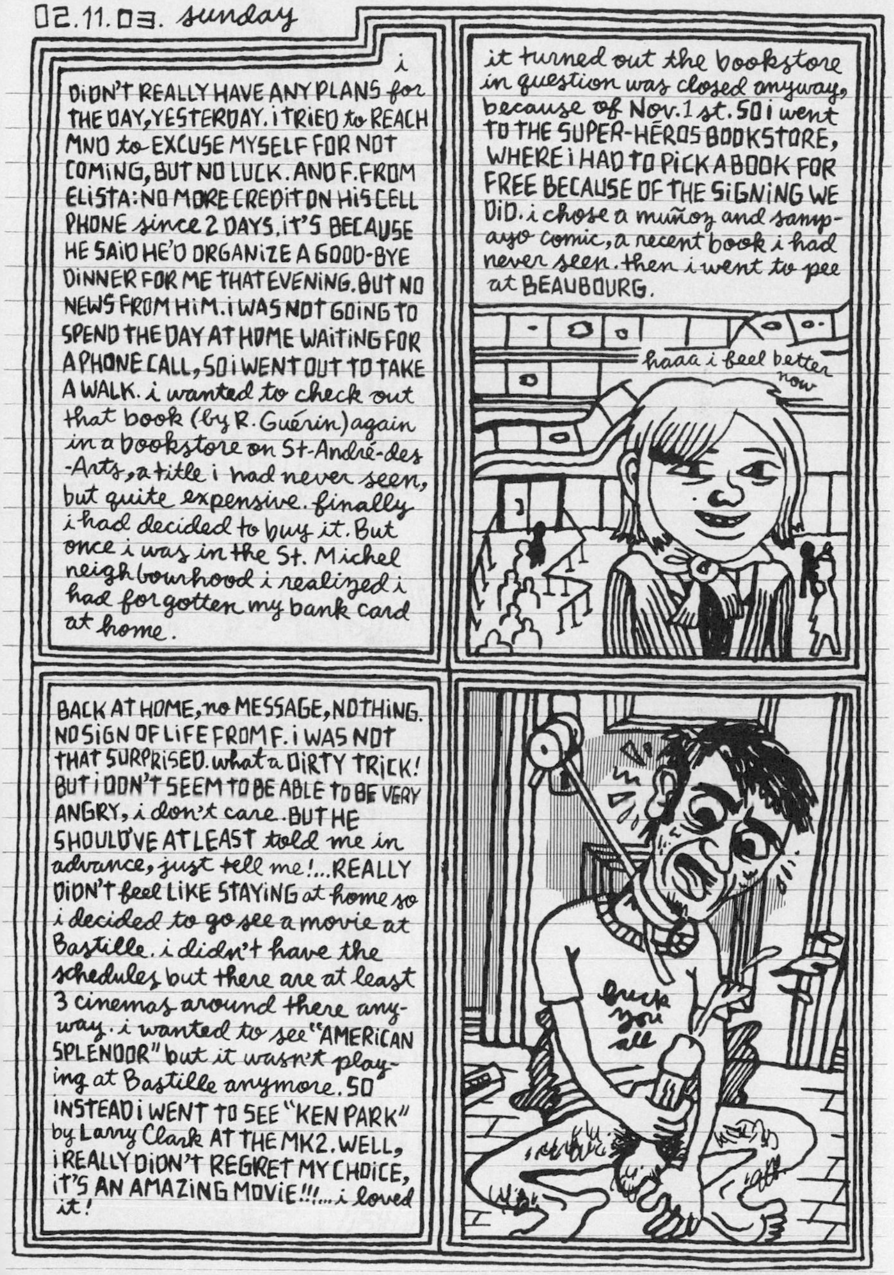
i didn't really have any plans for the day, yesterday. i tried to reach MND to excuse myself for not coming, but no luck. and F. from Elista: no more credit on his cell phone since 2 days. it's because he said he'd organize a good-bye dinner for me that evening. but no news from him. i was not going to spend the day at home waiting for a phone call, so i went out to take a walk. i wanted to check out that book (by R. Guérin) again in a bookstore on St-André-des-Arts, a title i had never seen, but quite expensive. finally i had decided to buy it. But once i was in the St. Michel neighbourhood i realized i had forgotten my bank card at home.
it turned out the bookstore in question was closed anyway, because of Nov. 1st. so i went to the Super-Héros bookstore, where i had to pick a book for free because of the signing we did. i chose a muñoz and sampayo comic, a recent book i had never seen. then i went to pee at Beaubourg.
haaa i feel better now
back at home, no message, nothing. no sign of life from F. i was not that surprised. what a dirty trick! but i don't seem to be able to be very angry, i don't care. but he should've at least told me in advance, just tell me!... really didn't feel like staying at home so i decided to go see a movie at Bastille. i didn't have the schedules but there are at least 3 cinemas around there anyway. i wanted to see "American Splendor" but it wasn't playing at Bastille anymore. so instead i went to see "Ken Park" by Larry Clark at the MK2. well, i really didn't regret my choice, it's an amazing movie!!!... i loved it!
fuck you all

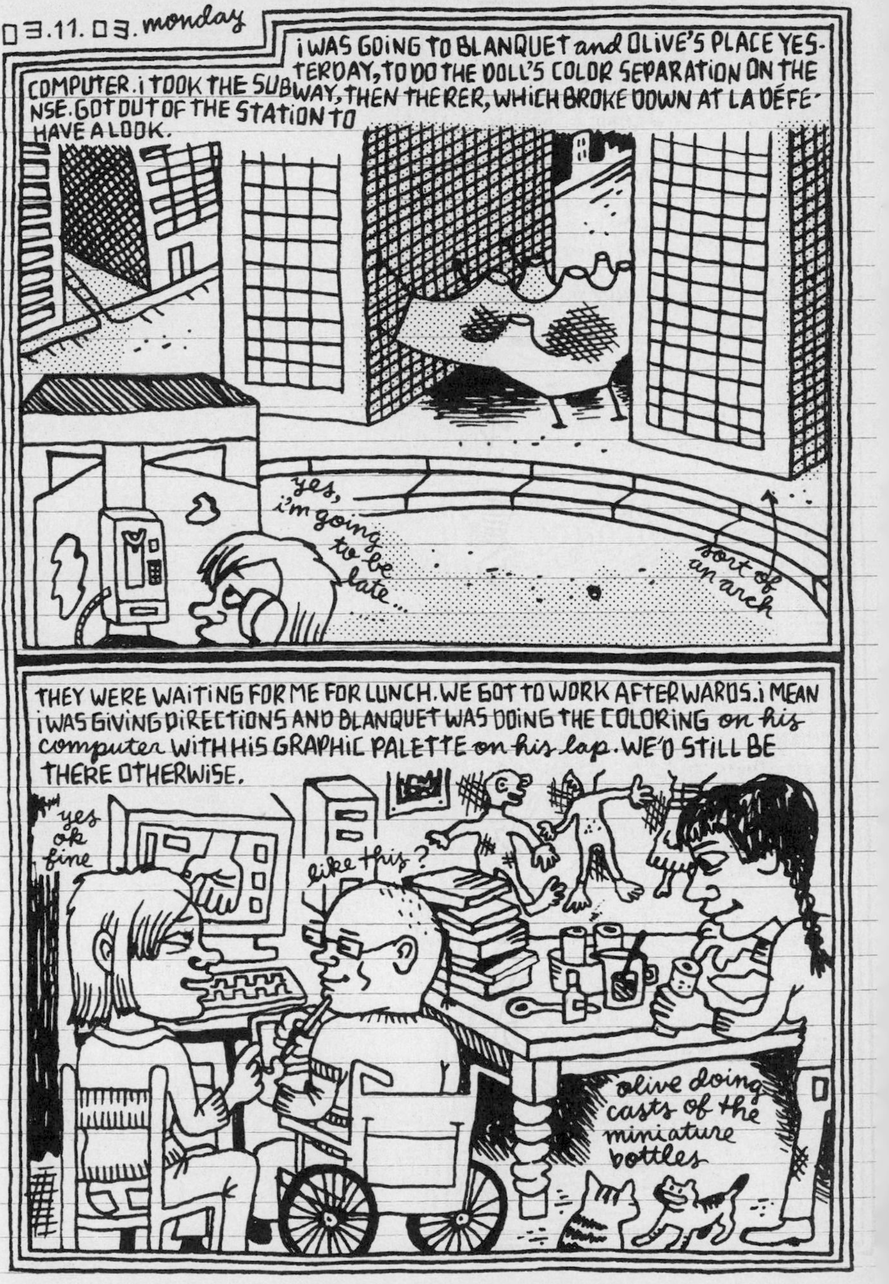
03.11.03. monday
i WAS GOING TO BLANQUET and OLIVE'S PLACE YESTERDAY, TO DO THE DOLL'S COLOR SEPARATION ON THE COMPUTER. i TOOK THE SUBWAY, THEN THE RER, WHICH BROKE DOWN AT LA DÉFENSE. GOT OUT OF THE STATION TO HAVE A LOOK.
yes, i'm going to be late...
sort of an arch
THEY WERE WAITING FOR ME FOR LUNCH. WE GOT TO WORK AFTERWARDS. i MEAN i WAS GIVING DIRECTIONS AND BLANQUET WAS DOING THE COLORING on his computer WITH HIS GRAPHIC PALETTE on his lap. WE'D STILL BE THERE OTHERWISE.
yes ok fine
like this?
olive doing casts of the miniature bottles

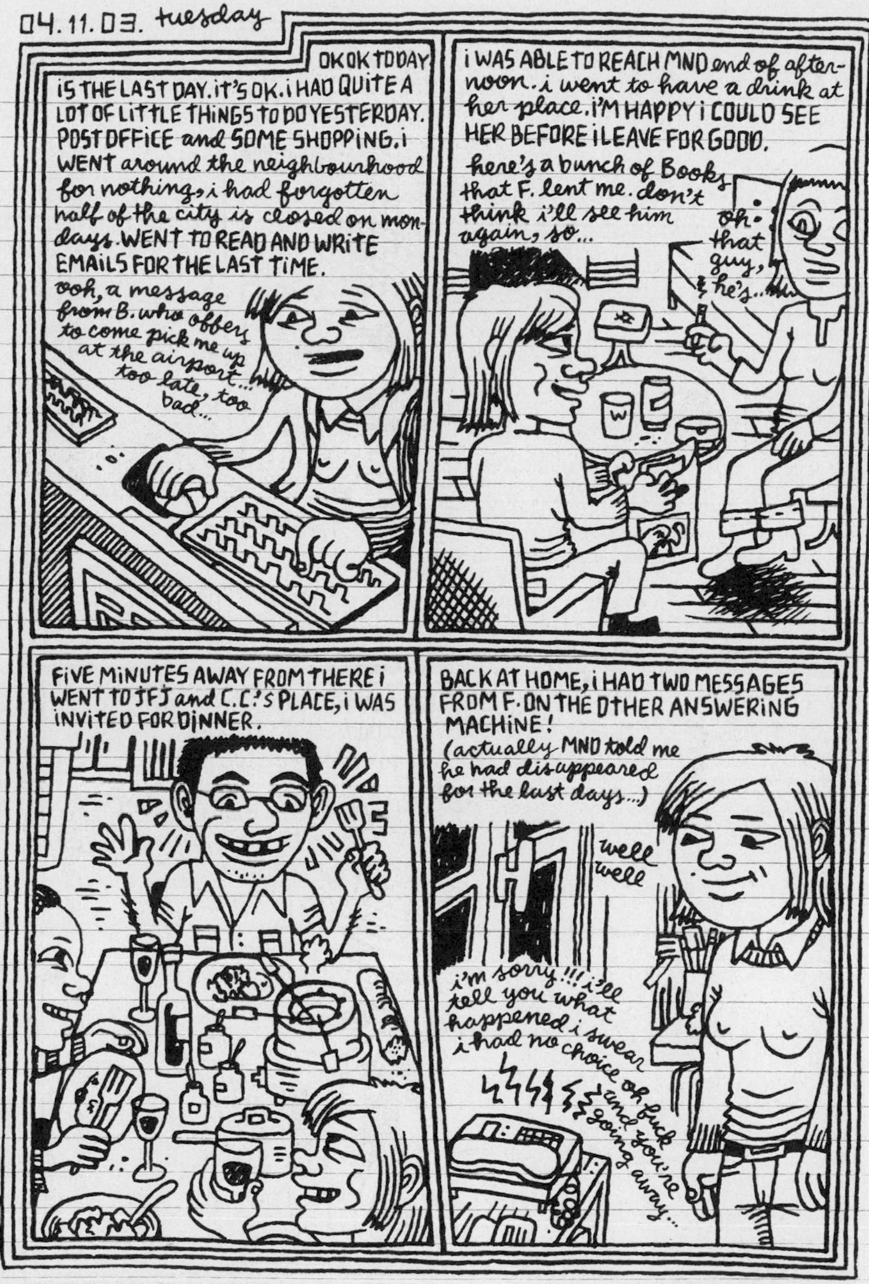
04.11.03. tuesday
OKOK TODAY IS THE LAST DAY. IT'S OK. I HAD QUITE A LOT OF LITTLE THINGS TO DO YESTERDAY. POST OFFICE and SOME SHOPPING. I WENT around the neighbourhood for nothing, i had forgotten half of the city is closed on mondays. WENT TO READ AND WRITE EMAILS FOR THE LAST TIME.
ooh, a message from B. who offers to come pick me up at the airport... too late, too bad...
I WAS ABLE TO REACH MND end of afternoon. i went to have a drink at her place. I'M HAPPY I COULD SEE HER BEFORE I LEAVE FOR GOOD.
here's a bunch of Books that F. lent me. don't think i'll see him again, so...
oh. that guy, he's...
FIVE MINUTES AWAY FROM THERE I WENT TO JFJ and C.C.'s PLACE, I WAS INVITED FOR DINNER.
BACK AT HOME, I HAD TWO MESSAGES FROM F. ON THE OTHER ANSWERING MACHINE!
(actually MND told me he had disappeared for the last days...)
well well
i'm sorry!!! i'll tell you what happened i swear i had no choice oh fuck and you're going away...

05.11.03. wednesday

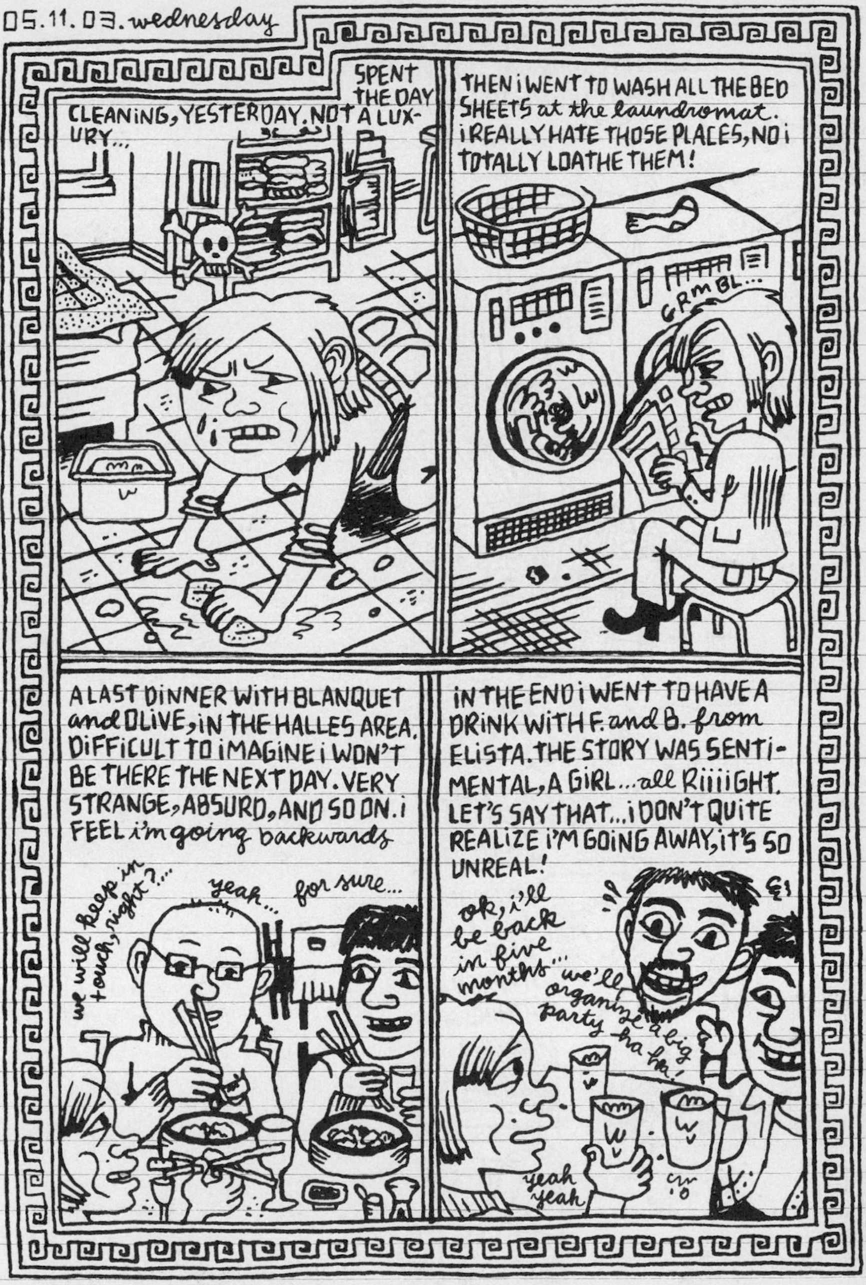
SPENT THE DAY CLEANING, YESTERDAY. NOT A LUXURY...
THEN i WENT TO WASH ALL THE BED SHEETS at the laundromat. i REALLY HATE THOSE PLACES, NO i TOTALLY LOATHE THEM!
GRMBL...
A LAST DINNER WITH BLANQUET and OLIVE, IN THE HALLES AREA. DIFFICULT TO iMAGINE i WON'T BE THERE THE NEXT DAY. VERY STRANGE, ABSURD, AND SO ON. i FEEL i'm going backwards
we will keep in touch, right?...
yeah...
for sure...
IN THE END i WENT TO HAVE A DRINK WITH F. and B. from ELiSTA. THE STORY WAS SENTIMENTAL, A GiRL... all RiiiiGHT. LET'S SAY THAT... i DON'T QUITE REALIZE i'M GOING AWAY, it's SO UNREAL!
ok, i'll be back in five months...
we'll organize a big party - ha ha!
yeah yeah

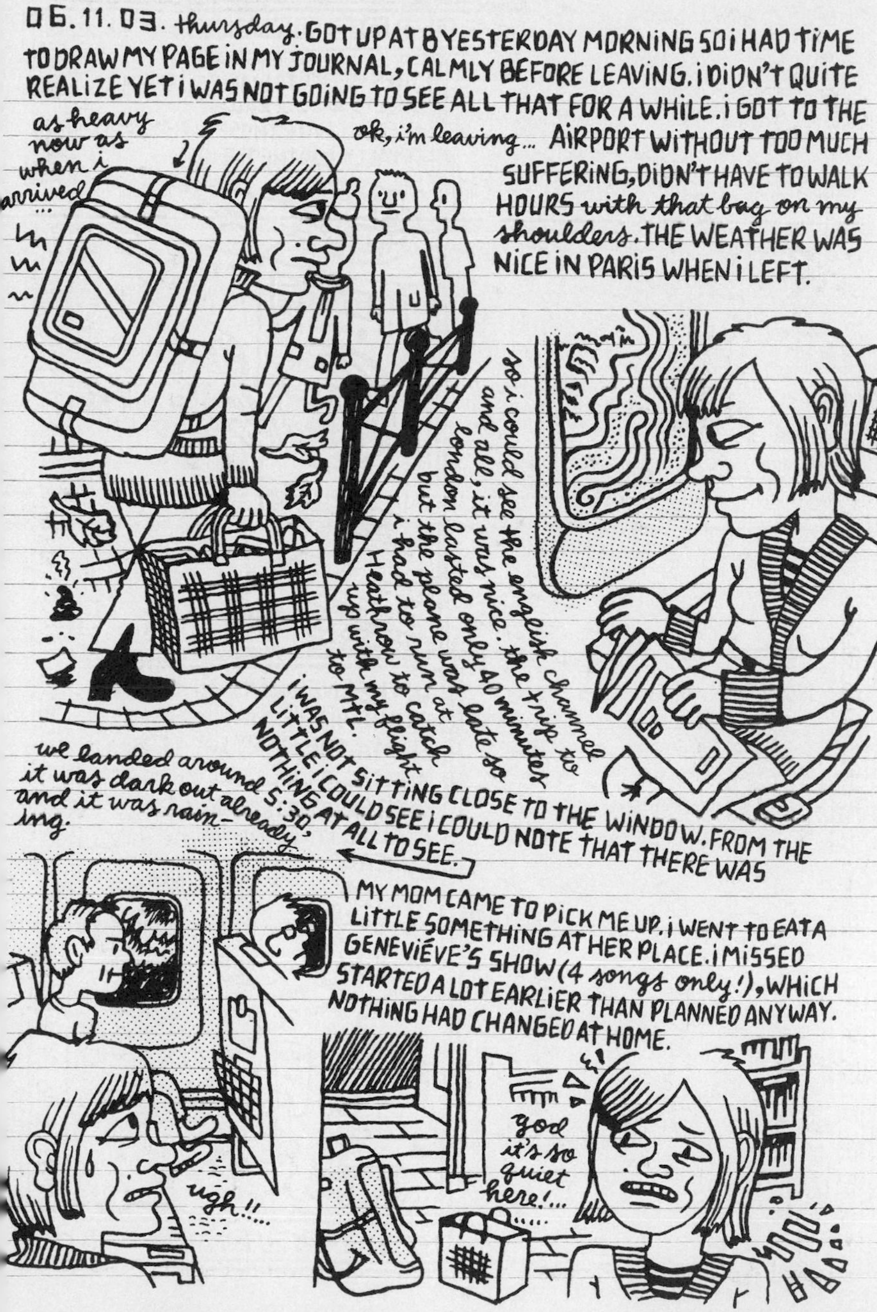

06.11.03. thursday. GOT UP AT 8 YESTERDAY MORNING SO I HAD TIME TO DRAW MY PAGE IN MY JOURNAL, CALMLY BEFORE LEAVING. I DIDN'T QUITE REALIZE YET I WAS NOT GOING TO SEE ALL THAT FOR A WHILE. I GOT TO THE AIRPORT WITHOUT TOO MUCH SUFFERING, DIDN'T HAVE TO WALK HOURS with that bag on my shoulders. THE WEATHER WAS NICE IN PARIS WHEN I LEFT.
as heavy now as when i arrived...
ok, i'm leaving...
so i could see the english channel and all, it was nice. the trip to london lasted only 40 minutes but the plane was late so i had to run at Heathrow to catch up with my flight to MTL.
I WAS NOT SITTING CLOSE TO THE WINDOW. FROM THE LITTLE I COULD SEE I COULD NOTE THAT THERE WAS NOTHING AT ALL TO SEE.
we landed around 5:30, it was dark out already and it was raining.
ugh!!....
MY MOM CAME TO PICK ME UP. I WENT TO EAT A LITTLE SOMETHING AT HER PLACE. I MISSED GENEVIÉVE'S SHOW (4 songs only!), WHICH STARTED A LOT EARLIER THAN PLANNED ANYWAY. NOTHING HAD CHANGED AT HOME.
god it's so quiet here!.....

... then **3**65 *More* day s **to** come in 20 07 **200** 8